Learning Java™

Other Java™ resources from O'Reilly

Related titles

Head First Java™
Head First Design Patterns
Head First Servlets and JSP™
Head First EJB™

Better, Faster, Lighter Java™
Java™ Cookbook™
Java™ in a Nutshell

Java Books Resource Center

java.oreilly.com is a complete catalog of O'Reilly's books on Java and related technologies, including sample chapters and code examples.

OnJava.com is a one-stop resource for enterprise Java developers, featuring news, code recipes, interviews, weblogs, and more.

Conferences

O'Reilly brings diverse innovators together to nurture the ideas that spark revolutionary industries. We specialize in documenting the latest tools and systems, translating the innovator's knowledge into useful skills for those in the trenches. Visit *conferences.oreilly.com* for our upcoming events.

Safari Bookshelf (*safari.oreilly.com*) is the premier online reference library for programmers and IT professionals. Conduct searches across more than 1,000 books. Subscribers can zero in on answers to time-critical questions in a matter of seconds. Read the books on your Bookshelf from cover to cover or simply flip to the page you need. Try it today with a free trial.

THIRD EDITION

Learning Java™

Patrick Niemeyer and Jonathan Knudsen

O'REILLY®

Beijing · Cambridge · Farnham · Köln · Paris · Sebastopol · Taipei · Tokyo

Learning Java™, Third Edition
by Patrick Niemeyer and Jonathan Knudsen

Published by O'Reilly Media, Inc., 1005 Gravenstein Highway North, Sebastopol, CA 95472.

O'Reilly books may be purchased for educational, business, or sales promotional use. Online editions are also available for most titles (*safari.oreilly.com*). For more information, contact our corporate/institutional sales department: (800) 998-9938 or *corporate@oreilly.com*.

Editors:	Mike Loukides and Debra Cameron
Production Editor:	Matt Hutchinson
Production Services:	Octal Publishing, Inc.
Cover Designer:	Hanna Dyer
Interior Designer:	David Futato

Printing History:

May 2000:	First Edition.
June 2002:	Second Edition.
May 2005:	Third Edition.

ISBN-10: 0-596-00873-2
ISBN-13: 978-0-596-00873-4
[M]   [05/07]

Table of Contents

Preface

This book is about the Java™ language and programming environment. Whether you are a software developer or just someone who uses the Internet in your daily life, you've undoubtedly heard about Java. Its introduction was one of the most exciting developments in the history of the Web and it hasn't slowed down much since. Java is now, arguably, the most popular programming language in the world, used by millions of developers on almost every kind of computer imaginable. In recent years Java has surpassed languages such as C++ and Visual Basic in terms of developer demand and become the de facto language for new development—especially for web-based applications and services. Most universities are now using Java in their introductory courses, alongside the other important modern languages. Perhaps you are using this text in one of your classes right now!

This book gives you a thorough grounding in Java fundamentals and APIs. *Learning Java*, Third Edition attempts to live up to its name by mapping out the Java language, its class libraries, programming techniques, and idioms. We'll dig deep into interesting areas and at least scratch the surface of the rest. Other titles from O'Reilly pick up where we leave off and provide more comprehensive information on specific areas and applications of Java.

Whenever possible, we provide compelling, realistic, and fun examples and avoid merely cataloging features. The examples are simple but hint at what can be done. We won't be developing the next great "killer app" in these pages, but we hope to give you a starting point for many hours of experimentation and inspired tinkering that will lead you to learn more on your own.

New Developments

This edition of *Learning Java* is actually the fifth edition—updated and retitled—of our original, popular *Exploring Java*. With each edition we've taken great care not only to add new material covering additional features, but to thoroughly revise and update the existing content to synthesize the coverage and add years of real-world perspective and experience to these pages.

One noticeable change in recent editions is that we've deemphasized the use of applets, reflecting their somewhat static role over the past couple of years in creating interactive web pages. In contrast, we've greatly expanded our coverage of server-side web applications and XML, which are now mature technologies.

We cover all of the important features of the latest release of Java, officially called Java 2 Standard Edition 5.0, JDK 1.5. Sun has changed the naming scheme many times over the years and this is the most confusing release ever! Sun coined the term "Java 2" to cover the major new features introduced in Java Version 1.2 and dropped the term JDK in favor of SDK. With this release Sun has skipped from Java Version 1.4 to the Java 5.0, but reprieved the term JDK and kept its numbering convention there. We've had no choice but to accept the term Java 5.0 into our vocabulary. You can't fight marketing.

This release of Java is targeted at developers and has the biggest set of language changes since Java's birth. We've tried to capture these new features and update every example in this book to reflect not only the current Java practice, but style.

New in This Edition

This edition of the book has been significantly reworked to be as complete and up to date as possible. New topics in this edition include:

- New Java 5.0 language features, including typesafe enumerations, variable-length argument lists (varargs), the enhanced for loop, autoboxing, static imports, and annotations (Chapters 4 through 7)
- A full chapter on generics and parameterized types (Chapter 8)
- Full coverage of the new Java concurrency package, including details on executors, thread pools, read/write locks, and more (Chapter 9)
- Printf-style text formatting and the new Scanner text-parsing API (Chapter 10)
- New Collections classes, including Queue and Concurrent collections (Chapter 11)
- Enhanced RMI (Chapter 13)
- Using and writing web services with the Java Web Services Developer Pack (Chapters 14 and 15)
- Coverage of NetBeans 4.x (Chapter 22)
- Major XML enhancements, including XML schema and validation, JAXB XML binding, XPath Expressions, and XInclude document processing (Chapter 24)
- Introduction to the Eclipse IDE 3.x (Appendix A) and Audience

This book is for computer professionals, students, technical people, and Finnish hackers. It's for everyone who has a need for hands-on experience with the Java language with an eye toward building real applications. This book could also be considered a crash course in object-oriented programming, networking, GUIs, and XML. As you learn about Java, you'll also learn a powerful and practical approach to software development beginning with a deep understanding of the fundamentals of Java and its APIs.

Superficially, Java looks like C or C++, so you'll have a tiny head start in using this book if you have some experience with one of these languages. If you do not, don't worry. Don't make too much of the syntactic similarities between Java and C or C++. In many respects, Java acts like more dynamic languages such as Smalltalk and Lisp. Knowledge of another object-oriented programming language should certainly help, although you may have to change some ideas and unlearn a few habits. Java is considerably simpler than languages such as C++ and Smalltalk. If you learn well from good, concise examples and personal experimentation, we think you'll like this book.

The last part of this book branches out to discuss Java in the context of web applications, web services, and XML processing, so you should be familiar with the basic ideas behind web browsers, servers, and documents.

Using This Book

This book is organized roughly as follows:

- Chapters 1 and 2 provide a basic introduction to Java concepts and a tutorial to give you a jump start on Java programming.
- Chapter 3 discusses fundamental tools for developing with Java (the compiler, the interpreter, and the JAR file package).
- Chapters 4 through 7 describe the Java language itself, beginning with the basic syntax and then covering classes and objects, exceptions, arrays, enumerations, annotations, and much more.
- Chapter 8 covers generics and parameterized types in Java.
- Chapter 9 covers the language's built-in thread facilities and the Java Concurrency package, which should be of particular interest to advanced programmers.
- Chapter 10 covers text processing, formatting, scanning, string utilities, and the powerful regular expressions API.
- Chapter 11 covers much of the core API including utilities and collections.
- Chapter 12 covers Java I/O, streams, files, and the NIO package.
- Chapters 13 and 14 cover Java networking, including sockets and NIO, URLs, and RMI.

- Chapter 15 covers web applications using servlets, servlet filters, and WAR files, as well as web services.

- Chapters 16 through 21 cover GUI development with the Abstract Window Toolkit (AWT) and Swing, which provide graphical user interface (GUI) and image support.

- Chapter 22 covers the JavaBeans™ component architecture and introduces the NetBeans IDE.

- Chapter 23 covers applets, the Java Plug-In, and JAR signing.

- Chapter 24 covers the Java APIs for working with XML and XSLT, including XML Schema, validation, XPath, and XInclude, as well as XML binding with JAXB.

- Appendix A covers using the Eclipse IDE with the examples in this book.

- Appendix B describes BeanShell, a lightweight scripting language for Java that I developed.

If you're like us, you don't read books from front to back. If you're really like us, you usually don't read the Preface at all. However, on the off chance that you will see this in time, here are a few suggestions:

- If you are an experienced programmer who has to learn Java in the next five minutes, you are probably looking for the examples. You might want to start by glancing at the tutorial in Chapter 2. If that doesn't float your boat, you should at least look at the information in Chapter 3, which explains how to use the compiler and interpreter, or Appendix A, which shows how to run the examples in the Eclipse IDE. This should get you started.

- Chapters 12 through 15 are essential if you are interested in writing advanced networked or web-based applications. This is one of the more interesting and important parts of Java.

- Chapters 16 though 22 discuss Java's graphics features and component architecture. You should read this if you are interested in writing graphical Java applications or applets.

- Chapter 23 covers the Applet API, including the Java plug-in for guaranteed browser compatibility and signed applets for advanced applications.

- Chapter 24 covers the Java APIs for working with XML, including SAX, DOM, DTDs, XML Schema, and using XSL to render output for the Web. XML technology is becoming key to cross-platform development. Read this chapter!

On the CD-ROM

The accompanying CD-ROM provides all you need to start working with Java immediately (view CD content online at *http://examples.oreilly.com/learnjava3/CD-ROM/*).

In addition to the full source code for all examples in the book, the CD contains the following software:

- Java 5 Standard Edition (also known as JDK 1.5)
- NetBeans (Version 4.1), a visual IDE for working with JavaBeans
- Eclipse (Version 3.1), one of the most popular Java IDEs
- Ant (Version 1.4.1), a universal Java build system from the Apache Project
- Tomcat (Version 4.0.3), a Java servlet and web services container from the Jakarta Project
- BeanShell (Version 2.0), a simple Java scripting language

Online Resources

There are many online sources for information about Java. Sun Microsystems's official web site for Java topics is *http://java.sun.com*; look here for the software, updates, and Java releases. This is where you'll find the JDK, which includes the compiler, the interpreter, and other tools (the JDK is also on the CD-ROM that comes with this book; view the CD content online at *http://examples.oreilly.com/learnjava3/CD-ROM/*).

You should also visit O'Reilly Media's Java site at *http://java.oreilly.com*. There you'll find information about other O'Reilly Java books, and a pointer to the home page for *Learning Java*, *http://www.oreilly.com/catalog/learnjava3/*, where you'll find the source code examples for this book.

Conventions Used in This Book

The font conventions used in this book are quite simple.

Italic is used for:

- Unix pathnames, filenames, and program names
- Internet addresses, such as domain names and URLs
- New terms where they are defined
- Program names, compilers, interpreters, utilities, and commands
- Threads

Constant width is used for:

- Anything that might appear in a Java program, including method names, variable names, and class names
- Tags that might appear in an HTML or XML document
- Keywords, objects, and environment variables

Constant width bold is used for:

- Text that is typed by the user on the command line

Constant width italic is used for:

- Replaceable items in code

This icon designates a note, which is an important aside to the nearby text.

This icon designates a warning relating to the nearby text.

In the main body of text, we always use a pair of empty parentheses after a method name to distinguish methods from variables and other creatures.

In the Java source listings, we follow the coding conventions most frequently used in the Java community. Class names begin with capital letters; variable and method names begin with lowercase. All the letters in the names of constants are capitalized. We don't use underscores to separate words in a long name; following common practice, we capitalize individual words (after the first) and run the words together. For example: thisIsAVariable, thisIsAMethod( ), ThisIsAClass, and THISISACONSTANT. Also, note that we differentiate between static and nonstatic methods when we refer to them. Unlike some books, we never write Foo.bar( ) to mean the bar( ) method of Foo unless bar( ) is actually static.

Using Code Examples

This book is here to help you get your job done. Generally, you may use the code in this book in your programs and documentation. You do not need to contact us for permission unless you're reproducing a significant portion of the code. For example, writing a program that uses several chunks of code from this book does not require permission. Selling or distributing a CD-ROM of examples from O'Reilly books *does* require permission. Answering a question by citing this book and quoting example code does not require permission. Incorporating a significant amount of example code from this book into your product's documentation *does* require permission.

We appreciate, but do not require, attribution. An attribution usually includes the title, author, publisher, and ISBN. For example: "*Learning Java*, Third Edition by Patrick Niemeyer and Jonathan Knudsen. Copyright 2005 O'Reilly Media, Inc., 0-596-00873-2."

If you feel your use of code examples falls outside fair use or the permission given above, feel free to contact us at *permissions@oreilly.com*.

Safari Enabled

 When you see a Safari® Enabled icon on the cover of your favorite technology book, it means the book is available online through the O'Reilly Network Safari Bookshelf.

Safari offers a solution that's better than e-books. It's a virtual library that lets you easily search thousands of top technology books, cut and paste code samples, download chapters, and find quick answers when you need the most accurate, current information. Try it for free at *http://safari.oreilly.com*.

How to Contact Us

Please address comments and questions concerning this book to the publisher:

O'Reilly Media, Inc.
1005 Gravenstein Highway North
Sebastopol, CA 95472
(800) 998-9938 (in the United States or Canada)
(707) 829-0515 (international or local)
(707) 829-0104 (fax)

We have a web page for this book, where we list errata, examples, or any additional information. You can access this page at:

http://www.oreilly.com/catalog/learnjava3

To comment or ask technical questions about this book, send email to:

bookquestions@oreilly.com

For more information about our books, conferences, Resource Centers, and the O'Reilly Network, see our web site at:

http://www.oreilly.com

Acknowledgments

Many people have contributed to putting this book together, both in its *Exploring Java* incarnation and in its current form as *Learning Java*. Foremost, we would like to thank Tim O'Reilly for giving us the opportunity to write this book. Thanks to Mike Loukides, the series editor, whose patience and experience helped us get started on this journey. Thanks to Paula Ferguson and John Posner, who contributed their organizational and editing abilities at various times. And a special thanks to Deb

Cameron, the tireless editor of this book, without whom the last two editions might never have been finished and certainly wouldn't have resembled English. We could not have asked for a more skillful or responsive team of people with whom to work.

Speaking of borrowings, the original version of the glossary came from David Flanagan's book, *Java in a Nutshell* (O'Reilly). We also borrowed several class hierarchy diagrams from David's book. These diagrams were based on similar diagrams by Charles L. Perkins.

Thanks also to Marc Wallace and Steven Burkett for reading the original work in progress and for the support of our friends at Washington University: Bryan O'Connor and Brian Gottlieb. Thanks also to Josh Peck, coauthor of the original book, *Exploring Java*. Thanks to all those who reviewed or answered questions: David Flanagan for generics; Henry Wong for the concurrency utilities; Jim Elliott, Marc Loy, and Brian Cole for Swing; Jack Shirazi for NIO; Tim Boudreau for NetBeans; Martin Aeschlimann, Jim Farley, and John Norman for Eclipse; Ed Howland for XML; and Ian Darwin for regular expressions. (Check out Ian's *Java Cookbook* [O'Reilly] for more examples.) Thanks also to Ray O'Leary, Mario Aquino, and Mark Volkmann for their reviews. And finally, thanks to my beautiful wife, Song Fang for putting up with me through all this work.

## CHAPTER 1

A Modern Language

The greatest challenges and most exciting opportunities for software developers today lie in harnessing the power of networks. Applications created today, whatever their intended scope or audience, will almost certainly be run on machines linked by a global network of computing resources. The increasing importance of networks is placing new demands on existing tools and fueling the demand for a rapidly growing list of completely new kinds of applications.

We want software that works—consistently, anywhere, on any platform—and that plays well with other applications. We want dynamic applications that take advantage of a connected world, capable of accessing disparate and distributed information sources. We want truly distributed software that can be extended and upgraded seamlessly. We want intelligent applications—such as autonomous agents that can roam the Net for us, ferreting out information and serving as electronic emissaries. We know, to some extent, what we want. So why don't we have it?

The problem, historically, has been that the tools for building these applications have fallen short. The requirements of speed and portability have been, for the most part, mutually exclusive, and security has been largely ignored or misunderstood. In the past, truly portable languages were bulky, interpreted, and slow. These languages were popular as much for their high-level functionality as for their portability. Fast languages usually provided speed by binding themselves to particular platforms, so they met the portability issue only halfway. There were even a few safe languages, but they were primarily offshoots of the portable languages and suffered from the same problems. Java is a modern language that addresses all three of these fronts: portability, speed, and security. This is why it has become dominant in the world of programming today.

Enter Java

The Java programming language, developed at Sun Microsystems under the guidance of Net luminaries James Gosling and Bill Joy, is designed to be a machine-independent programming language that is both safe enough to traverse networks and powerful enough to replace native executable code. Java addresses the issues raised here and helps us start building the kinds of applications we want.

Initially, most of the enthusiasm for Java centered on its capabilities for building embedded applications for the Web called *applets*. But in the early days, applets and other client-side GUI applications written in Java were limited. Today, Java has Swing, one of the most sophisticated toolkits for building graphical user interfaces (GUIs) in any language. This development has allowed Java to become a popular platform for developing traditional client-side application software.

Of even more importance in the past few years, Java has become the premier platform for web-based applications and web services. These applications use technologies including the Java Servlet API, Enterprise JavaBeans™, and many popular open source and commercial Java application servers and frameworks. Java's portability and speed make it the platform of choice for modern business applications.

This book will show you how to use Java to accomplish all of these real-world programming tasks. In the coming chapters we'll cover everything from text processing to networking, building rich client-side GUI applications with Swing and lightweight web-based applications with XML.

Java's Origins

The seeds of Java were planted in 1990 by Sun Microsystems patriarch and chief researcher, Bill Joy. At the time, Sun was competing in a relatively small workstation market while Microsoft was beginning its domination of the more mainstream, Intel-based PC world. When Sun missed the boat on the PC revolution, Joy retreated to Aspen, Colorado to work on advanced research. He was committed to the idea of accomplishing complex tasks with simple software and founded the aptly named Sun Aspen Smallworks.

Of the original members of the small team of programmers assembled in Aspen, James Gosling will be remembered as the father of Java. Gosling first made a name for himself in the early 80s as the author of Gosling Emacs, the first version of the popular Emacs editor that was written in C and ran under Unix. Gosling Emacs became popular but was soon eclipsed by a free version, GNU Emacs, written by Emacs's original designer. By that time, Gosling had moved on to design Sun's NeWS, which briefly contended with the X Window System for control of the Unix GUI desktop in 1987. Although some people would argue that NeWS was superior to X, NeWS lost because Sun kept it proprietary and didn't publish source code while the primary developers of X formed the X Consortium and took the opposite approach.

Designing NeWS taught Gosling the power of integrating an expressive language with a network-aware windowing GUI. It also taught Sun that the Internet programming community will ultimately refuse to accept proprietary standards, no matter how good they may be. The seeds of Java's licensing scheme and open (if not quite "open source") code were sown by NeWS's failure. Gosling brought what he had learned to Bill Joy's nascent Aspen project. In 1992, work on the project led to the founding of the Sun subsidiary, FirstPerson, Inc. Its mission was to lead Sun into the world of consumer electronics.

The FirstPerson team worked on developing software for information appliances, such as cellular phones and personal digital assistants (PDAs). The goal was to enable the transfer of information and real-time applications over cheap infrared and packet-based networks. Memory and bandwidth limitations dictated small, efficient code. The nature of the applications also demanded they be safe and robust. Gosling and his teammates began programming in C++, but they soon found themselves confounded by a language that was too complex, unwieldy, and insecure for the task. They decided to start from scratch, and Gosling began working on something he dubbed "C++ minus minus."

With the foundering of the Apple Newton, it became apparent that the PDA's ship had not yet come in, so Sun shifted FirstPerson's efforts to interactive TV (ITV). The programming language of choice for ITV set-top boxes was to be the near ancestor of Java, a language called Oak. Even with its elegance and ability to provide safe interactivity, Oak could not salvage the lost cause of ITV at that time. Customers didn't want it, and Sun soon abandoned the concept.

At that time, Joy and Gosling got together to decide on a new strategy for their innovative language. It was 1993, and the explosion of interest in the Web presented a new opportunity. Oak was small, safe, architecture-independent, and object-oriented. As it happens, these are also some of the requirements for a universal, Internet-savvy programming language. Sun quickly changed focus, and, with a little retooling, Oak became Java.

Growing Up

It would not be overdoing it to say that Java caught on like wildfire. Even before its first official release when Java was still a nonproduct, nearly every major industry player had jumped on the Java bandwagon. Java licensees included Microsoft, Intel, IBM, and virtually all major hardware and software vendors. That's not to say that everything was easy. Even with all this support, Java took a lot of knocks and had some growing pains during its first few years.

A series of breach of contract and antitrust lawsuits between Sun and Microsoft over the distribution of Java and its use in Internet Explorer has hampered its deployment on the world's most common desktop operating system—Windows. Microsoft's involvement with Java also become one focus of a larger federal lawsuit over serious anticompetitive practices at the company, with court testimony revealing concerted efforts by the software giant to undermine Java by introducing incompatibilities in its version of the language. Meanwhile, Microsoft introduced its own Java-like language called C# (C-sharp) as part of its .NET initiative and dropped Java from inclusion in the latest versions of Windows.

But Java continues to spread on both high- and low-end platforms. As we begin looking at the Java architecture, you'll see that much of what is exciting about Java comes from the self-contained, virtual machine environment in which Java applications run. Java has been carefully designed so that this supporting architecture can be implemented either in software, for existing computer platforms, or in customized hardware, for new kinds of devices. Sun and other industry giants are producing fast Java chips and microprocessors tailored to run media-rich Java applications. Hardware implementations of Java are currently used in smart cards and other embedded systems. Today you can buy "wearable" devices, such as rings and dog tags, that have Java interpreters embedded in them. Software implementations of Java are available for all modern computer platforms down to portable computing devices, such as the popular Palm PDA. Java is also becoming standard equipment on many new cell phones.

A Virtual Machine

Java is both a compiled and an interpreted language. Java source code is turned into simple binary instructions, much like ordinary microprocessor machine code. However, whereas C or C++ source is reduced to native instructions for a particular model of processor, Java source is compiled into a universal format—instructions for a *virtual machine*.

Compiled Java *bytecode* is executed by a Java runtime interpreter. The runtime system performs all the normal activities of a real processor, but it does so in a safe, virtual environment. It executes a stack-based instruction set and manages memory like an operating system. It creates and manipulates primitive data types and loads and invokes newly referenced blocks of code. Most importantly, it does all this in accordance with a strictly defined open specification that can be implemented by anyone who wants to produce a Java-compliant virtual machine. Together, the virtual machine and language definition provide a complete specification. There are no features of the base Java language left undefined or implementation-dependent. For example, Java specifies the sizes and mathematical properties of all its primitive data types rather than leaving it up to the platform implementation.

The Java interpreter is relatively lightweight and small; it can be implemented in whatever form is desirable for a particular platform. The interpreter may be run as a separate application, or it can be embedded in another piece of software, such as a web browser. Put together, this means that Java code is implicitly portable. The same Java application bytecode can run on any platform that provides a Java runtime environment, as shown in Figure 1-1. You don't have to produce alternative versions of your application for different platforms, and you don't have to distribute source code to end users.

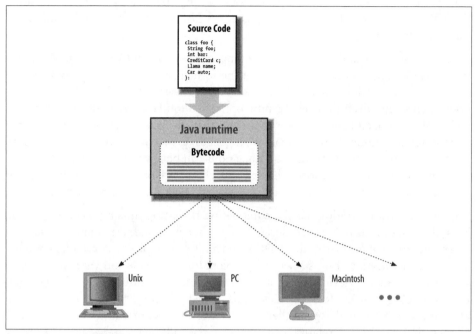

Figure 1-1. The Java runtime environment

The fundamental unit of Java code is the *class*. As in other object-oriented languages, classes are application components that hold executable code and data. Compiled Java classes are distributed in a universal binary format that contains Java bytecode and other class information. Classes can be maintained discretely and stored in files or archives locally or on a network server. Classes are located and loaded dynamically at runtime as they are needed by an application.

In addition to the platform-specific runtime system, Java has a number of fundamental classes that contain architecture-dependent methods. These *native methods* serve as the gateway between the Java virtual machine and the real world. They are implemented in a natively compiled language on the host platform and provide low-level access to resources such as the network, the windowing system, and the host filesystem. The vast majority of Java, however, is written in Java itself—bootstrapped from these basic primitives—and is therefore portable. This includes fundamental Java tools such as the Java compiler, web browser components, and the sophisticated GUI libraries, which are also written in Java and are therefore available on all Java platforms in exactly the same way without porting.

Historically, interpreters have been considered slow, but Java is not a traditional interpreted language. In addition to compiling source code down to portable bytecode,

Java has also been carefully designed so that software implementations of the runtime system can further optimize their performance by compiling bytecode to native machine code on the fly. This is called just-in-time (JIT) or dynamic compilation. With JIT compilation, Java code can execute as fast as native code and maintain its transportability and security.

This is an often misunderstood point among those who want to compare language performance. There is only one intrinsic performance penalty that compiled Java code suffers at runtime for the sake of security and virtual machine design—array bounds checking. Everything else can be optimized to native code just as it can with a statically compiled language. Going beyond that, the Java language includes more structural information than many other languages, providing more room for optimizations. Also remember that these optimizations can be made at runtime, taking into account the actual application behavior and characteristics. What can be done at compile time that can't be done better at runtime? Well, there is a tradeoff: time.

The problem with a traditional JIT compilation is that optimizing code takes time. So a JIT compiler can produce decent results but may suffer a significant latency when the application starts up. This is generally not a problem for long-running server-side applications but is a serious problem for client-side software and applications run on smaller devices with limited capabilities. To address this, Sun's compiler technology, called HotSpot, uses a trick called *adaptive compilation*. If you look at what programs actually spend their time doing, it turns out that they spend almost all their time executing a relatively small part of the code again and again. The chunk of code that is executed repeatedly may be only a small fraction of the total program, but its behavior determines the program's overall performance. Adaptive compilation also allows the Java runtime to take advantage of new kinds of optimizations that simply can't be done in a statically compiled language, hence the claim that Java code can run faster than C/C++ in some cases.

To take advantage of this fact, HotSpot starts out as a normal Java bytecode interpreter, but with a difference: it measures (profiles) the code as it is executing to see what parts are being executed repeatedly. Once it knows which parts of the code are crucial to performance, HotSpot compiles those sections into optimal native machine code. Since it compiles only a small portion of the program into machine code, it can afford to take the time necessary to optimize those portions. The rest of the program may not need to be compiled at all—just interpreted—saving memory and time. In fact, Sun's default Java VM can run in one of two modes: client and server, which tell it whether to emphasize quick startup time and memory conservation or flat out performance.

A natural question to ask at this point is, Why throw away all this good profiling information each time an application shuts down? Well, Sun has partially broached this topic with the release of Java 5.0 through the use of shared, read-only classes that are stored persistently in an optimized form. This significantly reduces both the startup time and overhead of running many Java applications on a given machine.

The technology for doing this is complex, but the idea is simple: optimize the parts of the program that need to go fast, and don't worry about the rest.

Java Compared with Other Languages

Java is a relatively new language, but it draws on many years of programming experience with other languages in its choice of features. It is worth taking a moment to compare Java at a high level with some other popular languages today, both for the benefit of those of you with other programming experience and for the newcomers who need to put things in context. We do not expect you to have a knowledge of any particular programming language in this book and when we refer to other languages by way of comparison we hope that the comments are self-explanatory.

At least three pillars are necessary to support a universal programming language today: portability, speed, and security. Figure 1-2 shows how Java compares to a couple of other languages.

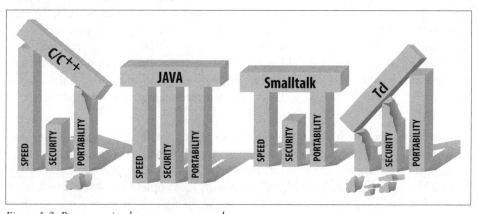

Figure 1-2. Programming languages compared

You may have heard that Java is a lot like C or C++, but that's really not true, except at a superficial level. When you first look at Java code, you'll see that the basic syntax looks like C or C++. But that's where the similarities end. Java is by no means a direct descendant of C or a next-generation C++. If you compare language features, you'll see that Java actually has more in common with highly dynamic languages such as Smalltalk and Lisp. In fact, Java's implementation is about as far from native C as you can imagine.

The surface-level similarities to these languages are worth noting, however. Java borrows heavily from C and C++ syntax, so you'll see terse language constructs, including an abundance of curly braces and semicolons. Java subscribes to the C philosophy that a good language should be compact; in other words, it should be sufficiently small and regular so a programmer can hold all the language's capabilities in his or her head at once. Just as C is extensible with libraries, packages of Java classes can be added to the core language components to extend its vocabulary.

C has been successful because it provides a reasonably feature-packed programming environment, with high performance and an acceptable degree of portability. Java also tries to balance functionality, speed, and portability, but it does so in a very different way. C trades functionality for portability; Java initially traded speed for portability. Java also addresses security issues while C doesn't.

In the early days before JIT and adaptive compilation, Java was slower than statically compiled languages and there was a constant refrain from detractors that it would never catch up. But as we described in the previous section, Java's performance is now comparable to C or C++ for equivalent tasks and those criticisms have generally fallen quiet. In fact, in 2004, ID Software's open source Quake2 video game engine was ported to Java. If Java is fast enough for first-person-shooter video games, it's certainly fast enough for business applications.

Scripting languages, such as Perl, Python, and Ruby, are very popular, and for good reason. There's no reason a scripting language can't be suitable for safe, networked applications. But most scripting languages are not designed for serious, large-scale programming. The attraction to scripting languages is that they are dynamic; they are powerful tools for rapid development. Some scripting languages such as Perl also provide powerful tools for text-processing tasks that more general-purpose languages find unwieldy. Scripting languages are also highly portable, albeit at the source-code level.

Not to be confused with Java, JavaScript is an object-based scripting language originally developed by Netscape for the web browser. It serves as a glue and an "in the document" language for dynamic, interactive HTML-based applications. JavaScript takes its name from its intended integration with Java applets and some similarity in syntax, but the comparison really ends there. While there have been applications of JavaScript outside of the browser, it has never really caught on as a general scripting language. For more information on JavaScript, check out *JavaScript: The Definitive Guide* by David Flanagan (O'Reilly).

The problem with scripting languages is that they are rather casual about program structure and data typing. Most scripting languages (with a hesitant exception for Python and later versions of Perl) are not object-oriented. They also have vastly simplified type systems and generally don't provide for sophisticated scoping of variables and functions. These characteristics make them unsuitable for building large, modular applications. Speed is another problem with scripting languages; the high-level, fully interpreted nature of these languages often makes them quite slow.

Advocates of individual scripting languages would take issue with some of these generalizations and no doubt they'd be right in some cases—scripting languages are growing up. But the fundamental tradeoff is undeniable: scripting languages were born as loose, less structured alternatives to systems programming languages and are generally not as suitable for large or complex projects for a variety of reasons, at least not today.

Java offers some of the essential advantages of a scripting language (it is highly dynamic), along with the added benefits of a lower-level language. Java 1.4 added a powerful Regular Expression API that competes with Perl for working with text and Java 5.0 has introduced new language features that streamline coding, such as "foreach"-style iteration over collections, variable argument lists, autoboxing and unboxing of primitives, and static imports of methods.

Incremental development with object-oriented components, combined with Java's simplicity, make it possible to develop applications rapidly and change them easily. Studies have found that development in Java is faster than in C or C++, strictly based on language features.[*] Java also comes with a large base of standard core classes for common tasks such as building GUIs and handling network communications. But along with these features, Java has the scalability and software-engineering advantages of more static languages. It provides a safe structure on which to build higher-level frameworks (and even other languages).

As we've already said, Java is similar in design to languages such as Smalltalk and Lisp. However, these languages are currently used mostly as research vehicles rather than for development of large-scale systems. One reason is that these languages never developed a standard portable binding to operating-system services, such as the C standard library or the Java core classes. Smalltalk is compiled to an interpreted bytecode format, and it can be dynamically compiled to native code on the fly, just like Java. But Java improves on the design by using a bytecode verifier to ensure the correctness of compiled Java code. This verifier gives Java a performance advantage over Smalltalk because Java code requires fewer runtime checks. Java's bytecode verifier also helps with security issues, something that Smalltalk doesn't address. Smalltalk is a mature language, though, and Java's designers took lessons from many of its features.

Throughout the rest of this chapter, we'll present a bird's-eye view of the Java language. We'll explain what's new and what's not-so-new about Java and why.

Safety of Design

You have no doubt heard a lot about the fact that Java is designed to be a safe language. But what do we mean by safe? Safe from what or whom? The security features that attract the most attention for Java are those features that make possible

---

[*] See, for example, G. Phipps, "Comparing Observed Bug and Productivity Rates for Java and C++," *Software—Practice & Experience*, Volume 29, 1999 (*http://www.spirus.com.au/papersAndTalks/javaVsC++.pdf*).

new types of dynamically portable software. Java provides several layers of protection from dangerously flawed code as well as more mischievous things such as viruses and Trojan horses. In the next section, we'll take a look at how the Java virtual machine architecture assesses the safety of code before it's run and how the Java *class loader* (the bytecode loading mechanism of the Java interpreter) builds a wall around untrusted classes. These features provide the foundation for high-level security policies that can allow or disallow various kinds of activities on an application-by-application basis.

In this section, though, we'll look at some general features of the Java programming language. Perhaps more important than the specific security features, although often overlooked in the security din, is the safety that Java provides by addressing common design and programming problems. Java is intended to be as safe as possible from the simple mistakes we make ourselves as well as those we inherit from legacy software. The goal with Java has been to keep the language simple, provide tools that have demonstrated their usefulness, and let users build more complicated facilities on top of the language when needed.

Simplify, Simplify, Simplify...

With Java, simplicity rules. Since Java started with a clean slate, it was able to avoid features that proved to be messy or controversial in other languages. For example, Java doesn't allow programmer-defined operator overloading (which in some languages allows programmers to redefine the meaning of basic symbols like + and -). Java doesn't have a source code preprocessor, so it doesn't have things like macros, #define statements, or conditional source compilation. These constructs exist in other languages primarily to support platform dependencies, so in that sense, they should not be needed in Java. Conditional compilation is also commonly used for debugging, but Java's sophisticated runtime optimizations and features such as *assertions* solve the problem more elegantly (we'll cover these in Chapter 4).

Java provides a well-defined *package* structure for organizing class files. The package system allows the compiler to handle some of the functionality of the traditional *make* utility (a tool for building executables from source code). The compiler can also work with compiled Java classes directly because all type information is preserved; there is no need for extraneous source "header" files, as in C/C++. All this means that Java code requires less context to read. Indeed, you may sometimes find it faster to look at the Java source code than to refer to class documentation.

Java also takes a different approach to some structural features that have been troublesome in other languages. For example, Java supports only a single inheritance class hierarchy (each class may have only one "parent" class) but allows multiple inheritance of interfaces. An *interface*, like an abstract class in C++, specifies the behavior of an object without defining its implementation. It is a very powerful mechanism that allows the developer to define a "contract" for object behavior that can be used and referred to independently of any particular object implementation. Interfaces in Java eliminate the need for multiple inheritance of classes and the associated problems.

It is only after many years of debate that, in Java 5.0, some major new language features have been added to the language. The latest release of Java added *generics*, which are an abstraction that allows Java classes to work with different types in a safe way that the compiler can understand. While generics can hardly be considered simple, their common usage and effect on the language will make code more maintainable and easier to read. Providing this without a major complication of the language has been an accomplishment.

As you'll see in Chapter 4, Java is a fairly simple and elegant programming language and that is still a large part of its appeal.

Type Safety and Method Binding

One attribute of a language is the kind of type checking it uses. Generally, languages are categorized as *static* or *dynamic*, which refers to the amount of information about variables known at compile time versus what is known while the application is running.

In a strictly statically typed language such as C or C++, data types are etched in stone when the source code is compiled. The compiler benefits from this by having enough information to catch many kinds of errors before the code is executed. For example, the compiler would not allow you to store a floating-point value in an integer variable. The code then doesn't require runtime type checking, so it can be compiled to be small and fast. But statically typed languages are inflexible. They don't support high-level constructs such as lists and collections as naturally as languages with dynamic type checking, and they make it impossible for an application to safely import new data types while it's running.

In contrast, a dynamic language such as Smalltalk or Lisp has a runtime system that manages the types of objects and performs necessary type checking while an application is executing. These kinds of languages allow for more complex behavior and are in many respects more powerful. However, they are also generally slower, less safe, and harder to debug.

The differences in languages have been likened to the differences among kinds of automobiles.* Statically typed languages such as C++ are analogous to a sports car—reasonably safe and fast—but useful only if you're driving on a nicely paved road. Highly dynamic languages such as Smalltalk are more like an off-road vehicle: they afford you more freedom but can be somewhat unwieldy. It can be fun (and sometimes faster) to

---

* The credit for the car analogy goes to Marshall P. Cline, author of the C++ FAQ.

go roaring through the back woods, but you might also get stuck in a ditch or mauled by bears.

Another attribute of a language is the way it binds method calls to their definitions. In a static language such as C or C++, the definitions of methods are normally bound at compile time, unless the programmer specifies otherwise. Languages like Smalltalk, on the other hand, are called "late binding" because they locate the definitions of methods dynamically at runtime. Early binding is important for performance reasons; an application can run without the overhead incurred by searching for methods at runtime. But late binding is more flexible. It's also necessary in an object-oriented language where new types can be loaded dynamically and only the runtime system can determine which method to run.

Java provides some of the benefits of both C++ and Smalltalk; it's a statically typed, late-binding language. Every object in Java has a well-defined type that is known at compile time. This means the Java compiler can do the same kind of static type checking and usage analysis as C++. As a result, you can't assign an object to the wrong type of variable or call nonexistent methods on an object. The Java compiler goes even further and prevents you from using uninitialized variables and creating unreachable statements (see Chapter 4).

However, Java is fully runtime-typed as well. The Java runtime system keeps track of all objects and makes it possible to determine their types and relationships during execution. This means you can inspect an object at runtime to determine what it is. Unlike C or C++, casts from one type of object to another are checked by the runtime system, and it's possible to use new kinds of dynamically loaded objects with a level of type safety. And since Java is a late-binding language, it's always possible for a subclass to override methods in its superclass, even a subclass loaded at runtime.

Incremental Development

Java carries all data-type and method-signature information with it from its source code to its compiled bytecode form. This means that Java classes can be developed incrementally. Your own Java source code can also be compiled safely with classes from other sources your compiler has never seen. In other words, you can write new code that references binary class files without losing the type safety you gain from having the source code.

Java does not suffer from the "fragile base class" problem. In languages such as C++, the implementation of a base class can be effectively frozen because it has many derived classes; changing the base class may require recompilation of all of the derived classes. This is an especially difficult problem for developers of class libraries. Java avoids this problem by dynamically locating fields within classes. As long as a class maintains a valid form of its original structure, it can evolve without breaking other classes that are derived from it or that make use of it.

Dynamic Memory Management

Some of the most important differences between Java and lower-level languages such as C and C++ involve how Java manages memory. Java eliminates ad hoc "pointers" that can reference arbitrary areas of memory and adds object garbage collection and high-level arrays to the language. These features eliminate many otherwise insurmountable problems with safety, portability, and optimization.

Garbage collection alone has saved countless programmers from the single largest source of programming errors in C or C++: explicit memory allocation and deallocation. In addition to maintaining objects in memory, the Java runtime system keeps track of all references to those objects. When an object is no longer in use, Java automatically removes it from memory. You can, for the most part, simply ignore objects you no longer use, with confidence that the interpreter will clean them up at an appropriate time.

Java uses a sophisticated garbage collector that runs intermittently in the background, which means that most garbage collecting takes place during idle times, between I/O pauses, mouse clicks, or keyboard hits. Advanced runtime systems, such as HotSpot, have more advanced garbage collection that can differentiate the usage patterns of objects (such as short-lived versus long-lived) and optimize their collection. The Java runtime can now tune itself automatically for the optimal distribution of memory for different kinds of applications, based on their behavior. With this kind of runtime profiling, automatic memory management can be much faster than the most diligently programmer-managed resources, something that some people still find hard to believe.

We've said that Java doesn't have pointers. Strictly speaking, this statement is true, but it's also misleading. What Java provides are references—a safe kind of pointer—and Java is rife with them. A reference is a strongly typed handle for an object. All objects in Java, with the exception of primitive numeric types, are accessed through references. You can use references to build all the normal kinds of data structures a C programmer would be accustomed to building with pointers, such as linked lists, trees, and so forth. The only difference is that with references you have to do so in a typesafe way.

Another important difference between a reference and a pointer is that you can't play games (pointer arithmetic) with references to change their values; they can point only to specific objects or elements of an array. A reference is an atomic thing; you can't manipulate the value of a reference except by assigning it to an object. References are passed by value, and you can't reference an object through more than a single level of indirection. The protection of references is one of the most fundamental aspects of Java security. It means that Java code has to play by the rules; it can't peek into places it shouldn't.

Java references can point only to class types. There are no pointers to methods. People sometimes complain about this missing feature, but you will find that tasks that call for pointers to methods can be accomplished more cleanly using interfaces and adapter classes instead. We should also mention that Java has a sophisticated Reflection API that actually allows you to reference and invoke individual methods. However this is not the normal way of doing things. We discuss reflection in Chapter 7.

Finally, we should mention that arrays in Java are true, first-class objects. They can be dynamically allocated and assigned like other objects. Arrays know their own size and type, and although you can't directly define or subclass array classes, they do have a well-defined inheritance relationship based on the relationship of their base types. Having true arrays in the language alleviates much of the need for pointer arithmetic, such as that used in C or C++.

Error Handling

Java's roots are in networked devices and embedded systems. For these applications, it's important to have robust and intelligent error management. Java has a powerful exception-handling mechanism, somewhat like that in newer implementations of C++. Exceptions provide a more natural and elegant way to handle errors. Exceptions allow you to separate error-handling code from normal code, which makes for cleaner, more readable applications.

When an exception occurs, it causes the flow of program execution to be transferred to a predesignated "catcher" block of code. The exception carries with it an object that contains information about the situation that caused the exception. The Java compiler requires that a method either declare the exceptions it can generate or catch and deal with them itself. This promotes error information to the same level of importance as argument and return types for methods. As a Java programmer, you know precisely what exceptional conditions you must deal with, and you have help from the compiler in writing correct software that doesn't leave them unhandled.

Threads

Today's applications require a high degree of parallelism. Even a very single-minded application can have a complex user interface—which requires concurrent activities. As machines get faster, users become more sensitive to waiting for unrelated tasks that seize control of their time. Threads provide efficient multiprocessing and distribution of tasks for both client and server applications. Java makes threads easy to use because support for them is built into the language.

Concurrency is nice, but there's more to programming with threads than just performing multiple tasks simultaneously. In most cases, threads need to be synchronized, which can be tricky without explicit language support. Java supports synchronization based on the *monitor* and *condition* model—a sort of lock and key system for accessing resources. The keyword synchronized designates methods and blocks of code for safe, serialized access within an object. There are also simple, primitive methods for explicit waiting and signaling between threads interested in the same object.

Java 5.0 introduced a new high-level concurrency package. This package provides powerful utilities that address common patterns in multithreaded programming, such as thread pools, coordination of tasks, and sophisticated locking. With the addition of the concurrency package, Java now provides some of the most advanced thread-related utilities of any language.

Although some developers may never have to write multithreaded code, learning to program with threads is an important part of mastering programming in Java and something all developers should grasp. See Chapter 9 for a discussion of this topic. For complete coverage of threads, refer to *Java Threads* by Scott Oaks and Henry Wong (O'Reilly).

Scalability

At the lowest level, Java programs consist of *classes*. Classes are intended to be small, modular components. They can be separated physically on different systems, retrieved dynamically, stored in a compressed format, and even cached in various distribution schemes. Over classes, Java provides *packages*, a layer of structure that groups classes into functional units. Packages provide a naming convention for organizing classes and a second tier of organizational control over the visibility of variables and methods in Java applications.

Within a package, a class is either publicly visible or protected from outside access. Packages form another type of scope that is closer to the application level. This lends itself to building reusable components that work together in a system. Packages also help in designing a scalable application that can grow without becoming a bird's nest of tightly coupled code.

Safety of Implementation

It's one thing to create a language that prevents you from shooting yourself in the foot; it's quite another to create one that prevents others from shooting you in the foot.

Encapsulation is the concept of hiding data and behavior within a class; it's an important part of object-oriented design. It helps you write clean, modular software. In most languages, however, the visibility of data items is simply part of the relationship between the programmer and the compiler. It's a matter of semantics, not an assertion about the actual security of the data in the context of the running program's environment.

When Bjarne Stroustrup chose the keyword private to designate hidden members of classes in C++, he was probably thinking about shielding you from the messy details of a class developer's code, not the issues of shielding that developer's classes and objects from attack by someone else's viruses and Trojan horses. Arbitrary casting and pointer arithmetic in C or C++ make it trivial to violate access permissions on classes without breaking the rules of the language. Consider the following code:

```
// C++ code
class Finances {
    private:
        char creditCardNumber[16];
        ...
};

main( ) {
    Finances finances;

    // Forge a pointer to peek inside the class
    char *cardno = (char *)&finances;
    printf("Card Number = %s\n", cardno);
}
```

In this little C++ drama, we have written some code that violates the encapsulation of the Finances class and pulls out some secret information. This sort of shenanigan—abusing an untyped pointer—is not possible in Java. If this example seems unrealistic, consider how important it is to protect the foundation (system) classes of the runtime environment from similar kinds of attacks. If untrusted code can corrupt the components that provide access to real resources, such as the filesystem, the network, or the windowing system, it certainly has a chance at stealing your credit card numbers.

If a Java application is to be able to dynamically download code from an untrusted source on the Internet and run it alongside applications that might contain confidential information, protection has to extend very deep. The Java security model wraps three layers of protection around imported classes, as shown in Figure 1-3.

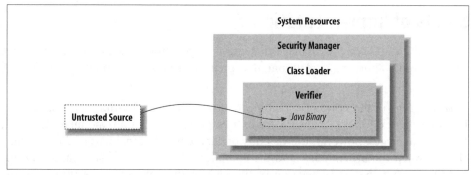

Figure 1-3. The Java security model

At the outside, application-level security decisions are made by a security manager in conjunction with a flexible security policy. A security manager controls access to system resources such as the filesystem, network ports, and the windowing environment. A security manager relies on the ability of a class loader to protect basic system classes. A class loader handles loading classes from local storage or the network. At the innermost level, all system security ultimately rests on the Java verifier, which guarantees the integrity of incoming classes.

The Java bytecode verifier is a fixed part of the Java runtime system. Class loaders and security managers (or *security policies* to be more precise), however, are components that may be implemented differently by different applications, such as applet viewers and web browsers. All three of these pieces need to be functioning properly to ensure security in the Java environment.*

The Verifier

Java's first line of defense is the *bytecode verifier*. The verifier reads bytecode before it is run and makes sure it is well-behaved and obeys the basic rules of the Java language. A trusted Java compiler won't produce code that does otherwise. However, it's possible for a mischievous person to deliberately assemble bad code. It's the verifier's job to detect this.

Once code has been verified, it's considered safe from certain inadvertent or malicious errors. For example, verified code can't forge references or violate access permissions on objects (as in our credit card example). It can't perform illegal casts or use objects in unintended ways. It can't even cause certain types of internal errors, such as overflowing or underflowing the operand stack. These fundamental guarantees underlie all of Java's security.

You might be wondering, isn't this kind of safety implicit in lots of interpreted languages? Well, while it's true that you shouldn't be able to corrupt the interpreter with bogus BASIC code, remember that the protection in most interpreted languages happens at a higher level. Those languages are likely to have heavyweight interpreters that do a great deal of runtime work, so they are necessarily slower and more cumbersome.

By comparison, Java bytecode is a relatively light, low-level instruction set. The ability to statically verify the Java bytecode before execution lets the Java interpreter run at full speed with full safety, without expensive runtime checks. This is what is fundamentally new about Java.

---

* You may have seen reports about various security flaws in Java. While these weaknesses are real, it's important to realize that they have been found in the various implementations of components, namely Sun's, Netscape's, and Microsoft's Java virtual machines, not in the basic security model itself. One of the reasons Sun has released the source code for Java is to encourage people to search for weaknesses so that they can be removed.

The verifier is a type of mathematical "theorem prover." It steps through the Java bytecode and applies simple, inductive rules to determine certain aspects of how the bytecode will behave. This kind of analysis is possible because compiled Java bytecode contains a lot more type information than the object code of other languages of this kind. The bytecode also has to obey a few extra rules that simplify its behavior. First, most bytecode instructions operate only on individual data types. For example, with stack operations, there are separate instructions for object references and for each of the numeric types in Java. Similarly, there is a different instruction for moving each type of value into and out of a local variable.

Second, the type of object resulting from any operation is always known in advance. No bytecode operations consume values and produce more than one possible type of value as output. As a result, it's always possible to look at the next instruction and its operands and know the type of value that will result.

Because an operation always produces a known type, by looking at the starting state it's possible to determine the types of all items on the stack and in local variables at any point in the future. The collection of all this type information at any given time is called the *type state* of the stack; this is what Java tries to analyze before it runs an application. Java doesn't know anything about the actual values of stack and variable items at this time, just what kind of items they are. However, this is enough information to enforce the security rules and to ensure that objects are not manipulated illegally.

To make it feasible to analyze the type state of the stack, Java places an additional restriction on how Java bytecode instructions are executed: all paths to the same point in the code have to arrive with exactly the same type state.*

Class Loaders

Java adds a second layer of security with a *class loader*. A class loader is responsible for bringing the bytecode for Java classes into the interpreter. Every application that loads classes from the network must use a class loader to handle this task.

After a class has been loaded and passed through the verifier, it remains associated with its class loader. As a result, classes are effectively partitioned into separate namespaces based on their origin. When a loaded class references another class

---

* The implications of this rule are of interest mainly to compiler writers. The rule means that Java bytecode can't perform certain types of iterative actions within a single frame of execution. A common example would be looping and pushing values onto the stack. This is not allowed because the path of execution would return to the top of the loop with a potentially different type state on each pass, and there is no way that a static analysis of the code can determine whether it obeys the security rules. This restriction makes it possible for the verifier to trace each branch of the code just once and still know the type state at all points. Thus, the verifier can ensure that instruction types and stack value types always correspond, without actually following the execution of the code. For a more thorough explanation of all this, see *The Java Virtual Machine* by Jon Meyer and Troy Downing (O'Reilly).

---

name, the location of the new class is provided by the original class loader. This means that classes retrieved from a specific source can be restricted to interact only with other classes retrieved from that same location. For example, a Java-enabled web browser can use a class loader to build a separate space for all the classes loaded from a given URL. Sophisticated security based on cryptographically signed classes can also be implemented using class loaders.

The search for classes always begins with the built-in Java system classes. These classes are loaded from the locations specified by the Java interpreter's *classpath* (see Chapter 3). Classes in the classpath are loaded by the system only once and can't be replaced. This means that it's impossible for an applet to replace fundamental system classes with its own versions that change their functionality.

Security Managers

A *security manager* is responsible for making application-level security decisions. A security manager is an object that can be installed by an application to restrict access to system resources. The security manager is consulted every time the application tries to access items such as the filesystem, network ports, external processes, and the windowing environment; the security manager can allow or deny the request.

Security managers are primarily of interest to applications that run untrusted code as part of their normal operation. For example, a Java-enabled web browser can run applets that may be retrieved from untrusted sources on the Net. Such a browser needs to install a security manager as one of its first actions. This security manager then restricts the kinds of access allowed after that point. This lets the application impose an effective level of trust before running an arbitrary piece of code. And once a security manager is installed, it can't be replaced.

In recent versions of Java, the security manager works in conjunction with an access controller that lets you implement security policies at a high level by editing a declarative security policy file. Access policies can be as simple or complex as a particular application warrants. Sometimes it's sufficient simply to deny access to all resources or to general categories of services, such as the filesystem or network. But it's also possible to make sophisticated decisions based on high-level information. For example, a Java-enabled web browser could use an access policy that lets users specify how much an applet is to be trusted or that allows or denies access to specific resources on a case-by-case basis. Of course, this assumes that the browser can determine which applets it ought to trust. We'll see how this problem is solved shortly.

The integrity of a security manager is based on the protection afforded by the lower levels of the Java security model. Without the guarantees provided by the verifier and the class loader, high-level assertions about the safety of system resources are meaningless. The safety provided by the Java bytecode verifier means that the interpreter can't be corrupted or subverted and that Java code has to use components as they are intended. This, in turn, means that a class loader can guarantee that an application is using the core Java system classes and that these classes are the only way to access basic system resources. With these restrictions in place, it's possible to centralize control over those resources at a high level with a security manager and user-defined policy.

Application and User-Level Security

There's a fine line between having enough power to do something useful and having all the power to do anything you want. Java provides the foundation for a secure environment in which untrusted code can be quarantined, managed, and safely executed. However, unless you are content with keeping that code in a little black box and running it just for its own benefit, you will have to grant it access to at least some system resources so that it can be useful. Every kind of access carries with it certain risks and benefits. For example, in the web browser environment, the advantages of granting an untrusted (unknown) applet access to your windowing system are that it can display information and let you interact in a useful way. The associated risks are that the applet may instead display something worthless, annoying, or offensive. Since most people can accept that level of risk, graphical applets and the Web in general are possible.

At one extreme, the simple act of running an application gives it a resource—computation time—that it may put to good use or burn frivolously. It's difficult to prevent an untrusted application from wasting your time or even attempting a "denial of service" attack. At the other extreme, a powerful, trusted application may justifiably deserve access to all sorts of system resources (e.g., the filesystem, process creation, network interfaces); a malicious application could wreak havoc with these resources. The message here is that important and sometimes complex security issues have to be addressed.

In some situations, it may be acceptable to simply ask the user to "okay" requests. With Sun's Java plug-in, web browsers can pop up a dialog box and ask the user's permission for an applet to access an otherwise restricted file. However, we can put only so much burden on our users. An experienced person will quickly grow tired of answering questions; an inexperienced user may not be able to answer the questions correctly. Is it okay for me to grant an applet access to something if I don't understand what that is?

Making decisions about what is dangerous and what is not can be difficult. Even ostensibly harmless access, such as displaying a window, can become a threat when paired with the ability of an untrusted application to communicate from your host. The Java Security Manager provides an option to flag windows created by an untrusted application with a special, recognizable border to prevent it from impersonating another application and perhaps tricking you into revealing your password or your secret recipe collection. There is also a grey area, in which an application can do devious things that aren't quite destructive. An applet that can mail a bug report can also mail-bomb your boss. The Java language provides the tools to implement whatever security policies you want. However, what these policies will be ultimately depends on who you are, what you are doing, and where you are doing it.

Signing Classes

Web browsers that run Java applets start by defining a few rules and some coarse levels of security that restrict where applets may come from and what system resources they may access. These rules are sufficient to keep a malicious applet from attacking you, but they aren't sufficient for applications you'd like to trust with sensitive information. To fully exploit the power of Java, we need to have some nontechnical basis on which to make reasonable decisions about what a program can be allowed to do. This nontechnical basis is trust; basically, you trust certain entities not to do anything that's harmful to you. For a home user, this may mean that you trust the "Bank of Boofa" to distribute applets that let you transfer funds between your accounts, or you may trust L.L. Bean to distribute an applet that debits your Visa account. For a company, this may mean you trust applets originating behind your firewall and perhaps applets from a few high-priority customers to modify internal databases. In all these cases, you don't need to know in detail what the program is going to do and give it permission for each operation. You only need to know that you trust the source.

This doesn't mean that there isn't a technical aspect to the problem of trust. Trusting your local bank when you walk up to the ATM means one thing; trusting some web page that claims to come from your local bank means something else entirely. It would be very difficult to impersonate the ATM two blocks down the street (though it has been known to happen), but, depending on your position on the Net, it's not all that difficult to impersonate a web site or to intercept data coming from a legitimate web site and substitute your own.

That's where cryptography comes in. *Digital signatures*, together with certificates, are techniques for verifying that data truly comes from the source it claims to have come from and hasn't been modified en route. If the Bank of Boofa signs its checkbook applet, your browser can verify that the applet actually came from the bank, not an imposter, and hasn't been modified. Therefore, you can tell your browser to trust applets that have the Bank of Boofa's signature. Java supports digital signatures; some of the details are covered in Chapter 23.

Java and the Web

The application-level safety features of Java make it possible to develop new kinds of applications that were not feasible before. A web browser that uses the Java runtime system can incorporate Java applets as executable content inside documents. This means that web pages can contain not only static textual information but also full-fledged interactive applications. The added potential for use of the Web is enormous. A user can retrieve and use software simply by navigating with a web browser. Formerly static information can be paired with portable software for interpreting and using the information. Instead of just providing some data for a spreadsheet, for example, a web document might contain a fully functional spreadsheet application embedded within it that allows users to view and manipulate the information. In recent years, some of this has started to happen, but the full potential has not yet been realized.

In addition to applets, a more recent model for Internet downloadable application content is Java Web Start. The Web Start API allows your web browser to install applications locally, with security still enforced by the Java runtime system. This system can also automatically update the software when it is used. We'll discuss this more in Chapter 23.

Applets

The term "applet" is used to mean a small, subordinate, or embeddable application. By "embeddable," we mean it's designed to be run and used within the context of a larger system. In that sense, most programs are embedded within a computer's operating system. An operating system manages its native applications in a variety of ways: it starts, stops, suspends, and synchronizes applications; it provides them with certain standard resources; and it protects them from one another by partitioning their environments.

As far as the web browser model is concerned, an applet is just another type of object to display; it's embedded into an HTML page with a special tag. Java-enabled web browsers can execute applets directly, in the context of a particular document, as shown in Figure 1-4. Browsers can also implement this feature using Sun's Java Plug-in, which runs Java just like other browser plug-ins display other kinds of content.

A Java applet is a compiled Java program, composed of classes just like any Java program. While a simple applet may consist of only a single class, most large applets consist of many classes. Classes may be stored in separate files on the server, allowing them to be retrieved as needed, but more generally they are packaged together into archives. Java defines a standard archive format—the JAR file—which is built on the common ZIP archive format.

An applet has a four-part life cycle. When an applet is initially loaded by a web browser, it's asked to initialize itself. The applet is then informed each time it's displayed and each time it's no longer visible to the user. Finally, the applet is told when it's no longer needed, so that it can clean up after itself. During its lifetime, an applet

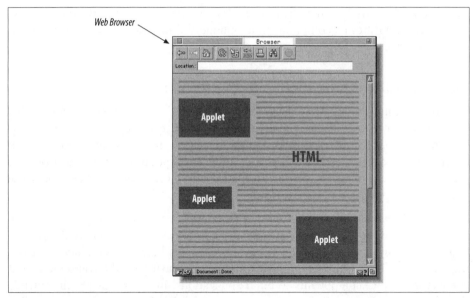

Figure 1-4. Applets in a web document

may start and suspend itself, do work, communicate with other applications, and interact with the web browser.

Applets are autonomous programs, but they are confined within the walls of a web browser or applet viewer and have to play by its rules. We'll be discussing the details of what applets can and can't do as we explore features of the Java language. However, under the most conservative security policies, an applet can interact only with the user and can communicate over the network only with the host from which it originated. Other types of activities, such as accessing files or interacting directly with outside applications, are typically prevented by the security manager that is part of the web browser or applet viewer. But aside from these restrictions, there is no fundamental difference between a Java applet and a standalone Java application.

New Kinds of Media

When it was first released, Java quickly achieved a reputation for multimedia capabilities. Frankly, this wasn't really deserved. At that point, Java provided facilities for doing simple animations and playing audio (which was leaps and bounds beyond static web pages). You could animate and play audio simultaneously, though you couldn't synchronize the two. Still, this was a significant advance for the Web, and people thought it was pretty impressive.

Java's multimedia capabilities have now taken shape. Java now has CD-quality sound, 3D animation, media players that synchronize audio and video, speech synthesis and recognition, and more. The Java Media Framework now supports most common audio and video file formats; the Java Sound API (part of the core classes) can record sound from a computer's microphone and play or record MIDI for musical instruments.

New Software Development Models

For many years, people have been using integrated development environments (IDEs) to create user interfaces. Some of these environments let you generate applications by moving components around on the screen, connecting components to each other, and so on. In short, designing a part of an application becomes a lot more like drawing a picture than like writing code. (Usually these tools also help you write code in the more traditional sense as well.)

For visual development environments to work well, you need to be able to create reusable software components. That's what the JavaBeans architecture is all about: it defines a way to package software as reusable building blocks. A graphical development tool can figure out a component's capabilities, customize the component, and connect it to other components to build applications. In theory, JavaBeans extends the idea of graphical development a step further. JavaBeans components, called beans, aren't limited to visible, user interface components: you can have beans that are entirely invisible and whose job is purely computational. For example, you can have a bean that does database access; you can connect this to a bean that lets the user request information from the database; and you can use another bean to display the result. You can also have a set of beans that implement the functions in a mathematical library; you can then do numerical analysis by connecting different functions to each other. In either case, the idea is that you can create programs without writing a great deal of code using beans from a variety of sources.

While this style of visual programming hasn't proven itself much outside of GUI development yet, elements of JavaBeans are seen throughout the Java libraries, especially in Swing. The JavaBeans APIs are a set of naming and design patterns that work with other Java capabilities—*reflection* and *serialization*—to allow tools to discover the capabilities of components and hook them together. The JavaBeans standard also specifies ways for individual beans to provide explicit information for these builder tools, including user-friendly names and appearance information, which allows for the more visual applications.

In this book, we'll take a look at the NetBeans open source IDE (*http://www. netbeans.org*) and see how to put together our own Java beans for use in its GUI builder. We also cover the popular Eclipse IDE (*http://eclipse.org*) later in the book. In addition to GUI building tools, both of these IDEs offer many advanced application building and testing features for Java. There has been a lot of evolution in the area of Java IDEs in recent years and in many ways IDEs are enhancing the productivity of Java programmers more than language innovations are.

Java as a General Application Language

Java was introduced to the world through the web browser and the Java applet API. However, Java is more than just a tool for building multimedia applications. Java is a powerful, general-purpose programming language that just happens to be safe and architecture-independent. Standalone Java applications are not subject to the restrictions placed on applets; they can perform the same jobs as do programs written in languages such as C and C++.

Any software that implements the Java runtime system can run Java applications. Applications written in Java can be large or small, standalone or component-like, as in other languages. Java applets are different from other Java applications only in that they expect to be managed by a larger application. They are also normally considered untrusted code. In this book, we will build examples of both applets and standalone Java applications. With the exception of the few things untrusted applets can't do, such as access files, all the tools we examine in this book apply to both applets and standalone Java applications.

A Java Road Map

With everything that's going on, it's hard to keep track of what's available now, what's promised, and what has been around for some time. The following sections comprise a road map that imposes some order on Java's past, present, and future.

The Past: Java 1.0–Java 1.4

Java 1.0 provided the basic framework for Java development: the language itself plus packages that let you write applets and simple applications. Although 1.0 is officially obsolete, there are still a lot of applets in existence that conform to its API.

Java 1.1 superseded 1.0, incorporating major improvements in the Abstract Window Toolkit (AWT) package (Java's original GUI facility), a new event pattern, new language facilities such as reflection and inner classes, and many other critical features. Java 1.1 is the version that was supported natively by most versions of Netscape and Microsoft Internet Explorer for many years. For various political reasons, the browser world was frozen in this condition for a long time. This version of Java is still considered a sort of baseline for applets, although even this will fall away as Microsoft drops support for Java in their platforms.

Java 1.2, dubbed "Java 2" by Sun, was a major release in December 1998. It provided many improvements and additions, mainly in terms of the set of APIs that were bundled into the standard distributions. The most notable additions were the inclusion of the Swing GUI package as a core API and a new, full-fledged 2D drawing API. Swing is Java's advanced user interface toolkit with capabilities far exceeding the old

AWT's. (Swing, AWT, and some other packages have been variously called the JFC, or Java Foundation Classes.) Java 1.2 also added a proper Collections API to Java.

Java 1.3, released in early 2000, added minor features but was primarily focused on performance. With Version 1.3, Java got significantly faster on many platforms and Swing received many bug fixes. In this timeframe, Java enterprise APIs such as Servlets and Enterprise JavaBeans also matured.

Java 1.4, released in 2002, integrated a major new set of APIs and many long-awaited features. This included language assertions, regular expressions, preferences and logging APIs, a new I/O system for high-volume applications, standard support for XML, fundamental improvements in AWT and Swing, and a greatly matured Java Servlets API for web applications.

The Present: Java 5.0

This book includes all the latest and greatest improvements through the final release of Java 5.0. This release provides many important and long-awaited language syntax enhancements including generics, typesafe enumerations, the enhanced for-loop, variable argument lists, static imports, autoboxing and unboxing of primitives, as well as advanced metadata on classes. A new concurrency API provides powerful threading capabilities and APIs for formatted printing and parsing similar to those in C have been added. RMI has also been overhauled to eliminate the need for compiled stubs and skeletons. There are also major additions in the standard XML APIs.

Here's a brief overview of the most important features of the current core Java API:

JDBC (Java Database Connectivity)
    A general facility for interacting with databases (introduced in Java 1.1).

RMI (Remote Method Invocation)
    Java's distributed objects system. RMI lets you call methods on objects hosted by a server running somewhere else on the network (introduced in Java 1.1).

Java Security
    A facility for controlling access to system resources, combined with a uniform interface to cryptography. Java Security is the basis for signed classes, which were discussed earlier.

JFC (Java Foundation Classes)
    A catch-all for a number of features, including the Swing user interface components; "pluggable look and feel," which means the ability of the user interface to adapt itself to the look and feel of the platform you're using; drag and drop; and accessibility, which means the ability to integrate with special software and hardware for people with disabilities.

Java 2D
    Part of JFC; enables high-quality graphics, font manipulation, and printing.

Internationalization

The ability to write programs that adapt themselves to the language the user wants to use; the program automatically displays text in the appropriate language (introduced in Java 1.1).

JNDI (Java Naming and Directory Interface)

A general service for looking up resources. JNDI unifies access to directory services, such as LDAP, Novell's NDS, and others.

The following "standard extension" APIs aren't necessarily part of the core Java distribution; you may have to download them separately:

JavaMail

A uniform API for writing email software.

Java 3D

A facility for developing applications with 3D graphics.

Java Media

Another catch-all that includes Java 2D, Java 3D, the Java Media Framework (a framework for coordinating the display of many different kinds of media), Java Speech (for speech recognition and synthesis), Java Sound (high-quality audio), Java TV (for interactive television and similar applications), and others.

Java Servlets

A facility that lets you write server-side web applications in Java.

Java Cryptography

Actual implementations of cryptographic algorithms. (This package was separated from Java Security for legal reasons.)

JavaHelp

A facility for writing help systems and incorporating them in Java programs.

Enterprise JavaBeans

A component architecture for building distributed server-side applications.

Jini

An interesting distributed component technology that is designed to enable distributed computing, discovery, and rendezvous of devices ranging from software tools to hardware and household appliances.

XML/XSL

Tools for creating and manipulating XML documents, validating them, mapping them to and from Java objects, and transforming them with stylesheets.

In this book, we'll try to give you a taste of as many features as possible; unfortunately for us (but fortunately for Java software developers), the Java environment has become so rich that it's impossible to cover everything in a single book.

The Future

Java shows no signs of slowing down and there are many areas where the growth of new technologies is now synonymous with the growth of the Java implementations of those technologies. This is especially true in the areas of web services, web application frameworks, and XML tools. Java continues to expand its role in web-based and server-side enterprise applications. What's old is also new again, and client-side Java is gaining momentum as well. There are now more desktop Java applications being used on a daily basis than ever before.

The area of small devices continues to be a rich one for Java. The Java "Java 2 Micro Edition" or J2ME is a subset of Java designed to fit on devices with limited capabilities. The reference platform for the J2ME architecture is the Palm PDA. Java is also now shipping in many cell phones, allowing downloadable applications and media.

Probably the most exciting areas of change in Java today are found in the trend toward lighter weight, simpler frameworks for business and the integration of the Java platform with dynamic languages for scripting web pages and extensions. There is much more interesting work to come.

Availability

You have several choices for Java development environments and runtime systems. Sun's Java development kit (JDK) is available for Windows and Linux and ships as standard equipment with Mac OS X and Solaris. Visit Sun's Java web site at *http://java.sun.com* for more information about obtaining the latest JDK (Version 5.0 is included on the accompanying CD-ROM; view CD content online at *http://examples.oreilly.com/learnjava3/CD-ROM/*). There are also Java ports for other platforms, including NetWare, HP-UX, OSF/1 (including Digital Unix), Silicon Graphics's IRIX, and various IBM operating systems (including AIX, OS/2, OS/390, and OS/400).

There are also a whole array of popular Java Integrated Development Environments. We'll discuss two in this book: IBM's Eclipse (*http://eclipse.org*) and the Sun-backed NetBeans IDE (*http://netbeans.org*). These all-in-one development environments let you write, test, and package software with advanced tools at your fingertips.

As for Java applets in web browsers, the world is generally too muddled to catalog specific versions of Java available on specific platforms. The answer, as we'll discuss later in this book, is to use the Java Plug-in in your pages, which adds up-to-date Java support for all browsers. With that said, the latest versions of the Netscape, FireFox, and Safari browsers generally do come with up-to-date Java runtimes. It is mainly Microsoft Internet Explorer that is the outlier.

## CHAPTER 2

A First Application

Before diving into our full discussion of the Java language, let's get our feet wet by jumping into some working code and splashing around a bit. In this chapter, we'll build a friendly little application that illustrates many of the concepts used throughout the book. We'll take this opportunity to introduce general features of the Java language and applications.

This chapter also serves as a brief introduction to the object-oriented and multithreaded aspects of Java. If these concepts are new to you, we hope that encountering them here in Java for the first time will be a straightforward and pleasant experience. If you have worked with another object-oriented or multithreaded programming environment, you should especially appreciate Java's simplicity and elegance. This chapter is intended only to give you a bird's eye view of the Java language and a feel for how it is used. If you have trouble with any of the concepts introduced here, rest assured they will be covered in greater detail later in the book.

We can't stress enough the importance of experimentation as you learn new concepts here and throughout the book. Don't just read the examples—run them. The source code for these examples and all of the examples in this book can be found on the accompanying CD-ROM and on our web site at *http://www.oreilly.com/catalog/learnjava3*. Compile the programs and try them. Then, turn our examples into your examples: play with them, change their behavior, break them, fix them, and hopefully have some fun along the way.

Java Tools and Environment

In this chapter, we concentrate on Java concepts and do not spend much time on tools. So we will refer only to the command-line java runtime and the javac compiler for Java 5.0. But we have also packaged all of the example code in this book to be run with the open-source Eclipse integrated development environment (IDE). If you would like to follow along with the examples using Eclipse, see Appendix A for an introduction to Eclipse and full instructions on loading the example project. You can then return here to follow along as we build the examples.

If you want to use the command line to follow our examples, you'll need to install the Sun Java Development Environment (JDK) before proceeding. As described at the end of Chapter 1, you can get the latest version online or find Java 5.0 on the CD accompanying this book. The Java 5.0 JDK is called, somewhat confusingly, JDK 1.5. The JDK comes with a standard installer. If you have problems running the command-line tools, turn to "Troubleshooting" at the end of this chapter for some guidance.

We'll show a Windows command prompt in this chapter. To follow along using the command line, simply open a command window. (Under Windows, select Start → Run. Type **command** and press Enter.) Type the given command, and press Enter.

```
C:\> javac HelloJava.java
```

The command you enter is identical on Unix, except where explicitly noted. Most other command-line examples throughout the book show a Unix shell prompt instead:

```
% javac HelloJava.java
```

HelloJava

In the tradition of introductory programming texts, we will begin with Java's equivalent of the archetypal "Hello World" application, HelloJava.

We'll end up taking four passes at this example before we're done (HelloJava, HelloJava2, etc.), adding features, and introducing new concepts along the way. But let's start with the minimalist version:

```
public class HelloJava {
    public static void main( String[] args ) {
        System.out.println("Hello, Java!");
    }
}
```

This five-line program declares a class called HelloJava and a method called main( ). It uses a predefined method called println( ) to write some text as output. This is a *command-line program*, which means that it runs in a shell or DOS window and prints its output there. That's a bit old school for our taste, so before we go any further, we're going to give HelloJava a *graphical user interface* (GUI). Don't worry about the code yet; just follow along with the progression here, and we'll come back for explanations in a moment.

In place of the line containing the `println( )` method, we're going to use something called a `JFrame` object to put a window on the screen. We can start by replacing the `println` line with the following three lines:

```
JFrame frame = new JFrame( "Hello, Java!" );
frame.setSize( 300, 300 );
frame.setVisible( true );
```

This snippet creates a `JFrame` object with the title "Hello, Java!" The `JFrame` is a graphical window. To display it, we simply configure its size on the screen using the `setSize( )` method and make it visible by calling the `setVisible( )` method.

If we stopped here, we would see an empty window on the screen with our "Hello, Java!" banner as its title. We'd like our message inside the window, not just scrawled on the top of it. To put something in the window, we need a couple more lines. The following, complete example adds a `JLabel` object to display the text centered in our window. The additional `import` line at the top is necessary to tell Java where to find the `JFrame` and `JLabel` classes (the definitions of the `JFrame` and `JLabel` objects that we're using).

```
import javax.swing.*;

public class HelloJava {
  public static void main( String[] args ) {
    JFrame frame = new JFrame( "Hello, Java!" );
    JLabel label = new JLabel("Hello, Java!", JLabel.CENTER );
    frame.getContentPane().add(label);
    frame.setSize( 300, 300 );
    frame.setVisible( true );
  }
}
```

Now that we've got something presentable, let's take a moment to compile and run this example. Place the text in a file called *HelloJava.java* (or locate the example file *ch02/HelloJava.java*).

Now to compile this source using the Java compiler, *javac*, type the following at a command prompt and press Enter:

```
C:\> javac HelloJava.java
```

This produces the Java bytecode binary class file *HelloJava.class*.

You can run the application with the Java virtual machine by specifying the class name (not the filename) as an argument. To do so, type the following command and press Enter:

```
C:\> java HelloJava
```

If you had a problem with either step, turn to the section "Trouble-shooting" at the end of this chapter for help. Alternatively, you may wish to run the examples using the Eclipse IDE (see Appendix A).

You should see the proclamation shown in Figure 2-1. Congratulate yourself: you have written your first application! Take a moment to bask in the glow of your monitor.

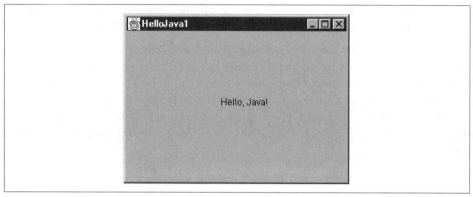

Figure 2-1. The HelloJava application

Be aware that when you click on the window's close box, the window goes away, but your program is still running. To stop Java and return control to the command line, type Ctrl-C or whatever key sequence stops a running application on your platform. We'll remedy this shortcoming in a later version of the example.

HelloJava may be a small program, but there is quite a bit going on behind the scenes. Those few lines represent the tip of an iceberg. What lies under the surface are the layers of functionality provided by the Java language and its foundation class libraries. Remember that in this chapter, we're going to cover a lot of ground quickly in an effort to show you the big picture. We'll try to offer enough detail for a good understanding of what is happening in each example but defer detailed explanations until the appropriate chapters. This holds for both elements of the Java language and the object-oriented concepts that apply to them. With that said, let's take a look now at what's going on in our first example.

Classes

The first example defines a class named HelloJava.

```
public class HelloJava {
    ...
```

Classes are the fundamental building blocks of most object-oriented languages. A *class* is a group of data items, with associated functions that can perform operations on that data. The data items in a class are called *variables* or sometimes *fields*; in

Java, functions are called *methods*. The primary benefits of an object-oriented language are this association between data and functionality in class units and also the ability of classes to *encapsulate* or hide details, freeing the developer from worrying about low-level details.

In an application, a class might represent something concrete, such as a button on a screen or the information in a spreadsheet, or it could be something more abstract, such as a sorting algorithm or perhaps the sense of ennui in a video game character. A class representing a spreadsheet might, for example, have variables that represent the values of its individual cells and methods that perform operations on those cells, such as "clear a row" or "compute values."

Our HelloJava class is an entire Java application in a single class. It defines just one method, main( ), which holds the body of our program:

```
public class HelloJava {
  public static void main( String[] args ) {
    ...
```

It is this main( ) method that is called first, when the application is started. The bit labeled String [] args allows us to pass *command-line arguments* to the application. We'll walk through the main( ) method in the next section. Finally, we'll note that although this version of HelloJava does not define any variables as part of its class, it does use two variables, frame and label, inside its main( ) method. We'll have more to say about variables soon as well.

The main( ) Method

As we saw when we ran our example, running a Java application means picking a particular class and passing its name as an argument to the Java virtual machine. When we did this, the java command looked in our HelloJava class to see if it contained the special method named main( ) of just the right form. It did, and so it was executed. If it had not been there, we would have received an error message. The main( ) method is the entry point for applications. Every standalone Java application includes at least one class with a main( ) method that performs the necessary actions to start the rest of the program.

Our main( ) method sets up a window (a JFrame) to hold the visual output of the HelloJava class. Right now, it's doing all the work in the application. But in an object-oriented application, we normally delegate responsibilities to many different classes. In the next incarnation of our example, we're going to perform just such a split—creating a second class—and we'll see that as the example subsequently evolves, the main( ) method remains more or less the same, simply holding the startup procedure.

Let's quickly walk through our main( ) method, just so we know what it does. First, main( ) creates a JFrame, the window that will hold our example:

```
JFrame frame = new JFrame("Hello, Java!");
```

The word new in this line of code is very important. JFrame is the name of a class that represents a window on the screen, but the class itself is just a template, like a building plan. The new keyword tells Java to allocate memory and actually create a particular JFrame object. In this case, the argument inside the parentheses tells the JFrame what to display in its title bar. We could have left out the "Hello, Java" text and used empty parentheses to create a JFrame with no title, but only because the JFrame specifically allows us to do that.

When frame windows are first created, they are very small. Before we show the JFrame, we set its size to something reasonable:

```
frame.setSize( 300, 300 );
```

This is an example of invoking a method on a particular object. In this case, the setSize() method is defined by the JFrame class, and it affects the particular JFrame object we've placed in the variable frame. Like the frame, we also create an instance of JLabel to hold our text inside the window:

```
JLabel label = new JLabel("Hello, Java!", JLabel.CENTER );
```

JLabel is much like a physical label. It holds some text at a particular position, in this case, on our frame. This is a very object-oriented concept: using an object to hold some text, instead of simply invoking some method to "draw" the text and moving on. The rationale for this will become clearer later.

Next, we have to place the label into the frame we created:

```
frame.getContentPane().add( label );
```

Here we're calling a method named add( )to place our label inside the JFrame.* The JFrame is a kind of container that can hold things. We'll talk more about that later. main( )'s final task is to show the frame window and its contents, which otherwise would be invisible. An invisible window makes for a pretty boring application.

```
frame.setVisible( true );
```

That's the whole main( ) method. As we progress through the examples in this chapter, it will remain mostly unchanged as the HelloJava class evolves around it.

Classes and Objects

A class is a blueprint for a part of an application; it holds methods and variables that make up that component. Many individual, working copies of a given class can exist while an application is active. These individual incarnations are called *instances* of the class or *objects*. Two instances of a given class may contain different data, but they always have the same methods.

---

* In versions of Java prior to 5.0, you must use the getContentPane( ) method to get the correct "pane" to hold items; you cannot add directly to the JFrame.

As an example, consider a Button class. There is only one Button class, but an application can create many different Button objects, each one an instance of the same class. Furthermore, two Button instances might contain different data, perhaps giving each a different appearance and performing a different action. In this sense, a class can be considered a mold for making the object it represents, something like a cookie cutter stamping out working instances of itself in the memory of the computer. As you'll see later, there's a bit more to it than that—a class can in fact share information among its instances—but this explanation suffices for now. Chapter 5 has the whole story on classes and objects.

The term *object* is very general and in some other contexts is used almost interchangeably with *class*. Objects are the abstract entities all object-oriented languages refer to in one form or another. We will use "object" as a generic term for an instance of a class. We might, therefore, refer to an instance of the Button class as a Button, a Button object, or, indiscriminately, as an object.

The main( ) method in the previous example creates a single instance of the JLabel class and shows it in an instance of the JFrame class. You could modify main( ) to create many instances of JLabel, perhaps each in a separate window.

Variables and Class Types

In Java, every class defines a new *type* (data type). A variable can be declared to be of this type and then hold instances of that class. A variable could, for example, be of type Button and hold an instance of the Button class, or of type SpreadSheetCell and hold a SpreadSheetCell object, just as it could be any of the simpler types such as int or float that represent numbers. The fact that variables have types and cannot simply hold any kind of object is another important feature of the language that ensures safety and correctness of code.

Ignoring the variables used inside the main( ) method for the moment, only one other variable is declared in our simple HelloJava example. It's found in the declaration of the main( ) method itself:

```
public void main( String [] args ) {
```

Just like functions in other languages, a method in Java declares a list of variables that it accepts as *arguments* or *parameters*, and it specifies the types of those variables. In this case, the main method is requiring that when it is invoked, it be passed a list of String objects in the variable named args. The String is the fundamental object representing text in Java. As we hinted earlier, Java uses the args parameter to pass any command-line arguments supplied to the Java virtual machine (VM) into your application. (We don't use them here.)

Up to this point, we have loosely referred to variables as holding objects. In reality, variables that have class types don't so much contain objects as point to them. Class-type variables are references to objects. A *reference* is a pointer to or a handle for an object. If you declare a class-type variable without assigning it an object, it doesn't point to anything. It's assigned the default value of null, meaning "no value." If you try to use a variable with a null value as if it were pointing to a real object, a runtime error, NullPointerException, occurs.

Of course, object references have to come from somewhere. In our example, we created two objects using the new operator. We'll examine object creation in more detail a little later in the chapter.

HelloComponent

Thus far our HelloJava example has contained itself in a single class. In fact, because of its simple nature, it has really served as just a single, large method. Although we have used a couple of objects to display our GUI message, our own code does not illustrate any object-oriented structure. Well, we're going to correct that right now by adding a second class. To give us something to build on throughout this chapter, we're going to take over the job of the JLabel class (bye bye JLabel!) and replace it with our own graphical class: HelloComponent. Our HelloComponent class will start simple, just displaying our "Hello, Java!" message at a fixed position. We'll add capabilities later.

The code for our new class is very simple, just a few more lines:

```
import java.awt.*;

class HelloComponent extends JComponent {
  public void paintComponent( Graphics g ) {
    g.drawString( "Hello, Java!", 125, 95 );
  }
}
```

You can add this text to the *HelloJava.java* file, or you can place it in its own file called *HelloComponent.java*. If you put it in the same file, you must move the new import statement to the top of the file, along with the other one. To use our new class in place of the JLabel, simply replace the two lines referencing the label with:

```
frame.add( new HelloComponent() );
```

This time when you compile *HelloJava.java,* you will see two binary class files: *HelloJava.class* and *HelloComponent.class* (regardless of how you arranged the source). Running the code should look much like the JLabel version, but if you resize the window, you'll notice that our class does not automatically adjust to center the code.

So what have we done, and why have we gone to such lengths to insult the perfectly good JLabel component? We've created our new HelloComponent class, *extending* a generic graphical class called JComponent. To extend a class simply means to add functionality to an existing class, creating a new one. We'll get into that in the next section. Here we have created a new kind of JComponent that contains a method called paintComponent( ), responsible for drawing our message. Our paintComponent( ) method takes one argument named (somewhat tersely) g, which is of type Graphics. When the paintComponent( ) method is invoked, a Graphics object is assigned to g, which we use in the body of the method. We'll say more about paintComponent( ) and the Graphics class in a moment. As for why, you'll see when we add all sorts of new features to our new component later on.

Inheritance

Java classes are arranged in a parent-child hierarchy in which the parent and child are known as the *superclass* and *subclass*, respectively. We'll explore these concepts fully in Chapter 6. In Java, every class has exactly one superclass (a single parent) but possibly many subclasses. The only exception to this rule is the Object class, which sits atop the entire class hierarchy; it has no superclass.

The declaration of our class in the previous example uses the keyword extends to specify that HelloComponent is a subclass of the JComponent class:

```
public class HelloComponent extends JComponent { ... }
```

A subclass may inherit some or all the variables and methods of its superclass. Through inheritance, the subclass can use those variables and methods as if it has declared them itself. A subclass can add variables and methods of its own, and it can also *override* or change the meaning of inherited methods. When we use a subclass, overridden methods are hidden (replaced) by the subclass's own versions of them. In this way, inheritance provides a powerful mechanism whereby a subclass can refine or extend the functionality of its superclass.

For example, the hypothetical spreadsheet class might be subclassed to produce a new scientific spreadsheet class with extra mathematical functions and special built-in constants. In this case, the source code for the scientific spreadsheet might declare methods for the added mathematical functions and variables for the special constants, but the new class automatically has all the variables and methods that constitute the normal functionality of a spreadsheet; they are inherited from the parent spreadsheet class. This also means the scientific spreadsheet maintains its identity as a spreadsheet, and we can use the extended version anywhere the simpler spreadsheet could be used. That last sentence has profound implications, which we'll explore throughout the book. It means that specialized objects can be used in place of more generic objects, customizing their behavior without changing the underlying application. This is called *polymorphism* and is one of the foundations of object-oriented programming.

Our HelloComponent class is a subclass of the JComponent class and inherits many variables and methods not explicitly declared in our source code. This is what allows our tiny class to serve as a component in a JFrame, with just a few customizations.

The JComponent Class

The JComponent class provides the framework for building all kinds of user interface components. Particular components, such as buttons, labels, and list boxes, are implemented as subclasses of JComponent.

We override methods in such a subclass to implement the behavior of our particular component. This may sound restrictive, as if we are limited to some predefined set of routines, but that is not the case at all. Keep in mind that the methods we are talking about are ways to interact with the windowing system. We don't have to squeeze our whole application in there. A realistic application might involve hundreds or thousands of classes, with legions of methods and variables and many threads of execution. The vast majority of these are related to the particulars of our job (these are called *domain objects*). The JComponent class and other predefined classes serve only as a framework on which to base code that handles certain types of user interface events and displays information to the user.

The paintComponent( ) method is an important method of the JComponent class; we override it to implement the way our particular component displays itself on the screen. The default behavior of paintComponent( ) doesn't do any drawing at all. If we hadn't overridden it in our subclass, our component would simply have been invisible. Here, we're overriding paintComponent( ) to do something only slightly more interesting. We don't override any of the other inherited members of JComponent because they provide basic functionality and reasonable defaults for this (trivial) example. As HelloJava grows, we'll delve deeper into the inherited members and use additional methods. We will also add some application-specific methods and variables just for the needs of HelloComponent.

JComponent is really the tip of another iceberg called Swing. Swing is Java's user interface toolkit, represented in our example by the import statement at the top; we'll discuss it in some detail in Chapters 16 through 18.

Relationships and Finger Pointing

We can correctly refer to HelloComponent as a JComponent because subclassing can be thought of as creating an "is a" relationship, in which the subclass "is a" kind of its superclass. HelloComponent is therefore a kind of JComponent. When we refer to a kind of object, we mean any instance of that object's class or any of its subclasses. Later, we will look more closely at the Java class hierarchy and see that JComponent is itself a subclass of the Container class, which is further derived from a class called Component, and so on, as shown in Figure 2-2.

In this sense, a HelloComponent object is a kind of JComponent, which is a kind of Container, and each of these can ultimately be considered to be a kind of Component. It's from these classes that HelloComponent inherits its basic GUI functionality and (as `java.lang` contains fundamental classes needed by the Java language itself; this package is imported automatically and that is why we didn't need an import statement to use class names such as `String` or `System` in our examples. The `java.awt` package contains classes of the older, graphical Abstract Window Toolkit; `java.net` contains the networking classes, and so on.

The paintComponent( ) Method

The source for our `HelloComponent` class defines a method, `paintComponent( )`, that overrides the `paintComponent( )` method of the `JComponent` class:

```
public void paintComponent( Graphics g ) {
    g.drawString( "Hello, Java!", 125, 95 );
}
```

The `paintComponent( )` method is called when it's time for our example to draw itself on the screen. It takes a single argument, a `Graphics` object, and doesn't return any type of value (`void`) to its caller.

Modifiers are keywords placed before classes, variables, and methods to alter their accessibility, behavior, or semantics. `paintComponent( )` is declared as `public`, which means it can be invoked (called) by methods in classes other than `HelloComponent`. In this case, it's the Java windowing environment that is calling our `paintComponent( )` method. A method or variable declared as `private` is accessible only from its own class.

The `Graphics` object, an instance of the `Graphics` class, represents a particular graphical drawing area. (It is also called a *graphics context*.) It contains methods that can be used to draw in this area, and variables that represent characteristics such as clipping or drawing modes. The particular `Graphics` object we are passed in the `paintComponent( )` method corresponds to our `HelloComponent`'s area of the screen, inside our frame.

The `Graphics` class provides methods for rendering shapes, images, and text. In `HelloComponent`, we invoke the `drawString( )` method of our `Graphics` object to scrawl our message at the specified coordinates. (For a description of the methods available in the `Graphics` class, see Chapter 20.)

As we've seen earlier, a method of an object is accessed by appending a dot (.) and its name to the object that holds it. We invoked the `drawString( )` method of the `Graphics` object (referenced by our g variable) in this way:

```
g.drawString( "Hello, Java!", 125, 95 );
```

It may be difficult to get used to the idea that our application is drawn by a method that is called by an outside agent at arbitrary times. How can we do anything useful with this? How do we control what gets done and when? These answers are forthcoming. For now, just think about how you would begin to structure applications that respond on command instead of by their own initiative.

HelloJava2: The Sequel

Now that we've got some basics down, let's make our application a little more interactive. The following minor upgrade, HelloJava2, allows us to drag the message text around with the mouse.

We'll call this example HelloJava2 rather than cause confusion by continuing to expand the old one, but the primary changes here and further on lie in adding capabilities to the HelloComponent class and simply making the corresponding changes to the names to keep them straight, e.g., HelloComponent2, HelloComponent3, etc. Having just seen inheritance at work, you might wonder why we aren't creating a subclass of HelloComponent and exploiting inheritance to build upon our previous example and extend its functionality. Well, in this case, that would not provide much advantage, and for clarity we simply start over.

Here is HelloJava2:

```
//file: HelloJava2.java
import java.awt.*;
import java.awt.event.*;
import javax.swing.*;

public class HelloJava2
{
  public static void main( String[] args ) {
    JFrame frame = new JFrame( "HelloJava2" );
    frame.getContentPane( ).add( new HelloComponent2("Hello, Java!") );
    frame.setDefaultCloseOperation( JFrame.EXIT_ON_CLOSE );
    frame.setSize( 300, 300 );
    frame.setVisible( true );
  }
}

class HelloComponent2 extends JComponent
    implements MouseMotionListener
{
  String theMessage;
  int messageX = 125, messageY = 95; // Coordinates of the message

  public HelloComponent2( String message ) {
    theMessage = message;
    addMouseMotionListener(this);
  }

  public void paintComponent( Graphics g ) {
    g.drawString( theMessage, messageX, messageY );
  }

  public void mouseDragged(MouseEvent e) {
    // Save the mouse coordinates and paint the message.
    messageX = e.getX( );
```

```
        messageY = e.getY( );
        repaint( );
    }

    public void mouseMoved(MouseEvent e) { }
}
```

Two slashes in a row indicates that the rest of the line is a comment. We've added a few comments to HelloJava2 to help you keep track of everything.

Place the text of this example in a file called *HelloJava2.java* and compile it as before. You should get new class files, *HelloJava2.class* and *HelloComponent2.class* as a result.

Run the example using the following command:

```
C:\> java HelloJava2
```

Feel free to substitute your own salacious comment for the "Hello, Java!" message and enjoy many hours of fun, dragging the text around with your mouse. Notice that now when you click the window's close button, the application exits; we'll explain that later when we talk about events. Now let's see what's changed.

Instance Variables

We have added some variables to the HelloComponent2 class in our example:

```
int messageX = 125, messageY = 95;
String theMessage;
```

messageX and messageY are integers that hold the current coordinates of our movable message. We have crudely initialized them to default values that should place the message somewhere near the center of the window. Java integers are 32-bit signed numbers, so they can easily hold our coordinate values. The variable theMessage is of type String and can hold instances of the String class.

You should note that these three variables are declared inside the braces of the class definition, but not inside any particular method in that class. These variables are called *instance variables,* and they belong to the class as a whole. Specifically, copies of them appear in each separate instance of the class. Instance variables are always visible to (and usable by) all the methods inside their class. Depending on their modifiers, they may also be accessible from outside the class.

Unless otherwise initialized, instance variables are set to a default value of 0, false, or null, depending on their type. Numeric types are set to 0, Boolean variables are set to false, and class type variables always have their value set to null, which means "no value." Attempting to use an object with a null value results in a runtime error.

Instance variables differ from method arguments and other variables that are declared inside the scope of a particular method. The latter are called *local variables*. They are effectively private variables that can be seen only by code inside the method. Java doesn't initialize local variables, so you must assign values yourself. If you try to use a local variable that has not yet been assigned a value, your code generates a compile-time error. Local variables live only as long as the method is executing and then disappear, unless something else saves their value. Each time the method is invoked, its local variables are recreated and must be assigned values.

We have used the new variables to make our previously stodgy paintComponent( ) method more dynamic. Now all the arguments in the call to drawString( ) are determined by these variables.

Constructors

The HelloComponent2 class includes a special kind of a method called a *constructor*. A constructor is called to set up a new instance of a class. When a new object is created, Java allocates storage for it, sets instance variables to their default values, and calls the constructor method for the class to do whatever application-level setup is required.

A constructor always has the same name as its class. For example, the constructor for the HelloComponent2 class is called HelloComponent2( ). Constructors don't have a return type, but you can think of them as creating an object of their class's type. Like other methods, constructors can take arguments. Their sole mission in life is to configure and initialize newly born class instances, possibly using information passed to them in these parameters.

An object is created with the new operator specifying the constructor for the class and any necessary arguments. The resulting object instance is returned as a value. In our example, a new HelloComponent2 instance is created in the main( ) method by this line:

```
frame.add( new HelloComponent2("Hello, Java!") );
```

This line actually does two things. We could write them as two separate lines that are a little easier to understand:

```
HelloComponent2 newObject = new HelloComponent2("Hello, Java!");
frame.add( newObject );
```

The first line is the important one, where a new HelloComponent2 object is created. The HelloComponent2 constructor takes a String as an argument and, as we have arranged it, uses it to set the message that is displayed in the window. With a little magic from the Java compiler, quoted text in Java source code is turned into a String object. (See Chapter 10 for a complete discussion of the String class.) The second line simply adds our new component to the frame to make it visible, as we did in the previous examples.

While we're on the topic, if you'd like to make our message configurable, you can change the constructor line to the following:

```
HelloComponent2 newobj = new HelloComponent2( args[0] );
```

Now you can pass the text on the command line when you run the application using the following command:

```
C:\> java HelloJava2 "Hello, Java!"
```

args[0] refers to the first command-line parameter. Its meaning will be clearer when we discuss arrays later in the book.

HelloComponent2's constructor then does two things: it sets the text of theMessage instance variable and calls addMouseMotionListener(). This method is part of the event mechanism, which we discuss next. It tells the system, "Hey, I'm interested in anything that happens involving the mouse."

```
public HelloComponent2(String message) {
    theMessage = message;
    addMouseMotionListener( this );
}
```

The special, read-only variable called this is used to explicitly refer to our object (the "current" object context) in the call to addMouseMotionListener(). A method can use this to refer to the instance of the object that holds it. The following two statements are therefore equivalent ways of assigning the value to theMessage instance variable:

```
theMessage = message;
```

or:

```
this.theMessage = message;
```

We'll normally use the shorter, implicit form to refer to instance variables, but we'll need this when we have to explicitly pass a reference to our object to a method in another class. We often do this so that methods in other classes can invoke our public methods or use our public variables.

Events

The last two methods of HelloComponent2, mouseDragged() and mouseMoved(), let us get information from the mouse. Each time the user performs an action, such as pressing a key on the keyboard, moving the mouse, or perhaps banging his or her head against a touch screen, Java generates an *event*. An event represents an action that has occurred; it contains information about the action, such as its time and location. Most events are associated with a particular GUI component in an application. A keystroke, for instance, can correspond to a character being typed into a particular text entry field. Pressing a mouse button can activate a particular button on the screen. Even just moving the mouse within a certain area of the screen can trigger effects such as highlighting or changing the cursor's shape.

To work with these events, we've imported a new package, java.awt.event, which provides specific Event objects that we use to get information from the user. (Notice that importing java.awt.* doesn't automatically import the event package. Packages don't really contain other packages, even if the hierarchical naming scheme would imply that they do.)

There are many different event classes, including MouseEvent, KeyEvent, and ActionEvent. For the most part, the meaning of these events is fairly intuitive. A MouseEvent occurs when the user does something with the mouse, a KeyEvent occurs when the user presses a key, and so on. ActionEvent is a little special; we'll see it at work later in this chapter in our third version of HelloJava. For now, we'll focus on dealing with MouseEvents.

GUI components in Java generate events for specific kinds of user actions. For example, if you click the mouse inside a component, the component generates a mouse event. Objects can ask to receive the events from one or more components by registering a *listener* with the event source. For example, to declare that a listener wants to receive a component's mouse-motion events, you invoke that component's addMouseMotionListener( ) method, specifying the listener object as an argument. That's what our example is doing in its constructor. In this case, the component is calling its own addMouseMotionListener( ) method, with the argument this, meaning "I want to receive my own mouse-motion events."

That's how we register to receive events. But how do we actually get them? That's what the two mouse-related methods in our class are for. The mouseDragged( ) method is called automatically on a listener to receive the events generated when the user drags the mouse—that is, moves the mouse with any button pressed. The mouseMoved( ) method is called whenever the user moves the mouse over the area without pressing a button. In this case, we've placed these methods in our HelloComponent2 class and had it register itself as the listener. This is entirely appropriate for our new text-dragging component. More generally, good design usually dictates that event listeners be implemented as *adapter classes* that provide better separation of GUI and "business logic." We'll discuss that in detail later in the book.

Our mouseMoved( ) method is boring: it doesn't do anything. We ignore simple mouse motions and reserve our attention for dragging. mouseDragged( ) has a bit more meat to it. This method is called repeatedly by the windowing system to give us updates on the position of the mouse. Here it is:

```
public void mouseDragged( MouseEvent e ) {
  messageX = e.getX( );
  messageY = e.getY( );
  repaint( );
}
```

The first argument to mouseDragged( ) is a MouseEvent object, e, that contains all the information we need to know about this event. We ask the MouseEvent to tell us the x and y coordinates of the mouse's current position by calling its getX( ) and getY( ) methods. We save these in the messageX and messageY instance variables for use elsewhere.

The beauty of the event model is that you have to handle only the kinds of events you want. If you don't care about keyboard events, you just don't register a listener for them; the user can type all she wants, and you won't be bothered. If there are no listeners for a particular kind of event, Java won't even generate it. The result is that event handling is quite efficient.[*]

While we're discussing events, we should mention another small addition we slipped into HelloJava2:

```
frame.setDefaultCloseOperation( JFrame.EXIT_ON_CLOSE );
```

This line tells the frame to exit the application when its close button is pressed. It's called the "default" close operation because this operation, like almost every other GUI interaction, is governed by events. We could register a window listener to get notification of when the user pushes the close button and take whatever action we like, but this convenience method handles the common cases.

Finally, we've danced around a couple of questions here: how does the system know that our class contains the necessary mouseDragged( ) and mouseMoved( ) methods (where do these names come from)? And why do we have to supply a mouseMoved( ) method that doesn't do anything? The answer to these questions has to do with interfaces. We'll discuss interfaces after clearing up some unfinished business with repaint( ).

The repaint( ) Method

Since we changed the coordinates for the message (when we dragged the mouse), we would like HelloComponent2 to redraw itself. We do this by calling repaint( ), which asks the system to redraw the screen at a later time. We can't call paintComponent( ) directly, even if we wanted to, because we don't have a graphics context to pass to it.

We can use the repaint( ) method of the JComponent class to request that our component be redrawn. repaint( ) causes the Java windowing system to schedule a call to our paintComponent( ) method at the next possible time; Java supplies the necessary Graphics object, as shown in Figure 2-4.

This mode of operation isn't just an inconvenience brought about by not having the right graphics context handy. The foremost advantage to this mode of operation is that the repainting behavior is handled by someone else while we are free to go about our business. The Java system has a separate, dedicated thread of execution that handles all repaint( ) requests. It can schedule and consolidate repaint( ) requests as necessary, which helps to prevent the windowing system from being overwhelmed

---

[*] Event handling in Java 1.0 was a very different story. Early on, Java did not have a notion of event listeners and all event handling happened by overriding methods in base GUI classes. This was both inefficient and led to poor design with a proliferation of highly specialized components.

Figure 2-4. Invoking the repaint() method

during painting-intensive situations like scrolling. Another advantage is that all the painting functionality must be encapsulated through our paintComponent() method; we aren't tempted to spread it throughout the application.

Interfaces

Now it's time to face the question we avoided earlier: how does the system know to call mouseDragged() when a mouse event occurs? Is it simply a matter of knowing that mouseDragged() is some magic name that our event-handling method must have? Not quite; the answer to the question touches on the discussion of interfaces, which are one of the most important features of the Java language.

The first sign of an interface comes on the line of code that introduces the HelloComponent2 class: we say that the class implements the MouseMotionListener interface.

```
class HelloComponent2 extends JComponent
    implements MouseMotionListener
{
```

Essentially, an interface is a list of methods that the class must have; this particular interface requires our class to have methods called mouseDragged() and mouseMoved(). The interface doesn't say what these methods have to do; indeed, mouseMoved() doesn't do anything. It does say that the methods must take a MouseEvent as an argument and return no value (that's what void means).

An interface is a contract between you, the code developer, and the compiler. By saying that your class implements the MouseMotionListener interface, you're saying that these methods will be available for other parts of the system to call. If you don't provide them, a compilation error will occur.

That's not the only way interfaces impact this program. An interface also acts like a class. For example, a method could return a MouseMotionListener or take a MouseMotionListener as an argument. When you refer to an object by an interface name in this way it means that you don't care about the object's actual class; the only requirement is that the class implements that interface. addMouseMotionListener() is such a method: its argument must be an object that implements the MouseMotionListener interface. The argument we pass is this, the HelloComponent2 object itself. The fact that it's an instance of JComponent is irrelevant; it could be a Cookie, an Aardvark, or any other class we dream up. What's important is that it implements MouseMotionListener and, thus, declares that it will have the two named methods. That's why we need a mouseMoved( ) method, even though the one we supplied doesn't do anything: the MouseMotionListener interface says we have to have one.

The Java distribution comes with many interfaces that define what classes have to do. This idea of a contract between the compiler and a class is very important. There are many situations like the one we just saw where you don't care what class something is, you just care that it has some capability, such as listening for mouse events. Interfaces give us a way of acting on objects based on their capabilities without knowing or caring about their actual type. They are a tremendously important concept in how we use Java as an object-oriented language, and we'll talk about them in detail in Chapter 4.

We'll also see shortly that interfaces provide a sort of escape clause to the Java rule that any new class can extend only a single class ("single inheritance"). A class in Java can extend only one class, but can implement as many interfaces as it wants; our next example implements two interfaces and the final example in this chapter implements three. In many ways, interfaces are almost like classes, but not quite. They can be used as data types, can extend other interfaces (but not classes), and can be inherited by classes (if class A implements interface B, subclasses of A also implement B). The crucial difference is that classes don't actually inherit methods from interfaces; the interfaces merely specify the methods the class must have.

HelloJava3: The Button Strikes!

Now we can move on to some fun stuff. HelloJava3 brings us a new graphical interface component: JButton.* In this example, we add a JButton component to our application that changes the color of our text each time the button is pressed. The draggable-message capability is still there, too. Our new code looks like this:

```
//file: HelloJava3.java
import java.awt.*;
import java.awt.event.*;
import javax.swing.*;

public class HelloJava3
{
```

---

* Why isn't it just called a Button? Button is the name that was used in Java's original GUI toolkit, AWT. AWT had some significant shortcomings, so it was extended and essentially replaced by Swing in Java 1.2. Since AWT already took the reasonable names, such as Button and MenuBar, and mixing them in code could be confusing, Swing user interface component names start with J, such as JButton and JMenuBar.

```
  public static void main( String[] args ) {
    JFrame frame = new JFrame( "HelloJava3" );
    frame.add( new HelloComponent3("Hello, Java!") );
    frame.setDefaultCloseOperation( JFrame.EXIT_ON_CLOSE );
    frame.setSize( 300, 300 );
    frame.setVisible( true );
  }
}

class HelloComponent3 extends JComponent
    implements MouseMotionListener, ActionListener
{
  String theMessage;
  int messageX = 125, messageY = 95;   // Coordinates of the message

  JButton theButton;

  int colorIndex;   // Current index into someColors
  static Color[] someColors = {
    Color.black, Color.red, Color.green, Color.blue, Color.magenta };

  public HelloComponent3( String message ) {
    theMessage = message;
    theButton = new JButton("Change Color");
    setLayout( new FlowLayout() );
    add( theButton );
    theButton.addActionListener( this );
    addMouseMotionListener( this );
  }

  public void paintComponent( Graphics g ) {
    g.drawString( theMessage, messageX, messageY );
  }

  public void mouseDragged( MouseEvent e ) {
    messageX = e.getX();
    messageY = e.getY();
    repaint();
  }

  public void mouseMoved( MouseEvent e ) {}

  public void actionPerformed( ActionEvent e ) {
    // Did somebody push our button?
    if (e.getSource() == theButton)
      changeColor();
  }

  synchronized private void changeColor(  ) {
    // Change the index to the next color, awkwardly.
    if (++colorIndex == someColors.length)
      colorIndex = 0;
    setForeground( currentColor() ); // Use the new color.
    repaint();
  }
```

```
    synchronized private Color currentColor( ) {
      return someColors[colorIndex];
    }
  }
```

Compile HelloJava3 in the same way as the other applications. Run the example, and you should see the display shown in Figure 2-5. Drag the text. Each time you press the button the color should change. Call your friends! Test yourself for color blindness!

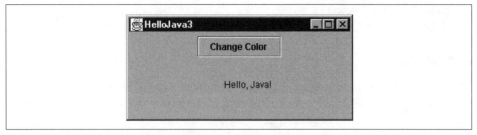

Figure 2-5. The HelloJava3 application

What have we added this time? Well, for starters, we have a new variable:

```
    JButton theButton;
```

The theButton variable is of type JButton and is going to hold an instance of the javax.swing.JButton class. The JButton class, as you might expect, represents a graphical button, like other buttons in your windowing system.

Three additional lines in the constructor create the button and display it:

```
    theButton = new JButton("Change Color");
    setLayout( new FlowLayout( ) );
    add( theButton );
```

In the first line, the new keyword creates an instance of the JButton class. The next line affects the way our component will be used as a container to hold the button. It tells HelloComponent3 how it should arrange components that are added to it for display—in this case, to use a scheme called a FlowLayout (more on that coming up). Finally, it adds the button to our component, just like we added HelloComponent3 to the content pane of the JFrame in the main( ) method.

Method Overloading

JButton has more than one constructor. A class can have multiple constructors, each taking different parameters and presumably using them to do different kinds of setup. When a class has multiple constructors, Java chooses the correct one based on the types of arguments used with them. We call the JButton constructor with a String argument, so Java locates the constructor method of the JButton class that takes a single String argument and uses it to set up the object. This is called *method overloading*. All methods in Java, not just constructors, can be overloaded; this is another aspect of the object-oriented programming principle of *polymorphism*.

Overloaded constructors generally provide a convenient way to initialize a new object. The JButton constructor we've used sets the text of the button as it is created:

```
theButton = new JButton("Change Color");
```

This is shorthand for creating the button and setting its label, like this:

```
theButton = new JButton( );
theButton.setText("Change Color");
```

Components

We have used the terms *component* and *container* somewhat loosely to describe graphical elements of Java applications, but these terms are used in the names of actual classes in the java.awt package.

Component is a base class from which all Java's GUI components are derived. It contains variables that represent the location, shape, general appearance, and status of the object as well as methods for basic painting and event handling. javax.swing.JComponent extends the base Component class and refines it for the Swing toolkit. The paintComponent( ) method we have been using in our example is inherited from the JComponent class. HelloComponent is a kind of JComponent and inherits all its public members, just as other GUI components do.

The JButton class is also derived from JComponent and therefore shares this functionality. This means that the developer of the JButton class had methods such as paintComponent( ) available with which to implement the behavior of the JButton object, just as we did when creating our example. What's exciting is that we are perfectly free to further subclass components such as JButton and override their behavior to create our own special types of user-interface components. JButton and HelloComponent3 are, in this respect, equivalent types of things.

Containers

The Container class is an extended type of Component that maintains a list of child components and helps to group them. The Container causes its children to be displayed and arranges them on the screen according to a particular layout strategy.

Because a Container is also a Component, it can be placed alongside other Component objects in other Containers, in a hierarchical fashion, as shown in Figure 2-6. Our HelloComponent3 class is a kind of Container (by virtue of the JComponent class) and can therefore hold and manage other Java components and containers, such as buttons, sliders, text fields, and panels.

Figure 2-6. Layout of Java containers and components

In Figure 2-6, the italicized items are Components, and the bold items are Containers. The keypad is implemented as a container object that manages a number of keys. The keypad itself is contained in the GizmoTool container object.

Since JComponent descends from Container, it can be both a component and a container. In fact, we've already used it in this capacity in the HelloComponent3 example. It does its own drawing and handles events, just like a component, but it also contains a button, just like a container.

Layout

Having created a JButton object, we need to place it in the container, but where? An object called a LayoutManager determines the location within the HelloComponent3 container at which to display the JButton. A LayoutManager object embodies a particular scheme for arranging components on the screen and adjusting their sizes. There are several standard layout managers to choose from, and we can, of course, create new ones. In our case, we specify one of the standard managers, a FlowLayout. The net result is that the button is centered at the top of the HelloComponent3 container. Our JFrame has another kind of layout, called BorderLayout. You'll learn more about layout managers in Chapter 19.

To add the button to the layout, we invoke the add( ) method that HelloComponent3 inherits from Container, passing the JButton object as a parameter:

```
add( theButton );
```

add( ) is a method inherited by our class from the Container class. It appends our JButton to the list of components the HelloComponent3 container manages. Thereafter, HelloComponent3 is responsible for the JButton: it causes the button to be displayed and it determines where in its window the button should be placed.

Subclassing and Subtypes

If you look up the add( ) method of the Container class, you'll see that it takes a Component object as an argument. In our example, we've given it a JButton object. What's going on?

As we've said, JButton is a subclass of the Component class. Because a subclass is a kind of its superclass and has, at minimum, the same public methods and variables, Java allows us to use an instance of a subclass anywhere we could use an instance of its superclass. JButton is a kind of Component, so any method that expects a Component as an argument will accept a JButton.

More Events and Interfaces

Now that we have a JButton, we need some way to communicate with it, that is, to get the events it generates. We could just listen for mouse clicks within the button and act accordingly, but that would require customization, via subclassing of the JButton, and we would be giving up the advantages of using a pre-fab component. Instead, we have the HelloComponent3 object listen for higher-level events, corresponding to button presses. A JButton generates a special kind of event called an ActionEvent when someone clicks on it with the mouse. To receive these events, we have added another method to the HelloComponent3 class:

```
public void actionPerformed( ActionEvent e ) {
  if ( e.getSource() == theButton )
    changeColor( );
}
```

If you followed the previous example, you shouldn't be surprised to see that HelloComponent3 now declares that it implements the ActionListener interface in addition to MouseMotionListener. ActionListener requires us to implement an actionPerformed( ) method that is called whenever an ActionEvent occurs. You also shouldn't be surprised to see that we added a line to the HelloComponent3 constructor, registering itself (this) as a listener for the button's action events:

```
theButton.addActionListener( this );
```

Note that this time we're registering our component as a listener with a different object—the button—whereas previously we were asking for our own events.

The actionPerformed( ) method takes care of any action events that arise. First, it checks to make sure that the event's source (the component generating the event) is what we think it should be: theButton. This may seem superfluous; after all, there is only one button. What else could possibly generate an action event? In this application, nothing, but it's a good idea to check because another application may have many buttons, and you may need to figure out which one has been clicked. Or you may add a second button to this application later, and you don't want it to break something. To check this, we call the getSource( ) method of the ActionEvent object, e. We then use the == operator to make sure the event source matches theButton.

 In Java, == is a test for *identity*, not equality; it is true if the event source and theButton are the same object. The distinction between equality and identity is important. We would consider two String objects to be equal if they have the same characters in the same sequence. However, they might not be the same object. In Chapter 7, we'll look at the equals( ) method, which tests for equality.

Once we establish that event e comes from the right button, we call our changeColor( ) method, and we're finished.

You may wonder why we don't have to change mouseDragged( ) now that we have a JButton in our application. The rationale is that the coordinates of the event are all that matter for this method. We are not particularly concerned if the event falls within an area of the screen occupied by another component. This means you can drag the text right through the JButton: try it and see! In this case, the arrangement of containers means that the button is on top of our component, so the text is dragged beneath it.

Color Commentary

To support HelloJava3's colorful side, we have added a couple of new variables and two helpful methods. We create and initialize an array of Color objects representing the colors through which we cycle when the button is pressed. We also declare an integer variable that serves as an index into this array, specifying the position of the current color:

```
int colorIndex;
static Color[] someColors = { Color.black, Color.red,
    Color.green, Color.blue, Color.magenta };
```

A number of things are going on here. First, let's look at the Color objects we are putting into the array. Instances of the java.awt.Color class represent colors; they are used by all classes in the java.awt package that deal with basic color graphics. Notice that we are referencing variables such as Color.black and Color.red. These look like examples of an object's instance variables, but Color is not an object, it's a class. What is the meaning of this? We'll discuss that next.

Static Members

A class can contain variables and methods that are shared among all instances of the class. These shared members are called *static variables* and *static methods*. The most common use of static variables in a class is to hold predefined constants or unchanging objects that all the instances can use.

This approach has two advantages. One advantage is that static values are shared by all instances of the class; the same value can be seen by all instances. More importantly, static members can be accessed even if no instances of the class exist. In this example, we use the static variable Color.red without having to create an instance of the Color class.

An instance of the Color class represents a visible color. For convenience, the Color class contains some static, predefined objects with friendly names such as green, red, and (the happy color) magenta. The variable green, for example, is a static member in the Color class. The data type of the variable green is Color. Internally, in Java-land, it is initialized like this:

```
public final static Color green = new Color(0, 255, 0);
```

The green variable and the other static members of Color cannot be modified (after they've been initialized) so that they are effectively constants and can be optimized as such by the Java VM. The alternative to using these predefined colors is to create a color manually by specifying its red, green, and blue (RGB) components using a Color class constructor.

Arrays

Next, we turn our attention to the array. We have declared a variable called someColors, which is an array of Color objects. In Java, arrays are *first-class* objects. This means that an array itself is a type of object—one that knows how to hold an indexed list of some other type of object. An array is indexed by integers; when you index an array, the resulting value is an object reference—that is, a reference to the object that is located in the array's specified slot. Our code uses the colorIndex variable to index someColors. It's also possible to have an array of simple primitive types, such as floats, rather than objects.

When we declare an array, we can initialize it using the curly brace construct. Specifying a comma-separated list of elements inside curly braces is a convenience that instructs the compiler to create an instance of the array with those elements and assign it to our variable. Alternatively, we could have just declared our someColors variable and, later, allocated an array object for it and assigned individual elements to that array's slots. See Chapter 5 for a complete discussion of arrays.

Our Color Methods

Now we have an array of Color objects and a variable with which to index the array. Two private methods do the actual work for us. The private modifier on these methods specifies that they can be called only by other methods in the same instance of the class. They cannot be accessed outside the object that contains them. We declare members to be private to hide the detailed inner workings of a class from the outside world. This is called *encapsulation* and is another tenet of object-oriented design as well as good programming practice. Private methods are created as helper functions for use solely in the class implementation.

The first method, currentColor( ), is simply a convenience routine that returns the Color object representing the current text color. It returns the Color object in the someColors array at the index specified by our colorIndex variable:

```
synchronized private Color currentColor() {
  return someColors[colorIndex];
}
```

We could just as readily have used the expression someColors[colorIndex] everywhere we use currentColor( ); however, creating methods to wrap common tasks is another way of shielding ourselves from the details of our class. In an alternative implementation, we might have shuffled off details of all color-related code into a separate class. We could have created a class that takes an array of colors in its constructor and then provided two methods: one to ask for the current color and one to cycle to the next color (just some food for thought).

The second method, changeColor( ), is responsible for incrementing the colorIndex variable to point to the next Color in the array. changeColor( ) is called from our actionPerformed( ) method whenever the button is pressed:

```
synchronized private void changeColor() {
    // Change the index to the next color, awkwardly.
    if ( ++colorIndex == someColors.length )
      colorIndex = 0;
    setForeground( currentColor() ); // Use the new color.
    repaint();
}
```

Here we increment colorIndex and compare it to the length of the someColors array. All array objects have a variable called length that specifies the number of elements in the array. If we have reached the end of the array, we wrap around to the beginning by resetting the index to 0. We've flagged this with a comment to indicate that we're doing something fishy here. But we'll come back to that in a moment. After changing the currently selected color, we do two things. First, we call the component's setForeground( ) method, which changes the color used to draw text in our component. Then we call repaint( ) to cause the component to be redrawn with the new color for the draggable message.

What is the synchronized keyword that appears in front of our currentColor( ) and changeColor( ) methods? Synchronization has to do with threads, which we'll examine in the next section. For now, all you need know is that the synchronized keyword indicates these two methods can never be running at the same time. They must always run in a mutually exclusive way.

The reason for this is related to the fishy way we increment our index. Notice that in changeColor( ), we increment colorIndex before testing its value. Strictly speaking, this means that for some brief period of time while Java is running through our code, colorIndex can have a value that is past the end of our array. If our currentColor( ) method happened to run at that same moment, we would see a runtime "array out of bounds" error. Now, it would be easy for us to fix the problem in this case with some simple arithmetic before changing the value, but this simple example is representative of more general synchronization issues we need to address. We'll use it to illustrate the use of the synchronized keyword. In the next section, you'll see that Java makes dealing with these problems relatively easy through language-level synchronization support.

HelloJava4: Netscape's Revenge

We have explored quite a few features of Java with the first three versions of the HelloJava application. But until now, our application has been rather passive; it has been completely *event-driven,* waiting patiently for events to come its way and responding to the whims of the user. Now our application is going to take some initiative—HelloJava4 will blink!* Here is the code for our latest version:

```java
//file: HelloJava4.java
import java.awt.*;
import java.awt.event.*;
import javax.swing.*;

public class HelloJava4
{
  public static void main( String[] args ) {
    JFrame frame = new JFrame( "HelloJava4" );
    frame.add( new HelloComponent4("Hello, Java!") );
    frame.setDefaultCloseOperation( JFrame.EXIT_ON_CLOSE );
    frame.setSize( 300, 300 );
    frame.setVisible( true );
  }
}

class HelloComponent4 extends JComponent
    implements MouseMotionListener, ActionListener, Runnable
{
  String theMessage;
  int messageX = 125, messageY = 95; // Coordinates of the message

  JButton theButton;

  int colorIndex; // Current index into someColors.
  static Color[] someColors = {
    Color.black, Color.red, Color.green, Color.blue, Color.magenta };

  boolean blinkState;
```

---

* The title of this section, "Netscape's Revenge," refers to the infamous <BLINK> HTML tag introduced with an early version of the Netscape web browser.

```java
public HelloComponent4( String message ) {
  theMessage = message;
  theButton = new JButton("Change Color");
  setLayout( new FlowLayout( ) );
  add( theButton );
  theButton.addActionListener( this );
  addMouseMotionListener( this );
  Thread t = new Thread( this );
  t.start( );
}

public void paintComponent( Graphics g ) {
  g.setColor(blinkState ? getBackground( ) : currentColor( ));
  g.drawString(theMessage, messageX, messageY);
}

public void mouseDragged(MouseEvent e) {
  messageX = e.getX( );
  messageY = e.getY( );
  repaint( );
}

public void mouseMoved(MouseEvent e) { }

public void actionPerformed( ActionEvent e ) {
  if ( e.getSource( ) == theButton )
    changeColor( );
}

synchronized private void changeColor( ) {
  if (++colorIndex == someColors.length)
    colorIndex = 0;
  setForeground( currentColor() );
  repaint( );
}

synchronized private Color currentColor( ) {
  return someColors[colorIndex];
}

public void run() {
  try {
    while(true) {
      blinkState = !blinkState; // Toggle blinkState.
      repaint( ); // Show the change.
      Thread.sleep(300);
    }
  } catch (InterruptedException ie) { }
}
}
```

Compile and run this version of HelloJava just like the others. You'll see that the text does, in fact, blink. Our apologies if you find this annoying—it's all in the name of education.

Threads

All the changes we've made in HelloJava4 have to do with setting up a separate thread of execution to make the text blink. Java is a *multithreaded* language, which means there can be many paths of execution, effectively running at the same time. A *thread* is a separate flow of control within a program. Conceptually, threads are similar to processes. Unlike processes, multiple threads share the same program space, which means that they can share variables and methods (but also have their own local variables). Threads are also quite lightweight in comparison to processes, so it's conceivable for a single application to be running many (perhaps hundreds or thousands) of threads concurrently.

Multithreading provides a way for an application to handle many different tasks at the same time. It's easy to imagine multiple things going on at the same time in an application like a web browser. The user could be listening to an audio clip while scrolling an image; at the same time, the browser can be downloading another image. Multithreading is especially useful in GUI-based applications because it improves the interactive performance of these applications.

Unfortunately for us, programming with multiple threads can be quite a headache. The difficulty lies in making sure routines are implemented so they can be run concurrently, by more than one thread at a time. If a routine changes the value of multiple state variables, for example, it may be important that those changes happen together, without overlapping changes affecting each other. Later in this section, we'll examine briefly the issue of coordinating multiple threads' access to shared data. In other languages, synchronization of threads can be extremely complex and error-prone. You'll see that Java gives you powerful tools that help you deal with many of these problems. See Chapter 9 for a detailed discussion of threads.

The Java runtime system creates and manages a number of threads. (Exactly how varies with the implementation.) We've already mentioned the repaint thread, which manages repaint( ) requests and event processing for GUI components that belong to the java.awt and javax.swing packages. Our example applications have done most of their work in one thread. Methods such as mouseDragged( ) and actionPerformed( ) are invoked by the windowing thread and run by its thread, on its time. Similarly, our HelloComponent constructor runs as part of the main application thread (the main( ) method). This means we are somewhat limited in the amount of processing we do within these methods. If we were, for instance, to go into an endless loop in our constructor, our application would never appear, because it would never finish initializing. If we want an application to perform any extensive processing, such as animation, a lengthy calculation, or communication, we should create separate threads for these tasks.

The Thread Class

As you might have guessed, threads are created and controlled as Thread objects. An instance of the java.lang.Thread class corresponds to a single thread. It contains methods to start, control, and interrupt the thread's execution. Our plan here is to create a Thread object to handle our blinking code. We call the Thread's start( ) method to begin execution. Once the thread starts, it continues to run until it completes its work, we interrupt it, or we stop the application.

So, how do we tell the thread which method to run? Well, the Thread object is rather picky; it always expects to execute a method called run( ) to perform the action of the thread. The run( ) method can, however, with a little persuasion, be located in any class we desire.

We specify the location of the run( ) method in one of two ways. First, the Thread class itself has a method called run( ). One way to execute some Java code in a separate thread is to subclass Thread and override its run( ) method to do our bidding. Invoking the start( ) method of the subclass object causes its run( ) method to execute in a separate thread.

It's not usually desirable to create a subclass of Thread to contain our run( ) method. The Thread class has a constructor that takes an object as its argument. If we create a Thread object using this constructor and call its start( ) method, the Thread executes the run( ) method of the argument object rather than its own. In order to accomplish this, Java needs a guarantee that the object we are passing it does indeed contain a compatible run( ) method. We already know how to make such a guarantee: we use an interface. Java provides an interface named Runnable that must be implemented by any class that wants to become a Thread.

The Runnable Interface

We've implemented the Runnable interface in HelloComponent4. To create a thread, the HelloComponent4 object passes itself (this) to the Thread constructor. This means that HelloComponent4 must implement the Runnable interface by implementing the run( ) method. This method is called automatically when the runtime system needs to start the thread.

We indicate that the class implements the interface in our class declaration:

```
public class HelloComponent4
    extends JComponent
    implements MouseMotionListener, ActionListener, Runnable {...}
```

At compile time, the Java compiler checks to make sure we abide by this statement. We have carried through by adding an appropriate run( ) method to HelloComponent4. It takes no arguments and returns no value. Our run( ) method accomplishes blinking by changing the color of our text a few times a second. It's a very short routine, but we're going to delay looking at it until we tie up some loose ends in dealing with the Thread itself.

Starting the Thread

We want the blinking to begin when the application starts, so we'll start the thread in the initialization code in HelloComponent4's constructor. It takes only two lines:

```
Thread t = new Thread(this);
t.start();
```

First, the constructor creates a new instance of Thread, passing it the object that contains the run( ) method to the constructor. Since HelloComponent4 itself contains our run( ) method, we pass the special variable this to the constructor. this always refers to our object. After creating the new Thread, we call its start( ) method to begin execution. This, in turn, invokes HelloComponent4's run( ) method in the new thread.

Running Code in the Thread

Our run( ) method does its job by setting the value of the variable blinkState. We have added blinkState, a Boolean variable that can have the value true or false, to represent whether we are currently blinking on or off:

```
boolean blinkState;
```

A setColor( ) call has been added to our paintComponent( ) method to handle blinking. When blinkState is true, the call to setColor( ) draws the text in the background color, making it disappear:

```
g.setColor(blinkState ? getBackground( ) : currentColor( ));
```

Here we are being very terse, using the C language–style ternary operator to return one of two alternative color values based on the value of blinkState. If blinkState is true, the value is the value returned by the getBackground( ) method. If it is false, the value is the value returned by currentColor( ).

Finally, we come to the run( ) method itself:

```
public void run( ) {
  try {
    while( true ) {
      blinkState = !blinkState;
      repaint( );
      Thread.sleep(300);
    }
  } catch (InterruptedException ie) {}
}
```

Basically, run( ) is an infinite while loop, which means the loop runs continuously until the thread is terminated by the application exiting (not a good idea in general, but it works for this simple example).

The body of the loop does three things on each pass:

- Flips the value of blinkState to its opposite value using the not operator (!)
- Calls repaint( ) to redraw the text
- Sleeps for 300 milliseconds (about a third of a second)

sleep( ) is a static method of the Thread class. The method can be invoked from any-where and has the effect of putting the currently running thread to sleep for the spec-ified number of milliseconds. The effect here is to give us approximately three blinks per second. The try/catch construct, described in the next section, traps any errors in the call to the sleep( ) method of the Thread class and, in this case, ignores them.

Exceptions

The try/catch statement in Java handles special conditions called *exceptions*. An exception is a message that is sent, normally in response to an error, during the exe-cution of a statement or a method. When an exceptional condition arises, an object is created that contains information about the particular problem or condition. Exceptions act somewhat like events. Java stops execution at the place where the exception occurred, and the exception object is said to be *thrown* by that section of code. Like an event, an exception must be delivered somewhere and handled. The section of code that receives the exception object is said to *catch* the exception. An exception causes the execution of the instigating section of code to stop abruptly and transfers control to the code that receives the exception object.

The try/catch construct allows you to catch exceptions for a section of code. If an exception is caused by any statement inside a try clause, Java attempts to deliver the exception to the appropriate catch clause. A catch clause looks like a method decla-ration with one argument and no return type.

```
try {
    ...
} catch ( SomeExceptionType e ) {
    ...
}
```

If Java finds a catch clause with an argument type that matches the type of the excep-tion, that catch clause is invoked. A try clause can have multiple catch clauses with different argument types; Java chooses the appropriate one in a way that is analo-gous to the selection of overloaded methods. You can catch multiple types of excep-tions from a block of code. Depending on the type of exception thrown, the appropriate catch clause is executed.

If there is no try/catch clause surrounding the code, or a matching catch clause is not found, the exception is thrown up to the calling method. If the exception is not caught there, it's thrown up to another level, and so on until the exception is handled or the Java VM prints an error and exits. This provides a very flexible error-handling mechanism so that exceptions in deeply nested calls can bubble up to the surface of the call stack for handling. As a programmer, you need to know what exceptions a particular statement can generate. For this reason, methods in Java are required to declare the exceptions they can throw. If a method doesn't handle an exception itself, it must specify that it can throw that exception so that its calling method knows that it may have to handle it. See Chapter 4 for a complete discussion of exceptions and the try/catch clause.

Why do we need a try/catch clause in the run( ) method? What kind of exception can Thread's sleep( ) method throw and why do we care about it when we don't seem to check for exceptions anywhere else? Under some circumstances, Thread's sleep( ) method can throw an InterruptedException, indicating that it was interrupted by another thread. Since the run( ) method specified in the Runnable interface doesn't declare it can throw an InterruptedException, we must catch it ourselves, or the compiler will complain. The try/catch statement in our example has an empty catch clause, which means that it handles the exception by ignoring it. In this case, our thread's functionality is so simple it doesn't matter if it's interrupted (and it won't be anyway). All the other methods we have used either handle their own exceptions or throw only general-purpose exceptions called RuntimeExceptions that are assumed to be possible everywhere and don't need to be explicitly declared.

Synchronization

At any given time we can have lots of threads running in an application. Unless we explicitly coordinate them, these threads will be executing methods without any regard for what the other threads are doing. Problems can arise when these methods share the same data. If one method is changing the value of some variables at the same time another method is reading these variables, it's possible that the reading thread might catch things in the middle and get some variables with old values and some with new. Depending on the application, this situation could cause a critical error.

In our HelloJava examples, both our paintComponent( ) and mouseDragged( ) methods access the messageX and messageY variables. Without knowing more about the implementation of the Java environment, we have to assume that these methods could conceivably be called by different threads and run concurrently. paintComponent( ) could be called while mouseDragged( ) is in the midst of updating messageX and messageY. At that point, the data is in an inconsistent state and if paintComponent( ) gets lucky, it could get the new x value with the old y value. Fortunately, Swing does not allow this to happen in this case because all event activity is handled by a single thread, and we probably would not even notice if it were to happen in this application anyway. We did, however, see another case, in our changeColor() and currentColor() methods, that is representative of the potential for a more serious "out of bounds" error.

The synchronized modifier tells Java to acquire a *lock* for the object that contains the method before executing that method. Only one method in the object can have the lock at any given time, which means that only one synchronized method in that object can be running at a time. This allows a method to alter data and leave it in a consistent state before a concurrently running method is allowed to access it. When the method is done, it releases the lock on the class.

Unlike synchronization in other languages, the synchronized keyword in Java provides locking at the language level. This means there is no way that you can forget to unlock a class. Even if the method throws an exception or the thread is terminated, Java will release the lock. This feature makes programming with threads in Java much easier than in other languages. See Chapter 9 for more details on coordinating threads and shared data.

Whew! Well, it's time to say goodbye to HelloJava. We hope that you have developed a feel for the major features of the Java language and that this will help you as you explore the details of programming with Java. If you are a bit bewildered by some of the material presented here, take heart. We'll be covering all the major topics presented here again in their own chapters throughout the book. This tutorial was meant to be something of a "trial by fire" to get the important concepts and terminology into your brain so that the next time you hear them you'll have a head start.

Troubleshooting

If you are having trouble with the *java* or *javac* commands, this section provides some guidance about what might be wrong. If you do not feel comfortable with the command line, you might prefer to run the examples in the Eclipse IDE. See Appendix A for an introduction to Eclipse and full instructions on running the example code.

Compilation (javac) Errors

If the *javac* command is not found, you may have installed the JRE (Java runtime environment) instead of the JDK. Install Java 5.0 (also known as JDK 1.5), as described in "Java Tools and Environment" at the beginning of this chapter.

If you are getting syntax error messages on the HelloJava examples, it is likely that your source code has a mistake or that the source file has become corrupted. The best way to eliminate this possibility is to copy the source directly from the ZIP file on the CD or download them from the examples link at the web site for this book, *http://www.oreilly.com/catalog/learnjava3/*.

Runtime (java) Errors

Most runtime errors are related to the Java CLASSPATH environment variable.

If you are getting `NoClassDefFound` or `ClassNotFound` errors when attempting to run the examples using the *java* command, you may have a classpath issue. By default there should be no value set in the environment variable CLASSPATH, but some untidy applications may set this value for you when you install them.

To display the value of CLASSPATH under Windows, use this command:

    C:\> set classpath

Use this command for Unix:

    % echo $CLASSPATH

To clear any CLASSPATH value, use this command under Windows:

    C:\> set classpath=

Use this command for Unix:

    % unset CLASSPATH; export CLASSPATH

Java Version Problems

To check the version of Java, use the *–version* switch with the *java* command. Type the following at the command prompt and press Enter:

    C:\> java -version

This should report "java version 5.0." If it doesn't, install Java 5.0 as described in "Java Tools and Environment" at the beginning of this chapter.

The getContentPane( ) Error

What if you get an error that says `Exception in thread "main" java.lang.Error: Do not use javax.swing.JFrame.add( ) use javax.swing.JFrame.getContentPane( ).add( )` instead? This error also indicates that you are using an earlier version of Java (prior to Java 5.0). Install Java 5.0.

## CHAPTER 3

Tools of the Trade

There are many options for Java development environments, ranging from the traditional text editor and command-line tools to a whole slew of advanced IDEs, including IBM's Eclipse, Sun's NetBeans, and Borland's JBuilder. (Both Eclipse and NetBeans are open source projects and can be downloaded for free as well as found on the CD-ROM accompanying this book.) The examples in this book were developed using Sun's no-frills Java Development Kit (JDK) on, at various times, Solaris, Windows, and Mac OS X platforms. The JDK includes the basic tools needed to compile, run, and package Java applications, and we will describe these tools in this chapter. But there is no reason you can't use your preferred IDE to follow along with the examples in this book. The source code for all of the examples can be found on the CD-ROM.

For an introduction to the Eclipse IDE and instructions for loading all of the examples in this book as an Eclipse project, see Appendix A. In Chapter 22, we introduce the NetBeans IDE with our discussion of the JavaBeans component architecture, so you will get little GUI development environment flavor there.

The Java VM

A Java virtual machine (VM) is software that implements the Java runtime system and executes Java applications. It can be a standalone application like the *java* program that comes with the JDK or part of a larger application like a browser. Usually the interpreter itself is a native application, supplied for each platform, which then bootstraps other tools written in the Java language. Tools such as Java compilers and IDEs are often implemented directly in Java to maximize their portability and extensibility. NetBeans, for example, is a pure-Java application.

The Java VM performs all the runtime activities of Java. It loads Java class files, verifies classes from untrusted sources, and executes the compiled bytecode. It manages memory and system resources. In implementations that support dynamic compilation, the interpreter also serves as a specialized compiler that turns Java bytecode into native machine instructions.

Throughout most of this book, we'll be building standalone Java programs, but we'll make frequent references to Java applets as well. Both are kinds of Java applications run by a Java VM. A standalone Java application is a complete program intended to be run independently. An applet is, conceptually, an embeddable component to be used in a larger application. Both technically and in usage there is not much difference between the two, other than the Java VM can't run an applet directly. To run an applet, you must use a web browser or the *appletviewer* tool that comes with the JDK.

Running Java Applications

A standalone Java application must have at least one class that contains a method called main( ), which contains the first code to be executed upon start up. To run the application, start the VM, specifying that class as an argument. You can also specify options to the interpreter as well as arguments to be passed to the application. Sun's Java VM is called *java*:

```
% java [interpreter options] class_name [program arguments]
```

The class should be specified as a fully qualified class name, including the package name, if any. Note, however, that you don't include the *.class* file extension. Here are a couple of examples:

```
% java animals.birds.BigBird
% java MyTest
```

The interpreter searches for the class in the *classpath*, a list of directories and archive files where classes are stored. We'll discuss the classpath in detail in the next section. The classpath can be specified either by an *environment variable* or with the command-line option -*classpath*. If both are present, the command-line option is used.

Alternately, the *java* command can be used to launch an "executable" Java archive (JAR) file:

```
% java -jar spaceblaster.jar
```

In this case, the JAR file is annotated with the name of the class containing the main( ) method and the classpath becomes the JAR file itself.

However it is launched, after loading the first class, the interpreter executes the class's main( ) method. From there, the application can reference other classes, start additional threads, and create its user interface or other structures, as shown in Figure 3-1.

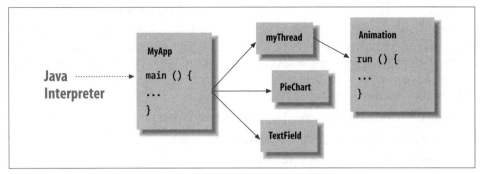

Figure 3-1. Starting a Java application

The main( ) method must have the right *method signature*. A method signature is the set of information that defines the method. It includes the method's name, argu-ments, and return type, as well as type and visibility modifiers. The main( ) method must be a public, static method that takes an array of String objects as its argu-ment and does not return any value (void):

```
public static void main ( String [] myArgs )
```

The fact that main( ) is a public and static method simply means that it is globally accessible and that it can be called directly by name. We'll discuss the implications of visibility modifiers such as public and the meaning of static in Chapters 4 through 6.

The main( ) method's single argument, the array of String objects, holds the com-mand-line arguments passed to the application. The name of the parameter doesn't matter; only the type is important. In Java, the content of myArgs is a true array. There's no need for an argument count parameter because arrays know how many arguments they contain and can happily provide that information:

```
int numArgs = myArgs.length;
```

myArgs[0] is the first command-line argument, and so on.[*]

The Java interpreter continues to run until the main( ) method of the initial class file returns and until any threads that it starts are complete. Special threads designated as daemon threads are automatically killed when the rest of the application has completed.

System Properties

Although it is possible to read host environment variables from Java, it is generally discouraged for application configuration. Instead, Java allows any number of *sys-tem property* values to be passed to the application when the VM is started. System

---

[*] Note that this differs from some languages, where argument zero is the name of the application.

properties are simply name-value string pairs that are available to the application through the static System.getProperty( ) method. You can use these properties as a more structured and portable alternative to command-line arguments and environment variables for providing general configuration information to your application at startup. Each system property is passed to the interpreter on the command line using the -D option followed by *name=value*. For example:

```
% java -Dstreet=sesame -Dscene=alley animals.birds.BigBird
```

The value of the street property is then accessible this way:

```
String street = System.getProperty("street");
```

An application can get its configuration in myriad ways, including via files or network configuration at runtime. In practice, Java applications make heavy use of system properties for basic configuration.

The Classpath

The concept of a *path* should be familiar to anyone who has worked on a DOS or Unix platform. It's an environment variable that provides an application with a list of places to look for some resource. The most common example is a path for executable programs. In a Unix shell, the PATH environment variable is a colon-separated list of directories that are searched, in order, when the user types the name of a command. The Java CLASSPATH environment variable, similarly, is a list of locations that are searched for Java class files. Both the Java interpreter and the Java compiler use the CLASSPATH when searching for packages and Java classes.

An element of the classpath can be a directory or JAR file. Java also supports archives in the conventional ZIP format, but JAR and ZIP are really the same format. JARs are simple archives that include extra files (metadata) that describe each archive's contents. JAR files are created with the JDK's *jar* utility; many tools for creating ZIP archives are publicly available and can be used to inspect or create JAR files. The archive format enables large groups of classes and their resources to be distributed in a single file; the Java runtime automatically extracts individual class files from an archive as needed.

The precise means and format for setting the classpath vary from system to system. On a Unix system (including Mac OS X), you set the CLASSPATH environment variable with a colon-separated list of directories and class archive files:

```
% CLASSPATH=/home/vicky/Java/classes:/home/josh/lib/foo.jar:.
% export CLASSPATH
```

This example specifies a classpath with three locations: a directory in the user's home, a JAR file in another user's directory, and the current directory, which is always specified with a dot (.). The last component of the classpath, the current directory, is useful when tinkering with classes.

On a Windows system, the CLASSPATH environment variable is set with a semicolon-separated list of directories and class archive files:

```
C:\> set CLASSPATH=D:\users\vicky\Java\classes;
```

The Java launcher and the other command-line tools know how to find the core classes, which are the classes included in every Java installation. The classes in the java.lang, java.io, java.net, and javax.swing packages, for example, are all core classes. You don't need to include these classes in your classpath; the Java interpreter and the other tools include them automatically.

To find other classes, the Java interpreter searches the elements of the classpath in order. The search combines the path location and the fully qualified class name. For example, consider a search for the class animals.birds.BigBird. Searching the classpath directory */usr/lib/java* means the interpreter looks for an individual class file at */usr/lib/java/animals/birds/BigBird.class*. Searching a ZIP or JAR archive on the classpath, say */home/vicky/Java/utils/classutils.jar*, means that the interpreter looks for component file *animals/birds/BigBird.class* within that archive.

For the Java runtime, *java*, and the Java compiler, *javac*, the classpath can also be specified with the *-classpath* option:

```
% javac -classpath /home/pat/classes:/utils/myutils.jar:. Foo.java
```

If you don't specify the CLASSPATH environment variable or command-line option, the classpath defaults to the current directory (.); this means that the files in your current directory are normally available. If you change the classpath and don't include the current directory, these files will no longer be accessible.

We suspect that about 80 percent of the problems that newcomers have when first learning Java are classpath-related. You may wish to pay particular attention to setting and checking the classpath when getting started. If you're working inside an IDE, it may remove some or all of the burden of managing the classpath. Ultimately, however, understanding the classpath and knowing exactly what is in it when your application runs is very important to your long-term sanity. The *javap* command, discussed next, can be useful in debugging classpath issues.

javap

A useful tool to know about is the *javap* command. With *javap*, you can print a description of a compiled class. You don't have to have the source code, and you don't even have to know exactly where it is, only that it is in your classpath. For example:

```
% javap java.util.Stack
```

prints the information about the java.util.Stack class:

```
Compiled from Stack.java
public class java.util.Stack extends java.util.Vector {
```

```
        public java.util.Stack( );
        public java.lang.Object push(java.lang.Object);
        public synchronized java.lang.Object pop( );
        public synchronized java.lang.Object peek( );
        public boolean empty( );
        public synchronized int search(java.lang.Object);
    }
```

This is very useful if you don't have other documentation handy and can also be helpful in debugging classpath problems. Using *javap* you can determine whether a class is in the classpath and possibly even which version you are looking at (many classpath issues involve duplicate classes in the classpath). If you are feeling really adventurous, you can try *javap* with the *-c* option, which causes it to also print the JVM instructions for each method in the class!

The Java Compiler

In this section, we'll say a few words about *javac*, the Java compiler in the JDK. The *javac* compiler is written entirely in Java, so it's available for any platform that supports the Java runtime system. *javac* turns Java source code into a compiled class that contains Java bytecode. By convention, source files are named with a *.java* extension; the resulting class files have a *.class* extension. Each source code file is considered a single compilation unit. As you'll see in Chapter 6, classes in a given compilation unit share certain features, such as package and import statements.

javac allows one public class per file and insists the file have the same name as the class. If the filename and class name don't match, *javac* issues a compilation error. A single file can contain multiple classes, as long as only one of the classes is public. Avoid packing too many classes into a single source file. Packing classes together in a *.java* file only superficially associates them. In Chapter 6 we'll talk about inner classes, classes that contain other classes and interfaces.

As an example, place the following source code in file *BigBird.java*:

```
package animals.birds;

public class BigBird extends Bird {
}
```

Next, compile it with:

```
% javac BigBird.java
```

Unlike the Java interpreter, which takes just a class name as its argument, *javac* needs a filename (with the *.java* extension) to process. The previous command produces the class file *BigBird.class* in the same directory as the source file. While it's nice to see the class file in the same directory as the source for this example, for most real applications, you need to store the class file in an appropriate place in the classpath.

You can use the *-d* option with *javac* to specify an alternative directory for storing the class files *javac* generates. The specified directory is used as the root of the class hierarchy, so *.class* files are placed in this directory or in a subdirectory below it, depending on whether the class is contained in a package. (The compiler creates intermediate subdirectories automatically, if necessary.) For example, we can use the following command to create the *BigBird.class* file at */home/vicky/Java/classes/animals/birds/BigBird.class*:

```
% javac -d /home/vicky/Java/classes BigBird.java
```

You can specify multiple *.java* files in a single *javac* command; the compiler creates a class file for each source file. But you don't need to list other classes your class references, as long as they are in the classpath in either source or compiled form. During compilation, Java resolves all other class references using the classpath.

The Java compiler is more intelligent than your average compiler, replacing some of the functionality of a *make* utility. For example, *javac* compares the modification times of the source and class files for all classes and recompiles them as necessary. A compiled Java class remembers the source file from which it was compiled, and as long as the source file is available, javac can recompile it if necessary. If, in the previous example, class BigBird references another class, animals.furry.Grover, *javac* looks for the source file *Grover.java* in an animals.furry package and recompiles it if necessary to bring the *Grover.class* class file up to date.

By default, however, *javac* checks only source files that are referenced directly from other source files. This means that if you have an out-of-date class file that is referenced only by an up-to-date class file, it may not be noticed and recompiled. You can force *javac* to walk the entire tree of objects using the -depend option, but this can increase compilation time significantly. This technique still won't help if you want to keep class libraries or other collections of classes up to date even if they aren't being referenced at all. For that and many other reasons, most projects use a real build utility such as Apache's Ant to manage builds, packaging, and more. We discuss Ant in Chapter 15.

Finally, it's important to note that *javac* can compile an application even if only the compiled (binary) versions of some of the classes are available. You don't need source code for all your objects. Java class files contain all the data type and method signature information that source files contain, so compiling against binary class files is as typesafe (and exception safe) as compiling with Java source code.

JAR Files

Java Archive (JAR) files are Java's suitcases. They are the standard and portable way to pack up all the parts of your Java application into a compact bundle for distribution or installation. You can put whatever you want into a JAR file: Java class files, serialized objects, data files, images, sounds, etc. As we'll see in Chapter 23, a JAR file can carry one or more digital signatures that attest to its integrity and authenticity. A signature can be attached to the file as a whole or to individual items in the file.

The Java runtime system understands JAR files and can load class files directly from an archive. So you can pack your application's classes in a JAR file and place it in your CLASSPATH, as described earlier. You can do the equivalent for applets by listing the JAR file in the ARCHIVE attribute of the HTML <applet> tag. Nonclass files (data, images, etc.) contained in your JAR file can also be retrieved from the classpath using the getResource( ) method (described in Chapter 12). Using this facility, your code doesn't have to know whether any resource is in a plain file or a member of a JAR archive. Whether a given class or datafile is an item in a JAR file, an individual file on the classpath, or an applet on a remote server, you can always refer to it in a standard way and let Java's class loader resolve the location.

File Compression

Items stored in JAR files are compressed with the standard ZIP file compression. Compression makes downloading classes over a network much faster. A quick survey of the standard Java distribution shows that a typical class file shrinks by about 40 percent when it is compressed. Text files such as arbitrary HTML or ASCII containing English words often compress to one-quarter their original size. (On the other hand, image files don't get much smaller when compressed; most of the common image formats have compression built in.)

Compression is not the only advantage that a JAR file has for transporting files over a network. Placing all the classes in a single JAR file enables them to be downloaded in a single transaction. Eliminating the overhead of making HTTP requests is likely to be a big savings, since individual class files tend to be small, and a complex applet could easily require many of them. On the downside, startup time could be increased if a large JAR file must be downloaded over a slow connection before the applet can start up.

Java 5.0 introduces a new archive format called Pack200, which is optimized specifically for Java class bytecode and can achieve over four-times greater compression of Java classes than ZIP alone. We'll talk about Pack200 later in this chapter.

The jar Utility

The *jar* utility provided with the JDK is a simple tool for creating and reading JAR files. Its user interface isn't particularly friendly. It mimics the Unix *tar* (tape archive) command. If you're familiar with *tar*, you'll recognize the following incantations:

jar -cvf jarFile path [path] [...]
> Create *jarFile* containing *path*(s).

jar -tvf jarFile [path] [...]
> List the contents of *jarFile*, optionally showing just *path*(s).

jar -xvf jarFile [path] [...]
> Extract the contents of *jarFile*, optionally extracting just *path*(s).

In these commands, the letters *c*, *t*, and *x* tell *jar* whether it is creating an archive, listing an archive's contents, or extracting files from an archive. The *f* means that the next argument is the name of the JAR file on which to operate. The *v* tells *jar* to be verbose when displaying information about files. In verbose mode, you get information about file sizes, modification times, and compression ratios.

Subsequent items on the command line (i.e., anything aside from the letters telling *jar* what to do and the file on which *jar* should operate) are taken as names of archive items. If you're creating an archive, the files and directories you list are placed in it. If you're extracting, only the filenames you list are extracted from the archive. (If you don't list any files, *jar* extracts everything in the archive.)

For example, let's say we have just completed our new game, *spaceblaster*. All the files associated with the game are in three directories. The Java classes themselves are in the *spaceblaster/game* directory, *spaceblaster/images* contains the game's images, and *spaceblaster/docs* contains associated game data. We can pack all this in an archive with this command:

```
% jar -cvf spaceblaster.jar spaceblaster
```

Because we requested verbose output, *jar* tells us what it is doing:

```
adding:spaceblaster/ (in=0) (out=0) (stored 0%)
adding:spaceblaster/game/ (in=0) (out=0) (stored 0%)
adding:spaceblaster/game/Game.class (in=8035) (out=3936) (deflated 51%)
adding:spaceblaster/game/Planetoid.class (in=6254) (out=3288) (deflated 47%)
adding:spaceblaster/game/SpaceShip.class (in=2295) (out=1280) (deflated 44%)
adding:spaceblaster/images/ (in=0) (out=0) (stored 0%)
adding:spaceblaster/images/spaceship.gif (in=6174) (out=5936) (deflated 3%)
adding:spaceblaster/images/planetoid.gif (in=23444) (out=23454) (deflated 0%)
adding:spaceblaster/docs/ (in=0) (out=0) (stored 0%)
adding:spaceblaster/docs/help1.html (in=3592) (out=1545) (deflated 56%)
adding:spaceblaster/docs/help2.html (in=3148) (out=1535) (deflated 51%)
```

jar creates the file *spaceblaster.jar* and adds the directory *spaceblaster*, adding the directories and files within *spaceblaster* to the archive. In verbose mode, *jar* reports the savings gained by compressing the files in the archive.

We can unpack the archive with this command:

```
% jar -xvf spaceblaster.jar
```

Likewise, we can extract an individual file or directory with:

```
% jar -xvf spaceblaster.jar filename
```

But you normally don't have to unpack a JAR file to use its contents; Java tools know how to extract files from archives automatically. We can list the contents of our JAR with the command:

```
% jar -tvf spaceblaster.jar
```

Here's the output; it lists all the files, their sizes, and creation times:

```
    0 Thu May 15 12:18:54 PDT 2003 META-INF/
 1074 Thu May 15 12:18:54 PDT 2003 META-INF/MANIFEST.MF
    0 Thu May 15 12:09:24 PDT 2003 spaceblaster/
    0 Thu May 15 11:59:32 PDT 2003 spaceblaster/game/
 8035 Thu May 15 12:14:08 PDT 2003 spaceblaster/game/Game.class
 6254 Thu May 15 12:15:18 PDT 2003 spaceblaster/game/Planetoid.class
 2295 Thu May 15 12:15:26 PDT 2003 spaceblaster/game/SpaceShip.class
    0 Thu May 15 12:17:00 PDT 2003 spaceblaster/images/
 6174 Thu May 15 12:16:54 PDT 2003 spaceblaster/images/spaceship.gif
23444 Thu May 15 12:16:58 PDT 2003 spaceblaster/images/planetoid.gif
    0 Thu May 15 12:10:02 PDT 2003 spaceblaster/docs/
 3592 Thu May 15 12:10:16 PDT 2003 spaceblaster/docs/help1.html
 3148 Thu May 15 12:10:02 PDT 2003 spaceblaster/docs/help2.html
```

JAR manifests

Note that the *jar* command automatically adds a directory called *META-INF* to our archive. The *META-INF* directory holds files describing the contents of the JAR file. It always contains at least one file: *MANIFEST.MF*. The *MANIFEST.MF* file can contain a "packing list" naming the files in the archive along with a user-definable set of attributes for each entry.

The manifest is a text file containing a set of lines in the form *keyword: value*. In Java 1.2 and later, the manifest is by default empty and contains only JAR file version information:

```
Manifest-Version: 1.0
Created-By: 1.2.1 (Sun Microsystems Inc.)
```

In Chapter 23, we'll discuss *signed* JAR files. When you sign a JAR file with a digital signature, digest (checksum) information is added to the manifest for each item in the archive. It looks like this:

```
Name: com/oreilly/Test.class
SHA1-Digest: dF2GZt8G11dXY2p4olzzIc5RjP3=
...
```

In the case of a signed JAR, the *META-INF* directory holds digital signature files for items in the archive. In Java 1.1, digest information was always added to the JAR.

But since it's really necessary only for signed JAR files, it is omitted by default when you create an archive in Java 1.2 and later.

You can add your own information to the manifest descriptions by specifying your own supplemental, manifest file when you create the archive. This is one possible place to store other simple kinds of attribute information about the files in the archive, perhaps version or authorship information.

For example, we can create a file with the following *keyword: value* lines:

```
Name: spaceblaster/images/planetoid.gif
RevisionNumber: 42.7
Artist-Temperament: moody
```

To add this information to the manifest in our archive, place it in a file called *myManifest.mf* and give the following *jar* command:

```
% jar -cvmf myManifest.mf spaceblaster.jar spaceblaster
```

We included an additional option, m, which specifies that *jar* should read additional manifest information from the file given on the command line. How does *jar* know which file is which? Because m is before f, it expects to find the manifest information before the name of the JAR file it will create. If you think that's awkward, you're right; get the names in the wrong order, and *jar* does the wrong thing. Be careful.

Although these attributes aren't automatically available to the application code, it's easy to retrieve them from a JAR file using the java.util.jar.Manifest class.

We'll see more examples of adding information to the JAR manifest in Chapter 22. The JavaBeans APIs use manifest information to designate which classes are "beans" using a Java-Bean attribute. This information is used by IDEs that work with JavaBeans.

Making a JAR file runnable

Aside from attributes, you can put a few special values in the manifest file. One of these, Main-Class, allows you to specify the class containing the primary main( ) method for an application contained in the JAR:

```
Main-Class: com.oreilly.Game
```

If you add this to your JAR file manifest (using the m option described earlier), you can run the application directly from the JAR:

```
% java -jar spaceblaster.jar
```

More importantly, under Mac OS X, Windows, and other GUI environments, you can simply click on the JAR file to launch the application. The interpreter looks for the Main-Class value in the manifest, then loads the named class as the application's initial class.

That's all on JAR files for now. Chapter 23 also picks up where this chapter leaves off in discussing cryptographically "signed" JAR files for trusted applets and application components.

The pack200 Utility

Pack200 is a new archive format introduced with Java 5.0 that is optimized for storing compiled Java class files. Pack200 is not a new form of compression but rather a super-efficient layout for class information that eliminates many types of waste and redundancy across many classes. It is effectively a bulk class file format that deconstructs many classes and reassembles their parts efficiently into one catalog. This then allows a standard compression format like ZIP to work at maximum efficiency on the archive, achieving four or more times greater compression. The Java runtime does not understand the Pack200 format, so you cannot place archives of this type into the classpath. Instead, it is mainly an intermediate format that is very useful for transferring application JARs over the network for applets and web-based applications. We'll talk about these in Chapter 23.

You can convert a JAR to and from Pack200 format with the *pack200* and *unpack200* commands supplied with the JDK.

For example, to convert *foo.jar* to *foo.pack.gz*, use the *pack200* command:

```
% pack200 foo.pack.gz foo.jar
```

To convert *foo.pack.gz* to *foo.jar*:

```
% unpack200 foo.pack.gz foo.jar
```

Note that the Pack200 process completely tears down and reconstructs your classes at the class level, so the resulting *foo.jar* file will not be byte-for-byte the same as the original.

Policy Files

One of the truly novel things about Java is that security is built into the language. As described in Chapter 1, the Java VM can verify class files and Java's security manager can impose limits on what classes do. In early versions of Java, it was necessary to implement security policies *programmatically* by writing a Java security manager class and using it in your application. A major shift occurred in Java 1.2, when a new *declarative* security system was added. This system allows you to write *policy files*— text-based descriptions of permissions—which are much simpler and don't require code changes. These policy files tell the security manager what to allow and disallow and for whom.

With security policies you can answer questions such as: "If I download a program from somewhere on the Internet, how can I prevent it from stealing information on my computer and sending it back to someone else?" "How can I prevent a malicious program from disabling my computer or erasing data on my disk?" Most computing platforms have no answer for these questions.

In early versions of Java, much of the buzz had to do with the security of applets. Applets generally run with security restrictions that prevent them from doing questionable things such as reading from or writing to the disk or contacting arbitrary computers on the network. With security policy files, it's just as easy to apply applet-style security to any application without modifying it. Furthermore, it's easy to fine-tune the access you grant. For example, you can allow an application to access only a specific directory on the disk, or you can allow network access to certain addresses.

Understanding security and security policies is important, so we'll cover it here. However, in practice, you probably won't use this facility yourself, unless you are writing a framework for running applications from many unknown sources. Java Web Start is an example of such a framework. It installs and updates Java applications over the Web with user-definable security restrictions.

The Default Security Manager

By default, no security manager is installed when you launch a Java application locally. You can turn on security using an option of the *java* interpreter to install a default security manager. The default security policy enforces many of the same rules as for applets. To see how this works, let's write a little program that does something questionable: it makes a network connection to some computer on the Internet. (We cover the specifics of network programming in Chapters 13 and 14.)

```
//file: EvilEmpire.java
import java.net.*;

public class EvilEmpire {
  public static void main(String[] args) throws Exception{
    try {
      Socket s = new Socket("207.46.131.13", 80);
      System.out.println("Connected!");
    }
    catch (SecurityException e) {
      System.out.println("SecurityException: could not connect.");
    }
  }
}
```

If you run this program with the Java interpreter, it makes the network connection:

```
C:\> java EvilEmpire
Connected!
```

But since this program is "evil," let's install the default security manager, like this:

```
C:\> java -Djava.security.manager EvilEmpire
SecurityException: could not connect.
```

That's better, but suppose that the application actually has a legitimate reason to make its network connection. We'd like to leave the default security manager in place, just to be safe, but we'd like to grant this application permission to make a network connection.

The policytool Utility

To permit our EvilEmpire example to make a network connection, we need to create a *policy file* that contains the appropriate permission. A handy utility called *policytool*, included with the JDK, helps make policy files. Fire it up from a command line like this:

```
C:\> policytool
```

You may get an error message when *policytool* starts up about not finding a default policy file. Don't worry about this; just click *OK* to make the message go away.

We now add a network permission for the EvilEmpire application. The application is identified by its origin, also called a *codebase*, described by a URL. In this case, it is a file: URL that points to the location of the EvilEmpire application on your disk.

If you started up *policytool*, you should see its main window, shown in Figure 3-2. Click on Add Policy Entry. Another window pops up, like the one shown in Figure 3-3 (but with the fields empty).

Figure 3-2. The policytool window

First, fill in the codebase with the URL of the directory containing EvilEmpire as shown in the figure. Then click on Add Permission. Yet another window pops up as shown in Figure 3-4.

Choose SocketPermission from the first combo box. Then fill out the second text field on the right side with the network address that EvilEmpire will connect to. Finally, choose connect from the third combo box. Click on OK; you should see the new permission in the policy entry window, as shown in Figure 3-3.

Figure 3-3. Adding a policy entry

Figure 3-4. Creating a new permission

Click on Done to finish creating the policy. Then choose Save As from the File menu and save the policy file as something memorable, such as *EvilEmpire.policy*. You can quit *policytool* now; we're all done with it.

There's nothing magical about the policy file you just created. Take a look at it with a text editor, which shows the simple syntax of the policy we created:

```
grant codeBase "file:/c:/Projects/Exploring/" {
  permission java.net.SocketPermission "207.46.131.13", "connect";
};
```

You can eschew *policytool* entirely and just create policy files with a text editor, if you're more comfortable that way.

Using a Policy File with the Default Security Manager

Now that we've gone to the trouble of creating a policy file, let's use it. You can tell the default security manager to use the policy file with another command-line option to the java interpreter:

```
C:\> java -Djava.security.manager -Djava.security.policy=EvilEmpire.policy EvilEmpire
Connected!
```

EvilEmpire can now make its socket connection because we have explicitly granted it permission with a policy file. The default security manager still protects us in other ways, however. EvilEmpire cannot write or read files on the disk except in the directory it came from, and it cannot make connections to any other network addresses except the one we specified. Take a moment and bask in this warm fuzzy feeling.

In Chapter 23, you'll see *policytool* again when we explain signed applets. In this chapter, codebases are identified by URLs, which isn't the most secure option. Through tricky network shenanigans, a clever forger may be able to give you code that appears to be from somewhere it's not. Cryptographically signed code is even more trustworthy; see Chapter 23 for details.

## CHAPTER 4

The Java Language

This chapter begins our introduction to the Java language syntax. Since readers come to this book with different levels of programming experience, it is difficult to set the right level for all audiences. We have tried to strike a balance between a thorough tour of the language syntax for beginners and providing enough background information so that a more experienced reader can quickly gauge the differences between Java and other languages. Since Java's syntax is derived from C, we make some comparisons to features of that language, but no special knowledge of C is necessary. We spend more time on aspects of Java that are different from other languages and less on elemental programming concepts. For example, we'll take a close look at arrays in Java because they are significantly different from those in other languages. We won't, on the other hand, spend as much time explaining basic language constructs such as loops and control structures. Chapters 5 through 7 will build on this chapter by talking about Java's object-oriented side and complete the discussion of the core language. Chapter 8 discusses generics, a Java 5.0 feature that enhances the way types work in the Java language, allowing you to write certain kinds of classes more flexibly and safely. After that, we dive into the Java APIs and see what we can do with the language. The rest of this book is filled with concise examples that do useful things and if you are left with any questions after these introductory chapters, we hope they'll be answered by real world usage.

Text Encoding

Java is a language for the Internet. Since the people of the Net speak and write in many different human languages, Java must be able to handle a large number of languages as well. One of the ways in which Java supports internationalization is through the Unicode character set. Unicode is a worldwide standard that supports the scripts of most languages.* Java bases its character and string data on the Unicode 4.0 standard, which uses 16 bits to represent each symbol.

Java source code can be written using Unicode and stored in any number of character encodings, ranging from its full 16-bit form to ASCII-encoded Unicode character values. This makes Java a friendly language for non-English-speaking programmers who can use their native language for class, method, and variable names just as they can for the text displayed by the application.

The Java char type and String objects natively support Unicode values. But if you're concerned about having to labor with two-byte characters, you can relax. The String API makes the character encoding transparent to you. Unicode is also very ASCII-friendly (ASCII is the most common character encoding for English). The first 256 characters are defined to be identical to the first 256 characters in the ISO 8859-1 (Latin-1) character set, so Unicode is effectively backward-compatible with the most common English character sets. Furthermore, the most common encoding for Unicode, called UTF-8, preserves ASCII values in their single byte form. This encoding is used in compiled Java class files, so for English text, storage remains compact.

Most platforms can't display all currently defined Unicode characters. As a result, Java programs can be written with special Unicode escape sequences. A Unicode character can be represented with this escape sequence:

```
\uxxxx
```

xxxx is a sequence of one to four hexadecimal digits. The escape sequence indicates an ASCII-encoded Unicode character. This is also the form Java uses to output (print) Unicode characters in an environment that doesn't otherwise support them. Java also comes with classes to read and write Unicode character streams in specific encodings, including UTF-8.

Comments

Java supports both C-style *block comments* delimited by /* and */ and C++-style *line comments* indicated by //:

```
/*  This is a
        multiline
            comment.    */

// This is a single-line comment
// and so // is this
```

---

* For more information about Unicode, see *http://www.unicode.org*. Ironically, one of the scripts listed as "obsolete and archaic" and not currently supported by the Unicode standard is Javanese—a historical language of the people of the Island of Java.

Block comments have both a beginning and end sequence and can cover large ranges of text. However, they cannot be "nested"; meaning that you can't have a block comment inside of a block comment without the compiler getting confused. Single-line comments have only a start sequence and are delimited by the end of a line; extra // indicators inside a single line have no effect. Line comments are useful for short comments within methods; they don't conflict with block comments, so you can still comment-out larger chunks of code including them.

Javadoc Comments

A block comment beginning with /** indicates a special *doc comment*. A doc comment is designed to be extracted by automated documentation generators, such as the JDK's *javadoc* program. A doc comment is terminated by the next */, just as with a regular block comment. Within the doc comment, lines beginning with @ are interpreted as special instructions for the documentation generator, giving it information about the source code. By convention, each line of a doc comment begins with a *, as shown in the following example, but this is optional. Any leading spacing and the * on each line are ignored:

```
/**
 * I think this class is possibly the most amazing thing you will
 * ever see. Let me tell you about my own personal vision and
 * motivation in creating it.
 * <p>
 * It all began when I was a small child, growing up on the
 * streets of Idaho. Potatoes were the rage, and life was good...
 *
 * @see PotatoPeeler
 * @see PotatoMasher
 * @author John 'Spuds' Smith
 * @version 1.00, 19 Dec 2006
 */
class Potato {
```

javadoc creates HTML documentation for classes by reading the source code and pulling out the embedded comments and @ tags. In this example, the tags cause author and version information to be presented in the class documentation. The @see tags produce hypertext links to the related class documentation.

The compiler also looks at the doc comments; in particular, it is interested in the @deprecated tag, which means that the method has been declared obsolete and should be avoided in new programs. The fact that a method is deprecated is noted in the compiled class file so a warning message can be generated whenever you use a deprecated feature in your code (even if the source isn't available).

Doc comments can appear above class, method, and variable definitions, but some tags may not be applicable to all of these. For example, the @exception tag can only be applied to methods. Table 4-1 summarizes the tags used in doc comments.

Table 4-1. Doc comment tags

Tag	Description	Applies to
@see	Associated class name	Class, method, or variable
@author	Author name	Class
@version	Version string	Class
@param	Parameter name and description	Method
@return	Description of return value	Method
@exception	Exception name and description	Method
@deprecated	Declares an item to be obsolete	Class, method, or variable
@since	Notes API version when item was added	Variable

Javadoc as metadata

Javadoc tags in doc comments represent *metadata* about the source code; that is, they add descriptive information about the structure or contents of the code that is not, strictly speaking, part of the application. In the past, some additional tools have extended the concept of Javadoc-style tags to include other kinds of metadata about Java programs. Java 5.0 introduced a new *annotations* facility that provides a more formal and extensible way to add metadata to Java classes, methods, and variables. We'll talk about annotations in Chapter 7. However, we should mention that there is an @deprecated annotation that has the same meaning as that of the Javadoc tag of the same name. Users of Java 5.0 will likely prefer it to the Javadoc form.

Types

The type system of a programming language describes how its data elements (variables and constants) are associated with storage in memory and how they are related to one another. In a statically typed language, such as C or C++, the type of a data element is a simple, unchanging attribute that often corresponds directly to some underlying hardware phenomenon, such as a register or a pointer value. In a more dynamic language such as Smalltalk or Lisp, variables can be assigned arbitrary elements and can effectively change their type throughout their lifetime. A considerable amount of overhead goes into validating what happens in these languages at runtime. Scripting languages such as Perl achieve ease of use by providing drastically simplified type systems in which only certain data elements can be stored in variables, and values are unified into a common representation, such as strings.

Java combines the best features of both statically and dynamically typed languages. As in a statically typed language, every variable and programming element in Java has a type that is known at compile time, so the runtime system doesn't normally have to check the validity of assignments between types while the code is executing. Unlike traditional C or C++, Java also maintains runtime information about objects and uses this to allow truly dynamic behavior. Java code may load new types at runtime and use them in fully object-oriented ways, allowing casting and full polymorphism (extending of types).

Java data types fall into two categories. *Primitive types* represent simple values that have built-in functionality in the language; they are fixed elements, such as literal constants and numbers. *Reference types* (or class types) include objects and arrays; they are called reference types because they "refer to" a large data type which is passed "by reference," as we'll explain shortly. In Java 5.0, *generic types* were introduced to the language, but they are really an extension of classes and are, therefore, actually reference types.

Primitive Types

Numbers, characters, and Boolean values are fundamental elements in Java. Unlike some other (perhaps more pure) object-oriented languages, they are not objects. For those situations where it's desirable to treat a primitive value as an object, Java provides "wrapper" classes. The major advantage of treating primitive values as special is that the Java compiler and runtime can more readily optimize their implementation. Primitive values and computations can still be mapped down to hardware as they always have been in lower-level languages. As of Java 5.0, the compiler can automatically convert between primitive values and their object wrappers as needed to partially mask the difference between the two. We'll explain what that means in more detail in the next chapter when we discuss *boxing* and *unboxing* of primitive values.

An important portability feature of Java is that primitive types are precisely defined. For example, you never have to worry about the size of an int on a particular platform; it's always a 32-bit, signed, two's complement number. Table 4-2 summarizes Java's primitive types.

Table 4-2. Java primitive data types

Type	Definition
boolean	true or false
char	16-bit, Unicode character
byte	8-bit, signed, two's complement integer
short	16-bit, signed, two's complement integer
int	32-bit, signed, two's complement integer
long	64-bit, signed, two's complement integer
float	32-bit, IEEE 754, floating-point value
double	64-bit, IEEE 754

Those of you with a C background may notice that the primitive types look like an idealization of C scalar types on a 32-bit machine, and you're absolutely right. That's how they're supposed to look. The 16-bit characters were forced by Unicode, and ad hoc pointers were deleted for other reasons. But overall, the syntax and semantics of Java primitive types are meant to fit a C programmer's mental habits.

Floating-point precision

Floating-point operations in Java follow the IEEE 754 international specification, which means that the result of floating-point calculations is normally the same on different Java platforms. However, since Version 1.3, Java has allowed for extended precision on platforms that support it. This can introduce extremely small-valued and arcane differences in the results of high-precision operations. Most applications would never notice this, but if you want to ensure that your application produces exactly the same results on different platforms, you can use the special keyword strictfp as a class modifier on the class containing the floating-point manipulation (we cover classes in the next chapter). The compiler then prohibits platform-specific optimizations.

Variable declaration and initialization

Variables are declared inside of methods or classes in C style, with a type followed by one or more comma-separated variable names. For example:

```
int foo;
double d1, d2;
boolean isFun;
```

Variables can optionally be initialized with an appropriate expression when they are declared:

```
int foo = 42;
double d1 = 3.14, d2 = 2 * 3.14;
boolean isFun = true;
```

Variables that are declared as members of a class are set to default values if they aren't initialized (see Chapter 5). In this case, numeric types default to the appropriate flavor of zero, characters are set to the null character (\0), and Boolean variables have the value false. Local variables, which are declared inside a method and live only for the duration of a method call, on the other hand, must be explicitly initialized before they can be used. As we'll see, the compiler enforces this rule so there is no danger of forgetting.

Integer literals

Integer literals can be specified in octal (base 8), decimal (base 10), or hexadecimal (base 16). A decimal integer is specified by a sequence of digits beginning with one of the characters 1–9:

```
int i = 1230;
```

Octal numbers are distinguished from decimal numbers by a leading zero:

```
int i = 01230;              // i = 664 decimal
```

A hexadecimal number is denoted by the leading characters 0x or 0X (zero "x"), followed by a combination of digits and the characters a–f or A–F, which represent the decimal values 10–15:

```
int i = 0xFFFF;             // i = 65535 decimal
```

Integer literals are of type int unless they are suffixed with an L, denoting that they are to be produced as a long value:

```
long l = 13L;
long l = 13;       // equivalent: 13 is converted from type int
```

(The lowercase letter l is also acceptable but should be avoided because it often looks like the number 1.)

When a numeric type is used in an assignment or an expression involving a "larger" type with a greater range, it can be *promoted* to the bigger type. In the second line of the previous example, the number 13 has the default type of int, but it's promoted to type long for assignment to the long variable. Certain other numeric and comparison operations also cause this kind of arithmetic promotion, as do mathematical expressions involving more than one type. For example, when multiplying a byte value by an int value, the compiler promotes the byte to an int first:

```
byte b = 42;
int i = 43;
int result = b * i;  // b is promoted to int before multiplication
```

A numeric value can never go the other way and be assigned to a type with a smaller range without an explicit cast, however:

```
int i = 13;
byte b = i;             // Compile-time error, explicit cast needed
byte b = (byte) i;   // OK
```

Conversions from floating-point to integer types always require an explicit cast because of the potential loss of precision.

Floating-point literals

Floating-point values can be specified in decimal or scientific notation. Floating-point literals are of type double unless they are suffixed with an f or F denoting that they are to be produced as a float value:

```
double d = 8.31;
double e = 3.00e+8;
float f = 8.31F;
float g = 3.00e+8F;
```

Character literals

A literal character value can be specified either as a single-quoted character or as an escaped ASCII or Unicode sequence:

```
char a = 'a';
char newline = '\n';
char smiley = '\u263a';
```

Reference Types

In an object-oriented language like Java, you create new, complex data types from simple primitives by creating a class. Each class then serves as a new type in the language. For example, if we create a new class called Foo in Java, we are also implicitly creating a new type called Foo. The type of an item governs how it's used and where it can be assigned. As with primitives, an item of type Foo can, in general, be assigned to a variable of type Foo or passed as an argument to a method that accepts a Foo value.

A type is not just a simple attribute. Classes can have relationships with other classes and so do the types that they represent. All classes exist in a parent-child hierarchy, where a child class or *subclass* is a specialized kind of its parent class. The corresponding types have the same relationship, where the type of the child class is considered a subtype of the parent class. Because child classes inherit all of the functionality of their parent classes, an object of the child's type is in some sense equivalent to or an extension of the parent type. An object of the child type can be used in place of an object of the parent's type. For example, if you create a new class, Cat, that extends Animal, the new type, Cat, is considered a subtype of Animal. Objects of type Cat can then be used anywhere an object of type Animal can be used; an object of type Cat is said to be assignable to a variable of type Animal. This is called *subtype polymorphism* and is one of the primary features of an object-oriented language. We'll look more closely at classes and objects in Chapter 5.

Primitive types in Java are used and passed "by value." In other words, when a primitive value like an int is assigned to a variable or passed as an argument to a method, it's simply copied. Reference types, on the other hand, are always accessed "by reference." A *reference* is simply a handle or a name for an object. What a variable of a reference type holds is a "pointer" to an object of its type (or of a subtype, as described earlier). When the reference is assigned or passed to a method, only the reference is copied, not the object it's pointing to. A reference is like a pointer in C or C++, except that its type is so strictly enforced that you can't mess with the reference itself—it's an atomic entity. The reference value itself can't be created or changed. A variable gets assigned a reference value only through assignment to an appropriate object.

Let's run through an example. We declare a variable of type Foo, called myFoo, and assign it an appropriate object:[*]

```
Foo myFoo = new Foo( );
Foo anotherFoo = myFoo;
```

myFoo is a reference-type variable that holds a reference to the newly constructed Foo object. (For now, don't worry about the details of creating an object; we'll cover that in Chapter 5.) We declare a second Foo type variable, anotherFoo, and assign it to the same object. There are now two identical references: myFoo and anotherFoo, but only one actual Foo object instance. If we change things in the state of the Foo object itself, we see the same effect by looking at it with either reference.

Object references are passed to methods in the same way. In this case, either myFoo or anotherFoo would serve as equivalent arguments:

```
myMethod( myFoo );
```

An important, but sometimes confusing, distinction to make at this point is that the reference itself is a value and that value is copied when it is assigned to a variable or passed in a method call. Given our previous example, the argument passed to a method (a local variable from the method's point of view) is actually a third copy of the reference, in addition to myFoo and anotherFoo. The method can alter the state of the Foo object itself through that reference (calling its methods or altering its variables), but it can't change the caller's notion of the reference to myFoo. That is, the method can't change the caller's myFoo to point to a different Foo object; it can change only its own reference. This will be more obvious when we talk about methods later. Java differs from C++ in this respect. If you need to change a caller's reference to an object in Java, you need an additional level of indirection. The caller would have to wrap the reference in another object so that both could share the reference to it.

Reference types always point to objects, and objects are always defined by classes. However, two special kinds of reference types, arrays and interfaces, specify the type of object they point to in a slightly different way.

Arrays in Java have a special place in the type system. They are a special kind of object automatically created to hold a collection of some other type of object, known as the *base type*. Declaring an array type reference implicitly creates the new class type, as you'll see in the next chapter.

Interfaces are a bit sneakier. An interface defines a set of methods and gives it a corresponding type. Any object that implements all methods of the interface can be treated as an object of that type. Variables and method arguments can be declared to

---

[*] The comparable code in C++ would be:

```
Foo& myFoo = *(new Foo( ));
Foo& anotherFoo = myFoo;
```

be of interface types, just like class types, and any object that implements the interface can be assigned to them. This allows Java to cross the lines of the class hierarchy and make objects that effectively have many types. We'll cover interfaces in the next chapter as well.

Finally, we should mention again that Java 5.0 made a major new addition to the language. *Generic types* or *parameterized types*, as they are called, are an extension of the Java class syntax that allows for additional abstraction in the way classes work with other Java types. Generics allow for specialization of classes by the user without changing any of the original class's code. We cover generics in detail in Chapter 8.

A Word About Strings

Strings in Java are objects; they are therefore a reference type. String objects do, however, have some special help from the Java compiler that makes them look more like primitive types. Literal string values in Java source code are turned into String objects by the compiler. They can be used directly, passed as arguments to methods, or assigned to String type variables:

```
System.out.println( "Hello, World..." );
String s = "I am the walrus...";
String t = "John said: \"I am the walrus...\"";
```

The + symbol in Java is overloaded to provide string concatenation as well as numeric addition. Along with its sister +=, this is the only overloaded operator in Java:

```
String quote = "Four score and " + "seven years ago,";
String more = quote + " our" + " fathers" +  " brought...";
```

Java builds a single String object from the concatenated strings and provides it as the result of the expression. We discuss the String class and all things text-related in great detail in Chapter 10.

Statements and Expressions

Java *statements* appear inside methods and classes; they describe all activities of a Java program. Variable declarations and assignments, such as those in the previous section, are statements, as are basic language structures such as if/then conditionals and loops.

```
int size = 5;
if ( size > 10 )
    doSomething();
for( int x = 0; x < size; x++ ) { ... }
```

Expressions produce values; an expression is evaluated to produce a result, to be used as part of another expression or in a statement. Method calls, object allocations, and, of course, mathematical expressions are examples of expressions. Technically, since variable assignments can be used as values for further assignments or operations (in somewhat questionable programming style), they can be considered to be both statements and expressions.

```
new Object( );
Math.sin( 3.1415 );
42 * 64;
```

One of the tenets of Java is to keep things simple and consistent. To that end, when there are no other constraints, evaluations and initializations in Java always occur in the order in which they appear in the code—from left to right, top to bottom. We'll see this rule used in the evaluation of assignment expressions, method calls, and array indexes, to name a few cases. In some other languages, the order of evaluation is more complicated or even implementation-dependent. Java removes this element of danger by precisely and simply defining how the code is evaluated. This doesn't mean you should start writing obscure and convoluted statements, however. Relying on the order of evaluation of expressions in complex ways is a bad programming habit, even when it works. It produces code that is hard to read and harder to modify.

Statements

Statements and expressions in Java appear within a *code block*. A code block is syntactically a series of statements surrounded by an open curly brace ({) and a close curly brace (}). The statements in a code block can include variable declarations and most of the other sorts of statements and expressions we mentioned earlier:

```
{
    int size = 5;
    setName("Max");
    ...
}
```

Methods, which look like C functions, are in a sense just code blocks that take parameters and can be called by their names—for example, the method setUpDog( ):

```
setUpDog( String name ) {
    int size = 5;
    setName( name );
    ...
}
```

Variable declarations are limited in scope to their enclosing code block. That is, they can't be seen outside of the nearest set of braces:

```
{
    int i = 5;
}

i = 6;              // Compile-time error, no such variable i
```

In this way, code blocks can be used to arbitrarily group other statements and variables. The most common use of code blocks, however, is to define a group of statements for use in a conditional or iterative statement.

if/else conditionals

Since a code block is itself collectively treated as a statement, we define a conditional like an if/else clause as follows:

```
if ( condition )
    statement;
[ else
    statement; ]
```

So, the if clause has the familiar (to C/C++ programmers) functionality of taking two different forms: a "one-liner" and a block. Here's one:

```
if ( condition )
    statement;
```

Here's the other:

```
if ( condition )  {
    [ statement; ]
    [ statement; ]
    [ ... ]
}
```

The *condition* is a Boolean expression. A Boolean expression is a true or false value or an expression that evaluates to one of those. For example i == 0 is a Boolean expression that tests whether the integer i holds the value 0.

In the second form, the statement is a code block, and all its enclosed statements are executed if the conditional succeeds. Any variables declared within that block are visible only to the statements within the successful branch of the condition. Like the if/else conditional, most of the remaining Java statements are concerned with controlling the flow of execution. They act for the most part like their namesakes in other languages.

do/while loops

The do and while iterative statements have the familiar functionality; their conditional test is also a Boolean expression:

```
while ( condition )
    statement;

do
    statement;
while ( condition );
```

For example:

```
while( queue.isEmpty( ) )
    wait( );
```

Unlike while or for loops (which we'll see next), that test their conditions first, a do-while loop always executes its statement body at least once.

The for loop

The most general form of the for loop is also a holdover from the C language:

```
for ( initialization; condition; incrementor )
    statement;
```

The variable initialization section can declare or initialize variables that are limited to the scope of the for statement. The for loop then begins a possible series of rounds in which the condition is first checked and, if true, the body is executed. Following each execution of the body, the incrementor expressions are evaluated to give them a chance to update variables before the next round begins:

```
for ( int i = 0; i < 100; i++ ) {
    System.out.println( i )
    int j = i;
    ...
}
```

This loop will execute 100 times, printing values from 0 to 99. If the condition of a for loop returns false on the first check, the body and incrementor section will never be executed.

You can use multiple comma-separated expressions in the initialization and incrementation sections of the for loop. For example:

```
for (int i = 0, j = 10; i < j; i++, j-- ) {
    ...
}
```

You can also initialize existing variables from outside the scope of the for loop within the initializer block. You might do this if you wanted to use the end value of the loop variable elsewhere:

```
int x;
for( x = 0; hasMoreValue( ); x++ )
  getNextValue( );
System.out.println( x );
```

The enhanced for loop

Java 5.0 introduced a new form of the for loop (auspiciously dubbed the "enhanced for loop"). In this simpler form, the for loop acts like a "foreach" statement in some other languages, iterating over a series of values in an array or other type of collection:

```
for ( varDeclaration : iterable )
    statement;
```

The enhanced for loop can be used to loop over arrays of any type as well as any kind of Java object that implements the java.lang.Iterable interface. This includes most of the classes of the Java Collections API. We'll talk about arrays in this and the next chapter; Chapter 11 covers Java Collections. Here are a couple of examples:

```
int [] arrayOfInts = new int [] { 1, 2, 3, 4 };

for( int i  : arrayOfInts )
    System.out.println( i );

List<String> list = new ArrayList<String>( );
list.add("foo");
list.add("bar");

for( String s : list )
    System.out.println( s );
```

Again, we haven't discussed arrays or the List class and special syntax in this example. What we're showing here is the enhanced for loop iterating over an array of integers and also a list of string values. In the second case, the List implements the Iterable interface and so can be a target of the for loop.

switch statements

The most common form of the Java switch statement takes an integer-type argument (or an argument that can be automatically promoted to an integer type) and selects among a number of alternative, integer constant case branches:

```
switch ( int expression )
{
    case int constantExpression :
        statement;
    [ case int constantExpression :
        statement;   ]
    ...
    [ default :
        statement;   ]
}
```

The case expression for each branch must evaluate to a different constant integer value at compile time. An optional default case can be specified to catch unmatched conditions. When executed, the switch simply finds the branch matching its conditional expression (or the default branch) and executes the corresponding statement. But that's not the end of the story. Perhaps counterintuitively, the switch statement then continues executing branches after the matched branch until it hits the end of the switch or a special statement called break. Here are a couple of examples:

```
int value = 2;

switch( value ) {
    case 1:
        System.out.println( 1 );
    case 2:
        System.out.println( 2 );
```

```
        case 3:
            System.out.println( 3 );
    }

    // prints 2, 3
```

Using break to terminate each branch is more common:

```
    int retValue = checkStatus( );

    switch ( retVal )
    {
        case MyClass.GOOD :
            // something good
            break;
        case MyClass.BAD :
            // something bad
            break;
        default :
            // neither one
            break;
    }
```

In this example, only one branch: GOOD, BAD, or the default is executed. The "fall through" behavior of the switch is justified when you want to cover several possible case values with the same statement, without resorting to a bunch of if-else statements:

```
    int value = getSize( );

    switch( value ) {
        case MINISCULE:
        case TEENYWEENIE:
        case SMALL:
            System.out.println("Small" );
            break;
        case MEDIUM:
            System.out.println("Medium" );
            break;
        case LARGE:
        case EXTRALARGE:
            System.out.println("Large" );
            break;
    }
```

This example effectively groups the six possible values into three cases.

Enumerations and switch statements. Java 5.0 introduced *enumerations* to the language. Enumerations are intended to replace much of the usage of integer constants for situations like the one just discussed with a type-safe alternative. Enumerations use objects as their values instead of integers but preserve the notion of ordering and comparability. We'll see in Chapter 5 that enumerations are declared much like classes and that the values can be "imported" into the code of your application to be used just like constants. For example:

```
    enum Size { Small, Medium, Large }
```

You can use enumerations in switches in Java 5.0 in the same way that the previous switch examples used integer constants. In fact, it is much safer to do so because the enumerations have real types and the compiler does not let you mistakenly add cases that do not match any value or mix values from different enumerations.

```java
// usage
Size size = ...;
switch ( size ) {
    case Small:
        ...
    case Medium:
        ...
    case Large:
        ...
}
```

Chapter 5 provides more details about enumerations as objects.

break/continue

The Java break statement and its friend continue can also be used to cut short a loop or conditional statement by jumping out of it. A break causes Java to stop the current block statement and resume execution after it. In the following example, the while loop goes on endlessly until the condition( ) method returns true, then it stops and proceeds at the point marked "after while."

```java
while( true ) {
    if ( condition() )
        break;
}
// after while
```

A continue statement causes for and while loops to move on to their next iteration by returning to the point where they check their condition. The following example prints the numbers 0 through 99, skipping number 33.

```java
for( int i=0; i < 100; i++ ) {
    if ( i == 33 )
        continue;
    System.out.println( i );
}
```

The break and continue statements should be familiar to C programmers, but Java's have the additional ability to take a label as an argument and jump out multiple levels to the scope of the labeled point in the code. This usage is not very common in day-to-day Java coding but may be important in special cases. Here is an outline:

```java
labelOne:
    while ( condition ) {
        ...
        labelTwo:
            while ( condition ) {
                ...
```

```
            // break or continue point
        }
    // after labelTwo
    }
// after labelOne
```

Enclosing statements, such as code blocks, conditionals, and loops, can be labeled with identifiers like labelOne and labelTwo. In this example, a break or continue without argument at the indicated position has the same effect as the earlier examples. A break causes processing to resume at the point labeled "after labelTwo"; a continue immediately causes the labelTwo loop to return to its condition test.

The statement break labelTwo at the indicated point has the same effect as an ordinary break, but break labelOne breaks both levels and resumes at the point labeled "after labelOne." Similarly, continue labelTwo serves as a normal continue, but continue labelOne returns to the test of the labelOne loop. Multilevel break and continue statements remove the main justification for the evil goto statement in C/C++.

There are a few Java statements we aren't going to discuss right now. The try, catch, and finally statements are used in exception handling, as we'll discuss later in this chapter. The synchronized statement in Java is used to coordinate access to statements among multiple threads of execution; see Chapter 9 for a discussion of thread synchronization.

Unreachable statements

On a final note, we should mention that the Java compiler flags "unreachable" statements as compile-time errors. An unreachable statement is one that the compiler determines won't be called at all. Of course, many methods may never actually be called in your code, but the compiler detects only those that it can "prove" are never called by simple checking at compile time. For example, a method with an unconditional return statement in the middle of it causes a compile-time error, as does a method with a conditional that the compiler can tell will never be fulfilled:

```
if (1 < 2)
    return;
// unreachable statements
```

Expressions

An expression produces a result, or value, when it is evaluated. The value of an expression can be a numeric type, as in an arithmetic expression; a reference type, as in an object allocation; or the special type, void, which is the declared type of a method that doesn't return a value. In the last case, the expression is evaluated only for its *side effects*, that is, the work it does aside from producing a value. The type of an expression is known at compile time. The value produced at runtime is either of this type or, in the case of a reference type, a compatible (assignable) subtype.

Operators

Java supports almost all standard C operators. These operators also have the same precedence in Java as they do in C, as shown in Table 4-3.

Table 4-3. Java operators

Precedence	Operator	Operand type	Description
1	++, --	Arithmetic	Increment and decrement
1	+, -	Arithmetic	Unary plus and minus
1	~	Integral	Bitwise complement
1	!	Boolean	Logical complement
1	(type)	Any	Cast
2	*, /, %	Arithmetic	Multiplication, division, remainder
3	+, -	Arithmetic	Addition and subtraction
3	+	String	String concatenation
4	<<	Integral	Left shift
4	>>	Integral	Right shift with sign extension
4	>>>	Integral	Right shift with no extension
5	<, <=, >, >=	Arithmetic	Numeric comparison
5	instanceof	Object	Type comparison
6	==, !=	Primitive	Equality and inequality of value
6	==, !=	Object	Equality and inequality of reference
7	&	Integral	Bitwise AND
7	&	Boolean	Boolean AND
8	^	Integral	Bitwise XOR
8	^	Boolean	Boolean XOR
9	|	Integral	Bitwise OR
9	|	Boolean	Boolean OR
10	&&	Boolean	Conditional AND
11	||	Boolean	Conditional OR
12	?:	N/A	Conditional ternary operator
13	=	Any	Assignment

We should also note that the percent (%) operator is not strictly a modulo, but a remainder, and can have a negative value.

Java also adds some new operators. As we've seen, the + operator can be used with String values to perform string concatenation. Because all integral types in Java are signed values, the >> operator performs a right-arithmetic-shift operation with sign extension. The >>> operator treats the operand as an unsigned number and performs a right-arithmetic-shift with no sign extension. The new operator, as in C++, is used to create objects; we will discuss it in detail shortly.

Assignment

While variable initialization (i.e., declaration and assignment together) is considered a statement, with no resulting value, variable assignment alone is an expression:

```
int i, j;          // statement
i = 5;             // both expression and statement
```

Normally, we rely on assignment for its side effects alone, but, as in C, an assignment can be used as a value in another part of an expression:

```
j = ( i = 5 );
```

Again, relying on order of evaluation extensively (in this case, using compound assignments in complex expressions) can make code obscure and hard to read. Do so at your own peril.

The null value

The expression null can be assigned to any reference type. It means "no reference." A null reference can't be used to reference anything and attempting to do so generates a NullPointerException at runtime.

Variable access

The dot (.) operator is used to select members of a class or object instance. It can retrieve the value of an instance variable (of an object) or a static variable (of a class). It can also specify a method to be invoked on an object or class:

```
int i = myObject.length;
String s = myObject.name;
myObject.someMethod( );
```

A reference-type expression can be used in compound evaluations by selecting further variables or methods on the result:

```
int len = myObject.name.length( );
int initialLen = myObject.name.substring(5, 10).length( );
```

Here we have found the length of our name variable by invoking the length( ) method of the String object. In the second case, we took an intermediate step and asked for a substring of the name string. The substring method of the String class also returns a String reference, for which we ask the length. Compounding operations like this is also called *chaining method calls*, which we'll mention later. One chained selection operation that we've used a lot already is calling the println( ) method on the variable out of the System class:

```
System.out.println("calling println on out");
```

Method invocation

Methods are functions that live within a class and may be accessible through the class or its instances, depending on the kind of method. Invoking a method means to execute its body, passing in any required parameter variables and possibly getting a value in return. A method invocation is an expression that results in a value. The value's type is the *return type* of the method:

```
System.out.println( "Hello, World..." );
int myLength = myString.length( );
```

Here, we invoked the methods println( ) and length( ) on different objects. The length( ) method returned an integer value; the return type of println( ) is void.

This is all pretty simple, but in Chapter 5 we'll see that it gets a little more complex when there are methods with the same name but different parameter types in the same class or when a method is redefined in a child class, as described in Chapter 6.

Object creation

Objects in Java are allocated with the new operator:

```
Object o = new Object( );
```

The argument to new is the constructor for the class. The *constructor* is a method that always has the same name as the class. The constructor specifies any required parameters to create an instance of the object. The value of the new expression is a reference of the type of the created object. Objects always have one or more constructors, though they may not always be accessible to you.

We look at object creation in detail in Chapter 5. For now, just note that object creation is a type of expression and that the result is an object reference. A minor oddity is that the binding of new is "tighter" than that of the dot (.) selector. So you can create a new object and invoke a method in it without assigning the object to a reference type variable if you have some reason to:

```
int hours = new Date( ).getHours( );
```

The Date class is a utility class that represents the current time. Here we create a new instance of Date with the new operator and call its getHours( ) method to retrieve the current hour as an integer value. The Date object reference lives long enough to service the method call and is then cut loose and garbage-collected at some point in the future (see Chapter 5 for details about garbage collection).

Calling methods in object references in this way is, again, a matter of style. It would certainly be clearer to allocate an intermediate variable of type Date to hold the new object and then call its getHours( ) method. However, combining operations like this is common.

The instanceof operator

The instanceof operator can be used to determine the type of an object at runtime. It tests to see if an object is of the same type or a subtype of the target type. This is the same as asking if the object can be assigned to a variable of the target type. The target type may be a class, interface, or array type as we'll see later. instanceof returns a boolean value that indicates whether the object matches the type:

```
Boolean b;
String str = "foo";
b = ( str instanceof String );   // true, str is a String
b = ( str instanceof Object );   // also true, a String is an Object
b = ( str instanceof Date );     // false, str is not a Date or subclass
```

instanceof also correctly reports whether the object is of the type of an array or a specified interface (as we'll discuss later):

```
if ( foo instanceof byte[] )
    ...
```

It is also important to note that the value null is not considered an instance of any object. The following test returns false, no matter what the declared type of the variable:

```
String s = null;
if ( s instanceof String )
    // false, null isn't an instance of anything
```

Exceptions

Java has its roots in embedded systems—software that runs inside specialized devices, such as hand-held computers, cellular phones, and fancy toasters. In those kinds of applications, it's especially important that software errors be handled robustly. Most users would agree that it's unacceptable for their phone to simply crash or for their toast (and perhaps their house) to burn because their software failed. Given that we can't eliminate the possibility of software errors, it's a step in the right direction to recognize and deal with anticipated application-level errors methodically.

Dealing with errors in a language such as C is entirely the responsibility of the programmer. The language itself provides no help in identifying error types and no tools for dealing with them easily. In C, a routine generally indicates a failure by returning an "unreasonable" value (e.g., the idiomatic -1 or null). As the programmer, you must know what constitutes a bad result and what it means. It's often awkward to work around the limitations of passing error values in the normal path of data flow.*

---

* The somewhat obscure setjmp( ) and longjmp( ) statements in C can save a point in the execution of code and later return to it unconditionally from a deeply buried location. In a limited sense, this is the functionality of exceptions in Java.

An even worse problem is that certain types of errors can legitimately occur almost anywhere, and it's prohibitive and unreasonable to explicitly test for them at every point in the software.

Java offers an elegant solution to these problems through *exceptions*. (Java exception handling is similar to, but not quite the same as, exception handling in C++.) An *exception* indicates an unusual condition or an error condition. Program control becomes unconditionally transferred or "thrown" to a specially designated section of code where it's caught and handled. In this way, error handling is orthogonal to (or independent of) the normal flow of the program. We don't have to have special return values for all our methods; errors are handled by a separate mechanism. Control can be passed a long distance from a deeply nested routine and handled in a single location when that is desirable, or an error can be handled immediately at its source. A few standard methods return -1 as a special value, but these are generally limited to situations where we are expecting a special value and the situation is not really out of bounds.*

A Java method is required to specify the exceptions it can throw (i.e., the ones that it doesn't catch itself), and the compiler makes sure that users of the method handle them. In this way, the information about what errors a method can produce is promoted to the same level of importance as its argument and return types. You may still decide to punt and ignore obvious errors, but in Java you must do so explicitly.

Exceptions and Error Classes

Exceptions are represented by instances of the class java.lang.Exception and its subclasses. Subclasses of Exception can hold specialized information (and possibly behavior) for different kinds of exceptional conditions. However, more often they are simply "logical" subclasses that serve only to identify a new exception type. Figure 4-1 shows the subclasses of Exception in the java.lang package. It should give you a feel for how exceptions are organized. Most other packages define their own exception types, which usually are subclasses of Exception itself or of its important subclass RuntimeException, which we'll discuss in a moment.

For example, an important exception class is IOException in the package java.io. The IOException class extends Exception and has many subclasses for typical I/O problems (such as a FileNotFoundException) and networking problems (such as a MalformedURLException). Network exceptions belong to the java.net package. Another important descendant of IOException is RemoteException, which belongs to the java.rmi package. It is used when problems arise during remote method

---

* For example, the getHeight( ) method of the Image class returns -1 if the height isn't known yet. No error has occurred; the height will be available in the future. In this situation, throwing an exception would be inappropriate.

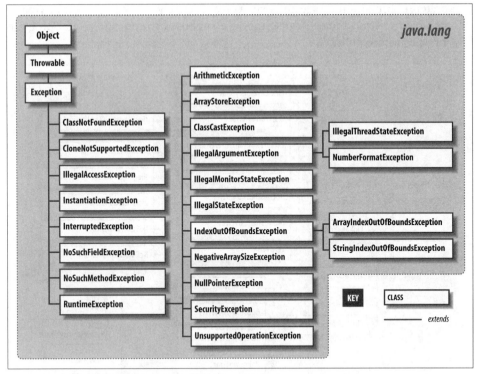

Figure 4-1. The java.lang.Exception subclasses

invocation (RMI). Throughout this book, we mention exceptions you need to be aware of as we encounter them.

An Exception object is created by the code at the point where the error condition arises. It can be designed to hold whatever information is necessary to describe the exceptional condition and also includes a full *stack trace* for debugging. (A stack trace is the list of all the methods called in order to reach the point where the exception was thrown.) The Exception object is passed as an argument to the handling block of code, along with the flow of control. This is where the terms "throw" and "catch" come from: the Exception object is thrown from one point in the code and caught by the other, where execution resumes.

The Java API also defines the java.lang.Error class for unrecoverable errors. The subclasses of Error in the java.lang package are shown in Figure 4-2. A notable Error type is AssertionError, which is used by the assert statement to indicate a failure (assertions are discussed later in this chapter). A few other packages define their own subclasses of Error, but subclasses of Error are much less common (and less useful) than subclasses of Exception. You generally needn't worry about these errors in your code (i.e., you do not have to catch them); they are intended to indicate fatal problems or virtual machine errors. An error of this kind usually causes the Java interpreter to display a message and exit. You are actively discouraged from trying to catch or recover from them because they are supposed to indicate a fatal program bug, not a routine condition.

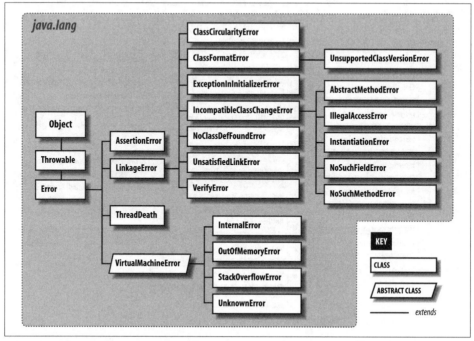

Figure 4-2. The java.lang.Error subclasses

Both Exception and Error are subclasses of Throwable. The Throwable class is the base class for objects which can be "thrown" with the throw statement. In general, you should extend only Exception, Error, or one of their subclasses.

Exception Handling

The try/catch guarding statements wrap a block of code and catch designated types of exceptions that occur within it:

```
try {
    readFromFile("foo");
    ...
}
catch ( Exception e ) {
    // Handle error
    System.out.println( "Exception while reading file: " + e );
    ...
}
```

In this example, exceptions that occur within the body of the try portion of the statement are directed to the catch clause for possible handling. The catch clause acts like a method; it specifies as an argument the type of exception it wants to handle and, if it's invoked, it receives the Exception object as an argument. Here, we receive the object in the variable e and print it along with a message.

A try statement can have multiple catch clauses that specify different types (subclasses) of Exception:

```
try {
    readFromFile("foo");
    ...
}
catch ( FileNotFoundException e ) {
    // Handle file not found
    ...
}
catch ( IOException e ) {
    // Handle read error
    ...
}
catch ( Exception e ) {
    // Handle all other errors
    ...
}
```

The catch clauses are evaluated in order, and the first assignable match is taken. At most, one catch clause is executed, which means that the exceptions should be listed from most to least specific. In the previous example, we anticipate that the hypothetical readFromFile( ) can throw two different kinds of exceptions: one for a file not found and another for a more general read error. Any subclass of Exception is assignable to the parent type Exception, so the third catch clause acts like the default clause in a switch statement and handles any remaining possibilities. We've shown it here for completeness, but in general you want to be as specific as possible in the exception types you catch.

One beauty of the try/catch scheme is that any statement in the try block can assume that all previous statements in the block succeeded. A problem won't arise suddenly because a programmer forgot to check the return value from some method. If an earlier statement fails, execution jumps immediately to the catch clause; later statements are never executed.

Bubbling Up

What if we hadn't caught the exception? Where would it have gone? Well, if there is no enclosing try/catch statement, the exception pops to the top of the method in which it appeared and is, in turn, thrown from that method up to its caller. If that point in the calling method is within a try clause, control passes to the corresponding catch clause. Otherwise, the exception continues propagating up the call stack, from one method to its caller. In this way, the exception bubbles up until it's caught, or until it pops out of the top of the program, terminating it with a runtime error message. There's a bit more to it than that because, in this case, the compiler might have reminded us to deal with it, but we'll get back to that in a moment.

Let's look at another example. In Figure 4-3, the method getContent( ) invokes the method openConnection( ) from within a try/catch statement. In turn, openConnection( ) invokes the method sendRequest( ), which calls the method write( ) to send some data.

Figure 4-3. Exception propagation

In this figure, the second call to write( ) throws an IOException. Since sendRequest( ) doesn't contain a try/catch statement to handle the exception, it's thrown again from the point where it was called in the method openConnection( ). Since openConnection( ) doesn't catch the exception either, it's thrown once more. Finally, it's caught by the try statement in getContent( ) and handled by its catch clause.

Stack Traces

Since an exception can bubble up quite a distance before it is caught and handled, we may need a way to determine exactly where it was thrown. It's also very important to know the context of how the point of the exception was reached; that is, which methods called which methods to get to that point. All exceptions can dump a stack trace that lists their method of origin and all the nested method calls it took to arrive there. Most commonly, the user sees a stack trace when it is printed using the printStackTrace( ) method.

```
try {
    // complex, deeply nested task
} catch ( Exception e ) {
    // dump information about exactly where the exception occurred
    e.printStackTrace( System.err );
    ...
}
```

For example, the stack trace for an exception might look like this:

```
java.io.FileNotFoundException: myfile.xml
        at java.io.FileInputStream.<init>(FileInputStream.java)
        at java.io.FileInputStream.<init>(FileInputStream.java)
        at MyApplication.loadFile(MyApplication.java:137)
        at MyApplication.main(MyApplication.java:5)
```

This stack trace indicates that the main( ) method of the class MyApplication called the method loadFile( ). The loadFile( ) method then tried to construct a FileInputStream, which threw the FileNotFoundException. Note that once the stack trace reaches Java system classes (like FileInputStream), the line numbers may be lost. This can also happen when the code is optimized by some virtual machines. Usually, there is a way to disable the optimization temporarily to find the exact line numbers. However, in tricky situations, changing the timing of the application can affect the problem you're trying to debug.

Prior to Java 1.4, stack traces were limited to a text output that was really suitable for printing and reading only by humans. Now methods allow you to retrieve the stack trace information programmatically, using the Throwable getStackTrace( ) method. This method returns an array of StackTraceElement objects, each of which represents a method call on the stack. You can ask a StackTraceElement for details about that method's location using the methods getFileName( ), getClassName( ), getMethodName( ), and getLineNumber( ). Element zero of the array is the top of the stack, the final line of code that caused the exception; subsequent elements step back one method call each until the original main( ) method is reached.

Checked and Unchecked Exceptions

We mentioned earlier that Java forces us to be explicit about our error handling, but it's not realistic to require that every conceivable type of error be handled in every situation. Java exceptions are therefore divided into two categories: *checked* and *unchecked*. Most application-level exceptions are checked, which means that any method that throws one, either by generating it itself (as we'll discuss later) or by ignoring one that occurs within it, must declare that it can throw that type of exception in a special throws clause in its method declaration. We haven't yet talked in detail about declaring methods (see Chapter 5). For now all you need to know is that methods have to declare the checked exceptions they can throw or allow to be thrown.

Again in Figure 4-3, notice that the methods openConnection( ) and sendRequest( ) both specify that they can throw an IOException. If we had to throw multiple types of exceptions, we could declare them separated with commas:

```
void readFile( String s ) throws IOException, InterruptedException {
    ...
}
```

The throws clause tells the compiler that a method is a possible source of that type of checked exception and that anyone calling that method must be prepared to deal with it. The caller may use a try/catch block to catch it, or, in turn, it may declare that it can throw the exception itself.

In contrast, exceptions that are subclasses of either the class java.lang.RuntimeException or the class java.lang.Error are unchecked. See Figure 4-1 for the subclasses of RuntimeException. (Subclasses of Error are generally reserved for serious class loading or runtime system problems.) It's not a compile-time error to ignore the possibility of these exceptions; methods also don't have to declare they can throw them. In all other respects, unchecked exceptions behave the same as other exceptions. We are free to catch them if we wish, but in this case we aren't required to.

Checked exceptions are intended to cover application-level problems, such as missing files and unavailable hosts. As good programmers (and upstanding citizens), we should design software to recover gracefully from these kinds of conditions. Unchecked exceptions are intended for system-level problems, such as "out of memory" and "array index out of bounds." While these may indicate application-level programming errors, they can occur almost anywhere and usually aren't possible to recover from. Fortunately, because they are unchecked exceptions, you don't have to wrap every one of your array-index operations in a try/catch statement.

To sum up, checked exceptions are problems a reasonable application should try to handle gracefully; unchecked exceptions (runtime exceptions or errors) are problems from which we would not normally expect our software to recover. Error types are those explicitly intended to be conditions that we should not normally try to handle or recover from.

Throwing Exceptions

We can throw our own exceptions, either instances of Exception, one of its existing subclasses, or our own specialized exception classes. All we have to do is create an instance of the Exception and throw it with the throw statement:

```
throw new IOException( );
```

Execution stops and is transferred to the nearest enclosing try/catch statement that can handle the exception type. (There is little point in keeping a reference to the Exception object we've created here.) An alternative constructor lets us specify a string with an error message:

```
throw new IOException("Sunspots!");
```

You can retrieve this string by using the Exception object's getMessage( ) method. Often, though, you can just print (or toString( )) the exception object itself to get the message and stack trace.

By convention, all types of `Exception` have a `String` constructor like this. The earlier `String` message is somewhat facetious and vague. Normally, you won't throw a plain old `Exception` but a more specific subclass. Here's another example:

```
public void checkRead( String s ) {
    if ( new File(s).isAbsolute() || (s.indexOf("..") != -1) )
        throw new SecurityException(
            "Access to file : "+ s +" denied.");
}
```

In this code, we partially implement a method to check for an illegal path. If we find one, we throw a `SecurityException`, with some information about the transgression.

Of course, we could include whatever other information is useful in our own specialized subclasses of `Exception`. Often, though, just having a new type of exception is good enough because it's sufficient to help direct the flow of control. For example, if we are building a parser, we might want to make our own kind of exception to indicate a particular kind of failure:

```
class ParseException extends Exception {
    ParseException( ) {
        super( );
    }
    ParseException( String desc ) {
        super( desc );
    }
}
```

See Chapter 5 for a full description of classes and class constructors. The body of our `Exception` class here simply allows a `ParseException` to be created in the conventional ways we've created exceptions previously (either generically or with a simple string description). Now that we have our new exception type, we can guard like this:

```
// Somewhere in our code
...
try {
    parseStream( input );
} catch ( ParseException pe ) {
    // Bad input...
} catch ( IOException ioe ) {
    // Low-level communications problem
}
```

As you can see, although our new exception doesn't currently hold any specialized information about the problem (it certainly could), it does let us distinguish a parse error from an arbitrary I/O error in the same chunk of code.

Chaining exceptions

Sometimes you'll want to take some action based on an exception and then turn around and throw a new exception in its place. This is common when building frameworks, where low-level detailed exceptions are handled and represented by higher-level exceptions that can be managed more easily. For example, you might want to catch an IOException in a communication package, possibly perform some cleanup, and ultimately throw a higher-level exception of your own, maybe something like LostServerConnection.

You can do this in the obvious way by simply catching the exception and then throwing a new one, but then you lose important information, including the stack trace of the original "causal" exception. To deal with this, you can use the technique of *exception chaining*. This means that you include the causal exception in the new exception that you throw. Java has explicit support for exception chaining. The base Exception class can be constructed with an exception as an argument or the standard String message and an exception:

```
throw new Exception( "Here's the story...", causalException );
```

You can get access to the wrapped exception later with the getCause( ) method. More importantly, Java automatically prints both exceptions and their respective stack traces if you print the exception or if it is shown to the user.

You can add this kind of constructor to your own exception subclasses (delegating to the parent constructor). However, since this API is a recent addition to Java (added in Version 1.4), many existing exception types do not provide this kind of constructor. You can still take advantage of this pattern by using the Throwable method initCause( ) to set the causal exception explicitly after constructing your exception and before throwing it:

```
try {
  // ...
} catch ( IOException cause ) {
  Exception e =
    new IOException("What we have here is a failure to communicate...");
  e.initCause( cause );
  throw e;
}
```

try Creep

The try statement imposes a condition on the statements that it guards. It says that if an exception occurs within it, the remaining statements are abandoned. This has consequences for local variable initialization. If the compiler can't determine whether a local variable assignment placed inside a try/catch block will happen, it won't let us use the variable. For example:

```
void myMethod( ) {
    int foo;

    try {
        foo = getResults( );
```

```
    }
    catch ( Exception e ) {
        ...
    }

    int bar = foo;  // Compile-time error -- foo may not have been initialized
```

In this example, we can't use foo in the indicated place because there's a chance it was never assigned a value. One obvious option is to move the assignment inside the try statement:

```
    try {
        foo = getResults( );

        int bar = foo;  // Okay because we get here only
                        // if previous assignment succeeds
    }
    catch ( Exception e ) {
        ...
    }
```

Sometimes this works just fine. However, now we have the same problem if we want to use bar later in myMethod( ). If we're not careful, we might end up pulling everything into the try statement. The situation changes, however, if we transfer control out of the method in the catch clause:

```
    try {
        foo = getResults( );
    }
    catch ( Exception e ) {
        ...
        return;
    }

    int bar = foo;  // Okay because we get here only
                    // if previous assignment succeeds
```

The compiler is smart enough to know that if an error had occurred in the try clause, we wouldn't have reached the bar assignment, so it allows us to refer to foo. Your code will dictate its own needs; you should just be aware of the options.

The finally Clause

What if we have some cleanup to do before we exit our method from one of the catch clauses? To avoid duplicating the code in each catch branch and to make the cleanup more explicit, use the finally clause. A finally clause can be added after a try and any associated catch clauses. Any statements in the body of the finally clause are guaranteed to be executed, no matter how control leaves the try body (whether an exception was thrown or not):

```
    try {
        // Do something here
```

```
    }
    catch ( FileNotFoundException e ) {
        ...
    }
    catch ( IOException e ) {
        ...
    }
    catch ( Exception e ) {
        ...
    }
    finally {
        // Cleanup here is always executed
    }
```

In this example, the statements at the cleanup point are executed eventually, no matter how control leaves the try. If control transfers to one of the catch clauses, the statements in finally are executed after the catch completes. If none of the catch clauses handles the exception, the finally statements are executed before the exception propagates to the next level.

If the statements in the try execute cleanly, or if we perform a return, break, or continue, the statements in the finally clause are still executed. To perform cleanup operations, we can even use try and finally without any catch clauses:

```
    try {
        // Do something here
        return;
    }
    finally {
        System.out.println("Whoo-hoo!");
    }
```

Exceptions that occur in a catch or finally clause are handled normally; the search for an enclosing try/catch begins outside the offending try statement, after the finally has been executed.

Performance Issues

Because of the way the Java virtual machine is implemented, guarding against an exception being thrown (using a try) is free. It doesn't add any overhead to the execution of your code. However, throwing an exception is not free. When an exception is thrown, Java has to locate the appropriate try/catch block and perform other time-consuming activities at runtime.

The result is that you should throw exceptions only in truly "exceptional" circumstances and avoid using them for expected conditions, especially when performance is an issue. For example, if you have a loop, it may be better to perform a small test on each pass and avoid throwing the exception rather than throwing it frequently. On the other hand, if the exception is thrown only once in a gazillion times, you may want to eliminate the overhead of the test code and not worry about the cost of throwing that exception. The general rule should be that exceptions are used for "out of bounds" or abnormal situations, not routine and expected conditions (such as the end of a file).

Assertions

An assertion is a simple pass/fail test of some condition, performed while your application is running. Assertions can be used to "sanity" check your code anywhere you believe certain conditions are guaranteed by correct program behavior. Assertions are distinct from other kinds of tests because they check conditions that should never be violated at a logical level: if the assertion fails, the application is to be considered broken and generally halts with an appropriate error message. Assertions are supported directly by the Java language and they can be turned on or off at runtime to remove any performance penalty of including them in your code.

Using assertions to test for the correct behavior of your application is a simple but powerful technique for ensuring software quality. It fills a gap between those aspects of software that can be checked automatically by the compiler and those more generally checked by "unit tests" and human testing. Assertions test assumptions about program behavior and make them guarantees (at least while they are activated).

Explicit support for assertions was added in Java 1.4. However, if you've written much code in any language, you have probably used assertions in some form. For example, you may have written something like the following:

```
if ( !condition )
    throw new AssertionError("fatal error: 42");
```

An assertion in Java is equivalent to this example but performed with the assert language keyword. It takes a Boolean condition and an optional expression value. If the assertion fails, an AssertionError is thrown, which usually causes Java to bail out of the application.

The optional expression may evaluate to either a primitive or object type. Either way, its sole purpose is to be turned into a string and shown to the user if the assertion fails; most often you'll use a string message explicitly. Here are some examples:

```
assert false;
assert ( array.length > min );
assert a > 0 : a  // shows value of a to the user
assert foo != null :  "foo is null!" // shows message to user
```

In the event of failure, the first two assertions print only a generic message, whereas the third prints the value of a and the last prints the foo is null! message.

Again, the important thing about assertions is not just that they are more terse than the equivalent if condition but that they can be enabled or disabled when you run the application. Disabling assertions means that their test conditions are not even evaluated, so there is no performance penalty for including them in your code (other than, perhaps, space in the class files when they are loaded).

Java 5.0 supports assertions natively. In Java 1.4 (the previous version in this crazy numbering scheme), code with assertions requires a compile-time switch:

```
% javac -source 1.4 MyApplication.java
```

Enabling and Disabling Assertions

Assertions are turned on or off at runtime. When disabled, assertions still exist in the class files but are not executed and consume no time. You can enable and disable assertions for an entire application or on a package-by-package or even class-by-class basis. By default, assertions are turned off in Java. To enable them for your code, use the java command flag -ea or -enableassertions:

```
% java -ea MyApplication
```

To turn on assertions for a particular class, append the class name:

```
% java -ea:com.oreilly.examples.Myclass  MyApplication
```

To turn on assertions just for particular packages, append the package name with trailing ellipses (. . .):

```
% java -ea:com.oreilly.examples...  MyApplication
```

When you enable assertions for a package, Java also enables all subordinate package names (e.g., com.oreilly.examples.text). However, you can be more selective by using the corresponding -da or -disableassertions flag to negate individual packages or classes. You can combine all this to achieve arbitrary groupings like this:

```
% java -ea:com.oreilly.examples... -da:com.oreilly.examples.text
    -ea:com.oreilly.examples.text.MonkeyTypewriters  MyApplication
```

This example enables assertions for the com.oreilly.examples package as a whole, excludes the package com.oreilly.examples.text, then turns exceptions on for just one class, MonkeyTypewriters, in that package.

Using Assertions

An assertion enforces a rule about something that should be unchanging in your code and would otherwise go unchecked. You can use an assertion for added safety anywhere you want to verify your assumptions about program behavior that can't be checked by the compiler.

A common situation that cries out for an assertion is testing for multiple conditions or values where one should always be found. In this case, a failing assertion as the default or "fall through" behavior indicates the code is broken. For example, suppose we have a value called `direction` that should always contain either the constant value LEFT or RIGHT:

```
if ( direction == LEFT )
    doLeft( );
else if ( direction == RIGHT )
    doRight( )
else
    assert false : "bad direction";
```

The same applies to the default case of a switch:

```
switch ( direction ) {
    case LEFT:
        doLeft( );
        break;
    case RIGHT:
        doRight( );
        break;
    default:
        assert false;
}
```

In general, you should not use assertions for checking the validity of arguments to methods because you want that behavior to be part of your application, not just a test for quality control that can be turned off. The validity of input to a method is called its *preconditions,* and you should usually throw an exception if they are not met; this elevates the preconditions to part of the method's "contract" with the user. However, checking the correctness of results of your methods with assertions before returning them is a good idea; these are called *post-conditions.*

Sometimes determining what is or is not a precondition depends on your point of view. For example, when a method is used internally within a class, preconditions may already be guaranteed by the methods that call it. Public methods of the class should probably throw exceptions when their preconditions are violated, but a private method might use assertions because its callers are always closely related code that should obey the correct behavior.

Finally, note that assertions cannot only test simple expressions but perform complex validation as well. Remember that anything you place in the condition expression of an `assert` statement is not evaluated when assertions are turned off. You can make helper methods for your assertions, containing arbitrary amounts of code. And, although it suggests a dangerous programming style, you can even use assertions that have side effects to capture values for use by later assertions—all of which will be disabled when assertions are turned off. For example:

```
int savedValue;
assert ( savedValue = getValue( )) != -1;
// Do work...
assert checkValue( savedValue );
```

Here, in the first assert, we use helper method getValue( ) to retrieve some information and save it for later. Then after doing some work, we check the saved value using another assertion, perhaps comparing results. When assertions are disabled, we'll no longer save or check the data. Note that it's necessary for us to be somewhat cute and make our first assert condition into a Boolean by checking for a known value. Again, using assertions with side effects is a bit dangerous because you have to be careful that those side effects are seen only by other assertions. Otherwise, you'll be changing your application behavior when you turn them off.

Arrays

An array is a special type of object that can hold an ordered collection of elements. The type of the elements of the array is called the *base type* of the array; the number of elements it holds is a fixed attribute called its *length*. Java supports arrays of all primitive and reference types.

The basic syntax of arrays looks much like that of C or C++. We create an array of a specified length and access the elements with the index operator, [ ]. Unlike other languages, however, arrays in Java are true, first-class objects. An array is an instance of a special Java array class and has a corresponding type in the type system. This means that to use an array, as with any other object, we first declare a variable of the appropriate type and then use the new operator to create an instance of it.

Array objects differ from other objects in Java in three respects:

- Java implicitly creates a special array class type for us whenever we declare a new type of array. It's not strictly necessary to know about this process in order to use arrays, but it helps in understanding their structure and their relationship to other objects in Java later.

- Java lets us use the [ ] operator to access array elements so that arrays look as we expect. We could implement our own classes that act like arrays, but we would have to settle for having methods such as get( ) and set( ) instead of using the special [ ] notation.

- Java provides a corresponding special form of the new operator that lets us construct an instance of an array with a specified length with the [ ] notation or initialize it directly from a structured list of values.

Array Types

An array type variable is denoted by a base type followed by the empty brackets, [ ]. Alternatively, Java accepts a C-style declaration, with the brackets placed after the array name.

The following are equivalent:

```
int [] arrayOfInts;  // preferred
int arrayOfInts [];  // C-style
```

In each case, `arrayOfInts` is declared as an array of integers. The size of the array is not yet an issue because we are declaring only the array type variable. We have not yet created an actual instance of the array class, with its associated storage. It's not even possible to specify the length of an array when declaring an array type variable. The size is strictly a function of the array object itself, not the reference to it.

An array of reference types can be created in the same way:

```
String [] someStrings;
Button [] someButtons;
```

Array Creation and Initialization

The new operator is used to create an instance of an array. After the new operator, we specify the base type of the array and its length, with a bracketed integer expression:

```
arrayOfInts = new int [42];
someStrings = new String [ number + 2 ];
```

We can, of course, combine the steps of declaring and allocating the array:

```
double [] someNumbers = new double [20];
Component [] widgets = new Component [12];
```

Array indices start with zero. Thus, the first element of `someNumbers[]` is 0, and the last element is 19. After creation, the array elements are initialized to the default values for their type. For numeric types, this means the elements are initially zero:

```
int [] grades = new int [30];
grades[0] = 99;
grades[1] = 72;
// grades[2] == 0
```

The elements of an array of objects are references to the objects, not actual instances of the objects. The default value of each element is therefore null until we assign instances of appropriate objects:

```
String names [] = new String [4];
names [0] = new String( );
names [1] = "Boofa";
names [2] = someObject.toString( );
// names[3] == null
```

This is an important distinction that can cause confusion. In many other languages, the act of creating an array is the same as allocating storage for its elements. In Java, a newly allocated array of objects actually contains only reference variables, each with the value null.* That's not to say that there is no memory associated with an empty array; memory is needed to hold those references (the empty "slots" in the array). Figure 4-4 illustrates the names array of the previous example.

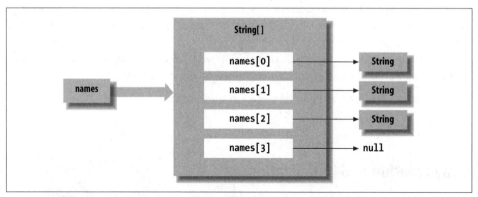

Figure 4-4. A Java array

names is a variable of type String[] (i.e., a string array). This particular String[] object contains four String type variables. We have assigned String objects to the first three array elements. The fourth has the default value null.

Java supports the C-style curly braces {} construct for creating an array and initializing its elements:

```
int [] primes = { 1, 2, 3, 5, 7, 7+4 };    // e.g., primes[2] = 3
```

An array object of the proper type and length is implicitly created, and the values of the comma-separated list of expressions are assigned to its elements. Note that we did not use the new keyword or the array type here. The type of the array was inferred from the assignment.

We can use the {} syntax with an array of objects. In this case, each expression must evaluate to an object that can be assigned to a variable of the base type of the array or the value null. Here are some examples:

```
String [] verbs = { "run", "jump", someWord.toString( ) };
Button [] controls = { stopButton, new Button("Forwards"),
    new Button("Backwards") };
// All types are subtypes of Object
Object [] objects = { stopButton, "A word", null };
```

---

* The analog in C or C++ is an array of pointers to objects. However, pointers in C or C++ are themselves two- or four-byte values. Allocating an array of pointers is, in actuality, allocating the storage for some number of those pointer objects. An array of references is conceptually similar, although references are not themselves objects. We can't manipulate references or parts of references other than by assignment, and their storage requirements (or lack thereof) are not part of the high-level Java language specification.

The following are equivalent:

```
Button [] threeButtons = new Button [3];
Button [] threeButtons = { null, null, null };
```

Using Arrays

The size of an array object is available in the public variable length:

```
char [] alphabet = new char [26];
int alphaLen = alphabet.length;              // alphaLen == 26

String [] musketeers = { "one", "two", "three" };
int num = musketeers.length;                 // num == 3
```

length is the only accessible field of an array; it is a variable, not a method. (Don't worry, the compiler tells you when you accidentally use parentheses as if it were a method; everyone does now and then.)

Array access in Java is just like array access in other languages; you access an element by putting an integer-valued expression between brackets after the name of the array. The following example creates an array of Button objects called keyPad and then fills the array with Button objects:

```
Button [] keyPad = new Button [ 10 ];
for ( int i=0; i < keyPad.length; i++ )
    keyPad[ i ] = new Button( Integer.toString( i ) );
```

Remember that we can also use the new enhanced for loop to iterate over array values. Here we'll use it to print all the values we just assigned:

```
for( int i : keyPad )
    System.out.println( i );
```

Attempting to access an element that is outside the range of the array generates an ArrayIndexOutOfBoundsException. This is a type of RuntimeException, so you can either catch and handle it yourself, if you really expect it, or ignore it, as we've already discussed:

```
String [] states = new String [50];

try {
    states[0] = "California";
    states[1] = "Oregon";
    ...
    states[50] = "McDonald's Land";  // Error: array out of bounds
}
catch ( ArrayIndexOutOfBoundsException err ) {
    System.out.println( "Handled error: " + err.getMessage() );
}
```

It's a common task to copy a range of elements from one array into another. Java supplies the arraycopy( ) method for this purpose; it's a utility method of the System class:

```
System.arraycopy( source, sourceStart, destination, destStart, length );
```

The following example doubles the size of the names array from an earlier example:

```
String [] tmpVar = new String [ 2 * names.length ];
System.arraycopy( names, 0, tmpVar, 0, names.length );
names = tmpVar;
```

A new array, twice the size of names, is allocated and assigned to a temporary variable tmpVar. The arraycopy( ) method is then used to copy the elements of names to the new array. Finally, the new array is assigned to names. If there are no remaining references to the old array object after names has been copied, it is garbage-collected on the next pass.

Anonymous Arrays

Often it is convenient to create "throw-away" arrays, arrays that are used in one place and never referenced anywhere else. Such arrays don't need a name because you never need to refer to them again in that context. For example, you may want to create a collection of objects to pass as an argument to some method. It's easy enough to create a normal, named array, but if you don't actually work with the array (if you use the array only as a holder for some collection), you shouldn't have to. Java makes it easy to create "anonymous" (i.e., unnamed) arrays.

Let's say you need to call a method named setPets( ), which takes an array of Animal objects as arguments. Provided Cat and Dog are subclasses of Animal, here's how to call setPets( ) using an anonymous array:

```
Dog pokey = new Dog ("gray");
Cat boojum = new Cat ("grey");
Cat simon = new Cat ("orange");
setPets ( new Animal [] { pokey, boojum, simon });
```

The syntax looks just like the initialization of an array in a variable declaration. We implicitly define the size of the array and fill in its elements using the curly-brace notation. However, since this is not a variable declaration, we have to explicitly use the new operator and the array type to create the array object.

Prior to Java 5.0, anonymous arrays were used frequently as a substitute for variable-length argument lists to methods, which are discussed in Chapter 5. With the introduction of variable-length argument lists in Java, the usefulness of anonymous arrays may diminish.

Multidimensional Arrays

Java supports multidimensional arrays in the form of arrays of array type objects. You create a multidimensional array with C-like syntax, using multiple bracket pairs, one for each dimension. You also use this syntax to access elements at various positions within the array. Here's an example of a multidimensional array that represents a chess board:

```
ChessPiece [][] chessBoard;
chessBoard = new ChessPiece [8][8];
chessBoard[0][0] = new ChessPiece.Rook;
chessBoard[1][0] = new ChessPiece.Pawn;
...
```

Here chessBoard is declared as a variable of type ChessPiece[][] (i.e., an array of ChessPiece arrays). This declaration implicitly creates the type ChessPiece[] as well. The example illustrates the special form of the new operator used to create a multidimensional array. It creates an array of ChessPiece[] objects and then, in turn, makes each element into an array of ChessPiece objects. We then index chessBoard to specify values for particular ChessPiece elements. (We'll neglect the color of the pieces here.)

Of course, you can create arrays with more than two dimensions. Here's a slightly impractical example:

```
Color [][][] rgbCube = new Color [256][256][256];
rgbCube[0][0][0] = Color.black;
rgbCube[255][255][0] = Color.yellow;
...
```

We can specify a partial index of a multidimensional array to get a subarray of array type objects with fewer dimensions. In our example, the variable chessBoard is of type ChessPiece[][]. The expression chessBoard[0] is valid and refers to the first element of chessBoard, which, in Java, is of type ChessPiece[]. For example, we can populate our chess board one row at a time:

```
ChessPiece [] homeRow = {
    new ChessPiece("Rook"), new ChessPiece("Knight"),
    new ChessPiece("Bishop"), new ChessPiece("King"),
    new ChessPiece("Queen"), new ChessPiece("Bishop"),
    new ChessPiece("Knight"), new ChessPiece("Rook")
};

chessBoard[0] = homeRow;
```

We don't necessarily have to specify the dimension sizes of a multidimensional array with a single new operation. The syntax of the new operator lets us leave the sizes of some dimensions unspecified. The size of at least the first dimension (the most significant dimension of the array) has to be specified, but the sizes of any number of trailing, less significant, array dimensions may be left undefined. We can assign appropriate array-type values later.

We can create a checkerboard of Boolean values (which is not quite sufficient for a real game of checkers either) using this technique:

```
boolean [][] checkerBoard;
checkerBoard = new boolean [8][];
```

Here, checkerBoard is declared and created, but its elements, the eight boolean[] objects of the next level, are left empty. Thus, for example, checkerBoard[0] is null until we explicitly create an array and assign it, as follows:

```
checkerBoard[0] = new boolean [8];
checkerBoard[1] = new boolean [8];
...
checkerBoard[7] = new boolean [8];
```

The code of the previous two examples is equivalent to:

```
boolean [][] checkerBoard = new boolean [8][8];
```

One reason we might want to leave dimensions of an array unspecified is so that we can store arrays given to us by another method.

Note that since the length of the array is not part of its type, the arrays in the checkerboard do not necessarily have to be of the same length. That is, multidimensional arrays don't have to be rectangular. Here's a defective (but perfectly legal to Java) checkerboard:

```
checkerBoard[2] = new boolean [3];
checkerBoard[3] = new boolean [10];
```

And here's how you could create and initialize a triangular array:

```
int [][] triangle = new int [5][];
for (int i = 0; i < triangle.length; i++) {
    triangle[i] = new int [i + 1];
    for (int j = 0; j < i + 1; j++)
        triangle[i][j] = i + j;
}
```

Inside Arrays

We said earlier that arrays are instances of special array classes in the Java language. If arrays have classes, where do they fit into the class hierarchy and how are they related? These are good questions, but we need to talk more about the object-oriented aspects of Java before answering them. That's the subject of the next chapter. For now, take it on faith that arrays fit into the class hierarchy.

Objects in Java

In this chapter, we get to the heart of Java and explore the object-oriented aspects of the language. The term *object-oriented design* refers to the art of decomposing an application into some number of objects, which are self-contained application components that work together. The goal is to break your problem down into a number of smaller problems that are simpler and easier to handle and maintain. Object-based designs have proven themselves over the years, and object-oriented languages such as Java provide a strong foundation for writing very small to very large applications. Java was designed from the ground up to be an object-oriented language, and all the Java APIs and libraries are built around solid object-based design patterns.

An object design "methodology" is a system or a set of rules created to help you break down your application into objects. Often this means mapping real-world entities and concepts (sometimes called the "problem domain") into application components. Various methodologies attempt to help you factor your application into a good set of reusable objects. This is good in principle, but the problem is that good object-oriented design is still more art than science. While you can learn from the various off-the-shelf design methodologies, none of them will help you in all situations. The truth is that there is no substitute for experience.

We won't try to push you into a particular methodology here; there are shelves full of books to do that.* Instead, we'll provide some common sense hints to get you started. The following general design guidelines will hopefully make more sense after you've read this chapter and the next:

- Hide as much of your implementation as possible. Never expose more of the internals of an object than you have to. This is key to building maintainable, reusable code. Avoid public variables in your objects, with the possible exception of

---

* Once you have some experience with basic object-oriented concepts, you might want to look at *Design Patterns: Elements of Reusable Object-Oriented Software* by Gamma, Helm, Johnson, and Vlissides (Addison-Wesley). This book catalogs useful object-oriented designs that have been refined over the years by experience. Many appear in the design of the Java APIs.

constants. Instead define *accessor* methods to set and return values (even if they are simple types). Later, when you need to, you'll be able to modify and extend the behavior of your objects without breaking other classes that rely on them.

- Specialize objects only when you have to—use *composition* instead of *inheritance*. When you use an object in its existing form, as a piece of a new object, you are *composing* objects. When you change or refine the behavior of an object (by *subclassing*), you are using *inheritance*. You should try to reuse objects by composition rather than inheritance whenever possible because when you compose objects, you are taking full advantage of existing tools. Inheritance involves breaking down the barrier of an object and should be done only when there's a real advantage. Ask yourself if you really need to inherit the whole public interface of an object (do you want to be a "kind" of that object) or whether you can just delegate certain jobs to the object and use it by composition.

- Minimize relationships between objects and try to organize related objects in packages. Classes that work closely together can be grouped using Java packages, which can hide those that are not of general interest. Only expose classes that you intend other people to use. The more loosely coupled your objects are, the easier it will be to reuse them later.

Classes

Classes are the building blocks of a Java application. A *class* can contain methods (functions), variables, initialization code, and, as we'll discuss later, other classes. It serves as a blueprint for making class *instances*, which are runtime objects that implement the class structure. You declare a class with the class keyword. Methods and variables of the class appear inside the braces of the class declaration:

```
class Pendulum {
    float mass;
    float length = 1.0;
    int cycles;

    float getPosition ( float time ) {
        ...
    }
    ...
}
```

The Pendulum class contains three variables: mass, length, and cycles. It also defines a method called getPosition( ), which takes a float value as an argument and returns a float value as a result. Variables and method declarations can appear in any order, but variable initializers can't make "forward references" to other variables that appear later. Once we've defined the Pendulum class, we can create a Pendulum object (an instance of that class) as follows:

```
Pendulum p;
p = new Pendulum( );
```

Recall that our declaration of the variable p doesn't create a Pendulum object; it simply creates a variable that refers to an object of type Pendulum. We still had to create the object, using the new keyword, as shown in the second line of the preceding code snippet. Now that we've created a Pendulum object, we can access its variables and methods, as we've already seen many times:

```
p.mass = 5.0;
float pos = p.getPosition( 1.0 );
```

Two kinds of variables can be defined in a class: *instance variables* and *static variables*. Every object instance has its own set of instance variables; the values of these variables in one instance of an object can differ from the values in another object. We'll talk about static variables later, which, in contrast, are shared among all instances of an object. In either case, if you don't initialize a variable when you declare it, it's given a default value appropriate for its type (null, zero, or false).

Figure 5-1 shows a hypothetical TextBook application that uses two instances of Pendulum through the reference-type variables bigPendulum and smallPendulum. Each of these Pendulum objects has its own copy of mass, length, and cycles. As with variables, methods defined in a class may be *instance methods* or *static methods*. An instance method is associated with an instance of the class, but the relationship isn't quite as simple as for variables. Instance methods are accessed through an object instance, but the object doesn't have its own "copy" of the methods (there is no duplication of code). Instead, the association means that instance methods can "see" and operate on the values of the instance variables of the object. As you'll see in Chapter 6 when we talk about subclassing, there's more to learn about how methods see variables. In that chapter, we'll also discuss how instance methods can be "overridden" in child classes—a very important feature of object-oriented design. Both aspects differ from static methods, which we'll see are really more like global functions—associated with a class by name only.

Accessing Fields and Methods

Inside a class, we can access variables and call methods of the class directly by name. Here's an example that expands on our Pendulum:

```
class Pendulum {
    ...
    void resetEverything( ) {
        mass = 1.0;
        length = 1.0;
        cycles = 0;
        ...
        float startingPosition = getPosition( 0.0 );
    }
    ...
}
```

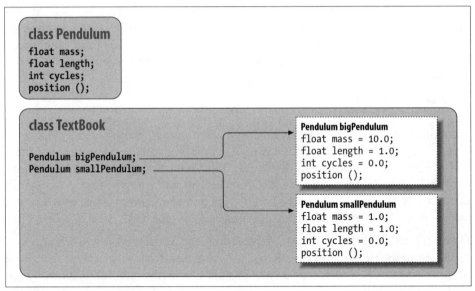

Figure 5-1. Instances of the Pendulum class

Other classes access members of an object through a reference, using the dot selector notation that we discussed in the last chapter:

```
class TextBook {
    ...
    void showPendulum( ) {
        Pendulum bob = new Pendulum( );
        ...
        int i = bob.cycles;
        bob.resetEverything( );
        bob.mass = 1.01;
        ...
    }
    ...
}
```

Here we have created a second class, TextBook, that uses a Pendulum object. It creates an instance in showPendulum( ) and then invokes methods and accesses variables of the object through the reference bob.

Several factors affect whether class members can be accessed from another class. You can use the visibility modifiers public, private, and protected to control access; classes can also be placed into a *package*, which affects their scope. The private modifier, for example, designates a variable or method for use only by other members of the class itself. In the previous example, we could change the declaration of our variable cycles to private:

```
class Pendulum {
    ...
    private int cycles;
    ...
```

Now we can't access cycles from TextBook:

```
class TextBook {
    ...
    void showPendulum( ) {
        ...
        int i = bob.cycles;  // Compile-time error
```

If we still need to access cycles in some capacity, we might add a public getCycles( ) method to the Pendulum class. (Creating accessor methods like this is a good design rule because it allows future flexibility in changing the type or behavior of the value.) We'll take a detailed look at packages, access modifiers, and how they affect the visibility of variables and methods in Chapter 6.

Static Members

As we've said, instance variables and methods are associated with and accessed through an instance of the class—i.e., through a particular object, like bob in the previous example. In contrast, members that are declared with the static modifier live in the class and are shared by all instances of the class. Variables declared with the static modifier are called *static variables* or *class variables*; similarly, these kinds of methods are called *static methods* or *class methods*. We can add a static variable to our Pendulum example:

```
class Pendulum {
    ...
    static float gravAccel = 9.80;
    ...
```

We have declared the new float variable gravAccel as static. That means if we change its value in any instance of a Pendulum, the value changes for all Pendulum objects, as shown in Figure 5-2.

Static members can be accessed like instance members. Inside our Pendulum class, we can refer to gravAccel like any other variable:

```
class Pendulum {
    ...
    float getWeight ( ) {
        return mass * gravAccel;
    }
    ...
}
```

However, since static members exist in the class itself, independent of any instance, we can also access them directly through the class. We don't need a Pendulum object to get or set the variable gravAccel; instead, we can use the class to select the variable:

```
Pendulum.gravAccel = 8.76;
```

This changes the value of gravAccel for any current or future instances. Why would we want to change the value of gravAccel? Well, perhaps we want to explore how

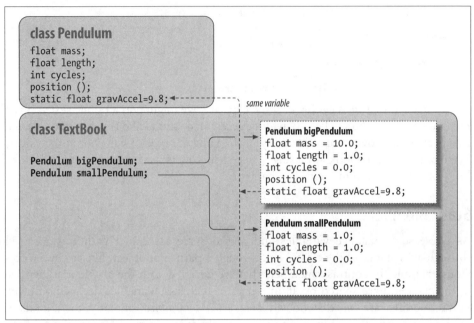

Figure 5-2. Static variables shared by all instances of a class

pendulums would work on different planets. Static variables are also very useful for other kinds of data shared among classes at runtime. For instance, you can create methods to register your object instances so that they can communicate, or so that you can keep track of all of them. It's also common to use static variables to define constant values. In this case, we use the static modifier along with the final modifier. So, if we cared only about pendulums under the influence of the Earth's gravitational pull, we might change Pendulum as follows:

```
class Pendulum {
    ...
    static final float EARTH_G = 9.80;
    ...
```

We have followed a common convention and named our constant with capital letters. The value of EARTH_G is a constant; it can be accessed through the class Pendulum or its instances, but its value can't be changed at runtime.

It's important to use the combination of static and final only for things that are really constant. That's because the compiler is allowed to "inline" such values within classes that reference them. This means that if you change a static final variable, you may have to recompile all code that uses that class (this is really the only case where you have to do that in Java). Static members are useful as flags and identifiers, which can be accessed from anywhere. They are also useful for values needed in the construction of an instance itself. In our example, we might declare a number of static values to represent various kinds of Pendulum objects:

```
class Pendulum {
    ...
    static int SIMPLE = 0, ONE_SPRING = 1, TWO_SPRING = 2;
    ...
```

We might then use these flags in a method that sets the type of a Pendulum or in a special constructor, as we'll discuss shortly:

```
Pendulum pendy = new Pendulum( );
pendy.setType( Pendulum.ONE_SPRING );
```

Again, inside the Pendulum class, we can use static members directly by name, as well; there's no need for the Pendulum. prefix:

```
class Pendulum {
    ...
    void resetEverything( ) {
        setType ( SIMPLE );
        ...
    }
    ...
}
```

Constants versus enumerations

In the previous section we saw two uses for static final variables (constants). The first was to create true constants; in that case, it was the numeric constant EARTH_G, but it could easily have been a String or Date value. The second usage was to create a fixed set of identifiers, SIMPLE, ONE_SPRING, etc., whose actual values were not as important as their uniqueness and, perhaps, particular order.

In Java 5.0, *enumerations* were added to replace this identifier usage with a mechanism that is both safer and, in some cases, more efficient. With Java 5.0, we could have declared our pendulum types as an enumeration like so:

```
public enum PendulumTypes { Simple, OneSpring, TwoSpring }
```

This enumeration creates not only the values, but also a new type, PendulumTypes, whose value is limited to one of the three discrete identifiers. Calling code can refer to the values as it did through our class: PendulumTypes.Simple. We've changed our case convention here to reflect the fact that these are not integer constants, but you can stick with uppercase if you prefer.

Later, when we talk about importing classes and packages, we'll discuss the new static import feature in Java 5.0, which allows us to import static identifiers and enumerations (which turn out to be related things) into a class so that we can use them by their simple names. For example:

```
new Pendulum( Simple );
```

We'll go into detail about enumerations later in this chapter after we've covered objects in more depth.

Methods

Methods appear inside class bodies. They contain local variable declarations and other Java statements that are executed when the method is invoked. Methods may return a value to the caller. They always specify a return type, which can be a primitive type, a reference type, or the type void, which indicates no returned value. Methods may take arguments, which are values supplied by the caller of the method.

Here's a simple example:

```
class Bird {
    int xPos, yPos;

    double fly ( int x, int y ) {
        double distance = Math.sqrt( x*x + y*y );
        flap( distance );
        xPos = x;
        yPos = y;
        return distance;
    }
    ...
}
```

In this example, the class Bird defines a method, fly( ), that takes as arguments two integers: x and y. It returns a double type value as a result, using the return keyword.

Prior to Java 5.0, the number and type of method arguments was fixed. Now Java has *variable-length argument lists* for methods, which allow a method to specify that it can take any number of arguments and sort them itself at runtime. We provide more details later in this chapter.

Local Variables

The fly( ) method declares a local variable called distance, which it uses to compute the distance flown. A local variable is temporary; it exists only within the scope of its method. Local variables are allocated when a method is invoked; they are normally destroyed when the method returns. They can't be referenced from outside the method itself. If the method is executing concurrently in different threads, each thread has its own version of the method's local variables. A method's arguments also serve as local variables within the scope of the method.

An object created within a method and assigned to a local variable may or may not persist after the method has returned. As with all objects in Java, it depends on whether any references to the object remain. If an object is created, assigned to a local variable, and never used anywhere else, that object is no longer referenced when the local variable disappears from scope, so garbage collection removes the object. If, however, we assign the object to an instance variable, pass it as an argument to another method, or pass it back as a return value, it may be saved by another variable holding its reference. We'll discuss object creation and garbage collection in more detail shortly.

Shadowing

If a local variable and an instance variable have the same name, the local variable *shadows* or hides the name of the instance variable within the scope of the method. In the following example, the local variables xPos and yPos hide the instance variables of the same name:

```
class Bird {
    int xPos, yPos;
    int xNest, yNest;
    ...
    double flyToNest() {
        int xPos = xNest;
        int yPos = yNest:
        return ( fly( xPos, yPos ) );
    }
    ...
}
```

When we set the values of the local variables in flyToNest( ), it has no effect on the values of the instance variables.

The "this" reference

You can use the special reference this any time you need to refer explicitly to the current object or a member of the current object. Often you don't need to use this, because the reference to the current object is implicit; such is the case when using unambiguously named instance variables inside a class. But we can use this to refer explicitly to instance variables in our object, even if they are shadowed. The following example shows how we can use this to allow argument names that shadow instance variable names. This is a fairly common technique because it saves having to make up alternative names. Here's how we could implement our fly( ) method with shadowed variables:

```
class Bird {
    int xPos, yPos;

    double fly ( int xPos, int yPos ) {
        double distance = Math.sqrt( xPos*xPos + yPos*yPos );
        flap( distance );
        this.xPos = xPos;  // instance var = local var
```

```
            this.yPos = yPos;
            return distance;
        }
        ...
    }
```

In this example, the expression this.xPos refers to the instance variable xPos and assigns it the value of the local variable xPos, which would otherwise hide its name. The only reason we need to use this in the previous example is because we've used argument names that hide our instance variables, and we want to refer to the instance variables. You can also use the this reference any time you want to pass a reference to "the current" enclosing object to some other method; we'll show examples of that later.

Static Methods

Static methods (class methods), like static variables, belong to the class and not to individual instances of the class. What does this mean? Well, foremost, a static method lives outside of any particular class instance. It can be invoked by name, through the class name, without any objects around. Because it is not bound to a particular object instance, a static method can directly access only other static members (static variables and other static methods) of the class. It can't directly see any instance variables or call any instance methods, because to do so we'd have to ask, "on which instance?" Static methods can be called from instances, just like instance methods, but the important thing is that they can also be used independently.

Our fly( ) method uses a static method: Math.sqrt( ), which is defined by the java.lang.Math class; we'll explore this class in detail in Chapter 11. For now, the important thing to note is that Math is the name of a class and not an instance of a Math object. (It so happens that you can't even make an instance of the Math class.) Because static methods can be invoked wherever the class name is available, class methods are closer to C-style functions. Static methods are particularly useful for utility methods that perform work that is useful either independently of instances or in working on instances. For example, in our Bird class, we could enumerate all of the available types of birds that can be created:

```
class Bird {
    ...
    static String [] getBirdTypes() { ... }

}
```

Here, we've defined a static method getBirdTypes( ) that returns an array of strings containing bird names. We can use getBirdTypes( ) from within an instance of Bird, just like an instance method. However, we can also call it from other classes, using the Bird class name:

```
String [] names = Bird.getBirdTypes( );
```

Perhaps a special version of the Bird class constructor accepts the name of a bird type. We could use this list to decide what kind of bird to create.

Static methods also play an important role in various design patterns, where you limit the use of the new operator for a class to one method—a static method called a *factory method*. We'll talk more about object construction later, but suffice it to say that it's common to see usage like this:

```
Bird bird = Bird.createBird( "pigeon" );
```

Initializing Local Variables

In the flyToNest( ) example, we made a point of initializing the local variables xPos and yPos. Unlike instance variables, local variables must be initialized before they can be used. It's a compile-time error to try to access a local variable without first assigning it a value:

```
void myMethod( ) {
    int foo = 42;
    int bar;

    bar += 1;  // compile-time error, bar uninitialized

    bar = 99;
    bar += 1;  // would be OK here
}
```

Notice that this doesn't imply local variables have to be initialized when declared, just that the first time they are referenced must be in an assignment. More subtle possibilities arise when making assignments inside conditionals:

```
void myMethod {
    int foo;
    if ( someCondition ) {
      foo = 42;
      ...
    }
    foo += 1;   // Compile-time error, foo may not be initialized
}
```

In this example, foo is initialized only if someCondition is true. The compiler doesn't let you make this wager, so it flags the use of foo as an error. We could correct this situation in several ways. We could initialize the variable to a default value in advance or move the usage inside the conditional. We could also make sure the path of execution doesn't reach the uninitialized variable through some other means, depending on what makes sense for our particular application. For example, we could simply make sure that we assign foo a value in both the if and else branch. Or we could return from the method abruptly:

```
int foo;
...
```

```
if ( someCondition ) {
    foo = 42;
    ...
} else
    return;

foo += 1;
```

In this case, there's no chance of reaching foo in an uninitialized state, so the compiler allows the use of foo after the conditional.

Why is Java so picky about local variables? One of the most common (and insidious) sources of errors in C or C++ is forgetting to initialize local variables, so Java tries to help us out. If it didn't, Java would suffer the same potential irregularities as C or C++.[*]

Argument Passing and References

In the beginning of Chapter 4 we described the distinction between primitive types, which are passed by value (by copying), and objects, which are passed by reference. Now that we've got a better handle on methods in Java, let's walk through an example:

```
void myMethod( int j, SomeKindOfObject o ) {
    ...
}

// use the method
int i = 0;
SomeKindOfObject obj = new SomeKindOfObject( );
myMethod( i, obj );
```

The chunk of code calls myMethod( ), passing it two arguments. The first argument, i, is passed by value; when the method is called, the value of i is copied into the method's parameter (a local variable to it) named j. If myMethod( ) changes the value of j, it's changing only its copy of the local variable.

In the same way, a copy of the reference to obj is placed into the reference variable o of myMethod( ). Both references refer to the same object, so any changes made through either reference affect the actual (single) object instance. If we change the value of, say, o.size, the change is visible either as o.size (inside myMethod( )) or as obj.size (in the calling method). However, if myMethod( ) changes the reference o itself—to point to another object—it's affecting only its local variable reference. It

---

[*] As with malloc'ed storage in C or C++, Java objects and their instance variables are allocated on a heap, which allows them default values once, when they are created. Local variables, however, are allocated on the Java virtual machine stack. As with the stack in C and C++, failing to initialize these could mean successive method calls could receive garbage values, and program execution might be inconsistent or implementation-dependent.

doesn't affect the caller's variable obj, which still refers to the original object. In this sense, passing the reference is like passing a pointer in C and unlike passing by reference in C++.

What if myMethod( ) needs to modify the calling method's notion of the obj reference as well (i.e., make obj point to a different object)? The easy way to do that is to wrap obj inside some kind of object. For example, we could wrap the object up as the lone element in an array:

```
SomeKindOfObject [] wrapper = new SomeKindOfObject [] { obj };
```

All parties could then refer to the object as wrapper[0] and would have the ability to change the reference. This is not aesthetically pleasing, but it does illustrate that what is needed is the level of indirection.

Another possibility is to use this to pass a reference to the calling object. In that case, the calling object serves as the wrapper for the reference. Let's look at a piece of code that could be from an implementation of a linked list:

```
class Element {
    public Element nextElement;

    void addToList( List list ) {
        list.addToList( this );
    }
}

class List {
    void addToList( Element element ) {
        ...
        element.nextElement = getNextElement();
    }
}
```

Every element in a linked list contains a pointer to the next element in the list. In this code, the Element class represents one element; it includes a method for adding itself to the list. The List class itself contains a method for adding an arbitrary Element to the list. The method addToList( ) calls addToList( ) with the argument this (which is, of course, an Element). addToList( ) can use the this reference to modify the Element's nextElement instance variable. The same technique can be used in conjunction with interfaces to implement callbacks for arbitrary method invocations.

Wrappers for Primitive Types

As we described in Chapter 4, there is a schism in the Java world between class types (i.e., objects) and primitive types (i.e., numbers, characters, and Boolean values). Java accepts this tradeoff simply for efficiency reasons. When you're crunching numbers, you want your computations to be lightweight; having to use objects for primitive types complicates performance optimizations. For the times you want to treat values as objects, Java supplies a standard wrapper class for each of the primitive types, as shown in Table 5-1.

Table 5-1. Primitive type wrappers

Primitive	Wrapper
Void	java.lang.Void
Boolean	java.lang.Boolean
Char	java.lang.Character
Byte	java.lang.Byte
Short	java.lang.Short
Int	java.lang.Integer
Long	java.lang.Long
Float	java.lang.Float
Double	java.lang.Double

An instance of a wrapper class encapsulates a single value of its corresponding type. It's an immutable object that serves as a container to hold the value and let us retrieve it later. You can construct a wrapper object from a primitive value or from a String representation of the value. The following statements are equivalent:

```
Float pi = new Float( 3.14 );
Float pi = new Float( "3.14" );
```

The wrapper constructors throw a NumberFormatException when there is an error in parsing a string.

Each of the numeric type wrappers implements the java.lang.Number interface, which provides "value" methods access to its value in all the primitive forms. You can retrieve scalar values with the methods doubleValue( ), floatValue( ), longValue( ), intValue( ), shortValue( ), and byteValue( ):

```
Double size = new Double ( 32.76 );

double d = size.doubleValue( );      // 32.76
float f = size.floatValue( );        // 32.76
long l = size.longValue( );          // 32
int i = size.intValue( );            // 32
```

This code is equivalent to casting the primitive double value to the various types.

The most common need for a wrapper is when you want to pass a primitive value to a method that requires an object. For example, in Chapter 11, we'll look at the Java Collections API, a sophisticated set of classes for dealing with object groups, such as lists, sets, and maps. All the Collections APIs work on object types, so primitives must be wrapped when stored in them. We'll see in the next section that Java 5.0 makes this wrapping process automatic. For now, let's do it ourselves. As we'll see, a

List is an extensible collection of Objects. We can use wrappers to hold numbers in a List (along with other objects):

```
// Simple Java code
List myNumbers = new ArrayList( );
Integer thirtyThree = new Integer( 33 );
myNumbers.add( thirtyThree );
```

Here we have created an Integer wrapper object so that we can insert the number into the List, using add( ). Later, when we are extracting elements from the List, we can recover the int value as follows:

```
// Simple Java code
Integer theNumber = (Integer)myNumbers.get(0);
int n = theNumber.intValue( );          // 33
```

In Java 5.0, the code is more concise and safer. The usage of the wrapper class is mostly hidden from us by the compiler, but it is still being used internally:

```
// Java code using autoboxing and generics
List<Integer> myNumbers = new ArrayList<Integer>( );
myNumbers.add( 33 );
int n = myNumbers.get( 0 );
```

This example will make more sense as you read on.

Autoboxing and Unboxing of Primitives

In Java 5.0, the compiler automatically wraps primitives in their wrapper types and unwraps them where appropriate. This process is called autoboxing and unboxing the primitive. It happens when primitives are used as arguments and return values in methods and on simple assignment to variables. For example:

```
// Simple assignments
Integer integer = 5;
int i = new Integer(5);

// Method arguments and return types
Double multiply( Double a, Double b ) {
    return a.doubleValue( ) * b.doubleValue( );
}

double d = multiply( 5.0, 5.0 );
```

In the first case, Java simply wrapped the value 5 into an Integer for us. In the second case, it unwrapped our (unnecessary) Integer object to its primitive value. Next, we have a method that multiplies two Double wrapper objects and returns the result as a Double wrapper. This example actually has three cases of boxing and one case of unboxing. First, the two double primitive values are boxed to Double types in order to call the method. Next, the return statement of the method is actually being called on a primitive double value, which the compiler turns into a Double before it leaves the method. Finally, the compiler unboxes the return value on assignment to the primitive double variable d. This example is not a compelling case, but it serves to exercise all of the features for us.

Performance implications of boxing

Gauging performance is tricky. For the vast majority of applications, the time it takes to perform tasks like creating a small object or calling a method is miniscule compared to other factors, such as I/O, user interaction, or the actual logic of the application. As a general rule, it's not wise to worry too much about these detailed performance issues until the application is mature (no premature optimization). However, we can anticipate that in performance-critical areas allowing Java to box and unbox primitives will not be as fast as using primitives directly. One aspect of this to consider is how many new objects are being created and reclaimed by the garbage collector. While in general Java may be forced to create a new object for each boxed primitive, there are optimizations for a small range of values. Java guarantees that the Boolean values true and false, "small" valued numeric types ranging from 0 to 127 for bytes and chars, and from −128 to 127 for shorts and integers are *interned*. Saying that they are interned means that instead of creating a new object each time, Java reuses the same object on subsequent boxings. This is safe because primitive wrappers are immutable and cannot be changed.

```
Integer i = 4;
Integer j = 4;
System.out.println( i == j ); // True only for small values.
```

The effect of this, as shown in this code snippet, is that for small identical values the boxed primitives are actually the same object. Java also attempts to intern string values in Java classes. We'll talk about that in Chapter 10.

Variable-Length Argument Lists

As we mentioned earlier, Java 5.0 introduced *variable-length argument lists* or "varargs" for methods. The most common example usage of varargs is for the new printf( ) style printing method, which allows any number of tags to be embedded in a string and takes an argument for each tag, to be printed. For example:

```
System.out.printf("My name is %s and my age is %s\n", "Bob", 21 );
System.out.printf("Get the %s out of %s before I %s\n", item, place, action );
```

Varargs allow the printf( ) method to accept any number of items to print (from zero to dozens, as awkward as that would be).

A method accepting a variable argument list is equivalent to a method accepting an array of some type of object. The difference is that the compiler makes the method call accept individual, comma-separated values, and then packs them into the array for us. The syntax for declaring the varargs method uses ellipses (...) where the square brackets of an array might go. For example:

```
void printObjects( Object ... list ) {
    // list is an Object []
    for( Object o : list )
        System.out.println( o );
}
```

Inside the printObjects( ) method, the variable list is actually an Object [] type. We could find out how many arguments were passed to us by asking the array for its length in the usual way:

```
System.out.println( "Number of arguments:" + list.length );
```

If the caller passed no arguments, the array will be empty.

In the case of our printObjects( ) method, we could pass a mix of primitive values as well as object types because the compiler would automatically box the primitives to their wrapper types for us before placing them into the Object [].

The variable argument list does not have to be of type Object. It can be of any type, including primitive types. For example:

```
printInts( int ... list ) {
    // list is an int []
}
// usage
printInts( 1, 2, 3, 4 );

printStrings( String ... list ) {
    // list is a String []
}
// usage
printStrings( "foo", "bar", "gee" );
```

The printInts( ) method receives an int [] array of primitive int values. The printStrings( ) method receives a String [] as its argument. The actual arguments must all be assignable (possibly after numeric promotion or boxing) to the type of the variable argument list. In other words, the printInts( ) method can only be called with numbers assignable to int, and the printStrings( ) method can only be called with Strings.

Varargs methods may also have any number of fixed arguments before the varargs declaration. This is how the printf( ) method guarantees that its first argument is the format string:

```
void printf( String format, Object ... args ) { ... }
```

Of course, a method can have only one varargs declaration and it must come last in the method signature.

Method Overloading

Method overloading is the ability to define multiple methods with the same name in a class; when the method is invoked, the compiler picks the correct one based on the arguments passed to the method. This implies that overloaded methods must have different numbers or types of arguments. (In Chapter 6, we'll look at *method overriding*, which occurs when we declare methods with identical signatures in different classes.)

Method overloading (also called *ad-hoc polymorphism*) is a powerful and useful feature. The idea is to create methods that act in the same way on different types of arguments. This creates the illusion that a single method can operate on many types of arguments. The print( ) method in the standard PrintStream class is a good example of method overloading in action. As you've probably deduced by now, you can print a string representation of just about anything using this expression:

```
System.out.print( argument )
```

The variable out is a reference to an object (a PrintStream) that defines nine different, "overloaded" versions of the print( ) method. The versions take arguments of the following types: Object, String, char[], char, int, long, float, double, and boolean.

```
class PrintStream {
    void print( Object arg ) { ... }
    void print( String arg ) { ... }
    void print( char [] arg ) { ... }
    ...
}
```

You can invoke the print( ) method with any of these types as an argument, and it's printed in an appropriate way. In a language without method overloading, this requires something more cumbersome, such as a uniquely named method for printing each type of object. In that case, it's your responsibility to remember what method to use for each data type.

In the previous example, print( ) has been overloaded to support two reference types: Object and String. What if we try to call print( ) with some other reference type? Say, a Date object? When there's not an exact type match, the compiler searches for an acceptable, *assignable* match. Since Date, like all classes, is a subclass of Object, a Date object can be assigned to a variable of type Object. It's therefore an acceptable match, and the Object method is selected.

What if there's more than one possible match? For example, we try to print a subclass of String called MyString. (The String class is final, so it can't really be subclassed, but let's use our imaginations.) MyString is assignable to either String or to Object. Here, the compiler makes a determination as to which match is "better" and selects that method. In this case, it's the String method.

The intuitive explanation is that the String class is closer to MyString in the inheritance hierarchy. It is a *more specific* match. A slightly more rigorous way of specifying it would be to say that a given method is more specific than another method if the argument types of the first method are all assignable to the argument types of the second method. In this case, the String method is more specific to a subclass of String than the Object method because type String is assignable to type Object. The reverse is not true.

If you're paying close attention, you may have noticed we said that the compiler resolves overloaded methods. Method overloading is not something that happens at runtime; this is an important distinction. It means that the selected method is chosen once, when the code is compiled. Once the overloaded method is selected, the choice is fixed until the code is recompiled, even if the class containing the called method is later revised and an even more specific overloaded method is added. This is in contrast to *overridden* methods, which are located at runtime and can be found even if they didn't exist when the calling class was compiled. We'll talk about method overriding later in the chapter.

Object Creation

Objects in Java are allocated on a system "heap" memory space. Unlike other languages, however, we needn't manage that memory ourselves. Java takes care of memory allocation and deallocation for you. Java explicitly allocates storage for an object when you create it with the new operator. More importantly, objects are removed by garbage collection when they're no longer referenced.

Constructors

Objects are allocated with the new operator using an *object constructor*. A constructor is a special method with the same name as its class and no return type. It's called when a new class instance is created, which gives the class an opportunity to set up the object for use. Constructors, like other methods, can accept arguments and can be overloaded (they are not, however, inherited like other methods; we'll discuss inheritance in Chapter 6).

```
class Date {
    long time;

    Date( ) {
        time = currentTime( );
    }

    Date( String date ) {
        time = parseDate( date );
    }
    ...
}
```

In this example, the class Date has two constructors. The first takes no arguments; it's known as the *default constructor*. Default constructors play a special role: if we don't define any constructors for a class, an empty default constructor is supplied for us. The default constructor is what gets called whenever you create an object by calling its constructor with no arguments. Here we have implemented the default constructor so that it sets the instance variable time by calling a hypothetical method, currentTime( ), which resembles the functionality of the real java.util.Date class. The second constructor takes a String argument. Presumably, this String contains a string representation of the time that can be parsed to set the time variable. Given the constructors in the previous example, we create a Date object in the following ways:

```
Date now = new Date( );
Date christmas = new Date("Dec 25, 2006");
```

In each case, Java chooses the appropriate constructor at compile time based on the rules for overloaded method selection.

If we later remove all references to an allocated object, it'll be garbage-collected, as we'll discuss shortly:

```
christmas = null;        // fair game for the garbage collector
```

Setting this reference to null means it's no longer pointing to the "Dec 25, 2006" string object. Setting the variable christmas to any other value would have the same effect. Unless the original string object is referenced by another variable, it's now inaccessible and can be garbage-collected. We're not suggesting that you have to set references to null to get the values garbage collected. Often this just happens naturally when local variables fall out of scope, but items referenced by instance variables of objects live as long as the object itself lives (through references to it) and static variables live effectively forever.

A few more notes: constructors can't be declared abstract, synchronized, or final (we'll define the rest of those terms later). Constructors can, however, be declared with the visibility modifiers public, private, or protected, just like other methods, to control their accessibility. We'll talk in detail about visibility modifiers in the next chapter.

Working with Overloaded Constructors

A constructor can refer to another constructor in the same class or the immediate superclass using special forms of the this and super references. We'll discuss the first case here and return to that of the superclass constructor after we have talked more about subclassing and inheritance. A constructor can invoke another, overloaded constructor in its class using the self-referential method call this( ) with appropriate

arguments to select the desired constructor. If a constructor calls another constructor, *it must do so as its first statement*:

```
class Car {
    String model;
    int doors;

    Car( String model, int doors ) {
        this.model = model;
        this.doors = doors;
        // other, complicated setup
        ...
    }

    Car( String model ) {
        this( model, 4 /* doors */ );
    }
    ...
}
```

In this example, the class `Car` has two constructors. The first, more explicit one,
accepts arguments specifying the car's model and its number of doors. The second
constructor takes just the model as an argument and, in turn, calls the first constructor with a default value of four doors. The advantage of this approach is that you can
have a single constructor do all the complicated setup work; other auxiliary constructors simply feed the appropriate arguments to that constructor.

The special call to `this( )` must appear as the first statement in our delegating constructor. The syntax is restricted in this way because there's a need to identify a clear
chain of command in the calling of constructors. At the end of the chain, Java
invokes the constructor of the superclass (if we don't do it explicitly) to ensure that
inherited members are initialized properly before we proceed.

There's also a point in the chain, just after invoking the constructor of the superclass, where the initializers of the current class's instance variables are evaluated.
Before that point, we can't even reference the instance variables of our class. We'll
explain this situation again in complete detail after we have talked about inheritance.

For now, all you need to know is that you can invoke a second constructor only as
the first statement of another constructor. For example, the following code is illegal
and causes a compile-time error:

```
Car( String m ) {
    int doors = determineDoors( );
    this( m, doors );   // Error: constructor call
                        // must be first statement
}
```

The simple model name constructor can't do any additional setup before calling the more explicit constructor. It can't even refer to an instance member for a constant value:

```
class Car {
    ...
    final int default_doors = 4;
    ...

    Car( String m ) {
        this( m, default_doors );  // Error: referencing
                                   // uninitialized variable
    }
    ...
}
```

The instance variable `defaultDoors` is not initialized until a later point in the chain of constructor calls setting up the object, so the compiler doesn't let us access it yet. Fortunately, we can solve this particular problem by using a static variable instead of an instance variable:

```
class Car {
    ...
    static final int DEFAULT_DOORS = 4;
    ...

    Car( String m ) {
        this( m, DEFAULT_DOORS );   // Okay!
    }
    ...
}
```

The static members of a class are initialized when the class is first loaded, so it's safe to access them in a constructor.

Static and Nonstatic Initializer Blocks

It's possible to declare a block of code (some statements within curly braces) directly within the scope of a class. This code block doesn't belong to any method; instead, it's executed once, at the time the object is constructed, or, in the case of a code block marked `static`, at the time the class is loaded. These blocks can be used to do additional setup for the class or an object instance and are called *initializer blocks*.

Instance initializer blocks can be thought of as extensions of instance variable initialization. They're called at the time the instance variable's initializers are evaluated (after superclass construction but before your constructor body), in the order in which they appear in the Java source:

```
class MyClass {
    Properties myProps = new Properties();
    // set up myProps
    {
```

```
        myProps.put("foo", "bar");
        myProps.put("boo", "gee");
    }
    int a = 5;
...
```

Normally, this kind of setup could be done just as well in the object's constructor. A notable exception is in the case of an anonymous inner class (see Chapter 6).

Similarly, you can use static initializer blocks to set up static class members. This more useful case allows the static members of a class to have complex initialization just like objects do with constructors:

```
class ColorWheel {
    static Hashtable colors = new Hashtable( );

    // set up colors
    static {
        colors.put("Red", Color.red );
        colors.put("Green", Color.green );
        colors.put("Blue", Color.blue );
        ...
    }
    ...
}
```

The class ColorWheel provides a variable colors that maps the names of colors to Color objects in a Hashtable. The first time the class ColorWheel is referenced and loaded, the static components of ColorWheel are evaluated in the order they appear in the source. In this case, the static code block simply adds elements to the colors table.

Object Destruction

Now that we've seen how to create objects, it's time to talk about their destruction. If you're accustomed to programming in C or C++, you've probably spent time hunting down memory leaks in your code. Java takes care of object destruction for you; you don't have to worry about traditional memory leaks, and you can concentrate on more important programming tasks.[*]

Garbage Collection

Java uses a technique known as *garbage collection* to remove objects that are no longer needed. The garbage collector is Java's grim reaper. It lingers in the background,

---

[*] It's still possible in Java to write code that holds onto objects forever, consuming more and more memory. This isn't really a leak so much as it is hoarding memory. It is also usually much easier to track down with the correct tools and techniques.

stalking objects and awaiting their demise. It finds and watches them, periodically counting references to them to see when their time has come. When all references to an object are gone and it's no longer accessible, the garbage-collection mechanism declares the object *unreachable* and reclaims its space back to the available pool of resources. An unreachable object is one that can no longer be found through any combination of "live" references in the running application.

Garbage collection uses a variety of different algorithms; the Java virtual machine architecture doesn't require a particular scheme. It's worth noting, however, how some implementations of Java have accomplished this task. In the beginning, Java used a technique called "mark and sweep." In this scheme, Java first walks through the tree of all accessible object references and marks them as alive. Java then scans the heap, looking for identifiable objects that aren't marked. In this technique, Java is able to find objects on the heap because they are stored in a characteristic way and have a particular signature of bits in their handles unlikely to be reproduced naturally. This kind of algorithm doesn't become confused by the problem of cyclic references, in which objects can mutually reference each other and appear alive even when they are dead (Java handles this problem automatically). This scheme wasn't the fastest method, however, and caused pauses in the program. Since Java 1.3, implementations have become much more sophisticated.

Modern Java garbage collectors effectively run continuously, without forcing any lengthy delay in execution of the Java application. Because they are part of a runtime system, they can also accomplish some things that could not be done statically. Sun's Java implementation divides the memory heap into several areas for objects with different estimated lifespans. Short-lived objects are placed on a special part of the heap, which reduces the time to recycle them drastically. Objects that live longer can be moved to other, less volatile parts of the heap. With the Java 5.0 implementation from Sun, the garbage collector can even "tune" itself by adjusting the size of parts of the heap based on the actual application performance. The improvement in Java's garbage collection since the early releases has been remarkable and is one of the reasons that Java is now roughly equivalent in speed to traditional compiled languages.

In general, you do not have to concern yourself with the garbage-collection process. But one garbage-collection method can be useful for debugging. You can prompt the garbage collector to make a clean sweep explicitly by invoking the System.gc( ) method. This method is completely implementation-dependent and may do nothing, but it can be used if you want some guarantee that Java has cleaned up before you do an activity.

Finalization

Before an object is removed by garbage collection, its finalize( ) method is invoked to give it a last opportunity to clean up its act and free other kinds of resources it may be holding. While the garbage collector can reclaim memory resources, it may not take care of things such as closing files and terminating network connections as gracefully or efficiently as could your code. That's what the finalize( ) method is for. An object's finalize( ) method is called once and only once before the object is garbage-collected. However, there's no guarantee when that will happen. Garbage collection may, in theory, never run on a system that is not short of memory. It is also interesting to note that finalization and collection occur in two distinct phases of the garbage-collection process. First, items are finalized, then they are collected. It is, therefore, possible that finalization can (intentionally or unintentionally) create a lingering reference to the object in question, postponing its garbage collection. The object is, of course, subject to collection later, if the reference goes away, but its finalize( ) method isn't called again.

The finalize( ) methods of superclasses are not invoked automatically for you. If you need to invoke the finalization routine of your parent classes, you should invoke the finalize( ) method of your superclass, using super.finalize( ). We discuss inheritance and overridden methods in Chapter 6.

Weak and Soft References

In general, as we've described, Java's garbage collector reclaims objects when they are unreachable. An unreachable object, again, is one that is no longer referenced by any variables within your application, one that is not reachable through any chain of references by any running thread. Such an object cannot be used by the application any longer and is, therefore, a clear case where the object should be removed.

In some situations, however, it is advantageous to have Java's garbage collector work with your application to decide when it is time to remove a particular object. For these cases, Java allows you to hold an object reference indirectly through a special wrapper object, a type of java.lang.ref.Reference. If Java then decides to remove the object, the reference the wrapper holds turns to null automatically. While the reference exists, you may continue to use it in the ordinary way and, if you wish, assign it elsewhere (using normal references), preventing its garbage collection.

There are two types of Reference wrappers that implement different schemes for deciding when to let their target references be garbage-collected. The first is called a WeakReference. *Weak references* are eligible for garbage collection immediately; they do not prevent garbage collection the way that ordinary "strong" references do. This means that if you have a combination of strong references and references contained in WeakReference wrappers in your application, the garbage collector waits until only WeakReferences remain and then collects the object. This is an essential feature that allows garbage collection to work with certain kinds of caching schemes. Often you'll want to cache an object reference for performance (to avoid creating it or looking it up). But unless you take specific action to remove unneeded objects from your cache, the cache keeps those objects alive forever by maintaining live references to them. By using weak references, you can implement a cache that automatically throws away references when the object would normally be garbage collected. In fact, an implementation of HashMap called WeakHashMap is provided that does just this (see Chapter 11 for details).

The second type of reference wrapper is called SoftReference. A *soft reference* is similar to a weak reference, but it tells the garbage collector to be less aggressive about reclaiming its contents. Soft-referenced objects are collected only when and if Java runs short of memory. This is useful for a slightly different kind of caching where you want to keep some content around unless there is a need to get rid of it. For example, a web browser can use soft references to cache images or HTML strings internally, thus keeping them around as long as possible until memory constraints come into play. (A more sophisticated application might also use its own scheme based on a "least recently used" marking of some kind.)

The java.lang.ref package contains the WeakReference and SoftReference wrappers, as well as a facility called ReferenceQueue that allows your application to receive a list of references that have been collected. It's important that your application use the queue or some other checking mechanism to remove the Reference objects themselves after their contents have been collected; otherwise, your cache will soon fill up with empty Reference object wrappers.

Enumerations

Now that we've covered the basics of classes, we can talk in more depth about one of the cool new features in Java 5.0, *enumerations*. An enumeration is an object type in the Java language that is limited to an explicit set of values. The values have an order, defined by their order of declaration in the code, and have a correspondence with a string name that is the same as their declared name in the source code.

We've already seen a couple of examples of enumerations used in place of static identifiers. For example:

```
enum Weekday { Sunday, Monday, Tuesday, Wednesday, Thursday, Friday, Saturday }

// usage
setDay( Weekday.Sunday );
```

Let's take a look at what the Java compiler is actually generating for the enum. It is a regular Java class, in this case named Weekday, so we can display it with the javap command like so:

```
% javap Weekday

public final class Weekday extends java.lang.Enum {
    public static final Weekday Sunday;
    public static final Weekday Monday;
    public static final Weekday Tuesday;
    public static final Weekday Wednesday;
    public static final Weekday Thursday;
```

```
    public static final Weekday Friday;
    public static final Weekday Saturday;

    public static final Weekday[] values();
    public static Weekday valueOf(java.lang.String);
}
```

Weekday is a subclass of the Enum type with seven static, final, "constant" object references corresponding to our seven enumerated values. Each of the enumerated values is of type Weekday. The Java compiler does not let us extend this class or create any other instances of this type. The only instances of Weekday that will ever exist are the seven enumerated values. This is what gives enumerations their type safety. A method expecting a Weekday can be given one of only seven values. Unlike a numeric constant identifier, no value other than a Weekday will work. As we saw in Chapter 4, enumerations (unlike most objects) can also be used in switch statements with all the same benefits.

Because enumerations are static values, they can be imported with the new Java static import, saving us some typing:

```
import mypackage.Weekday.*;
...
setDay( Friday );
setDeadline( Sunday );
```

We should also mention that enumerations can be declared not only at the "top level" alongside classes but within classes or interfaces as well. In this case, they act just like inner classes (see Chapter 6).

Enum Values

You can get the ordered list of enum values for a type with the static values() method.

```
Weekday [] weekdays = Weekday.values();
```

The compareTo() method of an enum compares an enum value to another value of the same enum type and returns an integer less than zero, zero, or greater than zero, indicating whether the target enum is "less than," "equal to," or "greater than" the order of the reference enum. This doesn't mean much for our Weekdays, but it might be useful for values that have a more numeric meaning or a (noncyclic) scale of some kind. For example:

```
Level level = Level.HIGH;
Level anotherLevel = Level.LOW;
if ( level.compareTo( anotherLevel ) > 0 ) // true
    doSomething();
```

We mentioned that enum values have a string correspondence for their names. You can get the string name of the value (which is exactly the same as it is declared in the source code) with the name() method. Going the other direction, you can "look up" any enum value by its class type and string name using the static `Enum.valueOf()` method:

```
String mondayString = Weekday.Monday.name( ); // "Monday"
Weekday mondayWeekday = Enum.valueOf( Weekday.class, "Monday" );
```

The `name()` value is also used by the `toString()` method of the value, so printing an enum value does what you'd expect.

Customizing Enumerations

We said that the `java.lang.Enum` type cannot be directly extended and that you can't create new instances of enum types. However, you can add things to the generated enumeration class when it's declared. For example, the enumeration `java.util.concurrent.TimeUnit`, which has identifiers for time units such as SECONDS, MILLI-SECONDS, and MICROSECONDS, has a `sleep()` method that interprets its argument in the correct time scale:

```
import static java.util.concurrent.TimeUnit.*;

SECONDS.sleep( 5 ); // sleep 5 seconds
```

Enumerations can have values with constructors, methods, and fields just like other classes. For the most part, this is straightforward; you just add a semicolon after the enum values and then add your additional class members. Let's add a "fun" value and accessor method to our weekdays:

```
public enum Weekday
{
    Sunday(8), Monday(0), Tuesday(1), Wednesday(2), Thursday(4),
        Friday(6), Saturday(10) ;

    int fun;

    Weekday( int fun ) { this.fun = fun; }

    public int getFun() { return fun; }
}
```

Here, we've added an instance variable, fun, to the Weekday class, as well as a constructor and accessor method that work with the value. The declaration of our enum values each now accepts the constructor value, much like a constructor call without the new keyword. Note that the semicolon at the end of the values is mandatory. Each Weekday now has a fun attribute.

There is an odd special feature of enums that we didn't show. In addition to adding features to the enum class as a whole (as in our example), we can add methods and variables to individual values of the enumeration by giving them a body with curly braces ({}). This is best served by an example:

```
enum Cat {
    Himilayan, Siamese, Caleco,
```

```
    Persian {
        public void someMethod( ) { ... }
    }
}
```

Now, only the Cat.Persian enum value has the method. In this case, the compiler generates a subclass of Cat as an inner class of the Persian type to hold the extra member. (We'll talk about inner classes in Chapter 6.) You could use this to have the Persian member override a method in the base enum class.

CHAPTER 6
Relationships Among Classes

So far in our exploration of Java, we have seen how to create Java classes and objects, which are instances of those classes. By themselves objects would be little more than a convention for organizing code. It is in the relationships between objects—their connections and privileges with respect to one another—that the power of an object-oriented language is really expressed.

That's what we'll cover in this chapter. In particular, we'll look at several kinds of relationships:

Inheritance relationships
> How a class inherits methods and variables from its parent class

Interfaces
> How to declare that a class implements certain behavior and define a type to refer to that behavior

Packaging
> How to organize objects into logical groups

Inner classes
> A generalization of classes that lets you nest a class definition inside another class definition

Subclassing and Inheritance

Classes in Java exist in a hierarchy. A class in Java can be declared as a *subclass* of another class using the extends keyword. A subclass *inherits* variables and methods from its *superclass* and can use them as if they were declared within the subclass itself:

```
class Animal {
    float weight;
    ...
    void eat() {
        ...
```

```
        }
        ...
    }

    class Mammal extends Animal {
        // inherits weight
        int heartRate;
        ...

        // inherits eat()
        void breathe() {
            ...
        }
    }
```

In this example, an object of type Mammal has both the instance variable weight and the method eat( ). They are inherited from Animal.

A class can extend only one other class. To use the proper terminology, Java allows *single inheritance* of class implementation. Later in this chapter, we'll talk about interfaces, which take the place of *multiple inheritance* as it's primarily used in other languages.

A subclass can be further subclassed. Normally, subclassing specializes or refines a class by adding variables and methods (you cannot remove or hide variables or methods by subclassing). For example:

```
    class Cat extends Mammal {
        // inherits weight and heartRate
        boolean longHair;
        ...

        // inherits eat( ) and breathe()
        void purr() {
            ...
        }
    }
```

The Cat class is a type of Mammal that is ultimately a type of Animal. Cat objects inherit all the characteristics of Mammal objects and, in turn, Animal objects. Cat also provides additional behavior in the form of the purr( ) method and the longHair variable. We can denote the class relationship in a diagram, as shown in Figure 6-1.

A subclass inherits all members of its superclass not designated as private. As we'll discuss shortly, other levels of visibility affect what inherited members of the class can be seen from outside of the class and its subclasses, but at a minimum, a subclass always has the same set of visible members as its parent. For this reason, the type of a subclass can be considered a *subtype* of its parent, and instances of the subtype can be used anywhere instances of the supertype are allowed. Consider the following example:

```
    Cat simon = new Cat();
    Animal creature = simon;
```

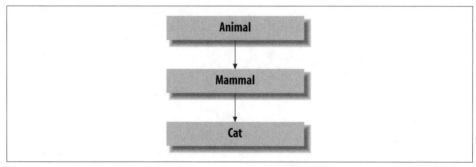

Figure 6-1. A class hierarchy

The Cat instance simon in this example can be assigned to the Animal type variable creature because Cat is a subtype of Animal. Similarly, any method accepting an Animal object would accept an instance of a Cat or any Mammal type as well. This is an important aspect of polymorphism in an object-oriented language such as Java. We'll see how it can be used to refine a class's behavior, as well as add new capabilities to it.

Shadowed Variables

In Chapter 5, we saw that a local variable of the same name as an instance variable *shadows* (hides) the instance variable. Similarly, an instance variable in a subclass can shadow an instance variable of the same name in its parent class, as shown in Figure 6-2.

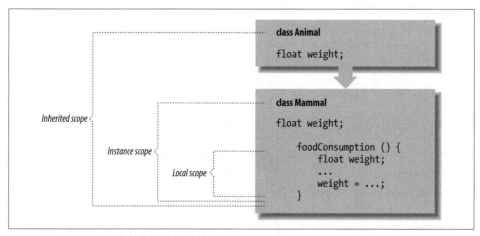

Figure 6-2. The scope of shadowed variables

In Figure 6-2, the variable weight is declared in three places: as a local variable in the method foodConsumption( ) of the class Mammal, as an instance variable of the class Mammal, and as an instance variable of the class Animal. The actual variable selected depends on the scope in which we are working.

In the previous example, all variables were of the same type. Just about the only reason to declare a variable with the same type in a subclass is to provide an alternate initializer.

A slightly more plausible use of shadowed variables involves changing their types. We could, for example, shadow an int variable with a double variable in a subclass that needs decimal values instead of integer values. We can do this without changing the existing code because, as its name suggests, when we shadow variables, we don't replace them but instead mask them. Both variables still exist; methods of the superclass see the original variable, and methods of the subclass see the new version. The determination of what variables the various methods see occurs at compile time.

Here's a simple example:

```
class IntegerCalculator {
    int sum;
    ...
}

class DecimalCalculator extends IntegerCalculator {
    double sum;
    ...
}
```

In this example, we shadow the instance variable sum to change its type from int to double.* Methods defined in the class IntegerCalculator see the integer variable sum while methods defined in DecimalCalculator see the floating-point variable sum. However, both variables actually exist for a given instance of DecimalCalculator, and they can have independent values. In fact, any methods that DecimalCalculator inherits from IntegerCalculator actually see the integer variable sum.

Since both variables exist in DecimalCalculator, we need a way to reference the variable inherited from IntegerCalculator. We do that using the super reference:

```
int s = super.sum;
```

Inside of DecimalCalculator, the super keyword used in this manner selects the sum variable defined in the superclass. We'll explain the use of super more fully in a bit.

Another important point about shadowed variables has to do with how they work when we refer to an object by way of a less derived type (a supertype). For example, we can refer to a DecimalCalculator object as an IntegerCalculator. If we do so and then access the variable sum, we get the integer variable, not the decimal one:

```
DecimalCalculator dc = new DecimalCalculator();
IntegerCalculator ic = dc;

int s = ic.sum;        // accesses IntegerCalculator sum
```

---

* Note that a better way to design our calculators would be to have an abstract Calculator class with two subclasses: IntegerCalculator and DecimalCalculator.

After this detailed explanation, you may still wonder what shadowed variables are good for. To be honest, the usefulness of shadowed variables is limited. It's much better to abstract the use of variables like this in other ways than to use tricky scoping rules. However, it's important to understand the concepts here before we talk about doing the same thing with methods. We'll see a different and more dynamic type of behavior when methods shadow other methods, or to use the correct terminology, *override* other methods.

Overriding Methods

In Chapter 5, we saw that we could declare *overloaded methods* (i.e., methods with the same name but a different number or type of arguments) within a class. Overloaded method selection works in the way we described on all methods available to a class, including inherited ones. This means that a subclass can define additional overloaded methods that add to the overloaded methods provided by a superclass.

A subclass can do more than that; it can define a method that has exactly the *same* method signature (name and argument types) as a method in its superclass. In that case, the method in the subclass *overrides* the method in the superclass and effectively replaces its implementation, as shown in Figure 6-3. Overriding methods to change the behavior of objects is called *subtype polymorphism*. It's the usage most people think of when they talk about the power of object-oriented languages.

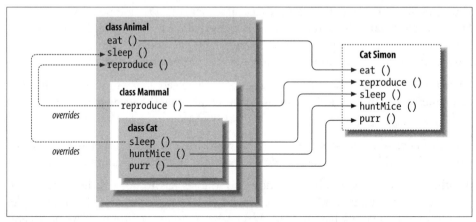

Figure 6-3. Method overriding

In Figure 6-3, `Mammal` overrides the `reproduce( )` method of `Animal`, perhaps to specialize the method for the peculiar behavior of mammals' giving live birth.* The `Cat` object's sleeping behavior is also overridden to be different from that of a general

---

* We'll ignore the platypus, which is an obscure nonvoviviparous mammal.

Animal, perhaps to accommodate cat naps. The Cat class also adds the more unique behaviors of purring and hunting mice.

From what you've seen so far, overridden methods probably look like they shadow methods in superclasses, just as variables do. But overridden methods are actually more powerful than that. When there are multiple implementations of a method in the inheritance hierarchy of an object, the one in the "most derived" class (the lowest one in the hierarchy) always overrides the others, even if we refer to the object through a reference of one of the superclass types.*

For example, if we have a Cat instance assigned to a variable of the more general type Animal, and we call its sleep() method, we still get the sleep() method implemented in the Cat class, not the one in Animal:

```
Cat simon = new Cat();
Animal creature = simon;
   ...
creature.sleep(  );        // accesses Cat sleep();
```

In other words, a Cat acts like a Cat, regardless of whether you know that you have one or not. In other respects, the variable creature may look like an Animal. As we explained earlier, access to a variable through an Animal reference would find the implementation in the Animal class, not the Cat class. However, because methods are located *dynamically*, searching subclasses first, the appropriate method in the Cat class is invoked, even though we are dealing with it as an Animal object. This means that the behavior of objects is dynamic. We can deal with specialized objects as if they were more general types of objects and still take advantage of their specialized implementations of behavior.

@Override

A common programming error in Java is to accidentally overload a method when trying to override it. Any difference in the number or type of arguments produces two overloaded methods instead of a single, overridden method. The new annotations syntax in Java 5.0 provides a way to get the compiler to help with this problem. An annotation, as we'll describe in Chapter 7, allows us to add special markers or metadata to source code that can be read by the compiler or runtime tools. One of the standard annotations that Java defines is called @Override and it tells the compiler that the method it marks is intended to override a method in the superclass. The compiler then warns if the method doesn't match. For example, we could specify that the sleep() method of our Cat class overrides one in a superclass like so:

```
class Cat extends Mammal {
    ...
    @Override void sleep() { ... }
}
```

* An overridden method in Java acts like a virtual method in C++.

Overridden methods and dynamic binding

In a previous section, we mentioned that *overloaded* methods are selected by the compiler at compile time. *Overridden* methods, on the other hand, are selected dynamically at runtime. Even if we create an instance of a subclass our code has never seen before (perhaps a new class loaded from the network), any overriding methods that it contains are located and used at runtime, replacing those that existed when we last compiled our code.

In contrast, if we load a new class that implements an additional, more specific, overloaded method, our code continues to use the implementation it discovered at compile time. Another effect of this is that casting (i.e., explicitly telling the compiler to treat an object as one of its assignable types) affects the selection of overloaded methods but not overridden methods.

Static method binding

Static methods don't belong to any object instance; they are accessed directly through a class name, so they are not dynamically selected at runtime like instance methods. That is why static methods are called "static"; they are always bound at compile time.

A static method in a superclass can be shadowed by another static method in a subclass, as long as the original method was not declared final. However, you can't "override" a static method with an instance method. In other words, you can't have a static method and instance method with the same signature in the same class hierarchy.

final methods and performance

In languages like C++, the default is for methods to act like shadowed variables, so you have to declare explicitly the methods you want to be dynamic (or, as C++ terms them, *virtual*). In Java, instance methods are, by default, dynamic. But you can use the final modifier to declare that an instance method can't be overridden in a subclass, and it won't be subject to dynamic binding.

We have seen final used with variables to effectively make them constants. When applied to a method, final means that its implementation is constant—no overriding allowed. final can also be applied to an entire class, which means the class can't be subclassed.

In the old days, dynamic method binding came with a significant performance penalty, and some people are still inclined to use the final modifier to guard against this. Modern Java runtime systems eliminate the need for this kind of fudging. A profiling runtime can determine which methods are not being overridden and "optimistically" inline them, treating them as if they were final until it becomes necessary to do otherwise. As a rule, you should use the final keyword when it is correct for your program's structure, not for performance considerations.

Compiler optimizations

In some older versions of Java, the *javac* compiler can be run with a *-O* switch, which tells it to perform certain optimizations, like inlining, statically. Most of these optimizations are now done at runtime by smarter VMs, so switches like this are generally not necessary.

Another kind of optimization allows you to include debugging code in your Java source without a size or performance penalty. Java doesn't have a preprocessor to explicitly control what source is included, but you can get some of the same effects by making a block of code conditional on a constant (i.e., static and final) variable. The Java compiler is smart enough to remove this code when it determines that it won't be called. For example:

```
static final boolean DEBUG = false;
...
final void debug (String message) {
    if (DEBUG) {
        System.err.println(message);
        // do other stuff
        ...
    }
}
```

In this case, the compiler can recognize that the condition on the DEBUG variable is always false, and the body of the debug( ) method will be optimized away. With a modern compiler the method call would be removed entirely. Of course, with the speed of modern machines, it's hard to imagine that a simple condition such as this would be significant anyway.

Note that this kind of debugging code is useful for purposes other than assertions, which we covered in Chapter 4. Assertions are supposed to be yes/no tests that guarantee the correctness of your program logic. While you could trick them into printing debugging information, it's not what they were intended for.

Method selection revisited

By now you should have a good, intuitive feel for how methods are selected from the pool of potentially overloaded and overridden method names of a class. If, however, you are dying for more detail, we'll provide it now.

In a previous section, we offered an inductive rule for overloaded method resolution. It said that a method is considered more specific than another if its arguments are assignable to the arguments of the second method. We can now expand this rule to include the resolution of overridden methods by adding the following condition: to be more specific than another method, the type of the class containing the method must also be assignable to the type of the class holding the second method.

What does that mean? Well, the only classes whose types are assignable are classes in the same inheritance hierarchy, meaning the set of all methods of the same name in a class or any of its parent or child classes. Since subclass types are assignable to super-class types, but not vice versa, the resolution is pushed, in the way that we expect, down the chain, toward the subclasses. This effectively adds a second dimension to the search, in which resolution is pushed down the inheritance tree toward more refined classes and, simultaneously, toward the most specific overloaded method within a given class.

Exceptions and overridden methods

An overriding method may change the behavior of an object, but in some ways, it must still fulfill the contract of the original method with the user. Specifically, an overriding method must adhere to the throws clause of the original method. The new method cannot throw new types of checked exceptions. It can only declare that it throws exception types assignable to those thrown by the method in the parent class. That is, it may declare that it throws the same types of exceptions or subtypes of those declared by the original method.

If the new method does not throw any of the checked exceptions of the original, it does not have to declare them and callers of the method via the subclass do not have to guard against them. The new method may also declare exactly the same checked exceptions as the original. The interesting thing is that the new method also has the option to refine those types by declaring that it throws more specific subtypes than the overridden method. This is not the same as just saying that the method can simply throw subtypes of its declared exceptions; any method can do that. The new method can actually redefine the throws clause of the method to be more specific. This technique is called *covariant* typing of the throws clause, which means that the exception types change to become more refined with the subtype.

Let's quickly review what the throws clause really means. If a method declares that it can throw an IOException, it is really saying that it can throw exceptions of type IOException or its subtypes. For example, FileNotFoundException is a type of IOException. A method declaring that it can throw IOException could actually throw FileNotFoundException or any other subtype of IOException at runtime:

```
public void readFile( ) throws IOException {
    ...
    if ( error ) throw new FileNotFoundException( filename );
}
```

When we call this method, the compiler will ensure that we allow for the possibility of any kind of IOException, using either a try/catch block or by throwing the exception from our own method.

When we override a method in a subclass, we get an opportunity to rewrite the throws clause of the method a bit. The new method must still be backward-compatible with the original, so any checked exceptions it throws must be assignable to those thrown by the overridden method. But we can be more specific if we want, refining the type of exception to go along with the new method's behavior. For example:

```
class MeatInedibleException extends InedibleException { ... }

class Animal {
    void eat( Food f ) throws InedibleException {
        ...
    }
}
class Herbivore extends Animal {
    void eat( Food f ) throws MeatInedibleException {
        if ( f instanceof Meat )
            throw new MeatInedibleException();
        ...
    }
}
```

In this code, Animal specifies that it can throw an InedibleException from its eat( ) method. Herbivore is a subclass of Animal, so its eat( ) method must also be able to throw an InedibleException. However, Herbivore's eat( ) method actually declares that it throws a more specific exception: MeatInedibleException. It can do this because MeatInedibleException is a subtype of InedibleException. If we are working with an Herbivore type directly, the compiler will allow us to catch just the MeatInedibleException and not require us to guard against the more general InedibleException:

```
Herbivore creature = ...
try {
    creature.eat( food );
} catch ( MeatInedibleException ) {
    // creature can't eat this food because it's meat
}
```

On the other hand, if we don't care why the food is inedible, we're free to guard for the more general InedibleException alone and treat it as any other Animal.

To sum up, an overriding method can refine not only the behavior of the parent method but also the type of checked exceptions it throws. Next, we'll talk about overridden methods that change their return type in exactly the same way.

Return types and overridden methods

For a method to qualify as an overridden method in a subclass, it must have exactly the same number and types of arguments. It must have the same "inputs," as it were. As we saw in the previous section, overriding methods may refine their "output" to some extent. Namely, they can narrow their throws clause by declaring that they throw subtypes of the original method's exception types. What about the main "output" of a method? Its return value? Can we change the return type of a method by overriding it? The answer used to be "no," but Java 5.0 gives us covariant return types on methods just as it does for exception types.

What this means is that, as of Java 5.0, when you override a method, you may change the return type to a subtype of the original method's return type. For example, if our Animal class has a factory method called create() that produces an instance of Animal, our Mammal class could refine the return type to Mammal:

```
class Animal {
    Animal create() { ... }
}
class Mammal extends Animal {
    Mammal create() { ... }
}
```

As we'll see later, this coding technique is very helpful because it eliminates runtime casting of objects.

Special References: this and super

The special references this and super allow you to refer to the members of the current object instance or to members of the superclass, respectively. We have seen this used elsewhere to pass a reference to the current object and to refer to shadowed instance variables. The reference super does the same for the parents of a class. You can use it to refer to members of a superclass that have been shadowed or overridden. Being able to invoke the original method of the superclass allows us to use it as part of our new method, delegating to its behavior before or after we perform additional work:

```
class Animal {
    void eat( Food f ) throws InedibleException {
        // consume food
    }
}

class Herbivore extends Animal {
    void eat( Food f ) throws MeatInedibleException {
        // check if edible
        ...
        super.eat( f );
    }
}
```

In this example, our Herbivore class overrides the Animal eat() method to first do some checking on the food object. After doing its job, it uses super.eat() to call the (otherwise overridden) implementation of eat() in its superclass.

super prompts a search for the method or variable to begin in the scope of the immediate superclass rather than the current class. The inherited method or variable found may reside in the immediate superclass or in a more distant one. The usage of the super reference when applied to overridden methods of a superclass is special; it tells the method resolution system to stop the dynamic method search at the superclass instead of at the most derived class (as it otherwise does). Without super, there would be no way to access overridden methods.

Casting

A *cast* explicitly tells the compiler to change the apparent type of an object reference. The main use for casts is when an object is temporarily assigned to a more general type. For example, if a String were assigned to a variable of type Object, to use it as a String again, we'd have to perform a cast to get it back. The compiler recognizes only the declared types of variables and doesn't know that we actually placed a String into it. In Java, casts are checked both at compile time and at runtime to make sure they are legal. At compile time the Java compiler will stop you from trying to perform a cast that cannot possibly work (such as turning a Date directly into a String). And at runtime Java will check that casts that are plausible (such as our String to String) are actually correct.

Attempting to cast an object to an incompatible type at runtime results in a ClassCastException. Only casts between objects in the same inheritance hierarchy (and, as we'll see later, to appropriate interfaces) are legal in Java and pass the scrutiny of the compiler and the runtime system. Casts in Java affect only the treatment of references; they never change the form of the actual object. This is an important rule to keep in mind. You never change the object pointed to by a reference by casting it; you change only the compiler's (or runtime system's) notion of it.

A cast can be used to *narrow* or *downcast* the type of a reference—to make it more specific. Often, we'll do this when we have to retrieve an object from a more general type of collection or when it has been previously used as a less derived type. (The prototypical example is using an object in a collection, as we'll see in Chapter 11.) Continuing with our Cat example:

```
Animal creature;
Cat simon;
// ...

creature = simon;        // OK
// simon = creature;      // Compile-time error, incompatible type
simon = (Cat)creature;    // OK
```

We can't reassign the reference in creature to the variable simon even though we know it holds an instance of a Cat (Simon). We have to perform the indicated cast to narrow the reference. Note that an implicit cast was performed when we went the other way to *widen* the reference simon to type Animal during the first assignment. In this case, an explicit cast would have been legal but superfluous.

What all this means is that you can't lie or guess about what an object is. If you have a Cat object, you can use it as an Animal or even Object because all Java classes are a subclass of Object. But if you have an Object you think is a Cat, you have to perform a cast to get it back to an Animal or a Cat. If you aren't sure whether the Object is a Cat or a Dog at runtime, you can check it with instanceof before you perform the cast. If you get the cast wrong, the runtime system throws a ClassCastException.

```
if ( creature instanceof Cat ) {
    Cat cat = (Cat)creature;
    cat.meow( );
}
```

As we mentioned earlier, casting can affect the selection of compile-time items such as variables and overloaded methods, but not the selection of overridden methods. Figure 6-4 shows the difference. As shown in the top half of the diagram, casting the reference simon to type Animal (widening it) affects the selection of the shadowed variable weight within it. However, as the lower half of the diagram indicates, the cast doesn't affect the selection of the overridden method sleep( ).

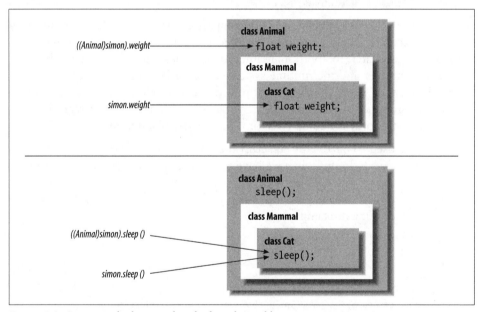

Figure 6-4. Casting and selection of methods and variables

Casting aspersions

Casting in Java is something that programmers strive to avoid. This is not only because it indicates a weakness in the static typing of the code, but because casts can also simply be tedious to use and make code less readable. Unfortunately, a great deal of code written in Java in the past has had no choice but to rely on casting so that it can work with any type of object the user requires. Java 5.0 introduced a major new language feature, generics, partly to address this issue. Generics allow Java code to be "typed" for a particular kind of object by the user, eliminating the need to cast in many situations. We'll cover generics in detail in Chapter 8 and see how they reduce the need for casts in most Java code.

Using Superclass Constructors

When we talked earlier about constructors, we discussed how the special statement this( ) invokes an overloaded constructor upon entry to another constructor. Similarly, the statement super( ) explicitly invokes the constructor of a superclass. Of course, we also talked about how Java makes a chain of constructor calls that includes the superclass's constructor, so why use super( ) explicitly? When Java makes an implicit call to the superclass constructor, it calls the default constructor. If we want to invoke a superclass constructor that takes arguments, we have to do so explicitly using super( ).

If we are going to call a superclass constructor with super( ), it must be the first statement of our constructor, just as this( ) must be the first call we make in an overloaded constructor. Here's a simple example:

```
class Person {
    Person ( String name ) {
        //  setup based on name
        ...
    }
    ...
}

class Doctor extends Person {
    Doctor ( String name, String specialty ) {
        super( name );
        // setup based on specialty
        ...
    }
    ...
}
```

In this example, we use super( ) to take advantage of the implementation of the superclass constructor and avoid duplicating the code to set up the object based on its name. In fact, because the class Person doesn't define a default (no arguments) constructor, we have no choice but to call super( ) explicitly. Otherwise, the compiler would complain that it couldn't find an appropriate default constructor to call. In other words, if you subclass a class whose constructors all take arguments, you have to invoke one of the superclass's constructors explicitly from at least one of your subclass's constructors.

Instance variables of the class are initialized upon return from the superclass constructor, whether that's due to an explicit call to super( ) or an implicit call to the default superclass constructor.

Full Disclosure: Constructors and Initialization

We can now tell the full story of how constructors are chained together and when instance variable initialization occurs. The rule has three parts and is applied repeatedly for each successive constructor that is invoked:

- If the first statement of a constructor is an ordinary statement—i.e., not a call to this( ) or super( )—Java inserts an implicit call to super( ) to invoke the default constructor of the superclass. Upon returning from that call, Java initializes the instance variables of the current class and proceeds to execute the statements of the current constructor.

- If the first statement of a constructor is a call to a superclass constructor via super( ), Java invokes the selected superclass constructor. Upon its return, Java initializes the current class's instance variables and proceeds with the statements of the current constructor.

- If the first statement of a constructor is a call to an overloaded constructor via this( ), Java invokes the selected constructor, and upon its return, simply proceeds with the statements of the current constructor. The call to the superclass's constructor has happened within the overloaded constructor, either explicitly or implicitly, so the initialization of instance variables has already occurred.

Abstract Methods and Classes

A method in Java can be declared with the abstract modifier to indicate that it's just a prototype. An abstract method has no body; it's simply a signature declaration followed by a semicolon. You can't directly use a class that contains an abstract method; you must instead create a subclass that implements the abstract method's body:

```
abstract void vaporMethod( String name );
```

In Java, a class that contains one or more abstract methods must be explicitly declared as an abstract class, also using the abstract modifier:

```
abstract class vaporClass {
    ...
    abstract void vaporMethod( String name );
    ...
}
```

An abstract class can contain other nonabstract methods and ordinary variable declarations, but it can't be instantiated. To be used, it must be subclassed and its abstract methods must be overridden with methods that implement a body. Not all abstract methods have to be implemented in a single subclass, but a subclass that doesn't override all its superclass's abstract methods with actual, concrete implementations must also be declared abstract.

Abstract classes provide a framework for classes that is to be "filled in" by the implementer. The java.io.InputStream class, for example, has a single abstract method called read( ). Various subclasses of InputStream implement read( ) in their own ways to read from their own sources. The rest of the InputStream class, however, provides extended functionality built on the simple read( ) method. A subclass of InputStream inherits these nonabstract methods to provide functionality based on the simple read( ) method that the subclass implements.

Interfaces

Java expands on the concept of abstract methods with *interfaces*. It's often desirable to specify a group of abstract methods defining some behavior for an object without tying it to any implementation at all. In Java, this is called an interface. An interface defines a set of methods that a class must implement. A class in Java can declare that it *implements* an interface if it implements the required methods. Unlike extending an abstract class, a class implementing an interface doesn't have to inherit from any particular part of the inheritance hierarchy or use a particular implementation.

Interfaces are kind of like Boy Scout or Girl Scout merit badges. A scout who has learned to build a birdhouse can walk around wearing a little sleeve patch with a picture of one. This says to the world, "I know how to build a birdhouse." Similarly, an interface is a list of methods that define some set of behavior for an object. Any class that implements each method listed in the interface can declare at compile time that it implements the interface and wear, as its merit badge, an extra type—the interface's type.

Interface types act like class types. You can declare variables to be of an interface type, you can declare arguments of methods to accept interface types, and you can specify that the return type of a method is an interface type. In each case, what is meant is that any object that implements the interface (i.e., wears the right merit badge) can fill that role. In this sense, interfaces are orthogonal to the class hierarchy. They cut across the boundaries of what kind of object an item *is* and deal with it only in terms of what it can *do*. A class can implement as many interfaces as it desires. In this way, interfaces in Java replace much of the need for multiple inheritance in other languages (and all its messy complications).

An interface looks, essentially, like a purely abstract class (i.e., a class with only abstract methods). You define an interface with the interface keyword and list its methods with no bodies, just prototypes (signatures):

```
interface Driveable {
    boolean startEngine( );
    void stopEngine( );
    float accelerate( float acc );
    boolean turn( Direction dir );
}
```

The previous example defines an interface called Driveable with four methods. It's acceptable, but not necessary, to declare the methods in an interface with the abstract modifier; we haven't done that here. More importantly, the methods of an interface are always considered public, and you can optionally declare them as so. Why public? Well, the user of the interface wouldn't necessarily be able to see them otherwise, and interfaces are generally intended to describe the behavior of an object, not its implementation.

Interfaces define capabilities, so it's common to name interfaces after their capabilities. Driveable, Runnable, and Updateable are good interface names. Any class that implements all the methods can then declare it implements the interface by using a special implements clause in its class definition. For example:

```
class Automobile implements Driveable {
    ...
    public boolean startEngine() {
        if ( notTooCold )
            engineRunning = true;
        ...
    }

    public void stopEngine() {
        engineRunning = false;
    }

    public float accelerate( float acc ) {
        ...
    }

    public boolean turn( Direction dir ) {
        ...
    }
    ...
}
```

Here, the class Automobile implements the methods of the Driveable interface and declares itself a type of Driveable using the implements keyword.

As shown in Figure 6-5, another class, such as Lawnmower, can also implement the Driveable interface. The figure illustrates the Driveable interface being implemented by two different classes. While it's possible that both Automobile and Lawnmower could derive from some primitive kind of vehicle, they don't have to in this scenario.

After declaring the interface, we have a new type, Driveable. We can declare variables of type Driveable and assign them any instance of a Driveable object:

```
Automobile auto = new Automobile();
Lawnmower mower = new Lawnmower();
Driveable vehicle;

vehicle = auto;
vehicle.startEngine();
vehicle.stopEngine();
```

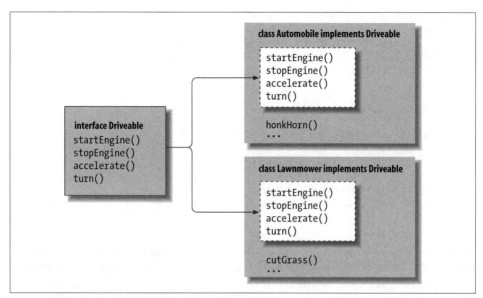

Figure 6-5. Implementing the Driveable interface

```
vehicle = mower;
vehicle.startEngine( );
vehicle.stopEngine( );
```

Both `Automobile` and `Lawnmower` implement `Driveable`, so they can be considered interchangeable objects of that type.

Interfaces as Callbacks

Interfaces can be used to implement "callbacks" in Java. This is when an object effectively passes a reference to one or more of its methods to another object. The callback occurs when the called object subsequently invokes one of the methods. In C or C++, this is prime territory for function pointers; Java uses interfaces instead. More generally, this concept is extended in Java to the concept of *events* in which listener objects register with event sources. We'll cover events in great detail in later chapters.

Consider two classes: a `TickerTape` class that displays data and a `TextSource` class that provides an information feed. We'd like our `TextSource` to send any new text data. We could have `TextSource` store a reference to a `TickerTape` object, but then we could never use our `TextSource` to send data to any other kind of object. Instead, we'd have to proliferate subclasses of `TextSource` that dealt with different types. A more elegant solution is to have `TextSource` store a reference to an interface type, `TextReceiver`:

```
interface TextReceiver {
    void receiveText( String text );
}
```

```
class TickerTape implements TextReceiver {
    public void receiveText( String text ) {
        System.out.println("TICKER:\n" + text + "\n");
    }
}

class TextSource {
    TextReceiver receiver;

    TextSource( TextReceiver r ) {
        receiver = r;
    }

    public void sendText( String s ) {
        receiver.receiveText( s );
    }
}
```

The only thing the TextSource really cares about is finding the right method to invoke in order to output some text. Using an interface establishes a "well-known" name, receiveText( ), for that method.

When the TextSource is constructed, a reference to the TickerTape (which implements the interface) is stored in an instance variable. This "registers" the TickerTape as the TextSource's "output device." Whenever it needs to output data, the TextSource calls the output device's receiveText( ) method. Later, we'll see that many APIs in Java use a model like this, but, in some cases, many "receivers" may register with the same source.

Interface Variables

Although interfaces mostly allow us to specify behavior without implementation, there's one exception. An interface can contain constants (static final variables), which can be referred to directly, through the interface name, and also appear in any class that implements the interface. This feature allows constants to be packaged for use with the methods of the interface:

```
interface Scaleable {
    static final int BIG = 0, MEDIUM = 1, SMALL = 2;
    void setScale( int size );
}
```

The Scaleable interface defines three integers: BIG, MEDIUM, and SMALL. All variables defined in interfaces are implicitly final and static; you don't have to use the modifiers, but, for clarity, we recommend you do. A class that implements Scaleable sees these constants:

```
class Box implements Scaleable {

    void setScale( int size ) {
        switch( size ) {
```

```
            case BIG:
                ...
            case MEDIUM:
                ...
            case SMALL:
                ...
        }
    }
    ...
}
```

While there is nothing technically wrong with using interfaces in this way, the main incentive is for the convenience of not having to qualify the references to all those constants within the class that uses them. This leads to the temptation to make interfaces just for that purpose. But this is bad because all of those public, static constants then appear in the public API of your class and can confuse the user of your class. What is worse, you can't remove them later because other code may rely on your class containing those values. In Java 5.0, it is better to use an enumeration or to put your constants in their own class and then use the new static import syntax to remove the hassle of referring to them. We'll discuss static import later in this chapter. This kind of usage is exactly what it is for:

```
enum SizeConstants { BIG, MEDIUM, SMALL }

// usage
static import mypackage.SizeConstants;
...
setSize( MEDIUM );
```

Flag interfaces

Sometimes completely empty interfaces serve as a marker that a class has a special property. The java.io.Serializeable interface is a good example. Classes that implement Serialize don't have to add any methods or variables. Their additional type simply identifies them to Java as classes that want to be able to be serialized.

Subinterfaces

An interface can extend another interface, just as a class can extend another class. Such an interface is called a *subinterface*. For example:

```
interface DynamicallyScaleable extends Scaleable {
    void changeScale( int size );
}
```

The interface DynamicallyScaleable extends our previous Scaleable interface and adds an additional method. A class that implements DynamicallyScaleable must implement all the methods of both interfaces.

Note here that we are using the term *extends* and not *implements* to subtype the interface. Interfaces can't implement anything! But an interface is allowed to extend as many interfaces as it wants. If you want to extend two or more interfaces, list them after the extends keyword, separated by commas:

```
interface DynamicallyScaleable extends Scaleable, SomethingElseable {
    ...
}
```

A class that implements this interface must also implement the other interfaces. Furthermore, interface subtypes are assignable to their supertypes in the same way that classes are, so an instance of DynamicallyScaleable can be assigned to a variable of type Scaleable, as you might expect.

Overlapping and conflicting methods

We should also note the possibility that when an interface extends two or more interfaces (or when a class implements two or more interfaces), there may be overlapping or conflicting methods in those interfaces. If two methods in different interfaces have exactly the same signature and return type, there is no problem and the implementation in the class satisfies both interfaces. If the methods differ in the way that overloaded methods do, the class must implement both method signatures. If the methods have the same name but differ in return or exception types, the class cannot implement both and compile-time errors occur.

Packages and Compilation Units

A *package* is a name for a group of related classes and interfaces. In Chapter 3, we discussed how Java uses package names to locate classes during compilation and at runtime. In this sense, packages are somewhat like libraries; they organize and manage sets of classes. Packages provide more than just source code–level organization. They create an additional level of scope for their classes and the variables and methods within them. We'll talk about the visibility of classes later in this section. In the next section, we discuss the effect that packages have on access to variables and methods among classes.

Compilation Units

The source code for a Java class is organized into *compilation units*. A simple compilation unit contains a single class definition and is named for that class. The definition of a class named MyClass, for instance, could appear in a file named *MyClass.java*. For most of us, a compilation unit is just a file with a *.java* extension, but theoretically in an integrated development environment, it could be an arbitrary entity. For brevity, we'll refer to a compilation unit simply as a file.

The division of classes into their own files is important because the Java compiler assumes much of the responsibility of a *make* utility. The compiler relies on the names of source files to find and compile dependent classes. It's possible to put more than one class definition into a single file, but there are some restrictions we'll discuss shortly.

A class is declared to belong to a particular package with the package statement. The package statement must appear as the first statement in a compilation unit. There can be only one package statement, and it applies to the entire file:

```
package mytools.text;

class TextComponent {
    ...
}
```

In this example, the class TextComponent is placed in the package mytools.text.

Package Names

Package names are constructed hierarchically, using a dot-separated naming convention. Package-name components construct a unique path for the compiler and runtime systems to locate files; however, they don't create relationships between packages in any other way. There is really no such thing as a "subpackage"; the package namespace is, in actuality, flat—not hierarchical. Packages under a particular part of a package hierarchy are related only by convention. For example, if we create another package called mytools.text.poetry (presumably for text classes specialized in some way to work with poetry), those classes won't be part of the mytools.text package; they won't have the access privileges of package members. In this sense, the package-naming convention can be misleading. One minor deviation from this notion is that assertions, which we described in Chapter 4, can be turned on or off for a package and all packages "under" it. But that is really just a convenience and not represented in the code structure.

Class Visibility

By default, a class is accessible only to other classes within its package. This means that the class TextComponent is available only to other classes in the mytools.text package. To be visible elsewhere, a class must be declared as public:

```
package mytools.text;

public class TextEditor {
    ...
}
```

The class TextEditor can now be referenced anywhere. A compilation unit can have only a single public class defined and the file must be named for that class.

By hiding unimportant or extraneous classes, a package builds a *subsystem* that has a well-defined interface to the rest of the world. Public classes provide a *facade* for the operation of the system. The details of its inner workings can remain hidden, as shown in Figure 6-6. In this sense, packages can hide classes in the way classes hide private members. Nonpublic classes within a package are sometimes called *package private* for this reason.

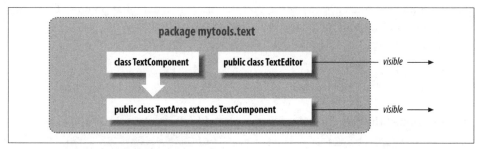

Figure 6-6. Packages and class visibility

Figure 6-6 shows part of the hypothetical mytools.text package. The classes TextArea and TextEditor are declared public so that they can be used elsewhere in an application. The class TextComponent is part of the implementation of TextArea and is not accessible from outside of the package.

Importing Classes

Classes within a package can refer to each other by their simple names. However, to locate a class in another package, we have to be more specific. Continuing with the previous example, an application can refer directly to our editor class by its *fully qualified name* of mytools.text.TextEditor. But we'd quickly grow tired of typing such long class names, so Java gives us the import statement. One or more import statements can appear at the top of a compilation unit, after the package statement. The import statements list the fully qualified names of classes and packages to be used within the file.

Like a package statement, an import statement applies to the entire compilation unit. Here's how you might use an import statement:

```
package somewhere.else;
import mytools.text.TextEditor;

class MyClass {
    TextEditor editBoy;
    ...
}
```

As shown in this example, once a class is imported, it can be referenced by its simple name throughout the code. It is also possible to import all the classes in a package using the * wildcard notation:

```
import mytools.text.*;
```

Now we can refer to all `public` classes in the `mytools.text` package by their simple names.

Obviously, there can be a problem with importing classes that have conflicting names. The compiler prevents you from explicitly importing two classes with the same name and gives you an error if you try to use an ambiguous class that could come from two packages imported with the package import notation. In this case, you just have to fall back to using fully qualified names to refer to those classes. You can either use the fully qualified name directly, or you can add an additional, single class `import` statement that disambiguates the class name. It doesn't matter whether this comes before or after the package import.

Other than the potential for naming conflicts, there's no penalty for importing many classes. Java doesn't carry extra baggage into the compiled class files. In other words, Java class files don't contain information about the imports; they only reference classes actually used in them.

One note about conventions: in our efforts to keep our examples short we'll sometimes import entire packages (.*) even when we use only a class or two from it. In practice, it's usually better to be specific when possible and list individual, fully qualified class imports if there are only a few of them. Some people (especially those using IDEs that do it for them) avoid using package imports entirely, choosing to list every imported class individually. Usually, a compromise is your best bet. If you are going to use more than two or three classes from a package, consider the package import.

The unnamed package

A class that is defined in a compilation unit that doesn't specify a package falls into the large, amorphous, unnamed package. Classes in this nameless package can refer to each other by their simple names. Their path at compile time and runtime is considered to be the current directory, so packageless classes are useful for experimentation and testing (and for brevity in examples in books about Java).

Static imports

The *static import* facility is new in Java 5.0. Using a variation of the `import` statement you can import static members of a class into the namespace of your file so that you don't have to qualify them when you use them. The best example of this is in working with the `java.lang.Math` class. With static import, we can get an illusion of built-in math "functions" and constants like so:

```
import static java.lang.Math.*;

// usage
double circumference = 2 * PI * radius;
double length = sin( theta ) * side;
int bigger = max( a, b );
int positive = abs( num );
```

This example imports all of the static members of the `java.lang.Math` class. We can also import individual members by name:

```
import static java.awt.Color.RED;
import static java.awt.Color.WHITE;
import static java.awt.Color.BLUE;

// usage
setField( BLUE );
setStripe( RED );
setStripe( WHITE );
```

To be precise, these static imports are importing a name, not a specific member into the namespace of our file. For example, importing the name "foo" would bring in any constants named `foo` as well as any methods named `foo( )` in the class.

Static imports are compelling and make life easier in Java 5.0. Using them too much, however, could quickly make your code difficult to read.

Visibility of Variables and Methods

One of the most important aspects of object-oriented design is *data hiding*, or *encapsulation*. By treating an object in some respects as a "black box" and ignoring the details of its implementation, we can write stronger, simpler code with components that can be easily reused.

Basic Access Modifiers

By default, the variables and methods of a class are accessible to members of the class itself and to other classes in the same package. To borrow from C++ terminology, classes in the same package are *friendly*. We'll call this the default level of visibility. As you'll see as we go on, the default visibility lies in the middle of the range of restrictiveness that can be specified.

The modifiers `public` and `private`, on the other hand, define the extremes. As we mentioned earlier, methods and variables declared as `private` are accessible only within their class. At the other end of the spectrum, members declared as `public` are accessible from any class in any package, provided the class itself can be seen. (The class that contains the methods must also be `public` to be seen outside of its package, as we discussed previously.) The `public` members of a class should define its most general functionality—what the black box is supposed to do.

Figure 6-7 illustrates the four simplest levels of visibility, continuing the example from the previous section. Public members in `TextArea` are accessible from anywhere. Private members are not visible from outside the class. The default visibility allows access by other classes in the package.

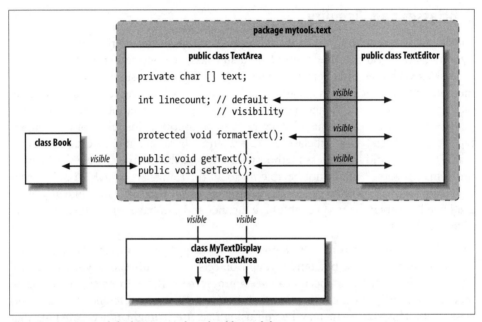

Figure 6-7. Private, default, protected, and public visibility

The protected modifier allows special access permissions for subclasses. Contrary to how it might sound, `protected` is slightly less restrictive than the default level of accessibility. In addition to the default access afforded classes in the same package, protected members are visible to subclasses of the class, even if they are defined in a different package. If you are a C++ programmer used to more restrictive meanings, this may rub you the wrong way.*

Table 6-1 summarizes the levels of visibility available in Java; it generally runs from most to least restrictive. Methods and variables are always visible within a declaring class itself, so the table doesn't addresses that scope.

---

* Early on, the Java language allowed for certain combinations of modifiers, one of which was `private protected`. The meaning of `private protected` was to limit visibility strictly to subclasses (and remove package access). This was later deemed confusing and overly complex. It is no longer supported.

Table 6-1. Visibility modifiers

Modifier	Visibility
private	None
None (default)	Classes in the package
protected	Classes in package and subclasses inside or outside the package
public	All classes

Subclasses and Visibility

Subclasses add two important (but unrelated) complications to the topic of visibility. First, when you override methods in a subclass, the overriding method must be at least as visible as the overridden method. While it is possible to take a private method and override it with a public method in a subclass, the reverse is not possible; you can't override a public method with a private method. This restriction makes sense if you recall that subtypes have to be usable as instances of their supertype (e.g., a Mammal is a subclass of Animal and, therefore, must be usable as an Animal). If we could override a method with a less visible method, we would have a problem: our Mammal might not be able to do all the things an Animal can. However, we can reduce the visibility of a variable. In this case, the variable acts like any other shadowed variable; the two variables are distinct and can have separate visibilities in different classes.

The next complication is a bit harder to follow: the protected variables of a class are visible to its subclasses, but only through objects of the subclass's type or its subtypes. In other words, a subclass can see a protected variable of its superclass as an inherited variable, but it can't access that same variable via a reference to the superclass itself. This statement may be confusing because it might not be obvious that visibility modifiers don't restrict access between instances of the same class in the same way they restrict access between instances of different classes. Two instances of the same class can access all of each other's members, including private ones, as long as they refer to each other as the correct type. Said another way: two instances of Cat can access all of each other's variables and methods (including private ones), but a Cat can't access a protected member in an instance of Animal unless the compiler can prove that the Animal is a Cat. That is, Cats have the special privileges of being an Animal only with respect to other Cats, not just any Animal. If you find this hard to follow, don't worry too much. If you run into this as a problem in the real world, you are probably trying to do something trickier than you should.

Interfaces and Visibility

Interfaces behave like classes within packages. An interface can be declared public to make it visible outside its package. Under the default visibility, an interface is visible only inside its package. Like classes, only one `public` interface can be declared in a compilation unit.

Arrays and the Class Hierarchy

Now we're going to shift gears a bit and return to the topic of arrays, considering them from the object point of view. At the end of Chapter 4, we mentioned that arrays have a place in the Java class hierarchy, but we didn't give you any details. Now that we've discussed the object-oriented aspects of Java, we can give you the whole story.

Array classes live in a parallel Java class hierarchy under the `Object` class. If a class is a direct subclass of `Object`, an array class for that base type also exists as a direct subclass of `Object`. Arrays of more derived classes are subclasses of the corresponding array classes. For example, consider the following class types:

```
class Animal { ... }
class Bird extends Animal { ... }
class Penguin extends Bird { ... }
```

Figure 6-8 illustrates the class hierarchy for arrays of these classes. Arrays of the same dimension are related to one another in the same manner as their base type classes. In our example, `Bird` is a subclass of `Animal`, which means that the `Bird[]` type is a subtype of `Animal[]`. In the same way a `Bird` object can be used in place of an `Animal` object, a `Bird[]` array can be assigned to a variable of type `Animal[]`:

```
Animal [][] animals;
Bird [][] birds = new Bird [10][10];
birds[0][0] = new Bird( );

// make animals and birds reference the same array object
animals = birds;
observe( animals[0][0] );              // processes Bird object
```

Because arrays are part of the class hierarchy, we can use `instanceof` to check the type of an array:

```
if ( birds instanceof Animal[][] )      // true
```

An array is a type of `Object` and so can be assigned to `Object` type variables:

```
Object obj = animals;
```

Since Java knows the actual type of all objects, you can also cast back if appropriate:

```
animals = (Animal [][])something;
```

ArrayStoreException

Because arrays have the property that an array of one type is assignable to an array of its supertype, it is possible to play games with the compiler and try to trick it into storing the wrong kind of object in an array. Java may not be able to check the types

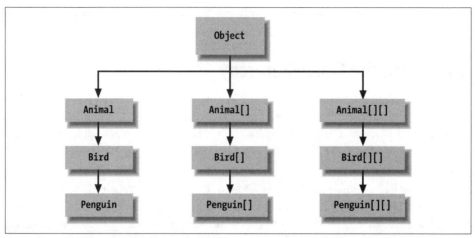

Figure 6-8. Arrays in the Java class hierarchy

of all objects you place into arrays at compile time. In those cases, it's possible to receive an ArrayStoreException at runtime if you try to assign the wrong type of object to an array element. For example:

```
String [] strings = new String [10];
Object [] objects = strings;  // alias String [] as Object []
object[0] = new Date(); // Runtime ArrayStoreException!
```

Here, we have "aliased" a String [] by assigning it to an Object []. By the third line, the compiler no longer knows the actual type of array stored in the object's variable and has no choice but to let us try whatever we want. Of course, at runtime the VM realizes that we are trying to put a Date object into an array of Strings and throws the ArrayStoreException for us. This type of problem shouldn't happen often for you in straightforward array use. We mention it here because the concept will come up again when we talk about generics in Chapter 8.

Inner Classes

All of the classes we've seen so far in this book have been *top-level*, "free standing" classes declared at the file and package level. But classes in Java can actually be declared at any level of scope, within any set of curly braces (i.e., almost anywhere that you could put any other Java statement). These *inner classes* belong to another class or method as a variable would and may have their visibility limited to its scope in the same way. Inner classes are a useful and aesthetically pleasing facility for structuring code. Their cousins, *anonymous inner classes*, are an even more powerful shorthand that make it seem as if you can create new kinds of objects dynamically within Java's statically typed environment. In Java, anonymous inner classes take the place of *closures* in other languages, giving the effect of handling state and behavior independently of classes.

However, as we delve into their inner workings, we'll see that inner classes are not quite as aesthetically pleasing or dynamic as they seem. Inner classes are pure syntactic sugar; they are not supported by the VM but are instead mapped to regular Java classes by the compiler. As a programmer, you may never need be aware of this; you can simply rely on inner classes like any other language construct. However, you should know a little about how inner classes work to better understand the compiled code and a few potential side effects.

Inner classes are essentially nested classes, for example:

```
Class Animal {
    Class Brain {
        ...
    }
}
```

Here, the class `Brain` is an inner class: it is a class declared inside the scope of class `Animal`. Although the details of what that means require a bit of explanation, we'll start by saying that Java tries to make the meaning, as much as possible, the same as for the other members (methods and variables) living at that level of scope. For example, let's add a method to the `Animal` class:

```
Class Animal {
    Class Brain {
        ...
    }
    void performBehavior( ) { ... }
}
```

Both the inner class `Brain` and the method `performBehavior( )` are within the scope of `Animal`. Therefore, anywhere within `Animal` we can refer to `Brain` and `performBehavior( )` directly, by name. Within `Animal`, we can call the constructor for `Brain` (new `Brain( )`) to get a `Brain` object or invoke `performBehavior( )` to carry out that method's function. But neither `Brain` nor `performBehavior( )` are generally accessible outside of the class `Animal` without some additional qualification.

Within the body of the inner `Brain` class and the body of the `performBehavior( )` method, we have direct access to all the other methods and variables of the `Animal` class. So, just as the `performBehavior( )` method could work with the `Brain` class and create instances of `Brain`, methods within the `Brain` class can invoke the `performBehavior( )` method of `Animal` as well as work with any other methods and variables declared in `Animal`. The `Brain` class "sees" all of the methods and variables of the `Animal` class directly in its scope.

That last bit has important consequences. From within `Brain` we can invoke the method `performBehavior( )`; that is, from within an instance of `Brain`, we can invoke the `performBehavior( )` method of an instance of `Animal`. Well, which instance of `Animal`? If we have several `Animal` objects around (say, a few `Cat`s and `Dog`s), we need to know whose `performBehavior( )` method we are calling. What does it mean for a class definition to be "inside" another class definition? The answer is that a `Brain` object always lives within a single instance of `Animal`: the one that it was told about when it was created. We'll call the object that contains any instance of `Brain` its *enclosing instance*.

A `Brain` object cannot live outside of an enclosing instance of an `Animal` object. Anywhere you see an instance of `Brain`, it will be tethered to an instance of `Animal`. Although it is possible to construct a `Brain` object from elsewhere (i.e., another class), `Brain` always requires an enclosing instance of `Animal` to "hold" it. We'll also say now that if `Brain` is to be referred to from outside of `Animal`, it acts something like an `Animal.Brain` class. And just as with the `performBehavior( )` method, modifiers can be applied to restrict its visibility. All of the usual visibility modifiers apply, and inner classes can also be declared `static`, as we'll discuss later.

We've said that within the `Animal` class we can construct a `Brain` in the ordinary way, using `new Brain( )`, for example. Although we'd probably never find a need to do it, we can also construct an instance of `Brain` from outside the class by referencing an instance of `Animal`. To do this requires that the inner class `Brain` be accessible and that we use a special form of the `new` operator designed just for inner classes:

```
Animal monkey = new Animal( );
Animal.Brain monkeyBrain = monkey.new Brain( );
```

Here, the `Animal` instance monkey is used to qualify the `new` operator on `Brain`. Again, this is not a very common thing to do and you can probably just forget that we said anything about it. Static inner classes are more useful. We'll talk about them a bit later.

Inner Classes as Adapters

A particularly important use of inner classes is to make *adapter classes*. An adapter class is a "helper" class that ties one class to another in a very specific way. Using adapter classes, you can write your classes more naturally, without having to anticipate every conceivable user's needs in advance. Instead, you provide adapter classes that marry your class to a particular interface. As an example, let's say that we have an `EmployeeList` object:

```
public class EmployeeList {
    private Employee [] employees = ... ;
    ...
}
```

`EmployeeList` holds information about a set of employees. Let's say that we would like to have `EmployeeList` provide its elements via an iterator. An iterator is a simple, standard interface to a sequence of objects. The `java.util.Iterator` interface has several methods:

```
public interface Iterator {
    boolean hasNext( );
```

```
        Object next( );
        void remove( );
    }
```

It lets us step through its elements, asking for the next one and testing to see if more remain. The iterator is a good candidate for an adapter class because it is an interface that our EmployeeList can't readily implement itself. Why can't the list implement the iterator directly? Because an iterator is a "one-way," disposable view of our data. It isn't intended to be reset and used again. It may also be necessary for there to be multiple iterators walking through the list at different points. We must, therefore, keep the iterator implementation separate from the EmployeeList itself. This is crying out for a simple class to provide the iterator capability. But what should that class look like?

Before we knew about inner classes, our only recourse would have been to make a new "top-level" class. We would probably feel obliged to call it EmployeeListIterator:

```
class EmployeeListIterator implements Iterator {
    // lots of knowledge about EmployeeList
    ...
}
```

Here we have a comment representing the machinery that the EmployeeListIterator requires. Think for just a second about what you'd have to do to implement that machinery. The resulting class would be completely coupled to the EmployeeList and unusable in other situations. Worse, to function, it must have access to the inner workings of EmployeeList. We would have to allow EmployeeListIterator access to the private array in EmployeeList, exposing this data more widely than it should be. This is less than ideal.

This sounds like a job for inner classes. We already said that EmployeeListIterator was useless without an EmployeeList; this sounds a lot like the "lives inside" relationship we described earlier. Furthermore, an inner class lets us avoid the encapsulation problem because it can access all the members of its enclosing instance. Therefore, if we use an inner class to implement the iterator, the array employees can remain private, invisible outside the EmployeeList. So let's just shove that helper class inside the scope of our EmployeeList:

```
public class EmployeeList {
    private Employee [] employees = ... ;
    ...

    class Iterator implements java.util.Iterator {
        int element = 0;

        boolean hasNext( ) {
            return  element < employees.length ;
        }

        Object next( ) {
            if ( hasMoreElements( ) )
```

```
                return employees[ element++ ];
            else
                throw new NoSuchElementException( );
        }

        void remove( ) {
            throw new UnsupportedOperationException( );
        }
    }
}
```

Now `EmployeeList` can provide a method like the following to let other classes work with the list:

```
Iterator getIterator( ) {
        return new Iterator( );
    }
```

One effect of the move is that we are free to be a little more familiar in the naming of our iterator class. Since it is no longer a top-level class, we can give it a name that is appropriate only within the `EmployeeList`. In this case, we've named it `Iterator` to emphasize what it does, but we don't need a name like `EmployeeIterator` that shows the relationship to the `EmployeeList` class because that's implicit. We've also filled in the guts of the `Iterator` class. As you can see, now that it is inside the scope of `EmployeeList`, `Iterator` has direct access to its private members, so it can directly access the employees array. This greatly simplifies the code and maintains compile-time safety.

Before we move on, we should note that inner classes can have constructors, variables, and initializers, even though we didn't need one in this example. They are, in all respects, real classes.

Inner Classes Within Methods

Inner classes may also be declared for "local" use within the body of a method. Returning to the `Animal` class, we can put `Brain` inside the `performBehavior( )` method if we decide that the class is useful only inside that method:

```
Class Animal {
    void performBehavior( ) {
        Class Brain {
            ...
        }
    }
}
```

In this situation, the rules governing what `Brain` can see are the same as in our earlier example. The body of `Brain` can see anything in the scope of `performBehavior( )` and above it (in the body of `Animal`). This includes local variables of `performBehavior( )` and its arguments. But because of the fleeting nature of a method invocation, there are a few limitations and additional restrictions, as described in the following sections. If you are thinking that inner classes within methods sounds arcane, bear with us until we talk about anonymous inner classes, which are tremendously useful.

Limitations on inner classes in methods

performBehavior( ) is a method, and method invocations have limited lifetimes. When they exit, their local variables normally disappear into the abyss. However, an instance of Brain (like any object created in the method) lives on as long as it is referenced. Java must make sure that any local variables used by instances of Brain created within an invocation of performBehavior( ) also live on. Furthermore, all the instances of Brain that we make within a single invocation of performBehavior( ) must see the same local variables. To accomplish this, the compiler must be allowed to make copies of local variables. Thus, their values cannot change once an inner class has seen them. This means that any of the method's local variables or arguments that are referenced by the inner class must be declared final. The final modifier means that they are constant once assigned. This is a little confusing and easy to forget, but the compiler will graciously remind you. For example:

```
void performBehavior( final boolean nocturnal )
{
class Brain {
        void sleep( ) {
            if ( nocturnal ) { ... }
        }
    }
}
```

In this code snippet, the argument nocturnal to the performBehavior( ) method must be marked final so that it can be referenced within the inner class Brain. This is just a technical limitation of how inner classes are implemented, ensuring that it's okay for the Brain class to keep a copy of the value.

Static inner classes

We mentioned earlier that the inner class Brain of the class Animal can, in some ways, be considered an Animal.Brain class. That is, it is possible to work with a Brain from outside the Animal class, using just such a qualified name: Animal.Brain. But, as we described, given that our Animal.Brain class always requires an instance of an Animal as its enclosing instance, it's not as common to work with them directly in this way.

However, there is another situation in which we want to use inner classes by name. An inner class that lives within the body of a top-level class (not within a method or another inner class) can be declared static. For example:

```
class Animal  {
    static class MigrationPattern {
```

```
            ...
    }
    ...
}
```

A static inner class such as this acts just like a new top-level class called `Animal.MigrationPattern`. We can use it just like any other class, without regard to any enclosing instances. Although this may seem strange, it is not inconsistent, since a static member never has an object instance associated with it. The requirement that the inner class be defined directly inside a top-level class ensures that an enclosing instance won't be needed. If we have permission, we can create an instance of the class using the qualified name:

```
Animal.MigrationPattern stlToSanFrancisco =
    new Animal.MigrationPattern( );
```

As you see, the effect is that `Animal` acts something like a mini package, holding the `MigrationPattern` class. Here, we have used the fully qualified name, but we could also import it like any other class:

```
import Animal.MigrationPattern;
```

This statement enables us to refer to the class simply as `MigrationPattern`. We can use all the standard visibility modifiers on inner classes, so a static inner class can have `private`, `protected`, `default`, or `public` visibility.

Here's another example. The Java 2D API uses static inner classes to implement specialized shape classes (i.e., the `java.awt.geom.Rectangle2D` class has two inner classes, `Float` and `Double`, that implement two different precisions). These shape classes are actually very simple subclasses; it would have been sad to have to multiply the number of top-level classes in that package by three to accommodate all of them. With inner classes, we can bundle them with their respective classes:

```
Rectangle2D.Float rect = new Rectangle2D.Float( );
```

Anonymous inner classes

Now we get to the best part. As a general rule, the more deeply encapsulated and limited in scope our classes are, the more freedom we have in naming them. We saw this in our earlier iterator example. This is not just a purely aesthetic issue. Naming is an important part of writing readable, maintainable code. We generally want to use the most concise, meaningful names possible. A corollary to this is that we prefer to avoid doling out names for purely ephemeral objects that are going to be used only once.

Anonymous inner classes are an extension of the syntax of the `new` operation. When you create an anonymous inner class, you combine a class declaration with the allocation of an instance of that class, effectively creating a "one-time only" class and a class instance in one operation. After the `new` keyword, you specify either the name of a class or an interface, followed by a class body. The class body becomes an inner class, which either extends the specified class or, in the case of an interface, is expected to implement the interface. A single instance of the class is created and returned as the value.

For example, we could do away with the declaration of the Iterator class in the EmployeeList example by using an anonymous inner class in the getIterator() method:

```
Iterator getIterator()
{
    return new Iterator() {
        int element = 0;
        boolean hasMore() {
            return  element < employees.length ;
        }
        Object next() {
            if ( hasMoreElements() )
                return employees[ element++ ];
            else
                throw new NoSuchElementException();
        }
        void remove() {
            throw new UnsupportedOperationException();
        }
    };
}
```

Here, we have simply moved the guts of Iterator into the body of an anonymous inner class. The call to new implicitly creates a class that implements the Iterator interface and returns an instance of the class as its result. Note the extent of the curly braces and the semicolon at the end. The getIterator() method contains a single statement, the return statement.

The previous example is a bit extreme and certainly does not improve readability. Inner classes are best used when you want to implement a few lines of code, but the verbiage and conspicuousness of declaring a separate class detracts from the task at hand. Here's a better example. Suppose that we want to start a new thread to execute the performBehavior() method of our Animal:

```
new Thread() {
    public void run() { performBehavior();  }
}.start();
```

Here, we have gone over to the terse side. We've allocated and started a new Thread, using an anonymous inner class that extends the Thread class and invokes our performBehavior() method in its run() method. The effect is similar to using a method pointer in some other language. However, the inner class allows the compiler to check type consistency, which would be more difficult (or impossible) with a true method pointer. At the same time, our anonymous adapter class with its three lines of code is much more efficient and readable than creating a new, top-level adapter class named AnimalBehaviorThreadAdapter.

While we're getting a bit ahead of the story, anonymous adapter classes are a perfect fit for event handling (which we cover fully in Chapter 16). Skipping a lot of explanation, let's say you want the method handleClicks( ) to be called whenever the user clicks the mouse. You would write code such as:

```
addMouseListener( new MouseInputAdapter() {
    public void mouseClicked(MouseEvent e) { handleClicks(e); }
} );
```

In this case, the anonymous class extends the MouseInputAdapter class by overriding its mouseClicked( ) method to call our method. A lot is going on in a very small space, but the result is clean, readable code. You assign method names that are meaningful to you while allowing Java to do its job of type checking.

Scoping of the "this" reference

Sometimes an inner class may want to get a handle on its "parent" enclosing instance. It might want to pass a reference to its parent or to refer to one of the parent's variables or methods that has been hidden by one of its own. For example:

```
class Animal {
    int size;
    class Brain {
        int size;
    }
}
```

Here, as far as Brain is concerned, the variable size in Animal is shadowed by its own version.

Normally, an object refers to itself using the special this reference (implicitly or explicitly). But what is the meaning of this for an object with one or more enclosing instances? The answer is that an inner class has multiple this references. You can specify which this you want by prefixing it with the name of the class. For instance (no pun intended), we can get a reference to our Animal from within Brain, like so:

```
class Brain {
    Animal ourAnimal = Animal.this;
    ...
}
```

Similarly, we could refer to the size variable in Animal:

```
class Brain {
    int animalSize = Animal.this.size;
    ...
}
```

How do inner classes really work?

Finally, let's get our hands dirty and take a look at what's really going on when we use an inner class. We've said that the compiler is doing all the things that we had hoped to forget about. Let's see what's actually happening. Try compiling this trivial example:

```
class Animal {
    class Brain {
    }
}
```

What you'll find is that the compiler generates two *.class* files: *Animal.class* and *Animal$Brain.class*.

The second file is the class file for our inner class. Yes, as we feared, inner classes are really just compiler magic. The compiler has created the inner class for us as a normal, top-level class and named it by combining the class names with a dollar sign. The dollar sign is a valid character in class names but is intended for use only by automated tools. (Please don't start naming your classes with dollar signs.) Had our class been more deeply nested, the intervening inner-class names would have been attached in the same way to generate a unique top-level name.

Now take a look at the class with the JDK's javap utility. In Java 5.0, you can refer to the inner class as Animal.Brain, but in earlier versions of Java, you may have to call the class by its real name, Animal$Brain:

```
% javap 'Animal$Brain'
class Animal$Brain extends java.lang.Object {
    Animal$Brain(Animal);
}
```

On a Windows system, it's not necessary to quote the argument, as we did on this Unix command line.

You'll see that the compiler has given our inner class a constructor that takes a reference to an Animal as an argument. This is how the real inner class gets the reference to its enclosing instance.

The worst thing about these additional class files is that you need to know they are there. Utilities such as *jar* don't automatically find them; when you're invoking such a utility, you need to specify these files explicitly or use a wildcard to find them:

```
% jar cvf animal.jar Animal*class
```

Security implications

Given what we just saw—that the inner class really does exist as an automatically generated top-level class—how does it get access to private variables? The answer, unfortunately, is that the compiler is forced to break the encapsulation of your object and insert accessor methods so that the inner class can reach them. The accessor methods are given package-level access, so your object is still safe within its package walls, but it is conceivable that this difference could be meaningful if people were allowed to create new classes within your package.

The visibility modifiers on inner classes also have some problems. Current implementations of the VM do not implement the notion of a private or protected class within a package, so giving your inner class anything other than public or default visibility is only a compile-time guarantee. It is difficult to conceive of how these security issues could be abused, but it is interesting to note that Java is straining a bit to stay within its original design.*

---

* Inner classes were added to Java in Version 1.1.

## CHAPTER 7

Working with Objects and Classes

In the previous two chapters, we came to know Java objects and their interrelationships. We will now climb the scaffolding of the Java class hierarchy to the very top and finish our study of the core language at the summit. In this chapter, we'll talk about the Object class itself, which is the "grandmother" of all classes in Java. We'll also describe the even more fundamental Class class (the class named "Class") that represents Java classes in the Java virtual machine. We'll discuss what you can do with these components in their own right. This will lead us to a more general topic: the Java Reflection API, which lets a Java program inspect and interact with (possibly unknown) objects dynamically, at runtime. Finally, we'll also talk about the Java Annotations API, new in Java 5.0, which allows developers to add metadata to their source code, for use by the compiler and runtime systems that look for it.

The Object Class

java.lang.Object is the ancestor of all objects; it's the primordial class from which all other classes are ultimately derived. Methods defined in Object are, therefore, very important because they appear in every instance of every class, throughout all of Java. At last count, there were nine public methods and two protected methods in Object. Five of these are versions of wait( ) and notify( ) that are used to synchronize threads on object instances, as we'll discuss in Chapter 9. The remaining four methods are used for basic comparison, conversion, and administration.

Every object has a toString( ) method that can be called when it's to be represented as a text value. PrintStream objects use toString( ) to print data, as discussed in Chapter 12. toString( ) is also used implicitly when an object is referenced in a string concatenation. Here are some examples:

```
MyObj myObject = new MyObj( );
Answer theAnswer = new Answer( );

System.out.println( myObject );
String s = "The answer is: " + theAnswer ;
```

To be friendly, a new kind of object can override toString( ) and implement its own version that provides appropriate information about itself. This is particularly helpful in debugging, where it is common to print the value of an object to see what is going on. Two other methods, equals( ) and hashCode( ), may also require specialization when you create a new class.

Equality and Equivalence

equals( ) determines whether two objects are equivalent. Precisely what that means for a particular class is something that you'll have to decide for yourself. Two String objects, for example, are considered equivalent if they hold precisely the same characters in the same sequence:

```
String userName = "Joe";
...
if ( userName.equals( suspectName ) )
    arrest( userName );
```

Using equals( ) is *not* the same as:

```
if ( userName == suspectName )        // Wrong!
```

This statement tests whether the two reference variables, userName and suspectName, refer to the same object. It is a test for *identity*, not equality. Two variables that are identical (point to the same object) will necessarily be equal, but the converse is not always true.

A class should override the equals( ) method if it needs to implement its own notion of equality. If you have no need to compare objects of a particular class, you don't necessarily need to override equals( ).

Watch out for accidentally overloading equals( ) if you mean to override it. With overloading, the method signatures differ; with overriding, they must be the same. The equals( ) method signature specifies an Object argument so that an object can be compared to any other kind of object, not only those of its own class type. You'll probably want to consider only objects of the same type for equivalence. But in order to override (not overload) equals( ), the method must specify its argument to be an Object.

Here's an example of correctly overriding an equals( ) method in class Shoes with an equals( ) method in subclass Sneakers. Using its own method, a Sneakers object can compare itself with any other object:

```
class Sneakers extends Shoes {
    public boolean equals( Object arg ) {
        if ( (arg != null) && (arg instanceof Sneakers) ) {
            // compare arg with this object to check equivalence
            // If comparison is okay...
            return true;
        }
```

```
        return false;
    }
    ...
}
```

If we specified public boolean equals(Sneakers arg) ... in the Sneakers class, we'd overload the equals( ) method instead of overriding it. If the other object happens to be assigned to a non-Sneakers variable, the method signature won't match. The result: superclass Shoes's implementation of equals( ) is called, which may or may not be what you intended.

Hashcodes

The hashCode( ) method returns an integer that is a hashcode for the object. A *hashcode* is like a signature or checksum for an object; it's a random-looking identifying number that is usually generated from the contents of the object. The hashcode should always be different for instances of the class that contain different data, but should be the same for instances that compare "equal" with the equals( ) method. Hashcodes are used in the process of storing objects in a Hashtable or a similar kind of collection. A random distribution of the hashcode values helps the Hashtable optimize its storage of objects by serving as an identifier for distributing them into storage evenly and quickly locating them later.

The default implementation of hashCode( ) in Object does not really implement this scheme. Instead it assigns each object instance a unique number. If you don't override this method when you create a subclass, each instance of your class will have a unique hashcode. This is sufficient for some objects. However, if your classes have a notion of equivalent objects (if you have overridden equals( )) and you want equal objects to serve as equivalent keys in a Hashtable, you should override hashCode( ) so that your equivalent objects generate the same hashcode value. We'll return to the topic of hashcodes in more detail in Chapter 11 when we discuss the Hashtable and HashMap classes.

Cloning Objects

Objects can use the clone( ) method of the Object class to make copies of themselves. A copied object is a new object instance, separate from the original. It may or may not contain exactly the same state (the same instance variable values) as the original; that is controlled by the object being copied. Just as important, the decision as to whether the object allows itself to be cloned at all is up to the object.

The Java Object class provides the mechanism to make a simple copy of an object including all of its state—a *bitwise* copy. But by default, this capability is turned off. (We'll show why in a moment.) To make itself cloneable, an object must implement the java.lang.Cloneable interface. This is a flag interface indicating to Java that the object wants to cooperate in being cloned (the interface does not actually contain any methods). If the object isn't cloneable, the clone( ) method throws a CloneNotSupportedException.

clone( ) is a protected method, so by default it can be called only by an object on itself, an object in the same package, or another object of the same type or a subtype. If we want to make an object cloneable by everyone, we have to override its clone( ) method and make it public.

Here is a simple, cloneable class—Sheep:

```java
import java.util.HashMap;

public class Sheep implements Cloneable {
    HashMap flock = new HashMap( );

    public Object clone( ) {
        try {
            return super.clone( );
        } catch (CloneNotSupportedException e ) {
            throw new Error("This should never happen!");
        }
    }
}
```

Sheep has one instance variable, a HashMap called flock (which the sheep uses to keep track of its fellow sheep). Our class implements the Cloneable interface, indicating that it is okay to copy Sheep, and it has overridden the clone( ) method to make it public. Our clone( ) simply returns the object created by the superclass's clone( ) method—a copy of our Sheep. Unfortunately, the compiler is not smart enough to figure out that the object we're cloning will never throw the CloneNotSupportedException, so we have to guard against it anyway. Our sheep is now cloneable. We can make copies like so:

```java
Sheep one = new Sheep( );
Sheep anotherOne = (Sheep)one.clone( );
```

The cast is necessary here because the return type of clone( ) is Object. In Java 5.0, we could change the return type of the clone( ) method in the subclass and move the cast into the clone( ) method itself, to make things a little easier on the users of the class:

```java
public Sheep clone( ) {
    try {
        return (Sheep)super.clone( );
    } catch (CloneNotSupportedException e ) {
        throw new Error("This should never happen!");
    }
}

// usage
Sheep one = new Sheep( );
Sheep anotherOne = one.clone( );
```

In either case, we now have two sheep instead of one. A properly implemented equals( ) method would tell us that the sheep are equivalent, but == tells us that they are, in fact, two distinct instances of Sheep. Java has made a *shallow copy* of our Sheep. What's so shallow about it? Java has simply copied the values of our variables. That means that the flock instance variable in each of our Sheep still holds the same information—that is, both sheep have a reference to the same HashMap. The situation looks like that shown in Figure 7-1.

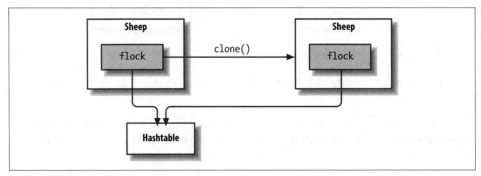

Figure 7-1. Shallow copy of an object

This may or may not be what you intended. If we instead want our Sheep to have separate copies of its full state (or something in between), we can take control ourselves. In the following example, DeepSheep, we implement a *deep copy*, duplicating our own flock variable:

```
public class DeepSheep implements Cloneable {
    HashMap flock = new HashMap( );

    public DeepSheep clone( ) {
        try {
            DeepSheep copy = (DeepSheep)super.clone( );
            copy.flock = (HashMap)flock.clone( );
            return copy;
        } catch (CloneNotSupportedException e ) {
            throw new Error("This should never happen!");
        }
    }
}
```

Our clone( ) method now clones the HashMap as well. Now, when a DeepSheep is cloned, the situation looks more like that shown in Figure 7-2.

Each DeepSheep now has its own full copy of the map. You can see now why objects are not cloneable by default. It would make no sense to assume that all objects can be sensibly duplicated with a shallow copy. Likewise, it makes no sense to assume that a deep copy is necessary, or even correct. In this case, we probably don't need a deep copy; the flock contains the same members no matter which sheep you're looking at,

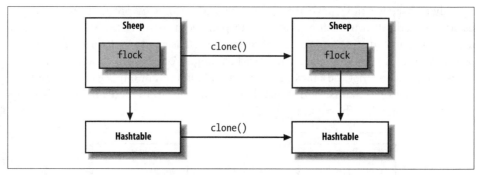

Figure 7-2. Deep copy of an object

so there's no need to copy the HashMap. But the decision depends on the object itself and its requirements.

The last method of Object we need to discuss is getClass( ). This method returns a reference to the Class object that produced the Object instance. We'll talk about it next.

The Class Class

A good measure of the complexity of an object-oriented language is the degree of abstraction of its class structures. We know that every object in Java is an instance of a class, but what exactly is a class? In languages like C++, objects are formulated by and instantiated from classes, but classes are really just artifacts of the compiler. In those languages, you see classes mentioned only in source code, not at runtime. By comparison, classes in Smalltalk are real, runtime entities in the language that are themselves described by "metaclasses" and "metaclass classes." Java strikes a happy medium between these two languages with what is effectively a two-tiered system that uses Class objects.

Classes in Java source code are represented at runtime by instances of the java.lang. Class class. There's a Class object for every object type you use; this Class object is responsible for producing instances of that type. But you don't generally have to worry about that unless you are interested in loading new kinds of classes dynamically at runtime or using a highly abstracted API that wants a "type" instead of an actual argument. The Class object is also the basis for "reflecting" on a class to find its methods and other properties, allowing you to find out about an object's structure or invoke its methods programmatically at runtime. We'll discuss reflection in the next section.

We get the Class associated with a particular object with the getClass( ) method:

```
String myString = "Foo!"
Class stringClass = myString.getClass( );
```

We can also get the Class reference for a particular class statically, using the .class notation:

```
Class stringClass = String.class;
```

The .class reference looks like a static field that exists in every class. However, it is really resolved by the compiler.

One thing we can do with the Class object is ask for its full name:

```
String s = "Boofa!";
Class stringClass = s.getClass();
System.out.println( stringClass.getName() );   // "java.lang.String"
```

Another thing that we can do with a Class is to ask it to produce a new instance of its type of object. Continuing with the previous example:

```
try {
    String s2 = (String)stringClass.newInstance();
}
catch ( InstantiationException e ) { ... }
catch ( IllegalAccessException e ) { ... }
```

Here, newInstance() has a return type of Object, so we have to cast it to a reference of the appropriate type. This is fine, but we'll see in the next chapter that the Class class is a generic class, which means that we can parameterize it to be more specific about the Java type we're dealing with. That is, we can get the newInstance() method to return the correct type directly without the cast. We'll show this here, but don't worry if it doesn't make any sense yet:

```
Class<String> stringClass = String.class;
try {
    String s2 = stringClass.newInstance(); // no cast necessary
}
catch ( InstantiationException e ) { ... }
catch ( IllegalAccessException e ) { ... }
```

A couple of exceptions can be thrown here. An InstantiationException indicates we're trying to instantiate an abstract class or an interface. IllegalAccessException is a more general exception that indicates we can't access a constructor for the object. Note that newInstance() can create only an instance of a class that has an accessible default constructor. It doesn't allow us to pass any arguments to a constructor. (In the next section, we'll learn how to do just that using the Reflection API.)

All this becomes more meaningful when we add the capability to look up a class by name. forName() is a static method of Class that returns a Class object given its name as a String:

```
try {
    Class sneakersClass = Class.forName("Sneakers");
} catch ( ClassNotFoundException e ) { ... }
```

A ClassNotFoundException is thrown if the class can't be located.

Combining these tools, we have the power to load new kinds of classes dynamically. When combined with the power of interfaces, we can use new data types loaded by a string name in our applications:

```java
interface Typewriter {
    void typeLine( String s );
    ...
}

class Printer implements Typewriter {
    ...
}

class MyApplication {
    ...
    String outputDeviceName = "Printer";

    try {
        Class newClass = Class.forName( outputDeviceName );
        Typewriter device = (Typewriter)newClass.newInstance( );
        ...
        device.typeLine("Hello...");
    }
    catch ( Exception e ) { ... }
}
```

Here, we have an application loading a class implementation (`Printer`, which implements the `Typewriter` interface) knowing only its name. Imagine the name was entered by the user or looked up from a configuration file. This kind of class loading is the basis for many kinds of configurable systems in Java.

Reflection

In this section, we'll take a look at the Java Reflection API, supported by the classes in the java.lang.reflect package. As its name suggests, reflection is the ability for a class or object to examine itself. Reflection lets Java code look at an object (more precisely, the class of the object) and determine its structure. Within the limits imposed by the security manager, you can find out what constructors, methods, and fields a class has, as well as their attributes. You can even change the value of fields, dynamically invoke methods, and construct new objects, much as if Java had primitive pointers to variables and methods. And you can do all this on objects that your code has never even seen before. In Java 5.0, the Annotations API also has the ability to preserve metadata about source code in the compiled classes and we can retrieve this information with the Reflection API.

We don't have room here to cover the Reflection API fully. As you might expect, the reflect package is complex and rich in details. But reflection has been designed so that you can do a lot with relatively little effort; 20% of the effort gives you 80% of the fun.

The Reflection API is used by JavaBeans to determine the capabilities of objects at runtime. It's also used at a lower level by object serialization to tear apart and build objects for transport over streams or into persistent storage. Obviously, the power to pick apart objects and see their internals must be zealously guarded by the security manager. The general rule is that your code is not allowed to do anything with the Reflection API that it couldn't do with static (ordinary, compiled) Java code. In short, reflection is a powerful tool, but it isn't an automatic loophole. By default, an object can't use it to work with fields or methods that it wouldn't normally be able to access (for example, another object's private fields), although those privileges can be granted, as we'll discuss later.

The three primary features of a class are its fields (variables), methods, and constructors. For purposes of describing and accessing an object, these three features are represented by separate classes in the Reflection API: java.lang.reflect.Field, java.lang.reflect.Method, and java.lang.reflect.Constructor. We can look up these members of a class through the Class object.

The Class class provides two pairs of methods for getting at each type of feature. One pair allows access to a class's public features (including those inherited from its superclasses) while the other pair allows access to any public or nonpublic item declared directly within the class (but not features that are inherited), subject to security considerations. Some examples:

- getFields() returns an array of Field objects representing all a class's public variables, including those it inherits.

- getDeclaredFields() returns an array representing all the variables declared in the class, regardless of their access modifiers, but not including inherited variables.

- For constructors, the distinction between "all constructors" and "declared constructors" is not meaningful (classes do not inherit constructors), so getConstructors() and getDeclaredConstructors() differ only in that the former returns public constructors while the latter returns all the class's constructors.

Each set of methods includes the methods for listing all the items at once (for example, getFields()) and an additional method for looking up a particular item by name and—for methods and constructors—by signature (for example, getField(), which takes the field name as an argument).

The following listing shows the methods in the Class class:

Field [] getFields();
> Get all public variables, including inherited ones.

Field getField(String name);
> Get the specified public variable, which may be inherited.

```
Field [] getDeclaredFields();
```
Get all public and nonpublic variables declared in this class (not including those inherited from superclasses).

```
Field getDeclaredField(String name);
```
Get the specified variable, public or nonpublic, declared in this class (inherited variables not considered).

```
Method [] getMethods();
```
Get all public methods, including inherited ones.

```
Method getMethod(String name, Class ... argumentTypes);
```
Get the specified public method whose arguments match the types listed in argumentTypes. The method may be inherited.

```
Method [] getDeclaredMethods();
```
Get all public and nonpublic methods declared in this class (not including those inherited from superclasses).

```
Method getDeclaredMethod(String name, Class ... argumentTypes);
```
Get the specified method, public or nonpublic, whose arguments match the types listed in argumentTypes, and which is declared in this class (inherited methods not considered).

```
Constructor [] getConstructors();
```
Get all public constructors of this class.

```
Constructor getConstructor(Class ... argumentTypes);
```
Get the specified public constructor of this class whose arguments match the types listed in argumentTypes.

```
Constructor [] getDeclaredConstructors();
```
Get all public and nonpublic constructors of this class.

```
Constructor getDeclaredConstructor(Class ... argumentTypes);
```
Get the specified constructor, public or nonpublic, whose arguments match the types listed in argumentTypes.

```
Class [] getDeclaredClasses();
```
Get all public and nonpublic inner classes declared within this class.

```
Constructor [] getInterfaces();
```
Get all interfaces implemented by this class, in the order that they are declared.

As you can see, the four getMethod( ) and getConstructor( ) methods take advantage of the Java 5.0 variable-length argument lists to allow you to pass in the argument types. In older versions of Java, you have to pass an array of Class types in their place. We'll show an example later.

As a quick example, we'll show how easy it is to list all the public methods of the java.util.Calendar class:

```
for ( Method method : Calendar.class.getMethods() )
    System.out.println( method );
```

Here, we have used the `.class` notation to get a reference to the `Class` of `Calendar`. Remember the discussion of the `Class` class; the reflection methods don't belong to a particular instance of `Calendar` itself; they belong to the `java.lang.Class` object that describes the `Calendar` class. If we wanted to start from an instance of `Calendar` (or, say, an unknown object), we could have used the `getClass()` method of the object instead:

```
Method [] methods = myUnknownObject.getClass().getMethods();
```

Modifiers and Security

All of the types of members of a Java class—fields, methods, constructors, and inner classes—have a method `getModifiers()` that returns a set of flags indicating whether the member is private, protected, default level, or publicly accessible. You can test for these with the `java.lang.reflect.Modifier` class, like so:

```
Method method = Object.class.getDeclaredMethod( "clone" ); // no arguments
int perms = method.getModifiers();
System.out.println( Modifier.isPublic( perms ) ); // false
System.out.println( Modifier.isProtected( perms ) ); // true
System.out.println( Modifier.isPrivate( perms ) ); // false
```

The `clone()` method in `Object` is protected.

Access to the Reflection API is governed by a security manager. A fully trusted application has access to all the previously discussed functionality; it can gain access to members of classes at the level of restriction normally granted code within its scope. It is, however, possible to grant special access to code so that it can use the Reflection API to gain access to private and protected members of other classes in a way that the Java language ordinarily disallows.

The `Field`, `Method`, and `Constructor` classes all extend from a base class called `AccessibleObject`. The `AccessibleObject` class has one important method called `setAccessible()`, which allows you to deactivate normal security when accessing that particular class member. That may sound too easy. It is indeed simple, but whether that method allows you to disable security or not is a function of the Java security manager and security policy. You can do this in a normal Java application running without any security policy, but not, for example, in an applet or other secure environment. For example, to be able to use the protected `clone()` method of the `Object` class, all we have to do (given no contravening security manager) is:

```
Method method = Object.class.getDeclaredMethod( "clone" );
method.setAccessible( true );
```

Accessing Fields

The class `java.lang.reflect.Field` represents static variables and instance variables. `Field` has a full set of overloaded accessor methods for all the base types (for example, getInt( ) and setInt( ), getBoolean( ) and setBoolean( )) and get( ) and set( ) methods for accessing fields that are reference types. Let's consider this class:

```
class BankAccount {
    public int balance;
}
```

With the Reflection API, we can read and modify the value of the public integer field balance:

```
BankAccount myBankAccount = ...;
...
try {
    Field balanceField = BankAccount.class.getField("balance");
    // read it
    int mybalance = balanceField.getInt( myBankAccount );
    // change it
    balanceField.setInt( myBankAccount, 42 );
} catch ( NoSuchFieldException e ) {
    ... // there is no "balance" field in this class
} catch ( IllegalAccessException e2) {
    ... // we don't have permission to access the field
}
```

In this example, we are assuming that we already know the structure of a BankAccount object. In general, we could gather that information from the object itself.

All the data access methods of Field take a reference to the particular object instance that we want to access. In this example, the getField( ) method returns a Field object that represents the balance of the BankAccount class; this object doesn't refer to any specific BankAccount. Therefore, to read or modify any specific BankAccount, we call getInt( ) and setInt( ) with a reference to myBankAccount, which is the particular object instance that contains the field we want to work with. For a static field, we'd use the value null here. An exception occurs if we try to access a field that doesn't exist, or if we don't have the proper permission to read or write to the field. If we make balance a private field, we can still look up the Field object that describes it, but we won't be able to read or write its value.

Therefore, we aren't doing anything that we couldn't have done with static code at compile time; as long as balance is a public member of a class that we can access, we can write code to read and modify its value. What's important is that we're accessing balance at runtime, and we could just as easily use this technique to examine the balance field in a class that was dynamically loaded or that we just discovered by iterating through the class's fields with the getDeclaredFields( ) method.

Accessing Methods

The class java.lang.reflect.Method represents a static or instance method. Subject to the normal security rules, a Method object's invoke( ) method can be used to call the underlying object's method with specified arguments. Yes, Java does have something like a method pointer!

As an example, we'll write a Java application called Invoke that takes as command-line arguments the name of a Java class and the name of a method to invoke. For simplicity, we'll assume that the method is static and takes no arguments (quite a limitation):

```
//file: Invoke.java
import java.lang.reflect.*;

class Invoke {
  public static void main( String [] args ) {
    try {
      Class clas = Class.forName( args[0] );

      Method method = clas.getMethod( args[1], new Class [] { } );
      Object ret =  method.invoke( null, null );
      // Java 5.0 with varargs
      // Method method = clas.getMethod( args[1] );
      // Object ret =  method.invoke( null );

      System.out.println(
          "Invoked static method: " + args[1]
          + " of class: " + args[0]
          + " with no args\nResults: " + ret );
    } catch ( ClassNotFoundException e ) {
      // Class.forName( ) can't find the class
    } catch ( NoSuchMethodException e2 ) {
      // that method doesn't exist
    } catch ( IllegalAccessException e3 ) {
      // we don't have permission to invoke that method
    } catch ( InvocationTargetException e4 ) {
      // an exception occurred while invoking that method
      System.out.println(
          "Method threw an: " + e4.getTargetException() );
    }
  }
}
```

We can run invoke to fetch the value of the system clock:

```
% java Invoke java.lang.System currentTimeMillis
Invoked static method: currentTimeMillis of class:
java.lang.System with no args
Results: 861129235818
```

Our first task is to look up the specified Class by name. To do so, we call the forName( ) method with the name of the desired class (the first command-line argument). We then ask for the specified method by its name. getMethod( ) has two arguments: the first is the method name (the second command-line argument), and the second is an array of Class objects that specifies the method's signature. (Remember that any method may be overloaded; you must specify the signature to make it clear which version you want.) Since our simple program calls only methods with no arguments, we create an anonymous empty array of Class objects. Had we wanted to invoke a method that takes arguments, we would have passed an array of the classes of their respective types, in the proper order. For primitive types, we would have used the standard wrappers (Integer, Float, Boolean, etc.) to hold the values. The classes of primitive types in Java are represented by special static TYPE fields of their respective wrappers; for example, use Integer.TYPE for the Class of an int. As shown in comments in the code, in Java 5.0, the getMethod( ) and invoke( ) methods now accept variable-length argument lists, which means that we can omit the arguments entirely and Java will make the empty array for us.

Once we have the Method object, we call its invoke( ) method. This calls our target method and returns the result as an Object. To do anything nontrivial with this object, you have to cast it to something more specific. Presumably, since we're calling the method, we know what kind of object to expect. But if we didn't, we could use the Method getReturnType( ) method to get the Class of the return type at runtime. If the returned value is a primitive type such as int or boolean, it will be wrapped in the standard wrapper class for its type. If the method returns void, invoke( ) returns a java.lang.Void object. This is the "wrapper" class that represents void return values.

The first argument to invoke( ) is the object on which we would like to invoke the method. If the method is static, there is no object, so we set the first argument to null. That's the case in our example. The second argument is an array of objects to be passed as arguments to the method. The types of these should match the types specified in the call to getMethod( ). Because we're calling a method with no arguments, we can pass null for the second argument to invoke( ). As with the return value, you must use wrapper classes for primitive argument types.

The exceptions shown in the previous code occur if we can't find or don't have permission to access the method. Additionally, an InvocationTargetException occurs if the method being invoked throws some kind of exception itself. You can find what it threw by calling the getTargetException( ) method of InvocationTargetException.

Accessing Constructors

The java.lang.reflect.Constructor class represents an object constructor in the same way that the Method class represents a method. You can use it, subject to the security manager, of course, to create a new instance of an object, even with constructors that require arguments. Recall that you can create instances of a class with Class.newInstance( ), but you cannot specify arguments with that method. This is the solution to that problem, if you really need to do it.

Here, we'll create an instance of java.util.Date,* passing a string argument to the constructor:

```
// Java 5.0 Code, using generic type and varargs
try {
    Constructor<Date> cons =
        Date.class.getConstructor( String.class );
    Date date = cons.newInstance( "Jan 1, 2006" );
    System.out.println( date );
} catch ( NoSuchMethodException e ) {
    // getConstructor() couldn't find the constructor we described
} catch ( InstantiationException e2 ) {
    // the class is abstract
} catch ( IllegalAccessException e3 ) {
    // we don't have permission to create an instance
} catch ( InvocationTargetException e4 ) {
    // the construct threw an exception
}
```

The story is much the same as with a method invocation; after all, a constructor is really no more than a method with some strange properties. We look up the appropriate constructor for our Date class—the one that takes a single String as its argument—by passing getConstructor( ) the String.class type. Here, we are using the Java 5.0 variable argument syntax. If the constructor required more arguments, we would pass additional Classes representing the class of each argument. We can then invoke newInstance( ), passing it a corresponding argument object. Again, to pass primitive types, we would wrap them in their wrapper types first. Finally, we print the resulting object to a Date. Note that we've slipped in another strange construct using generics here. The Constructor<Date> type here simply allows us to specialize the Constructor for the Date type, alleviating the need to cast the result of the newInstance( ) method, as before.

The exceptions from the previous example apply here, too, along with IllegalArgumentException and InstantiationException. The latter is thrown if the class is abstract and, therefore, can't be instantiated.

What About Arrays?

The Reflection API allows you to create and inspect arrays of base types using the java.lang.reflect.Array class. The process is very much the same as with the other classes, so we won't cover it in detail. The primary feature is a static method of Array called newInstance( ), which creates an array, allowing you to specify a base type and length. You can also use it to construct multidimensional array instances, by specifying an array of lengths (one for each dimension). For more information, look in your favorite Java language reference.

---

* This Date constructor is deprecated but will serve us for this example.

Accessing Generic Type Information

In Chapter 8, we'll discuss generics in Java 5.0. Generics is a major addition that adds new dimensions (literally) to the concept of types in the Java language. With the addition of generics, types are no longer simply one-to-one with Java classes and interfaces but can be parameterized on one or more types to create a new, generic type. To make matters more complicated, these new types do not actually generate new classes but instead are artifacts of the compiler. To keep the generic information, Java adds information to the compiled class files.

In Java 5.0, the Reflection API has been beefed up to accommodate all of this, mainly through the addition of the new `java.lang.reflect.Type` class, which is capable of representing generic types. Covering this in detail is a bit outside the scope of this book and since we won't even get to generics until Chapter 8, we won't devote much more space to this topic here. However, the following code snippets may guide you later if you return to the topic of accessing generic type information reflectively:

```
// public interface List<E> extends Collection<E> { ... }

TypeVariable [] tv = List.class.getTypeParameters();
System.out.println( tv[0].getName() ); // "E"
```

This snippet gets the type parameter of the `java.util.List` class and prints its name:

```
class StringList extends ArrayList<String> { }

Type type = StringList.class.getGenericSuperclass();

System.out.println( type );  //
// "java.util.ArrayList<java.lang.String>"


ParameterizedType pt = (ParameterizedType)type;
System.out.println( pt.getActualTypeArguments()[0] ); //
// "class java.lang.String"
```

This second snippet gets the `Type` for a class that extends a generic type and then prints the actual type on which it was parameterized.

Accessing Annotation Data

Later in this chapter, we discuss annotations, a new feature in Java 5.0 that allows metadata to be added to Java classes, methods, and fields. Annotations can optionally be retained in the compiled Java classes and accessed through the Reflection API. This is one of several intended uses for annotations, allowing code at runtime to see the metadata and provide special services for the annotated code. For example, a property on a Java object might be annotated to indicate that it is expecting a container application to set its value or export it in some way.

Covering this in detail is outside the scope of this book; however, getting annotation data through the Reflection API in Java 5.0 is easy. Java classes, as well as `Method` and `Field` objects, have the following pairs of methods (and some other related ones):

```
public <A extends Annotation> A getAnnotation(Class<A> annotationClass)
public Annotation[] getDeclaredAnnotations( )
```

These methods (the first is a generic method, as covered in Chapter 8) return `java.lang.annotation.Annotation` type objects that represent the metadata.

Dynamic Interface Adapters

Ideally, Java reflection would allow us to do everything at runtime that we can do at compile time (without forcing us to generate and compile source into bytecode). But that is not entirely the case. Although we can dynamically load and create instances of objects at runtime using the `Class.forName( )` method, there is no general way to create new types of objects—for which no class files preexist—on the fly.

The `java.lang.reflect.Proxy` class, however, takes a step toward solving this problem by allowing the creation of adapter objects that implement arbitrary Java interfaces at runtime. The `Proxy` class is a factory that can generate an adapter class, implementing any interface (or interfaces) you want. When methods are invoked on the adapter class, they are delegated to a single method in a designated `InvocationHandler` object. You can use this to create dynamic implementations of any kind of interface at runtime and handle the method calls anywhere you want. For example, using a `Proxy`, you could log all of the method calls on an interface, delegating them to a "real" implementation afterward. This kind of dynamic behavior is important for tools that work with Java beans, which must register event listeners. (We'll mention this again in Chapter 22.) It's also useful for a wide range of problems.

In the following snippet, we take an interface name and construct a proxy implementing the interface. It outputs a message whenever any of the interface's methods is invoked:

```
import java.lang.reflect.*;

InvocationHandler handler =
    new InvocationHandler( ) {
        Object invoke( Object proxy, Method method, Object[] args ) {
            System.out.println(
                "Method: "+ method.getName( ) +"( )"
                +" of interface: "+ interfaceName
                + " invoked on proxy!"
            );
            return null;
        }
    };

Class clas = Class.forName( MyInterface );
```

```
MyInterface interfaceProxy =
    (MyInterface)Proxy.newProxyInstance(
        clas.getClassLoader( ), new Class[] { class }, handler );

// use MyInterface
myInterface.anyMethod( ); // Method: anyMethod( ) ... invoked on proxy!
```

The resulting object, interfaceProxy, is cast to the type of the interface we want. It will call our handler whenever any of its methods are invoked.

First, we make an implementation of InvocationHandler. This is an object with an invoke( ) method that takes as its argument the Method being called and an array of objects representing the arguments to the method call. We then fetch the class of the interface that we're going to implement using Class.forName( ). Finally, we ask the proxy to create an adapter for us, specifying the types of interfaces (you can specify more than one) that we want implemented and the handler to use. invoke( ) is expected to return an object of the correct type for the method call. If it returns the wrong type, a special runtime exception is thrown. Any primitive types in the arguments or in the return value should be wrapped in the appropriate wrapper class. (The runtime system unwraps the return value, if necessary.)

What Is Reflection Good For?

Reflection, although in some sense a "backdoor" feature of the Java language, is finding more and more important uses. In this chapter, we mentioned that reflection is used to access runtime annotations in Java 5.0. In Chapter 22, we'll see how reflection is used to dynamically discover capabilities and features of JavaBean objects. Those are pretty specialized applications—what can reflection do for us in everyday situations?

We could use reflection to go about acting as if Java had dynamic method invocation and other useful capabilities; in Chapter 22, we'll see a dynamic adapter class that uses reflection to make calls for us. As a general coding practice however, dynamic method invocation is a bad idea. One of the primary features of Java (and what distinguishes it from some scripting languages) is its strong typing and safety. You abandon much of that when you take a dip in the reflecting pool. And although the performance of the Reflection API is very good, it is not precisely as fast as compiled method invocations in general.

More appropriately, you can use reflection in situations where you need to work with objects that you can't know about in advance. Reflection puts Java on a higher plane of programming languages, opening up possibilities for new kinds of applications. As we've mentioned, it makes possible one use of Java annotations at runtime, allowing us to inspect classes, methods, and fields for metadata. Another important and growing use for reflection is integrating Java with scripting languages. With reflection, you can write language interpreters in Java that can access the full Java APIs, create objects, invoke methods, modify variables, and do all the other things a

Java program can do at compile time, while the program is running. In fact, you could go so far as to reimplement the Java language in Java, allowing completely dynamic programs that can do all sorts of things. Sound crazy? Well, someone has already done this—one of the authors of this book! We'll explain next.

The BeanShell Java scripting language

I can't resist inserting a plug here for BeanShell—my free, open source, lightweight Java scripting language. BeanShell is just what I alluded to in the previous section—a Java application that uses the Reflection API to execute Java statements and expressions dynamically. You can use BeanShell interactively to quickly try out some of the examples in this book or take it further to start using Java syntax as a scripting language in your applications. BeanShell exercises the Java Reflection API to its fullest and serves as a demonstration of how dynamic the Java runtime environment really is.

You can find a copy of BeanShell on the CD-ROM that accompanies this book and the latest release and documentation at its own web site, *http://www.beanshell.org*. In recent years, BeanShell has become quite popular. It is now distributed with the Java Development Environment for Emacs (JDEE) and has been bundled with popular application environments including BEA's WebLogic server, NetBeans, and Sun's Java Studio IDE. See Appendix B for more information on getting started. I hope you find it both interesting and useful!

Annotations

As we mentioned in Chapter 4, Java for a long time has supported a limited kind of metadata in Java source code through the use of Javadoc comment tags. With Javadoc tags like @deprecated or @author, we can add some information to a class, method, or field. In this case, the information is mainly useful to the Javadoc documentation generator, because comments exist only in Java source code. However, developers have long wanted a way to generalize metadata for other purposes. And in fact, some tools have been developed over the years that read extended Javadoc-style tags in comments and do all sorts of things with them, including code generation and documentation. In Java 5.0, a new formal, extensible metadata system called annotations has been added to the language that provides the Javadoc-style, source-level functionality as well as new possibilities for using metadata at runtime.

Annotations allow you to add metadata to Java classes, methods, and fields. This metadata can be utilized by tools at compile time and optionally retained in the compiled Java classes for use at runtime as well. The availability of annotation data to the running program opens up new uses for metadata. For example, annotations cannot only be used at compile time to generate auxiliary classes or resources but also could be used by a server to provide special services to classes such as importing or exporting of values, security, or monitoring. Annotations will be used heavily in the Enterprise JavaBeans (EJB) Version 3 specification to simplify configuration and deployment information.

Technically, according to the spec, annotations are not supposed to "directly affect the semantics of a program." However, that admonition is a little vague and there is some fear in the Java community that this facility will open a Pandora's box of possible abuses. Hopefully, developers will use them with restraint.

Only a handful of "built-in" annotations are supplied with Java 5.0 and we'll summarize them in this section. Creating new annotations is syntactically easy, but implementing the behavior for them (via the compiler or a runtime system) is a bit beyond the scope of this book, so we won't cover that here. The Sun JDK provides a framework tool called *apt* that can be used to implement source-level annotations that generate and compile code or resource files. Accessing annotation data at runtime is done via the Reflection API as described earlier in this chapter.

Using Annotations

The @Deprecated annotation is an example of the simplest kind, a *marker* or *flag* annotation. A marker annotation indicates some semantics just by its presence. (In the case of @Deprecated it means that the member is deprecated and the compiler should generate warnings if it is used.) To use the @Deprecated annotation, we place it before a Java class, method, or field like this:

```
@Deprecated class OldClass { ... }

class AgingClass {
    @Deprecated public someMethod( ) { ... }
    ...
}
```

More generally, annotations may take "arguments" in an extended method-like syntax. Table 7-1 summarizes the possible variations.

Table 7-1. Use of arguments in annotations

Example	Description
@Deprecated	Marker annotation (no "data")
@WarningMessage("Something about...")	Single argument
@TestValues({ "one", "two" })	Array of arguments
@Author(first="Pat", last="Niemeyer")	Named arguments

(The first annotation in the table, @Deprecated, is a real annotation as described earlier; the remaining three are fictitious.) To accept multiple values, an annotation may either use the curly brace ({}) array syntax or the more novel named argument syntax listed in the final example. The named syntax allows arguments to be passed in any order.

Standard Annotations

Table 7-2 summarizes the application-level standard annotations supplied with Java 5.0.

Table 7-2. Standard annotations

Annotation	Description
@Deprecated	Deprecation warning on member
@Override	Indicates that the annotated method must override a method in the parent class or a compiler warning is issued
@SuppressWarnings(value="*type*")	Indicates that the specified warning types should be suppressed by the compiler for the annotated class or method

We have already discussed the @Deprecated and @Override annotations, the latter of which we discussed in the section "Overriding Methods" in Chapter 6. The @SuppressWarnings annotation is intended to have a compelling use in bridging legacy code with new generic code in Java 5.0, but at the time of this writing, it is not implemented.

Technically, four other standard annotations are supplied with Java 5.0, but they are part of the java.lang.annotations package and are used to annotate only other annotations (they are really meta-annotations). For example, the java.lang.annotation. Retention annotation sets the retention policy for an annotation, specifying whether it is retained in the compiled class and loaded at runtime.

The apt Tool

The Java 5.0 JDK from Sun ships with the command-line Annotation Processing Tool, *apt*, that is a sort of frontend to the *javac* compiler. *apt* uses pluggable annotation processors to process the annotations in source files before the code is compiled by *javac*. If you write your own source-level annotations, you can build a plug-in annotation processor for *apt* that will be invoked to process your annotation in the source code. Your annotation processor can be quite sophisticated, examining the structure of the source code (in a read-only fashion) through the supplied syntax tree (object model) and generating any additional files or actions that it wishes. If you generate new Java source files, they will be automatically compiled by *javac* for you. Running *apt* on a source file with no annotations simply falls through to *javac*.

CHAPTER 8

Generics

It's been almost 10 years since the introduction of the Java programming language (and the first edition of this book). In that time, the Java language has matured and come into its own. But only with Java 5.0, the sixth major release of Java, did the core language itself change in a significant way. Yes, there were subtle changes and drop-ins over the years. Inner classes, added very early on, were important. But no language improvements prior to this point have affected all Java code or all Java developers in the way that Java 5.0 will.

Generics are about abstraction. Generics let you create classes and methods that work in the same way on different types of objects. The term "generic" comes from the idea that we'd like to be able to write general algorithms that can be broadly reused for many types of objects rather than having to adapt our code to fit each circumstance. This concept is not new; it is the impetus behind object-oriented programming itself. Java generics do not so much add new capabilities to the language as they make reusable Java code easier to write and easier to read.

Generics take reuse to the next level by making the *type* of the objects we work with an explicit parameter of the generic code. For this reason, generics are also referred to as *parameterized types*. In the case of a generic class, the developer specifies a type as a parameter (an argument) whenever she uses the generic type. The class is parameterized by the supplied type, to which the code adapts itself.

In other languages, generics are sometimes referred to as *templates*, which is more of an implementation term. Templates are like intermediate classes, waiting for their type parameters so that they can be used. Java takes a different path, which has both benefits and drawbacks that we'll describe in detail in this chapter.

There is much to say about Java generics and some of the fine points may be a bit obscure at first. But don't get discouraged. The vast majority of what you'll do with generics is easy and intuitive. The rest will come with a little patience and tinkering.

We begin our discussion with the most compelling case for generics: container classes and collections. Next, we take a step back and look at the good, bad, and ugly of how Java generics work before getting into the details of writing generic classes. We then introduce generic methods, which intelligently infer their parameter types based upon how they are invoked. We conclude by looking at a couple of real-world generic classes in the Java API.

Containers: Building a Better Mousetrap

In an object-oriented programming language like Java, polymorphism means that objects are always to some degree interchangeable. Any child of a type of object can serve in place of its parent type and, ultimately, every object is a child of java.lang. Object, the object-oriented "Eve," so to speak. It is natural, therefore, for the most general types of *containers* in Java to work with the type Object so that they can hold most anything. By containers, we mean classes that hold instances of other classes in some way. The Java Collections Framework is the best example of containers. A List, for example, holds an ordered collection of elements of type Object. A Map holds an association of key-value pairs, with the keys and values also being of the most general type, Object. With a little help from wrappers for primitive types, this arrangement has served us well. But (not to get too Zen on you), in a sense, a "collection of any type" is also a "collection of no type," and working with Objects pushes a great deal of responsibility onto the user of the container.

It's kind of like a costume party for objects where everybody is wearing the same mask and disappears into the crowd of the collection. Once objects are dressed as the Object type the compiler can no longer see the real types and loses track of them. It's up to the user to pierce the anonymity of the objects later using a type cast. And like attempting to yank off a party-goer's fake beard, you'd better have the cast correct or you'll get an unwelcome surprise.

```
Date date = new Date( );
List list = new ArrayList( );
list.add( date );
...
Date firstElement = (Date)list.get(0); // Is the cast correct?  Maybe.
```

The List interface has an add( ) method that accepts any type of Object. Here, we assigned an instance of ArrayList, which is simply an implementation of the List interface, and added a Date object. Is the cast in this example correct? It depends on what happens in the elided "..." period of time.

Can Containers Be Fixed?

It's natural to ask if there is a way to make this situation better. What if we know that we are only going to put Dates into our list? Can't we just make our own list that only accepts Date objects, get rid of the cast, and let the compiler help us again? The answer, surprisingly perhaps, is no. At least, not in a very satisfying way.

Our first instinct may be to try to "override" the methods of ArrayList in a subclass. But of course, rewriting the add( ) method in a subclass would not actually override anything; it would add a new *overloaded* method.

```
public void add( Object o ) { ... }
public void add( Date d ) { ... } // overloaded method
```

The resulting object still accepts any kind of object—it just invokes different methods to get there.

Moving along, we might take on a bigger task. For example, we might write our own DateList class that does not extend ArrayList but delegates the guts of its methods to the ArrayList implementation. With a fair amount of tedious work, that would get us an object that does everything a List does but works with Dates. However, we've now shot ourselves in the foot because our container is no longer an implementation of List and we can't use it interoperably with all of the utilities that deal with collections, such as Collections.sort( ), or add it to another collection with the Collection addAll( ) method.

To generalize, the problem is that instead of refining the behavior of our objects, what we really want to do is to change their contract with the user. We want to adapt their API to a more specific type and polymorphism doesn't allow that. It would seem that we are stuck with Objects for our collections. But this is where generics come in.

Enter Generics

Generics in Java are an enhancement to the syntax of classes that allow us to specialize the class for a given type or set of types. A generic class requires one or more *type parameters* wherever we refer to the class type and uses them to customize itself.

If you look at the source or Javadoc for the List class, for example, you'll see it defined something like this:

```
public class List< E > {
    ...
    public void add( E element ) { ... }
    public E get( int i ) { ... }
}
```

The identifier E between the angle brackets (<>) is a *type variable*. It indicates that the class List is generic and requires a Java type as an argument to make it complete. The name E is arbitrary, but there are conventions that we'll see as we go on. In this case, the type variable E represents the type of elements we want to store in the list. The List class refers to the type variable within its body and methods as if it were a real type, to be substituted later. The type variable may be used to declare instance variables, arguments to methods, and the return type of methods. In this case, E is used as the type for the elements we'll be adding via the add( ) method and the return type of the get( ) method. Let's see how to use it.

The same angle bracket syntax supplies the type parameter when we want to use the List type:

```
List<String> listOfStrings;
```

In this snippet, we declared a variable called listOfStrings using the generic type List with a type parameter of String. String refers to the String class, but we could have specialized List with any Java class type. For example:

```
List<Date> dates;
List<java.math.BigDecimal> decimals;
List<Foo> foos;
```

Completing the type by supplying its type parameter is called *instantiating the type*. It is also sometimes called *invoking the type*, by analogy with invoking a method and supplying its arguments. Whereas with a regular Java type, we simply refer to the type by name, a generic type must be instantiated with parameters wherever it is used.* Specifically this means we must instantiate the type everywhere types can appear: as the declared type of a variable (as shown in this code snippet), as the type of a method argument, as the return type of a method, or in an object allocation expression using the new keyword.

Returning to our listOfStrings, what we have now is effectively a List in which the type String has been substituted for the type variable E in the class body:

```
public class List< String > {
    ...
    public void add( String element ) { ... }
    public String get( int i ) { ... }
}
```

We have specialized the List class to work with elements of type String and *only* elements of type String. This method signature is no longer capable of accepting an arbitrary Object type.

List is just an interface. To use the variable, we'll need to create an instance of some actual implementation of List. As we did in our introduction, we'll use ArrayList. As before, ArrayList is a class that implements the List interface, but, in this case, both List and ArrayList are generic classes. As such, they require type parameters to instantiate them where they are used. Of course, we'll create our ArrayList to hold String elements to match our List of Strings:

```
List<String> listOfStrings = new ArrayList<String>();
```

---

* That is, unless you want to use a generic type in a nongeneric way. We'll talk about "raw" types later in this chapter.

There is no new syntax in this example. As always, the new keyword takes a Java type and parentheses with possible arguments for the class's constructor. In this case, the type is ArrayList<String>—the generic ArrayList type instantiated with the String type.

We can now use our specialized List with strings. The compiler prevents us from even trying to put anything other than a String object (or a subtype of String if there were any) into the list and allows us to fetch them with the get( ) method without requiring any cast:

```
List<String> listOfStrings = new ArrayList<String>();
listOfStrings.add("eureka! ");
String s = listOfStrings.get(0); // "eureka! "

listOfStrings.add( new Date() ); // Compile-time Error!
```

Let's take another example from the Collections API. The Map interface provides a dictionary-like mapping that associates key objects with value objects. Keys and values do not have to be of the same type. The generic Map interface requires two type parameters: one for the key type and one for the value type. The Javadoc looks like this:

```
public class Map< K, V > {
    ...
    public V put( K key, V value ) { ... } // returns any old value
    public V get( K key ) { ... }
}
```

We can make a Map that stores Employee objects by Integer "employee id" numbers like this:

```
Map< Integer, Employee > employees = new HashMap< Integer, Employee >();
Integer bobsId = ...;
Employee bob = ...;

employees.put( bobsId, bob );
Employee employee = employees.get( bobsId );
```

Here, we used HashMap, which is a generic class that implements the Map interface, and instantiated both types with the type parameters Integer and Employee. The Map now works only with keys of type Integer and holds values of type Employee.

The reason we used Integer here to hold our number is that the type parameters to a generic class must be class types. We can't parameterize a generic class with a primitive type, such as int or boolean. Fortunately, autoboxing of primitives in Java 5.0 (see Chapter 5) makes it appear almost as if we can, by allowing us to use primitive types as if they were wrapper types:

```
employees.put( 42, bob );
Employee bob = employees.get( 42 );
```

Here, autoboxing converted the integer 42 to an Integer wrapper for us twice.

In Chapter 11, we'll see that all of the Java collection classes and interfaces have been made generic in Java 5.0. Furthermore, dozens of other APIs now use generics to let you adapt them to specific types. We'll talk about them as they occur throughout the book.

Talking About Types

Before we move on to more important things, we should say a few words about the way we describe a particular parameterization of a generic class. Since the most common and compelling case for generics is for container-like objects, it's common to think in terms of a generic type "holding" a parameter type. In our example, we called our List<String> a "list of strings" because, sure enough, that's what it was. Similarly, we might have called our employee map a "Map of employee ids to Employee objects." However, these descriptions focus a little more on what the classes *do* than on the type itself. Take instead a single object container called Trap< E > that could be instantiated on an object of type Mouse or of type Bear, that is, Trap<Mouse> or Trap<Bear>. Our instinct is to call the new type a "mouse trap" or "bear trap." Similarly, we could have thought of our list of strings as a new type: "string list" or our employee map as a new "integer employee object map" type. There is no harm in using whatever verbiage you prefer, but these latter descriptions focus more on the notion of the generic as a *type* and may help a little bit later when we have to discuss how generic types are related in the type system. There we'll see that the container terminology turns out to be a little counterintuitive.

In the following section, we'll carry on our discussion of generic types in Java from a different perspective. We've seen a little of what they can do; now we need to talk about how they do it.

"There Is No Spoon"

In the movie *The Matrix*,[*] the hero Neo is offered a choice. Take the blue pill and remain in the world of fantasy or take the red pill and see things as they really are. In dealing with generics in Java, we are faced with a similar ontological dilemma. We can go only so far in any discussion of generics before we are forced to confront the reality of how they are implemented. Our fantasy world is one created by the compiler to

---

[*] For those of you who might like some context for the title of this section, here is where it comes from:

> Boy: Do not try and bend the spoon. That's impossible. Instead only try to realize the truth.
>
> Neo: What truth?
>
> Boy: There is no spoon.
>
> Neo: There is no spoon?
>
> Boy: Then you'll see that it is not the spoon that bends, it is only yourself.
>
> —Wachowski, Andy and Larry. *The Matrix*. 1 videocassette (136 minutes). Warner Brothers, 1999.

make our lives writing code easier to accept. Our reality (though not quite the dysto-pian nightmare in the movie) is a harsher place, filled with unseen dangers and questions. Why don't casts and tests work properly with generics? Why can't I implement what appear to be two different generic interfaces in one class? Why is it that I can declare an array of generic types, even though there is no way in Java to create such an array?!? We'll answer these questions and more in this chapter, and you won't even have to wait for the sequel. Let's get started.

The design goals for Java generics were formidable: add a radical new syntax to the language that introduces parameterized types, safely, with no impact on perfor-mance and, oh, by the way, make it backward-compatible with all existing Java code and don't change the compiled classes in any serious way. It's actually fairly amazing that these conditions could be satisfied at all and no surprise that it took a while. But as always, the compromises lead to some headaches.

To accomplish this feat, Java employs a technique called *erasure*, which relates to the idea that since most everything we do with generics applies statically, at compile time, generic information does not really have to be carried over into the compiled classes. The generic nature of the classes, enforced by the compiler, can be "erased" in the compiled classes, allowing us to maintain compatibility with nongeneric code. While Java does retain information about the generic features of classes in the com-piled form, this information is used mainly by the compiler. The Java runtime does not actually know anything about generics at all.

Erasure

Let's take a look at a compiled generic class: our friend, List. We can do this easily with the *javap* command:

```
% javap java.util.List
```

```
public interface java.util.List extends java.util.Collection{
    ...
    public abstract boolean add(java.lang.Object);
    public abstract java.lang.Object get(int);
```

The result looks exactly like it did prior to Java generics, as you can confirm with any older version of the JDK. Notably, the type of elements used with the add( ) and get( ) methods is Object. Now, you might think that this is just a ruse and that when the actual type is instantiated, Java will create a new version of the class internally. But that's not the case. This is the one and only List class and it is the actual runtime type used by all parameterizations of List, for example, List<Date> and List<String>, as we can confirm:

```
List<Date> dateList  = new ArrayList<Date>();
System.out.println( dateList instanceof List ); // true!
```

But our generic dateList clearly does not implement the List methods just discussed:

```
dateList.add( new Object() ); // Compile-time Error!
```

This illustrates the somewhat schizophrenic nature of Java generics. The compiler believes in them, but the runtime says they are an illusion. What if we try something a little more sane looking and simply check that our dateList is a List<Date>:

```
System.out.println( dateList instanceof List<Date> ); // Compile-time Error!
// Illegal, generic type for instanceof
```

This time the compiler simply puts its foot down and says, "no." You can't test for a generic type in an instanceof operation. Since there are no actual differentiable classes for different parameterizations of List at runtime, there is no way for the instanceof operator to tell the difference between one incarnation of List and another. All of the generic safety checking was done at compile time and now we're just dealing with a single actual List type.

What has really happened is that the compiler has erased all of the angle bracket syntax and replaced the type variables in our List class with a type that can work at runtime with any allowed type: in this case, Object. We would seem to be back where we started, except that the compiler still has the knowledge to enforce our usage of the generics in the code at compile time and it can, therefore, handle the cast for us. If you decompile a class using a List<Date> (the *javap* command with the *-c* option shows you the bytecode, if you dare), you will see that the compiled code actually contains the cast to Date, even though we didn't write it ourselves.

We can now answer one of the questions we posed at the beginning of the section ("Why can't I implement what appear to be two different generic interfaces in one class?"). We can't have a class that implements two different generic List instantiations because they are really the same type at runtime and there is no way to tell them apart:

```
public abstract class DualList implements List<String>, List<Date> { }
// Error: java.util.List cannot be inherited with different arguments:
//     <java.lang.String> and <java.util.Date>
```

Raw Types

Although the compiler treats different parameterizations of a generic type as truly different types (with different APIs) at compile time, we have seen that only one real type exists at runtime. For example, the class of List<Date> and List<String> share the plain old Java class List. List is called the *raw type* of the generic class. Every generic has a raw type. It is the degenerate, "plain" Java form in which all of the generic type information has been removed and the type variables replaced by some general Java type like Object.

Java 5.0 has been carefully arranged such that the raw type of all of the generic classes works out to be exactly the same as the earlier, nongeneric types. So the raw type of a List in Java 5.0 is the same as the old, nongeneric List type that has been around since JDK 1.2. Since the vast majority of current Java code in existence today does not (and may never) use generics, this type equivalency and compatibility is very important.

It is still possible to use raw types in Java 5.0 just as before. The only difference is that the Java 5.0 compiler generates a new type of warning wherever they are used in an "unsafe" way. For example:

```
// nongeneric Java code using the raw type, same as always
List list = new ArrayList(); // assignment ok
list.add("foo"); // unchecked warning on usage of raw type
```

This snippet uses the raw List type just as any good old-fashioned Java code prior to Java 5.0 would have. The difference is that now the Java compiler issues an *unchecked warning* about the code if we attempt to insert an object into the list.

```
% javac MyClass.java
Note: MyClass.java uses unchecked or unsafe operations.
Note: Recompile with -Xlint:unchecked for details.
```

The compiler instructs us to use the –Xlint:unchecked option to get more specific information about the locations of unsafe operations:

```
% javac -Xlint:unchecked MyClass.java
warning: [unchecked] unchecked call to add(E) as a member of the raw type java.util.
List:    list.add("foo");
```

Note that creating and assigning the raw ArrayList do not generate a warning. It is only when we try to use an "unsafe" method (one that refers to a type variable) that we get the warning. This means that it's still okay to use older style nongeneric Java APIs that work with raw types. We only get warnings when we do something unsafe in our own code.

One more thing about erasure before we move on. In the previous examples, the type variables were replaced by the Object type, which could represent any type applicable to the type variable E. Later we'll see that this is not always the case. We can place limitations or *bounds* on the parameter types, and, when we do, the compiler can be more restrictive about the erasure of the type. We'll explain in more detail later after we discussed bounds, but, for example:

```
class Bounded< E extends Date > {
    public void addElement( E element ) { ... }
}
```

This parameter type declaration says that the element type E may be any subtype of the Date type. In this case, the erasure of the addElement() method can be more restrictive than Object, and the compiler uses Date:

```
public void addElement( Date element ) { ... }
```

Date is called the *upper bound* of this type, meaning that it is the top of the object hierarchy here and the type can be instantiated only on type Date or on "lower" (more derived) types.

Now that we have a handle on what generic types really are, we can go into a little more detail about how they behave.

Parameterized Type Relationships

We know now that parameterized types share a common, raw type. This is why our parameterized List<Date> is just a List at runtime. In fact, we can assign any instantiation of List to the raw type if we want:

```
List list = new ArrayList<Date>( );
```

We can even go the other way and assign a raw type to a specific instantiation of the generic type:

```
List<Date> dates = new ArrayList( ); // unchecked warning
```

This statement generates an unchecked warning on the assignment, but thereafter the compiler trusts you that the list contained only Dates prior to the assignment. It is also permissible, but pointless, to perform a cast in this statement. We'll talk about casting to generic types a bit later.

Whatever the runtime types, the compiler is running the show and does not let us assign things that are clearly incompatible:

```
List<Date> dates = new ArrayList<String>( ); // Compile-time Error!
```

Of course, the ArrayList<String> does not implement the methods of List<Date> conjured by the compiler, so these types are incompatible.

But what about more interesting type relationships? The List interface, for example, is a subtype of the more general Collection interface. Is a particular instantiation of the generic List also assignable to some instantiation of the generic Collection? Does it depend on the type parameters and their relationships? Clearly, a List<Date> is not a Collection<String>. But is a List<Date> a Collection<Date>? What about a List<Date> being a Collection<Object>?

We'll just blurt out the answer first, then walk through it and explain. The rule is that for the simple types of generic instantiations we've discussed so far in this chapter *inheritance applies only to the "base" generic type and not to the parameter types.* Furthermore, assignability applies only when the two generic types are instantiated on *exactly the same parameter type.* In other words, there is still one-dimensional inheritance, following the base generic class type, but with the catch that the parameter types must be identical.

For example, recalling that a List is a type of Collection, we can assign instantiations of List to instantiations of Collection when the type parameter is exactly the same:

```
Collection<Date> cd;
List<Date> ld = new ArrayList<Date>( );
cd = ld; // Ok!
```

This code snippet says that a List<Date> is a Collection<Date>—pretty intuitive. But trying the same logic on a variation in the parameter types fails:

```
List<Object> lo;
List<Date> ld = new ArrayList<Date>( );
lo = ld; // Compile-time Error!  Incompatible types.
```

Although our intuition tells us that the Dates in that List could all live happily as Objects in a List, the assignment is an error. We'll explain precisely why in the next section, but for now just note that the type parameters are not exactly the same and, as we've said, there is no inheritance relationship among the parameter types in generics. This is a case where thinking of the instantiation in terms of types and not in terms of what they do helps. These are not really a "list of dates" and a "list of objects" but more like a DateList and an ObjectList, the relationship of which is not immediately obvious.

Try to pick out what's okay and what's not okay in the following example:

```
Collection<Number> cn;
List<Integer> li = new ArrayList<Integer>( );
cn = li; // Compile-time Error!  Incompatible types.
```

It is possible for an instantiation of List to be an instantiation of Collection, but only if the parameter types are exactly the same. Inheritance doesn't follow the parameter types and this example fails.

One more thing: earlier we mentioned that this rule applies to the simple types of instantiations we've discussed so far in this chapter. What other types are there? Well, the kinds of instantiations we've seen so far where we plug in an actual Java type as a parameter are called *concrete type instantiations*. Later we'll talk about *wildcard instantiations*, which are akin to mathematical set operations on types. We'll see that it's possible to make more exotic instantiations of generics where the type relationships are actually two-dimensional, depending both on the base type and the parameterization. But don't worry, this doesn't come up very often and is not as scary as it sounds.

Why Isn't a List<Date> a List<Object>?

It's a reasonable question. Even with our brains thinking of arbitrary DateList and ObjectList types, we can still ask why they couldn't be assignable. Why shouldn't we be able to assign our List<Date> to a List<Object> and work with the Date elements as Object types?

The reason gets back to the heart of the rationale for generics that we discussed in the introduction: changing APIs. In the simplest case, supposing an ObjectList type extends a DateList type, the DateList would have all of the methods of ObjectList and we could still insert Objects into it. Now, you might object that generics let us change the APIs, so that doesn't apply anymore. That's true, but there is a bigger problem. If we could assign our DateList to an ObjectList variable, we would have to be able to use Object methods to insert elements of types other than Date into it. We could *alias* the DateList as an ObjectList and try to trick it into accepting some other type:

```
DateList dateList = new DateList();
ObjectList objectList = dateList;
objectList.add( new Foo() ); // should be runtime error!
```

We'd expect to get a runtime error when the actual DateList implementation was presented with the wrong type of object. And therein lies the problem. Java generics have no runtime representation. Even if this functionality were useful, there is no way with the current scheme for Java to know what to do at runtime. Another way to look at it is that this feature is simply dangerous because it allows for an error at runtime that couldn't be caught at compile time. In general, we'd like to catch type errors at compile time. By disallowing these assignments, Java can guarantee that your code is typesafe if it compiles with no unchecked warnings.

Actually, that last sentence is not entirely true, but it doesn't have to do with generics; it has to do with arrays. If this all sounds familiar to you, it's because we mentioned it already in relation to Java arrays. Array types have an inheritance relationship that allows this kind of aliasing to occur:

```
Date [] dates = new Date[10];
Object [] objects = dates;
objects[0] = "not a date"; // Runtime ArrayStoreException!
```

However, arrays have runtime representations as different classes and they check themselves at runtime, throwing an ArrayStoreException in just this case. So, in theory, Java code is not guaranteed typesafe by the compiler if you use arrays in this way.

Casts

We've now talked about relationships between generic types and even between generic types and raw types. But we haven't brought up the concept of a cast yet. No cast was necessary when we interchanged generics with their raw types. Instead, we just crossed a line that triggers unchecked warnings from the compiler:

```
List list = new ArrayList<Date>();
List<Date> dl = list; // unchecked warning
```

Normally, we use a cast in Java to work with two types that could be assignable. For example, we could attempt to cast an Object to a Date because it is plausible that the Object is a Date value. The cast then performs the check at runtime to see if we are correct. Casting between unrelated types is a compile-time error. For example, we can't even try to cast an Integer to a String. Those types have no inheritance relationship. What about casts between compatible generic types?

```
Collection<Date> cd = new ArrayList<Date>( );
List<Date> ld = (List<Date>)cd; // Ok!
```

This code snippet shows a valid cast from a more general Collection<Date> to a List<Date>. The cast is plausible here because a Collection<Date> is assignable from and could actually be a List<Date>. Similarly, the following cast catches our mistake where we have aliased a TreeSet<Date> as a Collection<Date> and tried to cast it to a List<Date>:

```
Collection<Date> cd = new TreeSet<Date>( );
List<Date> ld = (List<Date>)cd; // Runtime ClassCastException!
ld.add( new Date() );
```

There is one case where casts are not effective with generics, however, and that is when we are trying to differentiate the types based on their parameter types:

```
Object o = new ArrayList<String>( );
List<Date> ldfo = (List<Date>)o; // unchecked warning, ineffective
Date d = ldfo.get(0); // unsafe at runtime, implicit cast may fail
```

Here, we aliased an ArrayList<String> as a plain Object. Next, we cast it to a List<Date>. Unfortunately, Java does not know the difference between a List<String> and a List<Date> at runtime, so the cast is fruitless. The compiler warns us of this by generating an unchecked warning at the location of the cast; we should be aware that we might find out later when we try to use the cast object that it is incorrect. Casts are ineffective at runtime because of erasure and the lack of type information.

Writing Generic Classes

Now that we have (at least some of) the "end user" view of generics, let's try writing a few classes ourselves. In this section, we'll talk about how type variables are used in the definition of generic classes, where they may appear, and some of their limitations. We'll also talk about subclassing generic types.

The Type Variable

We've already seen the basics of how type variables are used in the declaration of a generic class. One or more type variables are declared in the angle bracket (<>) type declaration and used throughout the body and instance methods of the class. For example:

```
class Mouse { }
class Bear { }

class Trap< T >
{
    T trapped;

    public void snare( T trapped ) { this.trapped = trapped; }
    public T release() { return trapped; }
}
```

```
// usage
Trap<Mouse> mouseTrap = new Trap<Mouse>( );
mouseTrap.snare( new Mouse( ) );
Mouse mouse = mouseTrap.release( );
```

Here, we created a generic Trap class that can hold any type of object. We used the type variable T to declare an instance variable of the parameter type as well as in the argument type and return type of the two methods.

The scope of the type variable is the instance portion of the class, including methods and any instance initializer blocks. The static portion of the class is not affected by the generic parameterization, and type variables are not visible in static methods or static initializers. As you might guess, just as all instantiations of the generic type have only one actual class (the raw type), they have only one, shared, static context as well. You cannot even invoke a static method through a parameterized type. You must use the raw type or an instance of the object.

The type variable can also be used in the type instantiation of other generic types used by the class. For example, if we wanted our Trap to hold more than one animal, we could create a List for them like so:

```
List<T> trappedList = new ArrayList<T>( );
```

Just to cover all the bases, we should mention that instantiations of generic types on the type variable act just like any other type and can serve in all the places that other instantiations of a type can. For example, a method in our class can take a List<T> as an argument:

```
public void trapAll( List<T> list ) { ... }
```

The effective type of the trapAll( ) method in a Trap<Mouse> is then simply:

```
trapAll( List<Mouse> list ) { ... }
```

We should note that this is *not* what we mean by the term "generic method." This is just a regular Java method that happens to take a generic type as an argument. We'll talk about real generic methods, which can infer their types from arguments and assignment contexts later in this chapter. A type variable can also be used to parameterize a generic parent class, as we'll see in the next section.

Subclassing Generics

Generic types can be subclassed just like any other class, by either generic or nongeneric child classes. A nongeneric subclass must extend a particular instantiation of the parent type, filling in the required parameters to make it concrete:

```
class DateList extends ArrayList<Date> { }

DateList dateList = new DateList( );
dateList.add( new Date( ) );
List<Date> ld = dateList;
```

Here, we have created a nongeneric subclass, DateList, of the concrete generic instantiation ArrayList<Date>. The DateList is a type of ArrayList<Date> and inherits the particular instantiation of all of the methods, just as it would from any other parent. We can even assign it back to the parent type if we wish, as shown in this example.

A generic subtype of a generic class may extend either a concrete instantiation of the class, as in the previous example, or it may share a type variable that it "passes up" to the parent upon instantiation:

```
class AdjustableTrap< T > extends Trap< T > {
    public void setSize( int i ) { ... }
}
```

Here, the type variable T used to instantiate the AdjustableTrap class is passed along to instantiate the base class, Trap. When the user instantiates the AdjustableTrap on a particular parameter type, the parent class is instantiated on that type as well.

Exceptions and Generics

Types appear in the body of classes in another place—the throws clauses of methods. Type variables may be used to define the type of exceptions thrown by methods, but to do so we need to introduce the concept of bounds. We cover bounds more in the next section, but in this case, the usage is really simple. We just need to ensure that the type variable we want to use as our exception type is actually a type of Throwable. We can do that by adding an extends clause to the declaration of our type variable, like this:

```
< T extends Throwable >
```

Here is an example class, parameterized on a type that must be a kind of Throwable. Its test() method accepts an instance of that kind of object and throws it as a checked exception:

```
ExceptionTester< T extends Throwable > {
    public void test( T exception ) throws T { throw exception; }
}

try {
    new E<ClassNotFoundException>().test(
        new ClassNotFoundException() );
} catch ( ClassNotFoundException e ) { ... }
```

The addition of the bound imposes the restriction that the parameter type used to instantiate the class, T, must be a type of Throwable. And we referenced the type T in the throws clause. So, an ExceptionTester<ClassNotFoundException> can throw a ClassNotFoundException from its test() method. Note that this is a checked exception and that has not been lost on the compiler. The compiler enforces the checked exception type that it just applied.

No generic Throwables

We saw that a type variable can be used to specify the type of Throwable in the throws clause of a method. Perhaps ironically, however, we cannot use generics to create new types of exceptions. No generic subtypes of Throwable are allowed. If you think about this for a moment, you'll see that to be useful, generic Throwables would require try/catch blocks that can differentiate instantiations of Throwable. And since (once again) there is no runtime representation of generics, this isn't possible with erasure.

Parameter Type Limitations

We have seen the parameter types (type variables) of a generic class used to declare instance variables, method arguments, and return types as well as "passed along" to parameterize a generic superclass. One thing that we haven't talked about is the question of how or whether we can use the type variable of a generic class to construct instances of the parameter type or work with objects of the type in other concrete ways. We deliberately avoided this issue in our previous "exception tester" example by simply passing our exception object in as an argument. Could we have done away with this argument? The answer, unfortunately, is that due to the limitations of erasure, there really is no parameter-type information to work with at runtime. In this section, we'll look at this problem and a workaround.

Since the type variable T has faithfully served as our parameter type everywhere else, you might imagine that we could use it to construct an instance of T using the new keyword. But we can't:

```
T element = new T( ); // Error! Invalid syntax.
```

Remember that all type information is erased in the compiled class. The raw type does not have any way of knowing the type of object you want to construct at runtime. Nor is there any way to get at the Class of the parameter type through the type variable, for the same reason. So reflection won't help us here either. This means that, in general, generics are limited to working with parameter types in relatively hands-off ways (by reference only). This is one reason that generics are more useful for containers than for some other applications. This problem comes up often though and there is a solution, although it's not quite as elegant as we'd like.

Using Class<T>

The only real way to get the type information that we need at runtime is to have the user explicitly pass in a Class reference, generally as one of the arguments to a method. Then we can explicitly refer to the class using reflection and create instances or do whatever else is necessary. This may sound like a really bad solution, without much type safety and placing a big burden on the developer to do the right thing. Fortunately, we can use a trick of generics to enforce this contract with the user and make it safe. The basic idea again is to have one of our methods accept the Class of the parameter type so that we can use it at runtime. Following our "exception tester" example:

```
public void test( Class type ) throws T { ... }
```

This isn't much better than it was before. Specifically, it doesn't guarantee that the Class type passed to the method will match the parameterized type of the class (used in the throws clause here).

Fortunately, Java 5.0 introduced some changes in the Class class. Class is, itself, now a generic type. Specifically, all instances of the Class class created by the Java VM are instantiated with their own type as a parameter. The class of the String type, for example, is now Class<String>, not just some arbitrary instance of the raw Class type that happens to know about strings.

This has two side effects. First, we can specify a particular instantiation of Class using the parameter type in our class. And second, since the Class class is now generic, all of the reflective and instance creation methods can be typed properly and no longer require casts, so we can write our test( ) method like this:

```
public void test( Class<T> type ) throws T {
    throw type.newInstance( );
}
```

The only Class instance that can be passed to our test( ) method now is Class<T>, the Class for the parameter type, T, on which we instantiated ExceptionTester. So, although the user still has the burden of passing in this seemingly extraneous Class argument, at least the compiler will ensure that we do it and do it correctly:

```
ExceptionTester<ArithmeticException> et =
    new ExceptionTester<ArithmeticException>( );

et.test( ArithmeticException.class ); // no other .class will work
```

In this code snippet, attempting to pass any other Class argument to the test( ) method generates a compile-time error.

Bounds

In the process of discussing generics, we've already had to mention bounds a few times. A bound is a constraint on the type of a type parameter. Bounds use the extends keyword and some new syntax to limit the parameter types that may be applied to a generic type. In the case of a generic class, the bounds simply limit the type that may be supplied to instantiate it.

A type variable may extend a class or interface type, meaning that its instantiation must be of that type or a subtype:

```
class EmployeeList< T extends Employee > { ... }
```

Here, we made a generic `EmployeeList` type that can be instantiated only with `Employee` types. We could further require that the `Employee` type implement one or more interfaces using the special & syntax:

```
class EmployeeList< T extends Employee & Ranked & Printable > { ... }
```

The order of the & interface bounds is not significant, but only one class type can be specified and if there is one, it must come first. When a type has no specific bounds, the bound extends `Object` is implicit.

By applying bounds to our type, we not only limit the instantiations of the generic class but we make the type arguments more useful. Now that we know our type must extend some type or implement some set of interfaces, we can use variables and arguments declared with `T` by those other type names. Here is a somewhat contrived extension of our previous example:

```
class EmployeeList< T extends Employee & Ranked & Printable >
{
    Ranked ranking;
    List<Printable> printList = new ArrayList<Printable>();

    public void addEmployee( T employee ) {
        this.ranking = employee;  // T as Ranked
        printList.add( employee );  // T as Printable
    }
}
```

Type variables can also refer to other type variables within the type declaration:

```
class Foo <A, B extends A> { ... }
```

We'll see a particularly vicious example of this later when we talk about the definition of the `Enum` class. We'll also see a more convenient technique for declaring how individual elements of a generic class relate to the parameter type when we cover wildcards in the next section.

Erasure and Bounds (Working with Legacy Code)

We mentioned earlier in our discussion of erasure that the resulting type used in place of the type parameter in the raw type for the generic class is the bound of the type variable. Specifically, we have seen many generics with no explicit bounds that defaulted to a bound of type `Object`. We also showed a quick example of a type that imposed a bound of extends `Date` and said that the type of its methods would be `Date` instead of `Object`. We can now be a little more specific.

The type after erasure used for the parameter type of a generic class is the *leftmost bound*. That is, the first bound specified after extends becomes the type used in the erasure. This implies that if the type extends a class type, it is always the erased type because it must always come first. But if the type extends only interface types, the choice is up to us. This fine point is important for backward compatibility with nongeneric code. Often when creating generic versions of nongeneric APIs, we have the opportunity to "tighten up" the specification a bit. Being aware of the leftmost bound gives us a way to explicitly control the type of the erased class. For example, suppose we create a generic List class that we only want instantiated on Listable objects, but we'd prefer not to change the API of our old List class, which accepted Object type elements. Our initial attempt:

```
class List< E extends Listable > { ... }
```

produces a raw type that accepts only Listable. However, we can insert a somewhat gratuitous additional type, Object, as the leftmost bound in order to get back our old API, without changing the new generic bounds:

```
class List< E extends Object & Listable > { ... }
```

Inserting Object doesn't change the actual bounds of the generic class but does change the erased signature.

Wildcards

We mentioned earlier that the kinds of generic type instantiations discussed so far in this chapter have all been concrete type instantiations. We described this as meaning that all of the parameter arguments are real Java types. For example, List<String> and List<Date> are instantiations of the generic List class with the concrete types String and Date. Now we're going to look at another kind of generic type instantiation: *wildcard instantiation*.

As we'll see in this section, wildcards are Java's way of introducing polymorphism into the type parameter portion of the generic equation. A wildcard instantiation uses a question mark (?) in place of an actual type parameter at instantiation time and denotes that the type can be assigned any of a range of possible instantiations of the generic type. The ? wildcard by itself is called the *unbounded wildcard* and denotes that any type instantiation is acceptable (assignable to the type).

```
List<?> anyInstantiationOfList = new ArrayList<Date>( );
anyInstantiationOfList = new ArrayList<String>( ); // another instantiation
```

In this snippet, we declared a variable anyInstantiationOfList whose type is the unbounded wildcard instantiation of the generic List type. (What a mouthful.) This means that the type we instantiated can be assigned any particular concrete instantiation of the List type, whether Dates, Strings, or Foos. Here, we assigned it a List<Date> first and, subsequently, a List<String>.

A Supertype of All Instantiations

The unbounded wildcard instantiation is a kind of supertype of all of these concrete instantiations. In contrast to the generic type relationships that we saw earlier, which followed only raw, "base" generic types, wildcards let us implement polymorphism on the parameter types. The unbounded wildcard is to generic type parameters what the Object type is to regular Java types: a supertype of everything.

```
// A List<Object> is not a List<Date>!
List<Object> objectList = new ArrayList<Date>() // Error!

// A List<?> can be a List<Date>
List<?> anyList = new ArrayList<Date>(); // Yes!
```

We are reminded in this example that List<Object> is not a List<Date>; polymorphism doesn't flow that way with generic instantiations of concrete types. But List<?>, the unbounded wildcard instantiation, can be assigned any instantiation of List. As we go on, we'll see that wildcards add a new dimension to the assignability of generic types.

Bounded Wildcards

A *bounded wildcard* is a wildcard that uses the extends keyword just as a type variable would, to limit the range of assignable types. For example:

```
List<? extends Date> dateInstantiations = new ArrayList<Date>();
dateInstantiations = new ArrayList<MyDate>(); // another instantiation
```

Our dateInstantiations variable is limited to holding instantiations of List on parameter types of Date and its subclasses. So, we can assign it a List<Date> or a List<MyDate>. In the same way that the unbounded wildcard serves as a superclass for all instantiations of a generic type, bounded wildcards create more limited supertypes covering a narrower range of instantiations. In this case, our wildcard instantiation, List<? extends Date>, is the supertype of all instantiations of List on Date types. As with type parameter bounds, the bound Date is called the upper bound of the type.

Wildcard bounds may extend interfaces as well as use the & syntax to add interface requirements to the bound:

```
Trap< ? extends Catchable & Releaseable > trap;
```

In this case, the instantiation serves as a supertype of the set of instantiations on types implementing both the Catchable and Releaseable interfaces.

Thinking Outside the Container

Let's be clear about what the wildcard means in the context of a container type such as List. The unbounded wildcard instantiation may be assigned any type instantiation, but it does ultimately refer to *some particular type instantiation*. A wildcard instantiation serves as the type of a variable, and that variable eventually holds some actual concrete instantiation of the generic type:

```
List<?> someInstantiationOfList;
someInstantiationOfList = new ArrayList<Date>();
someInstantiationOfList = new ArrayList<String>();
```

In this example, our List<?> variable is either a List<String> or a List<Date>. It is *not* some new kind of List that can hold either String or Date elements.

In the same way, a wildcard with bounds ultimately holds one of the concrete instantiations assignable to its bounds. Imagine for a moment that we have a private class Foo with only one subclass Bar and no others. The expression Collection<? extends Foo> in this case means the set of two possibilities: either Collection<Foo> or Collection<Bar>. That is, either a Collection of elements with a common supertype of Foo or a collection of elements with a common supertype of Bar. Again, the wildcard instantiation matches either of those generic type instantiations. It does *not* create a new type of collection that can contain either Foos or Bars. (That is actually the job of Collection<Foo>, which can contain both Foo and Bar elements.)

For this reason, wildcard type instantiations are valid types for referencing an object, but they cannot be used as the type to create an instance of an object. In general, you cannot use a wildcard type with the new keyword to allocate an object instance because the wildcard denotes one or a possible set of objects. It doesn't make sense.

Lower Bounds

We saw the extends construct used to specify an upper bound for both type variables and wildcard instantiations. It implies a type that is "at the top" of the object hierarchy for the bound. Wildcard instantiations actually allow another type of bound called a *lower bound* as well. A lower bound is specified with the keyword super and, as you might guess, requires that instantiations be of a certain type or any of its supertypes, up to Object. For example:

```
List< ? super MyDate > listOfAssignableFromMyDate;
listOfAssignableFromMyDate = new ArrayList<MyDate>( );
listOfAssignableFromMyDate = new ArrayList<Date>( );
listOfAssignableFromMyDate = new ArrayList<Object>( );
```

This wildcard instantiation creates a type that can hold any instantiation of List on the type MyDate or any of its supertypes. In our example world, that means the wildcard type can be assigned one of only three types: List<MyDate>, List<Date>, or List<Object>. Here, we have cut off the object inheritance hierarchy after three generations. No further subclasses of MyDate can be used.

As we hinted in the example, it may help to read ? super MyDate as "Assignable from MyDate." Lower bounds are useful for cases where we want to be sure that a particular container instantiation can hold a particular element type, without limiting it to just the specific type of the element. We'll show a good example of this when we talk about generic methods later. For now, just try to digest this as complementary to upper bounds.

One last thing about lower bounds: only the wildcard instantiation syntax can use the super keyword to refer to lower bounds. Bounds of type variables in generic class declarations cannot have lower bounds. Erasure replaces all references to the type variables with their upper bounds, so runtime types have no way to enforce the contract.

Reading, Writing, and Arithmetic

We've glossed over an important issue so far in our discussion of wildcard types: namely, how can we use them? What kinds of types does the compiler enforce for variables and arguments which referred to the type variables in the generic class? For example, if we have a List<?> list of any instantiation type, what are the rules about putting objects into it and getting them back out? What is their type?

We have to take the two cases separately. Drawing on the analogy of a container, we'll call getting a return value from a method on an object as a specific type *reading the object as a type*. Conversely, we'll call passing arguments of a specific type to methods of the object *writing the object as a type*. So, for example, a List<Date> can be read and written as the Date type and a Trap<Mouse> has methods that can be read and written as the Mouse type.

To be more precise, though, we should say that List<Date> can be read as the Date type but can be written as any subtype of Date. After all, we could add a MyDate to a List<Date>. Let's look now at the wildcard instantiation List< ? extends Date >. We know it holds an instantiation of the List type on some type of Date. What more can we say about the elements of such a List, which could hold *any* instantiation of the Date type? Well, the elements will always be subtypes of Date. This means that, at a minimum, we should be able to read the object through our wildcard type as type Date:

```
List< ? extends Date > someDateList = new ArrayList<MyDate>( );
...
Date date = someDateList.get( 0 ); // read as Date
```

The compiler lets us assign the value directly to a Date because it knows that whatever the instantiation of the List, the elements must be a subtype of Date. (Of course, we could have read the object as type Object or any supertype of Date if we'd wanted as well.)

But what about going the other way and writing? If someDatelist could be an instantiation of List on any subclass of Date, how can we know what type of objects to write to it? (How can we safely call its add( ) method?) The answer is that we can't. Since we don't know the correct type, the compiler won't let us write anything to the List through our wildcard instantiation of the type:

```
List< ? extends Date > someDateList = new ArrayList<MyDate>( );
someDatelist.add( new Date() ); // Compile-time Error!
someDatelist.add( new MyDate() ); // Compile-time Error!
```

Another way to put this is that since our wildcard instantiation has an upper bound of Date, we can read the type as Date. We'll reiterate that in the form of a rule in a moment.

Recall that an unbounded wildcard is really just a wildcard with a bound of type Object <? extends Object>. Obviously, even an unbounded wildcard instantiation holds objects that can be assigned to Object, so it's okay to read an unbounded wildcard as the Object type:

```
List<?> someList = new ArrayList<String>();
...
Object object = someList.get( 0 ); // read as Object
```

But, of course, we cannot know the actual type of the elements, so we cannot write to the list through our unbounded wildcard type.

What about lower bounds? Well, the situation is neatly reversed with respect to reading and writing. Since we know that the elements of any instantiation matching our lower bounded wildcard must be a supertype of the lower bound, we can write to the object as the lower bound type through our wildcard:

```
List< ? super MyDate > listAssignableMyDate = new ArrayList<Date>();
listAssignableMyDate.add( new MyDate() );
listAssignableMyDate.add( new Date() ); // Compile-time Error!
```

But not knowing what supertype of MyDate the elements are, we cannot read the list as any specific type. Of course, the List must still hold some type of Object, so we can always read the lower bounded list as type Object through the wildcard. The type Object is the default upper bound:

```
Object obj = listAssignableMyDate.get( 0 ); // read as Object
```

Whew. Well, having gone through that explanation, we can now sum it up concisely in an easy-to-remember rule:

> Wildcard instantiations of generic types can be read as their upper bound and written as their lower bound.

To elaborate: all wildcard instantiations have an upper bound of Object even if none other is specified, so all wildcard instantiations can at least be read as type Object. But not all wildcards have a lower bound. Only those using the super construct have a lower bound and so only those wildcard instantiations can be written as a type more specific than Object.

<?>, <Object>, and the Raw Type

We've covered a lot of ground and the semantics can be a bit hard to follow. Let's exercise our knowledge by reviewing a few cases that may or may not have similarities.

Natural questions to ask are, What good is the unbounded wildcard anyway? Why not just use the raw type? How do unbounded wildcard instantiation and raw types compare? The first difference is that the compiler will issue unchecked warnings when we use methods of the raw type. But that's superficial. Why is the compiler warning us? It's because it cannot stop us from abusing our raw type by foisting the wrong type of objects on it. Using an unbounded wildcard is like putting on boxing gloves and saying that we want to play by the rules. Doing so comes at a cost. The compiler guarantees that we are safe by allowing us only the operations that it knows are safe, namely, reading as type Object (the upper bound of everything). The compiler does not let us write to an unbounded wildcard at all. So why use the unbounded wildcard? To play by the rules of generics and guarantee that we don't do anything unsafe.

Next, we can knock down any notion that an unbounded wildcard instantiation is similar to an instantiation on the type Object. Remember that a List<?> holds *some* instantiation of List. It could be a List<Date> for all we know. But a List<Object> is actually a list that holds concrete Object types. The List<Object> can be read and written as Object. The List<?> can only be read (not written) and only read as Object in a degenerate sense. The elements of List<?> are actually all of some unknown type. The elements of the unknown type list all have a common supertype that could be Object but could be some other common type more restrictive than Object. The knowledge of what "could be" in the List<?> doesn't do much for us in practice but means something completely different from List<Object>.

Finally, let's round out the comparisons by asking how List<Object> and the raw type compare. Now we're onto something. In fact, the raw type after erasure *is* effectively List<Object> as you'll recall. But in this case, we're telling the compiler that that is okay. Here, we are asking for a type with elements that can hold any type safely and the compiler obliges. The answer to the question of how List<Object> and the raw type List compare is that List<Object> is the "generic safe" version of the raw type of yesterday.

Wildcard Type Relationships

Before we leave our wild discussion of wildcard types, let's return one more time to the notion of wildcard type instantiations as types in the Java type system. Earlier in this chapter, we described how regular concrete instantiations of generic types are related by virtue of their "base" generic type inheritance, only with the proviso that their type parameters are exactly the same. Later, we tried to instill the idea that wildcard instantiations add an inheritance relationship to the type parameters, the other half of the generic instantiation. Now, we'll bring the two together. Things can get arcane pretty quickly, but the simple cases are easy to swallow.

The question is, If we have two different wildcard instantiations of a type or related types, how, if at all, are they related? For example, since an unbounded wildcard instantiation can hold any instantiation, can it be assigned a value with a more restrictive bound?

```
List< ? extends Date > dateLists = ...;
List< ? >  anylists;
anyLists = dateLists; // Ok!
```

The answer is yes. For purposes of assignability, wildcard instantiations can be considered as types with possible supertype or subtype relationships determined by their bounds. Let's spell out the unbounded wildcard instantiation as it really is, an instantiation with an upper bound of Object:

```
List< ? extends Date > dateLists = ...;
List< ? extends Object >  objectLists;
objectLists = dateLists; // Ok!
```

The rule is that if the "base" generic, raw type is assignable and the bounds of the wildcard instantiation are also assignable, the overall types are assignable. Let's look at another example:

```
List< ? extends Integer > intLists = ...;
Collection< ? extends Number > numCollections;
numCollections = intLists; // Ok!
```

What this effectively says is that some List of Integer types can be treated as some Collection of Number types through the wildcard instantiation. If you think about it, you'll see that there is no conflict here. A List is certainly a Collection. And all we're doing is widening the type by which we can read the elements from Integer to Number. In neither case could we have written to the collection via the wildcard instantiation anyway.

What all this ultimately means is that with the introduction of wildcard instantiations, the type relationships of Java generic classes becomes two-dimensional. There is the raw type relationship to consider and then the wildcard parameter relationship. In fact, if you consider that generic classes may have more than one type parameter, the relationships can get even more complicated (N-dimensional). Fortunately, none of this comes up very often in the real world.

Generic Methods

Thus far in this chapter, we've talked about generic types and the implementation of generic classes. Now, we're going to look at a different kind of generic animal: *generic methods*. Generic methods essentially do for individual methods what type parameters do for generic classes. But as we'll see, generic methods are smarter and can figure out their parameter types from their usage context, without having to be explicitly parameterized. (In reality, of course, it is the compiler that does this.) Generic methods can appear in any class (not just generic classes) and are very useful for a wide variety of applications.

First, let's quickly review the way that we've seen regular methods interact with generic types. We've seen that generic classes can contain methods that use type variables in their arguments and return types in order to adapt themselves to the parameterization of the class. We've also mentioned that generic types themselves can be used in most of the places that any other type can be used. So methods of generic or nongeneric classes can use generic types as argument and return types as well. Here are examples of those usages:

```
// Not generic methods

class GenericClass< T > {
    // method using generic class parameter type
    public void T cache( T entry ) { ... }
}
class RegularClass {
    // method using concrete generic type
    public List<Date> sortDates( List<Date> dates ) { ... }
    // method using wildcard generic type
    public List<?> reverse( List<?> dates ) { ... }
}
```

The cache( ) method in GenericClass accepts an argument of the parameter type T and also returns a value of type T. The sortDates( ) method, which appears in the nongeneric example class, works with a concrete generic type, and the reverse( ) method works with a wildcard instantiation of a generic type. These are examples of methods that work with generics, but they are not true generic methods.

Generic Methods Introduced

Like generic classes, generic methods have a parameter type declaration using the <> syntax. This syntax appears before the return type of the method:

```
// generic method
<T> T cache( T entry ) { ... }
```

This cache( ) method looks very much like our earlier example, except that it has its own parameter type declaration that defines the type variable T. This method is a generic method and can appear in either a generic or nongeneric class. The scope of T is limited to the method cache( ) and hides any definition of T in any enclosing generic class. As with generic classes, the type T can have bounds:

```
<T extends Entry & Cacheable > T cache( T entry ) { ... }
```

Unlike a generic class, it does not have to be instantiated with a specific parameter type for T before it is used. Instead, it infers the parameter type T from the type of its argument, entry. For example:

```
BlogEntry newBlogEntry = ...;
NewspaperEntry newNewspaperEntry = ...;

BlogEntry oldEntry = cache( newBlogEntry );
NewspaperEntry old = cache( newNewspaperEntry );
```

Here, our generic method cache( ) inferred the type BlogEntry (which we'll presume for the sake of the example is a type of Entry and Cacheable). BlogEntry became the type T of the return type and may have been used elsewhere internally by the method. In the next case, the cache( ) method was used on a different type of Entry and was able to return the new type in exactly the same way. That's what's powerful about generic methods: the ability to infer a parameter type from their usage context. We'll go into detail about that next.

Another difference with generic class components is that generic methods may be static:

```java
class MathUtils {
    public static <T extends Number> T max( T x, T y ) { ... }
}
```

Constructors for classes are essentially methods, too, and follow the same rules as generic methods, minus the return type.

Type Inference from Arguments

In the previous section, we saw a method infer its type from an argument:

```java
<T> T cache( T entry ) { ... }
```

But what if there is more than one argument? We saw just that situation in our last snippet, the static generic method max(x, y). All looks well when we give it two identical types:

```java
Integer max = MathUtils.max( new Integer(1), new Integer( 2 ) ) ;
```

But what does it make of the arguments in this invocation?

```java
MathUtils.max( new Integer(1), new Float( 2 ) ) ;
```

In this case, the Java compiler does something really smart. It climbs up the argument type parent classes, looking for the *nearest common supertype*. Java also identifies the *nearest common interfaces* implemented by both of the types. It identifies that both the Integer and the Float types are subtypes of the Number type. It also recognizes that each of these implements (a certain generic instantiation of) the Comparable interface. Java then effectively makes this combination of types the parameter type of T for this method invocation. The resulting type is, to use the syntax of bounds, Number & Comparable. What this means to us is that the result type T is assignable to anything matching that particular combination of types.

```java
Number max = MathUtils.max( new Integer(1), new Float( 2 ) );
Comparable max = MathUtils.max( new Integer(1), new Float( 2 ) );
```

In English, this statement says that we can work with our Integer and our Float at the same time only if we think of them as Numbers or Comparables, which makes sense. The return type has become a new type, which is effectively a Number that also implements the Comparable interface.

This same inference logic works with any number of arguments. But to be useful, the arguments really have to share some important common supertype or interface. If they don't have anything in common, the result will be their de facto common ancestor, the `Object` type. For example, the nearest common supertype of a `String` and a `List` is `Object` along with the `Serializeable` interface. There's not much a method could do with a type lacking real bounds anyway.

Type Inference from Assignment Context

We've seen a generic method infer its parameter type from its argument types. But what if the type variable isn't used in any of the arguments or the method has no arguments? Suppose the method only has a parametric return type:

```
<T> T foo() { ... }
```

You might guess that this is an error because the compiler would appear to have no way of determining what type we want. But it's not! The Java compiler is smart enough to look at the context in which the method is called. Specifically, if the result of the method is assigned to a variable, the compiler tries to make the type of that variable the parameter type. Here's an example. We'll make a factory for our `Trap` objects:

```
<T> Trap<T> makeTrap() { return new Trap<T>(); }

// usage
Trap<Mouse> mouseTrap = makeTrap();
Trap<Bear> bearTrap = makeTrap();
```

The compiler has, as if by magic, determined what kind of instantiation of `Trap` we want based on the assignment context.

Before you get too excited about the possibilities, there's not much you can do with a plain type parameter in the body of that method. For example, we can't create instances of any particular concrete type T, so this limits the usefulness of factories. About all we can do is the sort of thing shown here, where we create instances of generics parameterized correctly for the context.

Furthermore, the inference only works on assignment to a variable. Java does not try to guess the parameter type based on the context if the method call is used in other ways, such as to produce an argument to a method or as the value of a return statement from a method. In those cases, the inferred type defaults to type `Object`. (See the section "Explicit Type Invocation" for a solution.)

Explicit Type Invocation

Although it should not be needed often, a syntax does exist for invoking a generic method with specific parameter types. The syntax is a bit awkward and involves a class or instance object prefix, followed by the familiar angle bracket type list, placed before the actual method invocation. Here are some examples:

```
Integer i = MathUtilities.<Integer>max( 42,  42 );
String s = fooObject.<String>foo( "foo" );
String s = this.<String>foo( "foo" );
```

The prefix must be a class or object instance containing the method. One situation where you'd need to use explicit type invocation is if you are calling a generic method that infers its type from the assignment context, but you are not assigning the value to a variable directly. For example, if you wanted to pass the result of our makeTrap( ) method as a parameter to another method, it would otherwise default to Object.

Wildcard Capture

Generic methods can do one more trick for us involving taming wildcard instantiations of generic types. The term *wildcard capture* refers to the fact that generic methods can work with arguments whose type is a wildcard instantiation of a type, just as if the type were known:

```
<T> Set<T> listToSet( List<T> list ) {
    Set<T> set = new HashSet<T>( );
    set.addAll( list );
    return set;
}

// usage
List<?> list = new ArrayList<Date>( );
Set<?> set = listToSet( list );
```

The result of these examples is that we converted an unknown instantiation of List to an unknown instantiation of Set. The type variable T represents the actual type of the argument, list, for purposes of the method body. The wildcard instantiation must match any bounds of the method parameter type. But since we can work with the type variable only through its bounds types, the compiler is free to refer to it by this new name, T, as if it were a known type. That may not seem very interesting, but it is useful because it allows methods that accept wildcard instantiations of types to delegate to other generic methods to do their work.

Another way to look at this is that generic methods are a more powerful alternative to methods using wildcard instantiations of types. We'll do a little comparison next.

Wildcard Types Versus Generic Methods

You'll recall that trying to work with an object through a wildcard instantiation of its generic type limits us to "reading" the object. We cannot "write" types to the object because its parameter type is unknown. In contrast, because generic methods can infer or capture an actual type for their arguments, they allow us to do a lot more with broad ranges of types than we could with wildcard instantiations alone.

For example, suppose we wanted to write a utility method that swaps the first two elements of a list. Using wildcards, we'd like to write something like this:

```
// Bad implementation
List<?> swap( List<?> list ) {
    Object tmp = list.get(0);
    list.set( 0, list.get(1) ); // error, can't write
    list.set( 1, tmp ); // error, can't write
    return list;
}
```

But we are not allowed to call the set( ) method of our list because we don't know what type it actually holds. We are really stuck and there isn't much we can do. But the corresponding generic method gives us a real type to hang our hat on:

```
<T> List<T> swap( List<T> list ) {
    T tmp = list.get( 0 );
    list.set( 0, list.get(1) );
    list.set( 1, tmp );
    return list;
}
```

Here, we are able to declare a variable of the correct (inferred) type and write using the set( ) methods appropriately. It would seem that generic methods are the only way to go here. But there is a third path. Wildcard capture, as described in the previous section, allows us to delegate our wildcard version of the method to our actual generic method and use it as if the type were inferred, even though it's open-ended:

```
List<?> swap( List<?> list ) {
    return swap2( list ); // delegate to generic form
}
```

Here, we renamed the generic version as swap2( ) and delegated.

Arrays of Parameterized Types

There is one place where we haven't yet considered how generic types affect the Java language: array types. After everything we've seen, it would seem natural to expect that arrays of generic types would come along for the ride. But as we'll see, Java has a schizophrenic relationship with arrays of parameterized types.

The first thing we need to do is recall how arrays work for regular Java types. An array is a kind of built-in collection of some base type of element. Furthermore, array types (including all multidimensional variations of the array) are true types in the Java language and are represented at runtime by unique class types. This is where the trouble begins. Although arrays in Java act a lot like generic collections (they change their APIs to adopt a particular type for "reading" and "writing"), they do not behave like Java generics with respect to their type relationships. As we saw in Chapter 6, arrays exist in the Java class hierarchy stemming from Object and extending down parallel branches with the plain Java objects.

Arrays are *covariant subtypes* of other types of arrays, which means that, unlike concrete generic types, although they change their method signatures, they are still related to their parents. This means that Strings [] in Java is a subtype of Object []. This brings up the aliasing problem that we mentioned earlier. An array of Strings can be aliased as an array of Objects and we can attempt to put things into it illegally that won't be noticed until runtime:

```
String [] strings = new String[5];
Object [] objects = strings;
objects[0] = new Date( ); // Runtime ArrayStoreException!
```

To prevent disaster, Java must check every array assignment for the correct type at runtime. But recall that generic types do not have real representations at runtime; there is only the raw type. So Java would have no way to know the difference between a Trap<Mouse> and a Trap<Bear> element in an array once the array was aliased as, say, an Object []. For this reason, Java does not allow you to create arrays of generic types—at least not concrete ones. (More on that later in this chapter.)

Using Array Types

Now, since we just said that Java won't let you make any of these arrays, you'd expect that would be pretty much the end of the story. But no! Even though we don't have real array implementations that perform the needed runtime behavior, Java allows us to declare the array type anyway. The catch is that you have to break type safety to use them by using an array of the raw type as their implementation:

```
Trap<Mouse> [] tma = new Trap[10]; // unchecked warning
Trap<Mouse> tm = new Trap<Mouse>( );
tma[0] = tm;
Trap<Mouse> again = tma[0];
```

Here, we declared an array of a generic type, Trap<Mouse>. Assigning any value (other than null) to the variable tma results in an unchecked warning from the compiler at the point of the assignment.

What we are effectively telling the compiler here is to trust us to make sure that the array contains only the correct generic types and asking it to allow us to use it thereafter as if it were checked. We do not get warnings at each usage as we would with a raw type, only at the point where we assign the array. The catch is that the compiler can't prevent us from abusing the array. The unchecked warning at the point where we assign the array is just a representative warning that reminds us that it's possible to abuse the array later.

What Good Are Arrays of Generic Types?

Why does Java let us even declare arrays of generic types? One important usage is that it allows generic types to be used in variable-length argument methods. For example:

```
void useLists( List<String> ... lists ) {
        List<String> ls0 = lists[0];
}
```

Another answer is that it's an escape hatch to preserve our ability to use arrays when necessary. You might want to do this for at least two reasons. First, arrays are faster than collections in many cases. The Java runtime is very good at optimizing array access and sometimes it just might be worth it to you to eat the compiler warning to get the benefits. Second, there is the issue of interfacing generic code to legacy code in which only the Javadoc and your faith in the developer are your guarantees as to the contents. By assigning raw arrays to generic instantiations, we can at least ensure that in simple usage we don't abuse the types in the new code.

Wildcards in Array Types

In general, wildcard instantiations of generics can be used as the base type for arrays in the same way that concrete instantiations can. Let's look at an example:

```
ArrayList<?>[] arrayOfArrayLists = ...;
```

This type declaration is an array of unbounded wildcard instantiations of ArrayList. Each element of the array can hold an instance of the wildcard type, meaning in this case, that each element of the array could hold a different instantiation of ArrayList. For example:

```
arrayOfArrayLists[0] = new ArrayList<Date>();
arrayOfArrayLists[1] = new ArrayList<String>();
```

There is also a secret surprise we are going to spring on you relating to wildcard types in arrays. Although we said that Java won't let us create arrays of generic types, there is an exception to the rule. Java does allow us to create arrays of unbounded wildcard instantiations. Here are two examples:

```
ArrayList<?>[] arrayOfArrayLists = new ArrayList<?>[10];
arrayOfArrayLists[0] = new ArrayList<Date>();

Trap<?> [] arrayOfTraps = new Trap<?>[10];
arrayOfTraps[0] = new Trap<Mouse>();
```

Here, we not only declared two arrays of wildcard instantiations, but we allocated the arrays as well! The trick is that the arrays must be of the unbounded wildcard type. Why does this work? Because each element in the unbounded wildcard instantiation of the array can hold any instantiation, no runtime check of the generic portion of the type is necessary at runtime. Any instantiation of `ArrayList` is assignable to the element of type `ArrayList<?>`, so only the check of the raw type is required.

The term *reifiable type* is used to refer to any type that is unchanged by erasure. This includes plain Java concrete types, primitives, and unbounded wildcard instantiations. Reifiable types are kind of like the real people in *The Matrix:* they still exist when unplugged from the simulation.

Case Study: The Enum Class

If you take a look at the definition of the `java.lang.Enum` class in Java 5.0, you'll see a rather bizarre-looking generic type declaration:

```
Enum< E extends Enum<E> > { ... }
```

In trying to parse this, you may be hampered by two thoughts, which we'll try to dispel right away. First, upon quick inspection this may appear to be recursive. The type variable E seems to be defined as something that's not yet finished being defined. But it's not really. We often have mathematical equations of the form x = function(x) and they are not recursive. What they really call out for is a special value of x that satisfies the condition. Next, although it's pretty clear that E is a subtype of some formulation of the generic Enum type, you may jump to the conclusion that E itself must be a generic type. Remember that concrete types can extend generics just as well as generics can.

With these thoughts in mind, let's hunt for some arrangement that satisfies these bounds. Let's focus only on the bound for a moment:

```
E extends Enum<E>
```

E is a subclass of some parameterization of Enum and, in particular, the parameterization of Enum is on the subclass type itself. To say this again, what it does is to require that any invocations of the Enum type are by subclasses of some parameterization of the Enum type. And specifically, the parameterizations of the Enum type supply their own type as the type parameter to their parent, Enum. What kind of class satisfies this condition?

```
class Foo extends Enum<Foo> { }
```

This Foo class does. The declaration of Foo, in fact, reads just as the bound does. Foo is a plain concrete type that extends Enum parameterized by its own type.*

What does this accomplish exactly? The first implication of this arrangement is that Enum can be instantiated only by subclasses of itself. Next, we have the condition that the Enum must be instantiated with the child type as its parameter type. This means

---

* In real life, Java doesn't let us extend the Enum type; that's reserved for the enum keyword and the compiler. But the structure is as shown.

that any methods of the parent Enum class that refer to the type variable E will now refer to the *child* type. This peculiar bound has guaranteed that child types customize their parent with their own type. In fact, this is exactly what the Enum class in Java needs to make enums work. The compareTo( ) method of a Java enum refers to the type variable and is intended to be applicable only to other instances of the specific child enum type:

```
public int compareTo( E e ) { ... }
```

For example, a Dog enum type should be able to compare only types of Dog and comparing a Dog with a Cat should produce a compile-time error. The bound accomplishes just that by adapting the compareTo( ) method to the Dog type:

```
class Dog extends Enum<Dog> { ... }
```

Normally, a nonfinal base class, having no way to know what children it may have in the future, could only refer to its own type as a general supertype for all of the children when it wants to work with others of its own kind. Methods of a nongeneric Enum class could only supply methods that work on any Enum. But through the magic of generics, we can effectively change the API of the class based on how it is invoked with parameters. In this case, we arranged that all subclasses must supply themselves as the parameter for the base class, tailoring its methods to themselves and pushing the base type down a generation.

Case Study: The sort( ) Method

Poking around in the java.util.Collections class we find all kinds of static utility methods for working with collections. Among them is this goody—the static generic method sort( ):

```
<T extends Comparable<? super T>> void sort( List<T> list ) { ... }
```

Another nut for us to crack. Let's focus on the last part of the bound:

```
Comparable<? super T>
```

This is a wildcard instantiation of the Comparable interface, so we can read the extends as implements, if it helps. Comparable holds a compareTo( ) method for some parameter type. A Comparable<String> means that the compareTo( ) method takes type String. Therefore, Comparable<? super T> is the set of instantiations of Comparable on T and all of its superclasses. A Comparable<T> suffices and, at the other end, so does a Comparable<Object>. What this means in English is that the elements must be comparable to their own type or some supertype of their own type. This is sufficient to ensure that the elements can all be compared to one another, but not as restrictive as saying that they must all implement the compareTo( ) method themselves. Some of the elements may inherit the Comparable interface from a parent class that knows how to compare only to a supertype of T and that is exactly what is allowed here.

Conclusion

Java generics are a very powerful and useful addition to the language. Although some of the details we delved into later in this chapter may seem daunting, the common usage is very simple and compelling: generics make collections better. As you begin to write more code using generics you will find that your code becomes more readable and more understandable. Generics make explicit what previously had to be inferred from usage. They complete the promise of type safety in the Java language and make Java a better language, despite their idiosyncrasies.

## CHAPTER 9

Threads

At the heart of designing computer systems and software lies the problem of managing time. We take for granted that modern computer systems such as desktop computers can manage many applications running concurrently and produce the effect that the software is running simultaneously. Of course we know that, for the most part, our single processor computers can do only one thing at a time. The magic is performed by sleight of hand in the operating system (OS), which juggles applications and turns its attention from one to the next so quickly that they appear to run at once.

In the old days, the unit of concurrency for such systems was the application or *process*. To the OS, a process was more or less a black box that decided what do to on its own. If an application required greater concurrency, it could get it only by running multiple processes and communicating between them, but this was a heavyweight approach and not very elegant. Later, the concept of *threads* was introduced. Threads provide fine-grained concurrency within a process, under the application's own control. Threads have existed for a long time but have historically been tricky to use. In Java, support for threading is built into the language, making it easier to work with threads. In Java 5.0, a whole new set of utilities was introduced that address common patterns and practices in multithreaded applications and raise them to the level of tangible Java APIs. Collectively, this means that Java is a language that supports threading both natively and at a high level. It also means that Java's APIs take full advantage of threading, so it's important that you become familiar with these concepts early in your exploration of Java.

Threads are integral to the design of many Java APIs, especially those involved in client-side applications, graphics, and sound. For example, when we look at GUI programming later in this book, you'll see that a component's paint( ) method isn't called directly by the application but rather by a separate drawing thread within the Java runtime system. At any given time, many such background threads may be performing activities in parallel with your application. On the server side, writing code that does explicit thread handling is less common and actively discouraged in the context of application servers and web applications. In those scenarios, the server environment should control the allocation of time. However, Java threads are there, servicing every request and running your application components. It's important to understand how your code fits into that environment.

In this chapter, we'll talk about writing applications that create and use their own threads explicitly. We'll talk about the low-level thread support built into the Java language first and then discuss the new Java 5.0 java.util.concurrent thread utilities package in detail at the end of this chapter. Laying a foundation in Java threads will help you better understand the functionality that has been added in Java 5.0.

Introducing Threads

Conceptually, a *thread* is a flow of control within a program. A thread is similar to the more familiar notion of a process, except that threads within the same application are much more closely related and share much of the same state. It's kind of like a golf course, which many golfers use at the same time. The threads may cooperate to share a working area. They have access to the same objects including static and instance variables within their application. However, threads have their own copies of local variables, just as players share the golf course, but not personal things like clubs and balls.

Multiple threads in an application have the same problems as the golfers—in a word, synchronization. Just as you can't have two sets of players blindly playing the same green at the same time, you can't have several threads trying to access the same variables without some kind of coordination. Someone is bound to get hurt. A thread can reserve the right to use an object until it's finished with its task, just as a golf party gets exclusive rights to the green until it's done. And a thread that is more important can raise its priority, asserting its right to play through.

The devil is in the details, of course, and those details have historically made threads difficult to use. Fortunately, Java makes creating, controlling, and coordinating threads simpler by integrating some of these concepts directly into the language.

It is common to stumble over threads when you first work with them because creating a thread exercises many of your new Java skills all at once. You can avoid confusion by remembering that two players are always involved in running a thread: a Java language Thread object that represents the thread itself and an arbitrary target object that contains the method the thread is to execute. Later, you will see that it is possible to play some sleight of hand and combine these two roles, but that special case just changes the packaging, not the relationship.

The Thread Class and the Runnable Interface

All execution in Java is associated with a Thread object, beginning with a "main" thread that is started by the Java VM to launch your application. A new thread is born when we create an instance of the java.lang.Thread class. The Thread object represents a real thread in the Java interpreter and serves as a handle for controlling and coordinating its execution. With it, we can start the thread, wait for it to complete, cause it to sleep for a time, or interrupt its activity. The constructor for the Thread class accepts information about where the thread should begin its execution. Conceptually, we would like to simply tell it what method to run, but since there are no pointers to methods in Java (not in this sense anyway), we can't specify one directly. Instead, we have to take a short detour and use the java.lang.Runnable interface to create an object that contains a "runnable" method. Runnable defines a single, general-purpose method:

```
public interface Runnable {
    abstract public void run();
}
```

Every thread begins its life by executing the run() method in a Runnable object, the "target object" that was passed to the thread's constructor. The run() method can contain any code, but it must be public, take no arguments, have no return value, and throw no checked exceptions.

Any class that contains an appropriate run() method can declare that it implements the Runnable interface. An instance of this class is then a runnable object that can serve as the target of a new thread. If you don't want to put the run() method directly in your object (and very often you don't), you can always make an adapter class that serves as the Runnable for you. The adapter's run() method can then call any method it wants after the thread is started. We'll show examples of these options later.

Creating and starting threads

A newly born thread remains idle until we give it a figurative slap on the bottom by calling its start() method. The thread then wakes up and proceeds to execute the run() method of its target object. start() can be called only once in the lifetime of a thread. Once a thread starts, it continues running until the target object's run() method returns (or throws an unchecked exception of some kind). The start() method has a sort of evil twin method called stop(), which kills the thread permanently. However, this method is deprecated and should no longer be used. We'll explain why and give some examples of a better way to stop your threads later in this chapter. We will also look at some other methods you can use to control a thread's progress while it is running.

Let's look at an example. The following class, Animation, implements a run() method to drive its drawing loop:

```
class Animation implements Runnable {
    boolean animate = true;
```

```
    public void run( ) {
        while ( animate ) {
            // draw Frames
            ...
        }
    }
}
```

To use it, we create a Thread object, passing it an instance of Animation as its target object, and invoke its start( ) method. We can perform these steps explicitly:

```
Animation happy = new Animation("Mr. Happy");
Thread myThread = new Thread( happy );
myThread.start( );
```

We have created an instance of our Animation class and passed it as the argument to the constructor for myThread. When we call the start( ) method, myThread begins to execute Animation's run( ) method. Let the show begin!

This situation is not terribly object-oriented. More often, we want an object to handle its own threads, as shown in Figure 9-1, which depicts a Runnable object that creates and starts its own thread. We'll show our Animation class performing these actions in its constructor, although in practice it might be better to place them in a more explicit controller method (e.g., startAnimation( )):

```
class Animation implements Runnable {
    Thread myThread;
    Animation (String name) {
        myThread = new Thread( this );
        myThread.start( );
    }
    ...
}
```

Figure 9-1. Interaction between Animation and its thread

In this case, the argument we pass to the Thread constructor is this, the current object (which is a Runnable). We keep the Thread reference in the instance variable myThread in case we want to interrupt the show or exercise some other kind of control later.

A natural-born thread

The Runnable interface lets us make an arbitrary object the target of a thread, as we did in the previous example. This is the most important general usage of the Thread class. In most situations in which you need to use threads, you'll create a class (possibly a simple adapter class) that implements the Runnable interface.

However, we'd be remiss not to show you the other technique for creating a thread. Another design option is to make our target class a subclass of a type that is already runnable. As it turns out, the Thread class itself conveniently implements the Runnable interface; it has its own run( ) method, which we can override directly to do our bidding:

```
class Animation extends Thread {
    boolean animate = true;

    public void run( ) {
        while ( animate ) {
            // draw Frames
            ...
        }
    }
}
```

The skeleton of our Animation class looks much the same as before, except that our class is now a subclass of Thread. To go along with this scheme, the default constructor of the Thread class makes itself the default target. That is, by default, the Thread executes its own run( ) method when we call the start( ) method, as shown in Figure 9-2. Now our subclass can just override the run( ) method in the Thread class. (Thread itself defines an empty run( ) method.)

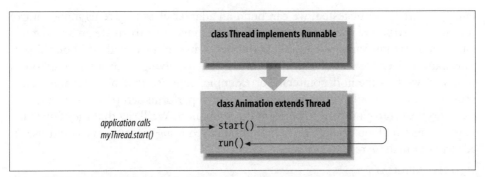

Figure 9-2. Animation as a subclass of Thread

Next, we create an instance of Animation and call its start( ) method (which it also inherited from Thread):

```
Animation bouncy = new Animation("Bouncy");
bouncy.start( );
```

Alternatively, we can have the Animation object start its thread when it is created, as before:

```
class Animation extends Thread {

    Animation (String name) {
        start( );
    }
    ...
}
```

Here, our Animation object just calls its own start( ) method when an instance is created. (It's probably better form to start and stop our objects explicitly after they're created rather than starting threads as a hidden side effect of object creation, but this serves the example well.)

Subclassing Thread may seem like a convenient way to bundle a thread and its target run( ) method. However, this approach often isn't the best design. If you subclass Thread to implement a thread, you are saying you need a new type of object that is a kind of Thread, which exposes all of the public API of the Thread class. While there is something satisfying about taking an object that's primarily concerned with performing a task and making it a Thread, the actual situations where you'll want to create a subclass of Thread should not be very common. In most cases, it is more natural to let the requirements of your program dictate the class structure and use Runnables to connect the execution and logic of your program. If you find you're subclassing Thread a lot, you may want to examine whether you are falling into the design trap of making objects that are really glorified functions.

Using an adapter

Finally, as we have suggested, we can build an adapter class to give us more control over how to structure the code. It is particularly convenient to create an anonymous inner class that implements Runnable and invokes an arbitrary method in our object. This almost gives the feel of starting a thread and specifying an arbitrary method to run, as if we had method pointers. For example, suppose that our Animation class provides a method called startAnimating( ), which performs setup (loads the images, etc.) and then starts a thread to perform the animation. We'll say that the actual guts of the animation loop are in a private method called drawFrames( ). We could use an adapter to run drawFrames( ) for us:

```
class Animation {

    public void startAnimating() {
        // do setup, load images, etc.
        ...
        // start a drawing thread
        Thread myThread = new Thread ( new Runnable() {
            public void run(  ) { drawFrames(); }
```

```
      } );
      myThread.start();
  }

  private void drawFrames() {
      // do animation ...
  }
}
```

In this code, the anonymous inner class implementing Runnable is generated for us by the compiler. We create a thread with this anonymous object as its target and have its run( ) method call our drawFrames( ) method. We have avoided implementing a generic run( ) method in our application code at the expense of generating an extra class.

Note that we could be even more terse in the previous example by simply having our anonymous inner class extend Thread rather than implement Runnable. We could also start the thread without saving a reference to it if we won't be using it later:

```
new Thread( ) {
    public void run( ) { drawFrames( ); }
}.start( );
```

Controlling Threads

We have seen the start( ) method used to bring a newly created thread to life. Several other instance methods let us explicitly control a thread's execution:

- The static Thread.sleep( ) method causes the currently executing thread to wait for a designated period of time, without consuming much (or possibly any) CPU time.
- The methods wait( ) and join( ) coordinate the execution of two or more threads. We'll discuss them in detail when we talk about thread synchronization later in this chapter.
- The interrupt( ) method wakes up a thread that is sleeping in a sleep( ) or wait( ) operation or is otherwise blocked on a long I/O operation.*

Deprecated methods

We should also mention three deprecated thread control methods: stop( ), suspend( ), and resume( ). The stop( ) method complements start( ); it destroys the thread. start( ) and the deprecated stop( ) method can be called only once in the thread's lifecycle. By contrast, the deprecated suspend( ) and resume( ) methods were used to arbitrarily pause and then restart the execution of a thread.

---

* interrupt( ) does not work in versions of Java prior to 1.1 and, historically, has not worked consistently in all Java implementations.

Although these deprecated methods still exist in the latest version of Java (and will probably be there forever), they shouldn't be used in new code development. The problem with both stop( ) and suspend( ) is that they seize control of a thread's execution in an uncoordinated, harsh way. This makes programming difficult; it's not always easy for an application to anticipate and properly recover from being interrupted at an arbitrary point in its execution. Moreover, when a thread is seized using one of these methods, the Java runtime system must release all its internal locks used for thread synchronization. This can cause unexpected behavior and, in the case of suspend( ), can easily lead to deadlock.

A better way to affect the execution of a thread—which requires just a bit more work on your part—is by creating some simple logic in your thread's code to use monitor variables (flags), possibly in conjunction with the interrupt( ) method, which allows you to wake up a sleeping thread. In other words, you should cause your thread to stop or resume what it is doing by asking it nicely rather than by pulling the rug out from under it unexpectedly. The thread examples in this book use this technique in one way or another.

The sleep( ) method

We often need to tell a thread to sit idle, or "sleep," for a fixed period of time. While a thread is asleep, or otherwise blocked from input of some kind, it doesn't consume CPU time or compete with other threads for processing. For this, we can call the static method Thread.sleep( ), which affects the currently executing thread. The call causes the thread to go idle for a specified number of milliseconds:

```
try {
    // The current thread
    Thread.sleep( 1000 );
} catch ( InterruptedException e ) {
    // someone woke us up prematurely
}
```

The sleep( ) method may throw an InterruptedException if it is interrupted by another thread via the interrupt( ) method. As you see in the previous code, the thread can catch this exception and take the opportunity to perform some action—such as checking a variable to determine whether or not it should exit—or perhaps just perform some housekeeping and then go back to sleep.

The join( ) method

Finally, if you need to coordinate your activities with another thread by waiting for it to complete its task, you can use the join( ) method. Calling a thread's join( ) method causes the caller to block until the target thread completes. Alternatively, you can poll the thread by calling join( ) with a number of milliseconds to wait. This is a very coarse form of thread synchronization. Later in this chapter, we'll look at a much more general and powerful mechanism for coordinating the activities of threads: wait( ), notify( ), and even higher-level APIs in the java.util.concurrent package.

The interrupt( ) method

Earlier we described the interrupt( ) method as a way to wake up a thread that is idle in a sleep( ), wait( ), or lengthy I/O operation. Any thread that is not running continuously (not a "hard loop") must enter one of these states periodically and so this is intended to be a point where the thread can be flagged to stop. When a thread is interrupted, its *interrupt status* flag is set. This can happen at any time, whether the thread is idle or not. The thread can test this status with the isInterrupted( ) method. isInterrupted(boolean), another form, accepts a Boolean value indicating whether or not to clear the interrupt status. In this way, a thread can use the interrupt status as a flag and a signal.

This is indeed the prescribed functionality of the method. However, historically, this has been a weak spot, and Java implementations have had trouble getting it to work correctly in all cases. In early Java VMs (prior to Version 1.1), interrupt did not work at all. More recent versions still have problems with interrupting I/O calls. By an I/O call, we mean when an application is blocked in a read( ) or write( ) method, moving bytes to or from a source such as a file or the network. In this case, Java is supposed to throw an InterruptedIOException when the interrupt( ) is performed. However, this has never been reliable across all Java implementations. To address this in Java 1.4, a new I/O framework (java.nio) was introduced with one of its goals being to specifically address these problems. When the thread associated with an NIO operation is interrupted, the thread wakes up and the I/O stream (called a "channel") is automatically closed. (See Chapter 12 for more about the NIO package.)

Death of a Thread

A thread continues to execute until one of the following happens:

- It explicitly returns from its target run( ) method.
- It encounters an uncaught runtime exception.
- The evil and nasty deprecated stop( ) method is called.

What happens if none of these things occurs, and the run( ) method for a thread never terminates? The answer is that the thread can live on, even after what is ostensibly the part of the application that created it has finished. This means we have to be aware of how our threads eventually terminate, or an application can end up leaving orphaned threads that unnecessarily consume resources.

In many cases, we really want to create background threads that do simple, periodic tasks in an application. The setDaemon( ) method can be used to mark a thread as a daemon thread that should be killed and discarded when no other nondaemon application threads remain. Normally, the Java interpreter continues to run until all threads have completed. But when daemon threads are the only threads still alive, the interpreter will exit.

Here's a devilish example using daemon threads:

```
class Devil extends Thread {
    Devil() {
        setDaemon( true );
        start();
    }
    public void run() {
        // perform evil tasks
    }
}
```

In this example, the Devil thread sets its daemon status when it is created. If any Devil threads remain when our application is otherwise complete, the runtime system kills them for us. We don't have to worry about cleaning them up.

Daemon threads are primarily useful in standalone Java applications and in the implementation of server frameworks, but not in component applications such as applets. Since an applet runs inside another Java application, any daemon threads it creates can continue to live until the controlling application exits—probably not the desired effect. A browser or any other application can use ThreadGroups to contain all the threads created by subsystems of an application and then clean them up if necessary.

One final note about killing threads gracefully. A very common problem new developers encounter the first time they create an application using an AWT or Swing component is that their application never exits; the Java VM seems to hang indefinitely after everything is finished. When working with graphics, Java has created an AWT thread to process input and painting events. The AWT thread is not a daemon thread, so it doesn't exit automatically when other application threads have completed, and the developer must call System.exit( ) explicitly. (If you think about it, this makes sense. Since most GUI applications are event-driven and simply wait for user input, they would otherwise simply exit after their startup code completed.)

Threading an Applet

Applets are embeddable Java applications that are expected to start and stop themselves on command, possibly many times in their lifetime. A Java-enabled web browser normally starts an applet when the applet is displayed and stops it when the user moves to another page or (in theory) when the user scrolls the applet out of view. To conform to this API, we would like an applet to cease its nonessential activity when it is stopped and resume it when started again. We'll talk about applets in Chapter 23, but it's not really essential to know about them here. We'll just use this as a more realistic example and as a transition to talk about our next topic, synchronization.

In this section, we will build UpdateApplet, a simple base class for an applet that maintains a thread to automatically update its display at regular intervals. UpdateApplet handles the basic creation and termination of the thread in the Applet's start( ) and stop( ) methods:

```java
public class UpdateApplet extends java.applet.Applet
    implements Runnable
{

    Thread thread;
    boolean running;
    int updateInterval = 1000;

    public void run( ) {
        while ( running )
        {
            repaint( );
            try {
                Thread.sleep( updateInterval );
            } catch ( InterruptedException e ) {
                System.out.println("interrupted...");
                return;
            }
        }
    }

    public void start( ) {
        System.out.println("starting...");
        if ( !running ) // naive approach
        {
            running = true;
            thread = new Thread(this);
            thread.start( );
        }
    }

    public void stop( ) {
        System.out.println("stopping...");
        thread.interrupt( );
        running = false;
    }
}
```

UpdateApplet is a Runnable object that alternately sleeps and calls its repaint( ) method. (There's nothing to paint, though, so running this applet is kind of boring. Later we'll subclass it to implement a digital clock.) It has two other public methods: start( ) and stop( ). These are methods of the Applet class we are overriding; don't confuse them with the similarly named methods of the Thread class. These start( ) and stop( ) methods are called by the web browser or applet viewer to tell the applet when it should and should not be running.

UpdateApplet illustrates an environmentally friendly way to deal with threads in a simple applet. UpdateApplet simply dismisses its thread each time the applet is stopped and recreates it if the applet is restarted. When UpdateApplet's start( ) method is called, we first check to make sure there is no currently running thread by checking the running flag. We then create one to begin our execution. When our applet is subsequently asked to stop, we set the flag indicating that it should stop and make sure the thread is awake by invoking its interrupt( ) method. In this way, we are sure to catch the thread either at the beginning of its next iteration or when it goes to sleep.

With UpdateApplet doing all the work for us, we can create the world's simplest clock applet with just a few lines of code. Figure 9-3 shows our Clock.

Clock

Tue Feb 01 17:48:40 CST 2005

Figure 9-3. The Clock applet

Here's the code:

```
//file: Clock.java
public class Clock extends UpdateApplet {
    public void paint( java.awt.Graphics g ) {
        g.drawString( new java.util.Date( ).toString( ), 10, 25 );
    }
}
```

The java.util.Date( ).toString( ) method creates a string that contains the current time.

Issues lurking

Our applet seems pretty straightforward and, in fact, works as advertised. But some things in it should concern us when we're thinking about threads. Let's look at that quick check of the running flag before we start our new thread:

```
if ( !running ) // naive approach
{
    running = true;
    ... /* start thread */
```

Now, an Applet's start( ) and stop( ) methods are guaranteed to be called in sequence and probably by the same controlling thread. As a result, this check for the existence of the running thread in start( ) may not seem necessary here. The stop( ) method should always be called before the start( ) method is invoked again. But, in the style of defensive programming the test seems like a good thing to do, right? That may be so, but, in general, it's not enough to prevent bad things from happening. The test may prevent a simple case of misaligned stop( ) and start( ) calls, but the bigger problem lurking here is what happens if start( ) and stop( ) were called repeatedly or in very quick succession in a multithreaded environment? In the extreme case, it would be possible for two threads to enter the test at about the same time and there is the chance that we could end up with multiple threads started and out of our control. What is needed is a real way to gain exclusive access to a resource (our flag) for a period of time. That's what synchronization is all about and we'll cover it in detail in the next section and throughout the rest of this chapter.

With synchronization, we might also consider more complex scenarios for our applet, such as keeping our thread alive but dormant while the applet is stopped. This would allow us to preserve expensive setup like network connections and clean them up later if necessary.

Synchronization

Every thread has a life of its own. Normally, a thread goes about its business without any regard for what other threads in the application are doing. Threads may be time-sliced, which means they can run in arbitrary spurts and bursts as directed by the operating system. On a multiprocessor system, it is even possible for many different threads to be running simultaneously on different CPUs. This section is about coordinating the activities of two or more threads so that they can work together and not collide in their use of the same variables and methods (coordinating their play on the golf course).

Java provides a few simple structures for synchronizing the activities of threads. They are all based on the concept of monitors, a widely used synchronization scheme (developed by C.A.R. Hoare). You don't have to know the details about how monitors work to be able to use them, but it may help you to have a picture in mind.

A monitor is essentially a lock. The lock is attached to a resource that many threads may need to access, but that should be accessed by only one thread at a time. It's very much like a restroom with a lock on the door. If the resource is not being used, the thread can acquire the lock and access the resource. That is, if the restroom is unlocked, you can enter and lock the door. When the thread is done, it relinquishes the lock, just as you unlock the door and leave it open for the next person. However, if another thread already has the lock for the resource, all other threads have to wait until the current thread finishes and releases the lock. This is just like when the restroom is occupied when you arrive: you have to wait until the current user is done and unlocks the door.

Fortunately, Java makes the process of synchronizing access to resources fairly easy. The language handles setting up and acquiring locks; all you have to do is specify which resources require synchronization.

Serializing Access to Methods

The most common need for synchronization among threads in Java is to serialize their access to some resource (an object)—in other words, to make sure that only one thread at a time can manipulate an object or variable.* In Java, every object has an associated lock. To be more specific, every class and every instance of a class has its own lock. The synchronized keyword marks places where a thread must acquire the lock before proceeding.

For example, suppose we implemented a SpeechSynthesizer class that contains a say( ) method. We don't want multiple threads calling say( ) at the same time, or we wouldn't be able to understand anything being said. So we mark the say( ) method as synchronized, which means that a thread has to acquire the lock on the SpeechSynthesizer object before it can speak:

```java
class SpeechSynthesizer {
    synchronized void say( String words ) {
        // speak
    }
}
```

Because say( ) is an instance method, a thread has to acquire the lock on the SpeechSynthesizer instance it is using before it can invoke the say( ) method. When say( ) has completed, it gives up the lock, which allows the next waiting thread to acquire the lock and run the method. It doesn't matter whether the thread is owned by the SpeechSynthesizer itself or some other object; every thread has to acquire the same lock, that of the SpeechSynthesizer instance. If say( ) were a class (static) method instead of an instance method, we could still mark it as synchronized. In this case, because no instance object is involved, the lock is on the class object itself.

Often, you want to synchronize multiple methods of the same class so that only one method modifies or examines parts of the class at a time. All static synchronized methods in a class use the same class object lock. By the same token, all instance methods in a class use the same instance object lock. In this way, Java can guarantee that only one of a set of synchronized methods is running at a time. For example, a SpreadSheet class might contain a number of instance variables that represent cell values as well as some methods that manipulate the cells in a row:

```java
class SpreadSheet {
    int cellA1, cellA2, cellA3;

    synchronized int sumRow( ) {
        return cellA1 + cellA2 + cellA3;
    }
```

---

* Don't confuse the term "serialize" in this context with Java object serialization, which is a mechanism for making objects persistent. The underlying meaning (to place one thing after another) does apply to both, however. In the case of object serialization, the object's data is laid out, byte for byte, in a certain order.

```
synchronized void setRow( int a1, int a2, int a3 ) {
    cellA1 = a1;
    cellA2 = a2;
    cellA3 = a3;
}
...
}
```

In this example, methods setRow( ) and sumRow( ) both access the cell values. You can see that problems might arise if one thread were changing the values of the variables in setRow( ) at the same moment another thread was reading the values in sumRow( ). To prevent this, we have marked both methods as synchronized. When threads are synchronized, only one runs at a time. If a thread is in the middle of executing setRow( ) when another thread calls sumRow( ), the second thread waits until the first one finishes executing setRow( ) before it runs sumRow( ). This synchronization allows us to preserve the consistency of the SpreadSheet. The best part is that all this locking and waiting is handled by Java; it's transparent to the programmer.

In addition to synchronizing entire methods, the synchronized keyword can be used in a special construct to guard arbitrary blocks of code. In this form, it also takes an explicit argument that specifies the object for which it is to acquire a lock:

```
synchronized ( myObject ) {
    // Functionality that needs to be synced
}
```

This code block can appear in any method. When it is reached, the thread has to acquire the lock on myObject before proceeding. In this way, we can synchronize methods (or parts of methods) in different classes in the same way as methods in the same class.

A synchronized instance method is, therefore, equivalent to a method with its statements synchronized on the current object. Thus:

```
synchronized void myMethod () {
    ...
}
```

is equivalent to:

```
void myMethod () {
    synchronized ( this ) {
        ...
    }
}
```

Accessing variables

In the SpreadSheet example, we guarded access to a set of instance variables with a synchronized method, which we did mainly so that we wouldn't change one of the variables while someone was reading the rest of them. We wanted to keep them coordinated. But what about individual variable types? Do they need to be synchronized?

Normally, the answer is no. Almost all operations on primitives and object reference types in Java happen *atomically*: they are handled by the VM in one step, with no opportunity for two threads to collide. You can't be in the middle of changing a reference and be only partially done when another thread looks at the reference.

But watch out—we did say almost. If you read the Java VM specification carefully, you will see that the double and long primitive types are not guaranteed to be handled atomically. Both of these types represent 64-bit values. The problem has to do with how the Java VM's stack handles them. It is possible that this specification will be beefed up in the future. But for now, to be strict, you should synchronize access to your double and long instance variables through accessor methods or use the volatile keyword or an atomic wrapper class, as we'll describe next.

Another issue, independent of the atomicity of the values, is the notion of different threads in the VM caching values for periods of time. That is, even though one thread may have changed the value, the Java VM may not be obliged to make that value appear until the VM reaches a certain state known as a "memory barrier." While this should not be a problem in most real-world programming cases, you can address this by declaring the variable with the volatile keyword. This keyword indicates to the VM that the value may be changed by external threads and effectively synchronizes access to it automatically.

Finally, Java 5.0 added a new package, java.util.concurrent.atomic that provides synchronized wrapper classes for all primitive types and references. These wrappers provide not only simple set( ) and get( ) operations on the values but also specialized "combo" operations, such as compareAndSet( ), that work atomically and can be used to build higher-level synchronized application components. The classes in this package were designed specifically to map down to hardware-level functionality in many cases and can be very efficient. We'll talk more about them later in this chapter.

Reentrant locking

The locks acquired by Java upon entering a synchronized method or block of code are *reentrant*, meaning that the thread holding onto the lock may acquire the same lock again any number of times and never blocks waiting for itself. In most cases, this means that the code behaves as you'd expect; a thread can call a synchronized method recursively and can itself call upon other synchronized methods within the same object.

The wait( ) and notify( ) Methods

With the synchronized keyword, we can serialize the execution of methods and blocks of code so that only one thread may be executing a synchronized item at a time. The wait( ) and notify( ) methods of the Object class extend this capability by allowing us to coordinate the waiting and running threads explicitly. Every object in Java is a subclass of Object, so every object inherits these methods. By using wait( ) and notify( ), a thread can effectively give up its hold on a lock at an arbitrary point and then wait for another thread to give it back before continuing. All of the coordinated activity still happens inside synchronized blocks, and still only one thread is executing at a given time.

By executing wait( ) from a synchronized block, a thread gives up its hold on the lock and goes to sleep. A thread might do this if it needs to wait for something to happen in another part of the application, as we'll see shortly. Later, when the necessary event happens, a thread that is running calls notify( ) from a block synchronized on the same object. Now, the first thread wakes up and begins trying to acquire the lock again. When the first thread manages to reacquire the lock, it continues from the point it left off. However, the thread that was waiting may not get the lock immediately (or perhaps ever). It depends on when the second thread eventually releases the lock and which thread manages to snag it next. The first thread won't wake up from the wait( ) unless another thread calls notify( ). An overloaded version of wait( ), however, allows us to specify a timeout period. If another thread doesn't call notify( ) in the specified period, the waiting thread automatically wakes up.

Let's look at a simple scenario to see what's going on. In the following example, we'll assume there are three threads—one waiting to execute each of the three synchronized methods of the MyThing class. We'll call them the *waiter*, *notifier*, and *related* threads. Here's a code fragment to illustrate:

```
class MyThing {
    synchronized void waiterMethod() {
        // do some stuff
        wait();   // now wait for notifier to do something
        // continue where we left off
    }
    synchronized void notifierMethod() {
        // do some stuff
        notify();  // notify waiter that we've done it
        // continue doing stuff
    }
    synchronized void relatedMethod() {
        // do some related stuff
    }
    ...
}
```

Let's assume *waiter* gets through the gate first and begins executing waiterMethod( ). The two other threads are initially blocked, trying to acquire the lock for the MyThing object. When *waiter* executes the wait( ) method, it relinquishes its hold on the lock and goes to sleep. Now, two viable threads are waiting for the lock. Which thread gets it depends on several factors, including chance and the priorities of the threads. (We'll discuss thread scheduling in the next section.)

Let's say that *notifier* is the next thread to acquire the lock, so it begins to run notifierMethod( ). *waiter* continues to sleep, and *related* languishes, waiting for its turn. When *notifier* executes the call to notify( ), the runtime system prods the *waiter* thread, effectively telling it something has changed. *waiter* wakes up and rejoins *related* in vying for the MyThing lock. It doesn't receive the lock automatically; it just changes from saying, "Leave me alone" to "I want the lock."

At this point, *notifier* still owns the lock and continues to hold it until the synchronized notifierMethod( ) returns—or perhaps executes a wait( ) itself. At that point, the other two methods get to fight over the lock. *waiter* would like to continue executing waiterMethod( ) from the point it left off, while *related*, which has been patient, would like to get started. We'll let you choose your own ending for the story.

For each call to notify( ), the runtime system wakes up just one thread that is asleep in a wait( ) call. The group of threads waiting on a lock is called the *wait set*. If multiple threads are waiting, Java picks a thread on an arbitrary basis, which may be implementation-dependent. The Object class also provides a notifyAll( ) call to wake up all waiting threads. In most cases, you'll probably want to use notifyAll( ) rather than notify( ). Keep in mind that notify( ) really means, "Hey, something related to this object has changed. The condition you are waiting for may have changed, so check it again." In general, there is no reason to assume only one thread at a time is interested in the change or able to act upon it. Different threads might look upon whatever has changed in different ways.

Wait conditions

In general, our *waiter* thread is waiting for a particular condition to change, and we will want it to sit in a loop like the following:

```
while ( condition != true )
    wait( );
```

This test is called the *wait condition*. Other synchronized threads call notify( ) or notifyAll( ) when they have modified the environment so that the condition can be checked again. It's important to use a loop on the wait condition to be sure that the thread has been awakened for the right reason. Threads may also use a timed version of wait( ) to do periodic work while checking the condition in this way. Using wait conditions like this is also an alternative to polling and sleeping, as you'll see in the following section.

Passing Messages

We'll next illustrate a classic interaction between two threads: a Producer and a Consumer. A producer thread creates messages and places them into a queue while a consumer reads and displays them. To be realistic, we'll give the queue a maximum depth. And to make things really interesting, we'll have our consumer thread be lazy and run much more slowly than the producer. This means that Producer occasionally has to stop and wait for Consumer to catch up. In Java 5.0, a BlockingQueue interface provides exactly this kind of functionality. But we'll build it ourselves here using basic synchronization techniques first and then take a look at Queues and all of the collection classes in Chapter 11.

Here are the Producer and Consumer classes:

```java
import java.util.*;

public class Consumer implements Runnable {
    Producer producer;

    Consumer( Producer producer ) {
        this.producer = producer;
    }

    public void run(  ) {
        while ( true ) {
            String message = producer.getMessage(  );
            System.out.println("Got message: " + message);
            try {
                Thread.sleep( 2000 );
            } catch ( InterruptedException e ) { }
        }
    }

    public static void main(String args[]) {
        Producer producer = new Producer( );
        new Thread( producer ).start( );
        Consumer consumer = new Consumer( producer );
        new Thread( consumer ).start( );
    }
}

public class Producer implements Runnable{
    static final int MAXQUEUE = 5;
    private List messages = new ArrayList( );

    public void run() {
        while ( true ) {
            putMessage();
            try {
                Thread.sleep( 1000 );
            } catch ( InterruptedException e ) { }
        }
    }

    private synchronized void putMessage(  )
    {
        while ( messages.size() >= MAXQUEUE )
            try {
                wait( );
            } catch( InterruptedException e ) { }
```

```
        messages.add( new java.util.Date( ).toString( ) );
        notify( );
    }

    // called by Consumer
    public synchronized String getMessage(   )
    {
        while ( messages.size( ) == 0 )
            try {
                notify( );
                wait( );
            } catch( InterruptedException e ) { }
        String message = (String)messages.remove(0);
        notify( );
        return message;
    }

}
```

For convenience, we have included a main( ) method in the Consumer class that runs the complete example. It creates a Consumer that is tied to a Producer and starts the two classes. You can run the example as follows:

% **java Consumer**

This produces the timestamp messages created by the Producer:

```
Got message: Sun Dec 19 03:35:55 CST 2006
Got message: Sun Dec 19 03:35:56 CST 2006
Got message: Sun Dec 19 03:35:57 CST 2006
...
```

The timestamps initially show a spacing of one second, although they appear every two seconds. Our Producer runs faster than our Consumer. Producer would like to generate a new message every second, while Consumer gets around to reading and displaying a message only every two seconds. Can you see how long it will take the message queue to fill up? What will happen when it does?

Let's look at the code. We are using a few new tools here. Producer and Consumer implement the Runnable interface, and each has a thread associated with it. The Producer and Consumer classes pass messages through an instance of a java.util.List object. We haven't discussed the List class yet, but it is essentially a dynamic array of elements. We use this one as a queue by simply adding and removing elements in first-in, first-out order. The List has no maximum capacity of its own, but we impose one with our own check.

The important activity is in the synchronized methods: putMessage( ) and getMessage( ). Although one of the methods is used by the Producer thread and the other by the Consumer thread, they both live in the Producer class so that we can coordinate them simply by declaring them synchronized. Here, they both implicitly use the Producer object's lock. If the queue is empty, the Consumer blocks in a call in the Producer, waiting for another message.

Another design option would implement the getMessage( ) method in the Consumer class and use a synchronized code block to synchronize explicitly on the Producer object. In either case, synchronizing on the Producer enables us to have multiple Consumer objects that feed on the same Producer. We'll do that later in this section.

putMessage( )'s job is to add a new message to the queue. It can't do this if the queue is already full, so it first checks the number of elements in messages. If there is room, it stuffs in another timestamp message. If the queue is at its limit, however, putMessage( ) has to wait until there's space. In this situation, putMessage( ) executes a wait( ) and relies on the consumer to call notify( ) to wake it up after a message has been read. Here, we have putMessage( ) testing the condition in a loop. In this simple example, the test might not seem necessary; we could assume that when putMessage( ) wakes up, there is a free spot. However, it's important to always test our wait condition in a loop like this when we synchronize threads because there is no other way to be certain why our thread has been awakened. Before it finishes, putMessage( ) calls notify( ) itself to prod any Consumer that might be waiting on an empty queue.

getMessage( ) retrieves a message for the Consumer. It enters a loop like that of putMessage( ), waiting for the queue to have at least one element before proceeding. If the queue is empty, it executes a wait( ) and expects the Producer to call notify( ) when more items are available. Notice that getMessage( ) makes its own calls to notify( ). It does this any time the queue is empty, to prod a producer that might be sleeping and also after it consumes a message, to give the producer the go ahead to fill the queue again. These scenarios are more plausible if there are more consumers, as we'll see next.

Let's add another consumer to the scenario, just to make things more interesting. Most of the necessary changes are in the Consumer class; here's the code for the modified class, now called NamedConsumer:

```java
public class NamedConsumer implements Runnable
{
    Producer producer;
    String name;

    NamedConsumer(String name, Producer producer) {
        this.producer = producer;
        this.name = name;
    }

    public void run( ) {
        while ( true ) {
            String message = producer.getMessage( );
            System.out.println(name + " got message: " + message);
            try {
                Thread.sleep( 2000 );
            } catch ( InterruptedException e ) { }
        }
    }
}
```

```
public static void main(String args[]) {
    Producer producer = new Producer();
    new Thread( producer ).start();

    NamedConsumer consumer = new NamedConsumer( "One", producer );
    new Thread( consumer ).start();
    consumer = new NamedConsumer( "Two", producer );
    new Thread( consumer ).start();
}
}
```

The NamedConsumer constructor takes a string name to identify each consumer. The run() method uses this name in the call to println() to identify which consumer received the message.

The only required modification to the Producer code is to change the notify() calls to notifyAll() calls in putMessage() and getMessage(). (We could have used notifyAll() in the first place.) Now, instead of the consumer and producer playing tag with the queue, we can have many players waiting for the condition of the queue to change. We might have a number of consumers waiting for a message, or we might have the producer waiting for a consumer to take a message. Whenever the condition of the queue changes, we prod all the waiting methods to reevaluate the situation by calling notifyAll().

Here is some sample output when two NamedConsumers are running, as in the main() method shown previously:

```
One got message: Sat Mar 18 20:00:01 CST 2006
Two got message: Sat Mar 18 20:00:02 CST 2006
One got message: Sat Mar 18 20:00:03 CST 2006
Two got message: Sat Mar 18 20:00:04 CST 2006
One got message: Sat Mar 18 20:00:05 CST 2006
Two got message: Sat Mar 18 20:00:06 CST 2006
One got message: Sat Mar 18 20:00:07 CST 2006
Two got message: Sat Mar 18 20:00:08 CST 2006
...
```

We see nice, orderly alternation between the two consumers as a result of the calls to sleep() in the various methods. Interesting things would happen, however, if we were to remove all calls to sleep() and let things run at full speed. The threads would compete, and their behavior would depend on whether the system is using time-slicing. On a time-sliced system, there should be a fairly random distribution between the two consumers while on a non-time-sliced system, a single consumer could monopolize the messages. We'll talk shortly about how threads compete for time when we discuss thread priority and scheduling.

Food for thought

Many things could be improved in this simple example. What we've tried to emphasize is a defensive style of programming with respect to notifications by threads. That is, you need to rely on real-world conditions that you can test when synchronizing threads; it's not robust to simply assume that you'll get the right notifications in the right place at the right time. With that said, our example does generate extraneous notifications that wake up threads at times when there may not be work for them. For example, we generate notifications both when the queue is empty and when it's full. A better design might split these cases and use two different object locks. Fortunately, most programmers won't have to deal with issues at this level, especially since Java 5.0 has introduced real Queues and other high-level synchronization constructs.

ThreadLocal Objects

A common issue that arises is the need to maintain some information or state on a per-thread basis. For example, we might want to carry some context with the current thread as it executes our application. Or we might simply want to have a value that is different for different threads in the same way that each thread "sees" its own local variables in a method. Java supports this through the ThreadLocal class. A ThreadLocal is an object wrapper that automatically maintains a separate value for any thread calling it. For example:

```
ThreadLocal userID = new ThreadLocal();
userID.set("Pat");  // called by thread 1
userID.set("Bob"); // called by thread 2
userID.get(); // thread 1 gets "Pat"
userID.get(); // thread 2 gets "Bob"
```

You can use an instance of ThreadLocal anywhere you might use a static or instance variable to automatically maintain separate values for each thread. You can also extend ThreadLocal and override its initialValue() method. The ThreadLocal will then use this method to initialize its value once, the first time get() is called:

```
class MyThreadLocalFactory extends ThreadLocal<Factory> {
    protected Factory initialValue() { return new MyFactory(); }
}
```

ThreadLocals are implemented using a Map attached to each Thread instance, so their values will disappear when the Thread is no longer used and garbage collected.

Scheduling and Priority

Java makes few guarantees about how it schedules threads. Almost all of Java's thread scheduling is left up to the Java implementation and, to some degree, the application. Although it might have made sense (and would certainly have made many developers happier) if Java's developers had specified a scheduling algorithm, a single scheduling algorithm isn't necessarily suitable for all the roles that Java can play. Instead, Sun decided to put the burden on you to write robust code that works whatever the scheduling algorithm, and let the implementation tune the algorithm for whatever is best.*

Therefore, the priority rules that we describe next are carefully worded in the Java language specification to be a general guideline for thread scheduling. You should be able to rely on this behavior overall (statistically), but it is not a good idea to write code that relies on very specific features of the scheduler to work properly. You should instead use the control and synchronization tools that we have described in this chapter to coordinate your threads.†

Every thread has a priority value. In general, any time a thread of a higher priority than the current thread becomes runnable (is started, stops sleeping, or is notified), it preempts the lower priority thread and begins executing. By default, threads with the same priority are scheduled round-robin, which means once a thread starts to run, it continues until it does one of the following:

- Sleeps, by calling `Thread.sleep( )` or `wait( )`
- Waits for a lock, in order to run a `synchronized` method
- Blocks on I/O, for example, in a `read( )` or `accept( )` call
- Explicitly yields control, by calling `yield( )`
- Terminates, by completing its target method or with a `stop( )` call (deprecated)

This situation looks something like Figure 9-4.

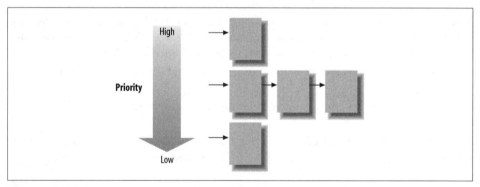

Figure 9-4. Priority preemptive, round-robin scheduling

---

* A notable alternative to this is the real-time Java specification that defines specialized thread behavior for certain types of applications. It was developed under the Java community process and can be found at *https://rtsj.dev.java.net/*.

† *Java Threads* by Scott Oaks and Henry Wong (O'Reilly) includes a detailed discussion of synchronization, scheduling, and other thread-related issues.

Thread State

At any given time, a thread is in one of five general states that encompass its lifecycle and activities. In Java 5.0, these states are made explicit through the Thread.State enumeration and the getState( ) method of the Thread class:

NEW

> The thread has been created but not yet started.

RUNNABLE

> The normal active state of a running thread, including the time when a thread is blocked in an I/O operation, like a read or write or network connection.

BLOCKED

> The thread is blocked, waiting to enter a synchronized method or code block. This includes the time when a thread has been awakened by a notify( ) and is attempting to reacquire its lock after a wait( ).

WAITING
TIMED_WAITING

> The thread is waiting for another thread via a call to wait( ) or join( ). In the case of TIMED_WAITING, the call has a timeout.

TERMINATED

> The thread has completed due to a return, an exception, or being stopped.

We can show the state of all threads in Java (in the current thread group) with the following snippet of code:

```
Thread [] threads = new Thread [ 64 ]; // max threads to show
int num = Thread.enumerate( threads );
for( int i = 0; i < num; i++ )
   System.out.println( threads[i] +":"+ threads[i].getState() );
```

You will probably not use this API in general programming, but it is interesting and useful for experimenting and learning about Java threads.

Time-Slicing

In addition to prioritization, all modern systems (with the exception of some embedded and "micro" Java environments) implement thread time-slicing. In a time-sliced system, thread processing is chopped up so that each thread runs for a short period of time before the context is switched to the next thread, as shown in Figure 9-5.

Higher-priority threads still preempt lower-priority threads in this scheme. The addition of time-slicing mixes up the processing among threads of the same priority; on a multiprocessor machine, threads may even be run simultaneously. This can introduce a difference in behavior for applications that don't use threads and synchronization properly.

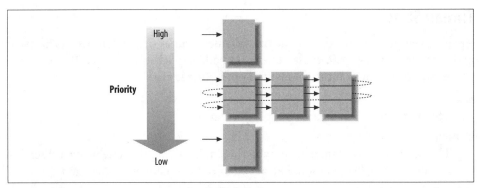

Figure 9-5. Priority preemptive, time-sliced scheduling

Strictly speaking, since Java doesn't guarantee time-slicing, you shouldn't write code that relies on this type of scheduling; any software you write should function under round-robin scheduling. If you're wondering what your particular flavor of Java does, try the following experiment:

```
public class Thready {
    public static void main( String args [] ) {
        new ShowThread("Foo").start( );
        new ShowThread("Bar").start( );
    }

    static class ShowThread extends Thread {
        String message;

        ShowThread( String message ) {
            this.message = message;
        }
        public void run( ) {
            while ( true )
                System.out.println( message );
        }
    }
}
```

The Thready class starts up two ShowThread objects. ShowThread is a thread that goes into a hard loop (very bad form) and prints its message. Since we don't specify a priority for either thread, they both inherit the priority of their creator, so they have the same priority. When you run this example, you will see how your Java implementation does its scheduling. Under a round-robin scheme, only "Foo" should be printed; "Bar" never appears. In a time-slicing implementation, you should occasionally see the "Foo" and "Bar" messages alternate (which is most likely what you will see).

Priorities

As we said before, the priorities of threads exist as a general guideline for how the implementation should allocate time among competing threads. Unfortunately, with the complexity of how Java threads are mapped to native thread implementations, the exact meaning of priorities cannot be relied upon. Instead you should only consider them a hint to the VM.

Let's play with the priority of our threads:

```
class Thready {
    public static void main( String args [] ) {
        Thread foo = new ShowThread("Foo");
        foo.setPriority( Thread.MIN_PRIORITY );
        Thread bar = new ShowThread("Bar");
        bar.setPriority( Thread.MAX_PRIORITY );
        bar.start( );
    }
}
```

We would expect that with this change to our Thready class, the Bar thread would take over completely. If you run this code on the Solaris implementation of Java 5.0, that's what happens. The same is not true on Windows or with some older versions of Java. Similarly, if you change the priorities to values other than min and max, you may not see any difference at all. The subtleties relating to priority and performance relate to how Java threads and priorities are mapped to real threads in the OS. For this reason, thread priorities should be reserved for system and framework development. It is not as useful in practice as simply implementing correct application-level control over processing using explicit synchronization.

Native Threads

A few times we mentioned the term *native threads*. This means that threads in the Java VM are tied directly or indirectly to threads in the underlying OS or hardware, which makes it possible for them to run truly independently and across multiprocessor machines. Older implementations of threading in Java (originally known as "green threads") effectively simulated threading within an individual process and had serious limitations blocking threads in I/O operations and with scalability. Again, all modern VMs (possibly excluding embedded environments) use native threads in one way or another. Some VMs may allow you to tune the mapping. In general, you shouldn't worry too much about how threads are implemented as long as you stick to the rules we've discussed and don't rely on peculiarities of scheduling or priorities.

Yielding

Whenever a thread sleeps, waits, or blocks on I/O, it gives up its time slot, and another thread is scheduled. As long as you don't write methods that use hard loops, all threads should get their due. However, a thread can also signal that it is willing to give up its time voluntarily at any point with the yield( ) call. We can change our previous example to include a yield( ) on each iteration:

```
...
static class ShowThread extends Thread {
    ...
    public void run() {
        while ( true ) {
            System.out.println( message );
            yield( );
        }
    }
}
```

You should see "Foo" and "Bar" messages strictly alternating. If you have threads that perform very intensive calculations or otherwise eat a lot of CPU time, you might want to find an appropriate place for them to yield control occasionally. Alternatively, you might want to drop the priority of your compute-intensive thread so that more important processing can proceed around it.

Unfortunately, the Java language specification is very weak with respect to yield( ). It is another one of those things you should consider an optimization hint rather than a guarantee. In the worst case, the runtime system may simply ignore calls to yield( ).

Thread Groups

The ThreadGroup class allows us to deal with threads wholesale: we can use it to arrange threads in groups and deal with the groups as a whole. A thread group can contain other thread groups, in addition to individual threads, so our arrangements can be hierarchical. Thread groups are particularly useful when we want to start a task that might create many threads of its own. By assigning the task a thread group, we can later identify and control all the task's threads. Thread groups are also the subject of restrictions that can be imposed by the Java Security Manager, so we can restrict a thread's behavior according to its thread group. For example, we can forbid threads in a particular group from interacting with threads in other groups. This is one way web browsers can prevent threads started by Java applets from stopping important system threads.

When we create a thread, it normally becomes part of the thread group to which the currently running thread belongs. To create a new thread group of our own, we can call the constructor:

```
ThreadGroup myTaskGroup = new ThreadGroup("My Task Group");
```

The ThreadGroup constructor takes a name, which a debugger can use to help you identify the group. (You can also assign names to the threads themselves.) Once we have a group, we can put threads in the group by supplying the ThreadGroup object as an argument to the Thread constructor:

```
Thread myTask = new Thread( myTaskGroup, taskPerformer );
```

Here, myTaskGroup is the thread group, and taskPerformer is the target object (the Runnable object that performs the task). Any additional threads that myTask creates also belong to the myTaskGroup thread group.

Working with ThreadGroups

The ThreadGroup class exists so that you can control threads in batches. It has methods that parallel the basic Thread control methods—even the deprecated stop( ), suspend( ), and resume( ). These methods operate on all the threads in a thread group. You can also mark a thread group as a "daemon"; a daemon thread group is automatically removed when all its children are gone. If a thread group isn't a daemon, you have to call destroy( ) to remove it when it is empty.

We can set the maximum priority for threads created in a thread group by calling setMaximumPriority( ). Thereafter, no threads can be created in the thread group with a priority higher than the maximum; threads that change their priority can't set their new priority higher than the maximum.

Finally, you can get a list of all threads in a group. The method activeCount( ) tells you how many threads are in the group; the method enumerate( ) gives you a list of them. We used the enumerate( ) method earlier when we showed the state of all threads in the default thread group using the static Thread.enumerate( )method. The argument to enumerate( ) is an array of Threads, which enumerate( ) fills in with the group's threads. Both activeCount( ) and enumerate( ) operate recursively on all thread groups the group contains.

Uncaught Exceptions

In Java, unchecked exceptions that are not caught by any method eventually bubble up to the run( ) method of the running thread and are thrown from there. By default, Java deals with these by simply printing them to the system error stream or log and terminating the thread. However, you can specify your own "catch all" behavior for these exceptions by subclassing ThreadGroup and overriding the uncaughtException( )

method. When an uncaught exception is generated, it is handed to this method, which can take some action or throw it again before the thread terminates.

In Java 5.0, this pattern was extended by defining an interface: `Thread.UncaughtExceptionHandler` and adding both per-thread and systemwide uncaught exception handlers in addition to the per-ThreadGroup exception handler. We can handle uncaught exceptions for a single thread like this:

```
Thread thread = new Thread( );
thread.setUncaughtExceptionHandler(
    new Thread.UncaughtExceptionHandler( ) {
        public void uncaughtException( Thread t, Throwable e ) {
            System.err.println( t + " threw exception: " + e );
        }
} );
```

This example prints the exception before the thread dies. We could have set the same handler on the `ThreadGroup` in the same way or assigned it for all exceptions using the static `Thread.setDefaultUncaughtExceptionHandler( )` method.

Thread Performance

The way that applications use threads and the associated costs and benefits have greatly impacted the design of many Java APIs. We will discuss some of the issues in detail in other chapters. But it is worth briefly mentioning some aspects of thread performance and how the use of threads has dictated the form and functionality of several recent Java packages.

The Cost of Synchronization

The act of acquiring locks to synchronize threads, even when there is no contention, takes time. In older implementations of Java, this time could be significant. With newer VMs, it is almost negligible.* However, unnecessary low-level synchronization can still slow applications by blocking threads where legitimate concurrent access otherwise could be allowed. Because of this, two important APIs, the Java Collections API and the Swing GUI API, were specifically crafted to avoid unnecessary synchronization, by placing it under the developer's control.

The `java.util` Collections API replaces earlier, simple Java aggregate types—namely `Vector` and `Hashtable`—with more fully featured and, notably, unsynchronized types (`List` and `Map`). The Collections API instead defers to application code to synchronize access to collections when necessary and provides special "fail fast"

---

* In a completely naive test (simple loop) using JDK 1.4.0 on a 400-MHz Sparc Ultra-60, we measured the cost of synchronization on an object to be about one-tenth of a microsecond. However, when the lock is contested, it is sure to be more expensive.

functionality to help detect concurrent access and throw an exception. It also provides synchronization "wrappers" that can provide safe access in the old style. In Java 5.0, special implementations of the Map and new Queue collections were added as part of the java.util.concurrent package. These implementations go even further in that they are written to allow a high degree of concurrent access without any user synchronization. We'll talk about these in Chapter 11.

The Java Swing GUI, which grew out of AWT, has taken a different approach to providing speed and safety. Swing dictates that modification of its components (with notable exceptions) must all be done by a single thread: the main event queue. Swing solves performance problems as well as nasty issues of determinism in event ordering by forcing a single super-thread to control the GUI. The application may access the event queue thread indirectly by pushing commands onto a queue through a simple interface.

Thread Resource Consumption

A fundamental pattern in Java, which will be illustrated in Chapters 12 and 13, is to start many threads to handle asynchronous external resources, such as socket connections. For maximum efficiency, a web server might be tempted to create a thread for each client connection it is servicing. With each client having its own thread, I/O operations may block and restart as needed. But as efficient as this may be in terms of throughput, it is a very inefficient use of server resources. Threads consume memory; each thread has its own "stack" for local variables, and switching between running threads (context switching) adds overhead to the CPU. While threads are relatively lightweight (in theory it is possible to have hundreds or thousands running on a large server), at a certain point, the resources consumed by the threads themselves start defeating the purpose of starting more threads. Often this point is reached with only a few dozen threads. Creating a thread per client is not a very scalable option.

An alternative approach is to create "thread pools" where a fixed number of threads pull tasks from a queue and return for more when they are finished. This recycling of threads makes for solid scalability, but it has historically been difficult to implement efficiently for servers in Java because stream I/O (for things like sockets) has not fully supported nonblocking operations. This changed with Java 1.4 and the introduction of the NIO (new I/O) package, java.nio. The NIO package introduces asynchronous I/O channels: nonblocking reads and writes plus the ability to "select" or test the readiness of streams for moving data. Channels can also be asynchronously closed, allowing threads to work gracefully. With the NIO package, it should be possible to create servers with much more sophisticated, scalable thread patterns.

With Java 5.0, thread pools and job "executor" services are codified as utilities as part of the new java.util.concurrent package, meaning you don't have to write these yourself any longer but can use or extend these base classes. We'll talk about them next when we discuss the concurrency utilities in Java 5.0.

Concurrency Utilities

So far in this chapter we've demonstrated how to create and synchronize threads at a low level, using Java language primitives. The java.util.concurrent package and subpackages introduced with Java 5.0 build on this functionality, adding important threading utilities and codifying some common design patterns by supplying standard implementations. Roughly in order of generality, these areas include:

Thread-aware Collections implementations
> The java.util.concurrent package augments the Java Collections API with several implementations for specific threading models. These include timed wait, blocking implementations of the Queue interface, as well as nonblocking, concurrent-access optimized implementations of the Queue and Map interfaces. The package also adds "copy on write" List and Set implementations for extremely efficient "almost always read" cases. These may sound complex, but actually cover some fairly simple cases very well. We'll cover the Collections API in Chapter 11.

Executors
> Executors run tasks, including Runnables, and abstract the concept of thread creation and pooling from the user. Executors are intended to be a high-level replacement for the idiom of creating new threads to service a series of jobs. Along with Executors, the Callable and Future interfaces are introduced, which expand upon Runnable to allow management, value return, and exception handling.

Locks
> The java.util.concurrent.locks package holds a set of classes including Lock and Condition that parallels the Java language-level synchronization primitives and promotes them to the level of a concrete API. The locks package also adds the concept of nonexclusive reader/writer locks, allowing for greater concurrency in synchronized data access.

High-level synchronization constructs
> This includes the classes CyclicBarrier, CountDownLatch, Semaphore, and Exchanger. These classes implement common synchronization patterns drawn from other languages and systems and can serve as the basis for new high-level tools.

Atomic operations (sounds very James Bond, doesn't it?)
> The java.util.concurrent.atomic package provides wrappers and utilities for atomic, "all-or-nothing" operations on primitive types and references. This includes simple combination atomic operations like testing a value before setting it and getting and incrementing a number in one operation.

With the possible exception of optimizations done by the Java VM for the atomic operations package, all of these utilities are implemented in pure Java, on top of the standard Java language synchronization constructs. This means that they are really just convenience utilities and don't truly add new capabilities to the language. Their main role is to offer standard patterns and idioms in Java threading and make them safer and more efficient to use. A good example of this is the Executor, which allows a user to manage a set of tasks in a predefined threading model without having to delve into creating threads at all. Higher level APIs like this both simplify coding and allow for greater optimization of the common cases.

We'll look at each of these areas in the remainder of this chapter, with the exception of the Collections implementations. We'll discuss those when we cover the Java Collections APIs in Chapter 11.

Before we dive in, we should mention that, while newly standardized in Java 5.0, the concurrency package that we'll describe has been around for some time as a product of the Java Community Process (JSR-166). The vast majority of it was originally written by Doug Lea, the author of *Concurrent Programming in Java* (Addison-Wesley), who deserves most of the credit for it.

Executors

In this chapter, we've created a lot of Threads and hopefully shown how to use them effectively. But in the grand scheme of things, threads are a fairly low-level programming tool and, without care, can be error-prone. When we recognize certain common patterns that developers reproduce over and over again using threads, it's natural to want to elevate a pattern to the level of an API. One such related pair of patterns is the concept of an *executor* service that manages tasks and that of a *thread pool* that services the tasks in an efficient way. The thread pool has been implemented and reimplemented by vast numbers of developers in one way or another over the years and when you add in features like scheduling different threading models, things can get quite complex.

To address these issues, the java.util.concurrent package includes interfaces for many default implementations of the executor pattern for common threading models. This includes sophisticated scheduling as well as asynchronous collection of results from the tasks, if they require it. In general, you can use an Executor as a replacement for creating one-off threads anywhere you need to execute Runnable objects. The advantage is that understanding and modifying the behavior of your code later is a lot easier when you work at this level.

For the simple case of running a number of tasks to completion, we can consider the base Executor interface, which executes Runnable objects for us. The neatest thing about Executor is that its companion utility class Executors is a factory for creating different kinds of Executor implementations. We'll talk about the various types it can produce in a bit, but for now let's use one called `newFixedThreadPool( )`, which, as its name suggests, returns an `Executor` that is implemented using a thread pool of a fixed size:

```
Executor executor = Executors.newFixedThreadPool( 3 ) ; // 3 threads

List<Runnable> runnables = ... ;
for( Runnable task : runnables )
    executor.execute( task );
```

Here, we are submitting a number of `Runnable` tasks to our `Executor`, which executes them using a pool with a maximum of three threads. If our list contains more than three tasks, then some of them will have to wait until a thread is free to service it. So, what happens when we submit the fourth item? The `Executor` interface doesn't specify that. It's up to the particular implementation to decide. `Executors` don't have to queue tasks, much less use a pool to service them. Some `Executor` implementations may block, or even execute the `Runnable` right on the `execute( )` call in the caller's thread. In this case (and for all `Executor` implementations created for us by the `Executors` factory methods), tasks are effectively put onto an unbounded queue. In the example, our loop submits all of the tasks immediately and they are queued by the executor until the threads have serviced them.

With just a line or two of code in our example, we've been able to throttle the concurrency of our task list and avoid the details of constructing any threads ourselves. Later, if we decide we'd rather execute the tasks one at a time, the change is trivial. Next, we'll take a step up and look at manageable tasks that produce values and executors that can schedule tasks for us.

Tasks with results: Callable and Future

Since the `Runnable` interface was created for `Threads` to consume, its API doesn't really allow for feedback to the caller. The new `Callable` interface, which is effectively a replacement for `Runnable`, rectifies this situation by providing a `call( )` method that both returns a result and can throw exceptions. `Callable` is a generic class that is parameterized by the type it returns. The following examples create a `Callable` that returns an integer:

```
class MyCallable implements Callable<Integer> {
    public Integer call() { return 2+2; }
}

// or anonymously
Callable<Integer> callable = new Callable<Integer>() {
    public Integer call() { return 2+2; }
};
```

There is also a convenience method for bridging Runnables to Callables in the Executors class. It takes a Runnable and a fixed value to return as a value when it completes:

```
Callable<Integer> callable = Executors.callable( runnable, 42/*return value*/ );
```

The new Future class is used with Callable and serves as a handle to wait for and retrieve the result of the task or cancel the task before it is executed. A Future is returned by the submit( ) methods of an ExecutorService, which is essentially a beefed up Executor. We'll discuss ExecutorServices in the next section.

```
Future<Integer> result = executorService.submit( callable );
int val = result.get( );  // blocks until ready
```

Future is also a generic interface, which is parameterized by its return type. This explains the somewhat cute name. For example a Future<Integer> could be read as "a future integer." Future has blocking and timed wait get( ) methods to retrieve the result when it is ready as well as an isDone( ) test method and a cancel( ) method to stop the task if it hasn't started yet. If the task has been cancelled, you get a CancellationException if you attempt to retrieve the result.

Enough said about these interfaces. Next, we'll look at the ExecutorService, which uses them.

ExecutorService

Our first Executor was little more than a sinkhole for Runnables and, as we described, required knowledge of the implementation to know how it would handle tasks at all. By contrast, an ExecutorService is intended to be an asynchronous task handler. Instead of an execute( ) method, it has submit( ) methods that accept a Callable (or Runnable) and return immediately with a Future object that can be used to manage the task and collect the result later. In addition to that, an ExecutorService has a lifecycle defined by its shutdown( ) method and related methods that can be used to stop the service gracefully after tasks are completed.

ExecutorService extends Executor and, in fact, all of the implementations returned by the Executors factory methods are actually ExecutorServices—including the one we used in our first example. We'll look at these factory methods to see what kind of services are offered.

Executors offers three types of ExecutorService implementations:

newFixedThreadPool(int)
> This is the classic thread pool with a specified maximum pool size and an unbounded queue for task submission. If a thread dies for some reason while handling a task, a new one will be created to replace it. Threads are never removed from the pool until the service is shut down.

newCachedThreadPool( )

This pool uses an open-ended number of threads that grows and shrinks with demand. The main advantage of this service is that threads are cached for a period of time and reused, eliminating the overhead of creating new threads for short-lived tasks. Threads that are not used for one minute are removed. Tasks are submitted directly to threads; there is no real queuing.

newSingleThreadExecutor( )

This ExecutorService uses a single thread to execute tasks from an unbounded queue. In this sense, it is identical to a fixed thread pool with a pool size of 1.

Let's look at a more realistic usage of an ExecutorService, drawn from the TinyHttpd example in Chapter 13. In that chapter, we create a mini web server to illustrate features of the networking APIs. Here, we won't show the networking details, but we'll implement the main request dispatching loop for the example using a thread pool executor service. (Flip to Chapter 13 to see the implementation of the Runnable client-connection handler class. But that class works equally well with both examples.) Here we go:

```
public class ExecutorHttpd
{
  ExecutorService executor = Executors.newFixedThreadPool(3);

  public void start( int port ) throws IOException
  {
    final ServerSocket ss = new ServerSocket( port );
    while ( !executor.isShutdown() )
      executor.submit( new TinyHttpdConnection( ss.accept() ) );
  }

  public void shutdown() throws InterruptedException {
    executor.shutdown();
    executor.awaitTermination( 30, TimeUnit.SECONDS );
    executor.shutdownNow();
  }

  public static void main( String argv[] ) throws Exception
  {
    new ExecutorHttpd().start( Integer.parseInt(argv[0]) );
  }
}
```

The ExecutorHttpd class holds an instance of a fixed thread pool ExecutorService with three threads to service client connections. In the start( ) method of our class, we create a ServerSocket that accepts incoming network connections. We then enter a loop that runs as long as our service is not flagged to shut down. Inside the loop, we create a new connection handler (a Runnable instance of TinyHttpdConnection) for each connection and submit it to the executor. The shutdown( ) method of our class illustrates a graceful termination. First, we call shutdown( ) on the executor, which causes the service to stop accepting new tasks and allow the currently running ones to complete. Then we wait a reasonable period of time for all web requests to finish (30 seconds) using the awaitTermination( ) method before trying a less graceful ending with shutdownNow( ). shutdownNow( ) attempts to interrupt or otherwise stop threads as quickly as possible. We leave things there, but the method actually returns a List of tasks that remain hung after the attempt. Finally, we have a main( ) method that exercises our example by creating an instance of ExecutorHttpd on a port specified as an argument to the program.

Collective tasks

In addition to its individual task submit( ) methods, ExecutorService also offers a set of collective invokeAll( ) and invokeAny( ) executor methods that submit multiple tasks as a group and return results either when they are all complete or when the first one completes, respectively. With this, we could reproduce our first example using a List of Callables like this:

```
List<Callable<Integer>> taskList = ...;
ExecutorService execService = Executors.newFixedThreadPool(3);
List<Future<Integer>> resultList = execService.invokeAll( taskList );
```

By contrast, the invokeAny( ) method returns just the first successfully completed task's result (canceling all the remaining unexecuted tasks):

```
int result = execService.invokeAny( taskList );
```

Both methods also offer timed wait versions that time out after a specified period of time.

Scheduled tasks

For tasks that you'd like to run at a future time or on a periodic basis, use the ScheduledExecutorService. ScheduledExecutorService is an ExecutorService with additional "schedule" methods that take a delay for a Runnable or Callable or a period specification for a Runnable. Two additional factory methods of Executors produce scheduled executors:

```
Executors.newScheduledThreadPool(int);
Executors.newSingleThreadScheduledExecutor( );
```

These are exactly like the similarly named methods for regular executor services.

To execute a task in the future, you specify a delay from the current time. For example:

```
ScheduledExecutorService exec = Executors.newScheduledThreadPool(3);

exec.schedule( runnable, 60, TimeUnit.SECONDS ); // run one minute in the future

// run at specified date and time
Calendar futureDate = ...; // convert calendar
Date date = futureDate.getTime( ); // to Date
long delay  = date.getTime( ) - System.currentTimeMillis( ); // to relative millis
exec.schedule( runnable, delay, TimeUnit.MILLISECONDS ); // run at specified date
```

For periodic work, there are two kinds of recurring schedules—fixed delay and fixed rate. *Fixed delay* means that a fixed amount of time elapses between the end of the task's execution and the beginning of the next execution. *Fixed rate* means that the task should begin execution at fixed time intervals, regardless of how long the task takes. The difference comes into play when the time to execute the task is long relative to the interval. The following snippet schedules a log file cleanup to occur in 12 hours and every 12 hours thereafter:

```
Runnable cleanup = new Runnable( ) {
    public void run( ) { cleanUpLogFiles( ); }
};

long period = 12*60*60, delay = period; // seconds

Future<?> logService = executionService.scheduleAtFixedRate(
    cleanup, delay, period, TimeUnit.SECONDS );
```

Since the task for periodic schedules is a Runnable, the Future object does not return a useful value (it returns null) so we don't specify a parameter type in its generic type instantiation. The Future is still useful for canceling the task at a later time if we wish:

```
logService.cancel( );
```

We should mention that the ScheduledExecutorService bears a great deal of similarity to the java.util.Timer class that we'll discuss in Chapter 11, especially with regard to the periodic schedules. A java.util.Timer is always single-threaded, however.

CompletionService

A CompletionService is a queue-like front end to an executor service. The CompletionService provides submit( ) methods, which delegate their tasks to a particular instance of Executor, and then provides take( ) and poll( ) methods for retrieving Future results for completed tasks. Think of a CompletionService as a babysitter for the Futures, allowing you to easily gather up only completed results. ExecutorCompletionService is a concrete implementation of CompletionService that takes an Executor in its constructor:

```
Executor executor = Executors.newFixedThreadPool(3);
CompletionService<Integer> completionService =
    new ExecutorCompletionService<Integer>( executor );

completionService.submit( callable );
completionService.submit( runnable, resultValue );

// poll for result
Future<Integer> result = completionService.poll( );
if ( result != null )
    // use value...
```

```
// block, waiting for result
Future<Integer> result = completionService.take( );
```

The ThreadPoolExecutor implementation

At various times in this chapter, we've referred to the different executor services produced by the Executors factory as different implementations of ExecutorService. But these implementations are just different configurations of a single, highly flexible implementation of ExecutorService called ThreadPoolExecutorService. You can use this implementation directly if you want; it offers some additional features. The primary constructor for ThreadPoolExecutorService allows you to specify both a "core" thread pool size and a maximum size, as well as a thread timeout value for removing idle threads. The core size is a minimum number of threads which, once created, are allowed to live indefinitely. The constructor also allows you to provide the task queue (an implementation of BlockingQueue) on which new tasks are placed. This last feature allows you to govern the queuing policy yourself. You could specify a queue with a limited capacity:

```
ExecutorService executorService = new ThreadPoolExecutor(
    corePoolSize, maximumPoolSize, keepAliveTime, timeUnit, taskQueue );
```

The ThreadPoolExecutor implementation also has methods that allow you to change the core and maximum pool size while the service is active or to "prestart" the core threads before the service is used.

Actually, these last features bring up an interesting issue. If we know that our executor service is an implementation of ThreadPoolExecutor, we can cast it at runtime to get access to these extra methods and do things like change the pool size. This may not be what the designers of some services had in mind; in fact, it could be downright dangerous in the wrong hands. For this reason, Executors offers a number of "unconfigurable" wrapper methods that act something like the "unmodifiable" collection methods we'll see in the Java Collections API. These methods wrap an executor service in a delegator object that does not expose the implementation to the caller:

```
ExecutorService tweakable = Executors.newFixedThreadPool( );
ExecutorService safe = Executors.unconfigurableExecutorService( tweakable );
```

An application server might, for example, wrap a service to protect itself from individual applications modifying a global service to suit their own needs.

Thread production

We said that the Executor pattern is a general replacement for using Threads to run simple tasks. Although Executors shield us from Thread creation, there still may be cases where we want some control over how the threads used in our various thread pool implementations are constructed or set up. For this reason and to standardize

Thread production in general, the concurrency package adds an explicit, factory API for thread creation.

The `ThreadFactory` interface provides a `newThread( )` method. One of these factories is used by all service implementations that create threads. All of the factory methods of `Executors` have an additional form that accepts an explicit `ThreadFactory` as an argument. You can get the default thread factory used by these with the `Executors.defaultThreadFactory( )` method. You could use your own `ThreadFactory` to perform custom setup, such as `ThreadLocal` values or priorities.

Locks

The `java.util.concurrent.locks` package holds classes that mimic and expand upon the built-in Java language synchronization primitives, adding "read/write" locks among other things. As we mentioned, these classes are just utilities written in Java and don't strictly add anything new to the language semantics. However, they do provide more flexible usage at the expense of some of the built-in safety of Java language synchronization.

At the heart of the locks package are the `Lock` and `Condition` interfaces. `Lock` represents the same concept as a Java lock (monitor) that is associated with each object and class for use with synchronized methods and blocks. The `Lock` class provides for exclusive access by the owner of the lock by allowing only one party to hold the lock at a time through the `lock( )` and `unlock( )` methods. In Java language synchronization, this is accomplished implicitly with the `synchronized` keyword:

```
// synchronized method
synchronized void writeData( ) { ... }

// synchronized block
synchronized ( someObject ) {
  ...
}
```

Upon entry to the synchronized method or block, Java acquires the lock and automatically releases it upon exiting. Even if an exception is thrown or the thread dies unexpectedly, Java automatically releases all of the locks it acquired. Using the `Lock` class instead requires us (or allows us, depending on how you look at it) to explicitly lock when we want the resource and remember to unlock it when we are through. The locking is not tied to any particular scope, such as a single method or code block. To reproduce the effect of the synchronized method in the example, we'd use something like:

```
Lock lock = new ReentrantLock( );

// method or block
lock.lock( );
try {
    // body of method or block ...
```

```
    } finally {
        lock.unlock( )
    }
```

The first caller to lock( ) acquires the lock and proceeds. Subsequent calls by other threads block until the lock is released. We perform the body of our locked operation in a try/finally block. This is generally important to ensure that no matter what happens—we always unlock before we leave, but you are free to implement arbitrary protocols at your own risk.

The lock implementation in this example is called ReentrantLock. The name implies that this kind of lock acts like Java locks do in that the lock is associated with the caller's thread. The owner of a lock may reacquire ("relock") the lock as many times as it wishes. For example, a recursive method that locks a resource upon entry is fine.

In addition to the standard-looking lock( ) method, the Lock interface has tryLock( ) methods that do not block or block for a specified period of time to acquire the lock. These conditional and timed wait locking forms are something that ordinary Java locks do not provide. The ReentrantLock implementation also has a notion of "fairness" that can be turned on or off when it is constructed. When fair is on, the lock attempts to hand out the lock to callers in the order in which they request it. Normal Java locks (and the default, unfair, policy of ReentrantLock) do not make this guarantee.

Read and write locks

The ReadWriteLock interface is a gateway to two different locks, one for reading and one for writing. The idea behind read/write locks is that for most resources it is okay for many "readers" to be viewing data, as long as it is not changing. Conversely, a writer of the data generally requires exclusive access to it. This is just what read/write locks do. Any number of readers may acquire the read lock as long as no write lock is in place. Only one party may hold the write lock, and no readers may hold read locks while the write lock is out. A writer may have to wait for readers to finish before acquiring the write lock, and readers may have to wait for a writer to finish before they are allowed to acquire read locks:

```
ReadWriteLock rwLock = new ReentrantReadWriteLock( fair );

// reader thread 1
rwLock.readLock( ).lock( );
// reader thread 2
rwLock.readLock( ).lock( );

// writer thread
rwLock.writeLock( ).lock( ); // blocks on threads 1 & 2
```

In this code snippet, two readers hold read locks while a writer blocks waiting on the write lock. When both readers have unlock( )ed their read locks, the writer gains exclusive access to the lock and any subsequent readers block until the writer is finished.

The owner of a write lock can acquire a read lock, too, if it wishes, but not vice-versa. Acquiring a read lock and then releasing the write lock is called *downgrading* the lock. Trying to acquire a write lock while holding a read lock (upgrading) is not allowed and causes a deadlock.

Conditions

To complete the picture of Lock as a parallel for Java language synchronization, we need an analogue to the wait( ), notify( ), and notifyAll( )mechanism. The Condition interface represents this functionality with its await( ), signal( ), and signalAll( ) methods. A Condition is associated with a Lock by the lock's newCondition( ) method. Unlike a normal Java lock, a Lock may have multiple Condition objects that represent multiple wait sets of threads.

The Condition await( ) method is used just like the wait( ) method of a Java object within a synchronized block:

```
Lock lock = ...
Condition condition = lock.newCondition( );
lock.lock( );
condition.await( ); // block, waiting for signal( )
lock.unlock( );

// meanwhile, in another thread...
lock.lock( );
condition.signal( );
lock.unlock( );
```

Like wait( ), the Condition await( ) method can be called only when the thread is the owner of the lock associated with the condition and the signal( ) method may be called only by another thread that has acquired the lock. Interestingly, though, in this case, these restrictions are implementation details of the java.util.concurrent package; some other implementation of these classes could conceivably change those restrictions in some way.

With the exception of the new reader/writer locks and some timed wait lock methods, it may not seem that the Locks package adds a great deal to Java. However, if you delve into it deeper, you'll find that it's also a toolkit for building new kinds of synchronization primitives and higher-level constructs. The locks package opens up a concrete implementation of Java's synchronization mechanism for all to tinker with and extend. A brief look at the implementation classes reveals nifty methods like getOwner( ) to tell you which thread owns a lock or getReadLockCount( ) to tell you how many readers are working on your data. Lots of things are possible with an open implementation like this, including specialized synchronization packages that do things like automatically detect deadlocks or tune themselves based on external information. There may also be cases where using the explicit lock API provided by this package performs better than language-level synchronization. But that probably doesn't justify the additional burden on developers except in special cases. Next, we'll move up a bit and look at some higher-level synchronization tools.

Synchronization Constructs

The `java.util.concurrent` package adds several high- and low-level synchronization utilities borrowed from other languages, including `CountDownLatch`, `Semaphore`, `CyclicBarrier`, and `Exchanger`.

CountDownLatch

The `CountDownLatch` is a very simple synchronization utility that allows any number of threads to block, waiting for a countdown value to reach 0 before being "released" to continue their activities. The `CountDownLatch` is initialized with the count when constructed. Thereafter, threads may block using the `await()` method or block for a limited period of time using the timed wait version of `await()`. Any running thread may decrement the counter at any time, whether threads are blocked or not. Once the counter reaches 0, all waiting threads unblock and continue. Thereafter, any calls to `await()` do not block and the `await()` method returns `false`, indicating that the count has passed. The count cannot be reset.

```
CountDownLatch latch = new CountDownLatch( 2 ); // count from 2

// thread 1
latch.await(); // blocks thread 1

// thread 2
latch.countDown(); // count is 1
latch.countDown(); // count is 0, thread 1 proceeds
```

Countdown latches are used in a wide variety of synchronization schemes to coordinate a number of threads on one result or cause a thread to wait for a number of other threads to produce results. Later we'll talk about a related utility, `CyclicBarrier`, that explicitly waits for a number of threads to synchronize to coordinate an action.

Semaphore

Semaphores are a very old synchronization construct that has been used in many other languages. Conceptually, a semaphore is a pool of *permits*—intangible permission slips to perform some activity. The semaphore is initialized with a specified number of permits. Callers can then use the `acquire()` and `release()` methods to take and return these permits. Calling `acquire()` when no permits are available causes the caller to block until one is released. In this way, for example, a semaphore could be used to limit access to some resource to a specified number of threads:

```
int concurrentReaders = 5;
boolean fair = true;
Semaphore sem = new Semaphore( concurrentReaders, fair );
```

```
Data readData( ) throws InterruptedException {
    sem.acquire( );
    // read data ...
    sem.release( );

    return data;
}
```

In this code snippet, readData( ) effectively limits itself to five concurrent reading threads at any given time. Additional threads are blocked in the acquire( ) method until a permit is free. In this sense, a semaphore is vaguely like a lock with multiple owners. This is where the similarity ends, however.

In actuality, a semaphore differs from a lock in several ways. First, the "pool of permits" is really just a number. No actual value is returned by acquire( ) and no association is made with the acquirer of the lock. This means that any actual locking behavior is strictly cooperative (by convention in the application). It also means that "permits" can be acquired and released by different callers without respect to who actually "acquired" them. It's really just incrementing or decrementing the number. Also, because there is no real association with an "owner," semaphores are not reentrant like real locks are. That is, if a thread calls acquire( ) multiple times, it simply decrements the counter multiple times. This behavior could be useful in some cases to count levels of recursion for security APIs, for example, but is not like a lock, in which one caller "owns" multiple permits. Finally, since the permits pool is really just a number, calling acquire( ) and release( ) out of sync can increase the permit pool beyond its starting point or decrement it below zero. It can even be initialized with a negative number if you wish to require releases before anyone may acquire a permit.

In addition to acquire( ), Semaphore has a tryAcquire( ) method that parallels the tryLock( ) method of Lock. It returns immediately, acquiring a permit if one was available and returning false otherwise. Another form of tryAcquire( ) accepts a timed wait period. Semaphores also have a notion of "fairness" in the ordering of acquire requests. By default, requests are not guaranteed to be ordered, but if the "fair" flag is set when the Semaphore is constructed, acquire( ) doles out permits in first-in-first-out (FIFO) order. The tradeoff is that ordering may impact performance a bit, depending on the implementation.

CyclicBarrier

The CyclicBarrier class is a synchronization point where a specified number of related threads meet after finishing their activities. When all of the threads have arrived, an optional, shared barrier action can be executed and then all of the threads are "released" to continue. The class is termed "cyclic" because it can then be used again in the case where the threads repeat their activities in this manner. CyclicBarrier is an alternative to using the join( ) method, which collects threads only when they have completed and returned from their run( ) method.

The following example, SiteTimer, accepts a number of URLs on the command line and times how long it takes to connect to each one, printing the results in sorted order. It performs the connections in parallel using a dedicated thread per site and uses a CyclicBarrier for the threads to rendezvous after each timing cycle and prints the results before they begin again. This example is a little longer than we'd normally present for a minor utility like this, but it illustrates a number of Java 5.0 features, such as generics, collections, formatted printing, autoboxing, as well as an inner class. Although we haven't yet discussed collections or the network portion of the example, the usage is fairly simple and you can return to the example after reading the relevant chapters later in this book.

```java
import java.util.*;
import java.util.concurrent.*;
import java.net.*;
import java.io.IOException;

public class SiteTimer
{
    CyclicBarrier barrier;
    List<Result> results = new ArrayList<Result>();

    private class Result implements Comparable<Result>
    {
        Long time;
        String site;
        Result( Long time, String site ) {
            this.time = time;
            this.site = site;
        }
        public int compareTo( Result r ) { return time.compareTo( r.time ); }
    }

    static long timeConnect( String site ) {
        long start = System.currentTimeMillis();
        try {
            new URL( site ).openConnection().connect();
        } catch ( IOException e ) {
            return -1;
        }
        return System.currentTimeMillis() - start;
    }

    void showResults() {
        Collections.sort( results );
        for( Result result : results )
            System.out.printf( "%-30.30s : %d\n", result.site, result.time );
        System.out.println("------------------");
    }
```

```
public void start( String [] args )
{
    Runnable showResultsAction = new Runnable() {
        public void run() {
            showResults();
            results.clear();
        } };
    barrier = new CyclicBarrier( args.length, showResultsAction );

    for ( final String site : args )
        new Thread() {
            public void run() {
                while( true ) {
                    long time = timeConnect( site );
                    results.add( new Result( time, site ) );
                    try {
                        barrier.await();
                    } catch ( BrokenBarrierException e ) { return;
                    } catch ( InterruptedException e ) { return; }
                }
            }
        }.start();
}

public static void main( String [] args ) throws IOException {
    new SiteTimer().start( args );
}
```

The start( ) method constructs the barrier, specifying the number of threads that must be present before the group has fully arrived and the action to perform when all of the threads are ready. For each site, a thread is created that loops, timing the connection to the site and adding a result object to the list before blocking on the barrier's await( ) method. When all of the threads reach the await( ) method, the barrier action fires, printing the results. All of the threads are then released to begin the next cycle.

If any of the waiting threads is interrupted or times out (using the timed wait version of the await( ) method) the barrier is said to be "broken" and all of the waiting threads receive a BrokenBarrierException. In theory, the barrier can be "fixed" by calling its reset( ) method, but this is complicated because only one thread from the group can reset the barrier properly. A reset( ) while any other thread is waiting causes the barrier to be broken and the waiting threads to receive the exception again, so it is probably best to start over at this point.

One more detail: the await( ) method returns an integer that indicates the order in which the threads arrived at the barrier. This can be used to divide up work for the next iteration of the threads. For example, if the threads' jobs are not identical, you could use the number to "elect" a leader thread or divide the threads into two or more groups.

Exchanger

The Exchanger is a synchronization point for a pair of threads to exchange data items. An item of the same type is passed in each direction using the exchange( ) method. The first method to arrive at the Exchanger blocks, waiting for its mate. When the second method arrives, they each receive the other's argument to the exchange( ) method. Any number of actual threads may be using the Exchanger and they are simply paired in some order when they arrive. Exchanger is a generic class that is parameterized by the type of object to be passed:

```
Exchanger<ByteBuffer> xchange = new Exchanger<ByteBuffer>( );

// thread 1
Buffer nextBuf = xchange.exchange( buffer1 ); // blocks

// thread 2
Buffer nextBuf = xchange.exchange( buffer2 );

// buffers exchanged, both threads continue...
```

The Exchanger pattern is primarily useful for reusing data objects or buffers between threads, as indicated in this code snippet. Say that you have a reader thread filling buffers with data and a writer thread writing the contents of the buffers somewhere. Using an Exchanger, the reader and writer can trade a pair of buffers back and forth without creating new ones. This may seem a bit arcane, but it has applications when using the NIO advanced I/O package, which we discuss in Chapters 12 and 13.

We should note that the Exchanger is similar to the SynchronousQueue, which we'll discuss in Chapter 11 when we cover the Collections API. The Exchanger, however, passes data in both directions, whereas SynchronousQueue simply passes elements in one direction.

Atomic Operations

The java.util.concurrent.atomic package holds an interesting set of wrapper classes for atomic, "all-or-nothing" operations on certain primitive types and reference values. An atomic operation is a kind of transaction where some sequence of events either completes or fails as a unit and there is no potential for any intermediate state to be seen. In this case, the transactions we're talking about are very simple operations that either set or get a value, possibly in combination with a simple test or mathematical operation. There are atomic wrapper classes for the following types: Booleans, integers, and long values as well as arrays of integers and longs and object references:

```
AtomicBoolean.java
AtomicInteger.java
AtomicIntegerArray.java
AtomicLong.java
AtomicLongArray.java
```

```
AtomicReference.java
AtomicReferenceArray.java
```

The AtomicBoolean class (which, by the way, has to compete with java.awt.Robot for coolest class name in Java) serves as a good example. At first glance, it seems like an oxymoron. After all, normal operations on Booleans in Java are atomic already. There is supposed to be no possible "in-between" state for a Boolean to be misread by any horribly mangled multithreaded code (as there theoretically could be for long and double values). Instead, the usefulness of the AtomicBoolean wrapper is in its combination operations: compareAndSet( ) and getAndSet( ):

```
AtomicBoolean bool = new AtomicBoolean( true );
bool.compareAndSet( expectedValue, newValue );
```

The compareAndSet( ) method first performs a comparison to an expected value (true or false in the case of a Boolean) and only if the value matches does it assign the new value. The interesting thing is that both of these operations happen "atomically," together. This means that there is no possibility of someone changing the value between the time that we checked it and assigned the new value. That may sound like a slim chance anyway, but it's very important for guaranteeing the semantics of flags. For example, suppose we have a master "shutdown" switch in our application and the thread that sets it wants to perform cleanup on the way out. Using compareAndSet( ) to test first, we can guarantee that only one thread can possibly set the flag and perform the procedure.

The getAndSet( ) method simply assigns the new value and returns the old value in the same, safe way. It's a little harder to see how this applies to a Boolean, so let's move on to AtomicInteger and AtomicLong. These numeric types have additional arithmetic combination operations:

```
int getAndIncrement( )
int getAndDecrement( )
int getAndAdd(int delta)
int incrementAndGet( )
int decrementAndGet( )
int addAndGet(int delta)
```

getAndIncrement( ) increments the value and then returns the previous value. incrementAndGet( ) does the converse, returning the new value. These operations are very useful for generating unique serial numbers. For example:

```
AtomicInteger serialNum = new AtomicInteger(0);

public int nextSerialNumber( ) {
    return serialNum.getAndIncrement( );
}
```

We could have accomplished the same thing by synchronizing the method, but this is, in some ways, simpler and may be much faster.

Object-type references can also be wrapped for atomic operations, including compareAndSet( ) and getAndSet( ). The AtomicReference class is generic and parameterized by the type of reference it wraps:

```
AtomicReference<Node> ref = new AtomicReference<Node>( node );
ref.compareAndSet( null, newNode );
```

Weak implementations

The compareAndSet( ) method has a strange twin named weakCompareAndSet( ), which has the dubious distinction that it simply may not work when called. It is, however, nice enough to tell you when it doesn't work by returning false. What's the point of this? Well, by allowing this fuzziness, Java may be able to make the implementation of the weak method much faster than the "certain" one. You can loop and retry the weak method instead and it may improve performance on some architectures. This is all because the Java VM may be able to map these kinds of atomic operations all the way down to the hardware level for performance, but restrictions may apply that make it difficult to guarantee.

Field updaters

The atomic package also supplies a set of "field update" utilities for each of the types that it can wrap. These utilities use reflection (see Chapter 7) to perform the kinds of atomic operations we described previously on "naked" primitive types that are not already wrapped in their atomic wrapper classes. The field updaters work on variables in an object by name and type. The catch is that atomicity is guaranteed only with respect to other callers that use the field updaters or the regular atomic wrapper classes. No guarantees are made with respect to other threads that address the variables in arbitrary ways.

Conclusion

Java was one of the first mainstream languages to provide support for threading at the language level and is now one of the first languages to standardize high-level threading utilities and APIs as well. In this chapter, we've covered both of these aspects. At this point, we've come to the end of our discussion of threads in Java and also, in a way, to the end of the first part of this book. In Chapters 1 through 9, we have discussed the Java language: its syntax and "built-in" features. In the rest of the book, we will focus mainly on the APIs and libraries that make up the rest of the Java platform. We will see that the real appeal of Java is the combination of this simple language married with powerful tools and standards.

## CHAPTER 10

Working with Text

If you've been reading this book sequentially, you've read all about the core Java language constructs, including the object-oriented aspects of the language and the use of threads. Now it's time to shift gears and start talking about the Java Application Programming Interface (API), the collection of classes that comprise the standard Java packages and come with every Java implementation. Java's core packages are one of its most distinguishing features. Many other object-oriented languages have similar features, but none has as extensive a set of standardized APIs and tools as Java does. This is both a reflection of and a reason for Java's success. Table 10-1 lists the most important packages in the API and shows which chapters discuss each of the packages.

Table 10-1. Java API packages

Package	Contents	Chapter
java.lang	Basic language classes	4–9
java.lang.reflect	Reflection	7
java.util.concurrent	Thread utilities	9
java.text java.util.regex	International text classes and regular expressions	10
java.util	Utilities and collections classes	10–12
java.io java.nio	Input and output	12
java.net	Networking and Remote Method Invocation classes	13–14
java.rmi	Remote Method Invocation classes	13
javax.servlet	Web applications	15
javax.swing java.awt	Swing GUI and 2D graphics	16–20
java.awt.image javax.imageio javax.media	Images, sound, and video	21

Table 10-1. Java API packages (continued)

Package	Contents	Chapter
java.beans	JavaBeans API	22
java.applet	The Applet API	23
javax.xml	The XML API	24

As you can see in Table 10-1, we have examined some classes in java.lang in earlier chapters while looking at the core language constructs. Starting with this chapter, we throw open the Java toolbox and begin examining the rest of the API classes, starting with text-related utilities, because they are fundamental to all kinds of applications.

Text-Related APIs

In this chapter, we cover most of the special-purpose, text-related APIs in Java, from simple classes for parsing words and numbers to advanced text formatting, internationalization, and regular expressions. But since so much of what we do with computers is oriented around text, classifying APIs as strictly text-related can be somewhat arbitrary. Some of the text-related packages we cover in the next chapter include the Java Calendar API, the Properties and User Preferences APIs, and the Logging API. But probably the most important new tools in the text arena are those for working with the Extensible Markup Language, XML. In Chapter 24, we cover this topic in detail, along with the XSL/XSLT stylesheet language. Together they provide a powerful framework for rendering documents.

Before we dive in, we should mention that one of the biggest developments in Java in a long time has been the introduction of *printf style* text formatting, introduced in Java 5.0. We call it "printf style" after the C language *printf* function, from which it was largely borrowed. Although this new formatting capability does not technically add many new features to Java, it is an important and highly anticipated addition that changes the "feel" of the language in a fundamental way. We'll show both the older and newer style tools in this chapter so that you can be familiar with both.

Strings

We'll start by taking a closer look at the Java String class (or, more specifically, java.lang.String). Since working with Strings is so fundamental, understanding the way Strings are implemented in Java and what you can do with them is very important. A String object encapsulates a sequence of Unicode characters. Internally, these characters are stored in a regular Java array, but the String object guards this array jealously and gives you access to it only through its own API. This is to support the idea that Strings are *immutable*; once you create a String object, you can't change its value. Lots of operations on a String object appear to change the characters or length of a string, but what they really do is return a new String object that copies or internally references the needed characters of the original. Java implementations make an effort to consolidate identical strings used in the same class into a shared-string pool and to share parts of Strings where possible.

The original motivation for all of this was performance. Immutable Strings can save memory and be optimized for speed by the Java VM. The flip side is that a programmer should have a basic understanding of the String class in order to avoid creating an excessive number of String objects in places where performance is an issue. That was especially true in the past, when VMs were slow and handled memory poorly. Nowadays string usage is not usually an issue in the overall performance of a real application.[*]

Constructing Strings

Literal strings, defined in your source code, are declared with double quotes and can be assigned to a String variable:

```
String quote = "To be or not to be";
```

Java automatically converts the literal string into a String object and assigns it to the variable.

Strings keep track of their own length, so String objects in Java don't require special terminators. You can get the length of a String with the length( ) method:

```
int length = quote.length( );
```

Strings can take advantage of the only overloaded operator in Java, the + operator, for string concatenation. The following code produces equivalent strings:

```
String name = "John " + "Smith";
String name = "John ".concat("Smith");
```

Literal strings can't span lines in Java source files, but we can concatenate lines to produce the same effect:

```
String poem =
    "'Twas brillig, and the slithy toves\n" +
    "   Did gyre and gimble in the wabe:\n" +
    "All mimsy were the borogoves,\n" +
    "   And the mome raths outgrabe.\n";
```

Embedding lengthy text in source code is not normally something you want to do. In this and the following chapter, we'll talk about ways to load Strings from files, special packages called resource bundles, and URLs. Technologies like Java Server Pages

---

[*] When in doubt, measure it! If your String-manipulating code is clean and easy to understand, don't rewrite it until someone proves to you that it is too slow. Chances are that they will be wrong. And don't be fooled by relative comparisons. A millisecond is 1000 times slower than a microsecond, but it still may be negligible to your application's overall performance.

and template engines also provide a way to factor out large amounts of text from your code. For example, in Chapter 14, we'll see how to load our poem from a web server by opening a URL like this:

```
InputStream poem = new URL(
    "http://myserver/~dodgson/jabberwocky.txt").openStream( );
```

In addition to making strings from literal expressions, you can construct a String directly from an array of characters:

```
char [] data = new char [] { 'L', 'e', 'm', 'm', 'i', 'n', 'g' };
String lemming = new String( data );
```

You can also construct a String from an array of bytes:

```
byte [] data = new byte [] { (byte)97, (byte)98, (byte)99 };
String abc = new String(data, "ISO8859_1");
```

In this case, the second argument to the String constructor is the name of a character-encoding scheme. The String constructor uses it to convert the raw bytes to standard 2-byte Unicode characters. If you don't specify a character encoding, the default encoding scheme on your system is used.[*]

Conversely, the charAt( ) method of the String class lets you access the characters of a String in an array-like fashion:

```
String s = "Newton";
for ( int i = 0; i < s.length( ); i++ )
    System.out.println( s.charAt( i ) );
```

This code prints the characters of the string one at a time. Alternately, we can get the characters all at once with toCharArray( ). Here's a way to save typing a bunch of single quotes and get an array holding the alphabet:

```
char [] abcs = "abcdefghijklmnopqrstuvwxyz".toCharArray( );
```

The notion that a String is a sequence of characters is also codified by the String class implementing the interface java.lang.CharSequence, which prescribes the methods length( ) and charAt( ) as well as a way to get a subset of the characters.

Strings from Things

Objects and primitive types in Java can be turned into a default textual representation as a String. For primitive types like numbers, the string should be fairly obvious; for object types it is under the control of the object itself. We can get the string representation of an item with the static String.valueOf( ) method. Various overloaded versions of this method accept each of the primitive types:

```
String one = String.valueOf( 1 ); // integer, "1"
String two = String.valueOf( 2.384f ); // float, "2.384"
String notTrue = String.valueOf( false ); // boolean, "false"
```

---

[*] In Windows, the default encoding is CP1252; in Solaris, it's ISO8859_1.

All objects in Java have a toString( ) method, inherited from the Object class. For many objects, this method returns a useful result that displays the contents of the object. For example, a java.util.Date object's toString( ) method returns the date it represents formatted as a string. For objects that do not provide a representation, the string result is just a unique identifier that can be used for debugging. The String.valueOf( ) method, when called for an object, invokes the object's toString( ) method and returns the result. The only real difference in using this method is that if you pass it a null object reference, it returns the String "null" for you, instead of producing a NullPointerException:

```
Date date = new Date( );
// Equivalent, e.g., "Sun Dec 19 05:45:34 CST 1969"
String d1 = String.valueOf( date );
String d2 = date.toString( );

date = null;
d1 = String.valueOf( date );  // "null"
d2 = date.toString( );   // NullPointerException!
```

String concatenation uses the valueOf( ) method internally, so if you "add" an object or primitive using the plus operator (+), you get a String:

```
String today = "Today's date is :" + date;
```

You'll sometimes see people use the empty string and the plus operator (+) as shorthand to get the string value of an object. For example:

```
String two = "" + 2.384f;
String today = "" + new Date( );
```

Comparing Strings

The standard equals( ) method can compare strings for *equality*; they contain exactly the same characters. You can use a different method, equalsIgnoreCase( ), to check the equivalence of strings in a case-insensitive way:

```
String one = "FOO";
String two = "foo";

one.equals( two );          // false
one.equalsIgnoreCase( two );  // true
```

A common mistake for novice programmers in Java is to compare strings with the == operator when they mean to use the equals( ) method. Remember that strings are objects in Java, and == tests for object *identity*, that is, whether the two arguments being tested are the same object. In Java, it's easy to make two strings that have the same characters but are not the same string object. For example:

```
String foo1 = "foo";
String foo2 = String.valueOf( new char [] { 'f', 'o', 'o' } );

foo1 == foo2        // false!
foo1.equals( foo2 )  // true
```

This mistake is particularly dangerous because it often works for the common case in which you are comparing literal strings (strings declared with double quotes right in the code). The reason for this is that Java tries to manage strings efficiently by combining them. At compile time, Java finds all the identical strings within a given class and makes only one object for them. This is safe because strings are immutable and cannot change. You can coalesce strings yourself in this way at runtime using the String intern( ) method. Interning a string returns an equivalent string reference that is unique across the VM.

The compareTo( ) method compares the lexical value of the String to another String, determining whether it sorts alphabetically earlier than, the same as, or later than the target string. It returns an integer that is less than, equal to, or greater than zero:

```
String abc = "abc";
String def = "def";
String num = "123";

if ( abc.compareTo( def ) < 0 )        // true
if ( abc.compareTo( abc ) == 0 )       // true
if ( abc.compareTo( num ) > 0 )        // true
```

The compareTo( ) method compares strings strictly by their characters' positions in the Unicode specification. This works for simple text but does not handle all language variations well. The Collator class, discussed next, can be used for more sophisticated comparisons.

The Collator class

The java.text package provides a sophisticated set of classes for comparing strings in specific languages. German, for example, has vowels with umlauts and another character that resembles the Greek letter beta and represents a double "s." How should we sort these? Although the rules for sorting such characters are precisely defined, you can't assume that the lexical comparison we used earlier has the correct meaning for languages other than English. Fortunately, the Collator class takes care of these complex sorting problems.

In the following example, we use a Collator designed to compare German strings. You can obtain a default Collator by calling the Collator.getInstance( ) method with no arguments. Once you have an appropriate Collator instance, you can use its compare( ) method, which returns values just like String's compareTo( ) method. The following code creates two strings for the German translations of "fun" and "later," using Unicode constants for these two special characters. It then compares them, using a Collator for the German locale. (Locales help you deal with issues relevant to particular languages and cultures; we'll talk about them in detail later in this chapter.) The result in this case is that "fun" (Spaß) sorts before "later" (später):

```
String fun = "Spa\u00df";
String later = "sp\u00e4ter";
```

```
Collator german = Collator.getInstance(Locale.GERMAN);
if (german.compare(fun, later) < 0) // true
```

Using collators is essential if you're working with languages other than English. In Spanish, for example, "ll" and "ch" are treated as unique characters and alphabetized separately. A collator handles cases like these automatically.

Searching

The String class provides several simple methods for finding fixed substrings within a string. The startsWith( ) and endsWith( ) methods compare an argument string with the beginning and end of the String, respectively:

```
String url = "http://foo.bar.com/";
if ( url.startsWith("http:") )  // true
```

The indexOf( ) method searches for the first occurrence of a character or substring and returns the starting character position, or -1 if the substring is not found:

```
String abcs = "abcdefghijklmnopqrstuvwxyz";
int i = abcs.indexOf( 'p' );     // 15
int i = abcs.indexOf( "def" );   // 3
int I = abcs.indexOf( "Fang" );  // -1
```

Similarly, lastIndexOf( ) searches backward through the string for the last occurrence of a character or substring.

Java 5.0 added a contains( ) method to handle the very common task of checking to see whether a given substring is contained in the target string:

```
String log = "There is an emergency in sector 7!";
if ( log.contains("emergency") ) pageSomeone( );

// equivalent to
if ( log.indexOf("emergency") != -1 ) ...
```

For more complex searching, you can use the Regular Expression API, which allows you to look for and parse complex patterns. We'll talk about regular expressions later in this chapter.

Editing

A number of methods operate on the String and return a new String as a result. While this is useful, you should be aware that creating lots of strings in this manner can affect performance. If you need to modify a string often or build a complex string from components, you should use the StringBuilder class, as we'll discuss shortly.

trim( ) is a useful method that removes leading and trailing whitespace (i.e., carriage return, newline, and tab) from the String:

```
String str = "   abc   ";
str = str.trim();  // "abc"
```

In this example, we have thrown away the original String (with excess whitespace), and it will be garbage-collected.

The toUpperCase( ) and toLowerCase( ) methods return a new String of the appropriate case:

```
String down = "FOO".toLowerCase( );      // "foo"
String up   = down.toUpperCase( );       // "FOO"
```

substring( ) returns a specified range of characters. The starting index is inclusive; the ending is exclusive:

```
String abcs = "abcdefghijklmnopqrstuvwxyz";
String cde = abcs.substring( 2, 5 ); // "cde"
```

The replace( ) method was added in Java 5.0, providing simple, literal string substitution. One or more occurrences of the target string are replaced with the replacement string, moving from beginning to end. For example:

```
String message = "Hello NAME, how are you?".replace( "NAME", "Penny" );
// "Hello Penny, how are you?"
String xy = "xxooxxxoo".replace( "xx", "X" );
// "XooXxoo"
```

The String class also has two methods that allow you to do more complex pattern substitution: replaceAll( ) and replaceFirst( ). Unlike the simple replace( ) method, these methods use regular expressions to describe the replacement pattern, which we'll cover later in this chapter.

String Method Summary

Table 10-2 summarizes the methods provided by the String class.

Table 10-2. String methods

Method	Functionality
charAt( )	Gets a particular character in the string
compareTo( )	Compares the string with another string
concat( )	Concatenates the string with another string
contains( )	Checks whether the string contains another string
copyValueOf( )	Returns a string equivalent to the specified character array
endsWith( )	Checks whether the string ends with a specified suffix
equals( )	Compares the string with another string
equalsIgnoreCase( )	Compares the string with another string, ignoring case
getBytes( )	Copies characters from the string into a byte array
getChars( )	Copies characters from the string into a character array
hashCode( )	Returns a hashcode for the string
indexOf( )	Searches for the first occurrence of a character or substring in the string

Table 10-2. String methods (continued)

Method	Functionality
intern( )	Fetches a unique instance of the string from a global shared-string pool
lastIndexOf( )	Searches for the last occurrence of a character or substring in a string
length( )	Returns the length of the string
matches( )	Determines if the whole string matches a regular expression pattern
regionMatches( )	Checks whether a region of the string matches the specified region of another string
replace( )	Replaces all occurrences of a character in the string with another character
replaceAll( )	Replaces all occurrences of a regular expression pattern with a pattern
replaceFirst( )	Replaces the first occurrence of a regular expression pattern with a pattern
split( )	Splits the string into an array of strings using a regular expression pattern as a delimiter
startsWith( )	Checks whether the string starts with a specified prefix
substring( )	Returns a substring from the string
toCharArray( )	Returns the array of characters from the string
toLowerCase( )	Converts the string to lowercase
toString( )	Returns the string value of an object
toUpperCase( )	Converts the string to uppercase
trim( )	Removes leading and trailing whitespace from the string
valueOf( )	Returns a string representation of a value

StringBuilder and StringBuffer

In contrast to the immutable string, the java.lang.StringBuilder class is a modifiable and expandable buffer for characters. You can use it to create a big string efficiently. StringBuilder and StringBuffer are twins; they have exactly the same API. StringBuilder was added in Java 5.0 as a drop-in, unsynchronized replacement for StringBuffer. We'll come back to that in a bit.

First, let's look at some examples of String construction:

```
// Could be better
String ball = "Hello";
ball = ball + " there.";
ball = ball + " How are you?";
```

This example creates an unnecessary String object each time we use the concatenation operator (+). Whether this is significant depends on how often this code is run and how big the string actually gets. Here's a more extreme example:

```
// Bad use of + ...
while( (line = readLine( )) != EOF )
    text += line;
```

This example repeatedly produces new String objects. The character array must be copied over and over, which can adversely affect performance. The solution is to use a StringBuilder object and its append( ) method:

```
StringBuilder sb = new StringBuilder("Hello");
sb.append(" there.");
sb.append(" How are you?");

StringBuilder text = new StringBuilder( );
while( (line = readline( )) != EOF )
    text.append( line );
```

Here, the StringBuilder efficiently handles expanding the array as necessary. We can get a String back from the StringBuilder with its toString( ) method:

```
String message = sb.toString( );
```

You can also retrieve part of a StringBuilder, as a String, using one of the substring( ) methods.

You might be interested to know that when you write a long expression using string concatenation, the compiler generates code that uses a StringBuilder behind the scenes:

```
String foo = "To " + "be " + "or";
```

It is really equivalent to:

```
String foo = new
    StringBuilder( ).append("To ").append("be ").append("or").toString( );
```

In this case, the compiler knows what you are trying to do and takes care of it for you.

The StringBuilder class provides a number of overloaded append( ) methods for adding any type of data to the buffer. StringBuilder also provides a number of overloaded insert( ) methods for inserting various types of data at a particular location in the string buffer. Furthermore, you can remove a single character or a range of characters with the deleteCharAt( ) and delete( ) methods. Finally, you can replace part of the StringBuilder with the contents of a String using the replace( ) method. The String and StringBuilder classes cooperate so that, in some cases, no copy of the data has to be made; the string data is shared between the objects.

You should use a StringBuilder instead of a String any time you need to keep adding characters to a string; it's designed to handle such modifications efficiently. You can convert the StringBuilder to a String when you need it, or simply concatenate or print it anywhere you'd use a String.

As we said earlier, StringBuilder was added in Java 5.0 as a replacement for StringBuffer. The only real difference between the two is that the methods of StringBuffer are synchronized and the methods of StringBuilder are not. This means that if you wish to use StringBuilder from multiple threads concurrently, you must synchronize the access yourself (which is easily accomplished). The reason for the change is that most simple usage does not require any synchronization and shouldn't have to pay the associated penalty (slight as it is).

Internationalization

The Java VM lets us write code that executes in the same way on any Java platform. But in a global marketplace, that is only half the battle. A big question remains: will the application content and data be understandable to end users worldwide? Must users know English to use your application? The answer is that Java provides thorough support for *localizing* the text of your application for most modern languages and dialects. In this section, we'll talk about the concepts of internationalization (often abbreviated "I18N") and the classes that support them.

The java.util.Locale Class

Internationalization programming revolves around the Locale class. The class itself is very simple; it encapsulates a country code, a language code, and a rarely used variant code. Commonly used languages and countries are defined as constants in the Locale class. (Maybe it's ironic that these names are all in English.) You can retrieve the codes or readable names, as follows:

```
Locale l = Locale.ITALIAN;
System.out.println(l.getCountry());          // IT
System.out.println(l.getDisplayCountry());   // Italy
System.out.println(l.getLanguage());         // it
System.out.println(l.getDisplayLanguage());  // Italian
```

The country codes comply with ISO 3166. You will find a complete list of country codes at *http://www.chemie.fu-berlin.de/diverse/doc/ISO_3166.html*. The language codes comply with ISO 639. A complete list of language codes is online at *http://www.ics.uci.edu/pub/ietf/http/related/iso639.txt*. There is no official set of variant codes; they are designated as vendor-specific or platform-specific. You can get an array of all supported Locales with the static getAvailableLocales() method (which you might use to let your users choose). Or you can retrieve the default Locale for the location where your code is running with the static Locale.getDefault() method and let the system decide for you.

Many classes throughout the Java API use a Locale to decide how to represent text. We ran into one earlier when talking about sorting text with the Collator class. We'll see more later in this chapter used to format numbers and currency strings, and again in the next chapter with the DateFormat class, which uses Locales to determine how to format and parse dates and times. Without getting into the details yet, here is a quick example:

```
System.out.printf( Locale.ITALIAN, "%f\n", 3.14 ); // "3,14"
```

The statement above uses the Italian Locale to indicate that the decimal number 3.14 should be formatted as it would in Italian, using a comma instead of a decimal point. We'll talk about formatting text in detail later in this chapter.

Resource Bundles

Before we move on to the details of formatting messages and values, we might take a step back and ask a bigger question: what about the messages themselves? How can we write and manage applications that are truly multilingual in their user interfaces and in all the messages they display to the user? We can discover our locale, but how do we manage all of the application text in our code? The ResourceBundle class offers a clean, flexible solution for factoring out the text and resources of your application into language-specific classes or text files.

A ResourceBundle is a collection of objects your application can access by name. It acts much like the Hashtable or Map collections we'll discuss in Chapter 11, looking up objects based on Strings that serve as keys. A ResourceBundle of a given name may be defined for many different Locales. To get a particular ResourceBundle, call the factory method ResourceBundle.getBundle( ), which accepts the name of the ResourceBundle and a Locale. The following example gets the ResourceBundle named "Message" for two Locales; from each bundle, it retrieves the message whose key is "HelloMessage" and prints the message:

```
import java.util.*;

public class Hello {
  public static void main(String[] args) {
    ResourceBundle bun;
    bun = ResourceBundle.getBundle("Message", Locale.ITALY);
    System.out.println(bun.getString("HelloMessage"));
    bun = ResourceBundle.getBundle("Message", Locale.US);
    System.out.println(bun.getString("HelloMessage"));
  }
}
```

The getBundle( ) method throws the runtime exception MissingResourceException if an appropriate ResourceBundle cannot be located.

You can provide ResourceBundles in two ways: either as compiled Java classes (hard-coded Java) or as simple property files. Resource bundles implemented as classes are either subclasses of ListResourceBundle or direct implementations of ResourceBundle. Resource bundles backed by a property file are represented at runtime by a PropertyResourceBundle object. ResourceBundle.getBundle( ) returns either a matching class or an instance of PropertyResourceBundle corresponding to a matching property file. The algorithm used by getBundle( ) is based on appending the country and language codes of the requested Locale to the name of the resource. Specifically, it searches for resources in this order:

```
name_language_country_variant
name_language_country
name_language
name
name_default-language_default-country_default-variant
name_default-language_default-country
name_default-language
```

In this example, when we try to get the ResourceBundle named Message, specific to Locale.ITALY, it searches for the following names (no variant codes are in the Locales we are using):

```
Message_it_IT
Message_it
Message
Message_en_US
Message_en
```

Let's define the Message_it_IT ResourceBundle as a hardcoded class, a subclass of ListResourceBundle:

```
import java.util.*;

public class Message_it_IT extends ListResourceBundle {
  public Object[][] getContents( ) {
    return contents;
  }

  static final Object[][] contents = {
    {"HelloMessage", "Buon giorno, world!"},
    {"OtherMessage", "Ciao."},
  };
}
```

ListResourceBundle makes it easy to define a ResourceBundle class; all we have to do is override the getContents( ) method. This method simply returns a two-dimensional array containing the names and values of its resources. In this example, contents[1][0] is the second key (OtherMessage), and contents [1][1] is the corresponding message (Ciao.).

Let's define a ResourceBundle for Locale.US. This time, we'll take the easy way and make a property file. Save the following data in a file called *Message_en_US.properties*:

```
HelloMessage=Hello, world!
OtherMessage=Bye.
```

So what happens if somebody runs your program in Locale.FRANCE, and no ResourceBundle is defined for that Locale? To avoid a runtime MissingResourceException, it's a good idea to define a default ResourceBundle. In our example, you can change the name of the property file to *Message.properties*. That way, if a language-or country-specific ResourceBundle cannot be found, your application can still run.

Parsing and Formatting Text

Parsing and formatting text is a large, open-ended topic. So far in this chapter, we've looked at only primitive operations on strings—creation, basic editing, searching, and turning simple values into strings. Now we'd like to move on to more structured forms of text. Java has a rich set of APIs for parsing and printing formatted strings, including numbers, dates, times, and currency values. We'll cover most of these topics in this chapter, but we'll wait to discuss date and time formatting until Chapter 11.

We'll start with parsing—reading primitive numbers and values as strings and chopping long strings into tokens. Then we'll go the other way and look at formatting strings and the java.text package. We'll revisit the topic of internationalization to see how Java can localize parsing and formatting of text, numbers, and dates for particular locales. Finally, we'll take a detailed look at regular expressions, the most powerful text-parsing tool Java offers. Regular expressions let you define your own patterns of arbitrary complexity, search for them, and parse them from text.

We should mention that you're going to see a great deal of overlap between the new formatting and parsing APIs (printf and Scanner) introduced in Java 5.0 and the older APIs of the java.text package. The new APIs effectively replace much of the old ones and in some ways are easier to use. Nonetheless, it's good to know about both because so much existing code uses the older APIs.

Parsing Primitive Numbers

In Java, numbers and Booleans are primitive types—not objects. But for each primitive type, Java also defines a *primitive wrapper* class. Specifically, the java.lang package includes the following classes: Byte, Short, Integer, Long, Float, Double, and Boolean. We'll talk about these in Chapter 1, but we bring them up now because these classes hold static utility methods that know how to parse their respective types from strings. Each of these primitive wrapper classes has a static "parse" method that reads a String and returns the corresponding primitive type. For example:

```
byte b = Byte.parseByte("16");
int n = Integer.parseInt( "42" );
long l = Long.parseLong( "99999999999" );
float f = Float.parseFloat( "4.2" );
double d = Double.parseDouble( "99.99999999" );
boolean b = Boolean.parseBoolean("true");
// Prior to Java 5.0 use:
boolean b = new Boolean("true").booleanValue( );
```

In Java 5.0, a new utility, `java.util.Scanner`, was introduced, which provides a single API for not only parsing individual primitive types from strings, but reading them from a stream of tokens. This example shows how to use it in place of the wrapper classes above:

```java
byte b = new Scanner("16").nextByte( );
int n = new Scanner("42").nextInt( );
long l = new Scanner("99999999999").nextLong( );
float f = new Scanner("4.2").nextFloat( );
double d = new Scanner("99.99999999").nextDouble( );
boolean b = new Scanner("true").nextBoolean( );
```

We'll see Scanner used to parse multiple values from a String or stream when we discuss tokenizing text later in this chapter.

Working with alternate bases

It's easy to parse integer type numbers (byte, short, int, long) in alternate numeric bases. You can use the parse methods of the primitive wrapper classes by simply specifying the base as a second parameter:

```java
long l = Long.parseLong( "CAFEBABE", 16 );  // l = 3405691582
byte b = Byte.parseByte ( "12", 8 ); // b = 10
```

All methods of the Java 5.0 Scanner class described earlier also accept a base as an optional argument:

```java
long l = new Scanner( "CAFEBABE" ).nextLong( 16 );  // l = 3405691582
byte b = new Scanner( "12" ).nextByte( 8 ); // b = 10
```

You can go the other way and convert a long or integer value to a string value in a specified base using special static `toString( )` methods of the Integer and Long classes:

```java
String s = Long.toString( 3405691582L, 16 );  // s = "cafebabe"
```

For convenience, each class also has a static `toHexString( )` method for working with base 16:

```java
String s = Integer.toHexString( 255 ).toUpperCase( );  // s = "FF";
```

Number formats

The wrapper class parser methods above handle the case of numbers formatted using only the simplest English conventions with no frills. If these parse methods do not understand the string, either because it's simply not a valid number or because the number is formatted in the convention of another language, they throw a `NumberFormatException`:

```java
// Italian formatting
double d = Double.parseDouble("1.234,56");  // NumberFormatException
```

The new Scanner API is much smarter and can use Locales to parse numbers in specific languages with more elaborate conventions. For example, the Scanner can handle comma-formatted numbers:

```
int n = new Scanner("99,999,999").nextInt( );
```

You can specify a Locale other than the default with the useLocale( ) method. Let's parse that value in Italian now:

```
double d = new Scanner("1.234,56").useLocale( Locale.ITALIAN ).nextDouble( );
```

If the Scanner cannot parse a string, it throws a runtime InputMismatchException:

```
double d = new Scanner("garbage").nextDouble( ); // InputMismatchException
```

If you can't use Java 5.0 yet, don't fret. Later in this chapter, we'll show you how to use the java.text package to accomplish the same thing with the NumberFormat class. The classes of the java.text package also allow you to parse additional types, such as dates, times, and localized currency values, that aren't handled by the Scanner.

Tokenizing Text

A common programming task involves parsing a string of text into words or "tokens" that are separated by some set of delimiter characters, such as spaces or commas. The first example contains words separated by single spaces. The second, more realistic problem involves comma-delimited fields.

```
Now is the time for all good men (and women)...

Check Number, Description,     Amount
4231,          Java Programming, 1000.00
```

Java has several (unfortunately overlapping) APIs for handling situations like this. The most powerful and useful are the String split( ) and Scanner APIs. Both utilize regular expressions to allow you to break the string on arbitrary patterns. We haven't talked about regular expressions yet, but in order to show you how this works we'll just give you the necessary magic and explain in detail later in this chapter. We'll also mention a legacy utility, java.util.StringTokenizer, which uses simple character sets to split a string. StringTokenizer is not as powerful, but doesn't require an understanding of regular expressions.

The String split( ) method accepts a regular expression that describes a delimiter and uses it to chop the string into an array of Strings:

```
String text = "Now is the time for all good men";
String [] words = text.split("\\s");
// words = "Now", "is", "the", "time", ...

String text = "4231,         Java Programming, 1000.00";
String [] fields = text.split("\\s*,\\s*");
// fields = "4231", "Java Programming", "1000.00"
```

In the first example, we used the regular expression \\s, which matches a single whitespace character (space, tab, or carriage return). The split( ) method returned an array of eight strings. In the second example, we used a more complicated regular expression, \\s*,\\s*, which matches a comma surrounded by any number of contiguous spaces (possibly zero). This reduced our text to three nice, tidy fields.

With the new Scanner API, we could go a step further and parse the numbers of our second example as we extract them:

```
String text = "4231,         Java Programming, 1000.00";
Scanner scanner = new Scanner( text ).useDelimiter("\\s*,\\s*");
int checkNumber = scanner.nextInt( ); // 4231
String description = scanner.next( ); // "Java Programming"
float amount = scanner.nextFloat( );  // 1000.00
```

Here, we've told the Scanner to use our regular expression as the delimiter and then called it repeatedly to parse each field as its corresponding type. The Scanner is convenient because it can read not only from Strings but directly from stream sources, such as InputStreams, Files, and Channels:

```
Scanner fileScanner = new Scanner( new File("spreadsheet.csv") );
fileScanner.useDelimiter( "\\s*,\\s* );
// ...
```

Another thing that you can do with the Scanner is to look ahead with the "hasNext" methods to see if another item is coming:

```
while( scanner.hasNextInt( ) ) {
  int n = scanner.nextInt( );
  ...
}
```

StringTokenizer

Although the StringTokenizer class that we mentioned is now a legacy item, it's good to know that it's there because it's been around since the beginning of Java and is used in a lot of code. StringTokenizer allows you to specify a delimiter as a set of characters and matches any number or combination of those characters as a delimiter between tokens. The following snippet reads the words of our first example:

```
String text = "Now is the time for all good men (and women)...";
StringTokenizer st = new StringTokenizer( text );

while ( st.hasMoreTokens( ) ) {
    String word = st.nextToken( );
    ...
}
```

We invoke the hasMoreTokens( ) and nextToken( ) methods to loop over the words of the text. By default, the StringTokenizer class uses standard whitespace characters— carriage return, newline, and tab—as delimiters. You can also specify your own set of delimiter characters in the StringTokenizer constructor. Any contiguous combination of the specified characters that appears in the target string is skipped between tokens:

```
String text = "4231,     Java Programming, 1000.00";
StringTokenizer st = new StringTokenizer( text, "," );

while ( st.hasMoreTokens( ) ) {
    String word = st.nextToken( );
    // word = "4231", "     Java Programming", "1000.00"
}
```

This isn't as clean as our regular expression example. Here we used a comma as the delimiter so we get extra leading whitespace in our description field. If we had added space to our delimiter string, the StringTokenizer would have broken our description into two words, "Java" and "Programming," which is not what we wanted.

Printf-Style Formatting

One of the most anticipated new features in Java 5.0 is printf-style string formatting. printf-style formatting utilizes special format strings embedded into text to tell the formatting engine where to place arguments and to give detailed specification about conversions, layout, and alignment. The printf formatting methods also make use of variable-length argument lists, which makes working with them much easier. Here is a quick example of printf-formatted output:

```
System.out.printf( "My name is %s and I am %d years old\n", name, age );
```

As we mentioned, printf formatting draws it name from the C language printf( ) function, so if you've done any C programming, this will look familiar. Java has extended the concept, adding some additional type safety and convenience features. Although Java has had some text formatting capabilities in the past (we'll discuss the java.text package and MessageFormat later), printf formatting was not really feasible until variable-length argument lists and autoboxing of primitive types were added in Java 5.0.

Formatter

The primary new tool in our text formatting arsenal is the java.util.Formatter class and its format( ) method. Several convenience methods can hide the Formatter object from you and you may not need to create a Formatter directly. First, the static String.format( ) method can be used to format a String with arguments (like the C language sprintf( ) method):

```
String message =
    String.format("My name is %s and I am %d years old.", name, age );
```

Next, the java.io.PrintStream and java.io.PrintWriter classes, which are used for writing text to streams, have their own format( ) method. We discuss streams in

Chapter 12, but this simply means that you can use this same printf-style formatting for writing strings to any kind of stream, whether it be to System.out standard console output, to a file, or to a network connection.

In addition to the format( ) method, PrintStream and PrintWriter also have a version of the format method that is actually called printf( ). The printf( ) method is identical to and, in fact, simply delegates to the format( ) method. It's there solely as a shout out to the C programmers and ex-C programmers in the audience.

The Format String

The syntax of the format string is compact and a bit cryptic at first, but not bad once you get used to it. The simplest format string is just a percent sign (%) followed by a conversion character. For example, the following text has two embedded format strings:

```
"My name is %s and I am %d years old."
```

The first conversion character is s, the most general format, which represents a string value, and the second is d, which represents an integer value. There are about a dozen basic conversion characters corresponding to different types and primitives and there are a couple of dozen more specifically used for formatting dates and times. We cover the basics here and return to date and time formatting in Chapter 11.

At first glance, some of the conversion characters may not seem to do much. For example, the %s general string conversion in our example above would actually have handled the job of displaying the numeric age argument just as well as %d. However, these specialized conversion characters accomplish three things. First, they add a level of type safety. By specifying %d, we ensure that only an integer type is formatted at that location. If we make a mistake in the arguments, we get a runtime IllegalFormatConversionException instead of garbage in our string. Second, the format method is Locale-sensitive and capable of displaying numbers, percentages, dates, and times in many different languages, just by specifying a Locale as an argument. By telling the Formatter the type of argument with type-specific conversion characters, printf can take into account language-specific localizations. Third, additional flags and fields can be used to govern layout with different meanings for different types of arguments. For example, with floating-point numbers, you can specify a precision in the format string.

The general layout of the embedded format string is as follows:

```
%[argument_index$][flags][width][.precision]conversion_type
```

Following the literal % are a number of optional items before the conversion type character. We'll discuss these as they come up, but here's the rundown. The argument index can be used to reorder or reuse individual arguments in the variable-length argument list by referring to them by number. The flags field holds one or more special flag characters governing the format. The `width` and `precision` fields control the size of the output for text and the number of digits displayed for floating-point numbers.

String Conversions

The conversion characters s represents the general string conversion type. Ultimately, all of the conversion types produce a `String`. What we mean is that the general string conversion takes the easy route to turning its argument into a string. Normally, this simply means calling `toString()` on the object. Since all of the arguments in the variable argument list are autoboxed, they are all `Objects`. Any primitives are represented by the results of calling `toString()` on their wrapper classes, which generally return the value as you'd expect. If the argument is null, the result is the `String` "null."

More interesting are objects that implement the `java.util.Formattable` interface. For these, the argument's `formatTo()` method is invoked, passing it the flags, width, and precision information and allowing it to return the string to be used. In this way, objects can control their own `printf` string representation, just as an object can with `toString()`.

Width, precision, and justification

For simple text arguments, you can think of the width and precision as a minimum and maximum number of characters to be output. As we'll see later, for floating-point numeric types, the precision changes meaning slightly and controls the number of digits displayed after the decimal point. We can see the effect on a simple string here:

```
System.out.printf("String is '%5s'\n", "A");
// String is '    A'
System.out.printf("String is '%.5s'\n", "Happy Birthday!");
// String is 'Happy'
```

In the first case, we specified a width of five characters, resulting in spaces being added to pad our argument. In the second example, we used the literal . followed by the precision value of 5 characters to limit the length of the string displayed, so our "Happy Birthday" string is truncated after the first five characters.

When our string was padded, it was right-justified (leading spaces added). You can control this with the flag character literal minus (-). Reversing our example:

```
System.out.printf("String is '%-5s'\n", "A");
// String is 'A    '
```

And, of course, we can combine all three, specifying a justification flag and a minimum and maximum width. Here is an example that prints words of varying lengths in two columns:

```
String [] words =
    new String [] { "abalone", "ape", "antidisestablishmentarianism" };
System.out.printf( "%-10s %s\n", "Word", "Length" );
for ( String word : words )
    System.out.printf "%-10.10s %s\n", word, word.length() );

// output
Word       Length
abalone    7
ape        3
antidisest 28
```

Uppercase

The s conversion's big brother S indicates that the output of the conversion should be forced to uppercase. Several other primitive and numeric conversion characters follow this pattern as we'll see later. For example:

```
String word = "abalone";
System.out.println(" The lucky word is: %S\n", word );
// The lucky word is: ABALONE
```

Numbered arguments

You can refer to an arbitrary argument by number from a format string using the %n$ notation. For example, the following uses the single argument three times:

```
System.out.println( "A %1$s is a %1$s is a %1$S...", "rose" );
 // A rose is a rose is a ROSE...
```

Numbered arguments are useful for two reasons. The first, shown here, is simply for reusing the same argument in different places and with different conversions. The usefulness of this becomes more apparent when we look at Date and Time formatting in Chapter 11, where we may refer to the same item half a dozen times to get individual fields. The second advantage is that numbered arguments give the message the flexibility to reorder the arguments. This is important when you're using formatting strings to lay out a message for internationalization or customization purposes.

```
log.format("Error %d : %s\n", errNo, errMsg );
// Error 42 : Low Power
log.format("%2$s (Error %1$d)\n", errNo, errMsg );
// Low Power (Error 42)
```

Primitive and Numeric Conversions

Table 10-3 shows character and Boolean conversion characters.

Table 10-3. Character and Boolean conversion characters

Conversion	Type	Description	Example output
c	Character	Formats the result as a Unicode character	a
b, B	Boolean	Formats result as Boolean	true, FALSE

The c conversion character produces a Unicode character:

```
System.out.printf("The first letter is: %c\n", 'a' );
```

The b and B conversion characters output the Boolean value of their arguments. If the argument is null, the output is false. Strangely, if the argument is of a type other than Boolean, the output is true. B is identical to b but forces the output to uppercase.

```
System.out.printf( "The door is open: %b\n", ( door.status( ) == OPEN ) );
```

As for String types, a width value can be specified on c and b conversions to pad the result to a minimum length.

Table 10-4 summarizes integer type conversion characters.

Table 10-4. Integer type conversion characters

Conversion	Type	Description	Example output
d	Integer	Formats the result as an integer.	999
x, X	Integer	Formats result as hexadecimal.	FF, 0xCAFE
o	Integer	Formats result as octal integer.	10, 010
h, H	Integer or object	Formats object as hexadecimal number. If object is not an integer, format its hashCode( ) value or "null" for null value.	7a71e498

The d, x, and o conversion characters handle the integer type values byte, short, int, and long. (The d apparently stands for decimal, which makes little sense in this context.) The h conversion is an oddity probably intended for debugging. Several important flags give additional control over the formatting of these numeric types. See the section "Flags" for details.

A width value can be specified on these conversions to pad the result. Precision values are not allowed on integer conversions.

Table 10-5 lists floating-point type conversion characters.

Table 10-5. Floating-point type conversion characters

Conversion	Type	Description	Example output
f	Floating point	Formats result as decimal number	3.14
e, E	Floating point	Formats result in scientific notation	3.000000e+08

Table 10-5. Floating-point type conversion characters (continued)

Conversion	Type	Description	Example output
g, G	Floating point	Formats result in either decimal or scientific notation depending on value and precision.	3.14, 10.0e-15
a, A	Floating point	Formats result as hexadecimal floating point number with significand and exponent.	0x1.fep7

The f conversion character is the primary floating-point conversion character. e and g conversions allow for values to be formatted in scientific notation. a complements the ability in Java 5.0 to assign floating-point values using hexadecimal significand and exponent notation, allowing bit-for-bit floating-point values to be displayed without ambiguity.

As always, a width value may be used to pad results to a minimum length. The precision value of the conversion, as its name suggests, controls the number of digits displayed after the decimal point for floating-point values. The value is rounded as necessary. If no precision value is specified, it defaults to six digits:

```
printf("float is %f\n",   1.23456789); // float is 1.234568
printf("float is %.3f\n", 1.23456789); // float is 1.235
printf("float is %.1f\n", 1.23456789); // float is 1.2
printf("float is %.0f\n", 1.23456789); // float is 1
```

The g conversion character determines whether to use decimal or scientific notation. First, the value is rounded to the specified precision. If the result is less than 10^{-4} (less than .0001) or if the result is greater than $10^{precision}$ (10 to the power of the precision value), it is displayed in scientific notation. Otherwise, decimal notation is displayed.

Flags

Table 10-6 summarizes supported flags to use in format strings.

Table 10-6. Flags for format strings

Flag	Arg types	Description	Example output
-	Any	Left-justifies result (pad space on the right)	'foo '
+	Numeric	Prefixes a + sign on positive results	+1
' '	Numeric	Prefixes a space on positive results (aligning them with negative values)	' 1'
0	Numeric	Pads number with leading zeros to accommodate width requirement	000001
,	Numeric	Formats numbers with commas or other Locale-specific grouping characters	1,234,567

Table 10-6. Flags for format strings (continued)

Flag	Arg types	Description	Example output
(	Numeric	Encloses negative numbers in parentheses (a convention used to show credits)	(42.50)
#	x,X,o	Uses an alternate form for octal and hexadecimal output	0xCAFE, 010

As mentioned earlier, the - flag can be used to left-justify formatted output. The remaining flags affect the display of numeric types as described.

The # alternate form flag can be used to print octal and hexadecimal values with their standard prefixes: 0x for hexadecimal or 0 for octal:

```
System.out.printf("%1$X, %1$#X", 0xCAFE, 0xCAFE ); // CAFE, 0xCAFE
System.out.printf("%1$o, %1$#o", 8, 8 ); // 10, 010
```

Miscellaneous

Table 10-7 lists the remaining formatting items.

Table 10-7. Miscellaneous formatting items

Conversion	Description
%	Produces a literal % character (Unicode \u0025)
n	Produces the platform-specific line separator (e.g., newline or carriage-return, newline)

Formatting with the java.text Package

The java.text package includes, among other things, a set of classes designed for generating and parsing string representations of objects. In this section, we'll talk about three classes: NumberFormat, ChoiceFormat, and MessageFormat. Chapter 11 describes the DateFormat class. As we said earlier, the classes of the java.text package overlap to a large degree with the capabilities of the Scanner and printf-style Formatter in Java 5.0. Despite these new features, a number of areas in the parsing of currencies, dates, and times can only be handled with the java.text package.

The NumberFormat class can be used to format and parse currency, percentages, or plain old numbers. NumberFormat is an abstract class, but it has several useful factory methods that produce formatters for different types of numbers. For example, to format or parse currency strings, use getCurrencyInstance( ):

```
double salary = 1234.56;
String here =     // $1,234.56
    NumberFormat.getCurrencyInstance( ).format(salary);
String italy =    // L 1.234,56
    NumberFormat.getCurrencyInstance(Locale.ITALY).format(salary);
```

The first statement generates an American salary, with a dollar sign, a comma to separate thousands, and a period as a decimal point. The second statement presents the same string in Italian, with a lire sign, a period to separate thousands, and a comma as a decimal point. Remember that NumberFormat worries about format only; it doesn't attempt to do currency conversion. (That would require, among other things, access to a dynamically updated table of exchange rates—a good opportunity for a Java bean but too much to ask of a simple formatter.) We can go the other way and parse a formatted value using the parse( ) method, as we'll see in the next example.

Likewise, getPercentInstance( ) returns a formatter you can use for generating and parsing percentages. If you do not specify a Locale when calling a getInstance( ) method, the default Locale is used:

```
double progress = 0.44;
NumberFormat pf = NumberFormat.getPercentInstance( );
System.out.println( pf.format(progress) );    // "44%"
try {
    System.out.println( pf.parse("77.2%") );  // "0.772"
}
catch (ParseException e) {}
```

And if you just want to generate and parse plain old numbers, use a NumberFormat returned by getInstance( ) or its equivalent, getNumberInstance( ):

```
NumberFormat guiseppe = NumberFormat.getInstance(Locale.ITALY);

// defaults to Locale.US
NumberFormat joe = NumberFormat.getInstance( );

try {
  double theValue = guiseppe.parse("34.663,252").doubleValue( );
  System.out.println(joe.format(theValue));  // "34,663.252"
}
catch (ParseException e) {}
```

We use guiseppe to parse a number in Italian format (periods separate thousands, comma is the decimal point). The return type of parse( ) is Number, so we use the doubleValue( ) method to retrieve the value of the Number as a double. Then we use joe to format the number correctly for the default (U.S.) locale.

Here's a list of the factory methods for text formatters in the java.text package. Again, we'll look at the DateFormat methods in the next chapter.

```
NumberFormat.getCurrencyInstance( )
NumberFormat.getCurrencyInstance(Locale inLocale)
NumberFormat.getInstance( )
NumberFormat.getInstance(Locale inLocale)
NumberFormat.getNumberInstance( )
NumberFormat.getNumberInstance(Locale inLocale)
NumberFormat.getPercentInstance( )
NumberFormat.getPercentInstance(Locale inLocale)
```

```
DateFormat.getDateInstance( )
DateFormat.getDateInstance(int style)
DateFormat.getDateInstance(int style, Locale aLocale)
DateFormat.getDateTimeInstance( )
DateFormat.getDateTimeInstance(int dateStyle, int timeStyle)
DateFormat.getDateTimeInstance(int dateStyle, int timeStyle, Locale aLocale)
DateFormat.getInstance( )
DateFormat.getTimeInstance( )
DateFormat.getTimeInstance(int style)
DateFormat.getTimeInstance(int style, Locale aLocale)
```

Thus far, we've seen how to format numbers as text. Now, we'll take a look at a class, ChoiceFormat, that maps numerical ranges to text. ChoiceFormat is constructed by specifying the numerical ranges and the strings that correspond to them. One constructor accepts an array of doubles and an array of Strings, where each string corresponds to the range running from the matching number up to (but not including) the next number in the array:

```
double[] limits = new double [] {0, 20, 40};
String[] labels = new String [] {"young", "less young", "old"};
ChoiceFormat cf = new ChoiceFormat(limits, labels);
System.out.println(cf.format(12)); // young
System.out.println(cf.format(26)); // less young
```

You can specify both the limits and the labels using a special string in an alternative ChoiceFormat constructor:

```
ChoiceFormat cf = new ChoiceFormat("0#young|20#less young|40#old");
System.out.println(cf.format(40)); // old
System.out.println(cf.format(50)); // old
```

The limit and value pairs are separated by vertical bars (|); the number sign (#) separates each limit from its corresponding value.

ChoiceFormat is most useful for handling pluralization in messages, enabling you to avoid hideous constructions such as, "you have one file(s) open." You can create readable error messages by using ChoiceFormat along with the MessageFormat class.

MessageFormat

MessageFormat is a string formatter that uses a pattern string in the same way that printf( ) formatting does. In Java 5.0, MessageFormat is largely replaced by printf( ), which has more options and is more widely used outside of Java. Nonetheless, some may still prefer MessageFormat's style, which is a bit less cryptic than that of printf( ). Prior to Java 5.0, MessageFormat accepted only arrays of arguments for its format method. With the introduction of varargs, it now offers a static formatting method, MessageFormat.format( ), paralleling the print-style formatting of String.format( ).

Arguments in a MessageFormat format string are delineated by curly brackets and may include information about how they should be formatted. Each argument consists of a number, an optional type, and an optional style, as summarized in Table 10-8.

Table 10-8. MessageFormat arguments

Type	Styles
Choice	*pattern*
Date	short, medium, long, full, *pattern*
Number	integer, percent, currency, *pattern*
Time	short, medium, long, full, *pattern*

Let's use an example to clarify this:

```
// Java 5.0
MessageFormat.format("You have {0} messages.", "no");

// or without varargs, use an Object []
MessageFormat mf = new MessageFormat("You have {0} messages.");
Object[] arguments = {"no"};
System.out.println(mf.format(arguments)); // "You have no messages."
```

The special incantation {0} means "use element zero of the arguments supplied to the format( ) method." When we generate a message by calling format( ), we pass in values to replace the placeholders ({0}, {1}, ...) in the template. In this case, we pass the string "no" as arguments[0], yielding the result, You have no messages.

Let's try this example again, but this time, we'll format a number and a date instead of a string argument:

```
MessageFormat mf = new MessageFormat(
    "You have {0, number, integer} messages on {1, date, long}.");

Object[] arguments = {new Integer(93), new Date()};

// "You have 93 messages on April 10, 2002."
System.out.println(mf.format(arguments));
```

In this example, we need to fill in two spaces in the template, so we need two elements in the arguments[] array. Element 0 must be a number and is formatted as an integer. Element 1 must be a Date and is printed in the long format. When we call format( ), the arguments[] array supplies these two values.

This is still sloppy. What if there is only one message? To make this grammatically correct, we can embed a ChoiceFormat-style pattern string in our MessageFormat pattern string:

```
MessageFormat mf = new MessageFormat(
  "You have {0, number, integer} message{0, choice, 0#s|1#|2#s}.");
Object[] arguments = {new Integer(1)};

// "You have 1 message."
System.out.println(mf.format(arguments));
```

In this case, we use element 0 of `arguments[]` twice: once to supply the number of messages and once to provide input to the `ChoiceFormat` pattern. The pattern says to add an `s` if argument 0 has the value `0` or is `2` or more.

When writing internationalized programs, you can use resource bundles to supply not only the text of messages, but the format strings for your `MessageFormat` objects, as well. In this way, you can automatically format messages that are in the appropriate language with dates and other language-dependent fields handled appropriately and in the appropriate order. Because arguments in the format string are numbered, you can refer to them in any location. For example, in English, you might say, "Disk C has 123 files"; in some other language, you might say, "123 files are on Disk C." You could implement both messages with the same set of arguments:

```
MessageFormat m1 = new MessageFormat(
    "Disk {0} has {1, number, integer} files.");
MessageFormat m2 = new MessageFormat(
    "{1, number, integer} files are on disk {0}.");
Object[] arguments = {"C", new Integer(123)};
```

In real life, the code could be more compact; you'd use only a single `MessageFormat` object, initialized with a string taken from a resource bundle. Or in Java 5.0, you'd likely want to use the static `format` method or switch to `printf( )` entirely.

Regular Expressions

Now, it's time to take a brief detour on our trip through Java and enter the land of *regular expressions*. A regular expression, or regex for short, describes a text pattern. Regular expressions are used with many tools—including the `java.util.regex` package, text editors, and many scripting languages—to provide sophisticated text-searching and powerful string-manipulation capabilities.

If you are already familiar with the concept of regular expressions and how they are used with other languages, you may wish to simply skim this section. At the very least, you'll need to look at the section "The java.util.regex API," later in this chapter, which covers the Java classes necessary to use them. On the other hand, if you've come to this point on your Java journey with a clean slate on this topic, and you're wondering exactly what regular expressions are, then pop open your favorite beverage and get ready. You are about to learn about the most powerful tool in the arsenal of text manipulation and what is, in fact, a tiny language within a language, all in the span of a few pages.

Regex Notation

A regular expression describes a pattern in text. By pattern, we mean just about any feature you can imagine identifying in text from the literal characters alone, without actually understanding their meaning. This includes features, such as words, word groupings, lines and paragraphs, punctuation, case, and more generally, strings and numbers with a specific structure to them, such as phone numbers, email addresses, and quoted phrases. With regular expressions you can search the dictionary for all the words that have the letter "q" without its pal "u" next to it, or words that start and end with the same letter. Once you have constructed a pattern, you can use simple tools to hunt for it in text or to determine if a given string matches it. A regex can also be arranged to help you dismember specific parts of the text it matched, which you could then use as elements of replacement text if you wish.

Write once, run away

Before moving on, we should say a few words about regular expression syntax in general. At the beginning of this section, we casually mentioned that we would be discussing a new language. Regular expressions do, in fact, comprise a simple form of programming language. If you think for a moment about the examples we cited earlier, you can see that something like a language is going to be needed to describe even simple patterns—such as email addresses—that have some variation in form.

A computer science textbook would classify regular expressions at the bottom of the hierarchy of computer languages, in terms of both what they can describe and what you can do with them. They are still capable of being quite sophisticated, however. As with most programming languages, the elements of regular expressions are simple, but they can be built up in combination to arbitrary complexity. And that is where things start to get sticky.

Since regexes work on strings, it is convenient to have a very compact notation that can be easily wedged between characters. But compact notation can be very cryptic, and experience shows that it is much easier to write a complex statement than to read it again later. Such is the curse of the regular expression. You may find that in a moment of late-night, caffeine-fueled inspiration, you can write a single glorious pattern to simplify the rest of your program down to one line. When you return to read that line the next day, however, it may look like Egyptian hieroglyphics to you. Simpler is generally better. If you can break your problem down and do it more clearly in several steps, maybe you should.

Escaped characters

Now that you're properly warned, we have to throw one more thing at you before we build you back up. Not only can the regex notation get a little hairy, but it is also somewhat ambiguous with ordinary Java strings. An important part of the notation is the escaped character, a character with a backslash in front of it. For example, the escaped d character, \d, is shorthand that matches any single digit character (0–9). However, you cannot simply write \d as part of a Java string, because Java uses the backslash for its own special characters and to specify Unicode character sequences (\uxxxx). Fortunately, Java gives us a replacement: an escaped backslash, which is two backslashes (\\), means a literal backslash. The rule is, when you want a backslash to appear in your regex, you must escape it with an extra one:

```
"\\d" // Java string that yields backslash "d"
```

And just to make things crazier, because regex notation itself uses backslash to denote special characters, it must provide the same "escape hatch" as well—allowing you to double up backslashes if you want a literal backslash. So if you want to specify a regular expression that includes a single literal backslash, it looks like this:

```
"\\\\"  // Java string yields two backslashes; regex yields one
```

Most of the "magic" operator characters you read about in this section operate on the character that precedes them, so these also must be escaped if you want their literal meaning. This includes such characters as ., *, +, braces {}, and parentheses ( ).

If you need to create part of an expression that has lots of literal characters in it, you can use the special delimiters \Q and \E to help you. Any text appearing between \Q and \E is automatically escaped. (You still need the Java String escapes—double backslashes for backslash, but not quadruple.) Java 5.0 added the static method Pattern.quote( ), which does the same thing, returning a properly escaped version of whatever string you give it.

Beyond that, my only suggestion to help maintain your sanity when working with these examples is to keep two copies—a comment line showing the naked regular expression and the real Java string, where you must double up all backslashes.

Characters and character classes

Now, let's dive into the actual regex syntax. The simplest form of a regular expression is plain, literal text, which means match that text exactly. This can be a single character or more. For example, in the following string, the pattern "s" can match the character s in the words rose and is:

```
"A rose is $1.99."
```

The pattern "rose" can match only the literal word rose. But this isn't very interesting. Let's crank things up a notch by introducing some special characters and the notion of character "classes."

Any character: dot (.)

The special character dot (.) matches any single character. The pattern ".ose" matches rose, nose, _ose (space followed by ose) or any other character followed by the sequence ose. Two dots match any two characters, and so on. The dot operator is not discriminating; it normally stops only for an end-of-line character (and, optionally, you can tell it not to; we discuss that later).

We can consider "." to represent the group or class of all characters. And regexes define more interesting character classes as well.

Whitespace or nonwhitespace character: \s, \S

> The special character \s matches a literal-space character or one of the following characters: \t (tab), \r (carriage return), \n (newline), \f (formfeed), and backspace. The corresponding special character \S does the inverse, matching any character except whitespace.

Digit or nondigit character: \d, \D

> \d matches any of the digits 0–9. \D does the inverse, matching all characters but digits.

Word or nonword character: \w, \W

> \w matches a "word" character, including upper- and lowercase letters A–Z, a–z, the digits 0–9, and the underscore character (_). \W matches everything except those characters.

Custom character classes

You can define your own character classes using the notation [...]. For example, the following class matches any of the characters a, b, c, x, y, or z:

    [abcxyz]

The special x–y range notation can be used as shorthand for the alphabetic characters. The following example defines a character class containing all upper- and lowercase letters:

    [A-Za-z]

Placing a caret (^) as the first character inside the brackets inverts the character class. For example:

    [^A-F]   // G, H, I, ..., a, b, c, ... etc.

matches any character except uppercase A–F.

Nesting character classes simply adds them:

    [A-F[G-Z]]   // A-Z

The && logical AND notation can be used to take the intersection (characters in common):

    [a-p&&[l-z]] // l, m, n, o, p
    [A-Z&&[^P]]   // A through Z except P

Position markers

The pattern "[Aa] rose" (including an upper- or lowercase A) matches three times in the following phrase:

    "A rose is a rose is a rose"

Position characters allow you to designate the relative location of a match. The most important are ^ and $, which match the beginning and end of a line, respectively:

```
^[Aa] rose  // matches "A rose" at the beginning of line
[Aa] rose$  // matches "a rose" at end of line
```

By default, ^ and $ match the beginning and end of "input," which is often a line. If you are working with multiple lines of text and wish to match the beginnings and endings of lines within a single large string, you can turn on "multiline" mode as described later in this chapter.

The position markers \b and \B match a word boundary or nonword boundary, respectively. For example, the following pattern matches rose and rosemary, but not primrose:

```
\brose
```

Iteration (multiplicity)

Simply matching fixed character patterns would not get us very far. Next, we look at operators that count the number of occurrences of a character (or more generally, of a pattern, as we'll see in "Capture groups"):

Any (zero or more iterations): asterisk (*)
> Placing an asterisk (*) after a character or character class means "allow any number of that type of character"—in other words, zero or more. For example, the following pattern matches a digit with any number of leading zeros (possibly none):
>
> ```
> 0*\d    // match a digit with any number of leading zeros
> ```

Some (one or more iterations): plus sign (+)
> The plus sign (+) means "one or more" iterations and is equivalent to XX* (pattern followed by pattern asterisk). For example, the following pattern matches a multiple-digit number with leading zeros:
>
> ```
> 0*\d+   // match a number (one or more digits) with leading zeros
> ```
>
> It may seem redundant to match the zeros at the beginning of expression because zero is, of course, a digit and is matched by the \d+ portion of the expression anyway. However, we'll show later how you can pick apart the string using a regex and get at just the pieces you want. In this case, you might want to strip off the leading zeros and keep only the digits.

Optional (zero or one iteration): question mark (?)
> The question mark operator (?) allows exactly zero or one iteration. For example, the following pattern matches a credit-card expiration date, which may or may not have a slash in the middle:
>
> ```
> \d\d/?\d\d // match four digits with an optional slash in the middle
> ```

Range (between x and y iterations, inclusive): {x,y}

The {x,y} curly-brace range operator is the most general iteration operator. It specifies a precise range to match. A range takes two arguments: a lower bound and an upper bound, separated by a comma. This regex matches any word with five to seven characters, inclusive:

```
\b\w{5,7}\b  // match words with at least 5 and at most 7 letters
```

At least x or more iterations (y is infinite): {x,}

If you omit the upper bound, simply leaving a dangling comma in the range, the upper bound becomes infinite. This is a way to specify a minimum of occurrences with no maximum.

Grouping

Just as in logical or mathematical operations, parentheses can be used in regular expressions to make subexpressions or to put boundaries on parts of expressions. This power lets us extend the operators we've talked about to work not only on characters, but on also words or other regular expressions. For example:

```
(yada)+
```

Here we are applying the + (one or more) operator to the whole pattern yada, not just one character. It matches yada, yadayada, yadayadayada, and so on.

Using grouping, we can start building more complex expressions. For example, while many email addresses have a three-part structure (e.g., *foo@bar.com*), the domain name portion can, in actuality, contain an arbitrary number of dot-separated components. To handle this properly, we can use an expression like this one:

```
\w+@\w+(\.\w)+   // Match an email address
```

This expression matches a word, followed by an @ symbol, followed by another word and then one or more literal dot-separated words—e.g., *pat@pat.net*, *friend@foo.bar.com*, or *mate@foo.bar.co.uk*.

Capture groups

In addition to basic grouping of operations, parentheses have an important, additional role: the text matched by each parenthesized subexpression can be separately retrieved. That is, you can isolate the text that matched each subexpression. There is then a special syntax for referring to each capture group within the regular expression by number. This important feature has two uses.

First, you can construct a regular expression that refers to the text it has already matched and uses this text as a parameter for further matching. This allows you to express some very powerful things. For example, we can show the dictionary example we mentioned in the introduction. Let's find all the words that start and end with the same letter:

```
\b(\w)\w*\1\b  // match words beginning and ending with the same letter
```

See the 1 in this expression? It's a reference to the first capture group in the expression, (\w). References to capture groups take the form \n where *n* is the number of the capture group, counting from left to right. In this example, the first capture group matches a word character on a word boundary. Then we allow any number of word characters up to the special reference \1 (also followed by a word boundary). The \1 means "the value matched in capture group one." Since these characters must be the same, this regex matches words that start and end with the same character.

The second use of capture groups is in referring to the matched portions of text while constructing replacement text. We'll show you how to do that a bit later when we talk about the Regular Expression API.

Capture groups can contain more than one character, of course, and you can have any number of groups. You can even nest capture groups. Next, we discuss exactly how they are numbered.

Numbering

Capture groups are numbered, starting at 1, and moving from left to right, by counting the number of open parentheses it takes to reach them. The special group number 0 always refers to the entire expression match. For example, consider the following string:

```
one ((two) (three (four)))
```

This string creates the following matches:

```
Group 0: one two three four
Group 1: two three four
Group 2: two
Group 3: three four
Group 4: four
```

Before going on, we should note one more thing. So far in this section we've glossed over the fact that parentheses are doing double duty: creating logical groupings for operations and defining capture groups. What if the two roles conflict? Suppose we have a complex regex that uses parentheses to group subexpressions and to create capture groups? In that case, you can use a special noncapturing group operator (?:) to do logical grouping instead of using parentheses. You probably won't need to do this often, but it's good to know.

Alternation

The vertical bar (|) operator denotes the logical OR operation, also called alternation or choice. The | operator does not operate on individual characters but instead applies to everything on either side of it. It splits the expression in two unless constrained by parentheses grouping. For example, a slightly naive approach to parsing dates might be the following:

```
\w+, \w+ \d+ \d+|\d\d/\d\d/\d\d  // pattern 1 or pattern 2
```

In this expression, the left matches patterns such as Fri, Oct 12, 2001, and the right matches 10/12/2001.

The following regex might be used to match email addresses with one of three domains (*net*, *edu*, and *gov*):

```
\w+@[\w.]*\.(net|edu|gov)  // email address ending in .net, .edu, or .gov
```

Special options

There are several special options that affect the way the regex engine performs its matching. These options can be applied in two ways:

- You can pass in one or more flags during the `Pattern.compile( )` step (discussed later in this chapter).
- You can include a special block of code in your regex.

We'll show the latter approach here. To do this, include one or more flags in a special block (`?x`), where *x* is the flag for the option we want to turn on. Generally, you do this at the beginning of the regex. You can also turn off flags by adding a minus sign (`?-x`), which allows you to apply flags to select parts of your pattern.

The following flags are available:

Case-insensitive: (`?i`)
> The (`?i`) flag tells the regex engine to ignore case while matching, for example:
>
> ```
> (?i)yahoo   // match Yahoo, yahoo, yahOO, etc.
> ```

Dot all: (`?s`)
> The (`?s`) flag turns on "dot all" mode, allowing the dot character to match anything, including end-of-line characters. It is useful if you are matching patterns that span multiple lines. The s stands for "single-line mode," a somewhat confusing name derived from Perl.

Multiline: (`?m`)
> By default, ^ and $ don't really match the beginning and end of lines (as defined by carriage return or newline combinations); they instead match the beginning or end of the entire input text. Turning on multiline mode with (`?m`) causes them to match the beginning and end of every line as well as the beginning and end of input. Specifically, this means the spot before the first character, the spot after the last character, and the spots just after and before line terminators inside the string.

Unix lines: (`?d`)
> The (`?d`) flag limits the definition of the line terminator for the ^, $, and . special characters to Unix-style newline only (\n). By default, carriage return newline (\r\n) is also allowed.

Greediness

We've seen hints that regular expressions are capable of sorting some complex patterns. But there are cases where what should be matched is ambiguous (at least to us, though not to the regex engine). Probably the most important example has to do with the number of characters the iterator operators consume before stopping. The .* operation best illustrates this. Consider the following string:

```
"Now is the time for <bold>action</bold>, not words."
```

Suppose we want to search for all the HTML-style tags (the parts between the < and > characters), perhaps because we want to remove them.

We might naively start with this regex:

```
</?.*>  // match <, optional /, and then anything up to >
```

We then get the following match, which is much too long:

```
<bold>action</bold>
```

The problem is that the .* operation, like all the iteration operators, is by default "greedy," meaning that it consumes absolutely everything it can, up until the last match for the terminating character (in this case, >) in the file or line.

There are solutions for this problem. The first is to "say what it is," that is, to be specific about what is allowed between the braces. The content of an HTML tag cannot actually include *anything*; for example, it cannot include a closing bracket (>). So we could rewrite our expression as:

```
</?\w*>  // match <, optional /, any number of word characters, then >
```

But suppose the content is not so easy to describe. For example, we might be looking for quoted strings in text, which could include just about any text. In that case, we can use a second approach and "say what it is not." We can invert our logic from the previous example and specify that anything *except* a closing bracket is allowed inside the brackets:

```
</?[^>]*>
```

This is probably the most efficient way to tell the regex engine what to do. It then knows exactly what to look for to stop reading. This approach has limitations, however. It is not obvious how to do this if the delimiter is more complex than a single character. It is also not very elegant.

Finally, we come to our general solution: the use of "reluctant" operators. For each of the iteration operators, there is an alternative, nongreedy form that consumes as few characters as possible, while still trying to get a match with what comes after it. This is exactly what we needed in our previous example.

Reluctant operators take the form of the standard operator with a "?" appended. (Yes, we know that's confusing.) We can now write our regex as:

```
</?.*?> // match <, optional /, minimum number of any chars, then >
```

We have appended ? to .* to cause .* to match as few characters as possible while still making the final match of >. The same technique (appending the ?) works with all the iteration operators, as in the two following examples:

```
.+?   // one or more, nongreedy
.{x,y}? // between x and y, nongreedy
```

Lookaheads and lookbehinds

In order to understand our next topic, let's return for a moment to the position marking characters (^, $, \b, and \B) that we discussed earlier. Think about what exactly these special markers do for us. We say, for example, that the \b marker matches a word boundary. But the word "match" here may be a bit too strong. In reality, it "requires" a word boundary to appear at the specified point in the regex. Suppose we didn't have \b; how could we construct it? Well, we could try constructing a regex that matches the word boundary. It might seem easy, given the word and nonword character classes (\w and \W):

```
\w\W|\W\w  // match the start or end of a word
```

But now what? We could try inserting that pattern into our regular expressions wherever we would have used \b, but it's not really the same. We're actually matching those characters, not just requiring them. This regular expression matches the two characters comprising the word boundary in addition to whatever else matches afterward whereas the \b operator simply *requires* the word boundary but doesn't match any text. The distinction is that \b isn't a matching pattern but a lookahead. A *lookahead* is a pattern that is required to match next in the string, but which is not consumed by the regex engine. When a lookahead pattern succeeds, the pattern moves on, and the characters are left in the stream for the next part of the pattern to use. If the lookahead fails, the match fails (or it backtracks and tries a different approach).

We can make our own lookaheads with the lookahead operator (?=). For example, to match the letter X at the end of a word, we could use:

```
(?=\w\W)X  // Find X at the end of a word
```

Here the regex engine requires the \W\w pattern to match but not consume the characters, leaving them for the next part of the pattern. This effectively allows us to write overlapping patterns (like the previous example). For instance, we can match the word "Pat" only when it's part of the word "Patrick," like so:

```
(?=Patrick)Pat  // Find Pat only in Patrick
```

Another operator (?!)–the *negative lookahead*—requires that the pattern not match. We can find all the occurrences of Pat not inside of a Patrick with this:

```
(?!Patrick)Pat  // Find Pat never in Patrick
```

It's worth noting that we could have written all of these examples in other ways, by simply matching a larger amount of text. For instance, in the first example we could have matched the whole word "Patrick." But that is not as precise, and if we wanted to use capture groups to pull out the matched text or parts of it later, we'd have to play games to get what we want. For example, suppose we wanted to substitute something for Pat (say, change the font). We'd have to use an extra capture group and replace the text with itself. Using lookaheads is easier.

In addition to looking ahead in the stream, we can use the (?<=) and (?<!) *lookbehind* operators to look backward in the stream. For example, we can find my last name, but only when it refers to me:

```
(?<=Pat )Niemeyer   // Niemeyer, only when preceded by Pat
```

Or we can find the string "bean" when it is not part of the phrase "Java bean":

```
(?<!Java *)bean    // The word bean, not preceded by Java
```

In these cases, the lookbehind and the matched text didn't overlap because the lookbehind was before the matched text. But you can place a lookahead or lookbehind at either point—before or after the match; for example, we could also match Pat Niemeyer like this:

```
Niemeyer(?<=Pat Niemeyer)
```

The java.util.regex API

Now that we've covered the theory of how to construct regular expressions, the hard part is over. All that's left is to investigate the Java API for applying regexes: searching for them in strings, retrieving captured text, and replacing matches with substitution text.

Pattern

As we've said, the regex patterns that we write as strings are, in actuality, little programs describing how to match text. At runtime, the Java regex package compiles these little programs into a form that it can execute against some target text. Several simple convenience methods accept strings directly to use as patterns. More generally, however, Java allows you to explicitly compile your pattern and encapsulate it in an instance of a Pattern object. This is the most efficient way to handle patterns that are used more than once, because it eliminates needlessly recompiling the string. To compile a pattern, we use the static method Pattern.compile():

```
Pattern urlPattern = Pattern.compile("\\w+://[\\w/]*");
```

Once you have a Pattern, you can ask it to create a Matcher object, which associates the pattern with a target string:

```
Matcher matcher = urlPattern.matcher( myText );
```

The matcher is what actually executes the matches. We'll talk about it next. But before we do, we'll just mention one convenience method of Pattern. The static method Pattern.matches() simply takes two strings—a regex and a target string—

and determines if the target matches the regex. This is very convenient if you want to do a quick test once in your application. For example:

```
Boolean match = Pattern.matches( "\\d+\\.\\d+f?", myText );
```

The previous line of code can test if the string myText contains a Java-style floating-point number such as "42.0f." Note that the string must match completely, to the end, to be considered a match.

The Matcher

A Matcher associates a pattern with a string and provides tools for testing, finding, and iterating over matches of the pattern against it. The Matcher is "stateful." For example, the find( ) method tries to find the next match each time it is called. But you can clear the Matcher and start over by calling its reset( ) method.

If you're just interested in "one big match"—that is, you're expecting your string to either match the pattern or not—you can use matches( ) or lookingAt( ). These correspond roughly to the methods equals( ) and startsWith( ) of the String class. The matches( ) method asks if the string matches the pattern in its entirety (with no string characters left over) and returns true or false. The lookingAt( ) method does the same, except that it asks only whether the string starts with the pattern and doesn't care if the pattern uses up all the string's characters.

More generally, you'll want to be able to search through the string and find one or more matches. To do this, you can use the find( ) method. Each call to find( ) returns true or false for the next match of the pattern and internally notes the position of the matching text. You can get the starting and ending character positions with the Matcher start( ) and end( ) methods, or you can simply retrieve the matched text with the group( ) method. For example:

```
import java.util.regex.*;

String text="A horse is a horse, of course of course...";
String pattern="horse|course";

Matcher matcher = Pattern.compile( pattern ).matcher( text );
while ( matcher.find( ) )
  System.out.println(
    "Matched: '"+matcher.group( )+"' at position "+matcher.start( ) );
```

The previous snippet prints the starting location of the words "horse" and "course" (four in all):

```
Matched: 'horse' at position 2
Matched: 'horse' at position 13
Matched: 'course' at position 23
Matched: 'course' at position 33
```

The method to retrieve the matched text is called group( ) because it refers to capture group zero (the entire match). You can also retrieve the text of other numbered capture groups by giving the group( ) method an integer argument. You can determine how many capture groups you have with the groupCount( ) method:

```
for (int i=1; i < matcher.groupCount(); i++)
System.out.println( matcher.group(i) );
```

Splitting and tokenizing strings

A very common need is to parse a string into a bunch of fields based on some delimiter, such as a comma. It's such a common problem that in Java 1.4, a method was added to the String class for doing just this. The method split( ) accepts a regular expression and returns an array of substrings broken around that pattern. For example:

```
String text = "Foo, bar ,   blah";
String [] fields = text.split( "\s*,\s*" );
```

yields a String array containing Foo, bar, and blah. You can control the maximum number of matches and also whether you get "empty" strings (for text that might have appeared between two adjacent delimiters) using an optional limit field.

If you are going to use an operation like this more than a few times in your code, you should probably compile the pattern and use its split( ) method, which is identical to the version in String. The String split( ) method is equivalent to:

```
Pattern.compile(pattern).split(string);
```

Another look at Scanner

As we mentioned when we introduced it, the Scanner class in Java 5.0 can use regular expressions to tokenize strings. You can specify a regular expression to use as the delimiter (instead of the default whitespace) either at construction time or with the useDelimiter( ) method. The Scanner next( ), hasNext( ), skip( ), and findInLine( ) methods all take regular expressions as well. You can specify these either as strings or with a compiled Pattern object.

You can use the findInLine( ) method of Scanner as an improved Matcher. For example:

```
Scanner scanner = new Scanner( "Quantity: 42 items, Price $2.34" );
scanner.findInLine("[Qq]uantity[:\\s]*");
int quantity=scanner.nextInt();
scanner.findInLine("[Pp]rice.*\\$");
float price=scanner.nextFloat();
```

The previous snippet locates the quantity and price values, allowing for variations in capitalization and spacing before the numbers.

Before we move on, we'll also mention a "Stupid Scanner Trick" that, while we don't recommend it, you might find amusing. Using the \A boundary marker, which denotes the beginning of input, as a delimiter, we can tell the Scanner to return the whole input as a single string. This is an easy way to read the contents of any stream into one large string:

```
InputStream source  = new URL("http://www.oreilly.com/").openStream( );
String text = new Scanner( source ).useDelimiter("\\A").next( );
```

This is probably not the most efficient or understandable way to do it, but it may save you a little typing in your experimentation.

Replacing text

A common reason that you'll find yourself searching for a pattern in a string is to change it to something else. The regex package not only makes it easy to do this but also provides a simple notation to help you construct replacement text using bits of the matched text.

The most convenient form of this API is Matcher's replaceAll( ) method, which substitutes a replacement string for each occurrence of the pattern and returns the result. For example:

```
String text = "Richard Nixon's social security number is: 567-68-0515.";
Matcher matcher =
Pattern.compile("\\d\\d\\d-\\d\\d\\-\\d\\d\\d\\d").matcher( text );
String output = matcher.replaceAll("XXX-XX-XXXX");
```

This code replaces all occurrences of U.S. government Social Security numbers with "XXX-XX-XXXX" (perhaps for privacy considerations).

Using captured text in a replacement. Literal substitution is nice, but we can make this more powerful by using capture groups in our substitution pattern. To do this, we use the simple convention of referring to numbered capture groups with the notation $n, where n is the group number. For example, suppose we wanted to show just a little of the Social Security number in the above example, so that the user would know if we were talking about him. We could modify our regex to catch, for example, the last four digits like so:

```
\d\d\d-\d\d-(\d\d\d\d)
```

We can then use that in the substitution text:

```
String output = matcher.replaceAll("XXX-XX-$1");
```

In Java 5.0, the static method Matcher.quoteReplacement( ) was added, which can be used to escape a literal string (so that it ignores the $ notation) before using it as replacement text.

Controlling the substitution. The replaceAll( ) method is useful, but you may want more control over each substitution. You may want to change each match to something different or base the change on the match in some programmatic way.

To do this, you can use the Matcher appendReplacement() and appendTail() methods. These methods can be used in conjunction with the find() method as you iterate through matches to build a replacement string. appendReplacement() and appendTail() operate on a StringBuffer that you supply. The appendReplacement() method builds a replacement string by keeping track of where you are in the text and appending all *nonmatched* text to the buffer for you as well as the substitute text that you supply. Each call to find() appends the intervening text from the last call, followed by your replacement, then skips over all the matched characters to prepare for the next one. Finally, when you have reached the last match, you should call appendTail(), which appends any remaining text after the last match. We'll show an example of this next, as we build a simple "template engine."

The simple template engine

Let's tie together what we've discussed in a nifty example. A common problem in Java applications is working with bulky, multiline text. In general, you don't want to store text messages in your application code, because it makes them difficult to edit or internationalize. But when you move them to external files or resources, you need a way for your application to plug in information at runtime. The best example of this is in Java servlets; a generated HTML page is often 99% static text with only a few "variable" pieces plugged in. Technologies such as JSP and XSL were developed to address this. But these are big tools, and we have a simple problem. So let's create a simple solution—a template engine.

Our template engine reads text containing special template tags and substitutes values that we provide it. And since generating HTML or XML is one of the most important applications of this, we'll be friendly to those formats by making our tags conform to the style of an XML comment. Specifically, our engine searches the text for tags that look like this:

```
<!--TEMPLATE:name  This is the template for the user name -->
```

XML-style comments start with <!-- and can contain anything up to a closing -->. We'll add the convention of requiring a TEMPLATE:name field to specify the name of the value we want to use. But aside from that, we'll still allow any descriptive text the user wants to include. To be friendly (and consistent), we'll allow any amount of whitespace to appear in the tags, including multiline text in the comments. We'll also ignore the text case of the "TEMPLATE" identifier, just in case. Now, we could do this all with low-level String commands, looping over whitespace and taking substrings a lot. But using the power of regexes, we can do it much more cleanly and with only about seven lines of relevant code. (We've rounded out the example with a few more to make it more useful.)

```
import java.util.*;
import java.util.regex.*;
```

```
public class Template
{
    Properties values = new Properties(  );
    Pattern templateComment =
        Pattern.compile("(?si)<!--\\s*TEMPLATE:(\\w+).*?-->");

    public void set( String name, String value ) {
        values.setProperty( name, value );
    }

    public String fillIn( String text ) {
        Matcher matcher = templateComment.matcher( text );

        StringBuffer buffer = new StringBuffer(  );
        while( matcher.find(  ) ) {
            String name = matcher.group(1);
            String value = values.getProperty( name );
            matcher.appendReplacement( buffer, value );
        }
        matcher.appendTail( buffer );
        return buffer.toString(  );
    }
}
```

You'd use the Template class like this:

```
String input = "<!-- TEMPLATE:name --> lives at "
    +"<!-- TEMPLATE:address -->";
Template template = new Template(  );
template.set("name", "Bob");
template.set("address", "1234 Main St.");
String output = template.fillIn( input );
```

In this code, input is a string containing tags for name and address. The set( )
method provides the values for those tags.

Let's start by picking apart the regex, templatePattern, in the example:

```
(?si)<!--\s*TEMPLATE:(\w+).*?-->
```

It looks scary, but it's actually very simple. Just start reading from left to right. First,
we have the special flags declaration (?si) telling the regex engine that it should be
in single-line mode, with .* matching all characters including newlines (s), and
ignoring case (i). Next, there is the literal <!-- followed by any amount of
whitespace (\s) and the TEMPLATE: identifier. After the colon, we have a capture
group (\w+), which reads our name identifier and saves it for us to retrieve later. We
allow anything (.*) up to the -->, being careful to specify that .* should be nongreedy (.*?). We don't want .* to consume other opening and closing comment tags
all the way to the last one but instead to find the smallest match (one tag).

Our fillIn( ) method does the work, accepting a template string, searching it, and
"replacing" the tag values with the values from set( ), which we have stored in a
Properties table. Each time fillIn( ) is called, it creates a Matcher to wrap the input

string and get ready to apply the pattern. It then creates a temporary `StringBuffer` to hold the output and loops, using the `Matcher` `find( )` method to get each tag. For each match, it retrieves the value of the capture group (group one) that holds the tag name. It looks up the corresponding value and replaces the tag with this value in the output string buffer using the `appendReplacement( )` method. (Remember that `appendReplacement( )` fills in the intervening text on each call, so we don't have to.) All that remains is to call `appendTail( )` at the end to get the remaining text after the last match and return the string value. That's it!

Regular expressions aren't new, but they are relatively new to Java (at least as a standard). We have shown you some of the power provided by these tools and (we hope) whetted your appetite for more. Regexes allow you to work in ways you may not have considered before. Especially now, when the software world is focused on textual representations of almost everything—from data to user interfaces—via XML and HTML, having powerful text-manipulation tools is fundamental. Just remember to keep those regexes simple so you can reuse them again and again.

CHAPTER 11

Core Utilities

In this chapter, we'll continue our look at the core Java APIs, covering more of the tools of the java.util package. The java.util package includes a wide range of utilities including tools for mathematical operations, working with dates and times, holding structured collections of objects, storing user preference data, and logging.

Math Utilities

Java supports integer and floating-point arithmetic directly in the language. Higher-level math operations are supported through the java.lang.Math class. As you may have seen by now, wrapper classes for primitive data types allow you to treat them as objects. Wrapper classes also hold some methods for basic conversions. Java provides the java.util.Random class for generating random numbers.

First, a few words about built-in arithmetic in Java. Java handles errors in integer arithmetic by throwing an ArithmeticException:

```
int zero = 0;

try {
    int i = 72 / zero;
} catch ( ArithmeticException e ) {
    // division by zero
}
```

To generate the error in this example, we created the intermediate variable zero. The compiler is somewhat crafty and would have caught us if we had blatantly tried to perform division by a literal zero.

Floating-point arithmetic expressions, on the other hand, don't throw exceptions. Instead, they take on the special out-of-range values shown in Table 11-1.

Table 11-1. Special floating-point values

Value	Mathematical representation
POSITIVE_INFINITY	1.0/0.0
NEGATIVE_INFINITY	-1.0/0.0
NaN	0.0/0.0

The following example generates an infinite result:

```
double zero = 0.0;
double d = 1.0/zero;

if ( d == Double.POSITIVE_INFINITY )
    System.out.println( "Division by zero" );
```

The special value NaN (not a number) indicates the result of dividing zero by zero. This value has the special mathematical distinction of not being equal to itself (NaN != NaN evaluates to true). Use Float.isNaN( ) or Double.isNaN( ) to test for NaN.

The java.lang.Math Class

The java.lang.Math class is Java's math library. It holds a suite of static methods covering all of the usual mathematical operations like sin( ), cos( ), and sqrt( ). The Math class isn't very object-oriented (you can't create an instance of Math). Instead it's really just a convenient holder for static methods that are more like global functions. As we saw in Chapter 6, it's possible to use the new Java 5.0 static import functionality to import the names of static methods and constants like this directly into the scope of our class and use them as if they were defined there.

Table 11-2 summarizes the methods in java.lang.Math.

Table 11-2. Methods in java.lang.Math

Method	Argument type(s)	Functionality
Math.abs(a)	int, long, float, double	Absolute value
Math.acos(a)	double	Arc cosine
Math.asin(a)	double	Arc sine
Math.atan(a)	double	Arc tangent
Math.atan2(a,b)	double	Angle part of rectangular-to-polar coordinate transform
Math.ceil(a)	double	Smallest whole number greater than or equal to a
Math.cbrt(a)	double	Cube root of a
Math.cos(a)	double	Cosine
Math.cosh(a)	double	Hyperbolic cosine
Math.exp(a)	double	Math.E to the power a
Math.floor(a)	double	Largest whole number less than or equal to a

Table 11-2. Methods in java.lang.Math (continued)

Method	Argument type(s)	Functionality
Math.hypot(a,b)	double	Precision calculation of the sqrt( ) of $a^2 + b^2$
Math.log(a)	double	Natural logarithm of a
Math.log10(a)	double	Log base 10 of a
Math.max(a, b)	int,long,float,double	The value a or b closer to Long.MAX_VALUE
Math.min(a, b)	int,long,float,double	The value a or b closer to Long.MIN_VALUE
Math.pow(a, b)	double	a to the power b
Math.random( )	None	Random-number generator
Math.rint(a)	double	Converts double value to integral value in double format
Math.round(a)	float,double	Rounds to whole number
Math.sin(a)	double	Sine
Math.sinh(a)	double	Hyperbolic sine
Math.sqrt(a)	double	Square root
Math.tan(a)	double	Tangent
Math.tanh(a)	double	Hyperbolic tangent

log( ), pow( ), and sqrt( ) can throw a runtime ArithmeticException. abs( ), max( ), and min( ) are overloaded for all the scalar values, int, long, float, or double, and return the corresponding type. Versions of Math.round( ) accept either float or double and return int or long, respectively. The rest of the methods operate on and return double values:

```
double irrational = Math.sqrt( 2.0 ); // 1.414...
int bigger = Math.max( 3, 4 );  // 4
long one = Math.round( 1.125798 ); // 1
```

For convenience, Math also contains the static final double values E and PI:

```
double circumference = diameter  * Math.PI;
```

The java.math Package

If the long and double types are not large or precise enough for you, the java.math package provides two classes, BigInteger and BigDecimal, that support arbitrary-precision numbers. These full-featured classes have a bevy of methods for performing arbitrary-precision math and precisely controlling rounding of remainders. In the following example, we use BigDecimal to add two very large numbers and then create a fraction with a 100-digit result:

```
long l1 = 9223372036854775807L; // Long.MAX_VALUE
long l2 = 9223372036854775807L;
System.out.println( l1 + l2 ); // -2 ! Not good.

try {
    BigDecimal bd1 = new BigDecimal( "9223372036854775807" );
```

```
        BigDecimal bd2 = new BigDecimal( 9223372036854775807L );
        System.out.println( bd1.add( bd2 ) ); // 18446744073709551614

        BigDecimal numerator = new BigDecimal(1);
        BigDecimal denominator = new BigDecimal(3);
        BigDecimal fraction =
            numerator.divide( denominator, 100, BigDecimal.ROUND_UP );
        // 100 digit fraction = 0.333333 ... 3334
    }
    catch (NumberFormatException nfe) { }
    catch (ArithmeticException ae) { }
```

If you implement cryptographic or scientific algorithms for fun, `BigInteger` is crucial. Other than that, you're not likely to need these classes.

Random Numbers

You can use the `java.util.Random` class to generate random values. It's a pseudorandom number generator that is initialized with a 48-bit seed.[*] Because it's a pseudorandom algorithm, you'll get the same series of values each time you use the same seed value. The default constructor uses the current time to produce a seed, but you can specify your own value in the constructor:

```
long seed = mySeed;
Random rnums = new Random( seed );
```

Once you have a generator, you can ask for one or more random values of various types using the methods listed in Table 11-3.

Table 11-3. Random number methods

Method	Range
nextBoolean( )	true or false
nextInt( )	−2147483648 to 2147483647
nextInt(int *n*)	0 to (n − 1) inclusive
nextLong( )	−9223372036854775808 to 9223372036854775807
nextFloat( )	0.0 inclusive to 1.0 exclusive
nextDouble( )	0.0 inclusive to 1.0 exclusive
nextGaussian( )	Gaussian distributed double with mean 0.0 and standard deviation of 1.0

By default, the values are uniformly distributed. You can use the `nextGaussian( )` method to create a Gaussian (bell curve) distribution of double values, with a mean of 0.0 and a standard deviation of 1.0. (Lots of natural phenomena follow a Gaussian distribution rather than a strictly uniform random one.)

---

[*] The generator uses a linear congruential formula. See *The Art of Computer Programming, Volume 2: Seminumerical Algorithms* by Donald Knuth (Addison-Wesley).

The static method `Math.random()` retrieves a random double value. This method initializes a `private` random number generator in the `Math` class the first time it's used, using the default `Random` constructor. Thus, every call to `Math.random()` corresponds to a call to `nextDouble()` on that random number generator.

Dates and Times

Working with dates and times without the proper tools can be a chore. Fortunately, Java has three classes that handle most of the work for you. The `java.util.Date` class encapsulates a point in time. The `java.util.GregorianCalendar` class, which extends the abstract `java.util.Calendar`, translates between a point in time and calendar fields like month, day, and year. Finally, the `java.text.DateFormat` class knows how to generate and parse string representations of dates and times in many languages.[*]

The separation of the `Date` and `GregorianCalendar` classes is analogous to having a class representing temperature and a class that translates that temperature to Celsius units. A `Date` represents an absolute point in time as defined by a number of milliseconds from the reference point: midnight, Jan 1, 1970, GMT. This is the same frame of reference used by the `System.currentTimeMillis()` call. A `Calendar` encapsulates a point in time and maps it to higher-level (and messier) notions like years, months, weeks, and days, and deals with discontinuities like leap years. Conceivably, we could define other subclasses of `Calendar`, say `JulianCalendar` or `LunarCalendar`, that map time using other sociological or cultural conventions.[†]

Working with Calendars

The default `GregorianCalendar` constructor creates a calendar initialized to the current time, in the current time zone:

```
GregorianCalendar now = new GregorianCalendar();
```

However, more generally we can just ask the `Calendar` class for an appropriate calendar instance without worrying about what type of calendar system the world is using this century:

```
Calendar now = Calendar.getInstance();
```

---

[*] Prior to Java 1.1, the `Date` class handled some of the functions of a calendar as well. Most of these methods have now been deprecated. Today, the only purpose of the `Date` class is to represent a point in time.

[†] Java's `GregorianCalendar` class is actually both a Julian and Gregorian calendar with a programmable cutover date. For a wealth of information about time and world time-keeping conventions, see *http://tycho.usno.navy.mil*, the U.S. Navy Directorate of Time.

In either case, all the real work is done through the main set( ) and get( ) methods of Calendar. These methods use static identifiers to refer to calendar fields and values. For example:

```
Calendar birthday = Calendar.getInstance( );
birthday.set( Calendar.YEAR, 1972 );
birthday.set( Calendar.MONTH, Calendar.MAY );
birthday.set( Calendar.DATE, 20 );
```

Here, we set the year, month, and day values on the calendar, altering the internal Date of the Calendar object. Any remaining fields that we did not set are left as they were initialized (to the current date and time when it was constructed). In this case, we did not really specify a full date and time; we simply overrode individual fields in the calendar.

The Calendar class contains identifiers for all of the standard date and time fields, as well as values such as days of the week and months of the year. The following are the most common identifiers:

- YEAR, MONTH
- WEEK_OF_YEAR, WEEK_OF_MONTH
- DATE, DAY_OF_YEAR, DAY_OF_MONTH, DAY_OF_WEEK
- HOUR, HOUR_OF_DAY, AM_PM
- MINUTE, SECOND, MILLISECOND
- ZONE_OFFSET, DST_OFFSET

DATE and DAY_OF_MONTH are synonymous. HOUR is a 12-hour clock that can be combined with AM_PM.

The values are just what you would expect, as shown in the following:

- SUNDAY, MONDAY, TUESDAY...
- JANUARY, FEBRUARY, MARCH...
- AM, PM

Don't forget that you can use the Java 5.0 import static construct to make your life a little easier when using a lot of static fields.

In addition to the set( ) method for changing field values, the Calendar class has two additional methods for performing date math, add( ) and roll( ). Using add( ) you can move a calendar forward or backward in any units of time easily, without having to calculate the other fields. For example, we can move our calendar forward four weeks:

```
Calendar cal = Calendar.getInstance( );
System.out.println( cal.getTime( ) );
// Thu Nov 04 16:39:06 CST 2004
```

```
cal.add( Calendar.WEEK_OF_YEAR, 4 );
System.out.println( cal.getTime() );
// Thu Dec 02 16:39:06 CST 2004
```

The roll( ) method, by contrast, does not alter the other fields of the calendar, but arbitrarily adjusts individual fields. See the Spinner example in Chapter 17 for additional information about adding and subtracting time periods using the add( ) method.

Finally, you can always get the internal Date of the Calendar object or reinitialize the calendar to a specific Date using the getTime( ) and setTime( ) method:

```
// Get the absolute time the Calendar references
Date date = calendar.getTime();

// Reinitialize this calendar to the current date and time
Date now = new Date();
calendard.setTime( now );
```

Time Zones

An instance of the TimeZone class represents a time zone and the knowledge of daylight savings time at that location. You can construct a time zone from a string specifier in a number of ways. The most general approach is to use an offset from GMT, but many human-readable formats are included. (For a list, use TimeZone.getAvailableIDs( ).)

```
TimeZone.getTimeZone("US/Central");       // CST
TimeZone.getTimeZone("GMT-06");           // CST
TimeZone.getTimeZone("America/Chicago");  // CST
```

A Calendar inherits the default time zone from the platform on which it was created. You can set a different time zone with the setTimeZone( ) method:

```
GregorianCalendar smokey = new GregorianCalendar();
smokey.setTimeZone( TimeZone.getTimeZone("US/Mountain") );
```

It's important to think about dates and time zones in the right way. Remember that a Date is an absolute point in time, while a Calendar translates that Date into localized fields that may depend on where you are. In a sense, it is meaningless to talk about the date "Nov 1, 2004," without specifying a time zone because at any given moment on earth "now" could be one of two different calendar days. Even specifying a date and time such as "Nov 1, 2004, 9:01 pm" is ambiguous, because that particular combination of calendar and time fields occurs at 24 separate times over the span of a day as the world turns (see Figure 11-1). Only a complete date, time, and time zone specifies an absolute point in time, such as "Nov 1, 2004, 9:01 pm EST." So it's important to remember that the Calendar class defaults all of these fields for you even if you haven't set them.

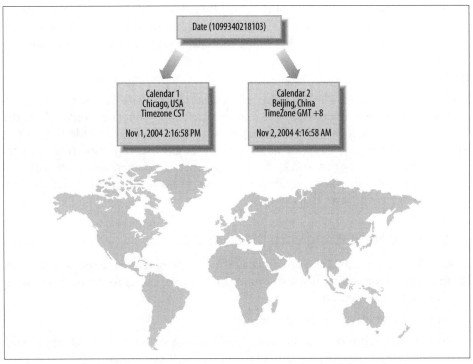

Figure 11-1. Calendars translate an absolute point in time to a localized data and time

The following example prints the day of the week for the same Date object in two different time zones:

```
Date date = new Date( ); // point in time

TimeZone CST = TimeZone.getTimeZone( "America/Chicago" );
Calendar usa = Calendar.getInstance( CST );
usa.setTime( date );
System.out.println( usa.get( Calendar.DAY_OF_WEEK ) );  // 1

TimeZone GMT8 = TimeZone.getTimeZone( "GMT+08"); // Beijing
Calendar china = Calendar.getInstance( GMT8 );
china.setTime( date );
System.out.println( china.get( Calendar.DAY_OF_WEEK ) ); // 2
```

In this example, we could also have simply changed the time zone on the calendar usa using the setTimeZone( ) method. Unlike the field set( ) methods, setting the time zone does not change the underlying Date value of the calendar, only the interpretation of the fields.

The meaning of the Date object and its relationship to Calendar become particularly important when dealing with APIs for things such as databases that construct dates from incomplete date and time fields. If, as is entirely possible, you end up sending your Date object from a client application in one part of the world to a server in another, you may be surprised that the calendar fields have changed. In these situations it's important to work with Calendars to translate the date fields and avoid the temptation to "fix" the problem by adding or subtracting real time from the date.

Locale

It should be clear now that Calendar is not just a fancy Date but is something in between a time-keeping device and a time-formatting device. This point is brought home by the fact that the Calendar class is also locale-sensitive. In addition to the notion of a time zone, a Calendar has a Locale that governs conventions such as on which day the week begins and ends. You can specify an alternate locale with the setLocale( ) method. Most locale-specific details, however, are handled by the DateFormat class, which we'll discuss next.

Parsing and Formatting with DateFormat

As its name suggests, the DateFormat class formats Date objects and not Calendars, so the first step in formatting dates and times from a Calendar is to get back to a Date with the getTime( ) method:

```
Date birthDate = calendar.getTime( );
```

To create string representations of dates and times, create a DateFormat object and apply its format( ) method to a Date object. Like the NumberFormat object we looked at in the previous chapter, DateFormat itself is abstract, but it has several static ("factory") methods that return useful DateFormat subclass instances. To get a default DateFormat, simply call getInstance( ):

```
DateFormat simple = DateFormat.getInstance( );
String now = simple.format( new Date( ) );        // 4/12/06 6:06 AM
```

You can generate a date string or a time string, or both, using the getDateInstance( ), getTimeInstance( ), and getDateTimeInstance( ) factory methods. The argument to these methods describes what level of detail you'd like to see. DateFormat defines four constants representing detail levels: they are SHORT, MEDIUM, LONG, and FULL. There is also a DEFAULT, which is the same as MEDIUM. The following code creates three DateFormat instances: one to format a date, one to format a time, and one to format a date and time together. getDateTimeInstance( ) requires two arguments: the first specifies how to format the date, the second how to format the time:

```
// 12-Apr-06
DateFormat df  = DateFormat.getDateInstance(DateFormat.DEFAULT);

// 9:18:27 AM
DateFormat tf  = DateFormat.getTimeInstance(DateFormat.DEFAULT);

// Wednesday, April 12, 2006 9:18:27 o'clock AM EDT
DateFormat dtf =
  DateFormat.getDateTimeInstance( DateFormat.FULL, DateFormat.FULL );
```

We're showing only how to create the DateFormat objects here; to actually generate a String from a date, you'll need to call the format( ) method of these objects, passing a Date as an argument.

Formatting dates and times for other countries is just as easy. Overloaded factory methods accept a Locale argument:

```
// 12 avr. 06
DateFormat df =
  DateFormat.getDateInstance( DateFormat.DEFAULT, Locale.FRANCE );

// 9:27:49
DateFormat tf =
  DateFormat.getTimeInstance( DateFormat.DEFAULT, Locale.GERMANY );

// mercoledi 12 aprile 2006 9.27.49 GMT-04:00
DateFormat dtf =
    DateFormat.getDateTimeInstance(
        DateFormat.FULL, DateFormat.FULL, Locale.ITALY );
```

To parse a string representing a date, we use the parse( ) method of the DateFormat class. The result is a Date object. The parsing algorithms are finicky, so it's safest to parse dates and times that are in the same format produced by the DateFormat. The parse( ) method throws a ParseException if it doesn't understand the string you give it. All of the following calls to parse( ) succeed except the last; we don't supply a time zone, but the format for the time is LONG. Other exceptions are occasionally thrown from the parse( ) method. To cover all the bases, catch NullPointerExceptions and StringIndexOutOfBoundsExceptions also:

```
try {
  Date d;
  DateFormat df;

  df = DateFormat.getDateTimeInstance(
          DateFormat.FULL, DateFormat.FULL);
  d = df.parse("Wednesday, April 12, 2006 2:22:22 o'clock PM EDT");

  df = DateFormat.getDateTimeInstance(
          DateFormat.MEDIUM, DateFormat.MEDIUM);
  d = df.parse("12-Apr-06 2:22:22 PM");

  df = DateFormat.getDateTimeInstance(
          DateFormat.LONG, DateFormat.LONG);
  d = df.parse("April 12, 2006 2:22:22 PM EDT");

  // throws a ParseException; detail level mismatch
  d = df.parse("12-Apr-06 2:22:22 PM");
}
catch (Exception e) { ... }
```

Printf-Style Date and Time Formatting

The printf-style formatting covered in Chapter 10 can render dates and times to strings in completely arbitrary ways, without having to resort to Calendar methods to get components.

All date and time format strings use the same conversion character, t or T, followed by a suffix character that identifies the actual format or date/time component to be generated. For example, the format string %tc turns a Date argument into the string equivalent of what you get with the standard Date toString( ) method:

```
System.out.printf( "The date is %tc\n", new Date() );
// The date is Thu Nov 04 22:32:00 CST 2004
```

As with other conversion characters, the only difference between t and T is that the latter forces all of the output to uppercase. All time and date formatting is locale-sensitive, including the names of days and months and the A.M./P.M. identifier. To format a Date for another language just pass the Locale as the first argument:

```
System.out.printf( Locale.ITALIAN, "The date is %tc\n", new Date() );
// The date is gio nov 04 22:32:00 CST 2004
```

There are two additional composite, date-only formats and three composite time-only formats, as shown in the following table. The format string description in the third column of Table 11-4 refers to date and time component formats discussed in Tables 11-5 and 11-6.

Table 11-4. Composite date and time formats

Format suffix	Example	Components
c	Thu Nov 04 22:32:00 CST 2004	%ta %tb %td %tT %tZ %tY
D	11/04/04	%tm/%td/%ty
F	2004-11-04	%tY-%tm-%td
r	10:32:00 PM	%tI:%tM:%tS %Tp
R	22:32	%tH:%tM
T	22:32:00	%tH:%tM:%tS

Table 11-5 lists formats for accessing date components.

Table 11-5. Date component formats

Format suffix	Examples	Description
a	Sun, Mon, Tue...	Abbreviated day of week
A	Sunday, Monday...	Full day of week
b	Jan, Feb, Mar, ...	Abbreviated month
B	January, February, ...	Full month
R	1999, 2004	Four-digit year

Table 11-5. Date component formats (continued)

Format suffix	Examples	Description
C	2004 = 20	High two digits of year
y	1999 = 99	Low two digits of year
j	001 … 366	Day of year
m	01 … 13	Month of year
d	01 … 31	Day of month
e	1 … 31	Day of month, no leading zeros

Table 11-6 lists formats for accessing time components.

Table 11-6. Time component formats

Format suffix	Examples	Description
H	00 … 23	24-hour clock
k	0 … 23	24-hour clock, no leading zeros
I	01 … 12	12-hour clock
l	1 … 12	12-hour clock, no leading zeros
M	00 … 59	Minute
S	00 … 60[a]	Second
L	000 … 999	Millisecond
p	am, pm	Morning or afternoon designator
Z	CST, EST	Time zone name
z	-0600	Time zone GMT offset

[a] The second value (60) is a convention used to support leap years.

Timers

Java includes two handy classes for timed code execution. If you write a clock application, for example, you might want to update the display every second. You might want to play an alarm sound at some predetermined time. You could accomplish these tasks using multiple threads and calls to Thread.sleep( ). But the java.util.Timer and java.util.TimerTask classes handle this for you.

The Timer class is a scheduler. Each instance of Timer has a single thread that runs in the background, watching the clock and executing one or more TimerTasks at appropriate times. You could, for example, schedule a task to run once, at a specific time like this:

```java
import java.util.*;

public class Y2K {
  public static void main(String[] args) {
    Timer timer = new Timer();
```

```
TimerTask task = new TimerTask( ) {
  public void run( ) {
    System.out.println("Y2K!");
  }
};

Calendar cal = new GregorianCalendar( 2000, Calendar.JANUARY, 1 );
timer.schedule( task, cal.getTime( ));
    }
  }
```

TimerTask implements the Runnable interface. To create a task, you can simply subclass TimerTask and supply a run( ) method. Here, we've created a simple anonymous subclass of TimerTask that prints a message to System.out. Using the schedule( )
method of Timer, we've asked that the task be run on January 1, 2000. If the scheduled time has already passed (as in our example), the task is run immediately.

There are some other varieties of schedule( ); you can run tasks once or at recurring
intervals. There are two kinds of recurring tasks—fixed delay and fixed rate. *Fixed
delay* means that a fixed amount of time elapses between the end of the task's execution and the beginning of the next execution. *Fixed rate* means that the task should
begin execution at fixed time intervals. The difference comes into play when the time
to execute the task is long relative to the interval. Keep in mind that tasks are executed by the Timer's single scheduler thread. If one task takes a very long time, other
tasks may be delayed, in which case, they run as soon as the thread becomes available.

You could, for example, update a clock display every second with code like this:

```
Timer timer = new Timer( );

TimerTask task = new TimerTask( ) {
    public void run( ) {
        repaint( ); // update the clock display
    }
};

timer.scheduleAtFixedRate( task, 0, 1000 );
```

A TimerTask can be canceled before its execution with its cancel( ) method.

Collections

Collections are fundamental to all kinds of programming. Anywhere we need to
keep a group of objects, we have some kind of collection. At the most basic level,
Java supports collections in the form of arrays. But since arrays have a fixed length,
they are awkward for groups of things that grow and shrink over the lifetime of an
application. Arrays also do not represent abstract relationships between objects
well. In the early days, the Java platform had only two basic classes to address these
needs: the java.util.Vector class, which represents a dynamic list of objects, and

the `java.util.Hashtable`, class which holds a map of key/value pairs. Today, Java has a more comprehensive approach to collections called the Collections Framework. The older classes still exist, but they have been retrofitted into the framework (with some eccentricities).

Though conceptually simple, collections are one of the most powerful parts of any programming language. Collections implement data structures that lie at the heart of managing complex information and relationships. A great deal of basic computer science is devoted to describing the most efficient ways to implement certain types of algorithms over collections. Having these tools at your disposal and understanding how to use them can make your code both much smaller and faster. It can also save you from reinventing the wheel.

Prior to Java 5.0, the Collections Framework had two major drawbacks. The first was that collections were, of necessity, untyped and worked only with anonymous `Objects` instead of real types like `Dates` and `Strings`. This meant that you had to perform a type cast every time you took an object out of a collection. In theory, this broke Java's compile-time type safety. In practice, this was less the problem than that it was just plain cumbersome and tedious. The second problem was that, for practical reasons, collections could work only with objects and not with primitive types. This meant that any time you wanted to put a number or other primitive type into a collection you had to store it in a wrapper class first and, of course, unpack it later upon retrieving it. The combination of these factors made code working with collections less readable and more dangerous to boot.

Two of the biggest new features in Java 5.0 (and the most basic changes to the core language in Java's lifetime) address these problems directly. First, the introduction of generic types, as we described in Chapter 8, have made it possible to have truly type-safe collections under the control of the programmer. Second, the introduction of autoboxing and unboxing of primitive types means that you can generally treat objects and primitives as equals as far as collections are concerned. The combination of these new features can significantly reduce the amount of code you write and add safety as well. As we'll see, all of the collections classes now take advantage of these features.

The Collections Framework is based around a handful of interfaces in the `java.util` package. These interfaces are divided into two hierarchies. The first hierarchy descends from the `Collection` interface. This interface (and its descendants) represents a container that holds other objects. The second, separate, hierarchy is based on the `Map` interface, which represents a group of key/value pairs.

The Collection Interface

The mother of all collections is an interface appropriately named `Collection`. It serves as a container that holds other objects, its *elements*. It doesn't specify exactly how the objects are organized; it doesn't say, for example, whether duplicate objects are allowed or whether the objects are ordered in any way. These kinds of details are left to child interfaces. Nevertheless, the Collection interface defines some basic operations common to all collections:

public boolean add(*element*)

This method adds the supplied object to this collection. If the operation succeeds, this method returns true. If the object already exists in this collection and the collection does not permit duplicates, false is returned. Furthermore, some collections are read-only. These collections throw an UnsupportedOperationException if this method is called.

public boolean remove(*element*)

This method removes the specified object from this collection. Like the add( ) method, this method returns true if the object is removed from the collection. If the object doesn't exist in this collection, false is returned. Read-only collections throw an UnsupportedOperationException if this method is called.

public boolean contains(*element*)

This method returns true if the collection contains the specified object.

public int size( )

Use this method to find the number of elements in this collection.

public boolean isEmpty( )

This method returns true if this collection has no elements.

public Iterator iterator( )

Use this method to examine all the elements in this collection. This method returns an Iterator, which is an object you can use to step through the collection's elements. We'll talk more about iterators in the next section.

Additionally, the methods addAll( ), removeAll( ), and containsAll( ) accept another Collection and add, remove, or test for all of the elements of the supplied collection.

Generics and collections

When using generics, the Collection type is parameterized with a specific type of element that the collection will hold. This makes a generic collection of "anything" into a specific collection of one type of element. The parameter type becomes the compile-time type of the element arguments in all of the methods of Collection (in this case, the add( ), remove( ), and contains( ) methods listed earlier). For example, in the following code, we create a Collection that works with Dates:

```
Collection<Date> dates = new ArrayList<Date>( );
dates.add( new Date( ) );
dates.add( "foo" ) // Error; string type where Date expected!!
```

ArrayList is just one type of Collection; we'll talk about it a bit later. The important thing is that we've declared the variable dates to be of the type Collection<Date>, that is, a collection of Dates, and we've allocated our ArrayList to match. Since our collection has been parameterized with the type Date, the add( ) method of the collection becomes add(Date date) and attempting to add any type of object other than a Date to the list would have caused a compile-time error.

If you are not using generics, you can simply substitute the type Object everywhere you see the element type and perform the appropriate casts. For example:

```
Collection dates = new ArrayList();
dates.add( new Date() );  // unchecked, compile-time warning
```

As we've described earlier in the book, this is essentially what the Java compiler is doing for us with generics. When using collections (or any generic classes) in this way under Java 5.0 or later, you will get compile-time warnings indicating that the usage is unchecked, meaning that it is possible to get an error at runtime if you have made a mistake. In this example, a mistake would not be caught until someone tried to retrieve the object from the collection and cast it to the expected type.

Runtime versus compile-time safety

With the introduction of generics, collections can now be made typesafe for a given type of element. However, a lot of existing Java code does not use generics and, in some cases, you may still simply wish to use plain Object collections. It's natural to ask if there isn't a way for us to simply subclass the existing collection classes to produce typesafe ones and, if so, why this wasn't done all along. Well, the answer is no. You can't get compile-time safety in this way because the new type-specific methods you would add would overload the general ones and not override them. (They wouldn't prevent the wider Object methods from being used.) However, you can implement runtime safety checks with special collections and this can be a reasonable thing to do. In fact, in support of generics migration, Java 5.0 supplies runtime-checked wrappers for all of the basic collection types. These wrappers enforce a specific Java element type at runtime by throwing ClassCastException if the wrong element is inserted. For example:

```
List list = new ArrayList();
list = Collections.checkedList( list, Date.class );
list.add( new Date() );
list.add( "foo" ); // Runtime ClassCastException!
```

Here, the static Collections.checkedList( ) method has wrapped our collection, list, in a wrapper that implements all of the methods of List, but checks that we are only holding Dates. The second argument to the method is the literal Date.class reference to the Class of Date. This serves to tell the wrapper what type we want to enforce. Corresponding "checked" collection methods exist for all of the basic collection interfaces that we'll see, including the base Collection, List, Set, and Map.

While they do not prevent mistakes from being made at compile time, runtime wrappers help catch errors quickly at runtime (on insertion rather than extraction of the element) and provide an additional level of confidence in the code.

Collections and arrays

Converting between collections and arrays is easy. As a special convenience, the elements of a collection can be placed into an array using the following methods:

```
public Object[] toArray( )
public <E> E[] toArray( E[] a )
// nongeneric equivalent
// public Object[] toArray( Object [] a )
```

The first method returns a plain Object array. With the second form, we can be more specific and get back an array of the correct element type. If we supply an array of sufficient size, it will be filled in with the values. But if the array is too short, a new array of the *same type* will be created, of the required length, and returned to us. If you don't want to bother creating the array, you can just pass in an empty array of the correct type like this:

```
String [] myStrings = myCollection( new String[0] ); // generic
```

(This trick is a little awkward and it would be nice if Java let us specify the type explicitly, using a Class reference, but for some reason, this isn't the case.) Going the other way, you can convert an array of objects to a List collection with the static asList( ) method of the java.util.Arrays class:

```
List list = Arrays.asList( myStrings );
```

Iteration

An *iterator* is an object that lets you step through a sequence of values. This kind of operation comes up so often that it is given a standard interface: java.util.Iterator. The Iterator interface has only two primary methods:

public Object next( )
> This method returns the next element of the associated collection.

public boolean hasNext( )
> This method returns true if you have not yet stepped through all the Collection's elements. In other words, it returns true if you can call next( ) to get the next element.

The following example shows how you could use an Iterator to print out every element of a collection:

```
public void printElements(Collection c, PrintStream out) {
    Iterator iterator = c.iterator();
    while ( iterator.hasNext() )
        out.println( iterator.next() );
}
```

In addition to the traversal methods, Iterator provides the ability to remove an element from a collection:

```
public void remove( )
```
> This method removes the last object returned from next( ) from the associated Collection.

Not all iterators implement remove( ). It doesn't make sense to be able to remove an element from a read-only collection, for example. If element removal is not allowed, an UnsupportedOperationException is thrown from this method. If you call remove( ) before first calling next( ), or if you call remove( ) twice in a row, you'll get an IllegalStateException.

For-loop over collections

Java 5.0 made iteration over collections even easier because, as we described in Chapter 4, the for-loop has been enhanced to operate over all types of Collection objects. For example, we can now step over all of the elements of a typed collection of Date objects like so:

```
Collection<Date> col = ...
for( Date date : collection )
    System.out.println( date );
```

The enhanced for-loop applies only to Collection type collections, not Maps. Maps are another type of beast that really contain two distinct sets of objects (keys and values), so it's not obvious what your intentions would be in such a loop.

java.util.Enumeration

Prior to the introduction of the Collections API there was another iterator interface: java.util.Enumeration. It used the slightly more verbose names: nextElement( ) and hasMoreElements( ) but accomplished the same thing. Many older classes provide Enumerations where they would now use Iterator. If you aren't worried about performance, you can just convert your Enumeration into a List with a static convenience method of the java.util.Collections class:

```
List list = Collections.list( enumeration );
```

Collection Types

The Collection interface has three child interfaces. Set represents a collection in which duplicate elements are not allowed. List is a collection whose elements have a specific order. The Queue interface, added in Java 5.0, is a buffer for objects with a notion of a "head" element that's next in line for processing.

Set

Set has no methods besides the ones it inherits from Collection. It simply enforces the no-duplicates rule. If you try to add an element that already exists in a Set, the add( ) method simply returns false. SortedSet adds only a few methods to Set. As you call add( ) and remove( ), the set maintains its order. You can retrieve subsets (which are also sorted) using the subSet( ), headSet( ), and tailSet( ) methods. The first( ), last( ), and comparator( ) methods provide access to the first element, the last element, and the object used to compare elements (more on this later).

List

The next child interface of Collection is List. The List is an ordered collection, similar to an array but with methods for manipulating the position of elements in the list:

public void add(E *element*)
> This method adds the specified element to the end of the list.

public void add(int *index,* E *element*)
> This method inserts the given object at the supplied position in the list. If the position is less than zero or greater than the list length, an IndexOutOfBoundsException will be thrown. The element that was previously at the supplied position, and all elements after it, are moved up one index position.

public void remove(int *index*)
> This method removes the element at the specified position. All subsequent elements move down one index position.

public E get(int *index*)
> This method returns the element at the given position.

public Object set(int *index,* E *element*)
> This method changes the element at the given position to the specified object. There must already be an object at the index or an IndexOutOfBoundsException is thrown.

The type E in these methods refers to the parameterized element type of the List class. Collection, Set, and List are all interface types. We'll look at concrete implementations of these shortly.

Queue

A Queue is a collection that acts like a buffer for elements. The queue maintains an ordering of items placed into it and has the notion of a "head" item for removal that can be queried or accepted:

public boolean offer(E element)
> This method attempts to place the element into the queue, returning true if successful. Different Queue types may have different limits or restrictions on element

types (including capacity). This method differs from the Collection method add( ) in that it returns a Boolean value instead of throwing an exception to indicate that the element cannot be accepted.

public E poll( )

This method removes the element at the head of the queue and returns it. If the queue is empty, null is returned.

public E peek( )

This method returns the head element without removing it from the queue. If the queue is empty, null is returned.

BlockingQueue

BlockingQueue is part of the java.util.concurrent package. It extends the Queue interface for queues that may have a fixed capacity and allows the user to block, waiting for space to insert an item or for an available item to retrieve. It adds timed wait versions of offer( ) and poll( ) and additional, blocking take( ) and put( ) methods:

public boolean offer(E element, long time, TimeUnit units)

This method attempts to place the element into the queue, just like the method of the base Queue interface, but blocks for up to the specified period of time as it waits for space to become available.

public E poll(long time, timeUnit unit)

This method attempts to remove the element at the head of the queue, just like the method of the base Queue interface, but blocks for up to the specified period of time as it waits for an element to become available.

public E take( )

This method retrieves the element at the head of the queue, blocking if necessary until one becomes available.

public void put(E element)

This method adds an element to the queue, blocking if necessary until space becomes available.

public boolean add(E element)

This method attempts to add an element to the queue immediately. If successful, it returns true. If no space is available, it throws an IllegalStateException. This method is useful for cases where you are not expecting the queue to ever reject an item.

The Map Interface

The Collections Framework also includes the java.util.Map, which is a collection of key/value pairs. Other names for map are "dictionary" or "associative array." Maps store and retrieve elements with key values; they are very useful for things like caches or minimalist databases. When you store a value in a map, you associate a key object with a value. When you need to look up the value, the map retrieves it using the key.

With generics, a Map type is parameterized with two types: one for the keys and one for the values. The following snippet uses a HashMap, which is an efficient type of map implementation that we'll discuss later:

```
Map<String, Date> dateMap = new HashMap<String, Date>( );
dateMap.put( "today", new Date( ) );
Date today = dateMap.get( "today" );

// nongeneric example
Map dateMap = new HashMap( );
dateMap.put( "today", new Date( ) );
Date today = (Date)dateMap.get( "today" );
```

Nongeneric maps simply map Object types to Object types and require the appropriate cast to retrieve values, as shown here.

The basic operations on Map are straightforward. In the following methods, the type K refers to the key parameter type and the type V refers to the value parameter type:

public V put(K *key,* V *value*)
> This method adds the specified key/value pair to the map. If the map already contains a value for the specified key, the old value is replaced and returned as the result.

public V get(K *key*)
> This method retrieves the value corresponding to key from the map.

public V remove(K *key*)
> This method removes the value corresponding to key from the map. The value removed is returned.

public int size( )
> Use this method to find the number of key/value pairs in this map.

You can retrieve all the keys or values in the map:

public Set keySet( )
> This method returns a Set that contains all the keys in this map.

public Collection values( )
> Use this method to retrieve all the values in this map. The returned Collection can contain duplicate elements.

Map has one child interface, SortedMap. A SortedMap maintains its key/value pairs sorted in a particular order according to the key values. It provides the subMap( ), headMap( ), and tailMap( ) methods for retrieving sorted map subsets. Like SortedSet, it also provides a comparator( ) method that returns an object that determines how the map keys are sorted. We'll talk more about that later.

Finally, we should make it clear that although related, Map is not a type of Collection (Map does not extend the Collection interface). You might wonder why. All of the methods of the Collection interface would appear to make sense for Map, except for iterator( ). A Map, again, has two sets of objects: keys and values, and separate iterators for each. This is why a Map is not a Collection.

One more note about maps: some map implementations (including Java's standard HashMap) allow null to be used as a key or value, but others may not.

ConcurrentMap

The ConcurrentMap interface is part of the java.util.concurrent package. It extends the base Map interface and adds atomic put, remove, and replace functionality that is useful for concurrent programming:

public V putIfAbsent(K key, V value)
> This method associates the value with the key only if the key was not already in use. If the key exists, no action is taken. If the key does not exist, it is created. The resulting value (existing or new) is returned.

public boolean remove(Object key, Object value)
> This method removes the mapping (key and value) only if the current value associated with the key equals the supplied value. It returns true if the value was removed, false if not.

public boolean replace(K key, V existingValue, V newValue)
> This method replaces the value associated with the key only if the existing value equals the existingValue argument. It returns true if the value was replaced.

public boolean replace(K key, V value)
> This method replaces the value associated with the key only if a mapping already exists for the key (i.e., it already has some value).

Collection Implementations

Up until this point, we've talked only about interfaces. But you can't instantiate interfaces; you need concrete implementations. Fortunately, the Collections Framework includes useful implementations of all of the collections interfaces. In some cases, there are several alternatives to choose from. To understand the tradeoffs between these implementations, it helps to have a basic understanding of the most common data structures used in all programming: arrays, linked lists, trees, and hash maps. Many books have been written about these data structures and we will not drag you into the mind-numbing details here. We'll hit the highlights briefly as a prelude to our discussion of the Java implementations. We should stress before we go on that the differences in the implementations of Java collections are only really significant when working with very large numbers of elements or with extreme time sensitivity. For the most part, they all behave well enough to be interchangeable.

Arrays

It should be fairly obvious that plain old Java arrays, shown in Figure 11-2, would be good at holding an ordered collections of elements. As we mentioned earlier however, one limitation of arrays is that they cannot grow. This means that to support a true Collection, arrays must be copied into larger arrays as capacity demands increase. Another problem with using arrays for lists is that inserting an element into the middle of an array or taking one out generally also involves copying large parts of the array to and fro, which is an expensive operation.

Figure 11-2. Array structure

Because of this, arrays are described as consuming *constant time* for retrieval, but *linear time* for insertion into or deletion from the body of the array. The term constant time here means that, in general, the time to retrieve an element stays roughly constant even as you add more elements to the array. Linear time means that the time to insert or delete an element takes longer and longer as the array adds elements; the time expense grows linearly with the number of elements. There are worse things too: exponential time, as you might imagine, means that an algorithm is useless for very large numbers of elements. All of the Java collection implementations work in linear time or better.

Arrays are useful when you are mostly reading or exclusively appending to the end of the collection.

Linked lists

A linked list, shown in Figure 11-3, holds its elements in a chain of *node*s, each referencing the node before and after it (if any). In this way, the linked list forms an ordered collection that looks something like an array. Unlike the magic of an array, however, to retrieve an element from a linked list, you must traverse the list from either the head or tail to reach the correct spot. As you might have guessed, this is a linear-time operation that gets more expensive as the number of elements grows. The flip-side is that once you're at the spot, inserting or deleting an element is a piece of cake: simply change the references and you're done. This means that insertions and deletions, at least near the head and tail of a linked list, are said to be in constant time.

Figure 11-3. Linked list structure

Linked lists are useful when you are doing a lot of insertions or deletions on a collection.

Trees

A tree is like a linked list in that it holds its elements in nodes that point to their neighbors. However, a tree, as its name suggests, does not have a linear structure, but instead arranges its elements in a cascade of branches like a family tree. The power of the tree structure is in sorting and searching elements that have a specified order. A *binary search tree*, as shown in Figure 11-4, arranges its elements such that the children divide up a range of values. One child holds values greater than the node and one child holds values lower. By applying this knowledge recursively on a properly "balanced" tree, we can rapidly find any value. The effort to search the tree is described as *log(n) time*, which means that it grows only with the logarithm of the number of elements, which is much better than the linear time it would take to check all of the elements by brute force.

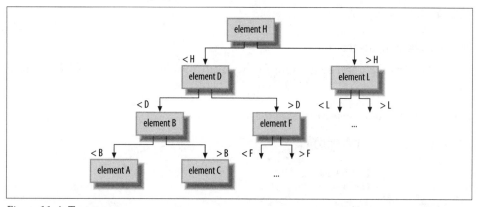

Figure 11-4. Tree structure

Trees are useful for maintaining or searching large collections of sorted elements.

Hash maps

Hash maps are strange and magical beasts. A hash map (or hash table as it is also called) uses a mathematical hash algorithm applied to its key value to distribute its element values into a series of "buckets." The algorithm relies on the hash algorithm to distribute the elements as uniformly (randomly) as possible. To retrieve an element by its key then simply involves searching the correct bucket. Because the hash calculation is fast and can have a large number of buckets, there are few elements to search and retrieval is very fast. As we described in Chapter 7, all Java Objects have a hash value as determined by the hashCode( ) method. We'll say a bit more about hash codes and key values for maps in a later section.

Hash map performance is governed by many factors, including the sophistication of the hash algorithm implemented by its elements (see Figure 11-5). In general, a good implementation can operate in linear time for putting and retrieving elements. Hash maps are fast at mapping unsorted collections.

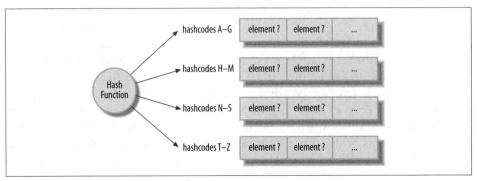

Figure 11-5. Hash map structure

Java Collections implementations

Table 11-7 lists the implementations of the Java Collections Framework by interface type.

Table 11-7. Collections Framework implementation classes

Interface	Implementation
Set	HashSet LinkedHashSet CopyOnWriteArraySet
SortedSet	TreeSet
List	ArrayList LinkedList Vector[a] CopyOnWriteArrayList
Map	HashMap LinkedHashMap IdentityHashMap Hashtable[a]
ConcurrentMap	ConcurrentHashMap
SortedMap	TreeMap
Queue	LinkedList PriorityQueue DelayQueue SynchronousQueue ConcurrentLinkedQueue

Table 11-7. Collections Framework implementation classes (continued)

Interface	Implementation
BlockingQueue	ArrayBlockingQueue
	LinkedBlockingQueue
	PriorityBlockingQueue

ᵃ Vector and Hashtable are legacy classes and should generally be avoided in favor of ArrayList and HashMap, respectively.

ArrayList and LinkedList provide the array and linked list implementations of the List interface described earlier. ArrayList is satisfactory for most purposes but use LinkedList when you plan to do a lot of insertions or deletions at various points in the list.

HashSet and HashMap provide a good hash map implementation of the Set and Map interfaces. The LinkedHashSet and LinkedHashMap implementations combine the hash algorithm with a linked list that maintains insertion order of the elements. (Note that these linked collections are ordered, but not sorted collections.)

TreeSet and TreeMap maintain sorted collections using a tree data structure. In the case of TreeMap, it is the key values that are sorted. The sorting is accomplished by a comparator object. We'll discuss sorting later in this chapter.

Queue is implemented both by LinkedList (which implements both List and Queue) and PriorityQueue. A PriorityQueue's prioritization comes from a sorting order determined by a comparator supplied with its constructor. Elements that sort "least" or "lowest" have the highest priority. The various implementations of BlockingQueue mirror these for concurrency-aware queues.

Finally, IdentityHashMap is an alternate type of HashMap that uses object identity instead of object equality to determine which keys match which objects. Normally any two objects that test equal with equals( ) operate as the same key in a Map. With IdentityHashMap, only the original object instance retrieves the element. We'll talk about hash codes and keys more in the next section.

We should also mention three specialized collections that we'll talk about later: EnumSet and EnumMap are specifically designed to work with Java enumerations. WeakHashMap uses weak references to cooperate with Java garbage collection.

Hash Codes and Key Values

The names Hashtable and HashMap refer to the object hash codes these map collections use to make their associations. Specifically, an element in a Hashtable or HashMap is not associated with a key strictly by the key object's identity but rather by the key's contents. This allows keys that are equivalent to access the same object. By "equivalent," we mean those objects that compare true with equals( ). If you store an object in a Hashtable using one object as a key, you can use any other object that equals( ) tells you is equivalent to retrieve the stored object.

It's easy to see why equivalence is important if you remember our discussion of strings. You may create two String objects that have the same text in them but that come from different sources in Java. In this case, the == operator tells you that the objects are different, but the equals( ) method of the String class tells you that they are equivalent. Because they are equivalent, if we store an object in a HashMap using one of the String objects as a key, we can retrieve it using the other.

The hash code of an object makes this association based on content. As we mentioned in Chapter 7, the hash code is like a fingerprint of the object's data content. HashMap uses it to store the objects so that they can be retrieved efficiently. The hash code is nothing more than a number (an integer) that is a function of the data. The number is always the same for identical data, but the hashing function is intentionally designed to generate as random a number as possible for different combinations of data. In other words, a very small change in the data should produce a big difference in the number. It should be unlikely that two similar datasets would produce the same hash code.

As we described earlier, internally, HashMap really just keeps a number of lists of objects, but it puts objects into the lists based on their hash code. When it wants to find the object again, it can look at the hash code and know immediately how to get to the appropriate list. The HashMap still might end up with a number of objects to examine, but the list should be short. For each object in the short list it finds, it does the following comparison to see if the key matches:

```
if ((keyHashcode == storedKeyHashcode) && key.equals(storedKey))
    return object;
```

There is no prescribed way to generate hash codes. The only requirement is that they be somewhat randomly distributed and reproducible (based on the data). This means that two objects that are not the same could end up with the same hash code by accident. This is unlikely (there are 2^{32} possible integer values); moreover, it shouldn't cause a problem because the HashMap ultimately checks the actual keys, as well as the hash codes, to see if they are equal. Therefore, even if two objects have the same hash code, they can still coexist in the HashMap as long as they don't test equal to one another as well.

Hash codes are computed by an object's hashCode( ) method, which is inherited from the Object class if it isn't overridden. The default hashCode( ) method simply assigns each object instance a unique number to be used as a hash code. If a class does not override this method, each instance of the class will have a unique hash code. This goes along well with the default implementation of equals( ) in Object, which only compares objects for identity using ==.

You must override equals( ) in any classes for which equivalence of different objects is meaningful. Likewise, if you want equivalent objects to serve as equivalent keys, you need to override the hashCode( ) method as well to return identical hash code values. To do this, you need to create some suitably complex and arbitrary function of the contents of your object. The only criterion for the function is that it should be almost certain to return different values for objects with different data, but the same value for objects with identical data.

Synchronized and Unsynchronized Collections

The java.util.Collections class contains important static methods that operate on Sets and Maps. Since all the static methods in Collections operate on interfaces, they work regardless of the actual implementation classes you're using. The first methods we'll look at involve creating synchronized versions of our collections.

Most of the default collection implementations are not synchronized; that is, they are not safe for concurrent access by multiple threads. The reason for this is performance. In many applications there is no need for synchronization, so the Collections API does not provide it by default. Instead, you can create a synchronized version of any collection using the following methods of the Collections class:

```
public static Collection synchronizedCollection(Collection c)
public static Set synchronizedSet(Set s)
public static List synchronizedList(List list)
public static Map synchronizedMap(Map m)
public static SortedSet synchronizedSortedSet(SortedSet s)
public static SortedMap synchronizedSortedMap(SortedMap m)
```

These methods return synchronized, threadsafe versions of the supplied collection, by wrapping them. For example, the following shows how to create a threadsafe List:

```
List list = new ArrayList( );
List syncList = Collections.synchronizedList(list);
```

Multiple threads can call methods on this list safely, blocking as necessary to wait for the other threads to complete.

In contrast to the norm, the older Hashtable and Vector collections are synchronized by default (and, therefore, may be a bit slower when that's not needed). The "copy on write" collection implementations that we'll talk about later also do not require synchronization for their special applications. Finally, the ConcurrentHashMap and ConcurrentLinkedQueue implementations that we'll cover later are threadsafe and designed specifically to support a high degree of concurrent access without incurring a significant penalty for their internal synchronization.

Synchronizing iterators

It's important to note that although synchronized collections are threadsafe, the Iterators returned from them are not. If you obtain an Iterator from a collection, you should do your own synchronization to ensure that the collection does not change as you're iterating through its elements. You can do this by synchronizing on the collection itself with the synchronized keyword:

```
synchronized(syncList) {
    Iterator iterator = syncList.iterator();
    // do stuff with the iterator here
}
```

If you do not synchronize on the collection while iterating and the collection changes, Java attempts to throw a ConcurrentModificationException. However, this is not guaranteed.

ConcurrentHashMap and ConcurrentLinkedQueue

Java 5.0 introduced the java.util.concurrent.ConcurrentHashMap class. This is part of the new thread utilities package and provides a Map that performs much better under multithreaded access. A ConcurrentHashMap is safe for access from multiple threads, but it does not necessarily block threads during operations. Instead, some degree of overlapping operations, such as concurrent reads, are permitted safely. The ConcurrentHashMap can even allow a limited number of concurrent writes to happen while reads are being performed. These operations and iterators over the map do not throw a ConcurrentModificationException, but no guarantees are made as to exactly when one thread will see another thread's work. All views of the map are based upon the most recently committed writes.

Similarly, the ConcurrentLinkedQueue implementation provides the same sort of benefits for a linked queue, allowing some degree of overlapping writes and reads by concurrent users.

Read-Only and Read-Mostly Collections

You can use the Collections class to create read-only versions of any collection:

```
public static Collection unmodifiableCollection(Collection c)
public static Set unmodifiableSet(Set s)
public static List unmodifiableList(List list)
public static Map unmodifiableMap(Map m)
public static SortedSet unmodifiableSortedSet(SortedSet s)
public static SortedMap unmodifiableSortedMap(SortedMap m)
```

Making unmodifiable versions of collections is a useful way to ensure that a collection handed off to another part of your code is not modified intentionally or inadvertently. Attempting to modify a read-only collection results in an UnsupportedOperationException.

Copy on write ("read-mostly") collections

The java.util.concurrent package contains the CopyOnWriteArrayList and CopyOnWriteArraySet List and Set implementations. These classes are threadsafe and do not require explicit synchronization, but are heavily optimized for read operations. Any write operation causes the entire data structure to be copied internally in a blocking operation. The advantage is that if you are almost always reading, these implementations are extremely fast and no synchronization is required.

WeakHashMap

In Chapter 5, we introduced the idea of weak references—object references that don't prevent their objects from being removed by the garbage collector. WeakHashMap is an implementation of Map that makes use of weak references in its keys and values. This means that you don't have to remove key/value pairs from a Map when you're finished with them. Normally, if you removed all references to a key object from the rest of your application, the Map would still contain a reference and keep the object "alive," preventing garbage collection. WeakHashMap changes this; once you remove references to a key object from the rest of the application, the WeakHashMap lets go of it, too.

EnumSet and EnumMap

EnumSet and EnumMap are collections designed to work specifically with the limited domain of objects defined by a Java enumerated type. (Enums are a new feature in Java 5.0. See Chapter 5.) Java enums are real Java objects and there is no reason you can't use them as keys or values in general collections. However, the EnumSet and EnumMap classes are highly optimized, taking advantage of the knowledge that the set, or keys in the map, respectively, may be one of only a few individual objects. With this knowledge, storage can be compact and fast using bit fields internally. The idea is to make using collection operations on enumerations efficient enough to replace the general usage pattern of bit-flags and make binary logic operations unnecessary. Instead of using:

```
int flags = getFlags();
if ( flags & ( Constants.ERROR | Constants.WARNING ) != 0 )
```

we could use set operations:

```
EnumSet flags = getFlags();
if ( flags.contains( Constants.Error) || flags.contains( Constants.Warning ) )
```

This code may not be as terse, but it is easier to understand and should be just as fast.

Sorting Collections

The Collections utilities include methods for performing common operations like sorting. Sorting comes in two varieties:

public static void sort(List *list*)

> This method sorts the given list. You can use this method only on lists whose elements implement the java.lang.Comparable interface. Luckily, many classes already implement this interface, including String, Date, BigInteger, and the wrapper classes for the primitive types (Integer, Double, etc.).

public static void sort(List *list,* Comparator *c*)

> Use this method to sort a list whose elements don't implement the Comparable interface. The supplied java.util.Comparator does the work of comparing elements. You might, for example, write an ImaginaryNumber class and want to sort a list of them. You would then create a Comparator implementation that knew how to compare two imaginary numbers.

The sorted collections we discussed earlier, SortedSet and SortedMap, maintain their collections in a specified order using the Comparable interface of their elements. If the elements do not implement Comparable, you must supply a Comparator object yourself in the constructor of the implementation. For example:

```
Comparator myComparator = ...
SortedSet mySet = new TreeSet( myComparator );
```

Collections give you some other interesting capabilities, too. If you're interested in learning more, check out the min( ), max( ), binarySearch( ), and reverse( ) methods.

A Thrilling Example

Collections is a bread-and-butter topic, which means it's hard to create exciting examples. The example in this section reads a text file, parses all its words, counts the number of occurrences, sorts them, and writes the results to another file. It gives you a good feel for how to use collections in your own programs. This example also shows new Java 5.0 features, including generics, autoboxing, and the Scanner API. The previous version of this example was about 30 percent longer.

```
Import java.io.*;
import java.util.*;

public class WordSort
{
  public static void main(String[] args) throws IOException
  {
    if ( args.length < 2 ) {
      System.out.println("Usage: WordSort inputfile outputfile");
      return;
    }
    String inputfile = args[0];
    String outputfile = args[1];
```

```
        /*  Create the word map. Each key is a word and each value is an
            Integer that represents the number of times the word occurs
            in the input file.
        */
        Map<String,Integer> map = new TreeMap<String,Integer>();

        Scanner scanner = new Scanner( new File(inputfile) );
        while ( scanner.hasNext() ) {
            String word = scanner.next();
            Integer count = map.get( word );
            count = ( count == null ? 1 : count +1 );
            map.put( word, count );
        }
        scanner.close();

        // get the map's keys
        List<String> keys = new ArrayList<String>( map.keySet() );

        // write the results to the output file
        PrintWriter out = new PrintWriter( new FileWriter(outputfile) );
        for ( String key : keys )
          out.println( key + " : " + map.get(key) );
        out.close();
    }
}
```

Suppose, for example, that you have an input file named *Ian Moore.txt*:

```
Well it was my love that kept you going
Kept you strong enough to fall
And it was my heart you were breaking
When he hurt your pride

So how does it feel
How does it feel
How does it feel
How does it feel
```

You could run the example on this file using the following command:

```
% java WordSort "Ian Moore.txt" count.txt
```

The output file, *count.txt*, looks like this:

```
And : 1
How : 3
Kept : 1
So : 1
Well : 1
When : 1
breaking : 1
does : 4
enough : 1
...
```

The results are case-sensitive: "How" and "how" are recorded separately. You could modify this behavior by converting words to all lowercase after retrieving them from the Scanner.

Properties

The java.util.Properties class is a specialized hash table for strings. Properties are generally used to hold textual configuration data. Examples of this are the Java System properties, which are passed to a Java application on the command line. We'll cover those later. More generally, you can use a Properties table to hold arbitrary configuration information for an application in an easily accessible format. The neat thing about a Properties table is that it can load and store its information in text format using streams (see Chapter 12 for information on streams). As of Java 5.0, Properties can also save themselves in XML format.

Any string values can be stored as key/value pairs in a Properties table. However, the convention is to use a dot-separated naming hierarchy to group property names into logical structures. (Unfortunately, this is just a convention, and you can't work with groups of properties in a hierarchical way as this might imply.) For example, you can create an empty Properties table and add String key/value pairs just as you could with a Map:

```
Properties props = new Properties( );
props.setProperty("myApp.xsize", "52");
props.setProperty("myApp.ysize", "79");
```

Thereafter, you can retrieve values with the getProperty( ) method:

```
String xsize = props.getProperty( "myApp.xsize" );
```

If the named property doesn't exist, getProperty( ) returns null. You can get an Enumeration of the property names with the propertyNames( ) method:

```
for ( Enumeration e = props.propertyNames( ); e.hasMoreElements; ) {
    String name = e.nextElement( );
    ...
}
```

When you create a Properties table, you can specify a second table for default property values:

```
Properties defaults = ...
Properties props = new Properties( defaults );
```

Now, when you call getProperty( ), the method searches the default table if it doesn't find the named property in the current table. An alternative version of getProperty( ) also accepts a default value; this value is returned instead of null if the property is not found in the current or default lists:

```
String xsize = props.getProperty( "myApp.xsize", "50" );
```

Loading and Storing

You can save a `Properties` table to an `OutputStream` using the save( ) method. The property information is output in a flat ASCII format. We'll talk about I/O in the next chapter, but bear with us for now. Continuing with the previous example, output the property information using the `System.out` stream as follows:

```
props.save( System.out, "Application Parameters" );
```

`System.out` is a standard output stream that prints to the console or command line of an application. We could also save the information to a file using a `FileOutputStream` as the first argument to save( ). The second argument to save( ) is a `String` that is used as a header for the data. The previous code outputs something like the following to `System.out`:

```
#Application Parameters
#Mon Feb 12 09:24:23 CST 2001
myApp.ysize=79
myApp.xsize=52
```

The load( ) method reads the previously saved contents of a `Properties` object from an `InputStream`:

```
FileInputStream fin;
...
Properties props = new Properties( )
props.load( fin );
```

The list( ) method is useful for debugging. It prints the contents to an `OutputStream` in a format that is more human-readable but not retrievable by load( ). It truncates long lines with an ellipsis (...).

Storing as XML

As of Java 5.0, the `Properties` class was enhanced with the storeToXML( ) and loadFromXML( ) methods. These operate just like the save( ) and load( ) methods but write an XML file like the following:

```
<?xml version="1.0" encoding="UTF-8"?>
<!DOCTYPE properties SYSTEM "http://java.sun.com/dtd/properties.dtd">
<properties>
<comment>My Properties</comment>
<entry key="myApp.ysize">79</entry>
<entry key="myApp.xsize">52</entry>
</properties>
```

We'll cover XML in detail in Chapter 24.

System Properties

The `java.lang.System` class provides access to basic system environment information through the static `System.getProperty( )` method. This method returns a `Properties` table that contains system properties. System properties take the place of environment variables in some programming environments. Table 11-8 summarizes system properties that are guaranteed to be defined in any Java environment.

Table 11-8. System properties

System property	Meaning
java.vendor	Vendor-specific string
java.vendor.url	URL of vendor
java.version	Java version
java.home	Java installation directory
java.class.version	Java class version
java.class.path	The classpath
os.name	Operating system name
os.arch	Operating system architecture
os.version	Operating system version
file.separator	File separator (such as / or \)
path.separator	Path separator (such as : or ;)
line.separator	Line separator (such as \n or \r\n)
user.name	User account name
user.home	User's home directory

Applets are, by current web browser conventions, prevented from reading the following properties: java.home, java.class.path, user.name, user.home, and user.dir. As you'll see later, these restrictions are implemented by a SecurityManager object.

Your application can set system properties with the static method System.setProperty( ). You can also set system properties when you run the Java interpreter, using the -D option:

```
% java -Dfoo=bar -Dcat=Boojum MyApp
```

Since it is common to use system properties to provide parameters such as numbers and colors, Java provides some convenience routines for retrieving property values and parsing them into their appropriate types. The classes Boolean, Integer, Long, and Color each come with a "get" method that looks up and parses a system property. For example, Integer.getInteger("foo") looks for a system property called foo and then returns it as an Integer. Color.getColor("foo") parses the property as an RGB value and returns a Color object.

The Preferences API

The Java Preferences API accommodates the need to store both system and per-user configuration data persistently across executions of the Java VM. The Preferences API is like a portable version of the Windows registry, a mini database in which you can keep small amounts of information, accessible to all applications. Entries are stored as name/value pairs, where the values may be of several standard types including strings, numbers, Booleans, and even short byte arrays. We should stress that the Preferences API is not intended to be used as a true database and you can't store large amounts of data in it. (That's not to say anything about how it's actually implemented.)

Preferences are stored logically in a tree. A preferences object is a node in the tree located by a unique path. You can think of preferences as files in a directory structure; within the file are stored one or more name/value pairs. To store or retrieve items, you ask for a preferences object for the correct path. Here is an example; we'll explain the node lookup shortly:

```
Preferences prefs = Preferences.userRoot().node("oreilly/learningjava");

prefs.put("author", "Niemeyer");
prefs.putInt("edition", 4);

String author = prefs.get("author", "unknown");
int edition = prefs.getInt("edition", -1);
```

In addition to the String and int type accessors, there are the following get methods for other types: getLong(), getFloat(), getDouble(), getByteArray(), and getBoolean(). Each of these get methods takes a key name and default value to be used if no value is defined. And, of course, for each get method, there is a corresponding "put" method that takes the name and a value of the corresponding type. Providing defaults in the get methods is mandatory. The intent is for applications to function even if there is no preference information or if the storage for it is not available, as we'll discuss later.

Preferences are stored in two separate trees: system preferences and user preferences. *System preferences* are shared by all users of the Java installation. But *user preferences* are maintained separately for each user; each user sees his or her own preference information. In our example, we used the static method userRoot() to fetch the root node (preference object) for the user preferences tree. We then asked that node to find the child node at the path *oreilly/learningjava*, using the node() method. The corresponding systemRoot() method provides the system root node.

The node() method accepts either a relative or an absolute path. A relative path asks the node to find the path relative to itself as a base. We also could have gotten our node this way:

```
Preferences prefs =
    Preferences.userRoot().node("oreilly").node("learningjava");
```

But node() also accepts an absolute path, in which case, the base node serves only to designate which tree the path is in. We could use the absolute path */oreilly/learningjava* as the argument to any node() method and reach our preferences object.

Preferences for Classes

Java is an object-oriented language, and so it's natural to wish to associate preference data with classes. In Chapter 12, we'll see that Java provides special facilities for loading resource files associated with class files. The Preferences API follows this pattern by associating a node with each Java package. Its convention is simple: the node path is just the package name with the dots (.) converted to slashes (/). All classes in the package share the same node.

You can get the preference object node for a class using the static `Preferences. userNodeForPackage( )` or `Preferences.systemNodeForPackage( )` methods, which take a `Class` as an argument and return the corresponding package node for the user and system trees, respectively. For example:

```
Preferences datePrefs = Preferences.systemNodeForPackage( Date.class );
Preferences myPrefs = Preferences.userNodeForPackage( MyClass.class );
Preferences morePrefs =
    Preferences.userNodeForPackage( myObject.getClass() );
```

Here, we've used the `.class` construct to refer to the `Class` object for the `Date` class in the system tree and to our own `MyClass` class in the user tree. The `Date` class is in the `java.util` package, so we'll get the node */java/util* in that case. You can get the `Class` for any object instance using the `getClass( )` method.

Preferences Storage

There is no need to "create" nodes. When you ask for a node, you get a preferences object for that path in the tree. If you write something to it, that data is eventually placed in persistent storage, called the backing store. The *backing store* is the implementation-dependent storage mechanism used to hold the preference data. All the put methods return immediately, and no guarantees are made as to when the data is actually stored. You can force data to the backing store explicitly using the `flush( )` method of the `Preferences` class. Conversely, you can use the `sync( )` method to guarantee that a preferences object is up to date with respect to changes placed into the backing store by other applications or threads. Both `flush( )` and `sync( )` throw a `BackingStoreException` if data cannot be read or written for some reason.

You don't have to create nodes, but you can test for the existence of a data node with the `nodeExists( )` method, and you can remove a node and all its children with the `removeNode( )` method. To remove a data item from a node, use the `remove( )` method, specifying the key; or you can remove all the data from a node with the `clear( )` method (which is not the same as removing the node).

Although the details of the backing store are implementation-dependent, the Preferences API provides a simple import/export facility that can read and write parts of a preference tree to an XML file. (The format for the file is available at *http://java.sun.com/ dtd/*.) A preference object can be written to an output stream with the `exportNode( )`

method. The exportSubtree( ) method writes the node and all its children. Going the other way, the static Preferences.importPreferences( ) method can read the XML file and populate the appropriate tree with its data. The XML file records whether it is user or system preferences, but user data is always placed into the current user's tree, regardless of who generated it.

It's interesting to note that since the import mechanism writes directly to the tree, you can't use this as a general data-to-XML storage mechanism; other current and forthcoming APIs play that role. Also, although we said that the implementation details are not specified, it's interesting how things really work in the current implementation. Java creates a directory hierarchy for each tree at *$JAVA_HOME/ jre/.systemPrefs* and *$HOME/.java/.userPrefs*, respectively. In each directory, there is an XML file called *prefs.xml* corresponding to that node.

Change Notification

Often your application should be notified if changes are made to the preferences while it's running. You can get updates on preference changes using the PreferenceChangeListener and NodeChangeListener interfaces. These interfaces are examples of *event listener* interfaces, and we'll see many examples of these in Chapters 16 through 18. We'll also talk about the general pattern later in this chapter in the section "Observers and Observables." For now, we'll just say that by registering an object that implements PreferenceChangeListener with a node, you can receive updates on added, removed, and changed preference data for that node. The NodeChangeListener allows you to be told when child nodes are added to or removed from a specific node. Here is a snippet that prints all the data changes affecting our */oreilly/learningjava* node:

```
Preferences prefs =
    Preferences.userRoot( ).node("/oreilly/learningjava");

prefs.addPreferenceChangeListener( new PreferenceChangeListener( ) {
    public void preferenceChange(PreferenceChangeEvent e) {
        System.out.println("Value: " + e.getKey( )
            + " changed to "+ e.getNewValue( ) );
    }
} );
```

In brief, this example listens for changes to preferences and prints them. If this example isn't immediately clear, it should be after you've read about events in Chapter 16 and beyond.

The Logging API

The java.util.logging package provides a highly flexible and easy to use logging framework for system information, error messages, and fine-grained tracing (debugging) output. With the logging package, you can apply filters to select log messages, direct their output to one or more destinations (including files and network services), and format the messages appropriately for their consumers.

Most importantly, much of this basic logging configuration can be set up externally at runtime through the use of a logging setup properties file or an external program. For example, by setting the right properties at runtime, you can specify that log messages are to be sent both to a designated file in XML format and also logged to the system console in a digested, human-readable form. Furthermore, for each of those destinations you can specify the level or priority of messages to be logged, discarding those below a certain threshold of significance. By following the correct source conventions in your code, you can even make it possible to adjust the logging levels for specific parts of your application, allowing you to target individual packages and classes for detailed logging without being overwhelmed by too much output. As of Java 5.0, the Logging API can even be controlled remotely via Java Management Extensions MBean APIs.

Overview

Any good logging API must have at least two guiding principles. First, performance should not inhibit the developer from using log messages freely. As with Java language assertions (discussed in Chapter 4), when log messages are turned off, they should not consume any significant amount of processing time. This means there's no performance penalty for including logging statements as long as they're turned off. Second, although some users may want advanced features and configuration, a logging API must have some simple mode of usage that is convenient enough for time-starved developers to use in lieu of the old standby System.out.println( ). Java's Logging API provides a simple model and many convenience methods that make it very tempting.

Loggers

The heart of the logging framework is the *logger*, an instance of java.util.logging. Logger. In most cases, this is the only class your code will ever have to deal with. A logger is constructed from the static Logger.getLogger( ) method, with a logger name as its argument. Logger names place loggers into a hierarchy, with a global, root logger at the top and a tree and children below. This hierarchy allows the configuration to be inherited by parts of the tree so that logging can be automatically configured for different parts of your application. The convention is to use a separate logger instance in each major class or package and to use the dot-separated package and/or class name as the logger name. For example:

```
package com.oreilly.learnjava;
public class Book {
    static Logger log = Logger.getLogger("com.oreilly.learnjava.Book");
```

The logger provides a wide range of methods to log messages; some take very detailed information, and some convenience methods take only a string for ease of use. For example:

```
log.warning("Disk 90% full.");
log.info("New user joined chat room.");
```

We cover methods of the logger class in detail a bit later. The names warning and info are two examples of logging levels; there are seven levels ranging from SEVERE at the top to FINEST at the bottom. Distinguishing log messages in this way allows us to select the level of information that we want to see at runtime. Rather than simply logging everything and sorting through it later (with negative performance impact) we can tweak which messages are generated. We'll talk more about logging levels in the next section.

We should also mention that for convenience in very simple applications or experiments, a logger for the name "global" is provided in the static field Logger.global. You can use it as an alternative to the old standby System.out.println( ) for those cases where that is still a temptation:

```
Logger.global.info("Doing foo...")
```

Handlers

Loggers represent the client interface to the logging system, but the actual work of publishing messages to destinations (such as files or the console) is done by *handler* objects. Each logger may have one or more Handler objects associated with it, which includes several predefined handlers supplied with the Logging API: ConsoleHandler, FileHandler, StreamHandler, and SocketHandler. Each handler knows how to deliver messages to its respective destination. ConsoleHandler is used by the default configuration to print messages on the command line or system console. FileHandler can direct output to files using a supplied naming convention and automatically rotate the files as they become full. The others send messages to streams and sockets, respectively. There is one additional handler, MemoryHandler, that can hold a number of log messages in memory. MemoryHandler has a circular buffer, which maintains a certain number of messages until it is triggered to publish them to another designated handler.

As we said, loggers can be set to use one or more handlers. Loggers also send messages up the tree to each of their parent logger's handlers. In the simplest configuration, this means that all messages end up distributed by the root logger's handlers. We'll see how to set up output using the standard handlers for the console, files, etc., shortly.

Filters

Before a logger hands off a message to its handlers or its parent's handlers, it first checks whether the logging level is sufficient to proceed. If the message doesn't meet the required level, it is discarded at the source. In addition to level, you can implement arbitrary filtering of messages by creating Filter classes that examine the log message before it is processed. A Filter class can be applied to a logger externally at runtime in the same way that the logging level, handlers, and formatters, discussed next, can be. A Filter may also be attached to an individual Handler to filter records at the output stage (as opposed to the source).

Formatters

Internally, messages are carried in a neutral format, including all the source information provided. It is not until they are processed by a handler that they are formatted for output by an instance of a Formatter object. The logging package comes with two basic formatters: SimpleFormatter and XMLFormatter. The SimpleFormatter is the default used for console output. It produces short, human-readable, summaries of log messages. XMLFormatter encodes all the log message details into an XML record format. The DTD for the format can be found at *http://java.sun.com/dtd/*.

Logging Levels

Table 11-9 lists the logging levels from most to least significant.

Table 11-9. Logging API logging levels

Level	Meaning
SEVERE	Application failure
WARNING	Notification of potential problem
INFO	Messages of general interest to end users
CONFIG	Detailed system configuration information for administrators
FINE FINER FINEST	Successively more detailed application tracing information for developers

These levels fall into three camps: end user, administrator, and developer. Applications often default to logging only messages of the INFO level and above (INFO, WARNING, and SEVERE). These levels are generally seen by end users and messages logged to them should be suitable for general consumption. In other words, they should be written clearly so they make sense to an average user of the application. Often these kinds of messages are presented to the end user on a system console or in a pop-up message dialog.

The CONFIG level should be used for relatively static but detailed system information that could assist an administrator or installer. This might include information about the installed software modules, host system characteristics, and configuration parameters. These details are important, but probably not as meaningful to an end user.

The FINE, FINER, and FINEST levels are for developers or others with knowledge of the internals of the application. These should be used for tracing the application at successive levels of detail. You can define your own meanings for these. We'll suggest a rough outline in our example, coming up next.

A Simple Example

In the following (admittedly very contrived) example, we use all the logging levels so that we can experiment with logging configuration. Although the sequence of messages is nonsensical, the text is representative of messages of that type.

```java
import java.util.logging.*;

public class LogTest {
    public static void main(String argv[])
    {
        Logger logger = Logger.getLogger("com.oreilly.LogTest");

        logger.severe("Power lost - running on backup!");
        logger.warning("Database connection lost, retrying...");
        logger.info("Startup complete.");
        logger.config("Server configuration: standalone, JVM version 1.5");
        logger.fine("Loading graphing package.");
        logger.finer("Doing pie chart");
        logger.finest("Starting bubble sort: value ="+42);
    }
}
```

There's not much to this example. We ask for a logger instance for our class using the static Logger.getLogger( ) method, specifying a class name. The convention is to use the fully qualified class name, so we'll pretend that our class is in a com.oreilly package.

Now, run LogTest. You should see output like the following on the system console:

```
Jan 6, 2002 3:24:36 PM LogTest main
SEVERE: Power lost - running on backup!
Jan 6, 2002 3:24:37 PM LogTest main
WARNING: Database connection lost, retrying...
Jan 6, 2002 3:24:37 PM LogTest main
INFO: Startup complete.
```

We see the INFO, WARNING, and SEVERE messages, each identified with a date and timestamp and the name of the class and method (LogTest main) from which they came. Notice that the lower-level messages did not appear. This is because the default logging level is normally set to INFO, meaning that only messages of severity INFO and above are logged. Also note that the output went to the system console and not to a log file somewhere; that's also the default. Now, we'll describe where these defaults are set and how to override them at runtime.

Logging Setup Properties

As we said in the introduction, probably the most important feature of the Logging API is the ability to configure so much of it at runtime through the use of external properties or applications. The default logging configuration is stored in the file *jre/lib/logging.properties* in the directory where Java is installed. It's a standard Java properties file (of the kind we described earlier in this chapter).

The format of this file is simple. You can make changes to it, but you don't have to. Instead you can specify your own logging setup properties file on a case-by-case basis, using a system property at runtime, as follows:

```
% java -Djava.util.logging.config.file=myfile.properties
```

In this command line, *myfile* is your properties file that contains directives we'll describe next. If you want to make this file designation more permanent, you can do so by setting the filename in the corresponding entry using the Java Preferences API described earlier in this chapter. You can go even further, and instead of specifying a setup file, supply a class that is responsible for setting up all logging configuration, but we won't get into that here.

A very simple logging properties file might look like this:

```
# Set the default logging level
.level = FINEST
# Direct output to the console
handlers = java.util.logging.ConsoleHandler
```

Here, we have set the default logging level for the entire application using the `.level` (that's dot-level) property. We have also used the `handlers` property to specify that an instance of the `ConsoleHandler` should be used (just like the default setup) to show messages on the console. If you run our application again, specifying this properties file as the logging setup, you will now see all our log messages.

But we're just getting warmed up. Next, let's look at a more complex configuration:

```
# Set the default logging level
.level = INFO

# Ouput to file and console
handlers = java.util.logging.FileHandler, java.util.logging.ConsoleHandler

# Configure the file output
java.util.logging.FileHandler.level = FINEST
java.util.logging.FileHandler.pattern = %h/Test.log
java.util.logging.FileHandler.limit = 25000
java.util.logging.FileHandler.count = 4
java.util.logging.FileHandler.formatter = java.util.logging.XMLFormatter

# Configure the console output
java.util.logging.ConsoleHandler.level = WARNING
```

```
# Levels for specific classes
com.oreilly.LogTest.level = FINEST
```

In this example, we have configured two log handlers: a `ConsoleHandler` with the logging level set to `WARNING` and also an instance of `FileHandler` that sends the output to an XML file. The file handler is configured to log messages at the `FINEST` level (all messages) and to rotate log files every 25,000 lines, keeping a maximum of four files.

The filename is controlled by the `pattern` property. Forward slashes in the filename are automatically localized to backslash (\) if necessary. The special symbol %h refers to the user home. You can use %t to refer to the system temporary directory. If filenames conflict, a number is appended automatically after a dot (starting at zero). Alternatively, you can use %u to indicate where a unique number should be inserted into the name. Similarly, when files rotate, a number is appended after a dot at the end. You can take control of where the rotation number is placed with the %g identifier.

In our example, we specified the `XMLFormatter` class. We could also have used the `SimpleFormatter` class to send the same kind of simple output to the console. The `ConsoleHandler` also allows us to specify any formatter we wish, using the `formatter` property.

Finally, we promised earlier that you could control logging levels for parts of your applications. To do this, set properties on your application loggers using their hierarchical names:

```
# Levels for specific logger (class) names
com.oreilly.LogTest.level = FINEST
```

Here, we've set the logging level for just our test logger, by name. The log properties follow the hierarchy, so we could set the logging level for all classes in the oreilly package with:

```
com.oreilly.level = FINEST
```

Logging levels are set in the order they are read in the properties file, so set the general ones first. Also note that the levels set on the handlers allow the file handler to filter only the messages being supplied by the loggers. So setting the file handler to `FINEST` won't revive messages squelched by a logger set to `SEVERE` (only the `SEVERE` messages will make it to the handler from that logger).

The Logger

In our example, we used the seven convenience methods named for the various logging levels. There are also three groups of general methods that can be used to provide more detailed information. The most general are:

```
log(Level level, String msg)
log(Level level, String msg, Object param1)
log(Level level, String msg, Object params[])
log(Level level, String msg, Throwable thrown)
```

These methods accept as their first argument a static logging level identifier from the Level class, followed by a parameter, array, or exception type. The level identifier is one of Level.SEVERE, Level.WARNING, Level.INFO, and so on.

In addition to these four methods, there are four corresponding methods named logp( ) that also take a source class and method name as the second and third arguments. In our example, we saw Java automatically determine that information, so why would we want to supply it? The answer is that Java may not always be able to determine the exact method name because of runtime dynamic optimization. The p in logp stands for "precise" and allows you to control this yourself.

There is yet another set of methods named logrb( ) (which probably should have been named logprb( )) that take both the class and method names and a resource bundle name. The resource bundle localizes the messages (see the section "Resource Bundles" in Chapter 10). More generally, a logger may have a resource bundle associated with it when it is created, using another form of the getLogger method:

```
Logger.getLogger("com.oreilly.LogTest", "logMessages");
```

In either case, the resource bundle name is passed along with the log message and can be used by the formatter. If a resource bundle is specified, the standard formatters treat the message text as a key and try to look up a localized message. Localized messages may include parameters using the standard message format notation and the form of log( ), which accepts an argument array.

Finally, there are convenience methods called entering( ), exiting( ), and throwing( ) which developers can use to log detailed trace information.

Performance

In the introduction, we said that performance is a priority of the Logging API. To that end we've described that log messages are filtered at the source, using logging levels to cut off processing of messages early. This saves much of the expense of handling them. However, it cannot prevent certain kinds of setup work that you might do before the logging call. Specifically, since we're passing things into the log methods, it's common to construct detailed messages or render objects to strings as arguments. Often this kind of operation is costly. To avoid unnecessary string construction, you should wrap expensive log operations in a conditional test using the Logger isLoggable( ) method to test whether you should carry out the operation:

```
if ( log.isLoggable( Level.CONFIG ) ) {
    log.config("Configuration: "+ loadExpensiveConfigInfo(  ) );
}
```

Observers and Observables

The `java.util.Observer` interface and `java.util.Observable` class are relatively small utilities, but they provide a glimpse of a fundamental design pattern in Java. Observers and observables are part of the MVC (Model-View-Controller) framework. It is an abstraction that lets a number of client objects (the *observers*) be notified whenever a certain object or resource (the *observable*) changes in some way. We will see this pattern used extensively in Java's event mechanism, covered in Chapters 16 through 19. Although these classes are not often used directly, it's worth looking at them to understand the pattern.

The `Observable` object has a method an `Observer` calls to register its interest. When a change happens, the `Observable` sends a notification by calling a method in each of the `Observers`. The observers implement the `Observer` interface, which specifies that notification causes an `Observer` object's `update( )` method to be called.

In the following example, we create a `MessageBoard` object that holds a `String` message. `MessageBoard` extends `Observable`, from which it inherits the mechanism for registering observers (`addObserver( )`) and notifying observers (`notifyObservers( )`). To observe the `MessageBoard`, we have `Student` objects that implement the `Observer` interface so that they can be notified when the message changes:

```java
//file: MessageBoard.java
import java.util.*;

public class MessageBoard extends Observable {
    private String message;

    public String getMessage() {
        return message;
    }
    public void changeMessage( String message ) {
        this.message = message;
        setChanged( );
        notifyObservers( message );
    }
    public static void main( String [] args ) {
        MessageBoard board = new MessageBoard( );
        Student bob = new Student( );
        Student joe = new Student( );
        board.addObserver( bob );
        board.addObserver( joe );
        board.changeMessage("More Homework!");
    }
} // end of class MessageBoard

class Student implements Observer {
    public void update(Observable o, Object arg) {
        System.out.println( "Message board changed: " + arg );
    }
}
```

Our MessageBoard object extends Observable, which provides a method called addObserver(). Each Student object registers itself using this method and receives updates via its update() method. When a new message string is set using the MessageBoard's changeMessage() method, the Observable calls the setChanged() and notifyObservers() methods to notify the observers. notifyObservers() can take as an argument an Object to pass along as an indication of the change. This object, in this case, the String containing the new message, is passed to the observer's update() method, as its second argument. The first argument to update() is the Observable object itself.

The main() method of MessageBoard creates a MessageBoard and registers two Student objects with it. Then it changes the message. When you run the code, you should see each Student object print the message as it is notified.

You can imagine how you could implement the observer/observable relationship yourself using a List to hold the list of observers. In Chapter 16 and beyond, we'll see that the Java AWT and Swing event model extends this design pattern to use strongly typed observables and observers, called events and event listeners. But for now, we turn our discussion of core utilities to another fundamental topic: I/O.

## CHAPTER 12

Input/Output Facilities

In this chapter, we continue our exploration of the Java API by looking at many of the classes in the java.io and java.nio packages. These packages offer a rich set of tools for basic I/O and also provide the framework on which all file and network communication in Java is built.

Figure 12-1 shows the class hierarchy of these packages.

We start by looking at the stream classes in java.io, which are subclasses of the basic InputStream, OutputStream, Reader, and Writer classes. Then we'll examine the File class and discuss how you can read and write files using classes in java.io. We also take a quick look at the data compression classes provided in java.util.zip. Finally, we begin our investigation of the java.nio package. The NIO, or "new" I/O, package (introduced in Java 1.4) adds significant new functionality for building high-performance services.

Streams

Most fundamental I/O in Java is based on *streams*. A stream represents a flow of data, or a channel of communication with (at least conceptually) a *writer* at one end and a *reader* at the other. When you are working with the java.io package to perform terminal input and output, reading or writing files, or communicating through sockets in Java, you are using various types of streams. Later in this chapter, we look at the NIO package, which introduces a similar concept called a *channel*. But for now, let's summarize the available types of streams:

InputStream
OutputStream

> Abstract classes that define the basic functionality for reading or writing an unstructured sequence of bytes. All other byte streams in Java are built on top of the basic InputStream and OutputStream.

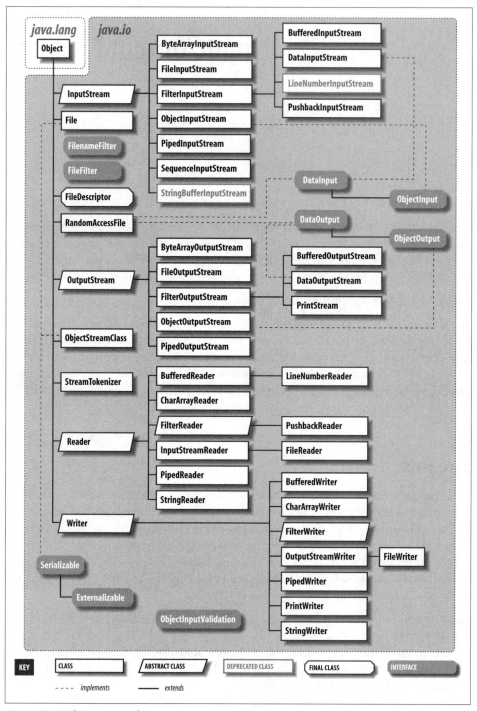

Figure 12-1. The java.io package

Reader

Writer

> Abstract classes that define the basic functionality for reading or writing a sequence of character data, with support for Unicode. All other character streams in Java are built on top of Reader and Writer.

InputStreamReader

OutputStreamWriter

> "Bridge" classes that convert bytes to characters and vice versa according to a specific character encoding scheme. Remember: in Unicode, a character is not a byte!

DataInputStream

DataOutputStream

> Specialized stream filters that add the ability to read and write simple data types, such as numeric primitives and String objects in a universal format.

ObjectInputStream

ObjectOutputStream

> Specialized stream filters that are capable of writing whole serialized Java objects and reconstructing them.

BufferedInputStream

BufferedOutputStream

BufferedReader

BufferedWriter

> Specialized stream filters that add buffering for additional efficiency.

PrintStream

PrintWriter

> Specialized streams that simplify printing text.

PipedInputStream

PipedOutputStream

PipedReader

PipedWriter

> "Loopback" streams used that can be used in pairs to move data within an application. Data written into a PipedOutputStream or PipedWriter is read from its corresponding PipedInputStream or PipedReader.

FileInputStream

FileOutputStream

FileReader

FileWriter

> Implementations of InputStream, OutputStream, Reader, and Writer that read from and write to files on the local filesystem.

Streams in Java are one-way streets. The java.io input and output classes represent the ends of a simple stream, as shown in Figure 12-2. For bidirectional conversations, you'll use one of each type of stream.

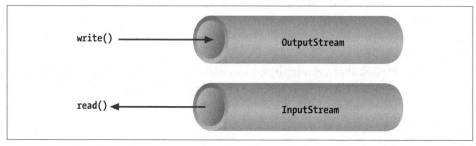

Figure 12-2. Basic input and output stream functionality

InputStream and OutputStream are abstract classes that define the lowest-level interface for all byte streams. They contain methods for reading or writing an unstructured flow of byte-level data. Because these classes are abstract, you can't create a generic input or output stream. Java implements subclasses of these for activities such as reading from and writing to files and communicating with sockets. Because all byte streams inherit the structure of InputStream or OutputStream, the various kinds of byte streams can be used interchangeably. A method specifying an InputStream as an argument can, of course, accept any subclass of InputStream. Specialized types of streams can also be layered to provide features, such as buffering, filtering, or handling higher-level data types.

Reader and Writer are very much like InputStream and OutputStream, except that they deal with characters instead of bytes. As true character streams, these classes correctly handle Unicode characters, which was not always the case with byte streams. Often, a bridge is needed between these character streams and the byte streams of physical devices, such as disks and networks. InputStreamReader and OutputStreamWriter are special classes that use a *character-encoding scheme* to translate between character and byte streams.

This section describes all the interesting stream types with the exception of FileInputStream, FileOutputStream, FileReader, and FileWriter. We postpone the discussion of file streams until the next section, where we cover issues involved with accessing the filesystem in Java.

Terminal I/O

The prototypical example of an InputStream object is the *standard input* of a Java application. Like stdin in C or cin in C++, this is the source of input to a command-line (non-GUI) program. It is an input stream from the environment—usually a terminal window or possibly the output of another command. The java.lang.System class, a general repository for system-related resources, provides a reference to standard input in the static variable System.in. It also provides a *standard output stream* and a *standard input stream* in the out and err variables, respectively.* The following example shows the correspondence:

```
InputStream stdin = System.in;
OutputStream stdout = System.out;
OutputStream stderr = System.err;
```

This example hides that System.out and System.err aren't really OutputStream objects, but more specialized and useful PrintStream objects. We'll explain these later, but for now we can reference out and err as OutputStream objects because they are a type of OutputStream as well.

We can read a single byte at a time from standard input with the InputStream's read( ) method. If you look closely at the API, you'll see that the read( ) method of the base InputStream class is an abstract method. What lies behind System.in is a particular implementation of InputStream that provides the real implementation of the read( ) method:

```
try {
    int val = System.in.read( );
} catch ( IOException e ) {
    ...
}
```

Although we said that the read( ) method reads a byte value, the return type in the example is int, not byte. That's because the read( ) method of basic input streams in Java use a convention from the C language to indicate the end of a stream with a special value. Byte values are returned (unsigned) as integers in the range 0 to 255 and the special value of integer -1 is used to indicate that end of stream has been reached. You'll need to test for this condition when using the simple read( ) method. You can then cast the value to a byte if needed. The following example reads each byte from an input stream and prints its value:

```
int val;
try {
    while( (val=System.in.read( )) != -1 )
        System.out.println((byte)val);
} catch ( IOException e ) { ... }
```

As we've shown in the examples, the read( ) method can also throw an IOException if there is an error reading from the underlying stream source. Various subclasses of IOException may indicate that a source such as a file or network connection has had an error. Additionally, higher-level streams that read data types more complex than a

---

* Standard error is a stream usually reserved for error-related text messages that should be shown to the user of a command-line application. It is differentiated from the standard output, which often might be redirected to a file or another application and not seen by the user.

single byte may throw EOFException, indicating an unexpected or premature end of stream.

An overloaded form of read( ) fills a byte array with as much data as possible up to the capacity of the array and returns the number of bytes read:

```
byte [] buff = new byte [1024];
int got = System.in.read( buff );
```

We can also check the number of bytes available for reading at a given time on an InputStream with the available( ) method. Using that information, we could create an array of exactly the right size:

```
int waiting = System.in.available();
if ( waiting > 0 ) {
    byte [] data = new byte [ waiting ];
    System.in.read( data );
    ...
}
```

However, the reliability of this technique depends on the ability of the underlying stream implementation to detect how much data can be retrieved. It generally works for files but should not be relied upon for all types of streams.

These read( ) methods block until at least some data is read (at least one byte). You must, in general, check the returned value to determine how much data you got and if you need to read more. (We look at nonblocking I/O later in this chapter.) The skip( ) method of InputStream provides a way of jumping over a number of bytes. Depending on the implementation of the stream, skipping bytes may be more efficient than reading them.

Finally, the close( ) method shuts down the stream and frees up any associated system resources. It's important for performance to remember to close streams when you are done with them. In some cases, streams may be closed automatically when objects are garbage-collected, but it is not a good idea to rely on this behavior. In Java 5.0, a new flag interface java.io.Closeable was added to identify all types of stream, channel, and related utility classes that can be closed.

Character Streams

In early versions of Java, some InputStream and OutputStream types included methods for reading and writing strings, but most of them operated by naively assuming that a 16-bit Unicode character was equivalent to an 8-bit byte in the stream. Unfortunately, this works only for Latin-1 (ISO 8859-1) characters and not for the world of other encodings used with different languages. In Chapter 10, we saw that the String class has a byte array constructor and a corresponding getBytes( ) method that each accept character encoding as an argument. In theory, we could use these as tools to transform arrays of bytes to and from Unicode characters so that we could work with byte streams that represent character data in any encoding format. Fortunately, however, we don't have to.

The java.io Reader and Writer character stream classes were introduced as streams that handle character data only. When you use these classes, you think only in terms of characters and string data and allow the underlying implementation to handle the conversion of bytes to a specific character encoding. As we'll see, some direct implementations of Reader and Writer exist, for example, for reading and writing files. But more generally, two special classes, InputStreamReader and OutputStreamWriter, bridge the gap between the world of character streams and the world of byte streams. These are, respectively, a Reader and a Writer that can be wrapped around any underlying byte stream to make it a character stream. An encoding scheme is used to convert between possibly multibyte encoded values and Java Unicode characters. An encoding scheme can be specified by name in the constructor of InputStreamReader or OutputStreamWriter. For convenience, the default constructor uses the system's default encoding scheme.

For example, let's parse a human-readable string from the standard input into an integer. We'll assume that the bytes coming from System.in use the system's default encoding scheme:

```
try {
    InputStreamReader converter = new InputStreamReader( System.in );
    BufferedReader in = new BufferedReader( converter );

    String line = in.readLine( );
    int i = NumberFormat.getInstance( ).parse( line ).intValue( );
} catch ( IOException e ) {
} catch ( ParseException pe ) { }
```

First, we wrap an InputStreamReader around System.in. This reader converts the incoming bytes of System.in to characters using the default encoding scheme. Then, we wrap a BufferedReader around the InputStreamReader. BufferedReader adds the readLine( ) method, which we can use to grab a full line of text (up to a platform-specific, line-terminator character combination) into a String. The string is then parsed into an integer using the techniques described in Chapter 10.

The important thing to note is that we have taken a byte-oriented input stream, System.in, and safely converted it to a Reader for reading characters. If we wished to use an encoding other than the system default, we could have specified it in the InputStreamReader's constructor like so:

```
InputStreamReader reader = new InputStreamReader( System.in, "UTF-8" );
```

For each character read from the reader, the InputStreamReader reads one or more bytes and performs the necessary conversion to Unicode.

In Chapter 13, we use an InputStreamReader and a Writer in our simple web server example, where we must use a character encoding specified by the HTTP protocol. We also return to the topic of character encodings when we discuss the java.nio.charset API, which allows you to query for and use encoders and decoders explicitly on buffers of characters and bytes. Both InputStreamReader and OutputStreamWriter can accept a Charset codec object as well as a character encoding name.

Stream Wrappers

What if we want to do more than read and write a sequence of bytes or characters? We can use a "filter" stream, which is a type of InputStream, OutputStream, Reader, or Writer that wraps another stream and adds new features. A filter stream takes the target stream as an argument in its constructor and delegates calls to it after doing some additional processing of its own. For example, you could construct a BufferedInputStream to wrap the system standard input:

```
InputStream bufferedIn = new BufferedInputStream( System.in );
```

The BufferedInputStream is a type of filter stream that reads ahead and buffers a certain amount of data. (We'll talk more about it later in this chapter.) The BufferedInputStream wraps an additional layer of functionality around the underlying stream. Figure 12-3 shows this arrangement for a DataInputStream, which is a type of stream that can read higher-level data types, such as Java primitives and strings.

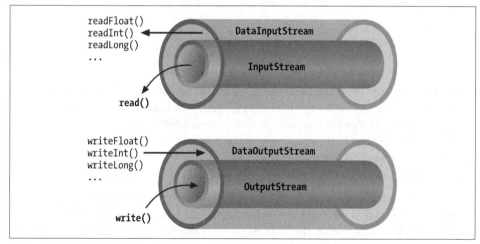

Figure 12-3. Layered streams

As you can see from the previous code snippet, the BufferedInputStream filter is a type of InputStream. Because filter streams are themselves subclasses of the basic stream types, they can be used as arguments to the construction of other filter streams. This allows filter streams to be layered on top of one another to provide different combinations of features. For example, we could first wrap our System.in with a

BufferedInputStream and then wrap the BufferedInputStream with a DataInputStream for reading special data types.

Java provides base classes for creating new types of filter streams: FilterInputStream, FilterOutputStream, FilterReader, and FilterWriter. These superclasses provide the basic machinery for a "no op" filter (a filter that doesn't do anything) by delegating all their method calls to their underlying stream. Real filter streams subclass these and override various methods to add their additional processing. We'll make an example filter stream later in this chapter.

Data streams

DataInputStream and DataOutputStream are filter streams that let you read or write strings and primitive data types comprised of more than a single byte. DataInputStream and DataOutputStream implement the DataInput and DataOutput interfaces, respectively. These interfaces define methods for reading or writing strings and all of the Java primitive types, including numbers and Boolean values. DataOutputStream encodes these values in a machine-independent manner and then writes them to its underlying byte stream. DataInputStream does the converse.

You can construct a DataInputStream from an InputStream and then use a method such as readDouble( ) to read a primitive data type:

```
DataInputStream dis = new DataInputStream( System.in );
double d = dis.readDouble( );
```

This example wraps the standard input stream in a DataInputStream and uses it to read a double value. readDouble( ) reads bytes from the stream and constructs a double from them. The DataInputStream methods expect the bytes of numeric data types to be in *network byte order*, a standard that specifies that the high-order bytes are sent first (also known as "big endian," as we discuss later).

The DataOutputStream class provides write methods that correspond to the read methods in DataInputStream. For example, writeInt( ) writes an integer in binary format to the underlying output stream.

The readUTF( ) and writeUTF( ) methods of DataInputStream and DataOutputStream read and write a Java String of Unicode characters using the UTF-8 "transformation format." UTF-8 is an ASCII-compatible encoding of Unicode characters commonly used for the transmission and storage of Unicode text. Not all encodings are guaranteed to preserve all Unicode characters, but UTF-8 does. You can also use UTF-8 with Reader and Writer streams by specifying it as the encoding name.

Buffered streams

The BufferedInputStream, BufferedOutputStream, BufferedReader, and BufferedWriter classes add a data buffer of a specified size to the stream path. A buffer can increase efficiency by reducing the number of physical read or write operations that correspond to read( ) or write( ) method calls. You create a buffered stream with an appropriate input or output stream and a buffer size. (You can also wrap another stream around a buffered stream so that it benefits from the buffering.) Here's a simple buffered input stream called bis:

```
BufferedInputStream bis =
  new BufferedInputStream(myInputStream, 4096);
...
bis.read(  );
```

In this example, we specify a buffer size of 4096 bytes. If we leave off the size of the buffer in the constructor, a reasonably sized one is chosen for us. On our first call to read( ), bis tries to fill the entire 4096-byte buffer with data, if it's available. Thereafter, calls to read( ) retrieve data from the buffer, which is refilled as necessary.

A BufferedOutputStream works in a similar way. Calls to write( ) store the data in a buffer; data is actually written only when the buffer fills up. You can also use the flush( ) method to wring out the contents of a BufferedOutputStream at any time. The flush( ) method is actually a method of the OutputStream class itself. It's important because it allows you to be sure that all data in any underlying streams and filter streams has been sent (before, for example, you wait for a response).

Some input streams such as BufferedInputStream support the ability to mark a location in the data and later reset the stream to that position. The mark( ) method sets the return point in the stream. It takes an integer value that specifies the number of bytes that can be read before the stream gives up and forgets about the mark. The reset( ) method returns the stream to the marked point; any data read after the call to mark( ) is read again.

This functionality could be useful when you are reading the stream in a parser. You may occasionally fail to parse a structure and so must try something else. In this situation, you can have your parser generate an error (a homemade ParseException) and then reset the stream to the point before it began parsing the structure:

```
BufferedInputStream input;
...
try {
    input.mark( MAX_DATA_STRUCTURE_SIZE );
    return( parseDataStructure( input ) );
}
catch ( ParseException e ) {
    input.reset( );
    ...
}
```

The BufferedReader and BufferedWriter classes work just like their byte-based counterparts but operate on characters instead of bytes.

PrintWriter and PrintStream

Another useful wrapper stream is `java.io.PrintWriter`. This class provides a suite of overloaded `print( )` methods that turn their arguments into strings and push them out the stream. A complementary set of `println( )` convenience methods appends a newline to the end of the strings. Java 5.0 added new `printf( )` (and identical `format( )`) methods that allow you to write printf-style formatted output to the stream.

`PrintWriter` is an unusual character stream because it can wrap either an `OutputStream` or another `Writer`. `PrintWriter` is the more capable big brother of the older `PrintStream` byte stream. The `System.out` and `System.err` streams are `PrintStream` objects; you have already seen such streams strewn throughout this book:

```
System.out.print("Hello, world...\n");
System.out.println("Hello, world...");
System.out.println("The answer is %d", 17 );
System.out.println( 3.14 );
```

`PrintWriter` and `PrintStream` have a strange, overlapping history. Early versions of Java did not have the `Reader` and `Writer` classes and streams such as `PrintStream`, which must of necessity convert bytes to characters; those versions simply made assumptions about the character encoding. As of Java 1.1, the `PrintStream` class was salvaged by having it translate characters to bytes using the system's default encoding scheme. For all new development, however, use a `PrintWriter` instead of a `PrintStream`. Because a `PrintWriter` can wrap an `OutputStream`, the two classes are more or less interchangeable.

When you create a `PrintWriter` object, you can pass an additional Boolean value to the constructor, specifying whether it should "auto-flush." If this value is true, the `PrintWriter` automatically performs a `flush( )` on the underlying `OutputStream` or `Writer` each time it sends a newline:

```
boolean autoFlush = true;
PrintWriter p = new PrintWriter( myOutputStream, autoFlush );
```

When this technique is used with a buffered output stream, it corresponds to the behavior of terminals that send data line by line.

The other big advantage that print streams have over regular character streams is that they shield you from exceptions thrown by the underlying streams. Unlike methods in other stream classes, the methods of `PrintWriter` and `PrintStream` do not throw `IOExceptions`. Instead they provide a method to explicitly check for errors on your own basis. This makes life a lot easier for printing text, which is a very common operation. You can check for errors with the `checkError( )` method:

```
System.out.println( reallyLongString );
if ( System.out.checkError( ) )                    // uh oh
```

Pipes

Normally, our applications are directly involved with one side of a given stream at a time. `PipedInputStream` and `PipedOutputStream` (or `PipedReader` and `PipedWriter`), however, let us create two sides of a stream and connect them, as shown in Figure 12-4. This can be used to provide a stream of communication between threads, for example, or as a loopback for testing. Most often it's used as a crutch to interface a stream-oriented API to a non-stream-oriented API.

Figure 12-4. Piped streams

To create a byte-stream pipe, we use both a `PipedInputStream` and a `PipedOutputStream`. We can simply choose a side and then construct the other side using the first as an argument:

```
PipedInputStream pin = new PipedInputStream( );
PipedOutputStream pout = new PipedOutputStream( pin );
```

Alternatively:

```
PipedOutputStream pout = new PipedOutputStream( );
PipedInputStream pin = new PipedInputStream( pout );
```

In each of these examples, the effect is to produce an input stream, pin, and an output stream, pout, that are connected. Data written to pout can then be read by pin. It is also possible to create the `PipedInputStream` and the `PipedOutputStream` separately and then connect them with the connect( ) method.

We can do exactly the same thing in the character-based world, using `PipedReader` and `PipedWriter` in place of `PipedInputStream` and `PipedOutputStream`.

Once the two ends of the pipe are connected, use the two streams as you would other input and output streams. You can use read( ) to read data from the `PipedInputStream` (or `PipedReader`) and write( ) to write data to the `PipedOutputStream` (or `PipedWriter`). If the internal buffer of the pipe fills up, the writer blocks and waits until space is available. Conversely, if the pipe is empty, the reader blocks and waits until some data is available.

One advantage to using piped streams is that they provide stream functionality in our code without compelling us to build new, specialized streams. For example, we can use pipes to create a simple logging or "console" facility for our application. We can send messages to the logging facility through an ordinary PrintWriter, and then it can do whatever processing or buffering is required before sending the messages off to their ultimate destination. Because we are dealing with string messages, we use the character-based PipedReader and PipedWriter classes. The following example shows the skeleton of our logging facility:

```java
//file: LoggerDaemon.java
import java.io.*;

class LoggerDaemon extends Thread {
    PipedReader in = new PipedReader( );

    LoggerDaemon( ) {
        start( );
    }

    public void run( ) {
        BufferedReader bin = new BufferedReader( in );
        String s;

        try {
            while ( (s = bin.readLine( )) != null ) {
                // process line of data
            }
        } catch (IOException e ) { }
    }

    PrintWriter getWriter( ) throws IOException {
        return new PrintWriter( new PipedWriter( in ) );
    }
}

class myApplication {
    public static void main ( String [] args ) throws IOException {
        PrintWriter out = new LoggerDaemon( ).getWriter( );

        out.println("Application starting...");
        // ...
        out.println("Warning: does not compute!");
        // ...
    }
}
```

LoggerDaemon reads strings from its end of the pipe, the PipedReader named in. LoggerDaemon also provides a method, getWriter( ), which returns a PipedWriter that is connected to its input stream. To begin sending messages, we create a new LoggerDaemon and fetch the output stream. In order to read strings with the readLine( )

method, LoggerDaemon wraps a BufferedReader around its PipedReader. For convenience, it also presents its output pipe as a PrintWriter rather than a simple Writer.

One advantage of implementing LoggerDaemon with pipes is that we can log messages as easily as we write text to a terminal or any other stream. In other words, we can use all our normal tools and techniques (including printf( )). Another advantage is that the processing happens in another thread, so we can go about our business while any processing takes place.

Streams from Strings and Back

StringReader is another useful stream class; it essentially wraps stream functionality around a String. Here's how to use a StringReader:

```
String data = "There once was a man from Nantucket...";
StringReader sr = new StringReader( data );

char T = (char)sr.read( );
char h = (char)sr.read( );
char e = (char)sr.read( );
```

Note that you will still have to catch IOExceptions thrown by some of the StringReader's methods.

The StringReader class is useful when you want to read data in a String as if it were coming from a stream, such as a file, pipe, or socket. Suppose you create a parser that expects to read from a stream, but you want to provide an alternative method that also parses a big string. You can easily add one using StringReader.

Turning things around, the StringWriter class lets us write to a character buffer via an output stream. The internal buffer grows as necessary to accommodate the data. When we are done, we can fetch the contents of the buffer as a String. In the following example, we create a StringWriter and wrap it in a PrintWriter for convenience:

```
StringWriter buffer = new StringWriter( );
PrintWriter out = new PrintWriter( buffer );

out.println("A moose once bit my sister.");
out.println("No, really!");

String results = buffer.toString( );
```

First, we print a few lines to the output stream to give it some data and then retrieve the results as a string with the toString( ) method. Alternately, we could get the results as a StringBuffer object using the getBuffer( ) method.

The StringWriter class is useful if you want to capture the output of something that normally sends output to a stream, such as a file or the console. A PrintWriter wrapped around a StringWriter is a viable alternative to using a StringBuffer to construct large strings piece by piece.

The `ByteArrayInputStream` and `ByteArrayOutputStream` work with bytes in the same way the previous examples worked with characters. You can write byte data to a `ByteArrayOutputStream` and retrieve it later with the `toByteArray()` method. Conversely, you can construct a `ByteArrayInputStream` from a byte array as `StringReader` does with a `String`. For example, if we want to see exactly what our `DataOutputStream` is writing when we tell it to encode a particular value, we could capture it with a byte array output stream:

```
ByteArrayOutputStream bao = new ByteArrayOutputStream( );
DataOutputStream dao = new DataOutputStream( bao );
dao.writeInt( 16777216 );
dao.flush( );

byte [] bytes = bao.toByteArray( );
for( byte b : bytes )
    System.out.println( b );  // 1, 0, 0, 0
```

The rot13InputStream Class

Before we leave streams, let's try making one of our own. We mentioned earlier that specialized stream wrappers are built on top of the `FilterInputStream` and `FilterOutputStream` classes. It's quite easy to create our own subclass of `FilterInputStream` that can be wrapped around other streams to add new functionality.

The following example, rot13InputStream, performs a *rot13* (rotate by 13 letters) operation on the bytes that it reads. *rot13* is a trivial obfuscation algorithm that shifts alphabetic characters to make them not quite human-readable (it simply passes over nonalphabetic characters without modifying them). rot13 *is* cute because it's symmetric; to "un-rot13" some text you simply rot13 it again. We use the rot13InputStream class in the "Content and Protocol Handlers" section of the expanded material on the CD that comes with this book (view CD content online at *http://examples.oreilly.com/learnjava3/CD-ROM/*). We've placed the class in the `learningjava.io` package to facilitate reuse. Here's our rot13InputStream class:

```
//file: rot13InputStream.java
package learningjava.io;
import java.io.*;

public class rot13InputStream extends FilterInputStream {

    public rot13InputStream ( InputStream i ) {
        super( i );
    }

    public int read( ) throws IOException {
        return rot13( in.read( ) );
    }

    // should override additional read( ) methods
```

```
    private int rot13 ( int c ) {
        if ( (c >= 'A') && (c <= 'Z') )
            c=(((c-'A')+13)%26)+'A';
        if ( (c >= 'a') && (c <= 'z') )
            c=(((c-'a')+13)%26)+'a';
        return c;
    }
}
```

The FilterInputStream needs to be initialized with an InputStream; this is the stream to be filtered. We provide an appropriate constructor for the rot13InputStream class and invoke the parent constructor with a call to super( ). FilterInputStream contains a protected instance variable, in, in which it stores a reference to the specified InputStream, making it available to the rest of our class.

The primary feature of a FilterInputStream is that it delegates its input tasks to the underlying InputStream. For instance, a call to FilterInputStream's read( ) method simply turns around and calls the read( ) method of the underlying InputStream to fetch a byte. The filtering happens when we do our extra work on the data as it passes through. In our example, the read( ) method fetches a byte from the underlying InputStream, in, and then performs the rot13 shift on the byte before returning it. The rot13( ) method shifts alphabetic characters while simply passing over all other values, including the end-of-stream value (-1). Our subclass is now a rot13 filter.

read( ) is the only InputStream method that FilterInputStream overrides. All other normal functionality of an InputStream, such as skip( ) and available( ), is unmodified, so calls to these methods are answered by the underlying InputStream.

Strictly speaking, rot13InputStream works only on an ASCII byte stream since the underlying algorithm is based on the Roman alphabet. A more generalized character-scrambling algorithm would have to be based on FilterReader to handle 16-bit Unicode classes correctly. (Anyone want to try rot32768?) We should also note that we have not fully implemented our filter: we should also override the version of read( ) that takes a byte array and range specifiers, perhaps delegating it to our own read. Unless we do so, a reader using that method would get the raw stream.

Files

Working with files in Java is easy but poses some conceptual problems. In the real world, the host filesystem lies outside of Java's virtual environment, and can, therefore, still suffer from architecture and implementation differences. Java tries to mask some of these differences by providing information to help an application tailor itself to the local environment; we'll mention these areas as they come up. Later, we'll show you how to avoid these issues for read-only application files and resources by using the Java classpath to insulate you from the filesystem entirely.

The java.io.File Class

The `java.io.File` class encapsulates access to information about a file or directory. It can be used to get attribute information about a file, list the entries in a directory, and perform basic filesystem operations, such as removing a file or making a directory. While the `File` object handles these "meta" operations, it doesn't provide the API for reading and writing file data; there are specialized streams for that purpose.

File constructors

You can create an instance of `File` from a `String` pathname:

```
File fooFile = new File( "/tmp/foo.txt" );
File barDir = new File( "/tmp/bar" );
```

You can also create a file with a relative path:

```
File f = new File( "foo" );
```

In this case, Java works relative to the current working directory of the Java interpreter. You can determine the current working directory by checking the `user.dir` property in the `System Properties` list:

```
System.getProperty("user.dir")); // e.g., /users/pat
```

An overloaded version of the `File` constructor lets you specify the directory path and filename as separate `String` objects:

```
File fooFile = new File( "/tmp", "foo.txt" );
```

With yet another variation, you can specify the directory with a `File` object and the filename with a `String`:

```
File tmpDir = new File( "/tmp" ); // File for directory /tmp
File fooFile = new File ( tmpDir, "foo.txt" );
```

None of these `File` constructors actually creates a file or directory, and it isn't an error to create a `File` object for a nonexistent file. The `File` object is just a handle for a file or directory whose properties you may wish to read, write, or test. For example, you can use the `exists( )` instance method to learn whether the file or directory exists.

Path localization

One of the reasons that working with files in Java is problematic is that pathnames are expected to follow the conventions of the local filesystem. The main differences are that the Windows filesystem uses "roots" or drive letters (for example, C:) and the backslash (\) instead of the forward slash (/) path separator.

On some systems, Java tries to compensate for the differences. For example, in the current implementation on Windows platforms, Java accepts paths with either forward slashes or backslashes. However, under Solaris, Java accepts only paths with forward slashes.

Your best bet is to make sure you follow the filename conventions of the host filesystem. If your application has a GUI that is opening and saving files at the user's request, you should be able to handle that functionality with the Swing JFileChooser class. This class encapsulates a graphical file-selection dialog box. The methods of the JFileChooser take care of system-dependent filename features for you.

If your application needs to deal with files on its own behalf, however, things get a little more complicated. The File class contains a few static variables to make this task possible. File.separator defines a String that specifies the file separator on the local host (e.g., / on Unix and Macintosh systems and \ on Windows systems); File.separatorChar provides the same information as a char.

You can use this system-dependent information in several ways. Probably the simplest way to localize pathnames is to pick a convention you use internally, for instance the forward slash (/), and do a String replace to substitute for the localized separator character:

```
// we'll use forward slash as our standard
String path = "mail/2004/june/merle";
path = path.replace('/', File.separatorChar);
File mailbox = new File( path );
```

Alternatively, you could work with the components of a pathname and build the local pathname when you need it:

```
String [] path = { "mail", "2004", "june", "merle" };

    StringBuffer sb = new StringBuffer(path[0]);
for (int i=1; i< path.length; i++)
    sb.append( File.separator + path[i] );
File mailbox = new File( sb.toString() );
```

One thing to remember is that Java interprets the backslash character (\) as an escape character when used in a String. To get a backslash in a String, you have to use \\.

To grapple with the issue of filesystems with multiple "roots" (for example, C:\ on Windows), the File class provides the static method listRoots( ), which returns an array of File objects corresponding to the filesystem root directories. Again, in a GUI application, a graphical file chooser dialogue shields you from this problem entirely.

File operations

Once we have a File object, we can use it to ask for information about the file or directory and to perform standard operations on it. A number of methods let us ask questions about the File. For example, isFile( ) returns true if the File represents a file while isDirectory( ) returns true if it's a directory. isAbsolute( ) indicates whether the

File encapsulates an *absolute path* or *relative path* specification. An absolute path is a system-dependent notion that means that the path doesn't depend on the application's working directory or any concept of a working root or drive.

Components of the File pathname are available through the following methods: getName( ), getPath( ), getAbsolutePath( ), and getParent( ). getName( ) returns a String for the filename without any directory information; getPath( ) returns the directory information without the filename. If the File has an absolute path specification, getAbsolutePath( ) returns that path. Otherwise, it returns the relative path appended to the current working directory. getParent( ) returns the parent directory of the File.

The string returned by getPath( ) or getAbsolutePath( ) may not follow the same case conventions as the underlying filesystem. You can retrieve the filesystem's own or "canonical" version of the file's path using the method getCanonicalPath( ). In Windows, for example, you can create a File object whose getAbsolutePath( ) is *C:\ Autoexec.bat* but whose getCanonical-Path( ) is *C:\AUTOEXEC.BAT*, both actually pointing to the same file. This is useful for comparing filenames that may have been supplied with different case conventions or for showing them to the user.

You can get or set the modification time of a file or directory with lastModified( ) and setLastModified( ) methods. The value is a long that is the number of milliseconds since the *epoch* (Jan 1, 1970, 00:00:00 GMT). We can also get the size of the file in bytes with length( ).

Here's a fragment of code that prints some information about a file:

```
File fooFile = new File( "/tmp/boofa" );

String type = fooFile.isFile( ) ? "File " : "Directory ";
String name = fooFile.getName( );
long len = fooFile.length( );
System.out.println( type + name + ", " + len + " bytes " );
```

If the File object corresponds to a directory, we can list the files in the directory with the list( ) method or the listFiles( ) method:

```
File tmpDir = new File("/tmp" );
String [] fileNames = tmpDir.list( );
File [] files = tmpDir.listFiles( );
```

list( ) returns an array of String objects that contains filenames. listFiles( ) returns an array of File objects. Note that in neither case are the files guaranteed to be in any kind of order (alphabetical, for example). You can use the Collections API to sort strings alphabetically like so:

```
List list = Arrays.asList( sa );
Collections.sort(l);
```

If the File refers to a nonexistent directory, we can create the directory with mkdir( ) or mkdirs( ). The mkdir( ) method creates at most a single directory level, so any intervening directories in the path must already exist. mkdirs( ) creates all directory levels necessary to create the full path of the File specification. In either case, if the directory cannot be created, the method returns false. Use renameTo( ) to rename a file or directory and delete( ) to delete a file or directory.

Although we can create a directory using the File object, this isn't the most common way to create a file; that's normally done implicitly when we intend to write data to it with a FileOutputStream or FileWriter, as we'll discuss in a moment. The exception is the createNewFile( ) method, which can be used to attempt to create a new zero-length file at the location pointed to by the File object. The useful thing about this method is that the operation is guaranteed to be "atomic" with respect to all other file creation in the filesystem. createNewFile( ) returns a Boolean value that tells you whether the file was created or not. This is sometimes used as a primitive locking feature—whoever creates the file first "wins." (The NIO package supports true file locks, as we'll see later). This is useful in combination with deleteOnExit( ), which flags the file to be automatically removed when the Java VM exits. Another file creation method related to the File class itself is the static method createTempFile( ), which creates a file in a specified location using an automatically generated unique name. This, too, is useful in combination with deleteOnExit( ).

The toURL( ) method converts a file path to a file: URL object. URLs are an abstraction that allows you to point to any kind of object anywhere on the Net. Converting a File reference to a URL may be useful for consistency with more general utilities that deal with URLs. See Chapter 14 for details.

Table 12-1 summarizes the methods provided by the File class.

Table 12-1. File methods

Method	Return type	Description
canRead( )	Boolean	Is the file (or directory) readable?
canWrite( )	Boolean	Is the file (or directory) writable?
createNewFile( )	Boolean	Creates a new file.
createTempFile (String *pfx*, String *sfx*)	File	Static method to create a new file, with the specified prefix and suffix, in the default temp file directory.
delete( )	Boolean	Deletes the file (or directory).
deleteOnExit( )	Void	When it exits, Java runtime system deletes the file.
exists( )	boolean	Does the file (or directory) exist?
getAbsolutePath( )	String	Returns the absolute path of the file (or directory).
getCanonicalPath( )	String	Returns the absolute, case-correct path of the file (or directory).
getName( )	String	Returns the name of the file (or directory).

Table 12-1. File methods (continued)

Method	Return type	Description
getParent( )	String	Returns the name of the parent directory of the file (or directory).
getPath( )	String	Returns the path of the file (or directory).
isAbsolute( )	boolean	Is the filename (or directory name) absolute?
isDirectory( )	boolean	Is the item a directory?
isFile( )	boolean	Is the item a file?
isHidden( )	boolean	Is the item hidden? (System-dependent.)
lastModified( )	long	Returns the last modification time of the file (or directory).
length( )	long	Returns the length of the file.
list( )	String []	Returns a list of files in the directory.
listFiles( )	File[]	Returns the contents of the directory as an array of File objects.
listRoots( )	File[]	Returns array of root filesystems if any (e.g., C:/, D:/).
mkdir( )	boolean	Creates the directory.
mkdirs( )	boolean	Creates all directories in the path.
renameTo(File *dest*)	boolean	Renames the file (or directory).
setLastModified( )	boolean	Sets the last-modified time of the file (or directory).
setReadOnly( )	boolean	Sets the file to read-only status.
toURL( )	java.net.URL	Generates a URL object for the file (or directory).

File Streams

OK, you're probably sick of hearing about files already and we haven't even written a byte yet! Well, now the fun begins. Java provides two specialized streams for reading from and writing to files: FileInputStream and FileOutputStream. These streams provide the basic InputStream and OutputStream functionality applied to reading and writing files. They can be combined with the filter streams described earlier to work with files in the same way as other stream communications.

You can create a FileInputStream from a String pathname or a File object:

```
FileInputStream in = new FileInputStream( "/etc/passwd" );
```

When you create a FileInputStream, the Java runtime system attempts to open the specified file. Thus, the FileInputStream constructors can throw a FileNotFoundException if the specified file doesn't exist or an IOException if some other I/O error occurs. You must catch these exceptions in your code. When the stream is first created, its available( ) method and the File object's length( ) method should return the same value. To save resources, you can call the close( ) method when you are done with the file.

To read characters from a file as a Reader, you can wrap an InputStreamReader around a FileInputStream. If you want to use the default character-encoding scheme for the platform, you can use the FileReader class instead, which is provided as a convenience. FileReader works just like FileInputStream, except that it is a character stream. (For some crazy reason, you can't specify a character encoding for the FileReader to use, so keep the InputStreamReader in mind.)

The following class, ListIt, is a small utility that sends the contents of a file or directory to standard output:

```java
//file: ListIt.java
import java.io.*;

class ListIt {
    public static void main ( String args[] ) throws Exception {
        File file =  new File( args[0] );

        if ( !file.exists( ) || !file.canRead() ) {
            System.out.println( "Can't read " + file );
            return;
        }

        if ( file.isDirectory() ) {
            String [] files = file.list();
            for ( String file : files )
                System.out.println( file );
        } else
            try {
                FileReader fr = new FileReader ( file );
                BufferedReader in = new BufferedReader( fr );
                String line;
                while ((line = in.readLine()) != null)
                    System.out.println(line);
            }
            catch ( FileNotFoundException e ) {
                System.out.println( "File Disappeared" );
            }
    }
}
```

ListIt constructs a File object from its first command-line argument and tests the File to see whether it exists and is readable. If the File is a directory, ListIt outputs the names of the files in the directory. Otherwise, ListIt reads and outputs the file, line by line.

For writing files, you can create a FileOutputStream from a String pathname or a File object. Unlike FileInputStream, however, the FileOutputStream constructors don't throw a FileNotFoundException. If the specified file doesn't exist, the

`FileOutputStream` creates the file. The `FileOutputStream` constructors can throw an `IOException` if some other I/O error occurs, so you still need to handle this exception.

If the specified file does exist, the `FileOutputStream` opens it for writing. When you subsequently call the `write( )` method, the new data overwrites the current contents of the file. If you need to append data to an existing file, you can use a form of the constructor that accepts a Boolean append flag:

```
FileInputStream fooOut =
    new FileOutputStream( fooFile ); // overwrite fooFile
FileInputStream pwdOut =
    new FileOutputStream( "/etc/passwd", true ); // append
```

Another way to append data to files is with `RandomAccessFile`, as we'll discuss shortly.

Just as with reading, to write characters (instead of bytes) to a file, you can wrap an `OutputStreamWriter` around a `FileOutputStream`. If you want to use the default character-encoding scheme, you can use instead the `FileWriter` class, which is provided as a convenience.

The following example reads a line of data from standard input and writes it to the file */tmp/foo.txt*:

```
String s = new BufferedReader(
    new InputStreamReader( System.in ) ).readLine( );
File out = new File( "/tmp/foo.txt" );
FileWriter fw = new FileWriter ( out );
PrintWriter pw = new PrintWriter( fw )
pw.println( s );
fw.close( );
```

Notice how we wrapped the `FileWriter` in a `PrintWriter` to facilitate writing the data. Also, to be a good filesystem citizen, we've called the `close( )` method when we're done with the `FileWriter`.

RandomAccessFile

The `java.io.RandomAccessFile` class provides the ability to read and write data at a specified location in a file. `RandomAccessFile` implements both the `DataInput` and `DataOutput` interfaces, so you can use it to read and write strings and primitive types at locations in the file just as if it were a `DataInputStream` and `DataOutputStream`. However, because the class provides random, rather than sequential, access to file data, it's not a subclass of either `InputStream` or `OutputStream`.

You can create a `RandomAccessFile` from a `String` pathname or a `File` object. The constructor also takes a second `String` argument that specifies the mode of the file.

Use r for a read-only file or rw for a read/write file. Here's how we would start to create a simple database to keep track of user information:

```
try {
    RandomAccessFile users =
        new RandomAccessFile( "Users", "rw" )
} catch (IOException e) { ... }
```

When you create a RandomAccessFile in read-only mode, Java tries to open the specified file. If the file doesn't exist, RandomAccessFile throws an IOException. If, however, you're creating a RandomAccessFile in read/write mode, the object creates the file if it doesn't exist. The constructor can still throw an IOException if another I/O error occurs, so you still need to handle this exception.

After you have created a RandomAccessFile, call any of the normal reading and writing methods, just as you would with a DataInputStream or DataOutputStream. If you try to write to a read-only file, the write method throws an IOException.

What makes a RandomAccessFile special is the seek( ) method. This method takes a long value and uses it to set the location for reading and writing in the file. You can use the getFilePointer( ) method to get the current location. If you need to append data to the end of the file, use length( ) to determine that location, then seek( ) to it. You can write or seek beyond the end of a file, but you can't read beyond the end of a file. The read( ) method throws an EOFException if you try to do this.

Here's an example of writing some data to our user database:

```
users.seek( userNum * RECORDSIZE );
users.writeUTF( userName );
users.writeInt( userID );
```

Of course, in this naive example we assume that the String length for userName, along with any data that comes after it, fits within the specified record size.

Applets and Files

Unless otherwise restricted, a Java application can read and write to the host filesystem with the same level of access as the user running the Java interpreter. For security reasons, untrusted applets and applications are not generally permitted to read from or write to arbitrary places in the filesystem. The ability of untrusted code to read and write files, as with any kind of system resource, is under the control of the system security policy, through a SecurityManager object. A security policy is set by the application that is running the untrusted code, such as appletviewer or a Java-enabled web browser. All filesystem access must first pass the scrutiny of the SecurityManager.

Most web browsers do not allow untrusted applets any access to the filesystem. However, as we'll see in Chapter 1, signed applets can be given arbitrary access to the filesystem, just like a standalone Java application. Currently, the only way for a filesystem-restricted Java program to save any real amount of data is through talking to its server via HTTP, or other network protocols. In Chapter 13, we'll take a detailed look at building networked applications with sockets. With the tools described in that chapter, it's possible to build powerful client/server applications.* A big part of packaging and deploying an application is dealing with all of the resource files that must go with it, such as configuration files, graphics, and application data. Java provides several ways to access these resources. One way is to simply open files and read the bytes. Another is to construct a URL pointing to a well-known location in the filesystem or over the network. (We'll discuss working with URLs in detail in Chapter 14.) The problem with these methods is that they generally rely on knowledge of the application's location and packaging, which could change or break if it is moved. What is really needed is a universal way to access resources associated with our application, regardless of how it's installed. The `Class` class's `getResource( )` method and the Java classpath provides just this. For example:

```
URL resource = MyApplication.class.getResource("/config/config.xml");
```

Instead of constructing a File reference or URL pointing to an absolute file path, or relying on composing information about an install directory, the `getResource( )` method provides a standard way to get resources relative to the classpath. A resource can be located either relative to a given class file or to the system classpath. `getResource( )` uses the classloader that loads the application's class files to load the data. This means that no matter where the application classes reside—a web server, the local filesystem, or even inside a JAR file or other archive—we can load resources packaged with them consistently.

Although we haven't discussed URLs yet, we can tell you that many APIs for loading data (for example, images) accept a URL directly. If you're reading the data yourself, you can ask the URL for an `InputStream` with the `URL openStream( )` method and treat it like any other stream. A convenience method called `getResourceAsStream( )` skips this step for you and returns an `InputStream` directly.

`getResource( )` takes as an argument a slash-separated *resource path* for the resource and returns a URL. There are two kinds of resource paths: absolute and relative. An absolute path begins with a slash (for example, */config/config.xml*). In this case, the search for the object begins at the "top" of the classpath. By the "top" of the classpath, we mean that Java looks within each element of the classpath (directory or JAR file) for the specified file. Given */config/config.xml*, it would check each directory or JAR file in the path for the file *config/config.xml*. In this case, it doesn't matter on which class `getResource( )` is called as long as it's from a classloader which has the resource file in its classpath. For example:

```
URL data = AnyClass.getResource("/config/config.xml");
```

---

* At one point, Sun introduced a Java extension called WebNFS, which allows applets and applications to work with files on an NFS server in much the same way as the ordinary File API. But this never took off.

A relative URL, on the other hand, does not begin with a slash (for example, simply *mydata.txt*). In this case, the search begins at the location of the class file on which getResource( ) is called. In other words, the path is relative to the package of the target class file. For example, if the class file *foo.bar.MyClass* is located at the path *foo/bar/MyClass.class* in some element of the classpath and the file *mydata.txt* is in the same directory (*foo/bar/mydata.txt*), we can request the file via *MyClass* with:

```
URL data = MyClass.getResource("mydata.txt");
```

In this case, the class and file come from the same logical directory. We say logical because the search is not limited only to the classpath element from which the class was loaded. Instead, the same relative path is searched in each element of the classpath, just as with an absolute path, until it is found. Although we'd expect the file *mydata.txt* to be packaged physically with *MyClass.class*, it might be found in another JAR file or directory at the same corresponding location.

For example, here's an application that looks up some resources:

```
//file: FindResources.java
package mypackage;
import java.net.URL;
import java.io.IOException;

public class FindResources {
  public static void main( String [] args ) throws IOException {
    // absolute from the classpath
    URL url = FindResources.class.getResource("/mypackage/foo.txt");
    // relative to the class location
    url = FindResources.class.getResource("foo.txt");
    // another relative document
    url = FindResources.class.getResource("docs/bar.txt");
  }
}
```

The FindResources class belongs to the mypackage package, so its class file will live in a *mypackage* directory somewhere on the classpath. FindResources locates the document *foo.txt* using an absolute and then a relative URL. At the end, FindResources uses a relative path to reach a document in the *mypackage/docs* directory. In each case we refer to the FindResources's Class object using the static .class notation. Alternatively, if we had an instance of the object, we could use its getClass( ) method to reach the Class object.

For an applet, the search is similar but occurs on the host from which the applet was loaded. getResource( ) first checks any JAR files loaded with the applet and then searches the normal remote applet classpath, constructed relative to the applet's codebase URL.

Again, getResource( ) returns a URL for whatever type of object you reference. This could be a text file or properties file that you want to read as a stream, or it might be an image or sound file or some other object. You can open a stream to the URL to

---

parse the data yourself or hand the URL over to an API that deals with URLs. We discuss URLs in depth in Chapter 14. We should also emphasize that loading resources in this way completely shields your application from the details of how it is packaged or deployed. You may start with your application in loose files and then package it into a JAR file and the resources will still be loaded. Applets may even load files in this way over the network since the applet classloader treats the server as part of its classpath.

Serialization

Using a DataOutputStream, you could write an application that saves the data content of your objects as simple types. However, Java provides an even more powerful mechanism called object serialization that does almost all the work for you. In its simplest form, *object serialization* is an automatic way to save and load the state of an object. However, object serialization has depths that we cannot plumb within the scope of this book, including complete control over the serialization process and interesting conundrums such as class versioning.

Basically, an instance of any class that implements the Serializable interface can be saved to and restored from a stream. Special stream subclasses, ObjectInputStream and ObjectOutputStream, are used to serialize primitive types and objects. Subclasses of Serializable classes are also serializable. The default serialization mechanism saves the value of all of the object's fields, except those that are static and those marked *transient*.

One of the most important (and tricky) things about serialization is that when an object is serialized, any object references it contains are also serialized. Serialization can capture entire "graphs" of interconnected objects and put them back together on the receiving end (we'll demonstrate this in an upcoming example). The implication is that any object we serialize must contain only references to other Serializable objects. We can take control by marking nonserializable variables as transient or overriding the default serialization mechanisms. The transient modifier can be applied to any instance variable to indicate that its contents are not useful outside of the current context and should never be saved.

In the following example, we create a Hashtable and write it to a disk file called *hash.ser*. The Hashtable object is already serializable because it implements the Serializable interface.

```
//file: Save.java
import java.io.*;
import java.util.*;

public class Save {
  public static void main(String[] args) {
    Hashtable hash = new Hashtable();
    hash.put("string", "Gabriel Garcia Marquez");
```

```
      hash.put("int", new Integer(26));
      hash.put("double", new Double(Math.PI));

      try {
        FileOutputStream fileOut = new FileOutputStream( "hash.ser" );
        ObjectOutputStream out = new ObjectOutputStream( fileOut );
        out.writeObject( hash );
        out.close( );
      }
      catch (Exception e) {
        System.out.println(e);
      }
    }
  }
```

First, we construct a Hashtable with a few elements in it. Then, in the lines of code inside the try block, we write the Hashtable to a file called *hash.ser*, using the writeObject( ) method of ObjectOutputStream. The ObjectOutputStream class is a lot like the DataOutputStream class, except that it includes the powerful writeObject( ) method.

The Hashtable we created has internal references to the items it contains. Thus, these components are automatically serialized along with the Hashtable. We'll see this in the next example when we deserialize the Hashtable.

```
//file: Load.java
import java.io.*;
import java.util.*;

public class Load {
  public static void main(String[] args) {
    try {
      FileInputStream fileIn = new FileInputStream("hash.ser");
      ObjectInputStream in = new ObjectInputStream(fileIn);
      Hashtable hash = (Hashtable)in.readObject( );
      System.out.println( hash.toString( ) );
    }
    catch (Exception e) {
      System.out.println(e);
    }
  }
}
```

In this example, we read the Hashtable from the *hash.ser* file, using the readObject( ) method of ObjectInputStream. The ObjectInputStream class is a lot like DataInputStream, except that it includes the readObject( ) method. The return type of readObject( ) is Object, so we need to cast it to a Hashtable. Finally, we print the contents of the Hashtable using its toString( ) method.

Initialization with readObject( )

Often simple deserialization alone is not enough to reconstruct the full state of an object. For example, the object may have had transient fields representing state that could not be serialized, such as network connections, event registration, or decoded image data. Objects have an opportunity to do their own setup after deserialization by implementing a special method named readObject( ).

Not to be confused with the readObject( ) method of the ObjectInputStream, this method is implemented by the serializable object itself. The readObject( ) method must have a specific signature, and it must be private. The following snippet is taken from an animated JavaBean that we'll talk about in Chapter 22:

```
private void readObject(ObjectInputStream s)
    throws IOException, ClassNotFoundException
{
    s.defaultReadObject(  );
    initialize( );
    if ( isRunning )
        start( );
}
```

When the readObject( ) method with this signature exists in an object, it is called during the deserialization process. The argument to the method is the ObjectInputStream doing the object construction. We delegate to its defaultReadObject( ) method to do the normal deserialization and then do our custom setup. In this case, we call one of our methods, named initialize( ), and optionally, a method called start( ).

We'll talk more about serialization in Chapter 22 when we discuss JavaBeans, and we'll see that it is possible to serialize a graphical GUI component currently in use and bring it back to life later.

SerialVersionUID

Java object serialization was designed to accommodate certain kinds of *compatible class changes* or evolution in the structure of classes. For example, changing the methods of a class does not necessarily mean that its serialized representation has to change since only the data of variables is stored. Nor would simply adding a new field to a class necessarily prohibit us from loading an old serialized version of the class. We could simply allow the new variable to take its default value. By default, however, Java is very picky and errs on the side of caution. If you make any kind of change to the structure of your class, by default you'll get an InvalidClassException when trying to read previously serialized forms of the class.

Java detects these versions by performing a hash function on the structure of the class and storing a 64-bit value, called the *Serial Version UID* (SUID), along with the serialized data. It can then compare the hash to the class when it is loaded.

Java allows us to take control of this process by looking for a special, magic field in our classes that looks like the following:

```
static final long serialVersionUID = -6849794470754667710L;
```

(The value is, of course, different for every class.) If it finds this static `serialVersionUID` long field in the class, it uses its value instead of performing the hash on the class. This value will be written out with serialized versions of the class and used for comparison when they are deserialized. This means that we are now in control of what versions of the class are compatible with what serialized representations. For example, we can create our serializable class from the beginning with our own SUID and then only increment it if we want to prevent older forms of the class from being loaded:

```
class MyDataObject implements Serializable {
    static final long serialVersionUID = 1; // Version 1
    ...
}
```

A utility called *serialver* that comes with the JDK allows you to calculate the hash that Java would use for the class yourself. This is necessary if you already have serialized objects stored and need to modify the class afterward. Running the *serialver* command on the class displays the SUID necessary to match the value already stored:

```
% serialver SomeObject
```

```
static final long serialVersionUID = -6849794470754667710L;
```

By placing this value into your class, you can "freeze" the SUID at the current value, allowing the class to change without being reloaded.

Data Compression

The `java.util.zip` package contains classes you can use for data compression. In this section, we'll talk about how to use these classes. We'll also present two useful example programs that build on what you have learned about streams and files. The classes in the `java.util.zip` package support two widespread compression formats: GZIP and ZIP.

Archives and Compressed Data

The `java.util.zip` package provides two filter streams for writing compressed data. The `GZIPOutputStream` is for writing data in GZIP compressed format. The `ZIPOutputStream` is for writing compressed ZIP archives, which can contain one or many files. To write compressed data in the GZIP format, simply wrap a

`GZIPOutputStream` around an underlying stream and write to it. The following is a complete example that shows how to compress a file using the GZIP format:

```java
//file: GZip.java
import java.io.*;
import java.util.zip.*;

public class GZip {
  public static int sChunk = 8192;

  public static void main(String[] args) {
    if (args.length != 1) {
      System.out.println("Usage: GZip source");
      return;
    }
    // create output stream
    String zipname = args[0] + ".gz";
    GZIPOutputStream zipout;
    try {
      FileOutputStream out = new FileOutputStream(zipname);
      zipout = new GZIPOutputStream(out);
    }
    catch (IOException e) {
      System.out.println("Couldn't create " + zipname + ".");
      return;
    }
    byte[] buffer = new byte[sChunk];
    // compress the file
    try {
      FileInputStream in = new FileInputStream(args[0]);
      int length;
      while ((length = in.read(buffer, 0, sChunk)) != -1)
        zipout.write(buffer, 0, length);
      in.close();
    }
    catch (IOException e) {
      System.out.println("Couldn't compress " + args[0] + ".");
    }
    try { zipout.close(); }
    catch (IOException e) {}
  }
}
```

First, we check to make sure we have a command-line argument representing a filename. We then construct a `GZIPOutputStream` wrapped around a `FileOutputStream` representing the given filename, with the *.gz* suffix appended. With this in place, we open the source file. We read chunks of data and write them into the `GZIPOutputStream`. Finally, we clean up by closing our open streams.

Writing data to a ZIP archive file is a little more involved but still quite manageable. While a GZIP file contains only one compressed file, a ZIP file is actually a collection of files, some (or all) of which may be compressed. Each item in the ZIP file is represented by a ZipEntry object. When writing to a ZipOutputStream, you'll need to call putNextEntry( ) before writing the data for each item. The following example shows how to create a ZipOutputStream. You'll notice it's just like creating a GZIPOutputStream:

```
ZipOutputStream zipout;
try {
  FileOutputStream out = new FileOutputStream("archive.zip");
  zipout = new ZipOutputStream(out);
}
catch (IOException e) {}
```

Let's say we have two files we want to write into this archive. Before we begin writing, we need to call putNextEntry( ). We create a simple entry with just a name. You can set other fields in ZipEntry, but most of the time, you won't need to bother with them.

```
try {
  ZipEntry entry = new ZipEntry("First");
  zipout.putNextEntry(entry);
  ZipEntry entry = new ZipEntry("Second");
  zipout.putNextEntry(entry);
    . . .
}
catch (IOException e) {}
```

Decompressing Data

To decompress data in the GZIP format, simply wrap a GZIPInputStream around an underlying FileInputStream and read from it. The following is a complete example that shows how to decompress a GZIP file:

```
//file: GUnzip.java
import java.io.*;
import java.util.zip.*;

public class GUnzip {
  public static int sChunk = 8192;
  public static void main(String[] args) {
    if (args.length != 1) {
      System.out.println("Usage: GUnzip source");
      return;
    }
    // create input stream
    String zipname, source;
    if (args[0].endsWith(".gz")) {
      zipname = args[0];
      source = args[0].substring(0, args[0].length( ) - 3);
    }
    else {
```

```
      zipname = args[0] + ".gz";
      source = args[0];
    }
    GZIPInputStream zipin;
    try {
      FileInputStream in = new FileInputStream(zipname);
      zipin = new GZIPInputStream(in);
    }
    catch (IOException e) {
      System.out.println("Couldn't open " + zipname + ".");
      return;
    }
    byte[] buffer = new byte[sChunk];
    // decompress the file
    try {
      FileOutputStream out = new FileOutputStream(source);
      int length;
      while ((length = zipin.read(buffer, 0, sChunk)) != -1)
        out.write(buffer, 0, length);
      out.close();
    }
    catch (IOException e) {
      System.out.println("Couldn't decompress " + args[0] + ".");
    }
    try { zipin.close(); }
    catch (IOException e) {}
  }
}
```

First, we check to make sure we have a command-line argument representing a filename. If the argument ends with *.gz*, we figure out what the filename for the uncompressed file should be. Otherwise, we use the given argument and assume the compressed file has the *.gz* suffix. Then we construct a GZIPInputStream wrapped around a FileInputStream, representing the compressed file. With this in place, we open the target file. We read chunks of data from the GZIPInputStream and write them into the target file. Finally, we clean up by closing our open streams.

Again, the ZIP archive presents a little more complexity than the GZIP file. When reading from a ZipInputStream, you should call getNextEntry() before reading each item. When getNextEntry() returns null, there are no more items to read. The following example shows how to create a ZipInputStream. You'll notice it's just like creating a GZIPInputStream:

```
ZipInputStream zipin;
try {
  FileInputStream in = new FileInputStream("archive.zip");
  zipin = new ZipInputStream(in);
}
catch (IOException e) {}
```

Suppose we want to read two files from this archive. Before we begin reading, we need to call getNextEntry( ). At the very least, the entry gives us a name of the item we are reading from the archive:

```
try {
  ZipEntry first = zipin.getNextEntry( );
}
catch (IOException e) {}
```

At this point, you can read the contents of the first item in the archive. When you come to the end of the item, the read( ) method returns -1. Now you can call getNextEntry( ) again to read the second item from the archive:

```
try {
  ZipEntry second = zipin.getNextEntry( );
}
catch (IOException e) {}
```

If you call getNextEntry( ) and it returns null, there are no more items and you have reached the end of the archive.

The NIO Package

The java.nio package was introduced in Java 1.4. The name NIO stands for "new I/O," which may seem to imply that it is to be a replacement for the java.io package. In fact, much of the NIO functionality overlaps with existing APIs. NIO was added primarily to address specific issues of scalability for large systems, especially in networked applications. That said, NIO also provides several new features Java lacked in basic I/O, so you'll want to look at some tools here even if you aren't planning to write any large or high-performance services. The following sections outline the primary features of NIO.

Asynchronous I/O

Most of the need for the NIO package was driven by the desire to add nonblocking and selectable I/O to Java. Prior to NIO, most read and write operations in Java were bound to threads and were forced to block for unpredictable amounts of time. Although certain APIs such as Sockets (which we'll see in Chapter 13) provided specific means to limit how long an I/O call could take, this was a workaround to compensate for the lack of a more general mechanism. Prior to the introduction of threads, in many languages I/O could still be done efficiently by setting I/O streams to a nonblocking mode and testing them for their readiness to send or receive data. In a nonblocking mode, a read or write does only as much work as can be done immediately—filling or emptying a buffer and then returning. Combined with the ability to test for readiness, this allows a single thread to continuously service many channels efficiently. The main thread "selects" a stream that is ready and works with it until it blocks and then moves to another. On a single-processor system, this is fundamentally equivalent to using multiple threads. Even now, this style of processing has scalability advantages when using a pool of threads (rather than just one). We'll discuss this in detail in Chapter 13 when we discuss networking and building servers that can handle many clients simultaneously.

In addition to nonblocking and selectable I/O, the NIO package enables closing and interrupting I/O operations asynchronously. As discussed in Chapter 9, prior to NIO there was no reliable way to stop or wake up a thread blocked in an I/O operation. With NIO, threads blocked in I/O operations always wake up when interrupted or when the channel is closed by anyone. Additionally, if you interrupt a thread while it is blocked in an NIO operation, its channel is automatically closed. (Closing the channel because the thread is interrupted might seem too strong, but usually it's the right thing to do.)

Performance

Channel I/O is designed around the concept of *buffers*, which are a sophisticated form of array, tailored to working with communications. The NIO package supports the concept of *direct buffers*—buffers that maintain their memory outside the Java VM in the host operating system. Since all real I/O operations ultimately have to work with the host OS, by maintaining the buffer space there, some operations can be made much more efficient. Data can be transferred without first copying it into Java and back out.

Mapped and Locked Files

NIO provides two general-purpose file-related features not found in java.io: memory-mapped files and file locking. We'll discuss memory-mapped files later, but suffice it to say that they allow you to work with file data as if it were all magically resident in memory. File locking supports the concept of shared and exclusive locks on regions of files—useful for concurrent access by multiple applications.

Channels

While java.io deals with streams, java.nio works with channels. A *channel* is an endpoint for communication. Although in practice channels are similar to streams, the underlying notion of a channel is more abstract and primitive. Whereas streams in java.io are defined in terms of input or output with methods to read and write bytes, the basic channel interface says nothing about how communications happen. It simply defines whether the channel is open or closed via the methods isOpen( ) and close( ). Implementations of channels for files, network sockets, or arbitrary devices then add their own methods for operations, such as reading, writing, or transferring data. The following channels are provided by NIO:

- `FileChannel`
- `Pipe.SinkChannel`, `Pipe.SourceChannel`
- `SocketChannel`, `ServerSocketChannel`, `DatagramChannel`

We'll cover `FileChannel` in this chapter. The `Pipe` channels are simply the channel equivalents of the `java.io` Pipe facilities. We'll talk about `Socket` and `Datagram` channels in Chapter 13.

All these basic channels implement the `ByteChannel` interface, designed for channels that have read and write methods such as I/O streams. `ByteChannels` read and write `ByteBuffers`, however, not byte arrays.

In addition to these native channels, you can bridge channels with `java.io` I/O streams and readers and writers for interoperability. However, if you mix these features, you may not get the full benefits and performance offered by the NIO package.

Buffers

Most of the utilities of the `java.io` and `java.net` packages operate on byte arrays. The corresponding tools of the NIO package are built around `ByteBuffers` (with another type of buffer, `CharBuffer`, serving the text world). Byte arrays are simple, so why are buffers necessary? They serve several purposes:

- They formalize the usage patterns for buffered data and they provide for things like read-only buffers and keep track of read/write positions and limits within a large buffer space. They also provide a mark/reset facility such as that of `BufferedInputStream`.

- They provide additional APIs for working with raw data representing primitive types. You can create buffers that "view" your byte data as a series of larger primitives, such as `shorts`, `ints`, or `floats`. The most general type of data buffer, `ByteBuffer`, includes methods that let you read and write all primitive types just like `DataOutputStream` does for streams.

- They abstract the underlying storage of the data, allowing for special optimizations by Java. Specifically, buffers may be allocated as direct buffers that use native buffers of the host operating system instead of arrays in Java's memory. The NIO `Channel` facilities that work with buffers can recognize direct buffers automatically and try to optimize I/O to use them. For example, a read from a file channel into a Java byte array normally requires Java to copy the data for the read from the host operating system into Java's memory. With a direct buffer, the data can remain in the host operating system, outside Java's normal memory space.

Buffer operations

A `Buffer` is a subclass of a `java.nio.Buffer` object. The base `Buffer` class is something like an array with state. It does not specify what type of elements it holds (that is for subtypes to decide), but it does define functionality common to all data buffers. A `Buffer` has a fixed size called its *capacity*. Although all the standard `Buffer`s provide "random access" to their contents, a `Buffer` expects to be read and written sequentially, so `Buffer`s maintain the notion of a *position* where the next element is read or written. In addition to position, a `Buffer` can maintain two other pieces of state information: a *limit*, which is a position that is a "soft" limit to the extent of a read or write, and a *mark*, which can be used to remember an earlier position for future recall.

Implementations of `Buffer` add specific, typed get and put methods that read and write the buffer contents. For example, `ByteBuffer` is a buffer of bytes and it has `get( )` and `put( )` methods that read and write bytes and arrays of bytes (along with many other useful methods we'll discuss later). Getting from and putting to the `Buffer` changes the position marker, so the `Buffer` keeps track of its contents somewhat like a stream. Attempting to read or write past the limit marker generates a `BufferUnderflowException` or `BufferOverflowException`, respectively.

The mark, position, limit, and capacity values always obey the formula:

mark ≤ position ≤ limit ≤ capacity

The position for reading and writing the `Buffer` is always between the mark, which serves as a lower bound, and the limit, which serves as an upper bound. The capacity represents the physical extent of the buffer space.

You can set the position and limit markers explicitly with the `position( )` and `limit( )` methods. Several convenience methods are provided for the common usage patterns. The `reset( )` method sets the position back to the mark. If no mark has been set, an `InvalidMarkException` is thrown. The `clear( )` method resets the position to 0 and makes the limit the capacity, readying the buffer for new data (the mark is discarded). The `clear( )` method does not actually do anything to the data in the buffer; it simply changes the position markers.

The `flip( )` method is used for the common pattern of writing data into the buffer and then reading it back out. `flip` makes the current position the limit and then resets the current position to 0 (any mark is thrown away), which saves having to keep track of how much data was read. Another method, `rewind( )`, simply resets the position to 0, leaving the limit alone. You might use it to write the same size data again. Here is a snippet of code that uses these methods to read data from a channel and write it to two channels:

```
ByteBuffer buff = ...
while ( inChannel.read( buff ) > 0 ) { // position = ?
    buff.flip( );     // limit = position; position = 0;
    outChannel.write( buff );
```

```
        buff.rewind( );  // position = 0
        outChannel2.write( buff );
        buff.clear( );   // position = 0; limit = capacity
    }
```

This might be confusing the first time you look at it because here the read from the Channel is actually a write to the Buffer and vice versa. Because this example writes all the available data up to the limit, either flip( ) or rewind( ) have the same effect in this case.

Buffer types

As stated earlier, various buffer types add get and put methods for reading and writing specific data types. Each of the Java primitive types has an associated buffer type: ByteBuffer, CharBuffer, ShortBuffer, IntBuffer, LongBuffer, FloatBuffer, and DoubleBuffer. Each provides get and put methods for reading and writing its type and arrays of its type. Of these, ByteBuffer is the most flexible. Because it has the "finest grain" of all the buffers, it has been given a full complement of get and put methods for reading and writing all the other data types as well as byte. Here are some ByteBuffer methods:

```
byte get( )
char getChar( )
short getShort( )
int getInt( )
long getLong( )
float getFloat( )
double getDouble( )

void put(byte b)
void put(ByteBuffer src)
void put(byte[] src, int offset, int length)
void put(byte[] src)
void putChar(char value)
void putShort(short value)
void putInt(int value)
void putLong(long value)
void putFloat(float value)
void putDouble(double value)
```

As we said, all the standard buffers also support random access. For each of the aforementioned methods of ByteBuffer, an additional form takes an index:

```
getLong( int index )
putLong( int index, long value )
```

But that's not all. ByteBuffer can also provide "views" of itself as any of the coarse-grained types. For example, you can fetch a ShortBuffer view of a ByteBuffer with the asShortBuffer( ) method. The ShortBuffer view is *backed* by the ByteBuffer, which means that they work on the same data, and changes to either one affect the other. The view buffer's extent starts at the ByteBuffer's current position, and its capacity is a function of the remaining number of bytes, divided by the new type's size. (For example, shorts consume two bytes each, floats four, and longs and doubles take eight.) View buffers are convenient for reading and writing large blocks of a contiguous type within a ByteBuffer.

CharBuffers are interesting as well, primarily because of their integration with Strings. Both CharBuffers and Strings implement the java.lang.CharSequence interface. This is the interface that provides the standard charAt( ) and length( ) methods. Because of this, newer APIs (such as the java.util.regex package) allow you to use a CharBuffer or a String interchangeably. In this case, the CharBuffer acts like a modifiable String with user-configurable start and end positions.

Byte order

Since we're talking about reading and writing types larger than a byte, the question arises: in what order do the bytes of multibyte values (e.g., shorts, ints) get written? There are two camps in this world: "big endian" and "little endian."* Big endian means that the most significant bytes come first; little endian is the reverse. If you're writing binary data for consumption by some native application, this is important. Intel-compatible computers use little endian, and many workstations that run Unix use big endian. The ByteOrder class encapsulates the choice. You can specify the byte order to use with the ByteArray order( ) method, using the identifiers ByteOrder.BIG_ENDIAN and ByteOrder.LITTLE_ENDIAN like so:

```
byteArray.order( ByteOrder.BIG_ENDIAN );
```

You can retrieve the native ordering for your platform using the static ByteOrder. nativeOrder( ) method. (I know you're curious.)

Allocating buffers

You can create a buffer either by allocating it explicitly using allocate( ) or by wrapping an existing plain Java array type. Each buffer type has a static allocate( ) method that takes a capacity (size) and also a wrap( ) method that takes an existing array:

```
CharBuffer cbuf = CharBuffer.allocate( 64*1024 );
```

A direct buffer is allocated in the same way, with the allocateDirect( ) method:

```
ByteBuffer bbuf = ByteBuffer.allocateDirect( 64*1024 );
```

As we described earlier, direct buffers can use operating system memory structures that are optimized for use with some kinds of I/O operations. The tradeoff is that allocating a direct buffer is a little slower than a plain buffer, so you should try to use

---

* The terms "big endian" and "little endian" come from Jonathan Swift's novel *Gulliver's Travels*, where it denoted two camps of Lilliputians: those who eat their eggs from the big end and those who eat them from the little end.

them for longer-term buffers. (For example, using Java 5.0 on a 400 MHz Sparc Ultra 60, it took about six milliseconds to allocate a 1 MB direct buffer versus two milliseconds for a plain buffer of the same size.)

Character Encoders and Decoders

Character encoders and decoders turn characters into raw bytes and vice versa, mapping from the Unicode standard to particular encoding schemes. Encoders and decoders have always existed in Java for use by Reader and Writer streams and in the methods of the String class that work with byte arrays. However, prior to Java 1.4, there was no API for working with encoding explicitly; you simply referred to encoders and decoders wherever necessary by name as a String. The java.nio.charset package formalizes the idea of a Unicode character set with the Charset class.

The Charset class is a factory for Charset instances, which know how to encode character buffers to byte buffers and decode byte buffers to character buffers. You can look up a character set by name with the static Charset.forName() method and use it in conversions:

```
Charset charset = Charset.forName("US-ASCII");
CharBuffer charBuff = charset.decode( byteBuff );  // to ascii
ByteBuffer byteBuff = charset.encode( charBuff );  // and back
```

You can also test to see if an encoding is available with the static Charset.isSupported() method.

The following character sets are guaranteed to be supplied:

- US-ASCII
- ISO-8859-1
- UTF-8
- UTF-16BE
- UTF-16LE
- UTF-16

You can list all the encoders available on your platform using the static availableCharsets() method:

```
Map map = Charset.availableCharsets();
Iterator it = map.keySet().iterator();
while ( it.hasNext() )
    System.out.println( it.next() );
```

The result of availableCharsets() is a map because character sets may have "aliases" and appear under more than one name.

In addition to the buffer-oriented classes of the java.nio package, the InputStreamReader and OutputStreamWriter bridge classes of the java.io package have been updated to work with Charset as well. You can specify the encoding as a Charset object or by name.

CharsetEncoder and CharsetDecoder

You can get more control over the encoding and decoding process by creating an instance of CharsetEncoder or CharsetDecoder (a codec) with the Charset newEncoder( ) and newDecoder( ) methods. In the previous snippet, we assumed that all the data was available in a single buffer. More often, however, we might have to process data as it arrives in chunks. The encoder/decoder API allows for this by providing more general encode( ) and decode( ) methods that take a flag specifying whether more data is expected. The codec needs to know this because it might have been left hanging in the middle of a multibyte character conversion when the data ran out. If it knows that more data is coming, it does not throw an error on this incomplete conversion. In the following snippet, we use a decoder to read from a ByteBuffer bbuff and accumulate character data into a CharBuffer cbuff:

```
CharsetDecoder decoder = Charset.forName("US-ASCII").newDecoder( );

boolean done = false;
while ( !done ) {
    bbuff.clear( );
    done = ( in.read( bbuff ) == -1 );
    bbuff.flip( );
    decoder.decode( bbuff, cbuff, done );
}
cbuff.flip( );
// use cbuff. . .
```

Here, we look for the end of input condition on the in channel to set the flag done. The encode( ) and decode( ) methods also return a special result object, CoderResult, that can determine the progress of encoding. The methods isError( ), isUnderflow( ), and isOverflow( ) on the CoderResult specify why encoding stopped: for an error, a lack of bytes on the input buffer, or a full output buffer, respectively.

FileChannel

Now that we've covered the basics of channels and buffers, it's time to look at a real channel type. The FileChannel is the NIO equivalent of the java.io.RandomAccessFile, but it provides several basic new features in addition to some performance optimizations. Use a FileChannel in place of a plain java.io file stream if you wish to use file locking, memory-mapped file access, or highly optimized data transfer between files or between file and network channels.

A FileChannel is constructed from a FileInputStream, FileOutputStream, or RandomAccessFile:

```
FileChannel readOnlyFc = new FileInputStream("file.txt").getChannel( );
FileChannel readWriteFc =
    new RandomAccessFile("file.txt", "rw").getChannel( );
```

FileChannels for file input and output streams are read-only or write-only, respectively. To get a read/write FileChannel, you must construct a RandomAccessFile with read/write permissions, as in the previous example.

Using a FileChannel is just like a RandomAccessFile, but it works with ByteBuffer instead of byte arrays:

```
bbuf.clear( );
readOnlyFc.position( index );
readOnlyFc.read( bbuf );
bbuf.flip( );
readWriteFc.write( bbuf );
```

You can control how much data is read and written either by setting buffer position and limit markers or using another form of read/write that takes a buffer starting position and length. You can also read and write to a random position using:

```
readWriteFc.read( bbuf, index )
readWriteFc.write( bbuf, index2 );
```

In each case, the actual number of bytes read or written depends on several factors. The operation tries to read or write to the limit of the buffer and the vast majority of the time that is what happens with local file access. The operation is guaranteed to block only until at least one byte has been processed. Whatever happens, the number of bytes processed is returned, and the buffer position is updated accordingly. This is one of the conveniences of working with buffers; they can manage the count for you. Like standard streams, the channel read( ) method returns –1 upon reaching the end of input.

The size of the file is always available with the size( ) method. It can change if you write past the end of the file. Conversely, you can truncate the file to a specified length with the truncate( ) method.

Concurrent access

FileChannels are safe for use by multiple threads and guarantee that data "viewed" by them is consistent across channels in the same VM. No guarantees are made about how quickly writes are propagated to the storage mechanism. If you need to be sure that data is safe before moving on, you can use the force( ) method to flush changes to disk. The force( ) method takes a Boolean argument indicating whether or not file metadata, including timestamp and permissions, must be written. Some systems keep track of reads on files as well as writes, so you can save a lot of updates if you set the flag to false, which indicates that you don't care about syncing that data immediately.

As with all Channels, a FileChannel may be closed by any thread. Once closed, all its read/write and position-related methods throw a ClosedChannelException.

File locking

FileChannels support exclusive and shared locks on regions of files through the lock( ) method:

```
FileLock fileLock = fileChannel.lock( );
int start = 0, len = fileChannel2.size( );
FileLock readLock = fileChannel2.lock( start, len, true );
```

Locks may be either shared or exclusive. An *exclusive* lock prevents others from acquiring a lock of any kind on the specified file or file region. A *shared* lock allows others to acquire overlapping shared locks but not exclusive locks. These are useful as write and read locks, respectively. When you are writing, you don't want others to be able to write until you're done, but when reading, you need only to block others from writing, not reading concurrently.

The simple lock( ) method in the previous example attempts to acquire an exclusive lock for the whole file. The second form accepts a starting and length parameter as well as a flag indicating whether the lock should be shared (or exclusive). The FileLock object returned by the lock( ) method can be used to release the lock:

```
fileLock.release( );
```

Note that file locks are a cooperative API; they do not necessarily prevent anyone from reading or writing to the locked file contents. In general, the only way to guarantee that locks are obeyed is for both parties to attempt to acquire the lock and use it. Also, shared locks are not implemented on some systems, in which case all requested locks are exclusive. You can test whether a lock is shared with the isShared( ) method.

Memory-mapped files

One of the most interesting features offered through FileChannel is the ability to map a file into memory. When a file is *memory-mapped*, like magic it becomes accessible through a single ByteBuffer—as if the entire file was read into memory at once. The implementation of this is extremely efficient, generally among the fastest ways to access the data. For working with large files, memory mapping can save a lot of resources and time.

This may seem counterintuitive; we're getting a conceptually easier way to access our data and it's also faster and more efficient? What's the catch? There really is no catch. The reason for this is that all modern operating systems are based on the idea of virtual memory. In a nutshell, that means the operating system makes disk space act like memory by continually paging (swapping 4-KB blocks called "pages") between memory and disk, transparent to the applications. Operating systems are very good at this; they efficiently cache the data the application is using and let go of what is not in use. Memory-mapping a file is really just taking advantage of what the OS is doing internally.

A good example of where a memory-mapped file would be useful is in a database. Imagine a 100 MB file containing records indexed at various positions. By mapping the file, we can work with a standard ByteBuffer, reading and writing data at arbitrary positions and let the native operating system read and write the underlying data in fine-grained pages, as necessary. We could emulate this behavior with RandomAccessFile or FileChannel, but we would have to explicitly read and write data into buffers first, and the implementation would almost certainly not be as efficient.

A mapping is created with the FileChannel map( ) method. For example:

```
FileChannel fc = new RandomAccessFile("index.db", "rw").getChannel();
MappedByteBuffer mappedBuff =
    fc.map( FileChannel.MapMode.READ_WRITE, 0, fc.size() );
```

The map( ) method returns a MappedByteBuffer, which is simply the standard ByteBuffer with a few additional methods relating to the mapping. The most important is force( ), which ensures that any data written to the buffer is flushed out to permanent storage on the disk. The READ_ONLY and READ_WRITE constant identifiers of the FileChannel.MapMode static inner class specify the type of access. Read/write access is available only when mapping a read/write file channel. Data read through the buffer is always consistent within the same Java VM. It may also be consistent across applications on the same host machine, but this is not guaranteed.

Again, a MappedByteBuffer acts just like a ByteBuffer. Continuing with the previous example, we could decode the buffer with a character decoder and search for a pattern like so:

```
CharBuffer cbuff = Charset.forName("US-ASCII").decode( mappedBuff );
Matcher matcher = Pattern.compile("abc*").matcher( cbuff );
while ( matcher.find() )
    System.out.println( matcher.start()+": "+matcher.group(0) );
```

Here, we have implemented something like the Unix *grep* command in about five lines of code (thanks to the Regular Expression API working with our CharBuffer as a CharSequence). Of course, in this example, the CharBuffer allocated by the decode( ) method is as large as the mapped file and must be held in memory. More generally, we can use the CharsetDecoder shown earlier to iterate through a large mapped space.

Direct transfer

The final feature of FileChannel that we'll look at is performance optimization. FileChannel supports two highly optimized data transfer methods: transferFrom( ) and transferTo( ), which move data between the file channel and another channel. These methods can take advantage of direct buffers internally to move data between the channels as fast as possible, often without copying the bytes into Java's memory space at all. The following example is currently the fastest way to implement a file copy in Java:

```java
import java.io.*;
import java.nio.*;
import java.nio.channels.*;

public class CopyFile {
    public static void main( String [] args ) throws Exception
    {
        String fromFileName = args[0];
        String toFileName = args[1];
        FileChannel in = new FileInputStream( fromFileName ).getChannel();
        FileChannel out = new FileOutputStream( toFileName ).getChannel();
        in.transferTo( 0, (int)in.size(), out );
        in.close();
        out.close();
    }
}
```

Scalable I/O with NIO

We've laid the groundwork for using the NIO package in this chapter, but left out some of the important pieces. In the next chapter, we'll see more of the real motivation for java.nio when we talk about nonblocking and selectable I/O. In addition to the performance optimizations that can be made through direct buffers, these capabilities make possible a design for network servers that uses fewer threads and can scale well to large systems. We'll also look at the other significant Channel types: SocketChannel, ServerSocketChannel, and DatagramChannel.

CHAPTER 13

Network Programming

The network is the soul of Java. Most of what is interesting about Java centers around the potential for dynamic, networked applications. As Java's networking APIs have matured, Java has also become the language of choice for implementing traditional client-server applications and services. In this chapter, we start our discussion of the java.net package, which contains the fundamental classes for communications and working with networked resources (we'll finish this discussion in Chapter 14). This chapter next discusses the java.rmi package, which provides Java's powerful, high-level, Remote Method Invocation (RMI) facilities. Finally, building on the material in Chapter 12, we complete our discussion of the java.nio package, which is highly efficient for implementing large servers.

The classes of java.net fall into two general categories: the Sockets API for working with low-level Internet protocols and higher-level, web-oriented APIs that work with uniform resource locators (URLs). Figure 13-1 shows the java.net package.

Java's Sockets API provides access to the standard network protocols used for communications between hosts on the Internet. Sockets are the mechanism underlying all other kinds of portable networked communications. Sockets are the lowest-level tool—you can use sockets for any kind of communications between client and server or peer applications on the Net, but you have to implement your own application-level protocols for handling and interpreting the data. Higher-level networking tools, such as remote method invocation, HTTP, and web services are implemented on top of sockets.

Java RMI is a powerful tool that leverages Java object serialization, allowing you to transparently work with objects on remote machines almost as if they were local. With RMI, it is easy to write distributed applications in which clients and servers work with each other's data as full-fledged Java objects rather than raw streams or packets of data. Technologies like Enterprise JavaBeans build on RMI and extend its semantics, so it is very important to understand the concepts involved.

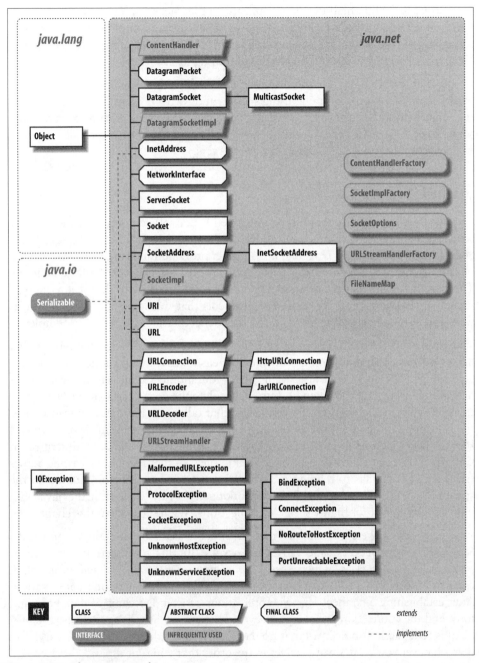

Figure 13-1. The java.net package

In contrast to RMI, which ties Java applications together in an object-to-object fashion, web services provide for more loosely coupled invocation of services on remote servers using web standards such as HTTP and XML. We talk about web services in Chapters 14 and 15 when we discuss programming for the Web.

In this chapter, we'll provide some simple, practical examples of both high- and low-level Java network programming using sockets and RMI. In Chapter 14, we'll look at the other half of the java.net package, which lets clients work with web servers and services via URLs. Chapter 15 covers Java servlets and the tools that allow you to write web applications and services for web servers.

Sockets

Sockets are a low-level programming interface for networked communications. They send streams of data between applications that may or may not be on the same host. Sockets originated in BSD Unix and are, in other programming languages, hairy, complicated things with lots of small parts that can break off and choke little children. The reason for this is that most socket APIs can be used with almost any kind of underlying network protocol. Since the protocols that transport data across the network can have radically different features, the socket interface can be quite complex.*

The java.net package supports a simplified, object-oriented socket interface that makes network communications considerably easier. If you have done network programming using sockets in other languages, you should be pleasantly surprised at how simple things can be when objects encapsulate the gory details. If this is the first time you've come across sockets, you'll find that talking to another application over the network can be as simple as reading a file or getting user input. Most forms of I/O in Java, including most network I/O, use the stream classes described in Chapter 12. Streams provide a unified I/O interface so that reading or writing across the Internet is similar to reading or writing on the local system. In addition to the stream-oriented interfaces, the Java networking APIs can work with the Java NIO buffer-oriented API for highly scalable applications. We'll see both in this chapter.

Java provides sockets to support three distinct classes of underlying protocols: Sockets, DatagramSockets, and MulticastSockets. In this first section, we look at Java's basic Socket class, which uses a *connection-oriented* and *reliable* protocol. A connection-oriented protocol provides the equivalent of a telephone conversation. After establishing a connection, two applications can send streams of data back and forth and the connection stays in place even when no one is talking. Because the protocol is reliable, it also ensures that no data is lost (resending data as necessary) and that whatever you send always arrives in the order that you sent it.

---

* For a discussion of sockets in general, see *Unix Network Programming* by Richard Stevens (Prentice-Hall).

In the next section, we look at the DatagramSocket class, which uses a connection-less, unreliable protocol. A *connectionless protocol* is more like the postal service. Applications can send short messages to each other, but no end-to-end connection is set up in advance and no attempt is made to keep the messages in order. It is not even guaranteed that the messages will arrive at all. A MulticastSocket is a variation of a DatagramSocket that performs multicasting, simultaneously sending data to mul-tiple recipients. Working with multicast sockets is very much like working with data-gram sockets. However, because multicasting is currently not widely supported across the Internet, we do not cover it here.

In theory, just about any protocol family can be used underneath the socket layer: Novell's IPX, Apple's AppleTalk, etc. But, in practice, there's only one important protocol family on the Internet, and only one protocol family that Java supports: the Internet Protocol (IP). The Socket class speaks TCP, the connection-oriented flavor of IP, and the DatagramSocket class speaks UDP, the connectionless kind. These pro-tocols are generally available on any system connected to the Internet.

Clients and Servers

When writing network applications, it's common to talk about clients and servers. The distinction is increasingly vague, but the side that initiates the conversation is usually considered the *client*. The side that accepts the request is usually the *server*. In the case where two peer applications use sockets to talk, the distinction is less important, but for simplicity we'll use this definition.

For our purposes, the most important difference between a client and a server is that a client can create a socket to initiate a conversation with a server application at any time while a server must be prepared in advance to listen for incoming conversations. The java.net.Socket class represents one side of an individual socket connection on both the client and server. In addition, the server uses the java.net.ServerSocket class to listen for new connections from clients. In most cases, an application acting as a server creates a ServerSocket object and waits, blocked in a call to its accept( ) method, until a connection arrives. When it arrives, the accept( ) method creates a Socket object the server uses to communicate with the client. A server may carry on conversations with multiple clients at once; in this case, there is still only a single ServerSocket, but the server has multiple Socket objects—one associated with each client, as shown in Figure 13-2.

At the socket level, a client needs two pieces of information to locate and connect to a server on the Internet: a *hostname* (used to find the host's network address) and a *port number*. The port number is an identifier that differentiates between multiple clients or servers on the same host. A server application listens on a prearranged port while waiting for connections. Clients select the port number assigned to the service they want to access. If you think of the host computers as hotels and the applications as

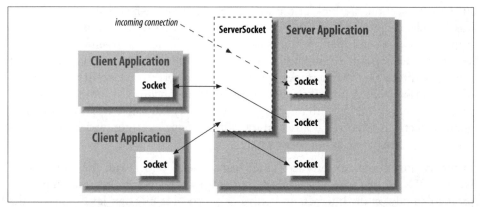

Figure 13-2. Clients and servers, Sockets and ServerSockets

guests, the ports are like the guests' room numbers. For one person to call another, he or she must know the other party's hotel name and room number.

Clients

A client application opens a connection to a server by constructing a Socket that specifies the hostname and port number of the desired server:

```
try {
    Socket sock = new Socket("wupost.wustl.edu", 25);
} catch ( UnknownHostException e ) {
    System.out.println("Can't find host.");
} catch ( IOException e ) {
    System.out.println("Error connecting to host.");
}
```

This code fragment attempts to connect a Socket to port 25 (the SMTP mail service) of the host *wupost.wustl.edu*. The client handles the possibility that the hostname can't be resolved (UnknownHostException) and that it might not be able to connect to it (IOException). The constructor can also accept a string containing the host's IP address:

```
Socket sock = new Socket("22.66.89.167", 25);
```

Once a connection is made, input and output streams can be retrieved with the Socket getInputStream( ) and getOutputStream( ) methods. The following (rather arbitrary) code sends and receives some data with the streams:

```
try {
    Socket server = new Socket("foo.bar.com", 1234);
    InputStream in = server.getInputStream( );
    OutputStream out = server.getOutputStream( );

    // write a byte
    out.write(42);
```

```
    // write a newline or carriage return delimited string
    PrintWriter pout = new PrintWriter( out, true );
    pout.println("Hello!");

    // read a byte
    byte back = (byte)in.read( );

    // read a newline or carriage return delimited string
    BufferedReader bin =
      new BufferedReader( new InputStreamReader( in ) );
    String response = bin.readLine( );

    // send a serialized Java object
    ObjectOutputStream oout = new ObjectOutputStream( out );
    oout.writeObject( new java.util.Date( ) );
    oout.flush( );

    server.close( );
}
catch (IOException e ) { ... }
```

In this exchange, the client first creates a Socket for communicating with the server. The Socket constructor specifies the server's hostname (*foo.bar.com*) and a prearranged port number (1234). Once the connection is established, the client writes a single byte to the server using the OutputStream's write( ) method. To send a string of text more easily, it then wraps a PrintWriter around the OutputStream. Next, it performs the complementary operations: reading a byte from the server using InputStream's read( ) method and then creating a BufferedReader from which to get a full string of text. Finally, we do something really funky and send a serialized Java object to the server, using an ObjectOutputStream. (We'll talk in depth about sending serialized objects later in this chapter.) The client then terminates the connection with the close( ) method. All these operations have the potential to generate IOExceptions; the catch clause is where our application would deal with these.

Servers

After a connection is established, a server application uses the same kind of Socket object for its side of the communications. However, to accept a connection from a client, it must first create a ServerSocket, bound to the correct port. Let's recreate the previous conversation from the server's point of view:

```
// Meanwhile, on foo.bar.com...
try {
    ServerSocket listener = new ServerSocket( 1234 );

    while ( !finished ) {
        Socket client = listener.accept( );  // wait for connection

        InputStream in = client.getInputStream( );
        OutputStream out = client.getOutputStream( );
```

```
      // read a byte
      byte someByte = (byte)in.read( );

      // read a newline or carriage-return-delimited string
      BufferedReader bin =
        new BufferedReader( new InputStreamReader( in ) );
      String someString = bin.readLine( );

      // write a byte
      out.write(43);

      // say goodbye
      PrintWriter pout = new PrintWriter( out, true );
      pout.println("Goodbye!");

      // read a serialized Java object
      ObjectInputStream oin = new ObjectInputStream( in );
      Date date = (Date)oin.readObject( );

      client.close( );
    }

    listener.close( );
  }
  catch (IOException e ) { ... }
  catch (ClassNotFoundException e2 ) { ... }
```

First, our server creates a ServerSocket attached to port 1234. On some systems, there are rules about what ports an application can use. Port numbers below 1024 are usually reserved for system processes and standard, *well-known* services, so we pick a port number outside of this range. The ServerSocket is created only once; thereafter, we can accept as many connections as arrive.

Next, we enter a loop, waiting for the accept( ) method of the ServerSocket to return an active Socket connection from a client. When a connection has been established, we perform the server side of our dialog, then close the connection and return to the top of the loop to wait for another connection. Finally, when the server application wants to stop listening for connections altogether, it calls the close( ) method of the ServerSocket.

This server is single-threaded; it handles one connection at a time, not calling accept( ) to listen for a new connection until it's finished with the current connection. A more realistic server would have a loop that accepts connections concurrently and passes them off to their own threads for processing. There is a lot to be said about implementing multithreaded servers. Later in this chapter, we'll create a tiny web server that starts a new thread for each connection and also a slightly more complex web server that uses the NIO package to handle many connections with a small number of threads.

Sockets and security

The previous examples presuppose that the client has permission to connect to the server and that the server is allowed to listen on the specified socket. If you're writing a general, standalone application, this is normally the case. However, applets and other untrusted applications run under the auspices of a security policy that can impose arbitrary restrictions on what hosts they may or may not talk to and whether or not they can listen for connections.

The security policy imposed on applets by the JDK `appletviewer` and most browsers allow untrusted applets to open socket connections only to the host that served them. That is, they can talk back only to the server from which their class files were retrieved. Untrusted applets are generally not allowed to open server sockets for incoming connections themselves. This doesn't mean that an untrusted applet can't cooperate with its server to communicate with anyone, anywhere. The applet's server could run a proxy that lets the applet communicate indirectly with anyone it likes. What this security policy prevents is malicious applets poking around inside corporate firewalls, making connections to trusted services. It places the burden of security on the originating server, not the client machine. Restricting access to the originating server limits the usefulness of Trojan applications that do annoying things from the client side. (You probably won't let your proxy spam people, because you'll be blamed.)

While fully trusted code and applications that are run without any security policy can perform any kind of activities, the default security policy that comes with Java 1.2 and later disallows most network access. If you are going to run your application under the default security manager (using the `-Djava.security.manager` option on the command line or by manually installing the security manager within your application), you must modify the policy file to grant the appropriate permissions to your code (see Chapter 3 for details). The following policy file fragment sets the socket permissions to allow connections to or from any host on any nonprivileged port:

```
grant {
  permission java.net.SocketPermission
    "*:1024-", "listen,accept,connect";
};
```

When starting the Java interpreter, you can install the security manager and use this file (call it *mysecurity.policy*):

```
% java -Djava.security.manager \
-Djava.security.policy=mysecurity.policy MyApplication
```

The DateAtHost Client

Many networked workstations run a time service that dispenses their clock's local time on a well-known port. This was a precursor of NTP, the more general Network Time Protocol. The next example, `DateAtHost`, includes a specialized subclass of java.util.Date that fetches the time from a remote host instead of initializing itself from the local clock. (See Chapter 11 for a complete discussion of the Date class.)

DateAtHost connects to the time service (port 37) and reads four bytes representing the time on the remote host. These four bytes have a peculiar specification that we decode to get the time. Here's the code:

```
//file: DateAtHost.java
import java.net.Socket;
import java.io.*;

public class DateAtHost extends java.util.Date {
    static int timePort = 37;
    // seconds from start of 20th century to Jan 1, 1970 00:00 GMT
    static final long offset = 2208988800L;

    public DateAtHost( String host ) throws IOException {
        this( host, timePort );
    }

    public DateAtHost( String host, int port ) throws IOException {
        Socket server = new Socket( host, port );
        DataInputStream din =
          new DataInputStream( server.getInputStream( ) );
        int time = din.readInt( );
        server.close( );

        setTime( (((1L << 32) + time) - offset) * 1000 );
    }
}
```

That's all there is to it. It's not very long, even with a few frills. We have supplied two possible constructors for DateAtHost. Normally we'd expect to use the first, which simply takes the name of the remote host as an argument. The second constructor specifies the hostname and the port number of the remote time service. (If the time service were running on a nonstandard port, we would use the second constructor to specify the alternate port number.) This second constructor does the work of making the connection and setting the time. The first constructor simply invokes the second (using the this( ) construct) with the default port as an argument. Supplying simplified constructors that invoke their siblings with default arguments is a common and useful technique; that is the main reason we've shown it here.

The second constructor opens a socket to the specified port on the remote host. It creates a DataInputStream to wrap the input stream and then reads a four-byte integer using the readInt( ) method. It's no coincidence that the bytes are in the right order. Java's DataInputStream and DataOutputStream classes work with the bytes of integer types in *network byte order* (most significant to least significant). The time protocol (and other standard network protocols that deal with binary data) also uses the network byte order, so we don't need to call any conversion routines. Explicit data conversions would probably be necessary if we were using a nonstandard protocol, especially when talking to a non-Java client or server. In that case, we'd have to read byte by byte and do some rearranging to get our four-byte value. After reading the data, we're finished with the socket, so we close it, terminating the connection to the server. Finally, the constructor initializes the rest of the object by calling Date's setTime( ) method with the calculated time value.

The four bytes of the time value are interpreted as an integer representing the number of seconds since the beginning of the 20th century. DateAtHost converts this to Java's notion of absolute time—the count of milliseconds since January 1, 1970 (an arbitrary date standardized by C and Unix). The conversion first creates a long value, which is the unsigned equivalent of the integer time. It subtracts an offset to make the time relative to the epoch (January 1, 1970) rather than the century, and multiplies by 1000 to convert to milliseconds. The converted time is used to initialize the object.

The DateAtHost class can work with a time retrieved from a remote host almost as easily as Date is used with the time on the local host. The only additional overhead is dealing with the possible IOException that can be thrown by the DateAtHost constructor:

```
try {
    Date d = new DateAtHost( "someserver.net" );
    System.out.println( "The time over there is: " + d );
}
catch ( IOException e ) { ... }
```

This example fetches the time at the host *someserver.net* and prints its value.

The TinyHttpd Server

Have you ever wanted to write your very own web server? Well, you're in luck. In this section, we're going to build TinyHttpd, a minimal but functional HTTP daemon. TinyHttpd listens on a specified port and services simple HTTP GET requests. GET requests are simple text commands that look something like this:

```
GET /path/filename [ optional stuff ]
```

Your web browser sends one or more of these requests for each document it retrieves from a web server. Upon reading a request, our server attempts to open the specified file and send its contents. If that document contains references to images or other items to be displayed inline, the browser follows up with additional GET requests. For best performance, TinyHttpd services each request in its own thread. Therefore, TinyHttpd can service several requests concurrently.

This example works, but it's a bit oversimplified. Remember that file pathnames are still somewhat architecture-dependent in Java. This example should work, as is, on most systems but could require some enhancement to work everywhere. It's possible to write slightly more elaborate code that uses the environmental information provided by Java to tailor itself to the local system. (Chapter 12 gives some hints about how.)

 Unless you have a firewall or other security in place, the next example serves files from your host without protection. Don't try this at work.

Now, without further ado, here's TinyHttpd:

```java
//file: TinyHttpd.java
import java.net.*;
import java.io.*;
import java.util.regex.*;
import java.util.concurrent.*;

public class TinyHttpd {
  public static void main( String argv[] ) throws IOException {
    Executor executor = Executors.newFixedThreadPool(3);
    ServerSocket ss = new ServerSocket( Integer.parseInt(argv[0]) );
    while ( true )
      executor.execute( new TinyHttpdConnection( ss.accept() ) );
  }
}

class TinyHttpdConnection implements Runnable {
  Socket client;
  TinyHttpdConnection ( Socket client ) throws SocketException {
    this.client = client;
  }
  public void run( ) {
    try {
      BufferedReader in = new BufferedReader(
        new InputStreamReader(client.getInputStream( ), "8859_1" ) );
      OutputStream out = client.getOutputStream( );
      PrintWriter pout = new PrintWriter(
        new OutputStreamWriter(out, "8859_1"), true );
      String request = in.readLine( );
      System.out.println( "Request: "+request);

      Matcher get = Pattern.compile("GET /?(\\S*).*").matcher( request );
      if ( get.matches( ) ) {
        request = get.group(1);
        if ( request.endsWith("/") || request.equals("") )
          request = request + "index.html";
        try {
          FileInputStream fis = new FileInputStream ( request );
          byte [] data = new byte [ 64*1024 ];
          for(int read; (read = fis.read( data )) > -1; )
              out.write( data, 0, read );
          out.flush( );
        } catch ( FileNotFoundException e ) {
          pout.println( "404 Object Not Found" ); }
```

```
        } else
          pout.println( "400 Bad Request" );
        client.close( );
      } catch ( IOException e ) {
        System.out.println( "I/O error " + e ); }
    }
  }
```

Compile TinyHttpd and place it in your classpath, as described in Chapter 3. Go to a directory with some interesting documents and start the daemon, specifying an unused port number as an argument. For example:

```
% java TinyHttpd 1234
```

You should now be able to use your web browser to retrieve files from your host. You'll have to specify the port number you chose in the URL. For example, if your hostname is *foo.bar.com*, and you started the server as shown, you could reference a file as in:

```
http://foo.bar.com:1234/welcome.html
```

Or if you're running both the server and your web browser on the same machine, you could reference a file as in:

```
http://localhost:1234/welcome.html
```

TinyHttpd looks for files relative to its current directory, so the pathnames you provide should be relative to that location. Retrieved some files? (Did you notice that when you retrieved an HTML file, your web browser automatically generated more requests for items like images that were contained within it?) Let's take a closer look.

The TinyHttpd application has two classes. The public TinyHttpd class contains the main( ) method of our standalone application. It begins by creating a ServerSocket, attached to the specified port. It then loops, waiting for client connections and creating instances of the second class, a TinyHttpdConnection, to service each request. The while loop waits for the ServerSocket accept( ) method to return a new Socket for each client connection. The Socket is passed as an argument to construct the TinyHttpdConnection that handles it. We use an Executor with a fixed pool size of three threads to service all of our connections.

TinyHttpdConnection is a Runnable object. For each connection we start a thread, which lives long enough to handle the single client connection and then dies. The body of TinyHttpdConnection's run( ) method is where all the magic happens. First, we fetch an OutputStream for talking back to our client. The second line reads the GET request from the InputStream into the variable request. This request is a single newline-terminated String that looks like the GET request we described earlier. For this, we use a BufferedInputStream wrapped around an InputStreamReader. (We'll say more about the InputStreamReader in a moment.)

We then parse the contents of request to extract a filename. Here, we are using the Regular Expression API (see Chapter 10 for a full discussion of regular expressions and the Regular Expression API). The pattern simply looks for the "GET " followed by an optional slash and then any string of non-whitespace characters. We add the ".*" at the end to cause the pattern to match the whole input, so that we can use the Matcher match( ) method to test if the whole request made sense to us or not. The part that matches the filename is in a capture group: "(\\S*)". This allows us to retrieve that text with the Matcher group( ) method. Finally, we check to see if the requested filename looks like a directory name (i.e., ends in a slash) or is empty. In these cases, we append the familiar default filename *index.html* as a convenience.

Once we have the filename, we try to open the specified file and send its contents using a large byte array. Here we loop, reading one buffer at a time and writing to the client via the OutputStream. If we can't parse the request or the file doesn't exist, we use the PrintStream to send a textual message. Then we return an appropriate HTTP error message. Finally, we close the socket and return from run( ), completing our task.

Do French web servers speak French?

In TinyHttpd, we explicitly created the InputStreamReader for our BufferedRead and the OutputStreamWriter for our PrintWriter. We do this so that we can specify the character encoding to use when converting to and from the byte representation of the HTTP protocol messages. (Note that we're not talking about the body of the file to be sent—that is simply a stream of raw bytes to us; rather we're talking about the GET and response messages.) If we didn't specify, we'd get the default character encoding for the local system. For many purposes that may be correct, but in this case, we are speaking of a well-defined international protocol, and we should be specific. The RFC for HTTP specifies that web clients and servers should use the ISO8859-1 character encoding. We specify this encoding explicitly when we construct the InputStreamReader and OutputStreamWriter. Now as it turns out, ISO8859-1 is just plain ASCII and conversion to and from Unicode should always leave ASCII values unchanged, so again we would probably not be in any trouble if we did not specify an encoding. But it's important to think about these things at least once—and now you have.

Taming the daemon

An important problem with TinyHttpd is that there are no restrictions on the files it serves. With a little trickery, the daemon would happily send any file in your filesystem to the client. It would be nice if we could enforce the restriction that TinyHttpd serve only files that are in the current working directory or a subdirectory, as it normally does. An easy way to do this is to activate the Java Security Manager. Normally, a security manager is used to prevent Java code downloaded over the Net from doing anything suspicious. However, we can press the security manager into service to restrict file access in our application as well.

You can use a policy like the simple one that we provided earlier in this chapter; it allows the server to accept connections on a specified range of sockets. Fortuitously, the default file-access security policy does just what we want: it allows an application access to files in its current working directory and subdirectories. So simply installing the security manager provides exactly the kind of file protection that we wanted in this case. (It would be easy to add additional permissions if you wish to extend the server's range to other well-defined areas.)

With the security manager in place, the daemon cannot access anything outside the current directory and its subdirectories. If it tries to, the security manager throws an exception and prevents access to the file. In that case, we should have TinyHttpd catch the SecurityException and return a proper message to the web browser. Add the following catch clause after the FileNotFoundException's catch clause:

```
...
} catch ( Security Exception e ) {
    pout.println("403 Forbidden");
}
```

Room for improvement

TinyHttpd still has quite a bit of room for improvement. Technically, it implements only an obsolete subset of the HTTP protocol (Version 0.9) in which the server expects only the GET request and returns just the content. All modern servers speak either HTTP 1.0 or 1.1, which allows for additional metadata in both the HTTP request and response and requires certain data (such as version number, content length). HTTP 1.1 also allows multiple requests to be sent over one socket connection.

Of course, real web servers can do all sorts of other things. For example, you might consider adding a few lines of code to read directories and generate linked HTML listings as most web servers do. Have fun with this example, and you can learn quite a bit.

Socket Options

As we've said, the Java Sockets API is a somewhat simplified interface to the general socket mechanisms. In other environments, where all the gory details of the network are visible to you, a lot of complex and sometimes esoteric options can be set on sockets to govern the behavior of the underlying protocols. Java gives us access to a few important ones. We'll refer to them by their standard (C language) names so that you can recognize them in other reading.

SO_TIMEOUT

The SO_TIMEOUT option sets a timer on all I/O methods of a socket that block so that you don't have to wait forever if they don't return. This works for operations such as accept() on server sockets and read() or write() on all sockets. If the timer expires before the operation would complete, an `InterruptedIOException` is thrown. You can catch the exception and continue to use the socket normally if it is appropriate, or you can take the opportunity to bail out of the operation. Multithreaded, blocking servers, such as `TinyHttpd`, can use this sort of technique for their shutdown logic:

```
serverSocket.setSoTimeout( 2000 ); // 2 seconds

while ( !shutdown ) {
    try {
        Socket client = serverSocket.accept( );
        handleClient( client );
    } catch ( InterruptedIOException e ) {
        // ignore the exception
    }

    // exit
}
```

You set the timer by calling the `setSoTimeout( )` method of the `Socket` class with the timeout period, in milliseconds, as an `int` argument. This works for regular `Sockets`, `ServerSockets` (TCP), and `DatagramSockets` (UDP), discussed later in this chapter. To find the current timeout value, call `getSoTimeout( )`.

This feature is a workaround for the fact that stream-oriented I/O operations in Java are blocking, and there is no way to test, or poll, them for activity. Later in this chapter, we'll complete our discussion of the NIO package, which provides full nonblocking I/O for all types of operations, including sockets.

TCP_NODELAY

This option turns off a feature of TCP called Nagle's algorithm, which tries to prevent certain interactive applications from flooding the network with very tiny packets. For example, in our very first network example we sent a single byte to the network in one write. With this option on, under certain conditions, the TCP implementation might have decided to hold that byte for a very brief period, hoping for more data to fill the next packet. You can turn this "delay" off if you have a fast network and you want all packets sent as soon as possible. The `Socket` `setTcpNoDelay( )` method takes a Boolean argument specifying whether the delay is on or off. To find out whether the `TCP_NODELAY` option is enabled, call `getTcpNoDelay( )`, which returns a `boolean`.

SO_LINGER

This option controls what happens to any unsent data when you perform a `close( )` on an active socket connection. Normally, the system blocks on the close and tries to deliver any network buffered data and close the connection gracefully. The setSoLinger( ) method of the Socket class takes two arguments: a boolean that enables or disables the option and an int that sets the time to wait (the *linger* value), in seconds. If you set the linger value to 0, any unsent data is discarded, and the TCP connection is aborted (terminated with a reset). To find the current linger value, call getSoLinger( ).

TCP_KEEPALIVE

This option can be enabled with the setKeepAlive( ) method. It triggers a feature of TCP that polls the other side every two hours if there is no other activity. Normally, when no data is flowing on a TCP connection, no packets are sent. This can make it difficult to tell whether the other side is simply being quiet or has disappeared. If one side of the connection closes properly, this is detected. But if the other side simply disappears, we don't know unless and until we try to talk to it. For this reason, servers often use TCP_KEEPALIVE to detect lost client connections (where they might otherwise only respond to requests, rather than initiate them). Keepalive is not part of the TCP specification; it's an add-on that's not guaranteed to be implemented everywhere. If you can, the best way to detect lost clients is to implement the polling as part of your own protocol.

Half-close

In TCP, it is technically possible to close one direction of a stream but not the other. In other words, you can shut down sending but not receiving, or vice versa. A few protocols use this to indicate the end of a client request by closing the client side of the stream, allowing the end of stream to be detected by the server. You can shut down either half of a socket connection with shutdownOutput( ) or shutdownInput( ).

Proxies and Firewalls

Most networks today are behind firewalls. Some firewalls not only prevent outsiders from getting in, but by default, prevent applications inside the firewall from opening direct socket-level connections to the outside network. Instead, firewalls that do this often provide a service called SOCKS (named for sockets) that acts as a proxy server for socket connections, giving the administrators more control over what connections are allowed. Firewalls may also be set up with direct proxies for higher-level protocols, such as HTTP and FTP, which allow even greater control and possibly screening of content. It's all about attempting to control who connects to whom and for what.

Java has built-in support for SOCKS as well as HTTP and FTP protocol proxies. All you have to do is set some system properties in your application (in an applet, this should be already taken care of for you through your browser configuration, because you wouldn't have authority to set those properties). To configure Java to use a SOCKS (Version 4 or 5) proxy server, set the following system properties:

socksProxyHost
> The SOCKS proxy server name

socksProxyPort
> The SOCKS proxy port number

If the SOCKS proxy requires a username and password, you can supply them in the additional properties java.net.socks.username and java.net.socks.password.

It's similar for HTTP and FTP proxies, which are set with separate properties:

http.proxyHost
ftp.proxyHost
> The proxy server name.

http.proxyPort
ftp.proxyPort
> The proxy port number.

http.nonProxyHosts
ftp.nonProxyHosts
> A list of hosts for which direct connections should always be made. Hosts in the list are separated by vertical bars (|) and may include asterisks (*) as wildcards. For example, myserver|*.mydomain.

You can set these properties on the command line using the Java interpreter's -D option or by calling the System.setProperty( ) method. The following command runs MyProgram using the HTTP proxy server at *foo.bar.com* on port 1234:

```
% java -Dhttp.proxyServer=foo.bar.com -Dhttp.proxyPort=1234 MyProgram
```

If the firewall does not allow any direct outside socket connections, even via SOCKS, your applet or application may still be able to communicate with the outside world by using HTTP to send and receive data in this way. See Chapter 14 for an example of how to perform HTTP POST and GET operations to send and retrieve data through firewalls allowing web traffic.

ProxySelector

Java 5.0 added an API to allow explicit control of Java's use of proxies. The java. net.ProxySelector class has a method that takes a uniform resource identifier (URI) object (a generalization of the URLs we use for web addresses; see Chapter 14) and returns a list of java.net.Proxy objects representing the proxies or direct connections to be used for the protocol specified. The default ProxySelector obeys the system properties we listed earlier. If required, you can create and install your own proxy selector to take control of the process. To see what decisions are being made, you can get the default selector with the static method ProxySelector.getDefault( )

and query it for various protocols with its select( ) method. The following example prints some string information about the preferred proxy (if any) for a specific HTTP URL:

```
ProxySelector ps = java.net.ProxySelector.getDefault( );
List list = ps.select( new URI("http://java.sun.com/") );
System.out.println( list.get(0) );//e.g. HTTP@myserver:1234
```

Detailed information can be gotten from the proxy object, which contains a type identifier specifying DIRECT, HTTP, or SOCKS and a proxy address. To query for a SOCKS socket proxy for a given host and port, use a URI string of the form socket://host:port.

Datagram Sockets

TinyHttpd used a Socket to create a connection to the client using the TCP protocol. In that example, the TCP protocol took care of data integrity; we didn't have to worry about data arriving out of order or incorrect. Now, let's take a walk on the wild side, building an applet that uses a java.net.DatagramSocket, which uses the UDP protocol. A datagram is sort of like a letter sent via the postal service: it's a discrete chunk of data transmitted in one packet. Unlike the previous example, where we could get a convenient OutputStream from our Socket and write the data as if writing to a file, with a DatagramSocket, we have to work one datagram at a time. (Of course, the TCP protocol was taking our OutputStream and slicing the data into packets, too, but we didn't have to worry about those details.)

UDP doesn't guarantee that the data is received. If the data packets are received, they may not arrive in the order in which they were sent; it's even possible for duplicate datagrams to arrive (under rare circumstances). Using UDP is something like cutting the pages out of the encyclopedia, putting them into separate envelopes, and mailing them to your friend. If your friend wants to read the encyclopedia, it's his or her job to put the pages in order. If some pages get lost in the mail, your friend has to send you a letter asking for replacements.

Obviously, you wouldn't use UDP to send a huge amount of data without error correction. However, it's significantly more efficient than TCP, particularly if you don't care about the order in which messages arrive or whether 100 percent of their arrival is guaranteed. For example, in a simple periodic database lookup, the client can send a query; the server's response itself constitutes an acknowledgment. If the response doesn't arrive within a certain time, the client can just send another query. It shouldn't be hard for the client to match responses to its original queries. Some important applications that use UDP are the Domain Name System (DNS) and Sun's Network File System (NFS).

The HeartBeat Applet

In this section, we build a simple applet, HeartBeat, that sends a datagram to its server each time it's started and stopped. We also build a simple standalone server application, Pulse, that receives these datagrams and prints them. Tracking the output gives you a crude measure of who is currently looking at your web page at any given time (assuming that firewalls do not block the UDP packets). This is an ideal application for UDP: we don't want the overhead of a TCP socket, and if the datagrams get lost, it's no big deal.

First, the HeartBeat applet:

```java
//file: HeartBeat.java
import java.net.*;
import java.io.*;

public class HeartBeat extends java.applet.Applet {
    String myHost;
    int myPort;

    public void init( ) {
        myHost = getCodeBase( ).getHost( );
        myPort = Integer.parseInt( getParameter("myPort") );
    }

    private void sendMessage( String message ) {
        try {
            byte [] data = message.getBytes("UTF-8");
            InetAddress addr = InetAddress.getByName( myHost );
            DatagramPacket packet =
              new DatagramPacket( data, data.length, addr, myPort );
            DatagramSocket ds = new DatagramSocket( );
            ds.send( packet );
            ds.close( );
        } catch ( IOException e ) {
            System.out.println( e );  // Error creating socket
        }
    }

    public void start( ) {
        sendMessage("Arrived");
    }
    public void stop( ) {
        sendMessage("Departed");
    }
}
```

Compile the applet and include it in an HTML document with an <applet> tag:

```html
<applet height="1 " width="1 " code="HeartBeat ">
    <param name="myPort" value="1234">
</applet>
```

Make sure to place the compiled *HeartBeat.class* file in the same directory as the HTML document. If you're not familiar with embedding applets in HTML documents, consult Chapter 23.

The myPort parameter should specify the port number on which our server application listens for data.

Next, the server-side application, Pulse:

```java
//file: Pulse.java
import java.net.*;
import java.io.*;

public class Pulse {
    public static void main( String [] argv ) throws IOException {
        DatagramSocket s =
          new DatagramSocket( Integer.parseInt(argv[0]) );

        while ( true ) {
            DatagramPacket packet =
              new DatagramPacket( new byte [1024], 1024 );
            s.receive( packet );
            String message = new String(
                packet.getData(), 0, packet.getLength(),"UTF-8" );
            System.out.println( "Heartbeat from: "
              + packet.getAddress( ).getHostName( )
              + " - " + message );
        }
    }
}
```

Compile Pulse and run it on your web server, specifying a port number as an argument:

```
% java Pulse 1234
```

The port number should be the same as the one you used in the myPort parameter of the <applet> tag for HeartBeat.

Now, pull up the web page in your browser. You won't see anything interesting there (a better application might do something visual as well), but you should get a blip from the Pulse application. Leave the page and return to it a few times. Each time the applet is started or stopped, it sends a message that Pulse reports:

```
Heartbeat from: foo.bar.com - Arrived
Heartbeat from: foo.bar.com - Departed
Heartbeat from: foo.bar.com - Arrived
Heartbeat from: foo.bar.com - Departed
...
```

Cool, eh? Just remember that the datagrams are not guaranteed to arrive (although it's highly unlikely you'll ever see them fail on a normal network), and it's possible that you could miss an arrival or a departure. Now let's look at the code.

The HeartBeat applet code

HeartBeat overrides the init( ), start( ), and stop( ) methods of the Applet class and implements one private method of its own, sendMessage( ), which sends a datagram. (We haven't covered applets yet, so if you want more details refer to Chapter 23.) HeartBeat begins its life in init( ), where it determines the destination for its messages. It uses the Applet getCodeBase( ) and getHost( ) methods to find the name of its originating host and fetches the correct port number from the myPort parameter of the <applet> tag. After init( ) has finished, the start( ) and stop( ) methods are called whenever the applet is started or stopped. These methods merely call sendMessage( ) with the appropriate message.

sendMessage( ) is responsible for sending a String message to the server as a datagram. It takes the text as an argument, constructs a datagram packet containing the message, and then sends the datagram. All the datagram information is packed into a java.net.DatagramPacket object, including the destination and port number. The DatagramPacket is like an addressed envelope, stuffed with our bytes. After the DatagramPacket is created, sendMessage( ) simply has to open a DatagramSocket and send it.

The first five lines of sendMessage( ) build the DatagramPacket:

```
try {
    byte [] data = message.getBytes("UTF-8");
    InetAddress addr = InetAddress.getByName( myHost );
    DatagramPacket pack =
        new DatagramPacket(data, data.length, addr, myPort );
```

First, the contents of message are placed into an array of bytes called data. Next a java.net.InetAddress object is created by looking up the hostname myHost. An InetAddress holds the network IP address for a host. This class also provides the static getByName( ) method for looking up an IP address by hostname using the system's *name service*. (We'll say more about InetAddress in the next section.) Finally, we call the DatagramPacket constructor with four arguments: the byte array containing our data, the length of the data, the destination address object, and the port number. We ask for the string to be encoded using the UTF-8 charset; we'll use the same character set to decode it.

The remaining lines construct a default client DatagramSocket and call its send( ) method to transmit the DatagramPacket. After sending the datagram, we close the socket:

```
DatagramSocket ds = new DatagramSocket( );
ds.send( pack );
ds.close( );
```

Two operations throw a type of IOException: the InetAddress.getByName( ) lookup and the DatagramSocket send( ) method. InetAddress.getByName( ) can throw an UnknownHostException, which is a type of IOException that indicates the hostname can't be resolved. If send( ) throws an IOException, it implies a serious client-side communication problem with the network. We need to catch these exceptions; our catch block simply prints a message telling us that something went wrong. If we get one of these exceptions, we can assume the datagram never arrived. However, we can't assume the inverse: even if we don't get an exception, we still don't know that the host is actually accessible or that the data actually arrived; with a DatagramSocket, we never find out from the API.

The Pulse server code

The Pulse server corresponds to the HeartBeat applet. First, it creates a DatagramSocket to listen on our prearranged port. This time, we specify a port number in the constructor; we get the port number from the command line as a string (argv[0]) and convert it to an integer with Integer.parseInt( ). Note the difference between this call to the constructor and the call in HeartBeat. In the server, we need to listen for incoming datagrams on a prearranged port, so we need to specify the port when creating the DatagramSocket. The client just sends datagrams, so we don't have to specify the port in advance; we build the port number into the DatagramPacket itself.

Second, Pulse creates an empty DatagramPacket of a fixed maximum size to receive an incoming datagram. This form of the constructor for DatagramPacket takes a byte array and a length as arguments. As much data as possible is stored in the byte array when it's received. (A practical limit on the size of a UDP datagram that can be sent over the Internet is 8K, although datagrams can be larger for local network use—theoretically up to 64K.) Finally, Pulse calls the DatagramSocket's receive( ) method to wait for a packet to arrive. When a packet arrives, its contents are printed by turning them to a string using UTF-8 encoding. We determine the actual number of received bytes from the packet's getLength( ) method.

As you can see, DatagramSockets are slightly more tedious than regular Sockets. With datagrams, it's harder to spackle over the messiness of the socket interface. The Java API rather slavishly follows the Unix interface, and that doesn't help. But all in all, it's not that hard to use datagrams for simple tasks.

InetAddress

The java.net.InetAddress class is the lowest-level Java API for working with IP addresses. Instances of InetAddress represent individual addresses and the InetAddress class provides the API for using the platform's name service to map a string hostname to a numeric IP address. Most of our networking examples showed the use of hostnames to identify remote servers, but under the covers, Java utilized the static InetAddress.getByName( ) method to map the name to a physical IP address. Java normally uses the DNS to perform this lookup (and it caches the results for efficiency). Most Java networking APIs (such as Sockets) will accept either a hostname or an InetAddress as a destination. The InetAddress class can also be used to perform reverse IP lookups (get a name for an IP address) as well as to find the primary address of the local host via the static InetAddress.getLocalHost() method.

Java 5.0 added an important feature to InetAddress. The method isReachable() attempts to use the ICMP *ping* protocol to determine whether a remote address can be reached over the network. The ping protocol is the standard mechanism used to check reachability and latency on networks. It is a low-level IP protocol (along with TCP and UDP) and is not guaranteed to be supported everywhere. If isReachable() can't use ICMP, it attempts to use TCP to reach the echo service (port 7) on the remote host. For example:

```
InetAddress server = InetAddress.getByName("myserver");
If ( !server.isReachable( timeout ) ) // milliseconds
    pageSomeone( );
```

Simple Serialized Object Protocols

Earlier in this chapter, we showed a hypothetical conversation in which a client and server exchanged some primitive data and a serialized Java object. Passing an object between two programs may not have seemed like a big deal at the time, but, in the context of Java as a portable bytecode language, it has profound implications. In this section, we show how a protocol can be built using serialized Java objects.

Before we move on, it's worth considering network protocols. Most programmers would consider working with sockets to be tedious and complex. Even though Java makes sockets much easier to use than many other languages, sockets still provide only an unstructured flow of bytes between their endpoints. If you want to do serious communications using sockets, the first thing you have to do is come up with a protocol that defines the data you are sending and receiving. The most complex part of that protocol usually involves how to marshal (package) your data for transfer over the Net and unpack it on the other side.

As we've seen, Java's DataInputStream and DataOuputStream classes solve this problem for simple data types. We can read and write numbers, Strings, and Java primitives in a standard format that can be understood on any other Java platform. To do real work, we need to be able to put simple types together into larger structures. Java object serialization solves this problem elegantly by allowing us to send our data in the state that we will use it—as Java objects. Serialization can even pack up entire graphs of interconnected objects and put them back together at a later time in another Java VM.

A Simple Object-Based Server

In the following example, a client sends a serialized object to the server, and the server responds in kind. The object sent by the client represents a request and the object returned by the server represents the response. The conversation ends when the client closes the connection. It's hard to imagine a simpler protocol. All the hairy details are taken care of by object serialization, which allows us to work with standard Java objects as we are used to.

To start, we define a class—Request—to serve as a base class for the various kinds of requests we make to the server. Using a common base class is a convenient way to identify the object as a type of request. In a real application, we might also use it to hold basic information, such as client names and passwords, timestamps, serial numbers, and so on. In our example, Request can be an empty class that exists so others can extend it:

```
//file: Request.java
public class Request implements java.io.Serializable {}
```

Request implements Serializable, so all its subclasses are serializable by default. Next, we create some specific kinds of Requests. The first, DateRequest, is also a trivial class. We use it to ask the server to send us a java.util.Date object as a response:

```
//file: DateRequest.java
public class DateRequest extends Request {}
```

Next, we create a generic WorkRequest object. The client sends a WorkRequest to get the server to perform some computation. The server calls the WorkRequest object's execute( ) method to do the work on the server side and then returns the resulting object as a response:

```
//file: WorkRequest.java
public abstract class WorkRequest extends Request {
    public abstract Object execute( );
}
```

For our application, we subclass WorkRequest to create MyCalculation, which adds code that performs a specific calculation; in this case, we just square a number:

```
//file: MyCalculation.java
public class MyCalculation extends WorkRequest {
    int n;

    public MyCalculation( int n ) {
        this.n = n;
    }
    public Object execute( ) {
        return new Integer( n * n );
    }
}
```

As far as data content is concerned, MyCalculation really doesn't do much; it only really transports an integer value for us. But keep in mind that a request object could hold lots of data, including references to many other objects in complex structures, such as arrays or linked lists. The only requirement is that all the objects to be sent must be serializable or must be able to be discarded by marking them as transient (see Chapter 12). Note that MyCalculation also contains behavior—the execute( ) operation. While Java object serialization sends only the data content of a class, in our discussion of RMI later in this chapter, we'll see how Java's ability to dynamically download bytecode for classes can make both the data content and behavior portable over the network.

It's also important to note that even without dynamically loading classes over the network (which is uncommon in practice), this design pattern, sometimes called the *command pattern*, is an important one. Using polymorphism to hide behavior details of tasks from the server allows the application to be easily extended. Polymorphism and Java object serialization are a powerful combination.

Now that we have our protocol, we need the server. The following Server class looks a lot like the TinyHttpd server we developed earlier in this chapter:

```
//file: Server.java
import java.net.*;
import java.io.*;

public class Server {
  public static void main( String argv[] ) throws IOException {
    ServerSocket ss = new ServerSocket( Integer.parseInt(argv[0]) );
    while ( true )
      new ServerConnection( ss.accept() ).start( );
  }
} // end of class Server

class ServerConnection extends Thread {
  Socket client;
  ServerConnection ( Socket client ) throws SocketException {
    this.client = client;
  }

  public void run( ) {
    try {
      ObjectInputStream in =
        new ObjectInputStream( client.getInputStream( ) );
      ObjectOutputStream out =
        new ObjectOutputStream( client.getOutputStream( ) );
      while ( true ) {
        out.writeObject( processRequest( in.readObject( ) ) );
        out.flush( );
      }
    } catch ( EOFException e3 ) { // Normal EOF
```

```
        try {
          client.close( );
        } catch ( IOException e ) { }
      } catch ( IOException e ) {
        System.out.println( "I/O error " + e ); // I/O error
      } catch ( ClassNotFoundException e2 ) {
        System.out.println( e2 ); // unknown type of request object
      }
    }

    private Object processRequest( Object request ) {
      if ( request instanceof DateRequest )
        return new java.util.Date( );
      else if ( request instanceof WorkRequest )
        return ((WorkRequest)request).execute( );
      else
        return null;
    }
  }
```

The Server handles each request in a separate thread. For each connection, the run( )
method creates an ObjectInputStream and an ObjectOutputStream, which the server
uses to receive the request and send the response. The processRequest( ) method
decides what the request means and comes up with the response. To figure out what
kind of request we have, we use the instanceof operator to look at the object's type.

Finally, we get to our Client, which is even simpler:

```
//file: Client.java
import java.net.*;
import java.io.*;

public class Client {
  public static void main( String argv[] ) {
    try {
      Socket server =
        new Socket( argv[0], Integer.parseInt(argv[1]) );
      ObjectOutputStream out =
        new ObjectOutputStream( server.getOutputStream( ) );
      ObjectInputStream in =
        new ObjectInputStream( server.getInputStream( ) );

      out.writeObject( new DateRequest() );
      out.flush( );
      System.out.println( in.readObject() );

      out.writeObject( new MyCalculation( 2 ) );
      out.flush( );
      System.out.println( in.readObject() );

      server.close( );
    } catch ( IOException e ) {
      System.out.println( "I/O error " + e ); // I/O error
```

```
      } catch ( ClassNotFoundException e2 ) {
        System.out.println( e2 ); // unknown type of response object
      }
    }
  }
```

Just like the server, Client creates the pair of object streams. It sends a DateRequest and prints the response; it then sends a MyCalculation object and prints the response. Finally, it closes the connection. On both the client and the server, we call the flush( ) method after each call to writeObject( ). This method forces the system to send any buffered data, ensuring that the other side sees the entire request before we wait for a response. When the client closes the connection, our server catches the EOFException that is thrown and ends the session. Alternatively, our client could write a special object, perhaps null, to end the session; the server could watch for this item in its main loop.

The order in which we construct the object streams is important. We create the output streams first because the constructor of an ObjectInputStream tries to read a header from the stream to make sure that the InputStream really is an object stream. If we tried to create both of our input streams first, we would deadlock waiting for the other side to write the headers.

Finally, we run the example, giving it a port number as an argument:

    % java Server 1234

Then we run the Client, telling it the server's hostname and port number:

    % java Client flatland 1234

The result should look something like this:

    Sun Mar 5 14:25:25 PDT 2006
    4

All right, the result isn't that impressive, but it's easy to think of more substantial applications. Imagine that you need to perform some complex computation on many large datasets. Using serialized objects makes maintenance of the data objects natural and sending them over the wire trivial. There is no need to deal with byte-level protocols at all.

Limitations

As we mentioned earlier, there is one catch in this scenario: both the client and server need access to the necessary classes. That is, all the Request classes—including MyCalculation, which is really the property of the Client—have to be deployed in the classpath on both the client and the server machines. In the next section, we'll see that it's possible to send the Java bytecode along with serialized objects to allow completely new kinds of objects to be transported dynamically over the network. We could create this solution on our own, adding to the earlier example using a network class loader to load the classes for us. But we don't have to: Java's RMI facility handles that for us. The ability to send both serialized data and class definitions over the network is not always needed, but it makes Java a powerful tool for developing advanced distributed applications.

Remote Method Invocation

The most fundamental means of communication in Java is method invocation. Mechanisms such as the Java event model are built on simple method invocations between objects in the same virtual machine. Therefore, when we want to communicate between virtual machines on different hosts, it's natural to want a mechanism with similar capabilities and semantics. Java's RMI mechanism does just that. It lets us get a reference to an object on a remote host and use it almost as if it were in our own virtual machine. RMI lets us invoke methods on remote objects, passing real Java objects as arguments and getting real Java objects as returned values.

Remote invocation is nothing new. For many years, C programmers have used remote procedure calls (RPC) to execute a C function on a remote host and return the results. The primary difference between RPC and RMI is that RPC, an offshoot of the C language, is primarily concerned with data structures. It's relatively easy to pack up data and ship it around, but for Java, that's not enough. In Java we don't just work with data structures; we work with objects that contain both data and methods for operating on the data. Not only do we have to be able to ship the state of an object (the data) over the wire, but the recipient has to be able to interact with the object (use its methods) after receiving it. With Java RMI, you can work with network services in an object-oriented fashion, using real, extensible types and pass "live" references between client and server.

It should be no surprise that RMI uses object serialization, which allows us to send graphs of objects (objects and all the connected objects that they reference). When necessary, RMI can also use dynamic class loading and the security manager to transport Java classes safely. In addition to making remote method calls almost as easy to use as local calls, RMI makes it possible to ship both data and behavior (code) around the Net.

Remote and Nonremote Objects

Before an object can be used remotely through RMI, it must be serializable. But that's not sufficient. Remote objects in RMI are real distributed objects. As the name suggests, a remote object can be an object on a different machine or an object on the local host. The term *remote* means that the object is used through a special kind of object interface that can be passed over the network. Like normal Java objects, remote objects are passed by reference. Regardless of where the reference is used, the method invocation occurs on the original object, which still lives on its original host. If a remote host returns a reference to one of its remote objects to you, you can call the object's methods; the actual method invocations happen on the remote host, where the object resides.

Nonremote objects are simpler; they're just normal serializable objects. (You can pass these over the network as we did in the previous section.) The catch is that when you pass a nonremote object over the network, it is simply copied, so references to the object on one host are not the same as those on the remote host. Nonremote objects are passed by value (copying) as opposed to by reference. This may be acceptable for many kinds of data holder objects on your host, such as the client requests and server responses in our previous example. These types of objects are sometimes called value objects or *data transfer objects* (DTOs).

Stubs and skeletons (be gone!)

No, we're not talking about a gruesome horror movie. Stubs and skeletons are used in the implementation of remote objects. When you invoke a method on a remote object (which could be on a different host), you are actually calling some local code behind the scenes that serves as a proxy for that object. This is the stub. (It is called a *stub* because it is something like a truncated placeholder for the object.) The *skeleton* is another proxy that lives with the real object on its original host. It receives remote method invocations from the stub and passes them to the object.

Prior to Java 5.0, it was necessary to explicitly generate the stub and skeleton classes for your remote objects and to deploy these classes with the corresponding parts of your application. If you are using only Java 5.0 clients and servers, you don't have to worry about that any longer, as Java now takes care of everything dynamically for you at runtime.

If you're using an older version of Java or require interoperability with older Java clients, you must still generate these classes as part of your build process. It's not a big deal and your code never has to reference them directly; they are hidden from you (in the closet, so to speak). Stubs and skeletons for your remote objects are created by running the *rmic* (RMI compiler) utility. After compiling your Java source files normally, you run *rmic* on the remote object classes as a second pass. It's easy; we'll show you how in the following examples.

Remote interfaces

Remote objects implement a special *remote interface* that specifies which of the object's methods can be invoked remotely. The remote interface is part of your application that you create by extending the java.rmi.Remote interface. Your remote object then implements its remote interface as it would any other Java interface. In your client-side code, you should then refer to the remote object as an instance of the remote interface—not as an instance of its implementation class. Because both the real object and stub that the client receives implement the remote interface, they are equivalent as far as we are concerned (for method invocation); locally, we never have to worry about whether we have a reference to a stub or to an actual object. This *type equivalence* means that we can use normal language features such as casting with remote objects. Of course, public fields (variables) of the remote object are not accessible through an interface, so you must make accessor methods if you want to manipulate the remote object's fields.

One additional requirement for remote objects distinguishes them from local objects. All methods in the remote interface must declare that they can throw the exception java.rmi.RemoteException. This exception (or one of its subclasses) is thrown when any kind of networking error happens (for example, a server crash, a network failure, or timeout). Some people see this as a limitation and try to paper over it in various ways. However, the RemoteException is there for a reason—remote objects can behave differently from local objects and your code needs to deal with that issue explicitly. There is no magic bullet (automatic retries, transactions) that truly makes the difference go away.

Here's a simple example of the remote interface that defines the behavior of RemoteObject; we give it two methods that can be invoked remotely, both of which return some kind of Value object:

```
import java.rmi.*;

public interface RemoteObject extends Remote {
    public Value doSomething( ) throws RemoteException;
    public Value doSomethingElse( ) throws RemoteException;
}
```

Exporting remote objects

You make a remote object available to the outside world by using the java.rmi.server.UnicastRemoteObject class. One way is simply to have the implementation of your remote object extend UnicastRemoteObject. When a subclass of UnicastRemoteObject is constructed, the RMI runtime system automatically "exports" it to start listening for network connections from clients. Like java.lang.Object, this superclass also provides implementations of equals( ), hashcode( ), and toString( ) that make sense for a remote object.

Here's a remote object class that implements the RemoteObject interface we showed earlier and extends UnicastRemoteObject; we haven't shown implementations for the two methods or the constructor:

```
public class MyRemoteObject implements RemoteObject
        extends java.rmi.UnicastRemoteObject
{
    public MyRemoteObject( ) throws RemoteException {...}
    public Value doSomething( ) throws RemoteException {...}
    public Value doSomethingElse( ) throws RemoteException {...}
    // nonremote methods
    private void doSomethingInternal() { ... }
}
```

Note that we have to supply a constructor that can throw a RemoteException (even if it does nothing) because UnicastRemoteObject's default constructor throws RemoteException and, even if it's not shown, the Java language always delegates to the superclass constructor. This class can have as many additional methods as it needs (presumably most of them will be private, but that isn't strictly necessary) but these nonremote methods are not required to throw the remote exception.

Now, what if we can't or don't want to make our remote object implementation a subclass of UnicastRemoteObject? Suppose, for example, that it has to be a subclass of BankAccount or some other special base type for our system. Well, we can simply take over the job of exporting the object ourselves, using the static method exportObject() of UnicastRemoteObject. The exportObject() method takes as an argument a Remote interface and accomplishes what the UnicastRemoteObject constructor normally does for us. It returns as a value the remote object's client stub. However, you will normally not do anything with this directly. In the next section, we'll discuss how clients actually find your service, through the RMI registry (a lookup service).

Normally, exported objects listen on individual *ephemeral* (randomly assigned) port numbers by default. (This is implementation-dependent.) You can control the port number allocation explicitly by exporting your objects using another form of UnicastRemoteObject.exportObject(), which takes both a Remote interface and a port number as arguments.

Finally, the name UnicastRemoteObject begs the question, "What other kinds of remote objects are there?" Right now, none. It's possible that Java could add remote objects using other protocols or multicast techniques in the future.

The RMI registry

The registry is RMI's phone book. You use the registry to look up a reference to a registered remote object on another host, using an application-specified name. We've already described how remote references can be passed back and forth by remote method calls. The registry is needed to bootstrap the process; the client needs some way of looking up an initial object.

The registry is implemented by a class called Naming and an application called rmiregistry. The rmiregistry application must be running on the local host before you start a Java program that uses the registry. You can then create instances of remote objects and bind them to particular names in the registry. A registry name can be anything you choose; it takes the form of a slash-separated path. When a client object wants to find your object, it constructs a special URL with the rmi: protocol, the hostname, and the object name. On the client, the RMI Naming class then talks to the registry and returns the remote object reference.

So, which objects need to register themselves with the registry? Initially this can be any object the client has no other way of finding. But a call to a remote method can return another remote object without using the registry. Likewise, a call to a remote method can have another remote object as its argument, without requiring the registry. You could design your system such that only one object registers itself and then serves as a factory for any other remote objects you need. In other words, it wouldn't be hard to build a simple object request "bouncer" (we won't say "broker") that returns references to all the remote objects your application uses. Depending on how you structure your application, this may happen naturally anyway.

The RMI registry is just one implementation of a lookup mechanism for remote objects. It is not very sophisticated, and lookups tend to be slow. It is not intended to be a general-purpose directory service but simply to bootstrap RMI communications. More generally, the Java Naming and Directory Interface (JNDI) can be used as a front end to other name services that can provide this functionality. JNDI is used with RMI as part of the Enterprise JavaBeans APIs.

An RMI Example

In our first example using RMI, we duplicate the simple serialized object protocol from the previous section. We make a remote RMI object called MyServer on which we can invoke methods to get a Date object or execute a WorkRequest object. First, we define our Remote interface:

```
//file: ServerRemote.java
import java.rmi.*;
import java.util.*;

public interface ServerRemote extends Remote {
    Date getDate( ) throws RemoteException;
    Object execute( WorkRequest work ) throws RemoteException;
}
```

The ServerRemote interface extends the java.rmi.Remote interface, which identifies objects that implement it as remote objects. We supply two methods that take the place of our old protocol: getDate( ) and execute( ).

Next, we implement this interface in a class called MyServer that defines the bodies of these methods. (Note that a more common convention for naming the implementation of remote interfaces is to append Impl to the class name. Using that convention, MyServer would instead be named something like ServerImpl.)

```
//file: MyServer.java
import java.rmi.*;
import java.util.*;

public class MyServer
    extends java.rmi.server.UnicastRemoteObject
    implements ServerRemote {

    public MyServer( ) throws RemoteException { }
```

```
        // implement the ServerRemote interface
        public Date getDate( ) throws RemoteException {
            return new Date( );
        }

        public Object execute( WorkRequest work )
          throws RemoteException {
            return work.execute( );
        }

        public static void main(String args[]) {
            try {
                ServerRemote server = new MyServer( );
                Naming.rebind("NiftyServer", server);
            } catch (java.io.IOException e) {
                // problem registering server
            }
        }
    }
```

MyServer extends UnicastRemoteObject, so when we create an instance of MyServer, it is automatically exported and starts listening to the network. We start by providing a constructor, which must throw RemoteException, accommodating errors that might occur in exporting an instance. Next, MyServer implements the methods of the remote interface ServerRemote. These methods are straightforward.

The last method in this class is main( ). This method lets the object set itself up as a server. main( ) creates an instance of the MyServer object and then calls the static method Naming.rebind( ) to place the object in the registry. The arguments to rebind( ) include the name of the remote object in the registry (NiftyServer)—which clients use to look up the object—and a reference to the server object itself. We could have called bind( ) instead, but rebind( ) handles the case where there's already a NiftyServer registered by replacing it.

We wouldn't need the main( ) method or this Naming business if we weren't expecting clients to use the registry to find the server. That is, we could omit main( ) and still use this object as a remote object. We would just be limited to passing the object in method invocations or returning it from method invocations—but that could be part of a factory registry, as we discussed before.

Now we need our client:

```
//file: MyClient.java
import java.rmi.*;
import java.util.*;

public class MyClient {

    public static void main(String [] args)
      throws RemoteException {
        new MyClient( args[0] );
    }
```

```
    public MyClient(String host) {
        try {
            ServerRemote server = (ServerRemote)
                Naming.lookup("rmi://"+host+"/NiftyServer");
            System.out.println( server.getDate( ) );
            System.out.println(
                server.execute( new MyCalculation(2) ) );
        } catch (java.io.IOException e) {
            // I/O Error or bad URL
        } catch (NotBoundException e) {
            // NiftyServer isn't registered
        }
    }
}
```

When we run MyClient, we pass it the hostname of the server on which the registry is running. The main( ) method creates an instance of the MyClient object, passing the hostname from the command line as an argument to the constructor.

The constructor for MyClient uses the hostname to construct a URL for the object. The URL looks like this: *rmi://hostname/NiftyServer*. (Remember, NiftyServer is the name under which we registered our ServerRemote.) We pass the URL to the static Naming.lookup( ) method. If all goes well, we get back a reference to a ServerRemote (the remote interface). The registry has no idea what kind of object it will return; lookup( ) therefore returns an Object, which we must cast to ServerRemote, the remote interface type.

Running the example

If you're using Java 5.0, all you have to do is compile your code and you're ready to go. You can run the client and server on the same machine or on different machines. First, make sure all the classes are in your classpath (or the current directory if there is no classpath) and then start the rmiregistry and MyServer on your server host:

```
% rmiregistry &    (on Windows: start rmiregistry)
% java MyServer
```

Next, run the client, passing the name of the server host (or "localhost"):

```
% java MyClient myhost
```

The client should print the date and the number 4, which the server graciously calculated. Hooray! With just a few lines of code, you have created a powerful client/server application.

If you are using an earlier version of Java or wish to explicitly generate the client stub, you just have to take an extra step after compiling the code. Run the *rmic* application to make the stub and skeleton files for MyServer:

```
% rmic MyServer
```

You should see some additional classes generated. Make sure these are deployed on both the client and server machines' classpaths; read on to learn about an alternative to distributing the classes on both client and server.

Dynamic class loading

Before running the example, we told you to distribute all the class files to both the client and server machines. However, RMI was designed to ship classes, in addition to data, around the network; you shouldn't have to distribute all the classes in advance. Let's go a step further and have RMI load classes for us as needed. This involves several steps.

First, we need to tell RMI where to find any other classes it needs. We can use the system property java.rmi.server.codebase to specify a URL on a web server (or FTP server) when we run our client or server. This URL specifies the location of a JAR file or a base directory where RMI begins its search for classes. When RMI sends a serialized object (i.e., an object's data) to some client, it also sends this URL. If the recipient needs the class file in addition to the data, it fetches the file at the specified URL. In addition to stub classes, other classes referenced by remote objects in the application can be loaded dynamically. Therefore, we don't have to distribute many class files to the client; we can let the client download them as necessary. In Figure 13-3, we see an example of MyClient going to the registry to get a reference to the ServerRemote object. Once there MyClient dynamically downloads the stub class for MyServer from a web server running on the server object's host.

We can now split our class files more logically between the server and client machines. For example, we could withhold the MyCalculation class from the server since it really belongs to the client. Instead, we can make the MyCalculation class available via a web server on some machine (probably our client's) and specify the URL when we run MyClient:

```
% java -Djava.rmi.server.codebase='http://myserver/foo/' ...
```

The trailing slash in the codebase URL is important: it says that the location is a base directory that contains the class files. In this case, we would expect that MyCalculation would be accessible at the URL *http://myserver/foo/MyCalculation.class*.

Next, we have to set up security. Since we are loading class files over the network and executing their methods, we must have a security manager in place to restrict the kinds of things those classes may do, at least when they are not coming from a trusted code source. RMI will not load any classes dynamically unless a security manager is installed. One easy way to meet this condition is to install the RMISecurityManager as the system security manager for your application. It is an example security manager that works with the default system policy and imposes some basic restrictions on what downloaded classes can do. To install the RMISecurityManager, simply add the following line to the beginning of the main( )

Figure 13-3. RMI applications and dynamic class loading

method of both the client and server applications (yes, we'll be sending code both ways in the next section):

```
main( ) {
    System.setSecurityManager( new RMISecurityManager( ) );
    ...
```

The RMISecurityManager works with the system security policy file to enforce restrictions. You have to provide a policy file that allows the client and server to do basic operations like make network connections. Unfortunately, allowing all the operations needed to load classes dynamically requires listing a lot of permission information and we don't want to get into that here. We suggest that for this example you simply grant the code all permissions. Here is an example policy file—call it *mysecurity.policy*:

```
grant {
    permission java.security.AllPermission ;
};
```

(It's exceedingly lame, not to mention risky, to install a security manager and then tell it to enforce no real security, but we're more interested in looking at the networking code at the moment.)

To run our MyServer application, we would use a command such as:

```
% java -Djava.rmi.server.codebase='http://myserver/foo/' \
    -Djava.security.policy=mysecurity.policy MyServer
```

Finally, one last magical incantation is required to enable dynamic class loading. As of the current implementation, the rmiregistry must be run without the classes that are to be loaded being in its classpath. If the classes are in the classpath of rmiregistry, it does not annotate the serialized objects with the URLs of their class files, and no classes are dynamically loaded. This limitation is really annoying; all we can say is to heed the warning for now.

If you follow these directions, you should be able to run our client with only the MyClient class and the ServerRemote remote interface in its classpath. All the other classes are loaded dynamically from the specified server as needed.

Passing remote object references

So far, we haven't done anything that we couldn't have done with the simple object protocol. We used only one remote object, MyServer, and we got its reference from the RMI registry. Now we extend our example to pass some remote references between the client and server, allowing additional remote calls in both directions. We'll add two methods to our remote ServerRemote interface:

```
public interface ServerRemote extends Remote {
    ...
    StringIterator getList( ) throws RemoteException;
    void asyncExecute( WorkRequest work, WorkListener listener )
        throws RemoteException;
}
```

getList( ) retrieves a new kind of object from the server: a StringIterator. The StringIterator we've created is a simple list of strings with some methods for accessing the strings in order. We make it a remote object so that implementations of StringIterator stay on the server.

Next, we spice up our work request feature by adding an asyncExecute( ) method. asyncExecute( ) lets us hand off a WorkRequest object as before, but it does the calculation on its own time. The return type for asyncExecute( ) is void because it doesn't actually return a value; we get the result later. Along with the request, our client passes a reference to a WorkListener object that is to be notified when the WorkRequest is done. We'll have our client implement WorkListener itself.

Because this is to be a remote object, our interface must extend Remote and its methods must throw RemoteExceptions:

```
//file: StringIterator.java
import java.rmi.*;
```

```
public interface StringIterator extends Remote {
    public boolean hasNext( ) throws RemoteException;
    public String next( ) throws RemoteException;
}
```

Next, we provide a simple implementation of StringIterator, called MyStringIterator:

```
//file: MyStringIterator.java
import java.rmi.*;

public class MyStringIterator
  extends java.rmi.server.UnicastRemoteObject
  implements StringIterator {

    String [] list;
    int index = 0;

    public MyStringIterator( String [] list )
      throws RemoteException {
        this.list = list;
    }
    public boolean hasNext( ) throws RemoteException {
        return index < list.length;
    }
    public String next( ) throws RemoteException {
        return list[index++];
    }
}
```

MyStringIterator extends UnicastRemoteObject. Its methods are simple: it can give you the next string in the list, and it can tell you if there are any strings you haven't seen yet.

Next, we discuss the WorkListener remote interface that defines how an object should listen for a completed WorkRequest. It has one method, workCompleted( ), which the server executing a WorkRequest calls when the job is done:

```
//file: WorkListener.java
import java.rmi.*;

public interface WorkListener extends Remote {
    public void workCompleted(WorkRequest request, Object result )
        throws RemoteException;
}
```

Let's add the new features to MyServer. We need to add implementations of the getList( ) and asyncExecute( ) methods, which we just added to the ServerRemote interface:

```
public class MyServer extends java.rmi.server.UnicastRemoteObject
                      implements ServerRemote {
    ...
    public StringIterator getList( ) throws RemoteException {
```

```
      return new MyStringIterator(
          new String [] { "Foo", "Bar", "Gee" } );
    }

    public void asyncExecute(
        WorkRequest request , WorkListener listener )
        throws java.rmi.RemoteException
    {
      new Thread( ) {
        public void run( ) {
          Object result = request.execute( );
          try {
            listener.workCompleted( request, result );
          } catch ( RemoteException e ) {
            System.out.println( e ); // error calling client
          }
        }
      }}.start( );
    }
  }
```

getList( ) just returns a StringIterator with some stuff in it. asyncExecute( ) calls a
WorkRequest's execute( ) method and notifies the listener when it's done.
asyncExecute( ) runs the request in a separate thread, allowing the remote method
call to return immediately. Later, when the work is done, the server uses the client's
WorkListener interface to return the result.

We have to modify MyClient to implement the remote WorkListener interface. This
turns MyClient into a remote object, so we will have it extend UnicastRemoteObject.
We also add the workCompleted( ) method the WorkListener interface requires.
Finally, we want MyClient to exercise the new features. We've put all of this in a new
version of the client called MyClientAsync:

```
//file: MyClientAsync.java
import java.rmi.*;
import java.util.*;

public class MyClientAsync
    extends java.rmi.server.UnicastRemoteObject implements WorkListener
{

    public MyClientAsync(String host) throws RemoteException
    {
        try {
            RemoteServer server = (RemoteServer)
                Naming.lookup("rmi://"+host+"/NiftyServer");

            server.asyncExecute( new MyCalculation( 100 ), this );
            System.out.println("call done...");
        } catch (java.io.IOException e) {
            // I/O Error or bad URL
        } catch (NotBoundException e) {
            // NiftyServer isn't registered
        }
    }
```

```
    public void workCompleted( WorkRequest request, Object result )
        throws RemoteException
    {
        System.out.println("Async result: "+result );
    }

    public static void main(String [] args) throws RemoteException {
        new MyClientAsync( args[0] );
    }

}
```

We use getList( ) to get the iterator from the server and then loop, printing the strings. We also call asyncExecute( ) to perform another calculation; this time, we square the number 100. The second argument to asyncExecute( ) is the WorkListener to notify when the data is ready; we pass a reference to ourselves (this).

If you're running Java 5.0, just compile and you're ready to go. But if you need to generate the stubs, run *rmic* to make the stubs for all our remote objects:

`% rmic MyClient MyServer MyStringIterator`

Restart the RMI registry and MyServer on your server, and run the client somewhere. You should get the following:

```
Sun Mar 5 23:57:19 PDT 2006
4
Foo
Bar
Gee
Async work result = 10000
```

If you are experimenting with dynamic class loading, you should be able to have the client download all the server's auxiliary classes (the stubs and the StringIterator) from a web server. And, conversely, you should be able to have MyServer fetch the Client stub and WorkRequest-related classes when it needs them.

We hope that this introduction has given you a feel for the tremendous power that RMI offers through object serialization and dynamic class loading. Java is one of the first programming languages to offer this kind of powerful framework for distributed applications. Although some of the advanced features are not used widely in business applications, RMI is the underpinning for the very widely used J2EE Enterprise JavaBeans architecture and is an important technology. For more information on RMI and J2EE, see *Java Enterprise in a Nutshell* (O'Reilly).

RMI Object Activation

One of the newer features of RMI is the ability to create remote objects that are persistent. They can save their state for arbitrary periods of inactivity and be reactivated when a request from a client arrives. This is an important feature for large systems with remote objects that must remain accessible across long periods of time. RMI activation effectively allows a remote object to be stored—in a database, for example—and automatically reincarnated when it is needed. RMI activation is not particularly easy to use and would not have benefited us in any of our simple examples; we won't delve into it here. Much of the functionality of objects that can be activated can be achieved by using factories of shorter-lived objects that know how to retrieve some state from a database (or other location). The primary users of RMI activation may be systems such as Enterprise JavaBeans, which need a generalized mechanism to save remotely accessible objects and revive them at later times.

RMI and CORBA

Java supports an important alternative to RMI, called CORBA (Common Object Request Broker Architecture). We won't say much about CORBA here, but you should know that it exists. CORBA is an older distributed object standard developed by the Object Management Group (OMG), of which Sun Microsystems is one of the founding members. Its major advantage is that it works across languages: a Java program can use CORBA to talk to objects written in other languages, like C or C++. This is may be a considerable advantage if you want to build a Java frontend for an older program that you can't afford to reimplement. CORBA also provides other services similar to those in the Java Enterprise APIs. CORBA's major disadvantages are that it's complex, inelegant, and somewhat arcane.

In recent years, Sun and IBM worked together to implement an OMG standard that bridges RMI and CORBA. Java RMI over IIOP uses the Internet Inter-Object Protocol to provide some RMI-to-CORBA interoperability. However, CORBA currently does not have many of the semantics necessary to support true RMI-style distributed objects, so this solution, though part of the JDK as of Version 1.3, is somewhat limited.

Scalable I/O with NIO

We'll now conclude the discussion of the NIO package we began in Chapter 12 by talking about nonblocking and selectable network communications. All our server examples in this chapter have used a thread-bound pattern (one thread per I/O operation). In Java this is very natural because of the ease with which we can create threads. It's also very efficient, within limits. Problems arise when you try to build very large-scale servers using this style of client handling. While on a large machine it's certainly possible to have hundreds or even thousands of threads (especially if they're mostly idle, waiting for I/O), this is a resource-hungry solution. Every thread you start in Java consumes memory for its internal stack, and the performance of managing this number of threads is highly system-dependent.

An alternative approach is to take a lesson from the old, dark days before threading was available and use nonblocking I/O operations to manage a lot of communications from a single thread. Better yet, our server uses a configurable pool of threads, taking advantage of machines with many processors.

At the heart of this process is the concept of selectable I/O. It's not good enough to simply have nonblocking I/O operations if you have no way to efficiently poll for work to be done. The NIO package provides for efficient polling using *selectable channels*. A selectable channel allows for the registration of a special kind of listener called a *selector* that can check the readiness of the channel for operations, such as reading and writing or accepting or creating network connections.

The selector and the selection process are not typical Java listeners of the kind we'll see elsewhere in this book but instead rather slavishly follow the conventions of C language systems. This is mainly for performance reasons; since this API is primarily intended for high-volume servers, it is bound very tightly to the traditional, underlying operating system facilities with less regard for ease of use. This, combined with the other details of using the NIO package, mean that this section is somewhat dense and the server we create here is one of the longer and more complex examples in the book. Don't be discouraged if you are a bit put off by this section. You can use the general techniques earlier in this chapter for most applications and reserve this knowledge for creating services that handle very high volumes of simultaneous client requests.

Selectable Channels

A selectable channel implements the SelectableChannel interface, which specifies that the channel can be set to a nonblocking mode and that it provides support for the select process that makes efficient polling possible. As of Java 1.4, the primary selectable channels are those for working with the network: SocketChannel, ServerSocketChannel, and DatagramChannel. The only other selectable channel is the Pipe (which can be used in an analogous way for intra-VM communication).

At the heart of the process is the Selector object, which knows about a particular set of selectable channels and provides a select( ) method for determining their readiness for I/O operations. Conceptually, the process is simple; you register one or more channels with a selector and then poll it, asking it to tell you which set of channels is ready to go. In actuality, there are a few additional pieces involved.

First, the Selector does not work directly with channels but instead operates on SelectionKey objects. A SelectionKey object is created implicitly when the channel is registered with the Selector. It encapsulates the selectable channel as well as information about what types of operations (e.g., read, write) we are interested in waiting for. That information is held in the SelectionKey in a set of flags called the *interest set*, which can be changed by the application at any time. SelectionKeys are also used to return the results of a select operation. Each call to select( ) returns the number of SelectionKeys that are ready for some type of I/O. The keys are then retrieved with the selectedKeys( ) method. Each key also has a set of flags called the *ready set* that indicates which operation of interest is actually ready (possibly more than one). For example, a SelectionKey interest set might indicate that we want to know when its channel is ready for reading or writing. After a select operation, if that key is in the set returned by the selector, we know that it is ready for one or more of those operations, and we can check the key's ready set to see which.

Before we go on, we should say that although we have been saying that channels are registered with selectors, the API is (confusingly) the other way around. Selectors are actually registered with the channels they manage, but it's better to mentally spackle over this and think of them the other way around.

Using Select

A Selector object is created using the Selector.open( ) method (Selector uses a factory pattern):

```
Selector selector = Selector.open( );
```

To register one or more channels with the selector, set them to nonblocking mode:

```
SelectableChannel channelA = // ...
channelA.configureBlocking( false );
```

Next, register the channels:

```
int interestOps = SelectionKey.OP_READ | SelectionKey.OP_WRITE;
SelectionKey key = channelA.register( selector, interestOps );
```

When we register the channel, we have an opportunity to set the initial interest operations (or "interest ops"). These are defined by constant fields in the SelectionKey class:

OP_READ
    Ready to read

OP_WRITE
    Ready to write

OP_CONNECT
    Client-socket connection ready

OP_ACCEPT
    Server-socket connection ready

These fields are bit flags; you can OR them together as in this example to express interest in more than one type of operation.

The result of the register( ) method is a SelectionKey object. We can use the key to change the interest ops at any time with the SelectionKey interestOps( ) method or to unregister the channel from the Selector with the key's cancel( ) method.

This same key is also returned as the result of selection operations when its channel is ready. When the SelectionKey is returned, its ready set holds flags for the operations that do not block if called. We can retrieve the value of the flags with the readySet( ) method. Convenience methods are available to test for each operation in the ready set: isReadable( ), isWritable( ), isConnectable( ), and isAcceptable( ).

Depending on how you structure your application, it may not be necessary to save the SelectionKey at registration time. In our example, we let the Selector keep track of the keys for us, simply using them when they are ready. In fact, we go even further and put the SelectionKey to work by asking it to hold a reference for us! The SelectionKey attach( ) method is a convenience method that can attach an arbitrary object to the key for use by our application. We show how this can be useful in a bit.

Once one or more channels are registered with the Selector, we can perform a select operation using one of its select( ) methods:

```
int readyCount = selector.select( );
```

Without arguments, the method blocks until at least one channel is ready for some operation or until the Selector's wakeup( ) method is called. Alternatively, you can use the form of select( ) that takes a timeout (in milliseconds) to wait for a ready channel before returning. There is also selectNow( ), which always returns immediately. Each of these returns the count of the number of ready channels.

You can use select( ) and wakeup( ) somewhat like wait( ) and notify( ). The wakeup is necessary because once a selection is started, it will not see any changes to its key's interest ops until the next invocation. If another thread changes the interest ops, it must use wakeup( ) to prompt the selecting thread to select( ) again. The Selector is also heavily synchronized; for example, calls to register new channels block until the select is finished. Often it's much easier to simply use select with a short timeout and a loop, like this:

```
while ( selector.select( 50 ) == 0 );
```

However, if another thread is allowed to change the interest ops, you still need to use wakeup( ) to maximize throughput. Otherwise, in the worst case, you could end up waiting the full select wait period on every iteration, even when there is work to be done.

Next, we can get the set of ready channels from the Selector with the selectedKeys( ) method and iterate through them, doing whatever our application dictates:

```
Set readySet = selector.selectedKeys( );
for( Iterator it = readySet.iterator( ); it.hasNext( ); ) {
    SelectionKey key = (SelectionKey)it.next( );
```

```
        it.remove( );  // remove the key from the ready set
    // use the key
    }
```

The ready set is returned to us as a java.util.Set, which we walk through with an Iterator (see Chapter 1). One important thing to note is that we've used the Iterator's remove( ) method to remove the key from the ready set. The select( ) methods add keys only to the ready set or add flags to keys already in the set; they never remove them, so we must clear the keys when we handle them. You can get the full set of keys a Selector is managing with the keys( ) method, but you should not attempt to remove keys from that set; use the cancel( ) method on individual keys instead. Or you can close the entire Selector with its close( ) method, unregistering all its keys.

LargerHttpd

Let's put this information to use. In this section, we create the big brother of TinyHttpd (our minimalist web server) called LargerHttpd. The LargerHttpd server is a nonblocking web server that uses SocketChannels and a pool of threads to service requests. In this example, a single thread executes a main loop that accepts new connections and checks the readiness of existing client connections for reading or writing. Whenever a client needs attention, it places the job in a queue where a thread from our thread pool waits to service it. As we said, this example is a bit longer than we would like, but it is really the minimum necessary to show a realistic usage of the APIs:

```
import java.io.*;
import java.util.*;
import java.util.concurrent.*;
import java.net.*;
import java.nio.*;
import java.nio.channels.*;
import java.nio.charset.*;
import java.util.regex.*;

public class LargerHttpd {
  Selector clientSelector;

  public void run( int port, int threads ) throws IOException
  {
    clientSelector = Selector.open( );
    ServerSocketChannel ssc = ServerSocketChannel.open( );
    ssc.configureBlocking(false);
    InetSocketAddress sa =
      new InetSocketAddress( InetAddress.getLocalHost( ), port );
    ssc.socket( ).bind( sa );
    ssc.register( clientSelector, SelectionKey.OP_ACCEPT );
    Executor executor = Executors.newFixedThreadPool( threads );
```

```
        while ( true )
        try {
          while ( clientSelector.select(100) == 0 );
          Set<SelectionKey> readySet = clientSelector.selectedKeys();
          for(Iterator<SelectionKey> it=readySet.iterator(); it.hasNext();) {
            final SelectionKey key = it.next();
            it.remove();
            if ( key.isAcceptable() )
              acceptClient( ssc );
            else {
              key.interestOps( 0 );
              executor.execute( new Runnable() {
                public void run() {
                  try {
                    handleClient( key );
                  } catch ( IOException e ) { System.out.println(e); }
                }
              } );
            }
          }
        } catch ( IOException e ) { System.out.println(e); }
      }

      void acceptClient( ServerSocketChannel ssc ) throws IOException {
        SocketChannel clientSocket = ssc.accept();
        clientSocket.configureBlocking(false);
        SelectionKey key =
          clientSocket.register( clientSelector, SelectionKey.OP_READ );
        HttpdConnection client = new HttpdConnection( clientSocket );
        key.attach( client );
      }

      void handleClient( SelectionKey key ) throws IOException {
        HttpdConnection client = (HttpdConnection)key.attachment();
        if ( key.isReadable() )
          client.read( key );
        else
          client.write( key );
        clientSelector.wakeup();
      }

      public static void main( String argv[] ) throws IOException {
        new LargerHttpd().run( Integer.parseInt(argv[0]), 3/*threads*/ );
      }
    }

    class HttpdConnection {
      static Charset charset = Charset.forName("8859_1");
      static Pattern httpGetPattern = Pattern.compile("(?s)GET /?(\\S*).*");
      SocketChannel clientSocket;
      ByteBuffer buff = ByteBuffer.allocateDirect( 64*1024 );
      String request;
      String response;
```

```
    FileChannel file;
    int filePosition;

    HttpdConnection ( SocketChannel clientSocket ) {
      this.clientSocket = clientSocket;
    }

    void read( SelectionKey key ) throws IOException {
      if ( request == null && (clientSocket.read( buff ) == -1
          || buff.get( buff.position( )-1 ) == '\n' ) )
        processRequest( key );
      else
        key.interestOps( SelectionKey.OP_READ );
    }

    void processRequest( SelectionKey key ) {
      buff.flip( );
      request = charset.decode( buff ).toString( );
      Matcher get = httpGetPattern.matcher( request );
      if ( get.matches( ) ) {
        request = get.group(1);
        if ( request.endsWith("/") || request.equals("") )
          request = request + "index.html";
        System.out.println( "Request: "+request);
        try {
          file = new FileInputStream ( request ).getChannel( );
        } catch ( FileNotFoundException e ) {
          response = "404 Object Not Found";
        }
      } else
        response = "400 Bad Request" ;

      if ( response != null ) {
        buff.clear( );
        charset.newEncoder( ).encode(
          CharBuffer.wrap( response ), buff, true );
        buff.flip( );
      }
      key.interestOps( SelectionKey.OP_WRITE );
    }

    void write( SelectionKey key ) throws IOException {
      if ( response != null ) {
        clientSocket.write( buff );
        if ( buff.remaining( ) == 0 )
          response = null;
      } else if ( file != null ) {
        int remaining = (int)file.size( )-filePosition;
        long sent = file.transferTo( filePosition, remaining, clientSocket);
        if ( sent >= remaining || remaining <= 0 ) {
          file.close( );
          file = null;
        } else
          filePosition += sent;
```

```
        }
        if ( response == null && file == null ) {
          clientSocket.close( );
          key.cancel( );
        } else
          key.interestOps( SelectionKey.OP_WRITE );
      }
    }
```

From a bird's eye view, the structure of LargerHttpd is the same as TinyHttpd. The main class, LargerHttpd, accepts connections, and a connection class, HttpdConnection, encapsulates a socket and handles the conversation with the client. However this time, instead of each connection object being a Runnable serviced in its own thread, its functionality is broken into two primary methods called read( ) and write( ). The job of our LargerHttpd is to accept new client socket connections, wrap them in an instance of HttpdConnection, and then watch the client's status with a Selector. Whenever we detect that a client is ready to send or receive data, we hand off a Runnable task to our Executor. The task calls read( ) or write( ) on the corresponding client, based on which operation is ready.

The HttpConnection object encapsulates the state of the conversation with the client. Since its interface is rather coarse, it must keep track of whether it is waiting to read more input, generate a response, or write file output. The HttpdConnection also manages the interest set of its key, so that it can effectively schedule itself to be woken up when it's ready for reading or writing. The association between the HttpdConnection and the key is made using the key's attach( ) and attachment( ) methods.

LargerHttpd's acceptClient( ) method does several things. First, it accepts the new socket connection. Next, it configures and registers it with the selector with an initial interest set for reading. Finally, it creates the HttpdConnection for the socket, and attaches the HttpdConnection object to the key for later retrieval.

The main loop of LargerHttpd is fairly straightforward. First, we set up the ServerSocketChannel. This is similar to setting up a plain ServerSocket, except that we must first create an InetSocketAddress object to hold the local address and port combination of our server socket and then explicitly bind our socket to that address with the ServerSocketChannel bind( ) method. We also configure the server socket to nonblocking mode and register it with our main Selector so that we can select for client connections in the same loop that we use to select for client read and write readiness.

In the main select loop, we check whether the key is ready for an accept operation and if so, we call acceptClient( ); if not, we set the key's interest set to zero with the interestOps( ) method and dispatch the key to our handleClient( ) method via a Runnable task. It's important that we change the interest set to zero to clear it before the next loop; otherwise, we'd be in a race to see whether the thread pool performed its maximum work before we detected another ready condition. Setting the interest ops to 0 and resetting it in the HttpdConnection object upon completion ensures that only one thread is handling a given client at a time.

For each operation that is ready, we dispatch a task to our Executor. The task calls handleClient( ), passing it the selection key. From the key, we retrieve the associated HttpdConnection object and call the appropriate service method based on whether the key is ready for reading or writing. After that, it's up to the connection object to do its job. Each call to the read( ) method simply does what would be one iteration of a read loop in a thread-bound application. Each read gets as much data as available and checks to see whether we've reached the end of a line (a \n newline character). Upon reaching the end of a line, we dispatch the call to the processRequest( ) method, which turns the byte buffer into text and uses the same techniques as our TinyHttpd to parse the request into a file pathname. On each incomplete call to read( ), we set the interest ops of our key back to OP_READ. Upon completing the read and processing the request, we switch to using OP_WRITE because we are now ready to send a response.

The write( ) method keeps track of whether it's sending a text response (error message) or a file, using the response and file instance variables. When sending a file, we use the FileChannel's transferTo( ) method to transfer bytes from the file directly to the network socket, without copying them into Java's memory space. (This is indeed an efficient little web server.) And that's about it. When we're done, we close the client socket and cancel our key, which causes it to be removed from the Selector's key set during the next select operation (discarding our HttpdConnection object with it).

Nonblocking Client-Side Operations

Our example showed SocketChannel used for nonblocking, selectable I/O in a typical server application. It's less common to need nonblocking I/O from a client, but there is certainly no reason you can't do it. Perhaps you're writing a peer-to-peer (P2P) application that manages many connections from both sides.

For the client side of communications, one additional tool is provided: a nonblocking socket-connect operation. The process of creating a TCP connection from the client side involves contacting the remote host in a two-phase acknowledgment. This process normally blocks until the connection is established. However, the NIO package provides an alternative that allows you to initiate the connection and then poll for its status. When set to nonblocking mode, a call to a SocketChannel's connect( ) method returns immediately. The connection is then attempted (and possibly succeeds or fails) in the background. Later, a Selector can be used, checking for the OP_CONNECT flag to see when the socket is ready to "finish connecting." The connection is finished by invoking the SocketChannel's finishConnect( ) method, which either returns or throws an IOException indicating the failure. The process of finishing the connection is really more about collecting the results of the asynchronous connection—acknowledging its success or failure—than about doing work.

## CHAPTER 14

Programming for the Web

When you think about the Web, you probably think of applications—web browsers, web servers—and the many kinds of content that those applications move around the network. But it's important to note that standards and protocols, not the applications themselves, have enabled the Web's growth. Since the earliest days of the Internet, there have been ways to move files from here to there, and document formats that were just as powerful as HTML, but there was not a unifying model for how to identify, retrieve, and display information nor was there a universal way for applications to interact with that data over the network. Since the web explosion began, HTML has reigned supreme as a common format for documents, and most developers have at least some familiarity with it. In this chapter, we're going to talk a bit about its cousin, HTTP, the protocol that handles communications between web clients and servers, and URLs, which provide a standard for naming and addressing objects on the Web. Java provides a very simple API for working with URLs to address objects on the Web. We'll discuss how to write web clients that can interact with the servers using the HTTP GET and POST methods and also say a bit about web services, which are the next step up the evolutionary chain. In Chapter 15, we'll jump over to the server side and take a look at servlets, Java programs that run on web servers and implement the other side of these conversations.

Uniform Resource Locators (URLs)

A URL points to an object on the Internet.[*] It's a text string that identifies an item, tells you where to find it, and specifies a method for communicating with it or retrieving it from its source. A URL can refer to any kind of information source. It might point to static data, such as a file on a local filesystem, a web server, or an FTP

---

[*] The term URL was coined by the Uniform Resource Identifier (URI) working group of the IETF to distinguish URLs from the more general notion of Uniform Resource Names or URNs (see RFC 2396), described later in this chapter.

site; or it can point to a more dynamic object such as an RSS news feed or a record in a database. URLs can even refer to less tangible resources such as Telnet sessions and email addresses.

Since there are many different ways to locate an item on the Net and different mediums and transports require different kinds of information, URLs can have many forms. The most common form has four components: a network host or server, the name of the item, its location on that host, and a protocol by which the host should communicate:

>   protocol://hostname/path/item-name

protocol (also called the "scheme") is an identifier such as http or ftp, *hostname* is usually an internet hostname, and the *path* and *item* components form a unique path that identifies the object on that host. Variants of this form allow extra information to be packed into the URL, specifying, for example, port numbers for the communications protocol and fragment identifiers that reference sections inside documents. Other more specialized types of URLs such as "mailto" URLs for email addresses or URLs for addressing things like database components may not follow this format precisely but do conform to the general notion of a protocol followed by a unique identifier.

Since most URLs have the notion of a hierarchy or path, we sometimes speak of a URL that is relative to another URL, called a *base URL*. In that case, we are using the base URL as a starting point and supplying additional information to target an object relative to that URL. For example, the base URL might point to a directory on a web server; a relative URL might name a particular file in that directory or in a subdirectory.

The URL Class

Bringing this down to a more concrete level is the Java URL class. The URL class represents a URL address and provides a simple API for accessing web resources, such as documents and applications on servers. It can use an extensible set of protocol and content handlers to perform the necessary communication and even data conversion. With the URL class, an application can open a connection to a server on the network and retrieve content with just a few lines of code. As new types of servers and new formats for content evolve, additional URL handlers can be supplied to retrieve and interpret the data without modifying your applications.

A URL is represented by an instance of the java.net.URL class. A URL object manages all the component information within a URL string and provides methods for retrieving the object it identifies. We can construct a URL object from a URL string or from its component parts:

```
try {
    URL aDoc =
        new URL( "http://foo.bar.com/documents/homepage.html" );
```

```
    URL sameDoc =
        new URL("http","foo.bar.com","documents/homepage.html");
    }
    catch ( MalformedURLException e ) { }
```

These two URL objects point to the same network resource, the *homepage.html* document on the server *foo.bar.com*. Whether the resource actually exists and is available isn't known until we try to access it. When initially constructed, the URL object contains only data about the object's location and how to access it. No connection to the server has been made. We can examine the various parts of the URL with the getProtocol( ), getHost( ), and getFile( ) methods. We can also compare it to another URL with the sameFile( ) method (which has an unfortunate name for something which may not point to a file). sameFile( ) determines whether two URLs point to the same resource. It can be fooled, but sameFile( ) does more than compare the URL strings for equality; it takes into account the possibility that one server may have several names as well as other factors. (It doesn't go as far as to fetch the resources and compare them, however.)

When a URL is created, its specification is parsed to identify just the protocol component. If the protocol doesn't make sense, or if Java can't find a protocol handler for it, the URL constructor throws a MalformedURLException. A *protocol handler* is a Java class that implements the communications protocol for accessing the URL resource. For example, given an http URL, Java prepares to use the HTTP protocol handler to retrieve documents from the specified web server.

As of Java 5.0, URL protocol handlers are guaranteed to be provided for http, https (secure HTTP), and ftp as well as local file URLs and jar URLs that refer to files inside JAR archives. Outside of that, it gets a little dicey. We'll talk more about the issues surrounding content and protocol handlers a bit later in this chapter.

Stream Data

The lowest level and most general way to get data back from a URL is to ask for an InputStream from the URL by calling openStream( ). Getting the data as a stream may also be useful if you want to receive continuous updates from a dynamic information source. The drawback is that you have to parse the contents of the byte stream yourself. Working in this mode is basically the same as working with a byte stream from socket communications, but the URL protocol handler has already dealt with all of the server communications and is providing you with just the content portion of the transaction. Not all types of URLs support the openStream( ) method because not all types of URLs refer to concrete data; you'll get an UnknownServiceException if the URL doesn't.

The following code prints the contents of an HTML file on a web server:

```
    try {
        URL url = new URL("http://server/index.html");
```

```
    BufferedReader bin = new BufferedReader (
        new InputStreamReader( url.openStream() ) );

    String line;
    while ( (line = bin.readLine()) != null )
        System.out.println( line );
} catch (Exception e) { }
```

We ask for an InputStream with openStream( ) and wrap it in a BufferedReader to read the lines of text. Because we specify the http protocol in the URL, we enlist the services of an HTTP protocol handler. Note that we haven't talked about content handlers yet. In this case, since we're reading directly from the input stream, no content handler (no transformation of the content data) is involved.

One note about applets. In the applet environment, you typically have additional security restrictions that limit the URLs to which you may communicate. To be sure that you can access the specified URL and use the correct protocol handler, you should construct URLs relative to the base URL that identifies the applet's *codebase*— the location of the applet code. This ensures that any data you load comes via the same protocol and from the same server as your applet. For example:

```
    new URL( getCodeBase(), "foo/bar.gif" );
```

Alternately, if you are just trying to get data files or media associated with an applet, there is a more general way; see the discussion of getResource( ) in Chapter 12.

Getting the Content as an Object

As we said previously, reading raw content from a stream is the most general mechanism for accessing data over the Web. openStream( ) leaves the parsing of data up to you. The URL class, however, supports a more sophisticated, pluggable, content-handling mechanism that we'll discuss now, but be aware that this is not widely used because of lack of standardization and limitations in how you can deploy new handlers. Although the Java community made some progress in Java 5.0 in standardizing a small set of protocol handlers, no such effort was made to standardize content handlers. This means that although this part of the discussion is interesting, its usefulness is limited.

The way it's supposed to work is that when Java knows the type of content being retrieved from a URL, and a proper content handler is available, you can retrieve the URL addresses as an appropriate Java object by calling the URL's getContent( ) method. In this mode of operation, getContent( ) initiates a connection to the host, fetches the data for you, determines the type of data, and then invokes a content handler to turn the bytes into a Java object. It acts sort of as if you had read a serialized Java object, as in Chapter 13. Java will try to determine the type of the content by looking at its MIME type, its file extension, or even by examining the bytes directly.

For example, given the URL *http://foo.bar.com/index.html*, a call to getContent( ) uses the HTTP protocol handler to retrieve data and might use an HTML content handler to turn the data into an appropriate document object. Similarly, a GIF file might be turned into an AWT Image or an ImageProducer object using a GIF content handler. If we access the GIF file using an FTP URL, Java would use the same content handler but a different protocol handler to receive the data.

Since the content handler must be able to return any type of object, the return type of getContent( ) is Object. This might leave us wondering what kind of object we got. In a moment, we'll describe how we could ask the protocol handler about the object's MIME type. Based on this, and whatever other knowledge we have about the kind of object we are expecting, we can cast the Object to its appropriate, more specific type. For example, if we expect an image, we might cast the result of getContent( ) to ImageProducer:

```
try {
    ImageProducer ip = (ImageProducer)myURL.getContent( );
} catch ( ClassCastException e ) { ... }
```

Various kinds of errors can occur when trying to retrieve the data. For example, getContent( ) can throw an IOException if there is a communications error. Other kinds of errors can occur at the application level: some knowledge of how the application-specific content and protocol handlers deal with errors is necessary. One problem that could arise is that a content handler for the data's MIME type wouldn't be available. In this case, getContent( ) invokes a special "unknown type" handler that returns the data as a raw InputStream (back to square one).

In some situations, we may also need knowledge of the protocol handler. For example, consider a URL that refers to a nonexistent file on an HTTP server. When requested, the server returns the familiar "404 Not Found" message. To deal with protocol-specific operations like this, we may need to talk to the protocol handler, which we'll discuss next.

Managing Connections

Upon calling openStream( ) or getContent( ) on a URL, the protocol handler is consulted and a connection is made to the remote server or location. Connections are represented by a URLConnection object, subtypes of which manage different protocol-specific communications and offer additional metadata about the source. The HttpURLConnection class, for example, handles basic web requests and also adds some HTTP-specific capabilities such as interpreting "404 Not Found" messages and other web server errors. We'll talk more about HttpURLConnection later in this chapter.

We can get a URLConnection from our URL directly with the openConnection( ) method. One of the things we can do with the URLConnection is ask for the object's content type, before reading data. For example:

```
URLConnection connection = myURL.openConnection( );
String mimeType = connection.getContentType( );
InputStream in = connection.getInputStream( );
```

Despite its name, a URLConnection object is initially created in a raw, unconnected state. In this example, the network connection was not actually initiated until we called the getContentType( ) method. The URLConnection does not talk to the source until data is requested or its connect( ) method is explicitly invoked. Prior to connection, network parameters and protocol-specific features can be set up. For example, as of Java 5.0, we can set timeouts on the initial connection to the server and on reads:

```
URLConnection connection = myURL.openConnection( );
connection.setConnectTimeout( 10000 ); // milliseconds
connection.setReadTimeout( 10000 ); // milliseconds
InputStream in = connection.getInputStream( );
```

As we'll see in the section "Using the POST Method," by casting the URLConnection to its specific subtype we can get at the protocol-specific information.

Handlers in Practice

The content- and protocol-handler mechanisms we've described are very flexible; to handle new types of URLs, you need only add the appropriate handler classes. One interesting application of this would be Java-based web browsers that could handle new and specialized kinds of URLs by downloading them over the Net. The idea for this was touted since the earliest days of Java. Unfortunately, it has never come to fruition. There is no API for dynamically downloading new content and protocol handlers. In fact, there is no standard API for determining what content and protocol handlers exist on a given platform.

Although Java 5.0 mandates protocol handlers for HTTP, HTTPS, FTP, FILE, and JAR, earlier versions of Java made no such guarantees. While in practice you will generally find these basic protocol handlers with all versions of Java, that's not entirely comforting and the story for content handlers is even less clear. The standard Java classes don't, for example, include content handlers for HTML, GIF, JPEG, or other common data types. Furthermore, although content and protocol handlers are part of the Java API and an intrinsic part of the mechanism for working with URLs, specific content and protocol handlers aren't defined. Even those protocol handlers that have been required in Java 5.0 are still packaged as part of the Sun implementation classes and are not truly part of the core API for all to see.

There are two real issues:

- There isn't a complete standard that says that certain types of handlers have to be provided in each environment along with the core Java API. Instead, we have to rely on the application to decide what kinds of data types it needs. This may make sense but is frustrating when it should be reasonable to expect certain basic types to be handled in all environments.

- No standard tells you what kind of object the content handler should return. Maybe GIF data should be returned as an `ImageProducer` object, but at the moment, that's an application-level decision. If you're writing your own application and your own content handlers, that isn't an issue: you can make any decision you want. (In practical terms, few developers take this approach.) But if you're writing content handlers for arbitrary applications, you need to know what they expect.

In summary, the Java content- and protocol-handler mechanism is a forward-thinking approach that never quite materialized. The promise of web browsers that dynamically extend themselves for new types of protocols and new content is, like flying cars, always just a few years away. Although the basic mechanics of the protocol-handler mechanism are useful (especially now with Java 5.0), for decoding content in your own applications you should probably turn to other, newer frameworks that have a bit more specificity.

Other Handler Frameworks

The idea of dynamically downloadable handlers could also be applied to other kinds of handler-like components. For example, the Java XML community is fond of referring to XML as a way to apply semantics to documents and to Java as a portable way to supply the behavior that goes along with those semantics. It's possible that an XML viewer could be built with downloadable handlers for displaying XML tags.

The JavaBeans APIs also touch upon this subject with the Java Activation Framework (JAF), which provides a way to detect the data stream type and "encapsulate access to it" in a Java bean. If this sounds suspiciously like the content handler's job, it is. Unfortunately, it looks like these APIs will not be merged and, outside of the Java Mail API, the JAF has not been widely used.

Fortunately, for working with URL streams of images, music, and video, very mature APIs are available. The Java Advanced Imaging API (JAI) includes a well-defined, extensible set of handlers for most image types, and the Java Media Framework (JMF) can play most common music and video types found online.

Writing Content and Protocol Handlers

Although content and protocol handlers are used fairly extensively in the internals of Java, they have not been leveraged much by developers for their own applications. We discussed some of the reasons for this earlier. But, if you're adventurous and want to try utilizing content and protocol handlers in your own applications or you have a need to retrofit an existing application, you can find out more in the *extras* folder on the CD accompanying this book. There you'll find a full chapter with examples covering everything you'll need to write your own content and protocol handlers.

Talking to Web Applications

Web browsers are the universal clients for web applications. They retrieve documents for display and serve as a user interface, primarily through the use of HTML forms and linked documents. Next, we show how to write client-side Java code that uses HTTP through the URL class to work with web applications directly using GET and POST operations to retrieve and send data. Later in this chapter, we'll begin a discussion of web services, which marry HTTP with XML to enable cross-platform application-to-application communications using web standards.

There are many reasons an application (or applet) might want to communicate via HTTP. For example, compatibility with another browser-based application might be important, or you might need to gain access to a server through a firewall where direct socket connections (and, hence, RMI or IIOP) are not available. HTTP is the lingua franca of the Net and despite its limitations (or more likely because of its simplicity), it has rapidly become one of the most widely supported protocols in the world. As for using Java on the client side, all the other reasons you would write a client GUI application (as opposed to a pure Web/HTML-based application) also present themselves. A client-side GUI can do sophisticated presentation and validation while, with the techniques presented here, still use web-enabled services over the network.

The primary task we discuss here is sending data to the server, specifically HTML form-encoded data. In a web browser, the name/value pairs of HTML form fields are encoded in a special format and sent to the server using one of two methods. The first method, using the HTTP GET command, encodes the user's input into the URL and requests the corresponding document. The server recognizes that the first part of the URL refers to a program and invokes it, passing along the information encoded in the URL as a parameter. The second method uses the HTTP POST command to ask the server to accept the encoded data and pass it to a web application as a stream. In Java, we can create a URL that refers to a server-side program and request or send it data using the GET and POST methods. (In Chapter 15, we'll see how to build web applications that implement the other side of this conversation.)

Using the GET Method

Using the GET method of encoding data in a URL is pretty easy. All we have to do is create a URL pointing to a server program and use a simple convention to tack on the encoded name/value pairs that make up our data. For example, the following code snippet opens a URL to a CGI program called *login.cgi* on the server *myhost* and passes it two name/value pairs. It then prints whatever text the CGI sends back:

```
URL url = new URL(
    // this string should be URL-encoded
    "http://myhost/cgi-bin/login.cgi?Name=Pat&Password=foobar");

BufferedReader bin = new BufferedReader (
  new InputStreamReader( url.openStream() ));

String line;
while ( (line = bin.readLine()) != null )
    System.out.println( line );
```

To form the URL with parameters, we start with the base URL of *login.cgi*; we add a question mark (?), which marks the beginning of the parameter data, followed by the first name/value pair. We can add as many pairs as we want, separated by ampersand (&) characters. The rest of our code simply opens the stream and reads back the response from the server. Remember that creating a URL doesn't actually open the connection. In this case, the URL connection was made implicitly when we called openStream( ). Although we are assuming here that our server sends back text, it could send anything. (In theory, we could use the getContentType( ) method of the URL to check the MIME type of any returned data and try to retrieve the data as an object using getContent( ) as well.)

It's important to point out that we have skipped a step here. This example works because our name/value pairs happen to be simple text. If any "nonprintable" or special characters (including ? or &) are in the pairs, they must be encoded first. The java.net.URLEncoder class provides a utility for encoding the data. We'll show how to use it in the next example.

Another important thing is that although this small example sends a password field, you should never send sensitive data using this simplistic approach. The data in this example is sent in clear text across the network (it is not encrypted). And in this case, the password field would appear anywhere the URL is printed as well (e.g., server logs and bookmarks). We'll talk about secure web communications later in this chapter and when we discuss writing web applications using servlets in Chapter 15.

Using the POST Method

Here's a small application that acts like an HTML form. It gathers data from two text fields—name and password—and posts the data to a specified URL using the HTTP

POST method. This Swing-based client application works with a server-side web-based application, just like a web browser.

Here's the code:

```java
//file: Post.java
import java.net.*;
import java.io.*;
import java.awt.*;
import java.awt.event.*;
import javax.swing.*;

public class Post extends JPanel implements ActionListener {
  JTextField nameField, passwordField;
  String postURL;

  GridBagConstraints constraints = new GridBagConstraints();
  void addGB( Component component, int x, int y ) {
    constraints.gridx = x;  constraints.gridy = y;
    add ( component, constraints );
  }

  public Post( String postURL ) {
    this.postURL = postURL;
    JButton postButton = new JButton("Post");
    postButton.addActionListener( this );
    setLayout( new GridBagLayout() );
    addGB( new JLabel("Name:"), 0,0 );
    addGB( nameField = new JTextField(20), 1,0 );
    addGB( new JLabel("Password:"), 0,1 );
    addGB( passwordField = new JPasswordField(20),1,1 );
    constraints.gridwidth = 2;
    addGB( postButton, 0,2 );
  }

  public void actionPerformed(ActionEvent e) {
    postData();
  }

  protected void postData() {
    StringBuffer sb = new StringBuffer();
    sb.append( URLEncoder.encode("Name") + "=" );
    sb.append( URLEncoder.encode(nameField.getText()) );
    sb.append( "&" + URLEncoder.encode("Password") + "=" );
    sb.append( URLEncoder.encode(passwordField.getText()) );
    String formData = sb.toString();

    try {
      URL url = new URL( postURL );
      HttpURLConnection urlcon =
          (HttpURLConnection) url.openConnection();
      urlcon.setRequestMethod("POST");
      urlcon.setRequestProperty("Content-type",
          "application/x-www-form-urlencoded");
```

```
        urlcon.setDoOutput(true);
        urlcon.setDoInput(true);
        PrintWriter pout = new PrintWriter( new OutputStreamWriter(
            urlcon.getOutputStream( ), "8859_1"), true );
        pout.print( formData );
        pout.flush( );

        // read results...
        if ( urlcon.getResponseCode( ) == HttpURLConnection.HTTP_OK )
          System.out.println("Posted ok!");
        else {
          System.out.println("Bad post...");
          return;
        }
        //InputStream in = urlcon.getInputStream( );
        // ...

      } catch (MalformedURLException e) {
        System.out.println(e);       // bad postURL
      } catch (IOException e2) {
        System.out.println(e2);      // I/O error
      }
    }

  public static void main( String [] args ) {
    JFrame frame = new JFrame("SimplePost");
    frame.getContentPane( ).add( new Post( args[0] ), "Center" );
    frame.pack( );
    frame.setVisible(true);
  }
}
```

When you run this application, you must specify the URL of the server program on the command line. For example:

```
% java Post http://www.myserver.example/cgi-bin/login.cgi
```

The beginning of the application creates the form; there's nothing here that won't be obvious after you've read Chapters 16 through 18, which cover the AWT and Swing GUI toolkits. All the magic happens in the protected postData( ) method. First, we create a StringBuffer and load it with name/value pairs, separated by ampersands. (We don't need the initial question mark when we're using the POST method because we're not appending to a URL string.) Each pair is first encoded using the static URLEncoder.encode( ) method. We run the name fields through the encoder as well as the value fields, even though we know that in this case they contain no special characters.

Next, we set up the connection to the server program. In our previous example, we didn't have to do anything special to send the data because the request was made by the simple act of opening the URL on the server. Here, we have to carry some of the weight of talking to the remote web server. Fortunately, the HttpURLConnection object does most of the work for us; we just have to tell it that we want to do a POST to the

URL and the type of data we are sending. We ask for the URLConnection object using the URL's openConnection( ) method. We know that we are using the HTTP protocol, so we should be able to cast it to an HttpURLConnection type, which has the support we need. As of Java 5.0, we can safely make this assumption because HTTP is always supported.

We then use setRequestMethod( ) to tell the connection we want to do a POST operation. We also use setRequestProperty( ) to set the Content-Type field of our HTTP request to the appropriate type—in this case, the proper MIME type for encoded form data. (This is necessary to tell the server what kind of data we're sending.) Finally, we use the setDoOutput( ) and setDoInput( ) methods to tell the connection that we want to both send and receive stream data. The URL connection infers from this combination that we are going to do a POST operation and expects a response. Next, we get an output stream from the connection with getOutputStream( ) and create a PrintWriter so we can easily write our encoded data.

After we post the data, our application calls getResponseCode( ) to see whether the HTTP response code from the server indicates the POST was successful. Other response codes (defined as constants in HttpURLConnection) indicate various failures. At the end of our example, we indicate where we could have read back the text of the response. For this application, we'll assume that simply knowing the post was successful is sufficient.

Although form-encoded data (as indicated by the MIME type we specified for the Content-Type field) is the most common, other types of communications are possible. We could have used the input and output streams to exchange arbitrary data types with the server program. The POST operation could send any kind of data; the server application simply has to know how to handle it. One final note: if you are writing an application that needs to decode form data, you can use the java.net. URLDecoder to undo the operation of the URLEncoder. If you use the Servlet API, this happens automatically, as you'll see in Chapter 15.

The HttpURLConnection

Other information from the request is available from the HttpURLConnection as well. We could use getContentType( ) and getContentEncoding( ) to determine the MIME type and encoding of the response. We could also interrogate the HTTP response headers using getHeaderField( ). (HTTP response headers are metadata name/value pairs carried with the response.) Convenience methods can fetch integer and date-formatted header fields, getHeaderFieldInt( ) and getHeaderFieldDate( ), which return an int and a long type, respectively. The content length and last modification date are provided through getContentLength( ) and getLastModified( ).

SSL and Secure Web Communications

The previous examples sent a field called `Password` to the server. However, standard HTTP doesn't provide encryption to hide our data. Fortunately, adding security for `GET` and `POST` operations like this is easy (trivial in fact, for the developer). Where available you simply have to use a secure form of the HTTP protocol—HTTPS:

```
https://www.myserver.example/cgi-bin/login.cgi
```

HTTPS is a version of the standard HTTP protocol run over Secure Sockets Layer (SSL), which uses public-key encryption techniques to encrypt the browser-to-server communications. Most web browsers and servers currently come with built-in support for HTTPS (or raw SSL sockets). Therefore, if your web server supports HTTPS, you can use a browser to send and receive secure data by specifying the `https` protocol in your URLs. There is much more to learn about SSL and related aspects of security such as authenticating whom you are actually talking to, but as far as basic data encryption goes, this is all you have to do. It is not something your code has to deal with directly. As of Java 1.4, the standard distribution from Sun is shipped with SSL and HTTPS support, and as of Java 5.0, all Java implementations must support HTTPS as well as HTTP for URL connections. This applies to applets using the Java Plug-in as well as applications. We'll discuss writing secure web applications in more detail in Chapter 15.

URLs, URNs, and URIs

Earlier, we discussed URLs and distinguished them from the concept of URNs. Whereas a URL points to a specific location on the Net and specifies a protocol or *scheme* for accessing its contents, a URN is simply a globally unique name. A URL is analogous to giving someone your phone number. But a URN is more like giving them your social security number. Your phone number may change, but your social security number uniquely identifies you forever.

While it's possible that some mechanism might be able to look at a given URN and tie it to a location (a URL), it is not necessarily so. URNs are intended only to be permanent, unique, abstract identifiers for an item, whereas a URL is a mechanism you can use to get in touch with a resource right now. You can use a phone number to contact me today, but you can use my social security number to uniquely identify me anytime.

An example of a URN is *http://www.w3.org/1999/XSL/Transform*, which is the identifier for a version of the Extensible Stylesheet Language, standardized by the W3C. Now, it happens that this is also a URL (you can go to that address and find information about the standard), but that is for convenience only. This URN's primary mission is to uniquely label the version of the programming language in a way that never changes.

Collectively, URLs and URNs are called Uniform Resource Identifiers or URIs. A URI is simply a URL or URN. So, URLs and URNs are kinds of URIs. The reason for this abstraction is that URLs and URNs, by definition, have some things in common. All URIs are supposed to be human-readable and "transcribable" (it should be possible to write them on the back of a napkin). They always have a hierarchical structure, and they are always unique. Both URLs and URNs also share some common syntax, which is described by RFC 2396.

The java.net.URI class formalizes these distinctions. The difference between the URI and URL classes is that the URI class does not try to parse the contents of the identifier and apply any "meaning." The URL class immediately attempts to parse the scheme portion of the URL and locate a protocol handler, whereas the URI class doesn't interpret its content. It serves only to allow us to work with the identifier as structured text, according to the general rules of URI syntax. With the URI class, you can construct the string, resolve relative paths, and perform equality or comparison operations, but no hostname or protocol resolution is done.

Web Services

Web services is a big, fast-moving topic and really the subject for another book entirely. However, since we have already covered so many of the basic networking concepts (and cover XML in detail in Chapter 24), we would be shirking our duties if we didn't provide an introduction to this important direction in application development. We conclude this chapter on client-side web communications with a small example of invoking a web service.

In contrast to regular web applications intended to be visited by web browsers, web services are application-level APIs intended to be invoked by other application components. The primary distinction from other types of interapplication communications mechanisms is that they use web standards and XML to maximize cross-platform interoperability. We will leave the analysis of when exactly this is important and the cost versus benefits tradeoffs out of our discussion here. But the value in this idea should be evident from the explosion of web-based business applications in the past few years. Web services allow web-based applications to provide well-defined, "hardened" interfaces for other web-based applications.

XML-RPC

The term web services means different things to different people and has spawned many (probably too many) new standards in recent years. However, the original concept is simple. Web services take the ubiquitous, universally understood, and easily implemented HTTP transaction and marry it with XML to define a standard for invoking application services over the Web. The process is a type of *remote procedure call* in which HTTP plays its traditional role as the basic communication provider and

XML adds a "business envelope" in which structured data is passed. This RPC-style web service interaction defines both the basic structure of an invocation request and also a set of XML encodings for marshaling the primitive data types, allowing data parameters and results to be exchanged in a truly cross-platform way. In contrast, another form of web services termed "document style" places more emphasis on the exchange of application-specific XML documents than on RPC-style data marshaling and unmarshaling. We will concentrate on RPC-style web services since they currently provide the tightest coupling to Java.

WSDL

A key component of web-services technology is the Web Services Description Language (WSDL). Using this standard, a structured XML document describes a web service, the individual functions (methods) it offers, and the XML data types for their respective arguments and return values. WSDL is a type of interface definition language (IDL) and plays that role for web services. However, a WSDL document can also specify the service location and other features.

For the client-side web-services developer, the WSDL document describing a service contains all of the information needed to generate the client-side code used to invoke the service from Java (or any other language). As we'll see in our example, it is not even necessary to have an understanding of WSDL to use the service. One can simply generate the client-side interfaces and use them from a Java language viewpoint. We'll see in Chapter 15 that we can generate the WSDL document for a new service directly from our own Java code as well.

The Tools

Sun's Java Web Services Developer Pack or JWSDP contains all of the tools and standard extension classes necessary to use, create, and work with web services in Java. Although most of the basic tools for working with XML are already packaged with the core Java distribution, the JWSDP adds the JAX-RPC classes necessary for remote calls as well as the development time *wscompile* tool. The *wscompile* tool reads a WSDL description file and generates the required Java interface and implementation classes to invoke it. The JWSDP can be downloaded at *http://java.sun.com/ webservices/*.

The JWSDP is by no means the only way to build and deploy web services. Most application servers provide their own mechanisms for deploying web services and generating client-side code. The Apache Axis project is another popular Java web services alternative.

Installation and environment

Using and, as we'll see in Chapter 15, writing web services is very easy. The only catch is that since the classes of the JWSDP are not yet part of the core Java distribution, a *lot* of external JAR files need to be in your classpath in order to use the code. The *wscompile* tool that reads the WSDL document and generates client-side classes is easy to run, but to use those classes currently requires a dozen additional JAR files. (Quite a mess.)

To make life easier for you, we're giving you two options for running the examples in this section. First, we're supplying you with a complete Ant *build.xml* file that can both generate the necessary classes and run the example for you. When you're working on a real project, using Ant is certainly the way to go. If you aren't yet comfortable with Ant or just prefer to play around with the examples directly, we've also provided scripts, *client-env.sh* and *client-env.bat*, that set the appropriate classpath (relative to the JWSDP) for you to run the client example. The *build.xml* file and scripts have been tested with JWSDP-1.5 and Java 5.0. You can find all of this and the source code for this section with the examples on the CD accompanying this book or online at *http://examples.oreilly.com/learnjava3/CD-ROM/*. In both cases, you must first set the location of your JWSDP install directory. For Ant, set the property in the *build.xml* file. For the shell scripts, set the environment variable JWSDP_HOME prior to running them.

There's one more thing: when you install the JWSDP, it may ask for the location of a server "container" (such as Tomcat) into which it should add the server-side components for running web services. It's not necessary for this chapter, but if you want to plan ahead for Chapter 15, you can go ahead and download Sun's reference Tomcat web services container from *http://java.sun.com/webservices/containers/ tomcat_for_JWSDP_1_5.html*. If you install it first (just unzip it to your preferred location), you can allow the JWSDP install to add its components now. If you don't want to do this yet, don't worry. We'll tell you how to add the components in Chapter 15.

The Temperature Service

This example shows just how easy it is to use a web service from client-side code. We're going to create a client for a web-based temperature lookup service. The service accepts a U.S. zip code as an argument and returns the actual temperature for that area as a result. Please note that the server-side component of this example is hosted by a web site called *xmethods.net*, which is a popular site for web services definitions and examples. Because this is a third-party educational site, we cannot guarantee that it will remain active. If for any reason *xmethods.net* takes this service down, you'll have to wait until Chapter 15, where we implement a simple web service ourselves.

Assuming you've installed the JWSDP classes, you can begin by downloading the WSDL file for the xmethods temperature service from *http://www.xmethods.net/sd/ 2001/TemperatureService.wsdl* or find it with the example code on the CD. This is one of the neat things about web services—you can usually ask the web service to give you its own WSDL description file. This means that about all you'd need to get started using someone's service is the appropriate URL. (Note that web browsers that don't display XML well may do odd things when you try to load this file. If you don't see the WSDL document, try using another browser such as FireFox or Microsoft Internet Explorer or fetch it from the CD.)

We'll walk through the steps for building and running the client code on the command line first. If you prefer to use the Ant build (which takes all the hassle out of it), we'll give you instructions later in this section. Before running the *wscompile* command, we must create a small configuration file telling it the location of the WSDL file and the name of the Java package into which to place the generated files. (This step is not part of the web services standard, just something the JWSDP implementation requires.) Place the following in a file called *client-config.xml* (or grab it from the CD):

```
<configuration xmlns="http://java.sun.com/xml/ns/jax-rpc/ri/config">
  <wsdl location="./TemperatureService.wsdl" packageName="temp"/>
</configuration>
```

Now we can run wscompile, found in *JWSDP_HOME/jaxrpc/bin*, like so:

```
% wscompile -gen client-config.xml
```

When *wscompile* completes, you should find a new directory named *temp* (for temperature) containing Java classes for the temperature service interface and an implementation class. This package contains an interface called TemperatureService as well as a TemperatureService_Impl implementation class and a service interface called TemperaturePortType. The "port" is WSDL terminology for a group of functions on a web service.

Our client application can now use these classes to invoke the service. The following code looks up the current temperature in the 63112 zip code:

```
import temp.*;

class TemperatureLookup {
    public static void main( String [] args ) throws Exception
    {
        TemperatureService impl = new TemperatureService_Impl();
        TemperaturePortType port = impl.getTemperaturePort();
        float temp = port.getTemp("63112");
        System.out.println("Temp = "+temp);
    }
}
```

To compile and run this example on the command line, first add the appropriate classpath using the appropriate client-env script and installation directory. On Windows, run these commands:

```
C:\> set JWSDP_HOME=install dir
C:\> client-env.bat
```

On Unix, run these commands instead:

```
% export JWSDP_HOME=install dir
% source client-env.sh
```

If you'd prefer to use the Ant build, just edit the *build.xml* file to set the jwsdphome property to your install directory and then run one of the targets: generate-client or run-client. The generate-client target calls *wscompile* in the same way that we showed earlier. The run-client target simply sets the appropriate classpath and runs the TemperatureLookup client.

```
% ant run-client
```

Since run-client automatically calls generate-client, that's all there is to it from the client side. The generated classes do all of the work. What we've demonstrated here is deceptively simple looking, but very powerful. From the WSDL document—an XML-based, completely language-neutral service description—we have generated a Java client-side API. From there, it took us just three lines of code to invoke the service. With similar tools, it should be possible to do the same from other languages as well. This is the appeal of web services.

We'll return to the topic of web services and implement our own web service in the next chapter, where we hop over to the server side of things and start building web applications.

## CHAPTER 15

Web Applications and Web Services

We're going to take a leap from the client side to the server side to learn how to write web-based Java applications and services. What distinguishes a web-based application or service from a regular Java program is that most of the code and logic reside on the server and the user utilizes a lightweight client or a web browser to access it. This is a very appealing model of software deployment and that is why it is spreading from interactive, browser-based, page-oriented web applications to more formal, application-to-application web services.

Most of this chapter is about the mechanics of the Java Servlet API, which is a framework for writing application components for servers, just as *applets* are client-side application components for web pages. The Servlet API is used in both Java web applications and in the implementation of web services. However, we'll deal with servlets directly only in the first part of this chapter, when writing web applications to be used from a web browser. Later, when we look at application-level web services, we'll be working with tools that shield us from this level of detail. Nonetheless, the two types of server-side applications still have things in common, including how they are deployed to the server using a Web Archive (WAR) file.

The Servlet API lives in the `javax.servlet` package, a standard Java API extension, so technically it isn't part of the core Java APIs. Similarly, the APIs used for building and deploying web services are bundled separately in the Java Web Services Developer Pack (JWSDP). In this book, we haven't talked about many standard extension packages, but these are particularly important. This chapter covers Java Servlet API 2.4 and JWSDP Version 1.5. Most web servers support the Java Servlet API either directly or indirectly through add-on modules. Most application servers now also offer a way to deploy web services, but this is not yet as standardized as servlets and web application deployment.

Servers that support the full set of Java Enterprise APIs (including servlets, JSPs, Enterprise JavaBeans, and usually web services) are called *application servers*. JBoss is a free, open source Java application server available from *http://www.jboss.org*, and BEA's WebLogic is a popular commercial application server. When we talk about highly modular application components, we often refer to their environment as a *container*. When we want to talk specifically about the part of these servers that runs servlets or web services, we can refer to them as the *servlet container* or *web services container*. We may also generically refer to them as servlet tools, servlet engines, or servlet runners.

We will try to avoid talking in too much detail about particular server environments, but we will use the Apache Project's Tomcat server for the examples in this book. Tomcat is a popular, free servlet and web application container that can be used by itself or in conjunction with other popular web servers. It is easy to configure and is a pure Java application, so you can use it on any platform that has a Java VM. You can download it from *http://jakarta.apache.org/tomcat/*. Tomcat has been adopted by Sun as part of the J2EE reference implementation, so it always has an up-to-date implementation of the specifications available in both source and binary form. Tomcat Version 5.x is required to support Java Servlet API Version 2.4, but, for our discussion, little else has changed from earlier versions of the server. For our web services example, we'll have to get the reference implementation of Tomcat from Sun, as this works best with the JWSDP.

Except where noted, all of our servlet examples will work equally well with the older Tomcat 4.x and the Servlet 2.3 API. The Servlet APIs and Java documentation can be downloaded directly from *http://java.sun.com/products/servlet/*. You might consider taking a look at the Java servlet specification white paper, also available at that location. It is a fairly readable specification document.

Web Application Technologies

Many different ways of writing server-side software for web applications have evolved over the years. Early on, the standard was CGI, usually in combination with a scripting language such as Perl. Various web servers also offered native-language APIs for pluggable software modules. Java, however—and in particular the Java Servlet API—is rapidly becoming the most popular architecture for building web-based applications. Java servlet containers are available for virtually every web server and servlets are becoming foundational for new levels of web infrastructure, such as web services.

Why has Java become so popular on the server side? Java is generally faster than scripting languages, especially in a server-side environment where long-running applications can be highly optimized by the VM. Servlets have an additional speed advantage over traditional CGI programs, because servlets execute in a multithreaded way within one instance of a VM. Older CGI applications required the server to start a separate process, pipe data to it, and receive the response as a stream. The unique runtime safety of Java also beats most native APIs in a production web-server environment, where it would be very bad to have an errant transaction bring down the server.

Java's portability also means that server-side applications can be scaled up rapidly across different types of hardware without significant porting issues. In many ways, Java has really proven itself in this "business environment" to a greater extent than in the Windows-dominated desktop world.

Speed and safety are factors, but perhaps the most important reason for using Java is that it makes writing large and complex applications much more manageable. Java servlets may not be quite as easy to write as scripts, but they are easier to update with new features, and servlets are far better at scaling for complex, high-volume applications. From servlet code, you can access all the standard Java APIs within the VM while your servlets are handling requests. This means that your Java servlet code can work well in a multitiered architecture, accessing "live" database connections with JDBC or communicating with other network services that have already been established. This kind of behavior has been hacked into CGI environments, but for Java, it is both robust and natural.

Before we move on, we should also mention servlets' relationships to other technologies: Java Server Pages (JSPs), XML/XSL, and application frameworks such as Struts and Java Server Faces (JSF). We'll talk more about the technologies involved in web services later in the chapter.

JSPs

JSPs are a document-centric way to write server-side applications. They consist of HTML content with specialized tag libraries and active Java-like syntax embedded within the pages. JSPs are compiled dynamically by the web server into Java servlets and can work with Java APIs directly and indirectly to generate dynamic content for the pages. Although all of the work still occurs on the server side, JSPs allow the developer to work as if he were writing code right in the page, which has both benefits and drawbacks. The benefit of this sort of "immediate mode" programming style is that it is easy to grasp and quick to crank out. The drawback is that it can lead to an unmanageable mix of business logic and presentation logic. The more code that appears mixed in with the static content, the greater the maintenance headache.

Most large-scale JSP projects today utilize tag libraries to minimize ad-hoc code in the pages. JSPs are also now routinely used in combination with *controller* servlets or other back-end framework controller components that do the heavy lifting of business logic for them. In this case, the term controller refers to the Model-View-Controller (MVC) separation of concerns that we introduced earlier when talking about Swing GUIs. Maintaining this separation leverages the advantages of JSP while avoiding its pitfalls.

XML

XML is a powerful set of standards for working with structured information in text form. The Extensible Stylesheet Language (XSL) is a language for transforming XML documents into other kinds of documents, including HTML. The combination of servlets that can generate XML content and XSL stylesheets that can transform content for presentation is a very exciting direction, covered in detail in Chapter 24. As we'll see later, web services use XML as their native data format, making them completely portable across platforms and languages.

Application Frameworks

One of the most popular frameworks for building web applications is the Apache Foundation's Struts Web Application Framework. Struts implements the Model-View-Controller paradigm by providing both a modular controller component architecture and an extensive tag library for JSP page development. Struts abstracts some of the mapping and navigation aspects required to glue together a web application through the use of an XML-based configuration file and also adds the ability to do declarative mapping of HTML forms to Java objects as well as automated validation of form fields.

Over the years, some of the value of Struts has been whittled away by big improvements in the underlying Servlet API. As we'll see in this chapter, the *web.xml* web application configuration file can accomplish a lot by itself and features such as servlet filters and declarative features such as security and login have added a great deal to the modularity of servlet-based applications. Struts can also be a bit awkward and is not quite as clean or easy to understand as one might wish. However, for now Struts is the 800-pound gorilla in the room and commands a lot of attention. Struts has a big following and for many people it is an invaluable piece of the web infrastructure. You can download Struts at *http://struts.apache.org/*.

JSF is Sun's response to Struts. Developed over the past few years by the Java Community Process (including some of the original Struts people) it is intended to become the "official" Java-sanctioned web-application framework. JSF builds upon lessons learned with Struts and refines the MVC model with server-side application components and more fine-grained navigation and event management. JSF is maturing after initially being received with mixed reviews. It is probably on track for wider adoption in the future. You can download the JSF APIs and learn more at *http://java.sun.com/j2ee/javaserverfaces/*.

Web Applications

So far we've used the term "web application" generically, referring to any kind of browser-based application that is located on a web server. Now we are going to have to be more precise with that term. In the context of the Java Servlet API, a web application is a collection of servlets, supporting Java classes, content such as HTML or JSP pages and images, and configuration information. For deployment (installation on a web server), a web application is bundled into a WAR file. We'll discuss WAR files in detail later, but suffice it to say that they are essentially JAR archives containing all the application files along with some deployment information. The important thing is that the standardization of WAR files means not only that the Java code is portable, but also that the process of deploying all the application's parts—its Java classes, resources, and configuration—is standardized.

At the heart of the WAR archive is the *web.xml* file. This XML configuration file describes which servlets and JSPs are to be deployed, their names and URL paths, their initialization parameters, and a host of other information, including security and authentication requirements.

Web applications, or web apps, also have a very well-defined runtime environment. Each web app has its own "root" path on the web server, meaning that all the URLs addressing its servlets and files start with a common unique prefix (e.g., *www.oreilly.com/someapplication/*). The web app's servlets are also isolated from those of other web applications. Web apps cannot directly access each other's files (although they may be allowed to do so through the web server, of course). Each web app also has its own servlet context. We'll discuss the servlet context in more detail, but in brief, it is a common area for servlets within an application to share information and get resources from the environment. The high degree of isolation between web applications is intended to support the dynamic deployment and updating of applications required by modern business systems and address security and reliability concerns. Web apps are intended to be coarse-grained, relatively complete applications—not to be tightly coupled with other web apps. Although there's no reason you can't make web apps cooperate at a high level, for sharing logic across applications, you might want to consider web services, which we'll discuss later in this chapter.

The Servlet Life Cycle

Let's jump ahead to the Servlet API itself so that we can get started building servlets right away. We'll fill in the gaps later when we discuss various parts of the APIs and WAR file structure in more detail. The Servlet API is very simple, almost exactly paralleling the Applet API. There are three life-cycle methods—init( ), service( ), and destroy( )—along with some methods for getting configuration parameters and servlet resources. Before a servlet is used the first time, it's initialized by the container through its init( ) method. Thereafter, the servlet spends its time handling service( ) requests and doing its job until (presumably) the server is shut down, and the servlet's destroy( ) method is called, giving it an opportunity to clean up.

Generally, only one instance of each deployed servlet class is instantiated per container. More precisely, it is one instance per servlet entry in the *web.xml* file, but we'll talk more about servlet deployment later. In the past, there was an exception to that rule when using the special, SingleThreadModel type of servlet. As of Servlet API 2.4, single-threaded servlets have been deprecated.

By default, servlets are expected to handle requests in a multithreaded way; that is, the servlet's service methods may be invoked by many threads at the same time. This means that you cannot store client-related data in instance variables of your servlet object. (Of course, you can store general data related to the servlet's operation, as long as it does not change on a per-request basis.) Per-client state information can be stored in a client *session* object on the server or in a client-side cookie, which persists across client requests. We'll talk about client state later as well.

The service( ) method of a servlet accepts two parameters: a servlet "request" object and a servlet "response" object. These provide tools for reading the client request and generating output; we'll talk about them in detail in the examples.

Servlets

There are actually two packages of interest in the Servlet API. The first is the javax.servlet package, which contains the most general Servlet APIs. The second important package is javax.servlet.http, which contains APIs specific to servlets that handle HTTP requests for web servers. In the rest of this section, we are going to discuss servlets as if all servlets were HTTP-related. In theory, you can write servlets for other protocols, but that's not what we're currently interested in.

The primary tool provided by the javax.servlet.http package is the HttpServlet base class. This is an abstract servlet that provides some basic implementation details related to handling an HTTP request. In particular, it overrides the generic servlet service( ) request and breaks it out into several HTTP-related methods, including doGet( ), doPost( ), doPut( ), and doDelete( ). The default service( ) method examines the request to determine what kind it is and dispatches it to one of these methods, so you can override one or more of them to implement the specific web server behavior you need.

doGet( ) and doPost( ) correspond to the standard HTTP GET and POST operations. GET is the standard request for retrieving a file or document at a specified URL. POST is the method by which a client sends an arbitrary amount of data to the server. HTML forms are the most common use for POST.

To round these out, HttpServlet provides the doPut( ) and doDelete( ) methods. These methods correspond to a poorly supported part of the HTTP protocol, meant to provide a way to upload and remove files. doPut( ) is supposed to be like POST but with different semantics; doDelete( ) would be its opposite. These aren't widely used.

HttpServlet also implements three other HTTP-related methods for you: doHead( ), doTrace( ), and doOptions( ). You don't normally need to override these methods. doHead( ) implements the HTTP HEAD request, which asks for the headers of a GET request without the body. HttpServlet implements this by default in the trivial way, by performing the GET method and then sending only the headers. You may wish to override doHead( ) with a more efficient implementation if you can provide one as an optimization. doTrace( ) and doOptions( ) implement other features of HTTP that allow for debugging and simple client/server capabilities negotiation. You shouldn't need to override these.

Along with HttpServlet, javax.servlet.http also includes subclasses of the ServletRequest and ServletResponse objects, HttpServletRequest and HttpServletRe-sponse. These subclasses provide, respectively, the input and output streams needed to read and write client data. They also provide the APIs for getting or setting HTTP header information and, as we'll see, client session information. Rather than document these dryly, we'll show them in the context of some examples. As usual, we'll start with the simplest possible example.

The HelloClient Servlet

Here's our servlet version of "Hello, World," HelloClient:

```
//file: HelloClient.java
import java.io.*;
import javax.servlet.ServletException;
import javax.servlet.http.*;

public class HelloClient extends HttpServlet {

    public void doGet(HttpServletRequest request,
                      HttpServletResponse response)
        throws ServletException, IOException {

        // must come first
        response.setContentType("text/html");
        PrintWriter out = response.getWriter();

        out.println(
            "<html><head><title>Hello Client</title></head><body>"
            + "<h1> Hello, Client </h1>"
            + "</body></html>" );
        out.close();
    }
}
```

If you want to try this servlet right away, skip ahead to "WAR Files and Deploy-ment," where we walk through the process of running this servlet. Simply package up the servlet class file along with a simple *web.xml* file that describes it and place it on your server. But for now, we're going to discuss just the servlet example code itself, which is pretty simple.

Let's have a look at the example. HelloClient extends the base HttpServlet class and overrides the doGet( ) method to handle simple requests. In this case, we want to respond to any GET request by sending back a one-line HTML document that says "Hello, Client." First, we tell the container what kind of response we are going to generate, using the setContentType( ) method of the HttpServletResponse object. Then, we get the output stream using the getWriter( ) method and print the message to it. Finally, we close the stream to indicate we're done generating output. (It shouldn't strictly be necessary to close the output stream, but we show it for completeness.)

ServletExceptions

The doGet( ) method of our example servlet declares that it can throw a ServletException. All of the service methods of the Servlet API may throw a ServletException to indicate that a request has failed. A ServletException can be constructed with a string message and an optional Throwable parameter that can carry any corresponding exception representing the root cause of the problem:

```
throw new ServletException("utter failure", someException );
```

By default, the web server determines exactly what is shown to the user when a ServletException is thrown, but often during development the exception and its stack trace are displayed. Using the *web.xml* file, you can designate custom error pages. (See the section "Error and Index Pages" later in this chapter for details.)

Alternatively, a servlet may throw an UnavailableException, a subclass of ServletException, to indicate that it cannot handle requests. This exception can be constructed to indicate that the condition is permanent or that it should last for a specified period of seconds.

Content type

Before fetching the output stream and writing to it, we must specify the kind of output we are sending by calling the response parameter's setContentType( ) method. In this case, we set the content type to text/html, which is the proper MIME type for an HTML document. In general, though, it's possible for a servlet to generate any kind of data, including sound, video, or some other kind of text. If we were writing a generic FileServlet to serve files like a regular web server, we might inspect the file-name extension and determine the MIME type from that or from direct inspection of the data. For writing binary data, you can use the getOutputStream( ) method to get an OutputStream as opposed to a Writer.

The content type is used in the Content-Type: header of the server's HTTP response, which tells the client what to expect even before it starts reading the result. This

---

allows your web browser to prompt you with the "Save File" dialog when you click on a ZIP archive or executable program. When the content-type string is used in its full form to specify the character encoding (for example, text/html; charset=ISO-8859-1), the information is also used by the servlet engine to set the character encoding of the PrintWriter output stream. As a result, you should always call the setContentType( ) method before fetching the writer with the getWriter( ) method. As of Java 5.0, the character encoding can also be set separately, via the servlet response object's setCharacterEncoding( ) method.

The Servlet Response

In addition to providing the output stream for writing content to the client, the HttpServletResponse object provides methods for controlling other aspects of the HTTP response, including headers, error result codes, redirects, and servlet container buffering.

HTTP headers are metadata name/value pairs sent with the response. You can add headers (standard or custom) to the response with the setHeader( ) and addHeader( ) methods (headers may have multiple values). There are also convenience methods for setting headers with integer and date values:

```
response.setIntHeader("MagicNumber", 42);
response.setDateHeader("CurrentTime", System.currentTimeMillis( ) );
```

When you write data to the client, the servlet container automatically sets the HTTP response code to a value of 200, which means OK. Using the sendError( ) method, you can generate other HTTP response codes. HttpServletResponse contains predefined constants for all of the standard codes. Here are a few common ones:

```
HttpServletResponse.SC_OK
HttpServletResponse.SC_BAD_REQUEST
HttpServletResponse.SC_FORBIDDEN
HttpServletResponse.SC_NOT_FOUND
HttpServletResponse.SC_INTERNAL_SERVER_ERROR
HttpServletResponse.SC_NOT_IMPLEMENTED
HttpServletResponse.SC_SERVICE_UNAVAILABLE
```

When you generate an error with sendError( ), the response is over, and you can't write any actual content to the client. You can specify a short error message, however, which may be shown to the client. (See the section "A Simple Filter" later in this chapter.)

An HTTP redirect is a special kind of response that tells the client web browser to go to a different URL. Normally this happens quickly and without any interaction from the user. You can send a redirect with the sendRedirect( ) method:

```
response.sendRedirect("http://www.oreilly.com/");
```

While we're talking about the response, we should say a few words about buffering. Most responses are buffered internally by the servlet container until the servlet service method has exited or a preset maximum size has been reached. This allows the container to set the HTTP content-length header automatically, telling the client how much data to expect. You can control the size of this buffer with the setBufferSize( ) method, specifying a size in bytes. You can even clear it and start over if no data has been written to the client. To clear the buffer, use isCommitted( ) to test whether any data has been set, then use resetBuffer( ) to dump the data if none has been sent. If you are sending a lot of data, you may wish to set the content length explicitly with the setContentLength( ) method.

Servlet Parameters

Our first example shows how to accept a basic request. Of course, to do anything really useful, we'll need to get some information from the user. Fortunately, the servlet engine handles this for us, interpreting both GET and POST form-encoded data from the client and providing it to us through the simple getParameter( ) method of the servlet request.

GET, POST, and the "extra path"

There are essentially two ways to pass information from your web browser to a servlet or CGI program. The most general is to "post" it, meaning that your client encodes the information and sends it as a stream to the program, which decodes it. Posting can be used to upload large amounts of form data or other data, including files. The other way to pass information is to somehow encode the information in the URL of your client's request. The primary way to do this is to use GET-style encoding of parameters in the URL string. In this case, the web browser encodes the parameters and appends them to the end of the URL string. The server decodes them and passes them to the application.

As we described in Chapter 14, GET-style encoding takes the parameters and appends them to the URL in a name/value fashion, with the first parameter preceded by a question mark (?) and the rest separated by ampersands (&). The entire string is expected to be *URL-encoded*: any special characters (such as spaces, ?, and & in the string) are specially encoded.

Another way to pass data in the URL is called *extra path*. This simply means that when the server has located your servlet or CGI program as the target of a URL, it takes any remaining path components of the URL string and hands it over as an extra part of the URL. For example, consider these URLs:

```
http://www.myserver.example/servlets/MyServlet
http://www.myserver.example/servlets/MyServlet/foo/bar
```

Suppose the server maps the first URL to the servlet called MyServlet. When subsequently given the second URL, the server still invokes MyServlet, but considers /foo/bar to be an "extra path" that can be retrieved through the servlet request getExtraPath( ) method.

Both GET and POST encoding can be used with HTML forms on the client by specifying get or post in the action attribute of the form tag. The browser handles the encoding; on the server side, the servlet engine handles the decoding.

The content type used by a client to post form data to a servlet is the same as that for any CGI: "application/x-www-form-urlencoded." The Servlet API automatically parses this kind of data and makes it available through the getParameter( ) method. However, if you do not call the getParameter( ) method, the data remains available in the input stream and can be read by the servlet directly.

GET or POST: which one to use?

To users, the primary difference between GET and POST is that they can see the GET information in the encoded URL shown in their web browser. This can be useful because the user can cut and paste that URL (the result of a search, for example) and mail it to a friend or bookmark it for future reference. POST information is not visible to the user and ceases to exist after it's sent to the server. This behavior goes along with the protocol's perspective that GET and POST are intended to have different semantics. By definition, the result of a GET operation is not supposed to have any side effects. That is, it's not supposed to cause the server to perform any persistent operations (such as making an e-commerce purchase). In theory, that's the job of POST. That's why your web browser warns you about reposting form data again if you hit reload on a page that was the result of a form posting.

The extra path method is not used for form data but would be useful for a servlet that retrieves files or handles a range of URLs in a human-readable way not driven by forms. Extra path information is often useful for URLs that the user must see or remember, because it looks like any other path.

The ShowParameters Servlet

Our first example didn't do anything interesting. This next example prints the values of any parameters that were received. We'll start by handling GET requests and then make some trivial modifications to handle POST as well. Here's the code:

```
//file: ShowParameters.java
import java.io.*;
import javax.servlet.ServletException;
import javax.servlet.http.*;
import java.util.Enumeration;

public class ShowParameters extends HttpServlet {

    public void doGet(HttpServletRequest request,
                      HttpServletResponse response)
```

```
        throws ServletException, IOException {
          showRequestParameters( request, response );
        }

    void showRequestParameters(HttpServletRequest request,
                               HttpServletResponse response)
      throws IOException {
        response.setContentType("text/html");
        PrintWriter out = response.getWriter( );

        out.println(
          "<html><head><title>Show Parameters</title></head><body>"
          + "<h1>Parameters</h1><ul>");

        for ( Enumeration e=request.getParameterNames( );
             e.hasMoreElements( ); ) {
          String name = (String)e.nextElement( );
          String value = request.getParameter( name );
          if (! value.equals("") )
              out.println("<li>"+ name +" = "+ value );
        }

        out.close( );
      }
    }
```

There's not much new here. As in the first example, we override the doGet( ) method. We delegate the request to a helper method that we've created, called showRequestParameters( ), a method that enumerates the parameters using the request object's getParameterNames( ) method and prints the names and values. (To make it pretty, we listed them in an HTML list by prefixing each with an <li> tag.)

As it stands, our servlet would respond to any URL that contains a GET request. Let's round it out by adding our own form to the output and also accommodating POST method requests. To accept posts, we override the doPost( ) method. The implementation of doPost( ) could simply call our showRequestParameters( ) method, but we can make it simpler still. The API lets us treat GET and POST requests interchangeably because the servlet engine handles the decoding of request parameters. So we simply delegate the doPost( ) operation to doGet( ).

Add the following method to the example:

```
    public void doPost( HttpServletRequest request,
                        HttpServletResponse response)
      throws ServletException, IOException {
        doGet( request, response );
    }
```

Now, let's add an HTML form to the output. The form lets the user fill in some parameters and submit them to the servlet. Add this line to the showRequestParameters( ) method before the call to out.close( ):

```
    out.println(
      "</ul><p><form method=\"POST\" action=\""
```

```
        + request.getRequestURI( ) + "\">"
        + "Field 1 <input name=\"Field 1\" size=20><br>"
        + "Field 2 <input name=\"Field 2\" size=20><br>"
        + "<br><input type=\"submit\" value=\"Submit\"></form>"
    );
```

The form's action attribute is the URL of our servlet so that the servlet will get the data. We use the getRequestURI( ) method to ask for the location of our servlet. For the method attribute, we've specified a POST operation, but you can try changing the operation to GET to see both styles.

So far, we haven't done anything terribly exciting. In the next example we'll add some power by introducing a user session to store client data between requests. But before we go on, we should mention a useful standard servlet, SnoopServlet, that is akin to our example above.

SnoopServlet

Most servlet containers come with some useful servlets that serve as examples or debugging aids. One of the most basic tools you have for debugging servlets is the "SnoopServlet." We place that name in quotes because you will find many different implementations of this with various names. But the original SnoopServlet came with the Java servlet development kit and an equivalent is supplied with the Tomcat server distribution. This very simple debugging tool displays everything about its environment and the incoming request, including all of the request parameters, just as our ShowParameters example did and more. There is a lot of useful information there. In the default Tomcat 4.x distribution, you can access the snoop servlet at *http://myserver:8080/examples/snoop*. In Tomcat 5.x, the servlet has been replaced by a JSP and is available at: *http://myserver:8080/jsp-examples/snp/snoop.jsp*.

User Session Management

One of the nicest features of the Servlet API is its simple mechanism for managing a user session. By a session, we mean that the servlet can maintain information over multiple pages and through multiple transactions as navigated by the user; this is also called maintaining state. Providing continuity through a series of web pages is important in many kinds of applications, such as handling a login process or tracking purchases in a shopping cart. In a sense, session data takes the place of instance data in your servlet object. It lets you store data between invocations of your service methods.

Session tracking is supported by the servlet container; you normally don't have to worry about the details of how it's accomplished. It's done in one of two ways: using client-side cookies or URL rewriting. *Client-side cookies* are a standard HTTP mechanism for getting the client web browser to cooperate in storing state information for you. A cookie is basically just a name/value attribute that is issued by the server, stored on the client, and returned by the client whenever it is accessing a certain group of URLs on a specified server. Cookies can track a single session or multiple user visits.

URL rewriting appends session-tracking information to the URL, using GET-style encoding or extra path information. The term "rewriting" applies because the server rewrites the URL before it is seen by the client and absorbs the extra information before it is passed back to the servlet. In order to support URL rewriting, a servlet must take the extra step to encode any URLs it generates in content (e.g., HTML links that may return to the page) using a special method of the HttpServletResponse object. We'll describe this later. You need to allow for URL rewriting by the server if you want your application to work with browsers that do not support cookies or have them disabled. Many sites simply choose not to work without cookies.

To the servlet programmer, state information is made available through an HttpSession object, which acts like a hashtable for storing whatever objects you would like to carry through the session. The objects stay on the server side; a special identifier is sent to the client through a cookie or URL rewriting. On the way back, the identifier is mapped to a session, and the session is associated with the servlet again.

The ShowSession Servlet

Here's a simple servlet that shows how to store some string information to track a session:

```java
//file: ShowSession.java
import java.io.*;
import javax.servlet.ServletException;
import javax.servlet.http.*;
import java.util.Enumeration;

public class ShowSession extends HttpServlet {

    public void doPost(
        HttpServletRequest request, HttpServletResponse response)
        throws ServletException, IOException
    {
        doGet( request, response );
    }

    public void doGet(
        HttpServletRequest request, HttpServletResponse response)
        throws ServletException, IOException
    {
        HttpSession session = request.getSession(  );
        boolean clear = request.getParameter("clear") != null;
        if ( clear )
            session.invalidate(  );
        else {
```

```
                String name = request.getParameter("Name");
                String value = request.getParameter("Value");
                if ( name != null && value != null )
                    session.setAttribute( name, value );
            }

            response.setContentType("text/html");
            PrintWriter out = response.getWriter( );
            out.println(
              "<html><head><title>Show Session</title></head><body>");

            if ( clear )
                out.println("<h1>Session Cleared:</h1>");
            else {
                out.println("<h1>In this session:</h1><ul>");
                Enumeration names = session.getAttributeNames( );
                while ( names.hasMoreElements( ) ) {
                    String name = (String)names.nextElement( );
                    out.println( "<li>"+name+" = " +session.getAttribute( name ) );
                }
            }

            out.println(
              "</ul><p><hr><h1>Add String</h1>"
              + "<form method=\"POST\" action=\""
              + request.getRequestURI( ) +"\">"
              + "Name: <input name=\"Name\" size=20><br>"
              + "Value: <input name=\"Value\" size=20><br>"
              + "<br><input type=\"submit\" value=\"Submit\">"
              + "<input type=\"submit\" name=\"clear\" value=\"Clear\"></form>"
            );
        }
    }
```

When you invoke the servlet, you are presented with a form that prompts you to enter a name and a value. The value string is stored in a session object under the name provided. Each time the servlet is called, it outputs the list of all data items associated with the session. You will see the session grow as each item is added (in this case, until you restart your web browser or the server).

The basic mechanics are much like our ShowParameters servlet. Our doGet( ) method generates the form, which points back to our servlet via a POST method. We override doPost( ) to delegate back to our doGet( ) method, allowing it to handle everything. Once in doGet( ), we attempt to fetch the user session object from the request object using getSession( ). The HttpSession object supplied by the request functions like a hashtable. There is a setAttribute( ) method, which takes a string name and an Object argument, and a corresponding getAttribute( ) method. In our example, we use the getAttributeNames( ) method to enumerate the values currently stored in the session and to print them.

By default, getSession( ) creates a session if one does not exist. If you want to test for a session or explicitly control when one is created, you can call the overloaded version getSession(false), which does not automatically create a new session and returns null if there is no session. Alternately, you can check to see if a session was just created with the isNew( ) method. To clear a session immediately, we can use the invalidate( ) method. After calling invalidate( ) on a session, we are not allowed to access it again, so we set a flag in our example and show the "Session Cleared" message. Sessions may also become invalid on their own by timing out. You can control session timeout in the application server or through the *web.xml* file (via the "session-timeout" value of the "session config" section). It is possible, through an interface we'll talk about later in this chapter, to find out when a session times out. In general, this appears to the application as either no session or a new session on the next request. User sessions are private to each web application and are not shared across applications.

We mentioned earlier that an extra step is required to support URL rewriting for web browsers that don't support cookies. To do this, we must make sure that any URLs we generate in content are first passed through the HttpServletResponse encodeURL( ) method. This method takes a string URL and returns a modified string only if URL rewriting is necessary. Normally, when cookies are available, it returns the same string. In our previous example, we should have encoded the server form URL retrieved from getRequestURI( ) before passing it to the client, if we wanted to allow for users without cookies.

The ShoppingCart Servlet

Now we build on the previous example to make a servlet that could be used as part of an online store. ShoppingCart lets users choose items and add them to their basket until checkout time. The page generated is not that pretty, but that's the sort of thing you'd introduce with proper separation of the presentation and business logic. Here we are just concentrating on the Servlet API;

```java
//file: ShoppingCart.java
import java.io.*;
import javax.servlet.ServletException;
import javax.servlet.http.*;
import java.util.Enumeration;

public class ShoppingCart extends HttpServlet {
    String [] items = new String [] {
        "Chocolate Covered Crickets", "Raspberry Roaches",
        "Buttery Butterflies", "Chicken Flavored Chicklets(tm)" };

    public void doPost(
        HttpServletRequest request, HttpServletResponse response)
        throws IOException, ServletException
    {
```

```
        doGet( request, response );
}

public void doGet(
    HttpServletRequest request, HttpServletResponse response)
    throws ServletException, IOException
{
    response.setContentType("text/html");
    PrintWriter out = response.getWriter(  );

    // get or create the session information
    HttpSession session = request.getSession(  );
    int [] purchases = (int [])session.getAttribute("purchases");
    if ( purchases == null ) {
        purchases = new int [ items.length ];
        session.setAttribute( "purchases", purchases );
    }

    out.println( "<html><head><title>Shopping Cart</title>"
                + "</title></head><body><p>" );

    if ( request.getParameter("checkout") != null )
        out.println("<h1>Thanks for ordering!</h1>");
    else {
        if ( request.getParameter("add") != null ) {
            addPurchases( request, purchases );
            out.println(
                "<h1>Purchase added.  Please continue</h1>");
        } else {
            if ( request.getParameter("clear") != null )
                for (int i=0; i<purchases.length; i++)
                    purchases[i] = 0;
            out.println("<h1>Please Select Your Items!</h1>");
        }
        doForm( out, request.getRequestURI(  ) );
    }
    showPurchases( out, purchases );
    out.close(  );
}

void addPurchases( HttpServletRequest request, int [] purchases ) {
    for (int i=0; i<items.length; i++) {
        String added = request.getParameter( items[i] );
        if ( added !=null && !added.equals("") )
            purchases[i] += Integer.parseInt( added );
    }
}

void doForm( PrintWriter out, String requestURI ) {
    out.println( "<form method=POST action="+ requestURI +">" );

    for(int i=0; i< items.length; i++)
        out.println( "Quantity <input name-\"" + items[i]
            + "\" value=0 size=3> of: " + items[i] + "<br>");
```

```
        out.println(
            "<p><input type=submit name=add value=\"Add To Cart\">"
          + "<input type=submit name=checkout value=\"Check Out\">"
          + "<input type=submit name=clear value=\"Clear Cart\">"
          + "</form>" );
    }

    void showPurchases( PrintWriter out, int [] purchases )
        throws IOException {

        out.println("<hr><h2>Your Shopping Basket</h2>");
        for (int i=0; i<items.length; i++)
            if ( purchases[i] != 0 )
                out.println( purchases[i] +"  "+ items[i] +"<br>" );
    }
}
```

ShoppingCart has some instance data: a String array that holds a list of products. We're making the assumption that the product selection is the same for all customers. If it's not, we'd have to generate the product list on the fly or put it in the session for the user. We cannot store any per-request or per-user data in instance variables.

We see the same basic pattern as in our previous servlets, with doPost( ) delegating to doGet( ), and doGet( ) generating the body of the output and a form for gathering new data. We've broken down the work using a few helper methods: doForm( ), addPurchases( ), and showPurchases( ). Our shopping cart form has three submit buttons: one for adding items to the cart, one for checkout, and one for clearing the cart. In each case, we display the contents of the cart. Depending on the button pressed (indicated by the name of the parameter), we add new purchases, clear the list, or show the results as a checkout window.

The form is generated by our doForm( ) method, using the list of items for sale. As in the other examples, we supply our servlet's address as the target of the form. Next, we have placed an integer array called purchases into the user session. Each element in purchases holds a count of the number of each item the user wants to buy. We create the array after retrieving the session simply by asking the session for it. If this is a new session, and the array hasn't been created, getAttribute( ) gives us a null value and we create an empty array to populate. Since we generate the form using the names from the items array, it's easy for addPurchases( ) to check for each name using getParameter( ) and increment the purchases array for the number of items requested. We also test for the value being equal to the empty string, because some broken web browsers send empty strings for unused field values. Finally, showPurchases( ) loops over the purchases array and prints the name and quantity for each item that the user has purchased.

Cookies

In our previous examples, a session lived only until you shut down your web browser or the server. You can do more long-term user tracking or identification that lasts beyond a single browser session by managing cookies explicitly. You can send a cookie to the client by creating a javax.servlet.http.Cookie object and adding it to the servlet response using the addCookie( ) method. Later, you can retrieve the cookie information from the servlet request and use it to look up persistent information in a database. The following servlet sends a "Learning Java" cookie to your web browser and displays it when you return to the page:

```java
//file: CookieCutter.java
import java.io.*;
import java.text.*;
import java.util.*;
import javax.servlet.*;
import javax.servlet.http.*;

public class CookieCutter extends HttpServlet {

    public void doGet(HttpServletRequest request,
                      HttpServletResponse response)
      throws IOException, ServletException {
        response.setContentType("text/html");
        PrintWriter out = response.getWriter( );

        if ( request.getParameter("setcookie") != null ) {
            Cookie cookie = new Cookie("Learningjava", "Cookies!");
            cookie.setMaxAge(3600);
            response.addCookie(cookie);
            out.println("<html><body><h1>Cookie Set...</h1>");
        } else {
            out.println("<html><body>");
            Cookie[] cookies = request.getCookies( );
            if ( cookies.length == 0 )
                out.println("<h1>No cookies found...</h1>");
            else
                for (int i = 0; i < cookies.length; i++)
                    out.print("<h1>Name: "+ cookies[i].getName( )
                              + "<br>"
                              + "Value: " + cookies[i].getValue( )
                              + "</h1>" );
            out.println("<p><a href=\""+ request.getRequestURI( )
                +"?setcookie=true\">"
                +"Reset the Learning Java cookie.</a>");
        }
        out.println("</body></html>");
        out.close( );
    }
}
```

This example simply enumerates the cookies supplied by the request object using the getCookies( ) method and prints their names and values. We provide a GET-style link that points back to our servlet with a parameter setcookie, indicating that we should set the cookie. In that case, we create a Cookie object using the specified name and value and add it to the response with the addCookie( ) method. We set the maximum age of the cookie to 3600 seconds, so it remains in the browser for an hour before being discarded (we'll talk about tracking a cookie across multiple sessions later). Specifying a negative time period indicates that the cookie should not be stored persistently and should be erased when the browser exits. A time period of 0 deletes any existing cookie immediately.

Two other Cookie methods are of interest: setDomain( ) and setPath( ). These methods allow you to specify the domain name and path component that determines where the client will send the cookie. If you're writing some kind of purchase applet for L.L. Bean, you don't want clients sending your cookies over to Eddie Bauer. In practice, however, this cannot happen. The default domain is the domain of the server sending the cookie. (You may not be able to specify other domains for security reasons.) The path parameter defaults to the base URL of the servlet, but you can specify a wider (or narrower) range of URLs on the server by manually setting this parameter.

The ServletContext API

Web applications have access to the server environment through the ServletContext API, a reference to which can be obtained from the HttpServlet getServletContext( ) method:

```
ServletContext context = getServletContext( );
```

Each web app has its own ServletContext. The context provides a shared space in which a web app's servlets may rendezvous and post objects. Objects may be placed into the context with the setAttribute( ) method and retrieved by name with the getAttribute( ) method:

```
context.setAttribute("myapp.statistics", myObject);
Object stats = context.getAttribute("myapp.statistics");
```

Attribute names beginning with "java." and "javax." are reserved for use by Java. Use the standard package-naming conventions for your attributes to avoid conflicts. One standard attribute that can be accessed through the servlet context is a reference to a private working directory represented by a java.io.File object. This temp directory is guaranteed unique to the web app. No guarantees are made about it being cleared upon exit, however, so you should use the temporary file API to create files here (unless you wish to try to keep them beyond the server exit). For example:

```
File tmpDir = (File)context.getAttribute("javax.servlet.context.tempdir");
File tmpFile = File.createTempFile( "appprefix", "appsuffix", tmpDir );
```

The servlet context also provides direct access to the web app's files from its root directory. The getResource( ) method is similar to the Class getResource( ) method (see Chapter 12). It takes a pathname and returns a special local URL for accessing that resource. In this case, it takes a path rooted in the servlet base directory (WAR file). The servlet may obtain references to files, including those in the *WEB-INF* directory, using this method. For example, a servlet may fetch an input stream for its own *web.xml* file:

```
InputStream in = context.getResourceAsStream("/WEB-INF/web.xml");
```

It could also use a URL reference to get one of its images:

```
URL bunnyURL = context.getResource("/images/happybunny.gif");
```

The method getResourcePaths( ) may be used to fetch a directory-style listing of all the resource files available matching a specified path. The return value is a java.util.Set collection of strings naming the resources available under the specified path. For example, the path / lists all files in the WAR; the path */WEB-INF/* lists at least the *web.xml* file and *classes* directory.

The ServletContext is also a factory for RequestDispatcher objects, which we won't cover here, but which allow for servlets to forward to or include the results of other servlets in their responses.

WAR Files and Deployment

As we described in the introduction to this chapter, a WAR file is an archive that contains all the parts of a web application: Java class files for servlets, JSPs, HTML pages, images, and other resources. The WAR file is simply a JAR file with specified directories for the Java code and one very important file: the *web.xml* file, which tells the application server what to run and how to run it. WAR files always have the extension *.war*, but they can be created and read with the standard *jar* tool.

The contents of a typical WAR might look like this, as revealed by the *jar* tool:

```
$ jar tvf shoppingcart.war

    index.html
    purchase.html
    receipt.html
    images/happybunny.gif
    WEB-INF/web.xml
    WEB-INF/classes/com/mycompany/PurchaseServlet.class
    WEB-INF/classes/com/mycompany/ReturnServlet.class
    WEB-INF/lib/thirdparty.jar
```

When deployed, the name of the WAR becomes, by default, the root path of the web application, in this case, *shoppingcart*. Thus, the base URL for this web app, if deployed on *http://www.oreilly.com*, is *http://www.oreilly.com/shoppingcart/*, and all references to its documents, images, and servlets start with that path. The top level of the WAR file becomes the document root (base directory) for serving files. Our *index.html* file appears at the base URL we just mentioned, and our *happybunny.gif* image is referenced as *http://www.oreilly.com/shoppingcart/images/happybunny.gif*.

The *WEB-INF* directory (all caps, hyphenated) is a special directory that contains all deployment information and application code. This directory is protected by the web server, and its contents are not visible to outside users of the application, even if you add *WEB-INF* to the base URL. Your application classes can load additional files from this area using getResource( ) on the servlet context, however, so it is a safe place to store application resources. The *WEB-INF* directory contains the all-important *web.xml* file, which we'll talk more about in the next section.

The *WEB-INF/classes* and *WEB-INF/lib* directories contain Java class files and JAR libraries, respectively. The *WEB-INF/classes* directory is automatically added to the classpath of the web application, so any class files placed here (using the normal Java package conventions) are available to the application. After that, any JAR files located in *WEB-INF/lib* are appended to the web app's classpath (the order in which they are appended is, unfortunately, not specified). You can place your classes in either location. During development, it is often easier to work with the "loose" *classes* directory and use the *lib* directory for supporting classes and third-party tools. It's also possible to install JAR files directly in the servlet container to make them available to all web apps running on that server. This is often done for common libraries that will be used by many web apps (such as the JWSDP libraries we'll use later when building web services). The location for placing the libraries, however, is not standard and any classes that are deployed in this way cannot be automatically reloaded if changed—a feature of WAR files that we'll discuss later. Servlet API 2.4 requires that each server provide a directory for these extension JARs and that the classes there will be loaded by a single classloader and made visible to the web application.

The web.xml File

The *web.xml* file is an XML file that lists the servlets to be run, the relative names (URL paths) under which to run them, their initialization parameters, and their deployment details, including security and authorization. We will assume that you have at least a passing familiarity with XML or that you can imitate the examples in a cut-and-paste fashion. (For details about working with Java and XML, see Chapter 24.) Let's start with a simple *web.xml* file for our HelloClient servlet example. It looks like this:

```
<web-app>
    <servlet>
        <servlet-name>helloclient1</servlet-name>
        <servlet-class>HelloClient</servlet-class>
    </servlet>
    <servlet-mapping>
        <servlet-name>helloclient1</servlet-name>
```

```
        <url-pattern>/hello</url-pattern>
    </servlet-mapping>
</web-app>
```

The top-level element of the document is called <web-app>. Many types of entries may appear inside the <web-app>, but the most basic are <servlet> declarations and <servlet-mapping> deployment mappings. The <servlet> declaration tag is used to declare an instance of a servlet and, optionally, to give it initialization and other parameters. One instance of the servlet class is instantiated for each <servlet> tag appearing in the *web.xml* file.

At minimum, the <servlet> declaration requires two pieces of information: a <servlet-name>, which serves as a handle to reference the servlet elsewhere in the *web.xml* file, and the <servlet-class> tag, which specifies the Java class name of the servlet. Here, we named the servlet helloclient1. We named it like this to emphasize that we could declare other instances of the same servlet if we wanted to, possibly giving them different initialization parameters, etc. The class name for our servlet is, of course, HelloClient. In a real application, the servlet class would likely have a full package name, such as com.oreilly.servlets.HelloClient.

A servlet declaration may also include one or more initialization parameters, which are made available to the servlet through the ServletConfig object's getInitParameter( ) method:

```
<servlet>
    <servlet-name>helloclient1</servlet-name>
    <servlet-class>HelloClient</servlet-class>
    <init-param>
        <param-name>foo</param-name>
        <param-value>bar</param-value>
    </init-param>
</servlet>
```

Next, we have our <servlet-mapping>, which associates the servlet instance with a path on the web server:

```
<servlet-mapping>
    <servlet-name>helloclient1</servlet-name>
    <url-pattern>/hello</url-pattern>
</servlet-mapping>
```

In older versions of the spec, servlet mapping entries must appear in the *web.xml* file after all the servlet declaration entries. In Servlet API 2.4, the order of elements under <web-app> is not restricted.[*]

Here we mapped our servlet to the path */hello*. If we later name our WAR *learning-java.war* and deploy it on *www.oreilly.com*, the full path to this servlet would be *http://www.oreilly.com/learningjava/hello*. Just as we could declare more than one

---

[*] This change corresponds with the change from XML DTDs to XML Schema for validation.

servlet instance with the `<servlet>` tag, we could declare more than one `<servlet-mapping>` for a given servlet instance. We could, for example, redundantly map the same helloclient1 instance to the paths */hello* and */hola*. The `<url-pattern>` tag provides some very flexible ways to specify the URLs that should match a servlet. We'll talk about this in detail in the next section.

Finally, we should mention that although the *web.xml* example listed earlier will work on some application servers, it is technically incomplete because it is missing formal information that specifies the version of XML it is using and the version of the *web.xml* file standard with which it complies. To make it fully compliant with the standards, add a line such as:

```
<?xml version="1.0" encoding="ISO-8859-1"?>
```

Following that is the matter of identifying the version of the *web.xml* content itself. In Servlet API 2.3 and earlier, the *web.xml* version information would take the form of a header like the following, which specifies an XML Document Type Definition (DTD):

```
<!DOCTYPE web-app
    PUBLIC "-//Sun Microsystems, Inc.//DTD Web Application 2.3//EN"
    "http://java.sun.com/dtd/web-app_2_3.dtd">
```

As of Servlet API 2.4, the *web.xml* version information has changed to take advantage of XML Schemas. (We'll talk about XML DTDs and XML Schemas in Chapter 24.) As of Version 2.4, the additional information is inserted into the `<web-app>` element itself:

```
<web-app xmlns="http://java.sun.com/xml/ns/j2ee"
    xmlns:xsi="http://www.w3.org/2001/XMLSchema-instance"
    xsi:schemaLocation="http://java.sun.com/xml/ns/j2ee
    http://java.sun.com/xml/ns/j2ee/web-app_2_4.xsd"
    version="2.4">
```

You can choose a format and copy and paste the appropriate lines in each *web.xml* file we use in this book. If you leave them out, the application may still run, but it will be harder for the servlet container to detect errors in your configuration and give you clear error messages.

URL Pattern Mappings

The `<url-pattern>` specified in the previous example was a simple string, /hello. For this pattern, only an exact match of the base URL followed by /hello would invoke our servlet. The `<url-pattern>` tag is capable of more powerful patterns, however, including wildcards. For example, specifying a `<url-pattern>` of /hello* allows our servlet to be invoked by URLs such as *www.oreilly.com/learningjava/helloworld* or *.../hellobaby*. You can even specify wildcards with extensions—e.g., *.html or *.foo, meaning that the servlet is invoked for any path that ends with those characters.

Using wildcards can result in more than one match. Consider URLs ending in /scooby* and /scoobydoo*. Which should be matched for a URL ending in .../scoobydoobiedoo? What if we have a third possible match because of a wildcard suffix extension mapping? The rules for resolving these are as follows.

First, any exact match is taken. For example, /hello matches the /hello URL pattern in our example regardless of any additional /hello*. Failing that, the container looks for the longest prefix match. So /scoobydoobiedoo matches the second pattern, /scoobydoo*, because it is longer and presumably more specific. Failing any matches there, the container looks at wildcard suffix mappings. A request ending in .foo matches a *.foo mapping at this point in the process. Finally, failing any matches there, the container looks for a default, catchall mapping named /*. A servlet mapped to /* picks up anything unmatched by this point. If there is no default servlet mapping, the request fails with a "404 not found" message.

Deploying HelloClient

Once you've deployed the HelloClient servlet, it should be easy to add examples to the WAR as you work with them in this chapter. In this section, we'll show you how to build a WAR by hand. In "Building WAR Files with Ant" later in this chapter, we'll show a more realistic way to manage your applications using the wonderful build tool, Ant. You can also grab the full set of examples, along with their source code, in the *learningjava.war* file on the CD-ROM that comes with this book or from this book's web site at *http://www.oreilly.com/catalog/learnjava3/*).

To create the WAR by hand, we first create the *WEB/INF* and *WEB-INF/classes* directories. Place *web.xml* into *WEB-INF* and *HelloClient.class* into *WEB-INF/classes*. Use the *jar* command to create *learningjava.war*:

```
$ jar cvf learningjava.war WEB-INF
```

You can also include some documents in the top level of this WAR by adding their names after the *WEB-INF* directory. This command produces the file *learningjava.war*. You can verify the contents using the *jar* command:

```
$ jar tvf learningjava.war
document1.html
WEB-INF/web.xml
WEB-INF/classes/HelloClient.class
```

Now all that is necessary is to drop the WAR into the correct location for your server. We assume you have downloaded and installed Tomcat. The location for WAR files is the path for your Tomcat installation, followed by */webapps*. Place your WAR here, and start the server. If Tomcat is configured with the default port number, you should be able to point to the HelloClient servlet with one of the following URLs: *http://localhost:8080/learningjava/hello* or *http://<yourserver>:8080/learningjava/hello*, where <yourserver> is the name or IP address of your server.

Reloading web apps

All servlet containers are supposed to provide a facility for reloading WAR files; many support reloading of individual servlet classes after they have been modified. Reloading WARs is part of the servlet specification and is especially useful during development. Support for reloading web apps varies from server to server. Normally, all that you have to do is drop a new WAR in place of the old one in the proper location (e.g., the *webapps* directory for Tomcat) and the container shuts down the old application and deploys the new version. This works in Tomcat 5.x when the "autoDeploy" attribute is set (it is on by default) and also in BEA's WebLogic application server, when it is configured in development mode.

Some servers, including Tomcat, "explode" WARs by unpacking them into a directory under the *webapps* directory, or they allow you explicitly to configure a root directory (or "context") for your unpacked web app through their own configuration files. In this mode, they may allow you to replace individual files, which can be especially useful for tweaking HTML or JSPs. Tomcat 5.x automatically reloads WAR files when they change (unless configured not to), so all you have to do is drop an updated WAR over the old one and it will redeploy it as necessary. Tomcat 4.x does not automatically reload WARs but can be made to reload classes and documents from an exploded web app via the Tomcat "manager." For example, you can prompt the server to reload the web app using a URL with the format *http://<yourserver>:8080/manager/reload?path=/learningjava*. However, even with that mechanism, it will not reload the *web.xml* file (you'll have to restart the server).

Tomcat 5.x also provides a client-side "deployer" package that integrates with Ant to automate building, deploying and redeploying applications. We'll discuss Ant later in this chapter.

Error and Index Pages

One of the finer points of writing a professional-looking web application is taking care to handle errors well. Nothing annoys a user more than getting a funny-looking page with some technical mumbo-jumbo error information on it when they expected the receipt for their Christmas present. Through the *web.xml* file, it is possible to specify documents or servlets to handle error pages shown for various conditions, as well as the special case of *welcome files* (index files) that are invoked for paths corresponding to directories. Let's start with error handling.

You can designate a page or servlet that can handle various HTTP error status codes, such as "404 Not Found" and "403 Forbidden," using one or more <error-page> declarations:

```
<web-app>
...
    <error-page>
        <error-code>404</error-code>
```

```
        <location>/notfound.html</location>
    </error-page>
    <error-page>
        <error-code>403</error-code>
        <location>/secret.html</location>
    </error-page>
```

Additionally, you can designate error pages based on Java exception types that may be thrown from the servlet. For example:

```
<error-page>
    <exception-type>java.lang.IOException</exception-type>
    <location>/ioexception.html</location>
</error-page>
```

This declaration catches any IOExceptions generated from servlets in the web app and displays the *ioexception.html* page. If no matching exceptions are found in the <error-page> declarations, and the exception is of type ServletException (or a subclass), the container makes a second try to find the correct handler. It looks for a wrapped exception (the "cause" exception) contained in the ServletException and attempts to match it to an error page declaration.

As we've mentioned, you can use a servlet to handle your error pages, just as you can use a static document. In fact, the container supplies several helpful pieces of information to an error-handling servlet, which the servlet can use in generating a response. The information is made available in the form of servlet request attributes through the method getAttribute( ):

```
Object requestAttribute = servletRequest.getAttribute("name");
```

Attributes are like servlet parameters, except that they can be arbitrary objects. We have seen attributes of the ServletContext in "The ServletContext API" section. In this case, we are talking about attributes of the request. When a servlet (or JSP or filter) is invoked to handle an error condition, the following string attributes are set in the request:

```
javax.servlet.error.servlet_name
javax.servlet.error.request_uri
javax.servlet.error.message
```

Depending on whether the <error-page> declaration was based on an <error-code> or <exception-type> condition, the request also contains one of the following two attributes:

```
// status code Integer or Exception object
javax.servlet.error.status_code
javax.servlet.error.exception
```

In the case of a status code, the attribute is an Integer representing the code. In the case of the exception type, the object is the actual instigating exception.

Indexes for directory paths can be designated in a similar way. Normally, when a user specifies a directory URL path, the web server searches for a default file in that directory to be displayed. The most common example of this is the ubiquitous *index.html* file. You can designate your own ordered list of files to look for by adding a `<welcome-file-list>` entry to your *web.xml* file. For example:

```
<welcome-file-list>
    <welcome-file>index.html</welcome-file>
    <welcome-file>index.htm</welcome-file>
</welcome-file-list>
```

`<welcome-file-list>` specifies that when a partial request (directory path) is received, the server should search first for a file named *index.html* and, if that is not found, a file called *index.htm*. If none of the specified welcome files is found, it is left up to the server to decide what kind of page to display. Servers are generally configured to display a directory-like listing or to produce an error message.

Security and Authentication

One of the most powerful features of web app deployment with the Servlet API is the ability to define *declarative security* constraints, meaning that you can spell out in the *web.xml* file exactly which areas of your web app (URL paths to documents, directories, servlets, etc.) are login-protected, the types of users allowed access to them, and the class of security protocol required for communications. It is not necessary to write code in your servlets to implement these basic security procedures.

There are two types of entries in the *web.xml* file that control security and authentication. First are the `<security-constraint>` entries, which provide authorization based on user roles and secure transport of data, if desired. Second is the `<login-config>` entry, which determines the kind of authentication used for the web application.

Assigning Roles to Users

Let's take a look at a simple example. The following *web.xml* excerpt defines an area called "Secret documents" with a URL pattern of */secret/** and designates that only users with the role "secretagent" may access them. It specifies the simplest form of login process: the BASIC authentication model, which causes the browser to prompt the user with a simple pop-up username and password dialog box:

```
<web-app>
...
    <security-constraint>
        <web-resource-collection>
            <web-resource-name>Secret documents</web-resource-name>
            <url-pattern>/secret/*</url-pattern>
        </web-resource-collection>
        <auth-constraint>
            <role-name>secretagent</role-name>
        </auth-constraint>
    </security-constraint>
```

```
<login-config>
    <auth-method>BASIC</auth-method>
</login-config>
```

In Servlet API 2.3 and prior, the security constraint entry comes after all servlet and filter-related entries in the *web.xml* file. Each `<security-constraint>` block has one `<web-resource-collection>` section that designates a named list of URL patterns for areas of the web app, followed by an `<auth-constraint>` section listing user roles that are allowed to access those areas. You can add the example setup to the *web.xml* file for the *learningjava.war* file and prepare to try it out. However, there is one additional step you'll have to take to get this working: create the user role "secretagent" and an actual user with this role in your application server environment.

Access to protected areas is granted to user roles, not individual users. A user role is effectively just a group of users; instead of granting access to individual users by name, access is granted to roles, and users are assigned one or more roles. A user role is an abstraction from users. Actual user information (name and password, etc.) is handled outside the scope of the web app, in the application server environment (possibly integrated with the host platform operating system). Generally, application servers have their own tools for creating users and assigning individuals (or actual groups of users) their roles. A given username may have many roles associated with it.

When attempting to access a login-protected area, the user's valid login will be assessed to see if she has the correct role for access. For the Tomcat server, adding users and assigning them roles is easy; simply edit the file *conf/tomcat-users.xml*. To add a user named "bond" with the "secretagent" role, you'd add an entry such as:

```
<user name="bond" password="007" roles="secretagent"/>
```

For other servers, you'll have to refer to the documentation to determine how to add users and assign security roles.

Secure Data Transport

Before we move on, there is one more piece of the security constraint to discuss: the transport guarantee. Each `<security-constraint>` block may end with a `<user-data-constraint>` entry, which designates one of three levels of transport security for the protocol used to transfer data to and from the protected area over the Internet. For example:

```
<security-constraint>
...
    <user-data-constraint>
        <transport-guarantee>CONFIDENTIAL</transport-guarantee>
    </user-data-constraint>
</security-constraint>
```

The three levels are NONE, INTEGRAL, and CONFIDENTIAL. NONE is equivalent to leaving out the section, indicating no special transport is required. This is the standard for normal web traffic, which is generally sent in plain text over the network. The INTEGRAL level of security specifies that any transport protocol used must guarantee the data sent is not modified in transit. This implies the use of digital signatures or some other method of validating the data at the receiving end but it does not require that the data be encrypted and hidden while it is transported. Finally, CONFIDENTIAL implies both INTEGRAL and encrypted. In practice, the only widely used secure transport used in web browsers is SSL. Requiring a transport guarantee other than NONE typically forces the use of SSL by the client browser.

Authenticating Users

The `<login-conf>` section determines exactly how a user authenticates himself or herself (logs in) to the protected area. The `<auth-method>` tag allows four types of login authentication to be specified: BASIC, DIGEST, FORM, and CLIENT-CERT. In our example, we showed the BASIC method, which uses the standard web browser login and password dialog. BASIC authentication sends the user's name and password in plain text over the Internet unless a transport guarantee has been used separately to start SSL and encrypt the data stream. DIGEST is a variation on BASIC that obscures the text of the password but adds little real security; it is not widely used. FORM is equivalent to BASIC, but instead of using the browser's dialog, we can use our own HTML form to post the username and password data to the container. The form data can come from a static HTML page or one generated by a servlet. Again, form data is sent in plain text unless otherwise protected by a transport guarantee (SSL). CLIENT-CERT is an interesting option. It specifies that the client must be identified using a client-side public key certificate. This implies the use of a protocol like SSL, which allows for secure exchange and mutual authentication using digital certificates. The exact method of setting up a client-side certificate is browser-dependent.

The FORM method is most useful because it allows us to customize the look of the login page (we recommend using SSL to secure the data stream). We can also specify an error page to use if the authentication fails. Here is a sample `<login-config>` using the form method:

```
<login-config>
    <auth-method>FORM</auth-method>
    <form-login-config>
        <form-login-page>/login.html</form-login-page>
        <form-error-page>/login_error.html</form-error-page>
    </form-login-config>
</login-config>
```

The login page must contain an HTML form with a specially named pair of fields for the name and password. Here is a simple *login.html* file:

```
<html>
<head><title>Login</title></head>
```

```
<body>
    <form method="POST" action="j_security_check">
        Username: <input type="text" name="j_username"><br>
        Password: <input type="password" name="j_password"><br>
        <input type="submit" value="submit">
    </form>
</body>
</html>
```

The username field is called j_username, the password field is called j_password, and the URL used for the form action attribute is j_security_check. There are no special requirements for the error page, but normally you will want to provide a "try again" message and repeat the login form.

As strange as it may seem, there is currently no API for explicitly logging out a user. However, it is specified that a user's login is no longer valid after the user session times out or is invalidated. Therefore, you can effectively log out the user by calling invalidate() on the session:

```
request.getSession().invalidate(); // log out
```

This is not quite the same thing as being logged out. What it means is that the user must log in again before performing another operation. Some servlet containers provide their own APIs for explicitly logging out a user. A portable logout API is expected to be included in Servlet API 2.5.

Procedural Security

We should mention that in addition to the declarative security offered by the *web. xml* file, servlets may perform their own active procedural (or programmatic) security using all the authentication information available to the container. We won't cover this in detail, but here are the basics.

The name of the authenticated user is available through the HttpServletRequest getRemoteUser() method, and the type of authentication provided can be determined with the getAuthType() method. Servlets can work with security roles using the isUserInRole() method. (To do this requires adding some additional mappings in the *web.xml* file allowing the servlet to refer to the security roles by reference names.)

For advanced applications, a java.security.Principal object for the user can be retrieved with the getUserPrincipal() method of the request. In the case where a secure transport like SSL was used, the method isSecure() returns true, and detailed information about how the principal was authenticated—the cipher type, key size, and certificate chain—is made available through request attributes. It is useful to note that the notion of being "logged in" to a web application, from the servlet container's point of view, is defined as there being a valid (non-null) value returned by the getUserPrincipal( ) method. This is what we meant when we said that there is no true API for logging out the user at this time, other than invalidating the session.

Servlet Filters

The servlet Filter API generalizes the Java Servlet API to allow modular component "filters" to operate on the servlet request and responses in a sort of pipeline. Filters are *chained*, meaning that when more than one filter is applied, the servlet request is passed through each filter in succession, with each having an opportunity to act upon or modify the request before passing it to the next filter. Similarly, upon completion, the servlet result is effectively passed back through the chain on its return trip to the browser. Servlet filters may operate on any requests to a web application, not just those handled by the servlets; they may filter static content, as well. As of Servlet API 2.4, you can also control whether filters are applied to error and welcome pages as well as pages forwarded or included using the request dispatcher.

Filters are declared and mapped to servlets in the *web.xml* file. There are two ways to map a filter: using a URL pattern like those used for servlets or by specifying a servlet by its instance name (<servlet-name>). Filters obey the same basic rules as servlets when it comes to URL matching, but when multiple filters match a path, they are all invoked.

The order of the chain is determined by the order in which matching filter mappings appear in the *web.xml* file, with <url-pattern> matches taking precedence over <servlet-name> matches. This is contrary to the way servlet URL matching is done, with specific matches taking the highest priority. Filter chains are constructed as follows. First, each filter with a matching URL pattern is called in the order in which it appears in the *web.xml* file; next, each filter with a matching servlet name is called, also in order of appearance. URL patterns take a higher priority than filters specifically associated with a servlet, so in this case, patterns such as /* have first crack at an incoming request.

The Filter API is very simple and mimics the Servlet API. A servlet filter implements the javax.servlet.Filter interface and implements three methods: init( ), doFilter( ), and destroy( ). The doFilter( ) method is where the work is performed. For each incoming request, the ServletRequest and ServletResponse objects are passed to doFilter( ). Here, we have a chance to examine and modify these objects—or even substitute our own objects for them—before passing them to the next filter and, ultimately, the servlet (or user) on the other side. Our link to the rest of the filter chain is another parameter of doFilter( ), the FilterChain object. With FilterChain, we can invoke the next element in the pipeline. The following section presents an example.

A Simple Filter

For our first filter, we'll do something easy but practical: create a filter that limits the number of concurrent connections to its URLs. We'll simply have our filter keep a counter of the active connections passing through it and turn away new requests when they exceed a specified limit:

```java
import java.io.*;
import javax.servlet.*;
import javax.servlet.http.*;

public class ConLimitFilter implements Filter
{
    int limit;
    int count;

    public void init( FilterConfig filterConfig )
        throws ServletException
    {
        String s = filterConfig.getInitParameter("limit");
        if ( s == null )
            throw new ServletException("Missing init parameter: "+limit);
        limit = Integer.parseInt( s );
    }

    public void doFilter (
        ServletRequest req, ServletResponse res, FilterChain chain )
            throws IOException, ServletException
    {
        if ( count > limit ) {
            HttpServletResponse httpRes = (HttpServletResponse)res;
            httpRes.sendError(
                httpRes.SC_SERVICE_UNAVAILABLE, "Too Busy.");
        } else {
            ++count;
            chain.doFilter( req, res );
            --count;
        }
    }

    public void destroy( ) { }
}
```

ConLimitFilter implements the three life-cycle methods of the Filter interface: init( ), doFilter( ), and destroy( ). In our init( ) method, we use the FilterConfig object to look for an initialization parameter named "limit" and turn it into an integer. Users can set this value in the section of the *web.xml* file where the instance of our filter is declared. The doFilter( ) method implements all our logic. First, it receives ServletRequest and ServletResponse object pairs for incoming requests. Depending on the counter, it then either passes them down the chain by invoking the next doFilter( ) method on the FilterChain object, or rejects them by generating its own response. We use the standard HTTP message "504 Service Unavailable" when we deny new connections.

Calling doFilter( ) on the FilterChain object continues processing by invoking the next filter in the chain or by invoking the servlet if ours is the last filter. Alternatively, when we choose to reject the call, we use the ServletResponse to generate our own response and then simply allow doFilter( ) to exit. This stops the processing chain at our filter, although any filters called before us still have an opportunity to intervene as the request effectively traverses back to the client.

Notice that ConLimitFilter increments the count before calling doFilter( ) and decrements it after. Prior to calling doFilter( ), we can work on the request before it reaches the rest of the chain and the servlet. After the call to doFilter( ), the chain to the servlet has completed, and the request is sent back to the client. This is our opportunity to do any post-processing of the response.

Finally, we should mention that although we've been talking about the servlet request and response as if they were HttpServletRequest and HttpServletResponse, the doFilter( ) method actually takes the more generic ServletRequest and ServletResponse objects as parameters. As filter implementers, we are expected to determine when it is safe to treat them as HTTP traffic and perform the cast as necessary (which we do here in order to use the sendError( ) HTTP response method).

A Test Servlet

Before we go on, here is a simple test servlet you can use to try out this filter and the other filters we'll develop in this section. It's called WaitServlet and, as its name implies, it simply waits. You can specify how long it waits as a number of seconds with the servlet parameter time.

```java
import java.io.*;
import javax.servlet.*;
import javax.servlet.http.*;

public class WaitServlet extends HttpServlet
{
    public void doGet( HttpServletRequest request, HttpServletResponse response)
        throws ServletException, IOException
    {
        String waitStr = request.getParameter("time");
        if ( waitStr == null )
            throw new ServletException("Missing parameter: time");
        int wait = Integer.parseInt(waitStr);

        try {
            Thread.sleep( wait * 1000 );
        } catch( InterruptedException e ) {
            throw new ServletException(e);
        }
```

```
            response.setContentType("text/html");
            PrintWriter out = response.getWriter(  );
            out.println(
                "<html><body><h1>WaitServlet Response</h1></body></html>");
            out.close(  );
        }
    }
```

By making multiple simultaneous requests to the WaitServlet, you can try out the ConLimitFilter. Be careful, though, because some web browsers (namely Opera) won't open multiple requests to the same URL. You may have to add extraneous parameters to trick the web browser. To try out in full, see the *learningjava.war* application.

Declaring and Mapping Filters

Filters are declared and mapped in the *web.xml* file much as servlets are. Like servlets, one instance of a filter class is created for each filter declaration in the *web.xml* file. A filter declaration looks like this:

```
<filter>
    <filter-name>defaultsfilter1</filter-name>
    <filter-class>RequestDefaultsFilter</filter-class>
</filter>
```

It specifies a filter handle name to be used for reference within the *web.xml* file and the filter's Java class name. Filter declarations may also contain <init-param> parameter sections, just like servlet declarations.

Filters are mapped to resources with <filter-mapping> declarations that specify the filter handle name and either the specific servlet handle name or a URL pattern, as we discussed earlier:

```
<filter-mapping>
    <filter-name>conlimitfilter1</filter-name>
    <servlet-name>waitservlet1</servlet-name>
 </filter-mapping>

<filter-mapping>
    <filter-name>conlimitfilter1</filter-name>
    <url-pattern>/*</url-pattern>
 </filter-mapping>
```

Filter mappings appear after all filter declarations in the *web.xml* file.

Filtering the Servlet Request

Our first filter example was not very exciting because it did not actually modify any information going to or coming from the servlet. Next, let's do some actual "filtering" by modifying the incoming request before it reaches a servlet. In this example, we'll create a request "defaulting" filter that automatically supplies default values for specified servlet parameters when they are not provided in the incoming request. Despite its simplicity, this example might be very useful. Here is the RequestDefaultsFilter:

```java
import java.io.*;
import javax.servlet.*;
import javax.servlet.http.*;

public class RequestDefaultsFilter implements Filter
{
    FilterConfig filterConfig;

    public void init( FilterConfig filterConfig ) throws ServletException
    {
        this.filterConfig = filterConfig;
    }

    public void doFilter (
        ServletRequest req, ServletResponse res, FilterChain chain )
            throws IOException, ServletException
    {
        WrappedRequest wrappedRequest =
            new WrappedRequest( (HttpServletRequest)req );
        chain.doFilter( wrappedRequest, res );
    }

    public void destroy(  ) { }

    class WrappedRequest extends HttpServletRequestWrapper
    {
        WrappedRequest( HttpServletRequest req ) {
            super( req );
        }

        public String getParameter( String name ) {
            String value = super.getParameter( name );
            if ( value == null )
                value = filterConfig.getInitParameter( name );
            return value;
        }
    }
}
```

To interpose ourselves in the data flow, we must do something drastic. We kidnap the incoming HttpServletRequest object and replace it with an evil twin that does our bidding. The technique, which we'll use here for modifying the request object and later for modifying the response, is to wrap the real request with an adapter, allowing us to override some of its methods. Here, we will take control of the HttpServletRequest's getParameter( ) method, modifying it to look for default values where it would otherwise return null.

Again, we implement the three life-cycle methods of Filter, but this time, before invoking doFilter( ) on the filter chain to continue processing, we wrap the incoming

HttpServletRequest in our own class, WrappedRequest. WrappedRequest extends a special adapter called HttpServletRequestWrapper. This wrapper class is a convenience utility that extends HttpServletRequest. It accepts a reference to a target HttpServletRequest object and, by default, delegates all of its methods to that target. This makes it very convenient for us to simply override one or more methods of interest to us. All we have to do is override getParameter( ) in our WrappedRequest class and add our functionality. Here, we simply call our parent's getParameter( ), and in the case where the value is null, we try to substitute a filter initialization parameter of the same name.

Try this example using the WaitServlet with a filter declaration and mapping as follows:

```
<filter>
    <filter-name>defaultsfilter1</filter-name>
    <filter-class>RequestDefaultsFilter</filter-class>
    <init-param>
        <param-name>time</param-name>
        <param-value>3</param-value>
    </init-param>
</filter>
...
<filter-mapping>
    <filter-name>defaultsfilter1</filter-name>
    <servlet-name>waitservlet1</servlet-name>
 </filter-mapping>
```

Now the WaitServlet receives a default time value of three seconds even when you don't specify one.

Filtering the Servlet Response

Filtering the request was fairly easy, and we can do something similar with the response object using exactly the same technique. There is a corresponding HttpServletResponseWrapper that we can use to wrap the response before the servlet uses it to communicate back to the client. By wrapping the response, we can intercept methods that the servlet uses to write the response, just as we intercepted the getParameter( ) method that the servlet used in reading the incoming data. For example, we could override the sendError( ) method of the HttpServletResponse object and modify it to redirect to a specified page. In this way, we could create a servlet filter that emulates the programmable error page control offered in the *web. xml* file. But the most interesting technique available to us, and the one we'll show here, involves actually modifying the data written by the servlet before it reaches the client. To do this we have to pull a double "switcheroo." We wrap the servlet response to override the getWriter( ) method and then create our own wrapper for the client's PrintWriter object supplied by this method, one that buffers the data written and allows us to modify it. This is a useful and powerful technique, but it can be tricky.

Our example, LinkResponseFilter, is an automatic hyperlink-generating filter that reads HTML responses and searches them for patterns supplied as regular expressions. When it matches a pattern, it turns it into an HTML link. The pattern and links are specified in the filter initialization parameters. You could extend this example with access to a database or XML file and add additional rules to make it into a very powerful site-management helper. Here it is:

```java
import java.io.*;
import java.util.*;
import javax.servlet.*;
import javax.servlet.http.*;

public class LinkResponseFilter implements Filter
{
    FilterConfig filterConfig;

    public void init( FilterConfig filterConfig )
        throws ServletException
    {
        this.filterConfig = filterConfig;
    }

    public void doFilter (
        ServletRequest req, ServletResponse res, FilterChain chain )
            throws IOException, ServletException
    {
        WrappedResponse wrappedResponse =
            new WrappedResponse( (HttpServletResponse)res );
        chain.doFilter( req, wrappedResponse );
        wrappedResponse.close(  );
    }

    public void destroy(  ) { }

    class WrappedResponse extends HttpServletResponseWrapper
    {
        boolean linkText;
        PrintWriter client;

        WrappedResponse( HttpServletResponse res ) {
            super( res );
        }

        public void setContentType( String mime ) {
            super.setContentType( mime );
            if ( mime.startsWith("text/html") )
                linkText = true;
        }
```

```
    public PrintWriter getWriter( ) throws IOException {
        if ( client == null )
            if ( linkText )
                client = new LinkWriter(
                    super.getWriter( ), new ByteArrayOutputStream( ) );
            else
                client = super.getWriter( );
        return client;
    }

    void close( ) {
        if ( client != null )
            client.close( );
    }
}

class LinkWriter extends PrintWriter
{
    ByteArrayOutputStream buffer;
    Writer client;

    LinkWriter( Writer client, ByteArrayOutputStream buffer ) {
        super( buffer );
        this.buffer = buffer;
        this.client = client;
    }

    public void close( ) {
        try {
            flush( );
            client.write( linkText( buffer.toString( ) ) );
            client.close( );
        } catch ( IOException e ) {
            setError( );
        }
    }

    String linkText( String text ) {
        Enumeration en = filterConfig.getInitParameterNames( );
        while ( en.hasMoreElements( ) ) {
            String pattern = (String)en.nextElement( );
            String value = filterConfig.getInitParameter( pattern );
            text = text.replaceAll(
                pattern, "<a href="+value+">$0</a>" );
        }
        return text;
    }
}
```

That was a bit longer than our previous examples, but the basics are the same. We have wrapped the HttpServletResponse object with our own WrappedResponse class using the HttpServletResponseWrapper helper class. Our WrappedResponse overrides two methods: getWriter( ) and setContentType( ). We override setContentType( ) in order to set a flag indicating whether the output is of type "text/html" (an HTML document). We don't want to be performing regular-expression replacements on binary data such as images, for example, should they happen to match our filter. We also override getWriter( ) to provide our substitute writer stream, LinkWriter. Our LinkWriter class is a PrintStream that takes as arguments the client PrintWriter and a ByteArrayOutputStream that serves as a buffer for storing output data before it is written. We are careful to substitute our LinkWriter only if the linkText Boolean set by setContent( ) is true. When we do use our LinkWriter, we cache the stream so that any subsequent calls to getWriter( ) return the same object. Finally, we have added one method to the response object: close( ). A normal HttpServletResponse does not have a close( ) method. We use ours on the return trip to the client to indicate that the LinkWriter should complete its processing and write the actual data to the client. We do this in case the client does not explicitly close the output stream before exiting the servlet service methods.

This explains the important parts of our filter-writing example. Let's wrap up by looking at the LinkWriter, which does the magic in this example. LinkWriter is a PrintStream that holds references to two other Writers: the true client PrintWriter and a ByteArrayOutputStream. The LinkWriter calls its superclass constructor, passing the ByteArrayOutputStream as the target stream, so all of its default functionality (its print( ) methods) writes to the byte array. Our only real job is to intercept the close( ) method of the PrintStream and add our text linking before sending the data. When LinkWriter is closed, it flushes itself to force any data buffered in its superclass out to the ByteArrayOutputStream. It then retrieves the buffered data (with the ByteArrayOutputStream toString( ) method) and invokes its linkText( ) method to create the hyperlinks before writing the linked data to the client. The linkText( ) method simply loops over all the filter initialization parameters, treating them as patterns, and uses the String replaceAll( ) method to turn them into hyperlinks. (See Chapter 1 for more about replaceAll( ).)

This example works, but it has limitations. First, we cannot buffer an infinite amount of data. A better implementation would have to make a decision about when to start writing data to the client, potentially based on the client-specified buffer size of the HttpServletResponse API. Next, our implementation of linkText( ) could probably be speeded up by constructing one large regular expression using alternation. You will no doubt find other ways it can be improved.

Building WAR Files with Ant

Thus far in this book, we have not become too preoccupied with special tools to help you construct Java applications. Partly, this is because it's outside the scope of this text, and partly it reflects a small bias of the authors against getting too entangled with particular development environments. There is, however, one universal tool that should be in the arsenal of every Java developer: the Jakarta Project's Ant. Ant is a project builder for Java, a pure Java application that fills the role that *make* does for C applications. Ant has many advantages over *make* when building Java code, not the least of which is that it comes with a wealth of special "targets" (declarative commands) to perform common Java-related operations such as building WAR files. Ant is fast, portable, and easy to install and use. Make it your friend.

We won't cover the usage of Ant in detail here. You can learn more and download it from its home page, *http://jakarta.apache.org/ant/* or grab it from the CD-ROM accompanying this book (view CD content online at *http://examples.oreilly.com/ learnjava3/CD-ROM/*). To get you started we give you a sample build file here. The Ant build file supplied with the examples for this chapter will compile the source and build the completed WAR file for you. You can find it with the example source.

A Development-Oriented Directory Layout

At the beginning of this chapter, we described the layout of a WAR, including the standard files and directories that must appear inside the archive. While this file organization is necessary for deployment inside the archive, it may not be the best way to organize your project during development. Maintaining *web.xml* and libraries inside a directory named *WEB-INF* under all of your content may be convenient for running the *jar* command, but it doesn't line up well with how those areas are created or maintained from a development perspective. Fortunately, with a simple Ant build file, we can create our WAR from an arbitrary project layout.

Let's choose a directory structure that is a little more oriented toward project development. For example:

```
myapplication
|
|-- src
|-- lib
|-- docs
|-- web.xml
```

We place our source-code tree under *src*, required library JAR files under *lib*, and our content under *docs*. We leave *web.xml* at the top where it's easy to tweak parameters, etc.

Here is a simple Ant *build.xml* file for constructing a WAR from the new directory structure:

```
<project name="myapplication" default="compile" basedir=".">

    <property name="war-file" value="${ant.project.name}.war"/>
    <property name="src-dir" value="src" />
    <property name="build-dir" value="classes" />
    <property name="docs-dir" value="docs" />
```

```
<property name="webxml-file" value="web.xml" />
<property name="lib-dir" value="lib" />

<target name="compile" depends="">
    <mkdir dir="${build-dir}"/>
    <javac srcdir="${src-dir}" destdir="${build-dir}"/>
</target>

<target name="war" depends="compile">
    <war warfile="${war-file}" webxml="${webxml-file}">
        <classes dir="${build-dir}"/>
        <fileset dir="${docs-dir}"/>
        <lib dir="${lib-dir}"/>
    </war>
</target>

<target name="clean">
    <delete dir="${build-dir}"/>
    <delete file="${war-file}"/>
</target>

</project>
```

A *build.xml* file such as this comes with the source code for the examples from this chapter. You can find it with the examples on the CD accompanying this book. You can use it to compile your code (the default target) simply by running ant, or you can compile and build the WAR by specifying the war target like this:

`% ant war`

Our *build.xml* file tells Ant to find all the Java files under the *src* tree that need building and compile them into a "build" directory named *classes*. Running *ant war* creates the file *myapplication.war*, placing all of the docs and the *web.xml* file in the correct locations. You can clean up everything and remove the generated *classes* directory and WAR by typing **ant clean** on the command line.

There is nothing really project-specific in this sample build file except the project name attribute in the first line, which you replace with your application's name. And we reference that name only to specify the name of the WAR to generate. You can customize the names of any of the files or directories for your own layout by changing the Ant <property> declarations. The *learningjava.war* file example for this chapter comes with a version of this Ant *build.xml* file. There are also Ant build files supplied with other chapters, to build some of the more complex examples. For example, Chapter 1 includes an Ant build file that automates the use of JAXB to generate Java classes from XML.

Deploying and Redeploying WARs with Ant

With Tomcat Version 5.x you can download a client-side "deployer" package, which provides Ant targets for deploying, redeploying, starting, stopping, and undeploying a web app on a running Tomcat server. The deployer package utilizes the Tomcat manager. Similar Ant tasks exist for other servers, such as WebLogic. Making these tasks part of your Ant build script can save a great deal of time and effort. The deployer package can be found along with the main Tomcat download at *http:// jakarta.apache.org/tomcat/*.

Implementing Web Services

Now that we've covered servlets and web applications in detail, we'd like to return to the topic of web services. In the previous chapter, we introduced the concept of a web service as an extension (formalization) of the basic HTTP web transaction, using XML content for application-to-application communication instead of consumption by a web browser client. In that chapter, we showed how easy it is to invoke an RPC-style web service, using client-side classes generated from a WSDL description file. In this section, we'll show the other side of that equation and demonstrate how to implement and deploy a web service.

The world of web services has been moving quickly and the APIs, buzzwords, and hype continue to proliferate. The appeal of this style of interapplication communication using simple web protocols has, to some extent, been tarnished by the design-by-committee approach of every standards body and competitor adding features and layers to the web services concept. The truth is that web services are (were) simple and elegant when compared to more elaborate protocols largely because they did not support all of the same semantics—state management, callbacks, transactions, authentication, and security. As these features are added, the complexity returns. We will not cover all aspects of web services in detail but instead focus on the original XML-RPC model that is appealing for a wide variety of simple applications. The future adoption or rejection of the bulk of web services standards will dictate how they affect us all in the coming years.

In Chapter 14, we walked through generating and running the client side of a web service (the Temperature service hosted at *xmethods.net*). In this chapter, we'll build and deploy our own web service, a simple façade called EchoService. We'll be using the JWSDP again and Tomcat as a web services container.

XML-RPC in Action

It's worth taking a moment to review what a web service really is. In this case, we are using the RPC-style web service, which means that both the client and server have well-defined API functions with known arguments and return types. That API is ultimately specified in a WSDL document that anyone can use to implement either side of the service. What's really at the heart of this kind of web service is the standardization of the way that the arguments and return values are marshaled (packed up) for their trip over the net, using XML. Most other kinds of RPC (such as Java RMI) use "native" protocols that may not be easy to implement in all languages. Web services use XML to send their data. Furthermore, the data is sent over the standard web protocol, HTTP, which means that it uses the same kind of request/response that your web browser does (and that we implemented in Chapter 13 with our own little web server).

Installation and Environment

In Chapter 14, we asked that you download and install JWSDP 1.5 from Sun and suggested that you might first want to install the Sun Tomcat reference web services container (in anticipation of using it in this chapter). If you haven't done one or both of those yet, please download the Tomcat container* now from *http://java.sun.com/webservices/containers/tomcat_for_JWSDP_1_5.html* and unpack it in a location of your choice. If you haven't installed the JWSDP yet, please do so now, downloading it from *http://java.sun.com/webservices/jwsdp*. The JWSDP installation program should ask you if you want to install components to the Tomcat server, and you should do so. If you previously installed JWSDP, you can install the components to Tomcat now by running the script installed in the directory where you installed JWSDP under *JWSDP_HOME/jwsdp-shared/bin/jwsdpontomcat.sh* (or *.bat*) and passing the location of your Tomcat installation as an argument.

As with our client-side example in Chapter 14, the actual coding of the example is very simple. A little complexity of the packaging and environment is the only difficulty in running these examples. Deploying a web service using JWSDP involves building a WAR, such as those we created earlier in this chapter. Before it can be deployed, however, the WAR requires an extra step that adds generated components to the archive. To simplify this and running of the client-side test, we'll do as we did in the last chapter and provide both a complete Ant build as well as command-line *client-env* scripts to help you. (Building the WAR does not require any special environment, but Ant makes that part easier.)

As always, the full example source and these build files can be found on the CD accompanying the book or online at *http://www.oreilly.com/catalog/learnjava3/*.

Defining the Service

To build our client-side API in Chapter 14, we began by downloading the WSDL description file for the (existing) Temperature service. The WSDL, again, is an XML file that describes the functions (methods) of the service and the types of arguments and return values they use. From this description, the *wscompile* command was able

---

* Unfortunately, at this writing only Sun's version of the Tomcat container works properly with the JWSDP 1.5, so you will have to install the package specified here. Fortunately, both of these are easy installs and uninstalls.

to generate the client-side classes that we needed to invoke the service remotely from Java.

In creating our own web service, we have (at least) two choices. We could follow a similar process and write a WSDL document describing our service, using it to generate the necessary server-side framework. However, we can take an easier path. The *wscompile* command is capable of reading a standard Java interface and automatically generating both the WSDL and the server-side framework for us. This means that all we really have to do is write a normal Java interface that describes the methods we want to expose, implement that interface in a regular Java object, and then run the tools appropriately. JWSDP and Tomcat will do the rest. When all goes well, it's really quite easy.

Our Echo Service

We'll begin by doing just what we described earlier, writing both an interface and implementation for our EchoService. The first requirement is that the interface must extend the java.rmi.Remote interface. Although we're not technically doing Java RMI here, this interface still serves as a flag for the "remote" nature of the service.[*] As with Java RMI, this necessitates declaring that all of the methods of the interface can throw java.rmi.RemoteException as well.

We'll create a simple service that echoes a few different kinds of values: an int, a String, and one of our own object types (a data holder object), MyObject. In the next section, we'll examine the data types, MyObject, and how they are handled in more detail. Here is the interface:

```
package learningjava;

public interface EchoService extends java.rmi.Remote
{
    public int echoInt( int value )
        throws java.rmi.RemoteException;
    public String echoString( String value )
        throws java.rmi.RemoteException;
    public MyObject echoMyObject( MyObject value)
        throws java.rmi.RemoteException;
}
```

We've named our echo methods individually to differentiate them because JAX-RPC doesn't handle overloaded methods. (If we'd had a name collision, JAX-RPC would have "numbered" our methods to distinguish them.) Here is the implementation:

```
package learningjava;

public class EchoServiceImpl implements EchoService
{
```

---

[*] The same interface is used in Enterprise JavaBeans to identify the remote interface of the beans.

```
    public int echoInt( int value ) { return value; }
    public String echoString( String value ) { return value; }
    public MyObject echoMyObject( MyObject value ) { return value; }
}
```

We've placed these into a `learningjava` package because it will be easier to work with the tools that way. Note again that the `EchoService` interface extends `Remote`, indicating that its methods are to be exposed via the service. Our `EchoServiceImpl` implements this interface and does the obvious, just returning the same values.

Data Types

As you might guess, since the data for our service has to be expressed as XML in a standard way, there are some limitations to the type of objects that can be transferred. JAX-RPC supports most of the common Java data types and many standard classes directly. It can also decompose JavaBeans-compliant data classes composed of these standard types so that you can use your own classes.

Standard types

Table 15-1 summarizes the directly supported types (those types that map directly to W3C Schema types [see Chapter 24] or for which JAX-RPC has a predefined mapping).

Table 15-1. Standard types

Category	Types
Primitives and their wrappers	`boolean`, `Boolean`, `byte`, `Byte`, `short`, `Short`, `float`, `Float`, `int`, `Integer`, `long`, `Long`, `double`, `Double`
Standard types	`java.lang.String`, `java.math.BigDecimal`, `java.math.BigInteger`, `java.util.Calendar`, `java.util.Date`
Collections	`ArrayList`, `LinkedList`, `Vector`, `Stack`, `HashMap`, `TreeMap`, `Hashtable`, `Properties`, `HashSet`, `TreeSet`

Standard Java arrays of all these types are also supported.

Value data objects

As we said, JAX-RPC can also work with our own object types, although there are several requirements and a caveat to mention. First, to be able to be marshaled, our objects must contain only fields that are supported data types (or further compositions of those). Next, our objects must follow two JavaBeans design patterns. It must have a public, no-args constructor and, if it contains any nonpublic fields, they must have "getter" and "setter" accessor methods. Chapter 22 provides more details about these issues.

Finally, unlike Java RMI, the simple way we're using XML-RPC here does not support the "behavior" or the real identity of our domain objects from end to end.

When a Java client uses our WSDL document to generate implementation classes, they will be getting simple data-holder replicas of the classes we specify. These "value objects" will pass along all the data content of our objects but are not related to the originals in any other way. Our server-side implementation will, of course, receive the data in the form of our own "real" domain objects. That is why they need to have available constructors so that the server-side framework can create and populate them for us to consume.

Here is our `MyObject` data holder class:

```java
package learningjava;

public class MyObject
{
    int intValue;
    String stringValue;

    public MyObject() { }

    public MyObject( int i, String s ) {
        this.intValue = i;
        this.stringValue = s;
    }

    public int getIntValue() { return intValue; }

    public void setIntValue( int intValue ) { this.intValue = intValue; }

    public String getStringValue() {
        return stringValue;
    }
    public void setStringValue( String stringValue ) {
        this.stringValue = stringValue;
    }
}
```

This class is a simple data holder that contains an `int` and `String` value. We've followed the rules, supplying get/set methods for our two variables and a default no-args constructor.

Deploying the Web Service

Let's get down to business (or open up for business, as it were) and deploy our web service to Tomcat. As we did in Chapter 14, we'll walk through the steps here as if you were doing all of this on the command line. But, of course, we've supplied an Ant build that will both generate the completed WAR and also run the client-side test class. We'll discuss the Ant setup at the end of this section.

The first step is to compile our application classes: *EchoService.java*, *EchoService-Impl.java*, and *MyObject.java*. The *wscompile* tool reads our interface directly from the compiled class binary.

Next, for the client-side code generation, the packaging tool requires a small configuration file to tell it some things about the deployment. A file called *jaxrpc-ri.xml* (supplied with the examples) includes the following lines of XML:

```
// File: jaxrpc-ri.xml
<?xml version="1.0" encoding="UTF-8"?>
<webServices
    xmlns="http://java.sun.com/xml/ns/jax-rpc/ri/dd" version="1.0"
    targetNamespaceBase="http://learningjava.com/wsdl"
    typeNamespaceBase="http://learningjava.com/types"
    urlPatternBase="/ws">

    <endpoint
        name="Echo"
        displayName="EchoService"
        description="Example Echo Service"
        interface="learningjava.EchoService"
        implementation="learningjava.EchoServiceImpl"
     />

    <endpointMapping endpointName="Echo" urlPattern="/echo"/>

</webServices>
```

As before, this file is not part of the web services standards but just a requirement of the JWSDP implementation tools. The `webServices` element tells the *wsdeploy* tool that we are going to use several things about our service. First, it defines namespaces to use for the WSDL document describing our service (see Chapter 24 for more on namespaces). These define what are essentially unique prefixes for our data element names in the WSDL document. The endpoint declaration describes the service by name, gives a description, and most importantly, identifies our interface and implementation classes. Finally, the `endpointMapping` element specifies the server URL mapping for our web service when it is deployed. We'll be calling our WAR *echo.war*, so our service will appear under an */echo/echo* path. As we'll see, you can hit this URL with your web browser to get information about the service, too.

Next, we'll create the "portable WAR" that serves as input to the deployment tool. This WAR contains our classes and *jaxrpc-ri.xml* description file as well as a base *web.xml* file for the application. As before, we'll need the a *web.xml* file for our WAR. In this case, the file will have entries added to it by the deployment tool. In a more advanced application, you might use *web.xml* to configure other aspects of the web services deployment, such as J2EE features of the container. You can just use an "empty" one such as this (supplied with the example code):

```
<?xml version="1.0" encoding="UTF-8"?>
<!DOCTYPE web-app
```

```
        PUBLIC "-//Sun Microsystems, Inc.//DTD Web Application 2.3//EN"
        "http://java.sun.com/j2ee/dtds/web-app_2_3.dtd">
<web-app>
</web-app>
```

Create the input WAR, placing the classes in the standard location and the *jaxrpc-ri.xml* file with *web.xml* (again, the Ant build will do this and the remaining steps for you). The WAR file should look like this:

```
WEB-INF/web.xml
WEB-INF/jaxrpc-ri.xml
WEB-INF/classes/learningjava/
WEB-INF/classes/learningjava/EchoService.class
WEB-INF/classes/learningjava/EchoServiceImpl.class
WEB-INF/classes/learningjava/MyObject.class
```

The next step will take the portable WAR as input and generate a deployable WAR as output. The resulting WAR contains additional generated server framework classes and the generated WSDL document for our service. Run the *wsdeploy* command, found in*/jaxrpc/bin* in the directory where you installed JWSDP under *<JWSDP_HOME>/jaxrpc/bin*, like this. Here's a sample command line:

```
% wsdeploy.sh -classpath classes -o echo.war echo-input.war
```

The *classes* argument is the classpath for your compiled classes (it can't read them from the JAR for some reason). The *–o* specifies the output WAR filename and the final argument is the input WAR filename.

If you wish the skip all that fun, you can build the completed WAR with the supplied Ant *build.xml* file simply by running Ant or invoking *ant build-war*:

```
% ant build-war
```

And we're ready to go! If you look inside the generated *echo.war* file, you'll see many additional classes now and also the *Echo.wsdl* document that has been generated for us. Deploy this WAR just as you would any other, by dropping it into the *webapps* directory of the Tomcat container that we installed earlier (under Tomcat 5.x, copy it to *tomcat50-jwsdp/webapps*). Monitor the log files in the *logs* directory for any problems.

Using the Service

After deploying the WAR, drive your web browser to the service URL. If you are running the server on the same machine, the URL should be *http://localhost:8080/echo/echo*. You should see a description of the service similar to the one shown in Figure 15-1.

This tells you that the service is active and gives you its configuration information. You can click on the WSDL link to download the WSDL description file that was generated for our service (contained in our WAR). The "Model" link provides a JWSDP specific description of the service in another XML format.

Figure 15-1. Web services description

We can use the WSDL to test our service, just as we did in Chapter 14. To do this on the command line, create a *client-config.xml* file with the following lines (or use the one supplied with the examples):

```
<configuration xmlns="http://java.sun.com/xml/ns/jax-rpc/ri/config">
    <wsdl location="Echo.wsdl" packageName="learningjava.impl"/>
</configuration>
```

Here, we've specified that the generated classes should go into a separate package, learningjava.impl, to avoid confusion between the generated MyObject and our original. Use the *wscompile* tool as we did before:

```
% wscompile -gen client-config.xml
```

Next, we'll create a small client that uses these classes to test the service:

```
import learningjava.impl.*;

public class EchoClient
{
    public static void main( String [] args ) throws java.rmi.RemoteException
    {
        Echo_Impl impl = new Echo_Impl();
        EchoService service = impl.getEchoServicePort();

        int i = service.echoInt( 42 );
        System.out.println( i == 42 );
```

```
            String s = service.echoString( "Hello!" );
            System.out.println( s.equals("Hello!") );
            MyObject myObj = service.echoMyObject( new MyObject(42, "Foo!") );
            System.out.println( myObj.getStringValue( ) );
        }
    }
```

To run this on the command line, use the appropriate *client-env* script to set your environment. (For Windows, you'll run the *.bat* file. For a Unix shell, you'll need to "source" the environment into your current shell using the source or . [dot] command.) Don't forget to set your JWSDP_HOME environment variable first. Then compile and run the EchoClient. You should see your values echoed back to you, including the value embedded in your value object.

Of course, if you don't want to go through all of those steps, you can use the supplied Ant build to generate and run EchoClient for you using the *generate-client* and *run-client* targets. If you just want to see the code, use *generate-client*. The *run-client* target will invoke the *generate-client* for you (a smarter build would not rebuild if it wasn't necessary). Remember to edit the *build.xml* file to specify the location of the jwsdphome property.

```
% ant run-client
```

And there we are. As we said in the introduction, the actual code required to implement and invoke our service is trivial. It's just the tools that are a little cumbersome, but they are improving every day.

Web services are indeed a fast-paced and exciting area for Java. As with most growing things, there are sure to be awkward stages and unfortunate missteps. The power of the example we've shown here lies not in its technical capabilities (other protocols offer more features), but in its open portability and the simplicity of the basic XML-RPC model. A developer using another language could implement the same service or client using only simple XML tools. Some will certainly complain in the beginning that XML is too slow or too fluffy and that more optimal, binary formats would better serve us. All we have to do is look back at the growth of the Web and HTTP for examples of simplicity and transparency reigning over optimization. We'll talk about some of these aspects in Chapter 24, when we cover XML in depth. The other side of the coin is that many people will jump on the web services bandwagon for no technical reason at all, where other protocols, such as Java RMI or even plain HTTP, would do just fine. As with all things, it's important to evaluate the real-world needs and to invest time to understand the technology to make a wise decision.

CHAPTER 16

Swing

Swing is Java's graphical user interface toolkit. The javax.swing package (and its numerous subpackages) contain classes representing interface items such as windows, buttons, combo boxes, trees, tables, and menus—everything you need to build a modern, rich client-side application.[*]

Swing is part of a larger collection of software called the Java Foundation Classes (JFC), which includes the following APIs:

- The Abstract Window Toolkit (AWT), the original user interface toolkit and base graphics classes

- Swing, the pure Java user interface toolkit

- Accessibility, which provides tools for integrating nonstandard input and output devices into your user interfaces

- The 2D API, a comprehensive set of classes for high-quality drawing

- Drag and Drop, an API that supports the drag-and-drop metaphor

JFC is one of the largest and most complex parts of the standard Java platform, so it shouldn't be any surprise that we'll take several chapters to discuss it. In fact, we won't even get to talk about all of it, just the most important parts—Swing and the 2D API. Here's the lay of the land:

- This chapter covers the basic concepts you need to understand how to build user interfaces with Swing.

- Chapter 17 discusses the basic components from which user interfaces are built: buttons, lists, text fields, checkboxes, and so on.

- Chapter 18 dives further into the Swing toolkit, describing text components, trees, tables, and other advanced components.

---

[*] Despite the javax prefix, which usually denotes a standard extension API, Swing is considered a core API and is included in all releases as of Java 1.2.

- Chapter 19 discusses layout managers, which are responsible for arranging components within a window.
- Chapter 20 discusses the fundamentals of drawing, including simple image display.
- Chapter 21 covers the image generation and processing tools of the `java.awt.image` package. We'll throw in audio and video for good measure.

We can't cover the full functionality of Swing in this book; if you want the whole story, see *Java Swing* by Marc Loy, Robert Eckstein, Dave Wood, Brian Cole, and James Elliott (O'Reilly). Instead, we'll cover the basic tools you are most likely to use and show some examples of what can be done with some of the more advanced features. Figure 16-1 shows the user interface component classes of the `javax.swing` package.

To understand Swing, it helps to understand its predecessor, AWT. As its name suggests, AWT is an abstraction. Like the rest of Java, it was designed to be portable; its functionality is the same for all Java implementations. However, people generally expect their applications to have a consistent look and feel and that is usually different on different platforms. So AWT was designed to provide the same functionality on all platforms, yet have the appearance of a native application. The idea is that you could choose to write your code under Windows, then run it on an X Window System or a Macintosh and get more or less the native look and feel on each platform for free.To achieve platform binding, AWT uses interchangeable *toolkits* that interact with the host windowing system to display user interface components. This shields the Java application from the details of the environment it's running in and keeps the APIs pure. Let's say you ask AWT to create a button. When your application or applet runs, a toolkit appropriate to the host environment renders the button appropriately: on Windows, you can get a button that looks like other Windows buttons; on a Macintosh, you can get a Mac button; and so on.

AWT had some serious shortcomings, however. The worst was that the use of platform-specific toolkits meant that AWT applications might be subtly incompatible on different platforms. Furthermore, AWT lacked advanced user interface components, such as trees and grids, that were not common to all environments. AWT provided the desired look and feel, but limited the features and true portability of Java GUI applications.

Swing takes a fundamentally different approach. Instead of using native toolkits to supply interface items, such as buttons and combo boxes, components in Swing are implemented in Java itself. This means that, whatever platform you're using, by default a Swing button (for example) looks the same. However, Swing also provides a powerful, pluggable look-and-feel API that allows the native operating system appearance to be rendered at the Java level. Working purely in Java makes Swing much less prone to platform-specific bugs, which were a problem for AWT. It also means that Swing components are much more flexible and can be extended and modified in your applications in ways that native components could never be.

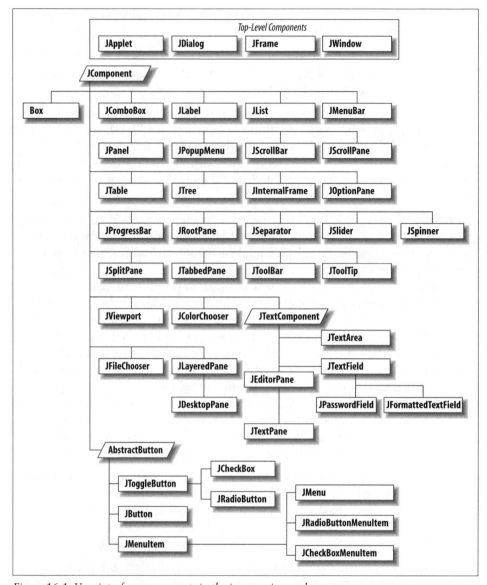

Figure 16-1. User interface components in the javax.swing package

Working with user interface components in Swing is meant to be easy. When building a user interface for your application, you'll be working with a large set of prefabricated components. It's easy to assemble a collection of user interface components (buttons, text areas, etc.) and arrange them inside containers to build complex layouts. However, when necessary, you can build upon these simple components to make entirely new kinds of interface gadgets that are completely portable and reusable.

Swing uses *layout managers* to arrange *components* inside *containers* and control their sizing and positioning. Layout managers define a strategy for arranging components instead of specifying absolute positions. For example, you can define a user interface with a collection of buttons and text areas and be reasonably confident that it will always display correctly, even if the user resizes the application window. It doesn't matter what platform or user interface look-and-feel you're using; the layout manager should still position them sensibly with respect to each other.

The next two chapters contain examples using most of the components in the javax.swing package. Before we dive into those examples, we need to spend some time talking about the concepts Swing uses for creating and handling user interfaces. This material should get you up to speed on GUI concepts and how they are used in Java.

Components

A *component* is the fundamental user interface object in Java. Everything you see on the display in a Java application is a component. This includes things like windows, panels, buttons, checkboxes, scrollbars, lists, menus, and text fields. To be used, a component usually must be placed in a *container*. Container objects group components, arrange them for display using a layout manager, and associate them with a particular display device. All Swing components are derived from the abstract javax.swing.JComponent class, as you saw in Figure 16-1. For example, the JButton class is a subclass of AbstractButton, which is itself a subclass of the JComponent class.

JComponent is the root of the Swing component hierarchy, but it descends from the AWT Container class. At this bottom level, Swing is based on AWT, so our conversation occasionally delves into the AWT package. Container's superclass is Component, the root of all AWT components, and Component's superclass is, finally, Object. Because JComponent inherits from Container, it has the capabilities of both a component and a container.

AWT and Swing, then, have parallel hierarchies. The root of AWT's hierarchy is Component, while Swing's components are based on JComponent. You'll find similar classes in both hierarchies, such as Button and JButton, List, and JList. But Swing is much more than a replacement for AWT—it contains sophisticated components as well as a real implementation of the Model-View-Controller (MVC) paradigm, which we'll discuss later.

For the sake of simplicity, we can split the functionality of the JComponent class into two categories: appearance and behavior. The JComponent class contains methods and variables that control an object's general appearance. This includes basic attributes, such as its visibility, its current size and location, and certain common graphical defaults, such as font and color, used by different subclasses in different ways. The JComponent class also contains graphics and event-handling methods which are overridden by subclasses to produce all of the different kinds of widgets that we will see.

When a component is first displayed, it's associated with a particular display device. The JComponent class encapsulates access to its display area on that device. It includes tools for rendering graphics, for working with off-screen resources, and for receiving user input.

When we talk about a component's behavior, we mean the way it responds to user-driven events. When the user performs an action (such as pressing the mouse button) within a component's display area, a Swing thread delivers an event object that describes what happened. The event is delivered to objects that have registered themselves as listeners for that type of event from that component. For example, when the user clicks on a button, the button generates an ActionEvent object. To receive those events, an object registers with the button as an ActionListener.

Events are delivered by invoking designated event-handler methods within the receiving object (the "listener"). A listener object receives specific types of events through methods of its listener interfaces (for example, through the actionPerformed( ) method of the ActionListener interface) for the types of events in which it is interested. Specific types of events cover different categories of component user interaction. For example, MouseEvents describe activities of the mouse within a component's area, KeyEvents describe key presses, and higher-level events (such as ActionEvents) indicate that a user interface component has done its job.

We will describe events thoroughly in this chapter because they are so fundamental to the way in which user interfaces function in Java. But they aren't limited to building user interfaces; they are an important interobject communications mechanism, which may be used by completely nongraphical parts of an application, as well. They are particularly important in the context of JavaBeans, which uses events as a generalized change-notification mechanism.

Swing's event architecture is very flexible. Instead of requiring every component to listen for and handle events for its own bit of the user interface, an application may register arbitrary event "handler" objects to receive the events for one or more components and "glue" those events to the correct application logic. A container might, for example, process some of the events relating to its child components.

In the graphical realm, the primary responsibility of a container is to lay out the components it contains visually, within its borders. A component informs its container when it does something that might affect other components in the container, such as changing its size or visibility. The container then tells its layout manager that it is time to rearrange the child components.

As we mentioned, Swing components are all fundamentally derived from Container. This doesn't mean that all Swing components can meaningfully contain arbitrary GUI elements within themselves. It does mean that the container-component relationship is built in at a low level. Containers can manage and arrange JComponent objects without knowing what they are or what they are doing. Components can be swapped and replaced with new versions easily and combined into composite user interface objects that can be treated as individual components themselves. This lends itself well to building larger, reusable user interface items.

Peers and Look-and-Feel

Swing components are sometimes referred to as *peerless*, or *lightweight*. These terms refer to the relationship that AWT has (and Swing does not have, respectively) with the native toolkits for rendering components on each platform. To get native components on the screen, AWT utilizes a set of peer objects that bridge the gap from pure Java to the host operating system.

At some level, of course, all our components have to talk to objects that contain native methods to interact with the host operating environment; the difference is at what level this occurs. AWT uses a set of peer interfaces. The peer interface makes it possible for a pure Java-language graphic component to use a corresponding real component—the peer object—in the native environment. With AWT, you don't generally deal directly with peer interfaces or the objects behind them; peer handling is encapsulated within the Component class.

AWT relies heavily on peers. For example, if you create a window and add eight buttons to it, AWT creates nine peers for you—one for the window and one for each of the buttons. As an application programmer, you don't have to worry about the peers, but they are always lurking under the surface, doing the real work of interacting with the operating system's windowing toolkit.

In Swing, by contrast, most components are *peerless*, or *lightweight*. This means that Swing components don't have any direct interaction with the underlying windowing system. They draw themselves in their parent container and respond to user events in pure Java, with no native code involved. In Swing, only the top-level (lowest API level) windows interact with the windowing system. These Swing containers descend from AWT counterparts, and, thus, still have peers. In Swing, if you create a window and add eight buttons to it, only one peer is created—for the window. Because it has fewer interactions with the underlying windowing system than AWT, Swing is less vulnerable to the peculiarities of any particular platform.

With lightweight components, it is easy to change their appearance. Since each component draws itself instead of relying on a peer, it can decide at runtime how to render itself. Accordingly, Swing supports different *look-and-feel* schemes, which can be changed at runtime. (A look-and-feel is the collected appearance of components in an application.) Look-and-feels based on Windows, Macintosh, and Motif are available (though licensing issues may encumber their use on various platforms), as well as several entirely original Java creations, including one called Metal. Java 5.0 added a default Java look-and-feel called Ocean, which has a slightly "flatter" and more modern look. Another new development in Java 5.0 is the addition of the Synth look-and-feel. Synth makes Java applications "skinnable" at a high level using an XML descriptor file and images as resources.

The MVC Framework

Before continuing our discussion of GUI concepts, we want to make a brief aside and talk about the MVC framework. MVC is a method of building reusable components that logically separates the structure, presentation, and behavior of a component into separate pieces. MVC is primarily concerned with building user interface components, but the basic ideas can be applied to many design issues; its principles can be seen throughout Java.

The fundamental idea behind MVC is the separation of the data model for an item from its presentation. For example, we can draw different representations of the data in a spreadsheet (e.g., bar graphs, pie charts). The data is the *model*; the particular representation is the *view*. A single model can have many views that present the data differently. A user interface component's *controller* defines and governs its behavior. Typically, this includes changes to the model, which, in turn, cause the view(s) to change. For a checkbox component, the data model could be a single Boolean variable, indicating whether it's checked or not. The behavior for handling mouse-click events would alter the model, and the view would examine that data when it draws the on-screen representation.

The way in which Swing objects communicate, by passing events from sources to listeners, is part of this MVC concept of separation. Event listeners are "observers" (controllers) and event sources are "observables" (models).* When an observable changes or performs a function, it notifies all its observers of the activity.

Swing components explicitly support MVC. Each component is actually composed of two pieces. One piece, called the UI-delegate, is responsible for the "view" and "controller" roles. It takes care of drawing the component and responding to user events. The second piece is the data model itself. This separation makes it possible for multiple Swing components to share a single data model. For example, a read-only text box and a drop-down list box could use the same list of strings as a data model.

---

* In Chapter 11 we described the Observer class and Observable interface of the java.util package. Swing doesn't use these classes directly, but it does use exactly the same design pattern for handling event sources and listeners.

Painting

In an event-driven environment such as Swing, components can be asked to draw themselves at any time. In a more procedural programming environment, you might expect a component to be involved in drawing only when first created or when it changes its appearance. In Java, however, components act in a way that is closely tied to the underlying behavior of the display environment. For example, when you obscure a component with another window and then re-expose it, a Swing thread may ask the component to redraw itself.

Swing asks a component to draw itself by calling its paint( ) method. paint( ) may be called at any time, but in practice, it's called when the object is first made visible, whenever it changes its appearance, or whenever some tragedy in the display system messes up its area. Because paint( ) can't generally make any assumptions about why it was called, it must redraw the component's entire display. The system may limit the drawing if only part of the component needs to be redrawn, but you don't have to worry about this. Swing is fairly smart and will do everything it can to avoid asking components to redraw themselves (including using "backing store" where applicable).

A component never calls its paint( ) method directly. Instead, if a component requires redrawing, it requests a call to paint( ) by invoking repaint( ). The repaint( ) method asks Swing to schedule the component for repainting. At some point after that, a call to paint( ) occurs. Swing is allowed to manage these requests in whatever way is most efficient. If there are too many requests to handle, or if there are multiple requests for the same component, the thread can collapse a number of repaint requests into a single call to paint( ). This means that you don't normally know exactly when paint( ) is called in response to a repaint( ); all you can expect is that it happens at least once, after you request it.

Calling repaint( ) is normally an implicit request to be updated as soon as possible. Another form of repaint( ) allows you to specify a time period within which you would like an update, giving the system more flexibility in scheduling the request. The system tries to repaint the component within the time you specify, but if you happen to make more than one repaint request within that time period, the system may simply condense them to carry out a single update within the time you specified. An application performing simple animation could use this method to govern its refresh rate (by specifying a period that is the inverse of the desired frame rate).

As we've mentioned, Swing components can act as containers, holding other components. Because every Swing component does its own drawing, Swing components are responsible for telling any contained components to draw themselves. Fortunately, this is all taken care of for you by a component's default paint( ) method. If you override this method, however, you have to make sure to call the superclass's implementation like this:

```
public void paint(Graphics g) {
    super.paint(g);
    ...
}
```

There's a cleaner way around this problem. All Swing components have a method called paintComponent( ). While paint( ) is responsible for drawing the component as well as its contained components, paintComponent( )'s sole responsibility is drawing the component itself. If you override paintComponent( ) instead of paint( ), you won't have to worry about drawing contained components.

Both paint( ) and paintComponent( ) receive a single argument: a Graphics object. The Graphics object represents the component's graphics context. It corresponds to the area of the screen on which the component can draw and provides the methods for performing primitive drawing and image manipulation. (We'll look at the Graphics class in detail in Chapter 18.)

Enabling and Disabling Components

Standard Swing components can be turned on and off by calling the setEnabled( ) method. When a component such as a JButton or JTextField is disabled, it becomes "ghosted" or "greyed-out" and doesn't respond to user input.

For example, let's see how to create a component that can be used only once. This requires getting ahead of the story; we won't explain some aspects of this example until later. Earlier, we said that a JButton generates an ActionEvent when it is pressed. This event is delivered to the listeners' actionPerformed( ) method. The following code disables whatever component generated the event:

```
public boolean void actionPerformed(ActionEvent e ) {
    ((JComponent)e.getSource( )).setEnabled(false);
}
```

This code calls getSource( ) to find out which component generated the event. We cast the result to JComponent because we don't necessarily know what kind of component we're dealing with; it might not be a button, because other kinds of components can generate action events. Once we know which component generated the event, we disable it.

You can also disable an entire container. Disabling a JPanel, for instance, disables all the components it contains.

Focus, Please

In order to receive keyboard events, a component has to have keyboard *focus*. The component with the focus is the currently *selected* component on the screen and is usually highlighted visually. It receives all keyboard event information until the focus changes to a new component. Typically, a component receives focus when the user clicks on it with the mouse or navigates to it using the keyboard. A component can ask for focus with the JComponent's requestFocus( ) method. You can configure whether a given component is eligible to receive focus with the setFocusable( ) method. By default most components, including things such as buttons and check-boxes, are "focusable." To make an entire window and its components nonfocus-able, use the Window setFocusableWindowState( ) method.

The control of focus is often at the heart of the user's experience with an application. Especially with text-entry fields and forms, users are accustomed to a smooth transfer of focus with the use of keyboard navigation cues (e.g., Tab and Shift-Tab for forward and backward field navigation). The management of focus in a large GUI with many components could be complex. Fortunately, in Java 1.4 and later, Swing handles almost all this behavior for you, so, in general, you don't have to implement code to specify how focus is transferred. Java 1.4 introduced an entirely new focus subsystem. The flexible KeyboardFocusManager API provides the expected common behavior by default and allows customization via FocusTraversalPolicy objects. We'll discuss focus-related events later in this chapter and focus navigation more in Chapter 18.

Other Component Methods

The JComponent class is very large; it has to provide the base-level functionality for all the various kinds of Java GUI objects. It inherits a lot of functionality from its parent Container and Component classes. We don't have room to document every method of the JComponent class here, but we'll flesh out our discussion by covering some of the more important ones:

Container getParent( )
> Return the container that holds this component.

String getName( )
void setName(String name)
> Get or assign the String name of this component. Naming a component is useful for debugging. The name is returned by toString( ).

void setVisible(boolean visible)
> Make the component visible or invisible, within its container. If you change the component's visibility, the container's layout manager automatically lays out its visible components.

```
Color getForeground( )
void setForeground(Color c)
void setBackground(Color c)
Color getBackground( )
```
Get and set the foreground and background colors for this component. The foreground color of any component is the default color used for drawing. For example, it is the color used for text in a text field as well as the default drawing color for the Graphics object passed to the component's paint( ) and paintComponent( ) methods. The background color is used to fill the component's area when it is cleared by the default implementation of update( ).

```
Dimension getSize( )
void setSize(int width, int height)
```
Get and set the current size of the component. Note that a layout manager may change the size of a component even after you've set its size yourself. To change the size a component "wants" to be, use setPreferredSize( ). There are other methods in JComponent to set its location, but this is normally the job of a layout manager.

```
Dimension getPreferredSize( )
void setPreferredSize(Dimension preferredSize)
```
Use these methods to examine or set the preferred size of a component. Layout managers attempt to set components to their preferred sizes. If you change a component's preferred size, you must call the method revalidate( ) on the component to get it laid out again.

```
Cursor getCursor( )
void setCursor(Cursor cursor)
```
Get or set the type of cursor (mouse pointer) used when the mouse is over this component's area. For example:

```
JComponent myComponent = ...;
Cursor crossHairs =
    Cursor.getPredefinedCursor( Cursor.CROSSHAIR_CURSOR );
myComponent.setCursor( crossHairs );
```

Containers

A container is a kind of component that holds and manages other components. Three of the most useful general container types are JFrame, JPanel, and JApplet. A JFrame is a top-level window on your display. JFrame is derived from java.awt.Window, which is pretty much the same but lacks a border (JWindow is the swing version of Window). A JPanel is a generic container element that groups components inside JFrames and other JPanels. The JApplet class is a kind of container that provides the foundation for applets that run inside web browsers. Like other containers, a JApplet can hold other user-interface components. You can also use the JComponent class directly, like a

JPanel, to hold components inside another container. With the exception of JFrame, JWindow, JApplet, and JDialog (another window-like container), which are derived from AWT components, all the components and containers in Swing are lightweight.

A container maintains the list of "child" components it manages and has methods for dealing with those components. Note that this child relationship refers to a visual hierarchy, not a subclass/superclass hierarchy. By themselves, most components aren't very useful until they are added to a container and displayed. The add( ) method of the Container class adds a component to the container. Thereafter, this component can be displayed in the container's display area and positioned by its layout manager. You can remove a component from a container with the remove( ) method.

Layout Managers

A *layout manager* is an object that controls the placement and sizing of components within the display area of a container. A layout manager is like a window manager in a display system; it controls where the components go and how big they are. Every container has a default layout manager, but you can install a new one by calling the container's setLayout( ) method.

Swing comes with a few layout managers that implement common layout schemes. The default layout manager for a JPanel is a FlowLayout, which tries to place objects at their preferred size from left to right and top to bottom in the container. The default for a JFrame is a BorderLayout, which places objects at specific locations within the window, such as NORTH, SOUTH, and CENTER. Another layout manager, GridLayout, arranges components in a rectangular grid. The most general (and difficult to use) layout manager is GridBagLayout, which lets you do the kinds of things you can do with HTML tables. (We'll get into the details of all these layout managers in Chapter 19.)

When you add a component to a container using a simple layout manager, you'll often use the version of add( ) that takes a single Component as an argument. However, if you're using a layout manager that uses "constraints," such as BorderLayout or GridBagLayout, you must specify additional information about where to put the new component. For that you can use the version that takes a constraint object. Here's how to place a component at the top edge of a container that uses a BorderLayout manager:

```
myContainer.add(myComponent, BorderLayout.NORTH);
```

In this case, the constraint object is the static member variable NORTH. GridBagLayout uses a much more complex constraint object to specify positioning.

Insets

Insets specify a container's margins; the space specified by the container's insets won't be used by a layout manager. Insets are described by an Insets object, which has four public int fields: top, bottom, left, and right. You normally don't need to worry about the insets; the container sets them automatically, taking into account extras like the menu bar that may appear at the top of a frame. To find the insets, call the component's getInsets( ) method, which returns an Insets object.

Z-Ordering (Stacking Components)

With the standard layout managers, components are not allowed to overlap. However, if you use custom-built layout managers or absolute positioning, components within a container may overlap. If they do, the order in which components were added to a container matters. When components overlap, they are "stacked" in the order in which they were added: the first component added to the container is on top, and the last is on the bottom. To give you more control over stacking, two additional forms of the add( ) method take an additional integer argument that lets you specify the component's exact position in the container's stacking order. Again, you don't normally need to think about this, but it's nice to know for completeness sake that it's there.

The revalidate( ) and doLayout( ) Methods

A layout manager arranges the components in a container only when asked to. Several things can mess up a container after it's initially laid out:

- Changing its size
- Resizing or moving one of its child components
- Adding, showing, removing, or hiding a child component

Any of these actions cause the container to be marked *invalid*. This means that it needs to have its child components readjusted by its layout manager. In most cases, Swing readjusts the layout automatically. All components, not just containers, maintain a notion of when they are valid or invalid. If the size, location, or internal layout of a Swing component changes, its revalidate( ) method is automatically called. Internally, the revalidate( ) method first calls the method invalidate( ) to mark the component and all its enclosing containers as invalid. It then validates the tree. Validation descends the hierarchy, starting at the nearest *validation root* container, recursively validating each child. Validating a child Container means invoking its doLayout( ) method, which asks the layout manager to do its job and then notes that the Container has been reorganized by setting its state to valid again. A validation root is a container that can accommodate children of any size such as JScrollPane (and, hence, can accommodate any possible changes in its child hierarchy without upsetting its own parents).

There are a few cases in which you may need to tell Swing to fix things manually. One example is when you change the preferred size of a component (as opposed to its actual onscreen size). To clean up the layout, call the revalidate( ) method. For example, if you have a small JPanel—say a keypad holding some buttons—and you change the preferred size of the JPanel by calling its setPreferredSize( ) method, you should also call revalidate( ) on the panel or its immediate container. The layout manager of the panel then rearranges its buttons to fit inside its new area.

Managing Components

There are a few additional tools of the Container class we should mention:

Component[ ] getComponents( )
>   Returns the container's components in an array.

void list(PrintWriter out, int indent)
>   Generates a list of the components in this container and writes them to the specified PrintWriter.

Component getComponentAt(int x, int y)
>   Tells you what component is at the specified coordinates in the container's coordinate system.

Listening for Components

You can use the ContainerListener interface to automate setting up a container's new components. A container that implements this interface can receive an event whenever it gains or loses a component. This facility makes it easy for a container to micromanage its components.

Windows and Frames

Windows and frames are the top-level containers for Java components. A JWindow is simply a plain, graphical screen that displays in your windowing system. Windows have no frills; they are mainly suitable for making "splash" screens and pop-up windows. JFrame, on the other hand, is a subclass of JWindow that has a border and can hold a menu bar. You can drag a frame around on the screen and resize it, using the ordinary controls for your windowing environment. Figure 16-2 shows a JFrame on the left and a JWindow on the right.

All other Swing components and containers must be held, at some level, inside a JWindow or JFrame. Applets are a kind of Container. Even applets must be housed in a frame or window, though normally you don't see an applet's parent frame because it is part of (or simply is) the browser or appletviewer displaying the applet.

Figure 16-2. A frame and a window

JFrames and JWindows are the only components that can be displayed without being added or attached to another Container. After creating a JFrame or JWindow, you can call the setVisible( ) method to display it. The following short application creates a JFrame and a JWindow and displays them side by side, just as in Figure 16-2.

```
//file: TopLevelWindows.java
import javax.swing.*;

public class TopLevelWindows {
  public static void main(String[] args) {
    JFrame frame = new JFrame("The Frame");
    frame.setSize(300, 300);
    frame.setLocation(100, 100);

    JWindow window = new JWindow( );
    window.setSize(300, 300);
    window.setLocation(500, 100);

    frame.setVisible(true);
    window.setVisible(true);
  }
}
```

The JFrame constructor can take a String argument that supplies a title, displayed in the JFrame's titlebar. (Or you can create the JFrame with no title and call setTitle( ) to supply the title later.) The JFrame's size and location on your desktop is determined by the calls to setSize( ) and setLocation( ). After creating the JFrame, we create a JWindow in almost exactly the same way. The JWindow doesn't have a titlebar, so there are no arguments to the JWindow constructor.

Once the JFrame and JWindow are set up, we call setVisible(true) to get them on the screen. The setVisible() method returns immediately, without blocking. Fortunately, our application does not exit, even though we've reached the end of the main() method, because the windows are still visible. You can close the JFrame by clicking on the close button in the titlebar. JFrame's default behavior is to hide itself when you click on the box by calling setVisible(false). You can alter this behavior by calling the setDefaultCloseOperation() method or by adding an event listener, which we'll cover later. Since we haven't arranged any other means here, you will have to hit Ctrl-C or whatever keystroke kills a process on your machine to stop execution of the TopLevelWindows application.

Other Methods for Controlling Frames

The setLocation() method of the Component class can be used on a JFrame or JWindow to set its position on the screen. The x and y coordinates are relative to the screen's origin (the top-left corner).

You can use the toFront() and toBack() methods to place a JFrame or JWindow in front of, or behind, other windows. By default, a user is allowed to resize a JFrame, but you can prevent resizing by calling setResizable(false) before showing the JFrame.

On most systems, frames can be "iconified"—that is, they can be shrunk down and represented by a little icon image. You can get and set a frame's icon image by calling getIconImage() and setIconImage(). As you can with all components, you can set the cursor by calling the setCursor() method.

Content Panes

Windows and frames have a little more structure than simple containers. Specifically, to support some of the fancier GUI features that require overlaying graphics (such as popups and menus), windows and frames actually consist of a number of separate overlapping container "panes" (as in glass) with names such as the root pane, layered pane, and glass pane. The primary pane of interest is usually the *content pane*. The content pane is just a Container that covers the visible area of the JFrame or JWindow; it is the container to which we actually want to add child components.

With simple containers, you can add child components with the add() method. In Java 5.0 and later, the same is true for JFrame and JWindow. Calling the add() method of one of these containers automatically places the child in the content pane container for you so that you don't really have to know about these other panes. In earlier versions of Java, you had to add child components to the content pane explicitly. It's not hard to do; we'll cover it now.

Whenever you create a new JFrame or JWindow, a content pane is automatically created for you. You can retrieve it with getContentPane( ). Here's an example that creates a JFrame and adds some components to its content pane explicitly:

```java
//file: MangoMango1.java
import java.awt.*;
import javax.swing.*;

public class MangoMango1 {
  public static void main(String[] args) {
    JFrame frame = new JFrame("The Frame");

    Container content = frame.getContentPane();
    content.setLayout(new FlowLayout());
    content.add(new JLabel("Mango"));
    content.add(new JButton("Mango"));

    frame.setLocation(100, 100);
    frame.pack();
    frame.setVisible(true);
  }
}
```

The call to JFrame's pack( ) method tells the frame window to resize itself to the minimum size required to hold all its components. Instead of having to determine the size of the JFrame, pack tells it to be "just big enough." If you do want to set the absolute size of the JFrame yourself, call setSize( ) instead.

Again, in Java 5.0 and later, we could omit the step of getting the content pane and simply set the layout on and add the buttons to the frame directly.

Another option is to create our own Container and make it the content pane of a JFrame or JWindow with setContentPane( ). Using this strategy, we could rewrite the previous example as follows:

```java
//file: MangoMango2.java
import java.awt.*;
import javax.swing.*;

public class MangoMango2 {
  public static void main(String[] args) {
    JFrame frame = new JFrame("The Frame");

    Container content = new JPanel();
    content.add(new JLabel("Mango"));
    content.add(new JButton("Mango"));
    frame.setContentPane(content);

    frame.setLocation(100, 100);
    frame.pack();
    frame.setVisible(true);
  }
}
```

We'll cover labels and buttons in Chapter 17 and layouts in Chapter 19. The important thing to remember is that prior to Java 5.0 you can't add components directly to a JFrame or JWindow. Instead, you must add them to the content pane or create an entirely new content pane. If you try to add components directly to one of these containers in an earlier version of Java, you get a runtime exception.

Events

We've spent a lot of time discussing the different kinds of objects in Swing—components, containers, and special containers such as frames and windows. Now it's time to discuss interobject communication in detail.

Swing objects communicate by sending events. The way we talk about events—"firing" them and "handling" them—makes it sound as if they are part of some special Java language feature. But they aren't. An event is simply an ordinary Java object that is delivered to its receiver by invoking an ordinary Java method. Everything else, however interesting, is purely convention. The entire Java event mechanism is really just a set of conventions for the kinds of descriptive objects that should be delivered; these conventions prescribe when, how, and to whom events should be delivered.

Events are sent from a single source object to one or more listeners. A listener implements prescribed event-handling methods that enable it to receive a type of event. It then registers itself with a source of that kind of event. Sometimes an adapter object may be interposed between the event source and the listener, but in any case, registration of a listener is always established before any events are delivered.

An event object is an instance of a subclass of java.util.EventObject; it holds information about something that's happened to its source. The EventObject parent class itself serves mainly to identify event objects; the only information it contains is a reference to the event source (the object that sent the event). Components don't normally send or receive EventObjects as such; they work with subclasses that provide more specific information.

AWTEvent is a subclass of java.awt.EventObject; further subclasses of AWTEvent provide information about specific event types. Swing has events of its own that descend directly from EventObject. For the most part, you'll just be working with specific event subclasses from the AWT or Swing packages.

ActionEvents correspond to a decisive "action" a user has taken with the component—like clicking a button or pressing Enter. An ActionEvent carries the name of an action to be performed (the *action command*) by the program. MouseEvents are generated when a user uses the mouse within a component's area. They describe the state of the mouse and, therefore, carry such information as the x and y coordinates and the state of your mouse buttons at the time the MouseEvent was created.

ActionEvent operates at a higher semantic level than MouseEvent: an ActionEvent lets us know that a component has performed its job; a MouseEvent simply confers a lot of information about the mouse at a given time. You could figure out that somebody clicked on a JButton by examining mouse events, but it is simpler to work with action events. The precise meaning of an event can also depend on the context in which it is received.

Event Receivers and Listener Interfaces

An event is delivered by passing it as an argument to the receiving object's event-handler method. ActionEvents, for example, are always delivered to a method called actionPerformed( ) in the receiver:

```
public void actionPerformed( ActionEvent e ) {
    ...
}
```

For each type of event, a corresponding listener interface prescribes the method(s) it must provide to receive those events. In this case, any object that receives ActionEvents must implement the ActionListener interface:

```
public interface ActionListener extends java.util.EventListener {
    public void actionPerformed( ActionEvent e );
}
```

All listener interfaces are subinterfaces of java.util.EventListener, which is an empty interface. It exists only to help Java-based tools such as IDEs identify listener interfaces.

Listener interfaces are required for a number of reasons. First, they help to identify objects that can receive a given type of event—they make event hookups "strongly typed." Event listener interfaces allow us to give the event-handler methods friendly, descriptive names and still make it easy for documentation, tools, and humans to recognize them in a class. Next, listener interfaces are useful because several methods can be specified for an event receiver. For example, the FocusListener interface contains two methods:

```
abstract void focusGained( FocusEvent e );
abstract void focusLost( FocusEvent e );
```

Although these methods each take a FocusEvent as an argument, they correspond to different reasons (contexts) for firing the event; in this case, whether the FocusEvent means that focus was received or lost. In this case, you could also figure out what happened by inspecting the event; all AWTEvents contain a constant specifying the event's type. But by using two methods, the FocusListener interface saves you the effort: if focusGained( ) is called, you know the event type was FOCUS_GAINED.

Similarly, the MouseListener interface defines five methods for receiving mouse events (and MouseMotionListener defines two more), each of which gives you some additional information about why the event occurred. In general, the listener interfaces group sets of related event-handler methods; the method called in any given situation provides a context for the information in the event object.

There can be more than one listener interface for dealing with a particular kind of event. For example, the MouseListener interface describes methods for receiving MouseEvents when the mouse enters or exits an area or a mouse button is pressed or released. MouseMotionListener is an entirely separate interface that describes methods to get mouse events when the mouse is moved (no buttons pressed) or dragged (buttons pressed). By separating mouse events into these two categories, Java lets you be a little more selective about the circumstances under which you want to receive MouseEvents. You can register as a listener for mouse events without receiving mouse motion events; because mouse motion events are extremely common, you don't want to handle them if you don't need to.

Two simple patterns govern the naming of Swing event listener interfaces and handler methods:

- Event-handler methods are public methods that return type void and take a single event object (a subclass of java.util.EventObject) as an argument.*
- Listener interfaces are subclasses of java.util.EventListener that are named with the suffix "Listener"—for example, MouseListener and ActionListener.

These may seem pretty obvious, but they are important because they are our first hint of a design pattern governing how to build components that work with events.

Event Sources

The previous section described the machinery an event receiver uses to listen for events. In this section, we'll describe how a receiver tells an event source to send it events, as they occur.

To receive events, an eligible listener must register itself with an event source. It does this by calling an "add listener" method in the event source and passing a reference to itself. (Thus, this scheme implements a *callback* facility.) For example, the Swing JButton class is a source of ActionEvents. Here's how a TheReceiver object might register to receive these events:

```
// receiver of ActionEvents
class TheReceiver implements ActionListener
{
    // source of ActionEvents
    JButton theButton = new JButton("Belly");
```

---

* This rule is not complete. The JavaBeans conventions (see Chapter 22) allows event-handler methods to take additional arguments when absolutely necessary and also to throw checked exceptions.

```
TheReceiver( ) {
   ...
   theButton.addActionListener( this );
}

public void actionPerformed( ActionEvent e ) {
   // Belly Button pushed...
}
```

TheReciever makes a call to the button's addActionListener( ) to receive ActionEvents from the button when they occur. It passes the reference this to register itself as an ActionListener.

To manage its listeners, an ActionEvent source (like the JButton) always implements two methods:

```
// ActionEvent source
public void addActionListener(ActionListener listener) {
    ...
}
public void removeActionListener(ActionListener listener) {
    ...
}
```

The removeActionListener( ) method removes the listener from the list so that it will not receive future events of that kind. Swing components supply implementations of both methods; normally, you won't need to implement them yourself. It's important to pay attention to how your application uses event sources and listeners. It's okay to throw away an event source without removing its listeners, but it isn't necessarily okay to throw away listeners without removing them from the source first because the event source might maintain references to them, preventing them from being garbage-collected.

You may be expecting some kind of "event source" interface listing these two methods and identifying an object as a source of this event type, but there isn't one. There are no event source interfaces in the current conventions. If you are analyzing a class and trying to determine what events it generates, you have to look for the paired add and remove methods. For example, the presence of the addActionListener( ) and removeActionListener( ) methods define the object as a source of ActionEvents. If you happen to be a human being, you can simply look at the documentation, but if the documentation isn't available, or if you're writing a program that needs to analyze a class (a process called *reflection*), you can look for this design pattern. (There is a utility, the java.beans.Introspector, which can do this for you.)

A source of FooEvent events for the FooListener interface must implement a pair of add/remove methods:

- addFooListener(FooListener *listener*)
- removeFooListener(FooListener *listener*)

If an event source can support only one event listener (unicast delivery), the add listener method can throw the java.util.TooManyListenersException.

What do all the naming patterns up to this point accomplish? For one thing, they make it possible for automated tools and integrated development environments to divine sources of particular events. Tools that work with JavaBeans will use the Java reflection and introspection APIs to search for these kinds of design patterns and identify the events that can be fired by a component.

At a more concrete level, it also means that event hookups are strongly typed, just like the rest of Java. So it's impossible to accidentally hook up the wrong kind of components; for example, you can't register to receive ItemEvents from a JButton because a button doesn't have an addItemListener( ) method. Java knows at compile time what types of events can be delivered to whom.

Event Delivery

Swing and AWT events are multicast; every event is associated with a single source but can be delivered to any number of receivers. When an event is fired, it is delivered individually to each listener on the list (see Figure 16-3).

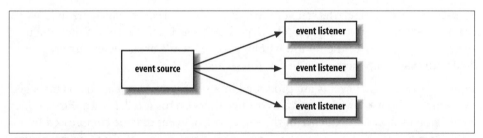

Figure 16-3. Event delivery

There are no guarantees about the order in which events are delivered. Nor are there any guarantees about what happens if you register yourself more than once with an event source; you may or may not get the event more than once. Similarly, you should assume that every listener receives the same event data. In general, events are immutable; they can't be changed by their listeners.

To be complete, we could say that event delivery is synchronous with respect to the event source, but that is because the event delivery is really just the invocation of a normal Java method. The source of the event calls the handler method of each listener. However, listeners shouldn't assume all the events will be sent in the same thread, unless they are AWT/Swing events, which are always sent serially by a global event dispatcher thread.

Event Types

All the events used by Swing GUI components are subclasses of java.util.EventObject. You can use or subclass any of the EventObject types for use in your own components. We describe the important event types here.

The events and listeners that are used by Swing fall into two packages: java.awt.event and javax.swing.event. As we've discussed, the structure of components has changed significantly between AWT and Swing. The event mechanism, however, is fundamentally the same, so the events and listeners in java.awt.event are used by Swing components. In addition, Swing has added event types and listeners in the javax.swing.event package.

java.awt.event.ComponentEvent is the base class for events that can be fired by any component. This includes events that provide notification when a component changes its dimensions or visibility as well as the other event types for mouse operations and key presses. ContainerEvents are fired by containers when components are added or removed.

The java.awt.event.InputEvent Class

MouseEvents, which track the state of the mouse, and KeyEvents, which are fired when the user uses the keyboard, are kinds of java.awt.event.InputEvents. When the user presses a key or moves the mouse within a component's area, the events are generated with that component identified as the source.

Input events and GUI events are processed in a special event queue that is managed by Swing. This gives Swing control over how all its events are delivered. First, under some circumstances, a sequence of the same type of event may be compressed into a single event. This is done to make some event types more efficient—in particular, mouse events and some special internal events used to control repainting. Perhaps more important to us, input events are delivered with extra information that lets listeners decide if the component itself should act on the event.

Mouse and Key Modifiers on InputEvents

InputEvents come with a set of flags for special modifiers. These let you detect whether the Shift, Control, or Alt keys were held down during a mouse button or key press, and, in the case of a mouse button press, distinguish which mouse button was involved. The following are the flag values contained in java.awt.event.InputEvent:

SHIFT_MASK
    Shift key with event

CTRL_MASK
    Control key with event

ALT_MASK

Windows Alt key or Mac Option/Alt with event; equivalent to BUTTON2_MASK

META_MASK

Mac Command key with event; equivalent to BUTTON3_MASK

BUTTON1_MASK

Mouse Button 1

BUTTON2_MASK

Mouse Button 2; equivalent to ALT_MASK

BUTTON3_MASK

Mouse Button 3; equivalent to META_MASK

To check for one or more flags, evaluate the bitwise AND of the complete set of modifiers and the flag or flags you're interested in. The complete set of modifiers involved in the event is returned by the InputEvent's getModifiers( ) method:

```
public void mousePressed (MouseEvent e) {
    int mods = e.getModifiers( );
    if ((mods & InputEvent.SHIFT_MASK) != 0) {
        // shifted Mouse Button press
    }
}
```

The three BUTTON flags can determine which mouse button was pressed on a two- or three-button mouse. BUTTON2_MASK is equivalent to ALT_MASK, and BUTTON3_MASK is equivalent to META_MASK. This means that pushing the second mouse button is equivalent to pressing the first (or only) button with the Alt key depressed, and the third button is equivalent to the first with the "Meta" key depressed. These provide some minimal portability even for systems that don't provide multibutton mice. However, for the most common uses of these buttons—pop-up menus—you don't have to write explicit code; Swing provides special support that automatically maps to the correct gesture in each environment (see the PopupMenu class in Chapter 17).

Mouse-wheel events

Java 1.4 added support for the mouse wheel, which is a scrolling device in place of a middle mouse button. By default, Swing handles mouse-wheel movement for scrollable components, so you should not have to write explicit code to handle this. Mouse-wheel events are handled a little differently from other events because the conventions for using the mouse wheel don't always require the mouse to be over a scrolling component. If the immediate target component of a mouse-wheel event is not registered to receive it, a search is made for the first enclosing container that wants to consume the event. This allows components enclosed in ScrollPanes to operate as expected.

If you wish to explicitly handle mouse-wheel events, you can register to receive them using the MouseWheelListener interface shown in Table 16-1 in the next section.

Mouse-wheel events encapsulate information about the amount of scrolling and the type of scroll unit, which on most systems may be configured externally to be fine-grained scroll units or large blocks. If you want a physical measure of how far the wheel was turned, you can get that with the getWheelRotation( ) method, which returns a number of clicks.

Focus Events

As we mentioned earlier, focus handling is largely done automatically in Swing applications and we'll discuss it further in Chapter 18. However, understanding how focus events are handled will help you understand and customize components.

As we described, a component can make itself eligible to receive focus using the JComponent setFocusable( ) method (Windows may use setFocusableWindowState( )). A component normally receives focus when the user clicks on it with the mouse. It can also programmatically request focus using the requestFocus( ) or requestFocusInWindow( ) methods. The requestFocusInWindow( ) method acts just like requestFocus( ) except that it does not ask for transfer across windows. (There are currently limitations on some platforms that prevent focus transfer from native applications to Java applications, so using requestFocusInWindow( ) guarantees portability by adding this restriction.)

Although a component can request focus explicitly, the only way to verify when a component has received or lost focus is by using the FocusListener interface (see Tables 16-1 and 16-2). You can use this interface to customize the behavior of your component when it is ready for input (e.g., the TextField's blinking cursor). Also, input components often respond to the loss of focus by committing their changes. For example, JTextFields and other components can be arranged to validate themselves when the user attempts to move to a new field and to prevent the focus change until the field is valid (as we'll see in Chapter 18).

Assuming that there is currently no focus, the following sequence of events happens when a component receives focus:

```
WINDOW_ACTIVATED
WINDOW_GAINED_FOCUS
FOCUS_GAINED
```

The first two are WindowEvents delivered to the component's containing Window, and the third is a FocusEvent, sent to the component itself. If a component in another window subsequently receives focus, the following complementary sequence will occur:

```
FOCUS_LOST
WINDOW_FOCUS_LOST
WINDOW_DEACTIVATED
```

These events carry a certain amount of context with them. The receiving component can determine from what component the focus is being transferred and from what Window. The yielding component and window are called "opposites" and are available with the FocusEvent getOppositeComponent( ) and WindowEvent getOppositeWindow( ) methods. If the opposite is part of a native non-Java application, then these values may be null.

Focus gained and lost events may also be marked as "temporary," as determined by the FocusEvent isTemporary( ) method. The concept of a temporary focus change is used for components such as pop-up menus, scrollbars, and window manipulation where control is expected to return to the primary component later. The distinction is made for components to "commit" or validate data upon losing focus. No commit should happen on a temporary loss of focus.

Event Summary

Tables 16-1 and 16-2 summarize commonly used Swing events, which Swing components fire them, and the methods of the listener interfaces that receive them. The events and listeners are divided between the java.awt.event and javax.swing.event packages.

Table 16-1. Swing component and container events

Event	Fired by	Listener interface	Handler methods
java.awt.event. ComponentEvent	All components	ComponentListener	componentResized( ) componentMoved( ) componentShown( ) componentHidden( )
java.awt.event. FocusEvent	All components	FocusListener	focusGained( ) focusLost( )
java.awt.event. KeyEvent	All components	KeyListener	keyTyped( ) keyPressed( ) keyReleased( )
java.awt.event. MouseEvent	All components	MouseListener	mouseClicked( ) mousePressed( ) mouseReleased( ) mouseEntered( ) mouseExited( )
		MouseMotionListener	mouseDragged( ) mouseMoved( )
java.awt.event. ContainerEvent	All containers	ContainerListener	componentAdded( ) componentRemoved( )

Table 16-2. Component-specific swing events

Event	Fired by	Listener interface	Handler method
java.awt.event. ActionEvent	JButton JCheckBoxMenuItem JComboBox JFileChooser JList JRadioButtonMenuItem JTextField JToggleButton	ActionListener	actionPerformed( )
java.awt.event. AdjustmentEvent	JScrollBar	Adjustment- Listener	adjustmentValue- Changed( )
javax.swing.event. CaretEvent	JTextComponent	CaretListener	caretUpdate( )
javax.swing.event. HyperlinkEvent	JEditorPane JTextPane	Hyperlink- Listener	hyperlinkUpdate( )
java.awt.event. InternalFrameEvent	JInternalFrame	InternalFrame- Listener	internalFrame- Activated( ) internalFrame- Closed( ) internalFrame- Closing( ) internalFrame- Deactivated( ) internalFrame- Deiconified( ) internalFrame- Iconified( ) internalFrame- Opened( )
java.awt.event. ItemEvent	JCheckBoxMenuItem JComboBox JRadioButtonMenuItem JToggleButton	ItemListener	itemStateChanged( )
javax.swing.event. ListDataEvent	ListModel	ListDataListener	contentsChanged( ) intervalAdded( ) intervalRemoved( )
javax.swing.event. ListSelectionEvent	JList ListSelectionModel	ListSelection- Listener	valueChanged( )
javax.swing.event. MenuEvent	JMenu	MenuListener	menuCanceled( ) menuDeselected( ) menuSelected( )
javax.swing.event. PopupMenuEvent	JPopupMenu	PopupMenu- Listener	popupMenuCanceled( ) popupMenuWill- BecomeInvisible( ) popupMenuWill- BecomeVisible( )

Table 16-2. Component-specific swing events (continued)

Event	Fired by	Listener interface	Handler method
javax.swing.event. MenuKeyEvent	JMenuItem	MenuKeyListener	menuKeyPressed( ) menuKeyReleased( ) menuKeyTyped( )
javax.swing.event. MenuDragMouseEvent	JMenuItem	MenuDragMouse- Listener	menuDragMouse- Dragged( ) menuDragMouse- Entered( ) menuDragMouse- Exited( ) menuDragMouse- Released( )
javax.swing.event. TableColumnModel- Event	TableColumnModel[a]	TableColumn- ModelListener	columnAdded( ) columnMargin- Changed( ) columnMoved( ) columnRemoved( ) columnSelection- Changed( )
javax.swing.event. TableModelEvent	TableModel	TableModel- Listener	tableChanged( )
javax.swing.event. TreeExpansionEvent	Jtree	TreeExpansion- Listener	treeCollapsed( ) treeExpanded( )
javax.swing.event. TreeModelEvent	TreeModel	TreeModel- Listener	treeNodesChanged( ) treeNodesInserted( ) treeNodesRemoved( ) treeStructure- Changed( )
javax.swing.event. TreeSelectionEvent	JTree TreeSelectionModel	TreeSelection- Listener	valueChanged( )
javax.swing.event. UndoableEditEvent	javax.swing.text. Document	UndoableEdit- Listener	undoableEdit- Happened( )
java.awt.event. WindowEvent	JDialog JFrame JWindow	WindowListener	windowOpened( ) windowClosing( ) windowClosed( ) windowIconified( ) windowDeiconified( ) windowActivated( ) windowDeactivated( )

[a] The TableColumnModel class breaks with convention in the names of the methods that add listeners. They are addColumnModelListener( ) and removeColumnModelListener( ).

In Swing, a component's model and view are distinct. Strictly speaking, components don't fire events; models do. When you press a JButton, for example, it's actually the button's data model that fires an ActionEvent, not the button itself. But JButton has a convenience method for registering ActionListeners; this method passes its argument through to register the listener with the button model. In many cases (as with JButtons), you don't have to deal with the data model separately from the view, so we can speak loosely of the component itself firing the events. InputEvents are, of course, generated by the native input system and fired for the appropriate component, although the listener responds as though they're generated by the component.

Adapter Classes

It's not ideal to have your application components implement a bunch of listener interfaces and receive events directly. Sometimes it's not even possible. Being an event receiver forces you to modify or subclass your objects to implement the appropriate event listener interfaces and add the code necessary to handle the events. And since we are talking about Swing events here, a more subtle issue is that you would be, of necessity, building GUI logic into parts of your application that shouldn't have to know anything about the GUI. Let's look at an example.

In Figure 16-4, we have drawn the plans for our Vegomatic food processor. Here we have made our Vegomatic object implement the ActionListener interface so that it can receive events directly from the three JButton components: Chop, Puree, and Frappe. The problem is that our Vegomatic object now has to know more than how to mangle food. It also has to be aware that it is driven by three controls—specifically, buttons that send action commands—and be aware of which methods it should invoke for those commands. Our boxes labeling the GUI and application code overlap in an unwholesome way. If the marketing people should later want to add or remove buttons or perhaps just change the names, we have to be careful. We may have to modify the logic in our Vegomatic object. All is not well.

An alternative is to place an adapter class between our event source and receiver. An *adapter* is a simple object whose sole purpose is to map an incoming event to an outgoing method.

Figure 16-5 shows a better design that uses three adapter classes, one for each button. The implementation of the first adapter might look like:

```
class VegomaticAdapter1 implements ActionListener {
    Vegomatic vegomatic;
    VegomaticAdapter1 ( Vegomatic vegomatic ) {
        this.vegomatic = vegomatic;
    }
    public void actionPerformed( ActionEvent e ) {
        vegomatic.chopFood( );
    }
}
```

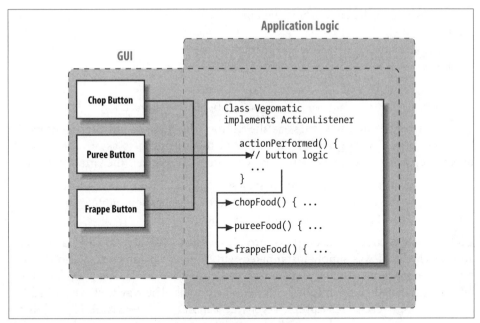

Figure 16-4. Implementing the ActionListener interface directly

Figure 16-5. Implementing the ActionListener interface using adapter classes

So, somewhere in the code where we build our GUI, we could register our listener like this:

```
Vegomatic theVegomatic = ...;
Button chopButton = ...;

// make the hookup
chopButton.addActionListener( new VegomaticAdapter1(theVegomatic) );
```

Instead of registering itself (this) as the Button's listener, the adapter registers the Vegomatic object (theVegomatic). In this way, the adapter acts as an intermediary, hooking up an event source (the button) with an event receiver (the virtual chopper).

We have completely separated the messiness of our GUI from the application code. However, we have added three new classes to our application, none of which does very much. Is that good? It depends on your vantage point.

Under different circumstances, our buttons may have been able to share a common adapter class that was simply instantiated with different parameters. Various trade-offs can be made between size, efficiency, and elegance of code. Adapter classes will often be generated automatically by development tools. The way we have named our adapter classes VegomaticAdapter1, VegomaticAdapter2, and VegomaticAdapter3 hints at this. More often, when hand-coding, you'll use an anonymous inner class, as we'll see in the next section. At the other extreme, we can forsake Java's strong typing and use the Reflection API to create a completely dynamic hookup between an event source and its listener.

Dummy Adapters

Many listener interfaces contain more than one event-handler method. Unfortunately, this means that to register yourself as interested in any one of those events, you must implement the whole listener interface. To accomplish this, you might find yourself typing dummy "stubbed-out" methods to complete the interface. There is nothing wrong with this, but it is a bit tedious. To save you some trouble, AWT and Swing provide some helper classes that implement these dummy methods for you. For each of the most common listener interfaces containing more than one method, there is an adapter class containing the stubbed methods. You can use the adapter class as a base class for your own adapters. When you need a class to patch together your event source and listener, you can subclass the adapter and override only the methods you want.

For example, the MouseAdapter class implements the MouseListener interface and provides the following minimalist implementation:

```
public void mouseClicked(MouseEvent e) {};
public void mousePressed(MouseEvent e) {};
public void mouseReleased(MouseEvent e) {};
public void mouseEntered(MouseEvent e) {};
public void mouseExited(MouseEvent e) {};
```

This isn't a tremendous time saver; it's simply a bit of sugar. The primary advantage comes into play when we use the MouseAdapter as the base for our own adapter in an anonymous inner class. For example, suppose we want to catch a mousePressed( ) event in some component and blow up a building. We can use the following to make the hookup:

```
someComponent.addMouseListener( new MouseAdapter( ) {
    public void MousePressed(MouseEvent e) {
        building.blowUp( );
    }
} );
```

We've taken artistic liberties with the formatting, but it's pretty readable. Moreover, we've avoided creating stub methods for the four unused event-handler methods. Writing adapters is common enough that it's nice to avoid typing those extra few lines and perhaps stave off the onset of carpal tunnel syndrome for a few more hours. Remember that any time you use an inner class, the compiler is generating a class for you, so the messiness you've saved in your source still exists in the output classes.

The AWT Robot!

This topic may not be of immediate use to everyone, but sometimes an API is just interesting enough that it deserves mentioning. In Java 1.3 a class with the intriguing name java.awt.Robot was added. The AWT robot provides an API for generating input events such as keystrokes and mouse gestures programmatically. It could be used to build automated GUI testing tools and the like. The following example uses the Robot class to move the mouse to the upper-left area of the screen and perform a series of events corresponding to a double click. On most Windows systems, this opens up the *My Computer* folder that lives in that region of the screen.

```
public class RobotExample
{
    public static void main( String [] args ) throws Exception
    {
        Robot r = new Robot(   );
        r.mouseMove(35,35);
        r.mousePress( InputEvent.BUTTON1_MASK );
        r.mouseRelease( InputEvent.BUTTON1_MASK );
        Thread.sleep(50);
        r.mousePress( InputEvent.BUTTON1_MASK );
        r.mouseRelease( InputEvent.BUTTON1_MASK );
    }
}
```

In addition to its magic fingers, the AWT Robot also has eyes! You can use the Robot class to capture an image of the screen or a rectangular portion of it, using the createScreenCapture( ) method. (Note that you can get the exact dimensions of the screen from the AWT's getScreenSize( ) method.)

Java 5.0 added a correspondingly useful API, java.awt.MouseInfo, which allows the gathering of mouse movement information from anywhere on the screen (not restricted to the area within the Java application's windows). The combination of Robot and MouseInfo should make it easier to record and play back events occurring anywhere on the screen from within Java.

Multithreading in Swing

An important compromise was made early in the design of Swing relating to speed, GUI consistency, and thread safety. To provide maximum performance and simplicity in the common case, Swing does not explicitly synchronize access to most Swing component methods. This means that most Swing components are, technically, not thread-safe for multithreaded applications. Now don't panic: it's not as bad as it sounds because there is a plan. All event processing in AWT/Swing is handled by a single system thread using a single system event queue. The queue serves two purposes. First, it eliminates thread-safety issues by making all GUI modifications happen in a single thread. Second, the queue imposes a strict ordering of all activity in Swing. Because painting is handled in Swing using events, all screen updating is also ordered with respect to all event handling.

What this means for you is that multithreaded programs need to be careful about how they update Swing components after they are *realized* (added to a visible container). If you make arbitrary modifications to Swing components from your own threads, you run the risk of malformed rendering on the screen and inconsistent behavior.

There are several conditions under which it is always safe to modify a Swing component. First, Swing components can be modified before they are realized. The term *realized* originates from the days when the component would have created its peer object. It is the point when it is added to a visible container or when it is made visible in the case of a window. Most of our examples in this book set up GUI components in their main( ) method, add them to a JFrame, and then, as their final action, cause the JFrame to be displayed using setVisible( ). This setup style is safe because components are not realized until the container is made visible. Actually, that last sentence is not entirely true. Technically, components can also be realized by the JFrame( ) pack( ) method. However, since no GUI is shown until the container is made visible, it is unlikely that any GUI activity can be mishandled.

Second, it's safe to modify Swing components from code that is already running from the system event handler's thread. Because all events are processed by the event queue, the methods of all Swing event listeners are normally invoked by the system event-handling thread. This means that event handler methods and, transitively, any methods called from those methods during the lifetime of that call, can freely modify Swing GUI components because they are already running in the system event-dispatching thread.

If you are unsure of whether some bit of code will ever be called outside the normal event thread, you can use the static method SwingUtilities.isEventDispatchThread( ) to test the identity of the current thread. You can then perform your activity using the event-queue mechanism we'll talk about next.

Finally, Swing components can be safely modified when the API documentation explicitly says that the method is threadsafe. Many important methods of Swing components are explicitly documented as threadsafe. These include the JComponent repaint( ) and revalidate( ) methods, many methods of Swing text components, and all listener add and remove methods.

If you can't meet any of the requirements for thread safety listed previously, you can use a simple API to get the system event queue to perform arbitrary activities for you on the event-handling thread. This is accomplished using the invokeAndWait( ) or invokeLater( ) static methods of the javax.swing.SwingUtilities class:

public static void invokeLater(Runnable doRun)
> Use this method to ask Swing to execute the run( ) method of the specified Runnable.

public static void invokeAndWait(Runnable
doRun)throwsInterruptedException,InvocationTargetException
> This method is just like invokeLater( ) except that it waits until the run( ) method has completed before returning.

You can put whatever activities you want inside a Runnable object and cause the event dispatcher to perform them using these methods. Often you'll use an inner class, for example:

```
SwingUtilities.invokeLater( new Runnable(  ) {
    public void run(  ) {
        MyComponent.setVisible(false);
    }
} );
```

You may find that you won't have to use the event dispatcher in simple GUI applications because most activity happens in response to user interface events where it is safe to modify components. However, consider these caveats when you create threads to perform long-running tasks such as loading data or communicating over the network.

CHAPTER 17

Using Swing Components

In the previous chapter, we discussed a number of concepts, including how Java's user interface facility is put together and how the fundamental pieces work. You should understand what components and containers are, how they work together to create a display, what events are, how components use them to communicate with the rest of your application, and what layout managers are.

Now that we're through with the general concepts and background, we'll get to the fun stuff: how to do things with Swing. We will cover most of the components that the Swing package supplies, how to use these components in applets and applications, and how to build your own components. We will have lots of code and lots of pretty examples to look at.

There's more material on this topic than fits in a single chapter. In this chapter, we'll cover all the basic user interface components. In the next chapter, we'll cover some of the more involved topics: text components, trees, tables, and creating your own components.

Buttons and Labels

We'll start with the simplest components: buttons and labels. Frankly, there isn't much to say about them. If you've seen one button, you've seen them all, and you've already seen buttons in the applications in Chapter 2 (`HelloJava3` and `HelloJava4`). A button generates an `ActionEvent` when the user presses it. To receive these events, your program registers an `ActionListener`, which must implement the `actionPerformed( )` method. The argument passed to `actionPerformed( )` is the event itself.

There's one more thing worth saying about buttons, which applies to any component that generates an action event. Java lets us specify an "action command" string for buttons (and other components, like menu items, that can generate action events). The action command is less interesting than it sounds. It is just a `String` that serves to identify the component that sent the event. By default, the action command of a `JButton` is the same as its label; it is included in action events so that you could use it to figure out which button an event came from. However, often you'll know this from the context of your event listener.

To get the action command from an action event, call the event's getActionCommand( ) method. The following code checks whether the user pressed the button labeled *Yes*:

```
public void actionPerformed(ActionEvent e){
    if (e.getActionCommand( ).equals("Yes") {
        //the user pressed "Yes"; do something
        ...
    }
}
```

Yes is a string, not a command per se. You can change the action command by calling the button's setActionCommand( ) method. The following code changes button myButton's action command to "confirm":

```
myButton.setActionCommand("confirm");
```

It's a good idea to get used to setting action commands explicitly; this helps to prevent your code from breaking when you or some other developer internationalizes it or otherwise changes the button's label. If you rely on the button's label, your code stops working as soon as that label changes; a French user might see the label Oui rather than Yes.

Swing buttons can have an image in addition to a label. The JButton class includes constructors that accept an Icon object, which knows how to draw itself. You can create buttons with captions, images, or both. A handy class called ImageIcon takes care of loading an image for you and can be used to add an image to a button. The following example shows how this works:

```
//file: PictureButton.java
import java.awt.*;
import java.awt.event.*;
import javax.swing.*;

public class PictureButton {
  public static void main(String[] args)
  {
    JFrame frame = new JFrame( );
    Icon icon = new ImageIcon("rhino.gif");
    JButton button = new JButton(icon);

    button.addActionListener( new ActionListener( ) {
      public void actionPerformed(ActionEvent ae) {
        System.out.println("Urp!");
      }
    });
```

```
        frame.getContentPane( ).add( button );
        frame.pack( );
        frame.setDefaultCloseOperation( JFrame.EXIT_ON_CLOSE );
        frame.setVisible(true);
    }
}
```

The example creates an ImageIcon from the *rhino.gif* file. Then, a JButton is created from the ImageIcon. The whole thing is displayed in a JFrame. This example also shows the idiom of using an anonymous inner class as an ActionListener.

There's even less to be said about JLabel components. They're just text strings or images housed in a component. There aren't any special events associated with labels; about all you can do is specify the text's alignment, which controls the position of the text within the label's display area. As with buttons, JLabels can be created with Icons if you want to create a picture label. The following code creates some labels with different options:

```
// default alignment (CENTER)
JLabel label1 = new JLabel("Lions");

// left aligned
JLabel label2 = new JLabel("Tigers", SwingConstants.LEFT);

//label with no text, default alignment
JLabel label3 = new JLabel( );

// create image icon
Icon icon = new ImageIcon("rhino.gif");

// create image label
JLabel label4 = new JLabel(icon);

// assigning text to label3
label3.setText("and Bears");

// set alignment
label3.setHorizontalAlignment(SwingConstants.RIGHT);
```

The alignment constants are defined in the SwingConstants interface.

We've built several labels, using a variety of constructors and several of the class's methods. To display the labels, just add them to a container by calling the container's add( ) method.

You can set other label characteristics, such as changing their font or color, using the methods of the Component class, JLabel's distant ancestor. For example, you can call setFont( ) and setColor( ) on a label, as with any other component.

Given that labels are so simple, why do we need them at all? Why not find a way to draw a text string directly on the container object? Remember that a JLabel is a JComponent. That means that labels have the normal complement of methods for setting fonts and colors that we mentioned earlier as well as the ability to be persistently and sensibly managed by a layout manager. Therefore, they're much more flexible than a text string drawn procedurally at an arbitrary location within a container. Speaking of layouts—if you use the setText( ) method to change the text of your label, the label's preferred size may change. But the label's container automatically lays out its components when this happens, so you don't have to worry about it.

HTML Text in Buttons and Labels

A neat feature of Swing is that it can interpret HTML-formatted text in JLabel and JButton labels. The following example shows how to create a button with some HTML-formatted text:

```
JButton button = new JButton(
  "<html>"
  + "S<font size=-1>MALL<font size=+0> "
  + "C<font size=-1>APITALS");
```

Older versions of Java may not render complex HTML very well. But as of JDK 1.4, most basic HTML features are supported, including crazy things such as images and tables.

Figure 17-1 uses an HTML table to arrange its text.

Figure 17-1. Button using HTML table

Figure 17-2 uses an HTML image tag to display an image.

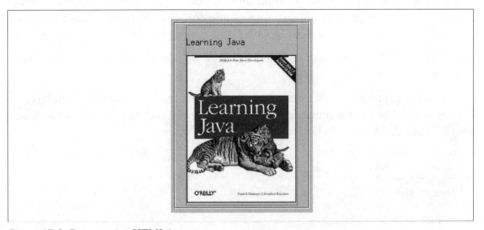

Figure 17-2. Button using HTML img tag

The code for the two figures looks like this:

```
String html=
    "<html><table border=1>"
    +"<tr><td>One</td><td>Two</td></tr>"
    +"<tr><td>Three</td><td>Four</td></tr>"
    +"</table>";
JButton button = new JButton(html);

String html2=
    "<html><h3>Learning Java</h3>"
    +"<img src=\"http://www.oreilly.com/catalog/covers/learnjava3.s.gif\">";
Jbutton button2 = new JButton(html2);
```

Checkboxes and Radio Buttons

A checkbox is a labeled toggle switch. Each time the user clicks it, its state toggles between checked and unchecked. Swing implements the checkbox as a special kind of button. Radio buttons are similar to checkboxes, but they are normally used in groups. Clicking on one radio button in the group automatically turns the others off. They are named for the mechanical preset buttons on old car radios (like some of us had in high school).

Checkboxes and radio buttons are represented by instances of JCheckBox and JRadioButton, respectively. Radio buttons can be tethered together using an instance of another class called ButtonGroup. By now you're probably well into the swing of things (no pun intended) and could easily master these classes on your own. We'll use an example to illustrate a different way of dealing with the state of components and to show off a few more things about containers.

A JCheckBox sends ItemEvents when it's pushed. Because a checkbox is a kind of button, it also fires ActionEvents when checked. For something like a checkbox, we might want to be lazy and check on the state of the buttons only at some later time, such as when the user commits an action. For example, when filling out a form you may only care about the user's choices when the submit button is finally pressed.

The next application, DriveThrough, lets us check off selections on a fast food menu, as shown in Figure 17-3.

DriveThrough prints the results when you press the Place Order button. Therefore, we can ignore all the events generated by our checkboxes and radio buttons and listen only for the action events generated by the submit button:

```
//file: DriveThrough.java
import java.awt.*;
import java.awt.event.*;
import javax.swing.*;

public class DriveThrough
{
```

Figure 17-3. The DriveThrough application

```java
public static void main(String[] args) {
  JFrame frame = new JFrame("Lister v1.0");

  JPanel entreePanel = new JPanel();
  final ButtonGroup entreeGroup = new ButtonGroup();
  JRadioButton radioButton;
  entreePanel.add(radioButton = new JRadioButton("Beef"));
  radioButton.setActionCommand("Beef");
  entreeGroup.add(radioButton);
  entreePanel.add(radioButton = new JRadioButton("Chicken"));
  radioButton.setActionCommand("Chicken");
  entreeGroup.add(radioButton);
  entreePanel.add(radioButton = new JRadioButton("Veggie", true));
  radioButton.setActionCommand("Veggie");
  entreeGroup.add(radioButton);

  final JPanel condimentsPanel = new JPanel();
  condimentsPanel.add(new JCheckBox("Ketchup"));
  condimentsPanel.add(new JCheckBox("Mustard"));
  condimentsPanel.add(new JCheckBox("Pickles"));

  JPanel orderPanel = new JPanel();
  JButton orderButton = new JButton("Place Order");
  orderPanel.add(orderButton);

  Container content = frame.getContentPane(); // unnecessary in 5.0+
  content.setLayout(new GridLayout(3, 1));
  content.add(entreePanel);
  content.add(condimentsPanel);
  content.add(orderPanel);

  orderButton.addActionListener(new ActionListener() {
    public void actionPerformed(ActionEvent ae) {
      String entree =
        entreeGroup.getSelection().getActionCommand();
      System.out.println(entree + " sandwich");
      Component[] components = condimentsPanel.getComponents();
      for ( Component c : components ) {
        JCheckBox cb = (JCheckBox)c;
          if (cb.isSelected())
            System.out.println("With " + cb.getText());
```

```
          }
        }
      });

      frame.setDefaultCloseOperation( JFrame.EXIT_ON_CLOSE );
      frame.setSize(300, 150);
      frame.setVisible(true);
    }
  }
```

DriveThrough lays out three panels. The radio buttons in the entreePanel are tied together through a ButtonGroup object. We add( ) the buttons to a ButtonGroup to make them mutually exclusive. The ButtonGroup object is an odd animal. One might expect it to be a container or a component, but it isn't; it's simply a helper object that allows only one RadioButton to be selected at a time.

In this example, the button group forces you to choose a beef, chicken, or veggie entree, but not more than one. The condiment choices, which are JCheckBoxes, aren't in a button group, so you can request any combination of ketchup, mustard, and pickles on your sandwich.

When the *Place Order* button is pushed, we receive an ActionEvent in the actionPerformed( ) method of our inner ActionListener. At this point, we gather the information in the radio buttons and checkboxes and print it. actionPerformed( ) simply reads the state of the various buttons. We could have saved references to the buttons in a number of ways; this example demonstrates two. First, we find out which entree was selected. To do so, we call the ButtonGroup's getSelection( ) method. This returns a ButtonModel, upon which we immediately call getActionCommand( ). This returns the action command as we set it when we created the radio buttons. The action commands for the buttons are the entrée names, which is exactly what we need.

To find which condiments were selected, we use a more complicated procedure. The problem is that condiments aren't mutually exclusive, so we don't have the convenience of a ButtonGroup. Instead, we ask the condiments JPanel for a list of its components. The getComponents( ) method returns an array of references to the container's child components. We'll use this to loop over the components and print the results. We cast each element of the array back to JCheckBox and call its isSelected( ) method to see if the checkbox is on or off. If we were dealing with different types of components in the array, we could determine each component's type with the instanceof operator. Or, more generally, we could maintain references to the elements of our form in some explicit way (a map by name, perhaps).

Lists and Combo Boxes

JLists and JComboBoxes are a step up on the evolutionary chain from JButtons and JLabels. Lists let the user choose from a group of alternatives. They can be configured to force a single selection or allow multiple choices. Usually, only a small group of choices is displayed at a time; a scrollbar lets the user move to the choices that aren't visible. The user can select an item by clicking on it. She can expand the selection to a range of items by holding down Shift and clicking on another item. To make discontinuous selections, the user can hold down the Control key instead of the Shift key (on a Mac, this is the Command key).

A combo box is a cross-breed between a text field and a list. It displays a single line of text (possibly with an image) and a downward pointing arrow on one side. If you click on the arrow, the combo box opens up and displays a list of choices. You can select a single choice by clicking on it. After a selection is made, the combo box closes up; the list disappears, and the new selection is shown in the text field.

Like other components in Swing, lists and combo boxes have data models that are distinct from visual components. The list also has a selection model that controls how selections may be made on the list data.

Lists and combo boxes are similar because they have similar data models. Each is simply an array of acceptable choices. This similarity is reflected in Swing, of course: the type of a JComboBox's data model is a subclass of the type used for a JList's data model. The next example demonstrates this relationship.

The following example creates a window with a combo box, a list, and a button. The combo box and the list use the same data model. When you press the button, the program writes out the current set of selected items in the list (see Figure 17-4).

Figure 17-4. A combo box and a list using the same data model

Here's the code for the example:

```
//file: Lister.java
import java.awt.*;
import java.awt.event.*;
import javax.swing.*;

public class Lister {
  public static void main(String[] args) {
    JFrame frame = new JFrame("Lister v1.0");
```

```
    // create a combo box
    String [] items = { "uno", "due", "tre", "quattro", "cinque",
                        "sei", "sette", "otto", "nove", "deici",
                        "undici", "dodici" };
    JComboBox comboBox = new JComboBox(items);
    comboBox.setEditable(true);

    // create a list with the same data model
    final JList list = new JList(comboBox.getModel());

    // create a button; when it's pressed, print out
    // the selection in the list
    JButton button = new JButton("Per favore");
    button.addActionListener(new ActionListener() {
      public void actionPerformed(ActionEvent ae) {
        Object[] selection = list.getSelectedValues();
        System.out.println("-----");
        for ( Object o : selection )
          System.out.println( o );
      }
    });

    // put the controls the content pane
    Container c = frame.getContentPane();   // unnecessary  in 5.0+
    JPanel comboPanel = new JPanel();
    comboPanel.add(comboBox);
    c.add(comboPanel, BorderLayout.NORTH);
    c.add(new JScrollPane(list), BorderLayout.CENTER);
    c.add(button, BorderLayout.SOUTH);

    frame.setSize(200, 200);
    frame.setDefaultCloseOperation( JFrame.EXIT_ON_CLOSE );
    frame.setVisible(true);
  }
}
```

The combo box is created from an array of strings. This is a convenience—behind the scenes, the JComboBox constructor creates a data model from the strings you supply and sets the JComboBox to use that data model. Our list is then created using the data model of the combo box. This works because JList expects to use a ListModel for its data model, and the ComboBoxModel used by the JComboBox is a subclass of ListModel.

The button's action event handler simply prints out the selected items in the list, which are retrieved with a call to getSelectedValues(). This method actually returns an object array, not a string array. List and combo box items, like many other things in Swing, are not limited to text. You can use images, drawings, or some combination of text and images. We simply print the result as a String.

You might expect that selecting one item in the combo box would select the same item in the list. In Swing components, selection is controlled by a selection model. The combo box and the list have distinct selection models; after all, you can select only one item from the combo box while it's possible to select multiple items from the list. Thus, while the two components share a data model, they have separate selection models.

We've made the combo box editable. By default, it would not be editable: the user could choose only one item in the drop-down list. With an editable combo box, the user can type in a selection, as if it were a text field. Noneditable combo boxes are useful if you just want to offer a limited set of choices; editable combo boxes are handy when you want to accept any input but offer some common choices.

There's a great class tucked away in the last example that deserves some recognition. It's JScrollPane. In Lister, you'll notice we created one when we added the List to the main window. JScrollPane simply wraps itself around another Component and provides scrollbars as necessary. The scrollbars show up if the contained Component's preferred size (as returned by getPreferredSize( )) is greater than the size of the JScrollPane itself. In the previous example, the scrollbars show up whenever the size of the List exceeds the available space.

You can use JScrollPane to wrap any Component, including components with drawings, images, or complex user interface panels. We'll discuss JScrollPane in more detail later in this chapter, and we'll use it frequently with the text components in Chapter 18.

The Spinner

JList and JComboBox are two ways to let the user choose from a set of values. A JComboBox has added flexibility when it is made editable, but, in general, both of these components are limited in that they can only prompt the user from a fixed set of choices. In Java 1.4, Swing added a component called JSpinner that is useful for large or open-ended sequences of values such as numbers or dates. The JSpinner is a cousin of the JComboBox; it displays a value in a field, but instead of providing a drop-down list of choices, it gives the user a small pair of up and down arrows for moving over a range of values (see Figure 17-5). Like the combo box, a JSpinner can also be made editable, allowing the user to type a valid value directly into the field.

Figure 17-5. Image of DateSelector application

Swing provides three basic types of Spinners, represented by three different data models for the JSpinner component: SpinnerListModel, SpinnerNumberModel, and SpinnerDateModel.

The SpinnerListModel acts like a combo box, specifying a fixed set of objects:

```
String [] options = new String [] { "small", "medium", "large", "huge" };
SpinnerListModel model = new SpinnerListModel( options );
JSpinner spinner = new JSpinner( model );
```

You can retrieve the current value from the model at any time:

```
String value = (String)model.getValue( );
```

Alternatively, you can register a ChangeListener to receive updates as the user changes values. With a SpinnerListModel, if the spinner is editable and the user enters a value directly, it is validated against the set of choices before being accepted. This behavior is a little different from the other types of SpinnerModels, which when editable, accept any valid value of the correct type (e.g., a number or date).

The SpinnerNumberModel displays numeric values. It can be configured with initial, minimum, and maximum values:

```
double initial=5.0, min=0.0, max=10.0, increment=0.1;
SpinnerNumberModel model =
    new SpinnerNumberModel( initial, min, max, increment );
JSpinner spinner = new JSpinner(model);
```

Here we have constructed a spinner with an initial value of 5.0 that allows the user to change the value to between 0 and 10.0 in increments of 0.1. The SpinnerNumberModel getNumber( ) method retrieves the current value.

Perhaps the most interesting feature of the JSpinner is the SpinnerDateModel, which allows the user to choose calendar dates by moving in specified increments of time. The SpinnerDateModel accepts a range, such as the SpinnerNumberModel, but the values are Date objects, and the increment is a java.util.Calendar constant field such as Calendar.DAY, Calendar.WEEK, and so on. The following example, DateSelector, creates a JSpinner showing the current date and time. It allows the user to change the date in increments of one week, over a range of one year (six months forward or back). A ChangeListener is registered with the model to display the values as they are modified:

```
import java.awt.*;
import java.awt.event.*;
import javax.swing.*;
import javax.swing.event.*;
import java.util.*;

public class DateSelector {
  public static void main(String[] args)
  {
    JFrame frame = new JFrame("DateSelector v1.0");

    Calendar now = Calendar.getInstance( );
    Calendar earliest = (Calendar)now.clone( );
    earliest.add( Calendar.MONTH, -6 );
    Calendar latest = (Calendar)now.clone( );
```

```
latest.add( Calendar.MONTH, 6 );
SpinnerModel model = new SpinnerDateModel(
    now.getTime( ), earliest.getTime( ), latest.getTime( ),
    Calendar.WEEK_OF_YEAR);
final JSpinner spinner = new JSpinner(model);

model.addChangeListener( new ChangeListener( ) {
    public void stateChanged(ChangeEvent e) {
        System.out.println( ((SpinnerDateModel)e.getSource()).getDate() );
    }
} );

frame.getContentPane( ).add( "North", new JLabel("Choose a week") );
frame.getContentPane( ).add( "Center", spinner );
frame.pack( );
frame.setDefaultCloseOperation( JFrame.EXIT_ON_CLOSE );
frame.setVisible(true);
    }
}
```

As we said, the SpinnerCalendarModel acts just like the SpinnerNumberModel, except that it works with Date objects and uses the special Calendar constants as increments. To create dates, we construct a Calendar object for the correct time and use its getTime( ) method. In this example, we used the Calendar's add( ) method to set the minimum and maximum values six months in each direction. Table 17-1 shows values for increments in the Calendar.

Table 17-1. Calendar field values

Field value	Increment
Calendar.MILLISECOND	One millisecond
Calendar.SECOND	One second
Calendar.MINUTE	One minute
Calendar.HOUR Calendar.HOUR_OF_DAY	One hour
Calendar.AM_PM	A.M. or P.M.
Calendar.DAY_OF_WEEK Calendar.DAY_OF_MONTH Calendar.DAY_OF_YEAR	One day
Calendar.MONTH	One month
Calendar.YEAR	One year
Calendar.ERA	B.C. or A.D. in the Gregorian Calendar

The SpinnerDateModel uses the Calendar add( ) method with a value of 1 or –1 and the corresponding constant value to increment or decrement the value. Increments of one have the same effect on several of the constants, as indicated in Table 17-1.

Borders

Any Swing component can have a decorative border. JComponent includes a method called setBorder( ); all you have to do is call it, passing it an appropriate implementation of the Border interface.

Swing provides many useful Border implementations in the javax.swing.border package. You could create an instance of one of these classes and pass it to a component's setBorder( ) method, but there's an even simpler technique.

The BorderFactory class creates any kind of border for you using static "factory" methods. Creating and setting a component's border, then, is simple:

```
JLabel labelTwo = new JLabel("I have an etched border.");
labelTwo.setBorder(BorderFactory.createEtchedBorder( ));
```

Every component has a setBorder( ) method, from simple labels and buttons right up to the fancy text and table components we cover in Chapter 18.

BorderFactory is convenient, but it does not offer every option of every border type. For example, if you want to create a raised EtchedBorder instead of the default lowered border, you'll need to use EtchedBorder's constructor, like this:

```
JLabel labelTwo = new JLabel("I have a raised etched border.");
labelTwo.setBorder( new EtchedBorder(EtchedBorder.RAISED) );
```

The Border implementation classes are listed and briefly described here:

BevelBorder
> This border draws raised or lowered beveled edges, giving an illusion of depth.

SoftBevelBorder
> This border is similar to BevelBorder, but thinner.

EmptyBorder
> Doesn't do any drawing, but does take up space. You can use it to give a component a little breathing room in a crowded user interface.

EtchedBorder
> A lowered etched border gives the appearance of a rectangle that has been chiseled into a piece of stone. A raised etched border looks like it is standing out from the surface of the screen.

LineBorder
> Draws a simple rectangle around a component. You can specify the color and width of the line in LineBorder's constructor.

MatteBorder
> A souped-up version of LineBorder. You can create a MatteBorder with a certain color and specify the size of the border on the left, top, right, and bottom of the component. MatteBorder also allows you to pass in an Icon that will be used to

draw the border. This could be an image (ImageIcon) or any other implementation of the Icon interface.

TitledBorder

A regular border with a title. TitledBorder doesn't actually draw a border; it just draws a title in conjunction with another border object. You can specify the locations of the title, its justification, and its font. This border type is particularly useful for grouping different sets of controls in a complicated interface.

CompoundBorder

A border that contains two other borders. This is especially handy if you want to enclose a component in an EmptyBorder and then put something decorative around it, such as an EtchedBorder or a MatteBorder.

The following example shows off some different border types. It's only a sampler, though; many more border types are available. Furthermore, the example only encloses labels with borders. You can put a border around any component in Swing. The example is shown in Figure 17-6.

Figure 17-6. A bevy of borders

Here is the source code:

```
//file: Borders.java
import java.awt.*;
import java.awt.event.*;
import javax.swing.*;
import javax.swing.border.*;

public class Borders {
  public static void main(String[] args) {
    // create a JFrame to hold everything
    JFrame frame = new JFrame("Borders");
```

```
    // Create labels with borders.
    int center = SwingConstants.CENTER;
    JLabel labelOne = new JLabel("raised BevelBorder", center);
    labelOne.setBorder(
        BorderFactory.createBevelBorder(BevelBorder.RAISED));
    JLabel labelTwo = new JLabel("EtchedBorder", center);
    labelTwo.setBorder(BorderFactory.createEtchedBorder());
    JLabel labelThree = new JLabel("MatteBorder", center);
    labelThree.setBorder(
        BorderFactory.createMatteBorder(10, 10, 10, 10, Color.pink));
    JLabel labelFour = new JLabel("TitledBorder", center);
    Border etch = BorderFactory.createEtchedBorder();
    labelFour.setBorder(
        BorderFactory.createTitledBorder(etch, "Title"));
    JLabel labelFive = new JLabel("TitledBorder", center);
    Border low = BorderFactory.createLoweredBevelBorder();
    labelFive.setBorder(
        BorderFactory.createTitledBorder(low, "Title",
        TitledBorder.RIGHT, TitledBorder.BOTTOM));
    JLabel labelSix = new JLabel("CompoundBorder", center);
    Border one = BorderFactory.createEtchedBorder();
    Border two =
        BorderFactory.createMatteBorder(4, 4, 4, 4, Color.blue);
    labelSix.setBorder(BorderFactory.createCompoundBorder(one, two));

    // add components to the content pane
    Container c = f.getContentPane();  // unnecessary  in 5.0+
    c.setLayout(new GridLayout(3, 2));
    c.add(labelOne);
    c.add(labelTwo);
    c.add(labelThree);
    c.add(labelFour);
    c.add(labelFive);
    c.add(labelSix);

    frame.setDefaultCloseOperation( JFrame.EXIT_ON_CLOSE );
    frame.pack();
    frame.setVisible(true);
  }
}
```

Menus

A JMenu is a standard pull-down menu with a fixed name. Menus can hold other menus as submenu items, enabling you to implement complex menu structures. In Swing, menus are first-class components, just like everything else. You can place them wherever a component would go. Another class, JMenuBar, holds menus in the conventional horizontal bar. Menu bars are real components, too, so you can place them wherever you want in a container: top, bottom, or middle. But in the middle of a container, it usually makes more sense to use a JComboBox rather than some kind of menu.

Menu items may have associated images and shortcut keys; there are even menu items that look like checkboxes and radio buttons. Menu items are really a kind of button. Like buttons, menu items fire action events when they are selected. You can respond to menu items by registering action listeners with them.

There are two ways to use the keyboard with menus. The first is called *mnemonics*. A mnemonic is one character in the menu name. If you hold down the Alt key and type a menu's mnemonic, the menu drops down, just as if you had clicked on it with the mouse. Menu items may also have mnemonics. Once a menu is dropped down, you can select individual items in the same way.

Menu items may also have accelerators. An *accelerator* is a key combination that selects the menu item, whether or not the menu that contains it is showing. A common example is the accelerator Ctrl-C, which is frequently used as a shortcut for the Copy item in the Edit menu.

The next example demonstrates several different features of menus. It creates a menu bar with three different menus. The first, Utensils, contains several menu items, a submenu, a separator, and a Quit item that includes both a mnemonic and an accelerator. The second menu, Spices, contains menu items that look and act like checkboxes. Finally, the Cheese menu demonstrates radio button menu items.

The application is shown in Figure 17-7 with one of its menus dropped down. Choosing Quit from the Utensils menu (or pressing Ctrl-Q) removes the window.

```java
//file: DinnerMenu.java
import java.awt.*;
import java.awt.event.*;
import javax.swing.*;

public class DinnerMenu
{
  public static void main(String[] args) {
    JFrame frame = new JFrame("Dinner Menu");

    // create the Utensils menu
    JMenu utensils = new JMenu("Utensils");
    utensils.setMnemonic(KeyEvent.VK_U);
    utensils.add(new JMenuItem("Fork"));
    utensils.add(new JMenuItem("Knife"));
    utensils.add(new JMenuItem("Spoon"));
    JMenu hybrid = new JMenu("Hybrid");
    hybrid.add(new JMenuItem("Spork"));
    hybrid.add(new JMenuItem("Spife"));
    hybrid.add(new JMenuItem("Knork"));
    utensils.add(hybrid);
    utensils.addSeparator();

    // do some fancy stuff with the Quit item
    JMenuItem quitItem = new JMenuItem("Quit");
    quitItem.setMnemonic(KeyEvent.VK_Q);
```

```
quitItem.setAccelerator(
    KeyStroke.getKeyStroke(KeyEvent.VK_Q, Event.CTRL_MASK));
quitItem.addActionListener(new ActionListener() {
  public void actionPerformed(ActionEvent e) { System.exit(0); }
});
utensils.add(quitItem);

// create the Spices menu
JMenu spices = new JMenu("Spices");
spices.setMnemonic(KeyEvent.VK_S);
spices.add(new JCheckBoxMenuItem("Thyme"));
spices.add(new JCheckBoxMenuItem("Rosemary"));
spices.add(new JCheckBoxMenuItem("Oregano", true));
spices.add(new JCheckBoxMenuItem("Fennel"));

// create the Cheese menu
JMenu cheese = new JMenu("Cheese");
cheese.setMnemonic(KeyEvent.VK_C);
ButtonGroup group = new ButtonGroup();
JRadioButtonMenuItem rbmi;
rbmi = new JRadioButtonMenuItem("Regular", true);
group.add(rbmi);
cheese.add(rbmi);
rbmi = new JRadioButtonMenuItem("Extra");
group.add(rbmi);
cheese.add(rbmi);
rbmi = new JRadioButtonMenuItem("Blue");
group.add(rbmi);
cheese.add(rbmi);

// create a menu bar and use it in this JFrame
JMenuBar menuBar = new JMenuBar();
menuBar.add(utensils);
menuBar.add(spices);
menuBar.add(cheese);
frame.setJMenuBar(menuBar);

frame.setDefaultCloseOperation( JFrame.EXIT_ON_CLOSE );
frame.setSize(200,200);
frame.setVisible(true);
  }
}
```

Yes, we know. Quit doesn't belong in the Utensils menu. If it's driving you crazy, you can go back and add a File menu as an exercise when we're through.

Creating menus is pretty simple work. You create a JMenu object, specifying the menu's title. Like the text of JButtons and JLabels, menu labels can contain simple HTML. Then you just add JMenuItems to the JMenu. You can also add JMenus to a JMenu; they show up as submenus. This is shown in the creation of the Utensils menu:

```
JMenu utensils = new JMenu("Utensils");
utensils.setMnemonic(KeyEvent.VK_U);
```

Figure 17-7. The DinnerMenu application

```
utensils.add(new JMenuItem("Fork"));
utensils.add(new JMenuItem("Knife"));
utensils.add(new JMenuItem("Spoon"));
JMenu hybrid = new JMenu("Hybrid");
hybrid.add(new JMenuItem("Spork"));
hybrid.add(new JMenuItem("Spife"));
hybrid.add(new JMenuItem("Knork"));
utensils.add(hybrid);
```

In the second line, we set the mnemonic for this menu using a constant defined in the KeyEvent class, which has static identifiers for all keys on the keyboard.

You can add those pretty separator lines with a single call:

```
utensils.addSeparator();
```

The Quit menu item has some bells and whistles we should explain. First, we create the menu item and set its mnemonic, just as we did before for the Utensils menu:

```
JMenuItem quitItem = new JMenuItem("Quit");
quitItem.setMnemonic(KeyEvent.VK_Q);
```

Now we want to create an accelerator for the menu item. We do this with the help of a class called KeyStroke:

```
quitItem.setAccelerator(
    KeyStroke.getKeyStroke(KeyEvent.VK_Q, Event.CTRL_MASK));
```

Finally, to actually do something in response to the menu item, we register an action listener:

```
quitItem.addActionListener(new ActionListener() {
    public void actionPerformed(ActionEvent e) { System.exit(0); }
});
```

Our action listener exits the application when the Quit item is selected.

Creating the Spices menu is just as easy, except that we use JCheckBoxMenuItems instead of regular JMenuItems. The result is a menu full of items that behave like checkboxes.

The next menu, Cheese, is a little more tricky. We want the items to be radio buttons, but we need to place them in a ButtonGroup to ensure they are mutually exclusive. Each item, then, is created, added to the button group, and added to the menu itself.

The final step is to place the menus we've just created in a JMenuBar. This is simply a component that lays out menus in a horizontal bar. We have two options for adding it to our JFrame. Since the JMenuBar is a real component, we could add it to the content pane of the JFrame. Instead, we use a convenience method called setJMenuBar( ), which automatically places the JMenuBar at the top of the frame's content pane. This saves us the trouble of altering the layout or size of the content pane; it is adjusted to coexist peacefully with the menu bar.

Pop-up Menus

One of Swing's nifty components is JPopupMenu, a context menu that appears at the mouse location when you press the appropriate mouse button or keystroke. (On a two-button mouse, clicking the right mouse button invokes a pop-up menu. On a single-button Mac, you Command-click.) Which button you press depends on the platform you're using; fortunately, from the code's point of view you don't have to care—Swing figures it out for you.

The care and feeding of JPopupMenu is basically the same as any other menu. You use a different constructor (JPopupMenu( )) to create it, but otherwise, you build a menu and add elements to it the same way. The big difference is that you don't attach it to a JMenuBar. Instead, just pop up the menu whenever and wherever you need it. Prior to Java 5.0, this process is a little cumbersome; you have to register to receive the appropriate mouse events, check them to see if they are the pop-up trigger and then pop the menu manually. With Java 5.0, the process is simplified by having components manage their own pop-up menus.

First, we'll show an example of explicit pop-up handling. The following example, PopupColorMenu, contains three buttons. You can use a JPopupMenu to set the color of each button or the background frame itself, depending on where you clickthe mouse.

```java
//file: PopUpColorMenu.java
import java.awt.*;
import java.awt.event.*;
import javax.swing.*;

public class PopUpColorMenu implements ActionListener
{
  Component selectedComponent;

  public PopUpColorMenu( ) {
    JFrame frame = new JFrame("PopUpColorMenu v1.0");
```

```
    final JPopupMenu colorMenu = new JPopupMenu("Color");
    colorMenu.add(makeMenuItem("Red"));
    colorMenu.add(makeMenuItem("Green"));
    colorMenu.add(makeMenuItem("Blue"));

    MouseListener mouseListener = new MouseAdapter() {
      public void mousePressed(MouseEvent e) { checkPopup(e); }
      public void mouseClicked(MouseEvent e) { checkPopup(e); }
      public void mouseReleased(MouseEvent e) { checkPopup(e); }
      private void checkPopup(MouseEvent e) {
        if (e.isPopupTrigger()) {
          selectedComponent = e.getComponent();
          colorMenu.show(e.getComponent(), e.getX(), e.getY());
        }
      }
    };

    Container content = frame.getContentPane(); // unnecessary  in 5.0+
    content.setLayout(new FlowLayout());
    JButton button = new JButton("Uno");
    button.addMouseListener(mouseListener);
    content.add(button);
    button = new JButton("Due");
    button.addMouseListener(mouseListener);
    content.add(button);
    button = new JButton("Tre");
    button.addMouseListener(mouseListener);
    content.add(button);

    frame.getContentPane().addMouseListener(mouseListener);

    frame.setSize(200,50);
    frame.setDefaultCloseOperation( JFrame.EXIT_ON_CLOSE );
    frame.setVisible(true);
  }

  public void actionPerformed(ActionEvent e) {
    String color = e.getActionCommand();
    if (color.equals("Red"))
      selectedComponent.setBackground(Color.red);
    else if (color.equals("Green"))
      selectedComponent.setBackground(Color.green);
    else if (color.equals("Blue"))
      selectedComponent.setBackground(Color.blue);
  }

  private JMenuItem makeMenuItem(String label) {
    JMenuItem item = new JMenuItem(label);
    item.addActionListener( this );
    return item;
  }
}
```

```
    public static void main(String[] args) {
        new PopUpColorMenu( );
    }
}
```

Figure 17-8 shows the example in action; the user is preparing to change the color of the bottom button.

Figure 17-8. The PopupColorMenu application

Because the pop-up menu is triggered by mouse events (in this example), we need to register a MouseListener for any of the components to which it applies. In this example, all three buttons and the content pane of the frame are eligible for the color pop-up menu. Therefore, we add a mouse-event listener for all these components explicitly. The same instance of an anonymous inner MouseAdapter subclass is used in each case. In this class, we override the mousePressed( ), mouseReleased( ), and mouseClicked( ) methods to display the pop-up menu when we get an appropriate event. How do we know what an "appropriate event" is? Fortunately, we don't need to worry about the specifics of our user's platform; we just need to call the event's isPopupTrigger( ) method. If this method returns true, we know the user has done whatever normally displays a pop-up menu on his system.

Once we know that the user wants to raise a pop-up menu, we display it by calling its show( ) method with the mouse event coordinates as arguments.

If we want to provide different menus for different types of components or the background, we create different mouse listeners for each different kind of component. The mouse listeners invoke different kinds of pop-up menus as appropriate.

The only thing left is to handle the action events from the pop-up menu items. We use a helper method called makeMenuItem( ) to register the PopUpColorMenu window as an action listener for every item we add. The example implements ActionListener and has the required actionPerformed( ) method. This method reads the action command from the event, which is equal to the selected menu item's label by default. It then sets the background color of the selected component appropriately.

Component-Managed Pop-ups

Things get a bit easier in Java 5.0, using the new pop-up menu API for components. In Java 5.0, any JComponent can manage a JPopupMenu directly with the setComponentPopupMenu( ) method. JComponents can also be told to simply inherit their parent container's pop-up menu via the setInheritsPopupMenu( ) method. This combination makes it very simple to implement a context menu that should appear in many components within a container.

Unfortunately, this doesn't lend itself well to our previous example (PopupColorMenu) for two reasons. First, we need to know which component the mouse was in when the pop-up was triggered and we don't get that information using this API. The pop-up handling is actually delegated to the container, not inherited. Second, not all types of components are registered to receive mouse events by default.* As a result, we'll create a new example that is more appropriate for a "one context menu to rule them all" application. The following example, ContextMenu, shows a TextArea and TextField that both inherit the same JPopupMenu from their JPanel container. When you select a menu item, the action is displayed in the text area.

```java
import java.awt.*;
import java.awt.event.*;
import javax.swing.*;

public class ContextMenu implements ActionListener
{
  JTextArea textArea = new JTextArea( );

  public ContextMenu( )
  {
    final JPopupMenu contextMenu = new JPopupMenu("Edit");
    contextMenu.add(makeMenuItem("Save"));
    contextMenu.add(makeMenuItem("Save As"));
    contextMenu.add(makeMenuItem("Close"));

    JFrame frame = new JFrame("ContextMenu v1.0");
    JPanel panel = new JPanel( );
    panel.setLayout( new BorderLayout( ) );
    frame.add( panel );
    panel.setComponentPopupMenu( contextMenu );

    textArea.setInheritsPopupMenu( true );
    panel.add( BorderLayout.CENTER, textArea );
```

---

* Components such as JPanel and JLabel by default do not expect to handle mouse events. When you register a listener such as MouseListener, it registers itself internally to begin processing these events. Unfortunately, at the time of this writing, using setInheritsPopupMenu( ) does not trigger this functionality. As a workaround, you could register a dummy mouse listener with these components to prompt them to expect mouse events and properly trigger context menus if you want them.

```
        JTextField textField = new JTextField( );
        textField.setInheritsPopupMenu( true );
        panel.add( BorderLayout.SOUTH, textField );

        frame.setDefaultCloseOperation( JFrame.EXIT_ON_CLOSE );
        frame.setSize(400,200);
        frame.setVisible(true);
    }

    public void actionPerformed( ActionEvent e ) {
        textArea.append( e.getActionCommand( ) +"\n" );
    }

    private JMenuItem makeMenuItem(String label) {
        JMenuItem item = new JMenuItem(label);
        item.addActionListener( this );
        return item;
    }

    public static void main(String[] args) {
        new ContextMenu( );
    }
}
```

We've constructed our JPopupMenu as before, but this time we are not responsible for listening for mouse clicks or triggering the pop-up explicitly. Instead we use the setComponentPopupMenu( ) method to ask the JPanel to handle it for us. We use setInheritsPopupMenu( ) on both the JTextArea and JTextField so that they will both delegate pop-up trigger mouse clicks to the JPanel automatically.

The JScrollPane Class

We used JScrollPane earlier in this chapter without explaining much about it. In this section, we'll remedy the situation.

A JScrollPane is a container that can hold one component. Said another way, a JScrollPane *wraps* another component. By default, if the wrapped component is larger than the JScrollPane itself, the JScrollPane supplies scrollbars. JScrollPane handles the events from the scrollbars and displays the appropriate portion of the contained component.

Technically, JScrollPane is a Container, but it's a funny one. It has its own layout manager, which can't be changed, and it accommodates only one component at a time. This isn't really a limitation. If you want to put a lot of stuff in a JScrollPane, just collect your components in a JPanel, with whatever layout manager you like, and put that panel into the JScrollPane.

When you create a JScrollPane, you specify the conditions under which its scrollbars are displayed. This is called the *scrollbar display policy*; a separate policy is used for the horizontal and vertical scrollbars. The following constants can be used to specify the policy for each of the scrollbars:

`HORIZONTAL_SCROLLBAR_AS_NEEDED`
`VERTICAL_SCROLLBAR_AS_NEEDED`

> Displays a scrollbar only if the wrapped component doesn't fit.

`HORIZONTAL_SCROLLBAR_ALWAYS`
`VERTICAL_SCROLLBAR_ALWAYS`

> Always shows a scrollbar, regardless of the contained component's size.

`HORIZONTAL_SCROLLBAR_NEVER`
`VERTICAL_SCROLLBAR_NEVER`

> Never shows a scrollbar, even if the contained component won't fit. If you use this policy, you should provide some other way to manipulate the `JScrollPane`.

By default, the policies are `HORIZONTAL_SCROLLBAR_AS_NEEDED` and `VERTICAL_SCROLLBAR_AS_NEEDED`.

Support for scrolling with mouse wheels is automatic as of Java 1.4. You do not have to do anything explicit in your application to get this to work.

The following example uses a `JScrollPane` to display a large image (see Figure 17-9). The application itself is very simple; all we do is place the image in a `JLabel`, wrap a `JScrollPane` around it, and put the `JScrollPane` in a `JFrame`'s content pane.

Figure 17-9. The ScrollPaneFrame application

Here's the code:

```
//file: ScrollPaneFrame.java
import java.awt.*;
import java.awt.event.*;
import javax.swing.*;
```

```
public class ScrollPaneFrame
{
  public static void main(String[] args) {
    String filename = "Piazza di Spagna.jpg";
    if (args.length > 0)
      filename = args[0];

    JFrame frame = new JFrame("ScrollPaneFrame v1.0");
    JLabel image = new JLabel( new ImageIcon(filename) );
    frame.getContentPane( ).add( new JScrollPane(image) );

    frame.setSize(300, 300);
    frame.setDefaultCloseOperation( JFrame.EXIT_ON_CLOSE );
    frame.setVisible(true);
  }
}
```

To hold the image, we have used a JLabel and ImageIcon. The ImageIcon class pre-loads the image using a MediaTracker and determines its dimensions. It's also possible to have the ImageIcon show the image as it loads or to ask it for information on the status of loading the image. We'll discuss image management in Chapter 21.

The JSplitPane Class

A *split pane* is a special container that holds two components, each in its own sub-pane. A *splitter bar* adjusts the sizes of the two subpanes. In a document viewer, for example, you might use a split pane to show a table of contents next to a page of text.

The following example uses two JLabels containing ImageIcons, like the previous example. It displays the two labels, wrapped in JScrollPanes, on either side of a JSplitPane (see Figure 17-10). You can drag the splitter bar back and forth to adjust the sizes of the two contained components.

```
//file: SplitPaneFrame.java
import java.awt.*;
import java.awt.event.*;
import javax.swing.*;
import javax.swing.border.*;

public class SplitPaneFrame {
  public static void main(String[] args) {
    String fileOne = "Piazza di Spagna.jpg";
    String fileTwo = "L1-Light.jpg";
    if (args.length > 0) fileOne = args[0];
    if (args.length > 1) fileTwo = args[1];

    JFrame frame = new JFrame("SplitPaneFrame");

    JLabel leftImage = new JLabel( new ImageIcon( fileOne ) );
    Component left = new JScrollPane(leftImage);
```

```
      JLabel rightImage = new JLabel( new ImageIcon( fileTwo ) );
      Component right = new JScrollPane(rightImage);

      JSplitPane split =
        new JSplitPane(JSplitPane.HORIZONTAL_SPLIT, left, right);
      split.setDividerLocation(100);
      frame.getContentPane( ).add(split);

      frame.setDefaultCloseOperation( JFrame.EXIT_ON_CLOSE );
      frame.setSize(300, 200);
      frame.setVisible(true);
    }
  }
```

Figure 17-10. Using a split pane

The JTabbedPane Class

If you've ever right-clicked on the desktop to set your Display Properties in Windows, you already know what a JTabbedPane is. It's a container with labeled tabs (e.g., Themes, Screen Saver, Appearance). When you click on a tab, a new set of controls is shown in the body of the JTabbedPane. In Swing, JTabbedPane is simply a specialized container.

Each tab has a name. To add a tab to the JTabbedPane, simply call addTab( ). You'll need to specify the name of the tab as well as a component that supplies the tab's contents. Typically, it's a container holding other components.

Even though the JTabbedPane only shows one set of components at a time, be aware that all the components on all the pages are alive and in memory at one time. If you have components that hog processor time or memory, try to put them into some "sleep" state when they are not showing.

The following example shows how to create a JTabbedPane. It adds standard Swing components to a tab named Controls. The second tab is filled with a scrollable image, which was presented in the previous examples.

```java
//file: TabbedPaneFrame.java
import java.awt.*;
import java.awt.event.*;
import javax.swing.*;
import javax.swing.border.*;

public class TabbedPaneFrame {
  public static void main(String[] args)
  {
    JFrame frame = new JFrame("TabbedPaneFrame");
    JTabbedPane tabby = new JTabbedPane( );

    // create the controls pane
    JPanel controls = new JPanel( );
    controls.add(new JLabel("Service:"));
    JList list = new JList(
        new String[] { "Web server", "FTP server" });
    list.setBorder(BorderFactory.createEtchedBorder( ));
    controls.add(list);
    controls.add(new JButton("Start"));

    // create an image pane
    String filename = "Piazza di Spagna.jpg";
    JLabel image = new JLabel( new ImageIcon(filename) );
    JComponent picture = new JScrollPane(image);
    tabby.addTab("Controls", controls);
    tabby.addTab("Picture", picture);

    frame.getContentPane( ).add(tabby);

    frame.setSize(200, 200);
    frame.setDefaultCloseOperation( JFrame.EXIT_ON_CLOSE );
    frame.setVisible(true);
  }
}
```

The code isn't especially fancy, but the result is an impressive-looking user interface. The first tab is a JPanel that contains some other components, including a JList with an etched border. The second tab simply contains the JLabel with ImageIcon wrapped in a JScrollPane. The running example is shown in Figure 17-11.

Our example has only two tabs, and they fit quite easily, but in a realistic application it is easy to run out of room. By default, when there are too many tabs to display in a single row, JTabbedPane automatically wraps them into additional rows. This behavior fits with the tab notion quite well, giving the appearance of a filing cabinet, but it also necessitates that when you select a tab from the back row, the tabs must be rearranged to bring the selected tab to the foreground. Many users find this confusing, and it violates a principal of user interface design that says that controls should

Figure 17-11. Using a tabbed pane

remain in the same location. Alternatively the tabbed pane can be configured to use a single, scrolling row of tabs by specifying a scrolling tab layout policy like this:

```
setTabLayoutPolicy( JTabbedPane.SCROLL_TAB_LAYOUT );
```

Scrollbars and Sliders

JScrollPane is such a handy component that you may not ever need to use scrollbars by themselves. In fact, if you ever do find yourself using a scrollbar by itself, chances are you really want to use another component called a *slider*.

There's not much point in describing the appearance and functionality of scrollbars and sliders. Instead, let's jump right in with an example that includes both components. Figure 17-12 shows a simple example with both a scrollbar and a slider.

Figure 17-12. Using a scrollbar and a slider

Here is the source code for this example:

```
//file: Slippery.java
import java.awt.*;
import java.awt.event.*;
import javax.swing.*;
import javax.swing.event.*;

public class Slippery {
  public static void main(String[] args)
```

```
  {
    JFrame frame = new JFrame("Slippery v1.0");
    Container content = frame.getContentPane();  // unnecessary  in 5.0+

    JPanel main = new JPanel(new GridLayout(2, 1));
    JPanel scrollBarPanel = new JPanel();
    final JScrollBar scrollBar =
        new JScrollBar(JScrollBar.HORIZONTAL, 0, 48, 0, 255);
    int height = scrollBar.getPreferredSize().height;
    scrollBar.setPreferredSize(new Dimension(175, height));
    scrollBarPanel.add(scrollBar);
    main.add(scrollBarPanel);

    JPanel sliderPanel = new JPanel();
    final JSlider slider =
        new JSlider(JSlider.HORIZONTAL, 0, 255, 128);
    slider.setMajorTickSpacing(48);
    slider.setMinorTickSpacing(16);
    slider.setPaintTicks(true);
    sliderPanel.add(slider);
    main.add(sliderPanel);

    content.add(main, BorderLayout.CENTER);

    final JLabel statusLabel =
        new JLabel("Welcome to Slippery v1.0");
    content.add(statusLabel, BorderLayout.SOUTH);

    // wire up the event handlers
    scrollBar.addAdjustmentListener(new AdjustmentListener() {
      public void adjustmentValueChanged(AdjustmentEvent e) {
        statusLabel.setText("JScrollBar's current value = "
                            + scrollBar.getValue());
      }
    });

    slider.addChangeListener(new ChangeListener() {
      public void stateChanged(ChangeEvent e) {
        statusLabel.setText("JSlider's current value = "
                            + slider.getValue());
      }
    });

    frame.pack();
    frame.setDefaultCloseOperation( JFrame.EXIT_ON_CLOSE );
    frame.setVisible(true);
  }
}
```

All we've really done here is added a JScrollBar and a JSlider to our main window.
If the user adjusts either of these components, the current value of the component is
displayed in a JLabel at the bottom of the window.

The JScrollBar and JSlider are both created by specifying an orientation, either HORIZONTAL or VERTICAL. You can also specify the minimum and maximum values for the components, as well as the initial value. The JScrollBar supports one additional parameter, the *extent*. The extent simply refers to what range of values is represented by the slider within the scroll bar. For example, in a scrollbar that runs from 0 to 255, an extent of 128 means that the slider will be half the width of the scrollable area of the scrollbar.

JSlider supports the idea of *tick marks*, lines drawn at certain values along the slider's length. *Major tick marks* are slightly larger than *minor tick marks*. To draw tick marks, just specify an interval for major and minor tick marks, and then paint the tick marks:

```
slider.setMajorTickSpacing(48);
slider.setMinorTickSpacing(16);
slider.setPaintTicks(true);
```

JSlider also supports labeling the ticks with text strings, using the setLabelTable( ) method.

Responding to events from the two components is straightforward. The JScrollBar sends out AdjustmentEvents every time something happens; the JSlider fires off ChangeEvents when its value changes. In our simple example, we display the new value of the changed component in the JLabel at the bottom of the window.

Dialogs

A dialog is another standard feature of user interfaces. Dialogs are frequently used to present information to the user ("Your fruit salad is ready.") or to ask a question ("Shall I bring the car around?"). Dialogs are used so commonly in GUI applications that Swing includes a handy set of prebuilt dialogs. These are accessible from static methods in the JOptionPane class. Many variations are possible; JOptionPane groups them into four basic types:

Message dialog
    Displays a message to the user, usually accompanied by an OK button.

Confirmation dialog
    Ask a question and displays answer buttons, usually Yes, No, and Cancel.

Input dialog
    Asks the user to type in a string.

Option dialogs
    The most general type. You pass it your own components, which are displayed in the dialog.

A confirmation dialog is shown in Figure 17-13.

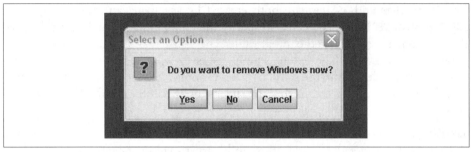

Figure 17-13. Using a confirmation dialog

Let's look at examples of each kind of dialog. The following code produces a message dialog:

```
JOptionPane.showMessageDialog(frame, "You have mail.");
```

The first parameter to showMessageDialog( ) is the parent component (in this case, frame, an existing JFrame). The dialog will be centered on the parent component. If you pass null for the parent component, the dialog is centered in your screen. The dialogs that JOptionPane displays are *modal*, which means they block other input to your application while they are showing.

Here's a slightly fancier message dialog. We've specified a title for the dialog and a message type, which affects the icon that is displayed:

```
JOptionPane.showMessageDialog(frame, "You are low on memory.",
        "Apocalyptic message", JOptionPane.WARNING_MESSAGE);
```

Here's how to display the confirmation dialog shown in Figure 17-13:

```
int result = JOptionPane.showConfirmDialog(null,
        "Do you want to remove Windows now?");
```

In this case, we've passed null for the parent component and it will be displayed centered on the screen. Special values are returned from showConfirmDialog( ) to indicate which button was pressed. A full example later in this section shows how to use this return value.

Sometimes you need to ask the user to type some input. The following code puts up a dialog requesting the user's name:

```
String name = JOptionPane.showInputDialog(null,
        "Please enter your name.");
```

Whatever the user types is returned as a String or null if the user presses the Cancel button.

The most general type of dialog is the option dialog. You supply an array of objects you wish to be displayed; JOptionPane takes care of formatting them and displaying the dialog. The following example displays a text label, a JTextField, and a JPasswordField. (Text components are described in the next chapter.)

```
JTextField userField = new JTextField( );
JPasswordField passField = new JPasswordField( );
String message = "Please enter your user name and password.";
result = JOptionPane.showOptionDialog(frame,
    new Object[] { message, userField, passField },
    "Login", JOptionPane.OK_CANCEL_OPTION,
    JOptionPane.QUESTION_MESSAGE,
    null, null, null);
```

We've also specified a dialog title ("Login") in the call to showOptionDialog( ). We want OK and Cancel buttons, so we pass OK_CANCEL_OPTION as the dialog type. The QUESTION_MESSAGE argument indicates we'd like to see the question-mark icon. The last three items are optional: an Icon, an array of different choices, and a current selection. Since the icon parameter is null, a default is used. If the array of choices and the current selection parameters were not null, JOptionPane might try to display the choices in a list or combo box.

The following application includes all the examples we've covered:

```java
import javax.swing.*;

public class ExerciseOptions {
  public static void main(String[] args) {
    JFrame frame = new JFrame("ExerciseOptions v1.0");
    frame.setSize(200, 200);
    frame.setVisible(true);

    JOptionPane.showMessageDialog(frame, "You have mail.");
    JOptionPane.showMessageDialog(frame, "You are low on memory.",
        "Apocalyptic message", JOptionPane.WARNING_MESSAGE);

    int result = JOptionPane.showConfirmDialog(null,
        "Do you want to remove Windows now?");
    switch (result) {
      case JOptionPane.YES_OPTION:
        System.out.println("Yes"); break;
      case JOptionPane.NO_OPTION:
        System.out.println("No"); break;
      case JOptionPane.CANCEL_OPTION:
        System.out.println("Cancel"); break;
      case JOptionPane.CLOSED_OPTION:
        System.out.println("Closed"); break;
    }

    String name = JOptionPane.showInputDialog(null,
        "Please enter your name.");
    System.out.println(name);

    JTextField userField = new JTextField( );
    JPasswordField passField = new JPasswordField( );
    String message = "Please enter your user name and password.";
    result = JOptionPane.showOptionDialog(frame,
        new Object[] { message, userField, passField },
```

```
            "Login", JOptionPane.OK_CANCEL_OPTION,
            JOptionPane.QUESTION_MESSAGE,
            null, null, null);
      if (result == JOptionPane.OK_OPTION)
        System.out.println(userField.getText( ) +
            " " + new String(passField.getPassword( )));

      System.exit(0);
    }
  }
```

File Selection Dialog

A JFileChooser is a standard file-selection box. As with other Swing components, JFileChooser is implemented in pure Java, so it can look and act the same on different platforms or take on the native appearance of the operating system, depending on what look and feel is in effect.

Selecting files all day can be pretty boring without a greater purpose, so we'll exercise the JFileChooser in a mini-editor application. Editor provides a text area in which we can load and work with files. (The JFileChooser created by Editor is shown in Figure 17-14.) We'll stop just shy of the capability to save and let you fill in the blanks (with a few caveats).

Figure 17-14. Using a JFileChooser

Here's the code:

```
import java.awt.*;
import java.awt.event.*;
```

```java
import java.io.*;
import javax.swing.*;

public class Editor extends JFrame implements ActionListener
{
  private JEditorPane textPane = new JEditorPane( );

  public Editor( ) {
    super("Editor v1.0");
    Container content = getContentPane( );  // unnecessary in 5.0+
    content.add(new JScrollPane(textPane), BorderLayout.CENTER);
    JMenu menu = new JMenu("File");
    menu.add(makeMenuItem("Open"));
    menu.add(makeMenuItem("Save"));
    menu.add(makeMenuItem("Quit"));
    JMenuBar menuBar = new JMenuBar( );
    menuBar.add(menu);
    setJMenuBar(menuBar);
    setSize(300, 300);
    setDefaultCloseOperation( JFrame.EXIT_ON_CLOSE );
  }

  public void actionPerformed(ActionEvent e) {
    String command = e.getActionCommand( );
    if (command.equals("Quit")) System.exit(0);
    else if (command.equals("Open")) loadFile( );
    else if (command.equals("Save")) saveFile( );
  }

  private void loadFile ( ) {
    JFileChooser chooser = new JFileChooser( );
    int result = chooser.showOpenDialog(this);
    if (result == JFileChooser.CANCEL_OPTION) return;
    try {
      File file = chooser.getSelectedFile( );
      java.net.URL url = file.toURL( );
      textPane.setPage(url);
    }
    catch (Exception e) {
      textPane.setText("Could not load file: " + e);
    }
  }

  private void saveFile( ) {
    JFileChooser chooser = new JFileChooser( );
    chooser.showSaveDialog(this);
    // Save file data...
  }

  private JMenuItem makeMenuItem( String name ) {
    JMenuItem m = new JMenuItem( name );
    m.addActionListener( this );
    return m;
  }
```

```
    public static void main(String[] s) {
  new Editor().setVisible(true);
    }
  }
```

Editor is a JFrame that lays itself out with a JEditorPane (which is covered in Chapter 18) and a pull-down menu. From the pull-down File menu, we can Open, Save, or Quit. The actionPerformed() method catches the events associated with these menu selections and takes the appropriate action.

The interesting parts of Editor are the private methods loadFile() and saveFile(). The loadFile() method creates a new JFileChooser and calls its showOpenDialog() method.

A JFileChooser does its work when the showOpenDialog() method is called. This method blocks the caller until the dialog completes its job, at which time the file chooser disappears. After that, we can retrieve the designated file with the getFile() method. In loadFile(), we convert the selected File to a URL and pass it to the JEditorPane, which displays the selected file. As you'll learn in the next chapter, JEditorPane can display HTML and RTF files.

You can fill out the unfinished saveFile() method if you wish, but it would be prudent to add the standard safety precautions. For example, you could use one of the confirmation dialogs we just looked at to prompt the user before overwriting an existing file.

The Color Chooser

Swing is chock full of goodies. JColorChooser is yet another ready-made dialog supplied with Swing; it allows your users to choose colors. The following brief example shows how easy it is to use JColorChooser:

```
import java.awt.*;
import java.awt.event.*;
import javax.swing.*;

public class LocalColor {
  public static void main(String[] args) {
    final JFrame frame = new JFrame("LocalColor v1.0");
    final Container content = frame.getContentPane();  // unnecessary in 5.0+
    content.setLayout(new GridBagLayout());
    JButton button = new JButton("Change color...");
    content.add(button);

    button.addActionListener(new ActionListener() {
      public void actionPerformed(ActionEvent e) {
        Color c = JColorChooser.showDialog(frame,
            "Choose a color", content.getBackground());
        if (c != null) content.setBackground(c);
      }
    });
```

```
        frame.setSize(200, 200);
        frame.setDefaultCloseOperation( JFrame.EXIT_ON_CLOSE );
        frame.setVisible(true);
    }
}
```

This example shows a frame window with a single button. When you click on the button, a color chooser pops up. After you select a color, it becomes the background color of the frame window.

Basically, all we have to do is call JColorChooser's static method showDialog( ). In this example, we specified a parent component, a dialog title, and an initial color value. But you can get away with just specifying a parent component. Whatever color the user chooses is returned; if the user presses the Cancel button, null is returned.

## CHAPTER 18

More Swing Components

In the previous chapter, we described most of the components that Swing offers for building user interfaces. In this chapter, you'll find out about the rest. These include Swing's text components, trees, and tables. These types of components have considerable depth but are quite easy to use if you accept their default options. We'll show you the easy way to use these components and start to describe the more advanced features of each. Later in this chapter, we'll also give an example of how to implement your own, custom components in Swing.

Text Components

Swing offers sophisticated text components, from plain-text entry boxes to HTML interpreters. For full coverage of Swing's text capabilities, see O'Reilly's *Java Swing*. In that encyclopedic book, several meaty chapters are devoted to text. It's a huge subject; we'll just scratch the surface here.

Let's begin by examining the simpler text components. JTextField is a single-line text editor and JTextArea is a simple, multiline text editor. Both JTextField and JTextArea derive from the JTextComponent class, which provides the functionality they have in common. This includes methods for setting and retrieving the displayed text, specifying whether the text is "editable" or read-only, manipulating the cursor position within the text, and manipulating text selections.

Observing changes in text components requires an understanding of how the components implement the Model-View-Controller (MVC) architecture. You may recall from the last chapter that Swing components implement a true MVC architecture. It's in the text components that you first get an inkling of a clear separation between the M and VC parts of the MVC architecture. The model for text components is an object called a Document. When you add or remove text from a JTextField or a JTextArea, the corresponding Document is changed. It's the document itself, not the visual components, that generates text-related events when something changes. To receive notification of JTextArea changes, therefore, you register with the underlying Document, not with the JTextArea component itself:

```
JTextArea textArea = new JTextArea( );
Document doc = textArea.getDocument( );
doc.addDocumentListener(someListener);
```

As you'll see in an upcoming example, you can easily have more than one visual text component use the same underlying Document data model.

In addition, JTextField components generate ActionEvents whenever the user presses the Return key within the field. To get these events, just implement the ActionListener interface and register your listener using the addActionListener( ) method.

The next sections contain a couple of simple applications that show you how to work with text areas and fields.

The TextEntryBox Application

Our first example, TextEntryBox, creates a JTextArea and ties it to a JTextField, as you can see in Figure 18-1.

Figure 18-1. The TextEntryBox application

When the user hits Return in the JTextField, we receive an ActionEvent and add the line to the JTextArea's display. Try it out. You may have to click your mouse in the JTextField to give it focus before typing in it. If you fill up the display with lines, you can test-drive the scrollbar:

```
//file: TextEntryBox.java
import java.awt.*;
import java.awt.event.*;
import javax.swing.*;

public class TextEntryBox {

    public static void main(String[] args) {
        JFrame frame = new JFrame("Text Entry Box");
```

```
final JTextArea area = new JTextArea();
area.setFont(new Font("Serif", Font.BOLD, 18));
area.setText("Howdy!\n");
final JTextField field = new JTextField();

Container content = frame.getContentPane(); // unnecessary  in 5.0+
content.add(new JScrollPane(area), BorderLayout.CENTER);
content.add(field, BorderLayout.SOUTH);
field.requestFocus();

field.addActionListener(new ActionListener() {
  public void actionPerformed(ActionEvent ae) {
    area.append(field.getText() + '\n');
    field.setText("");
  }
});

frame.setDefaultCloseOperation( JFrame.EXIT_ON_CLOSE );
frame.setSize(200, 300);
frame.setVisible(true);
    }
  }
```

TextEntryBox is exceedingly simple; we've done a few things to make it more interesting. We give the text area a bigger font using Component's setFont() method; fonts are discussed in Chapter 20. Finally, we want to be notified whenever the user presses Return in the text field, so we register an anonymous inner class as a listener for action events.

Pressing Return in the JTextField generates an action event, and that's where the fun begins. We handle the event in the actionPerformed() method of our inner ActionListener implementation. Then, we use the getText() and setText() methods to manipulate the text the user has typed. These methods can be used for JTextField and JTextArea since these components are both derived from the JTextComponent class and, therefore, have some common functionality.

The event handler, actionPerformed(), calls field.getText() to read the text that the user typed into our JTextField. It then adds this text to the JTextArea by calling area.append(). Finally, we clear the text field by calling the method field. setText(""), preparing it for more input.

Remember, the text components really are distinct from the text data model, the Document. When you call setText(), getText(), or append(), these methods are shorthand for operations on an underlying Document.

By default, JTextField and JTextArea are editable; you can type and edit in both text components. They can be changed to output-only areas by calling setEditable(false). Both text components also support *selections*. A selection is a range of text that is highlighted for copying, cutting, or pasting in your windowing system. You select text by dragging the mouse over it; you can then cut, copy, and paste it into other text windows using the default keyboard gestures. On most systems these are Ctrl-C for copy, Ctrl-V for paste, and Ctrl-X for cut (on the Mac it's Command-C, Command-V, and Command-X). You can also programmatically manage these operations using the JTextComponent's cut( ), copy( ), and paste( ) methods. You could, for example, create a pop-up menu with the standard cut, copy, and paste options using these methods. The current text selection is returned by getSelectedText( ), and you can set the selection using selectText( ), which takes an index range or selectAll( ).

Notice how JTextArea fits neatly inside a JScrollPane. The scroll pane gives us the expected scrollbars and scrolling behavior if the text in the JTextArea becomes too large for the available space.

Formatted Text

The JFormattedTextField component provides explicit support for editing complex formatted values such as numbers and dates. JFormattedTextField acts somewhat like a JTextField, except that it accepts a format-specifying object in its constructor and manages a complex object type (such as Date or Integer) through its setValue( ) and getValue( ) methods. The following example shows the construction of a simple form with different types of formatted fields:

```java
import java.text.*;
import javax.swing.*;
import javax.swing.text.*;
import java.util.Date;

public class FormattedFields
{
    public static void main( String[] args ) throws Exception {
        Box form = Box.createVerticalBox( );
        form.add( new JLabel("Name:") );
        form.add( new JTextField("Joe User") );

        form.add( new JLabel("Birthday:") );
        JFormattedTextField birthdayField =
            new JFormattedTextField(new SimpleDateFormat("mm/dd/yy"));
        birthdayField.setValue( new Date() );
        form.add( birthdayField );

        form.add( new JLabel("Age:") );
        form.add(new JFormattedTextField(new Integer(32)));

        form.add( new JLabel("Hairs on Body:") );
        JFormattedTextField hairsField
            = new JFormattedTextField( new DecimalFormat("###,###") );
        hairsField.setValue(new Integer(100000));
        form.add( hairsField );
```

```
        form.add( new JLabel("Phone Number:") );
        JFormattedTextField phoneField =
            new JFormattedTextField( new MaskFormatter("(###)###-####") );
        phoneField.setValue("(314)555-1212");
        form.add( phoneField );

        JFrame frame = new JFrame("User Information");
        frame.getContentPane( ).add(form);
        frame.pack( );
        frame.setDefaultCloseOperation( JFrame.EXIT_ON_CLOSE );
        frame.setVisible(true);
    }
}
```

JFormattedTextField can be constructed in a variety of ways. You can use a plain instance of java.lang.Number (e.g., Integer and Float) as a prototype or set the layout explicitly using a formatting object from the java.text package: java.text.NumberFormat, java.text.DateFormat, or the more arbitrary java.text.MaskFormatter. The NumberFormat and DateFormat classes of the java.text package are discussed in Chapters 10 and 11. MaskFormatter allows you to construct arbitrary physical layout conventions. In a moment, we'll discuss input filtering and component validation, which also allow you to restrict the kinds of characters that could fill the fields or perform arbitrary checks on the data. Finally, we should mention that in this example we've used a Box container. A Box is just a Swing container that uses a BoxLayout, which we'll discuss more in Chapter 19.

After construction you can set a valid value using setValue( ) and retrieve the last valid value with getValue( ). To do this, you'll have to cast the value back to the correct type based on the format you are using. For example, this statement retrieves the date from our birthday field:

```
Date bday = (Date)birthdayField.getValue( );
```

JFormattedTextField validates its text when the user attempts to shift focus to a new field (either by clicking with the mouse outside of the field or using keyboard navigation). By default, JFormattedTextField handles invalid input by simply reverting to the last valid value. If you wish to allow invalid input to remain in the field for further editing, you can set the setFocusLostBehavior( ) method with the value JFormattedTextField.COMMIT (the default is COMMIT_OR_REVERT). In any case, invalid input does not change the value property retrieved by getValue( ).

Filtering Input

JFormattedTextField does not know about all format types itself; instead it uses AbstractFormatter objects that know about particular format types. The AbstractFormatters, in turn, provide implementations of two interfaces: DocumentFilter and NavigationFilter. A DocumentFilter attaches to implementations of Document and allows you to intercept editing commands, modifying them as you wish. A NavigationFilter can be attached to JTextComponents to control the movement of the cursor (as in a mask-formatted field). You can implement your own AbstractFormatters for use with JFormattedTextField, and, more generally, you can use the DocumentFilter interface to control how documents are edited in any type of text component. For example, you could create a DocumentFilter that maps characters to uppercase or strange symbols. DocumentFilter provides a low-level, edit-by-edit means of controlling or mapping user input. We will show an example of this now. In the following section, we discuss how to implement higher-level field *validation* that ensures the correctness of data after it is entered, in the same way that the formatted text field did for us earlier.

DocumentFilter

The following example, DocFilter, applies a document filter to a JTextField. Our DocumentFilter simply maps any input to uppercase. Here is the code:

```
import java.text.*;
import javax.swing.*;
import javax.swing.text.*;

public class DocFilter
{
    public static void main( String[] args ) throws Exception
    {
        JTextField field = new JTextField(30);

        ((AbstractDocument)(field.getDocument( ))).setDocumentFilter(
            new DocumentFilter( )
        {
            public void insertString(
                FilterBypass fb, int offset, String string, AttributeSet attr)
                    throws BadLocationException
                {
                    fb.insertString( offset, string.toUpperCase( ), attr );
                }

            public void replace(
                FilterBypass fb, int offset, int length, String string,
                AttributeSet attr) throws BadLocationException
                {
                    fb.replace( offset, length, string.toUpperCase( ), attr );
                }
        } );

        JFrame frame = new JFrame("User Information");
        frame.getContentPane( ).add( field );
        frame.pack( );
        frame.setDefaultCloseOperation( JFrame.EXIT_ON_CLOSE );
        frame.setVisible(true);
    }
}
```

The methods insertString( ) and replace( ) of the DocumentFilter are called when text is added to the document or modified. Within them, we have an opportunity to filter the text before passing it on. When we are ready to apply the text, we use the FilterBypass reference to pass it along. FilterBypass has the same set of methods, which apply the changes directly to the document. The DocumentFilter remove( ) method can also be used to intercept edits to the document that remove characters. One thing to note in our example is that not all Documents have a setDocumentFilter( ) method. Instead, we have to cast our document to an AbstractDocument. Only document implementations that extend AbstractDocument accept filters (unless you implement your own). This sad state of affairs is because that the Document Filter API was added in Java 1.4, and it was decided that changes could not be made to the original Document interface.

Validating Data

Low-level input filtering prevents you from doing such things as entering a number where a character should be. In this section, we're going to talk about high-level validation, which accounts for things like February having only 28 days or a credit-card number being for a Visa or MasterCard. Whereas character filtering prevents you from entering incorrect data, field validation happens after data has been entered. Normally, validation occurs when the user tries to change focus and leave the field, either by clicking the mouse or through keyboard navigation. Java 1.4 added the InputVerifier API, which allows you to validate the contents of a component before focus is transferred. Although we are going to talk about this in the context of text fields, an InputVerifier can actually be attached to any JComponent to validate its state in this way.

The following example creates a pair of text fields. The first allows any value to be entered, while the second accepts only numbers between 0 and 100. When both fields are happy, you can freely move between them. However, when you enter an invalid value in the second field and try to leave, the program just beeps and selects the text. The focus remains trapped until you correct the problem.

```
import javax.swing.*;

public class Validator
{
    public static void main( String[] args ) throws Exception {
        Box form = Box.createVerticalBox( );
        form.add( new JLabel("Any Value") );
        form.add( new JTextField("5000") );

        form.add( new JLabel("Only 0-100") );
        JTextField rangeField = new JTextField("50");
        rangeField.setInputVerifier( new InputVerifier( ) {
            public boolean verify( JComponent comp ) {
                JTextField field = (JTextField)comp;
```

```
                    boolean passed = false;
                    try {
                        int n = Integer.parseInt(field.getText( ));
                        passed = ( 0 <= n && n <= 100 );
                    } catch (NumberFormatException e) { }
                    if ( !passed ) {
                        comp.getToolkit( ).beep( );
                        field.selectAll( );
                    }
                    return passed;
                }
            } );
            form.add( rangeField );

            JFrame frame = new JFrame("User Information");
            frame.getContentPane( ).add(form);
            frame.setDefaultCloseOperation( JFrame.EXIT_ON_CLOSE );
            frame.pack( );
            frame.setVisible(true);
        }
    }
```

We have created an anonymous inner class extending InputVerifier with this code.
The API is very simple; at validation time our verify( ) method is called, and we are
passed a reference to the component needing checking. Here we cast to the correct
type (we know what we are verifying, of course) and parse the number. If it is out of
range, we beep and select the text. We then return true or false indicating whether
the value passes validation.

You can use an InputVerifier in combination with a JFormattedTextField to both
guide user input into the correct format and validate the semantics of what the user
entered.

Say the Magic Word

Before we move on from our discussion of formatted text, we should mention that
Swing includes a class just for typing passwords, called JPasswordField. A
JPasswordField behaves just like a JTextField (it's a subclass), except every character
typed is echoed as the same, obfuscating character, typically an asterisk. Figure 18-2
shows the option dialog example that was presented in Chapter 17. The example
includes a JTextField and a JPasswordField.

The creation and use of JPasswordField is basically the same as for JTextField. If you
find asterisks distasteful, you can tell the JPasswordField to use a different character
using the setEchoChar( ) method.

Normally, you would use getText( ) to retrieve the text typed into the
JPasswordField. This method, however, is deprecated; you should use getPassword( )
instead. The getPassword( ) method returns a character array rather than a String
object. This is done because character arrays are a little less vulnerable than Strings

Figure 18-2. Using a JPasswordField in a dialog

to discovery by memory-snooping password sniffer programs and they can be erased directly and easily. If you're not that concerned, you can simply create a new String from the character array. Note that methods in the Java cryptographic classes accept passwords as character arrays, not strings, so you can pass the results of a getPassword( ) call directly to methods in the cryptographic classes without ever creating a String.

Sharing a Data Model

Our next example shows how easy it is to make two or more text components share the same Document; Figure 18-3 shows what the application looks like.

Figure 18-3. Three views of the same data model

Anything the user types into any text area is reflected in all of them. All we had to do is make all the text areas use the same data model, like this:

```
JTextArea areaFiftyOne = new JTextArea( );
JTextArea areaFiftyTwo = new JTextArea( );
areaFiftyTwo.setDocument(areaFiftyOne.getDocument( ));
JTextArea areaFiftyThree = new JTextArea( );
areaFiftyThree.setDocument(areaFiftyOne.getDocument( ));
```

We could just as easily make seven text areas sharing the same document or seventy. While this example may not look very useful, keep in mind that you can scroll different text areas to different places in the same document. That's one of the beauties of putting multiple views on the same data; you get to examine different parts of it. Another useful technique is viewing the same data in different ways. You could, for example, view some tabular numerical data as both a spreadsheet and a pie chart. The MVC architecture that Swing uses means that it's possible to do this in an intelligent way so that if numbers in a spreadsheet are updated, a pie chart that uses the same data is automatically updated, too.

This example works because, behind the scenes, there are a lot of events flying around. When you type in one of the text areas, the text area receives the keyboard events. It calls methods in the document to update its data. In turn, the document sends events to the other text areas telling them about the updates so that they can correctly display the document's new data. But don't worry about any of this; you just tell the text areas to use the same data, and Swing takes care of the rest:

```
//file: SharedModel.java
import java.awt.*;
import java.awt.event.*;
import javax.swing.*;

public class SharedModel {
    public static void main(String[] args) {
    JFrame frame = new JFrame("Shared Model");

    JTextArea areaFiftyOne = new JTextArea( );
    JTextArea areaFiftyTwo = new JTextArea( );
    areaFiftyTwo.setDocument(areaFiftyOne.getDocument( ));
    JTextArea areaFiftyThree = new JTextArea( );
    areaFiftyThree.setDocument(areaFiftyOne.getDocument( ));

    Container content = frame.getContentPane( );
    content.setLayout(new GridLayout(3, 1));
    content.add(new JScrollPane(areaFiftyOne));
    content.add(new JScrollPane(areaFiftyTwo));
    content.add(new JScrollPane(areaFiftyThree));

    frame.setDefaultCloseOperation( JFrame.EXIT_ON_CLOSE );
    frame.setSize(300, 300);
    frame.setVisible(true);
    }
}
```

Setting up the display is simple. We use a GridLayout (discussed in the next chapter) and add three text areas to the layout. Then, all we have to do is tell the text areas to use the same Document.

HTML and RTF for Free

Most user interfaces will use only two subclasses of JTextComponent. These are the simple JTextField and JTextArea classes that we just covered. That's just the tip of the iceberg, however. Swing offers sophisticated text capabilities through two other subclasses of JTextComponent: JEditorPane and JTextPane.

The first of these, JEditorPane, can display HTML and Rich Text Format (RTF) documents. It also fires one more type of event, a HyperlinkEvent. Subtypes of this event are fired off when the mouse enters, exits, or clicks on a hyperlink. Combined with JEditorPane's HTML display capabilities, it's easy to build a simple browser. The following browser, as shown in Figure 18-4, has only about 70 lines of code.

```
//file: CanisMinor.java
import java.awt.*;
import java.awt.event.*;
import java.net.*;
import javax.swing.*;
import javax.swing.event.*;

public class CanisMinor extends JFrame {
  protected JEditorPane mEditorPane;
  protected JTextField mURLField;

  public CanisMinor(String urlString) {
    super("CanisMinor v1.0");
    createGUI(urlString);
  }

  protected void createGUI( String urlString ) {
    Container content = getContentPane( );
    content.setLayout(new BorderLayout( ));

    JToolBar urlToolBar = new JToolBar( );
    mURLField = new JTextField(urlString, 40);
    urlToolBar.add(new JLabel("Location:"));
    urlToolBar.add(mURLField);
    content.add(urlToolBar, BorderLayout.NORTH);

    mEditorPane = new JEditorPane( );
    mEditorPane.setEditable(false);
    content.add(new JScrollPane(mEditorPane), BorderLayout.CENTER);

    openURL(urlString);

    mURLField.addActionListener(new ActionListener( ) {
      public void actionPerformed(ActionEvent ae) {
```

```
      openURL(ae.getActionCommand( ));
    }
  });

  mEditorPane.addHyperlinkListener(new LinkActivator( ));

  setSize(500, 600);
  setDefaultCloseOperation( JFrame.EXIT_ON_CLOSE );
}

protected void openURL(String urlString) {
  try {
    URL url = new URL(urlString);
    mEditorPane.setPage(url);
    mURLField.setText(url.toExternalForm( ));
  }
  catch (Exception e) {
    System.out.println("Couldn't open " + urlString + ":" + e);
  }
}

class LinkActivator implements HyperlinkListener {
  public void hyperlinkUpdate(HyperlinkEvent he) {
    HyperlinkEvent.EventType type = he.getEventType( );
    if (type == HyperlinkEvent.EventType.ACTIVATED)
      openURL(he.getURL( ).toExternalForm( ));
  }
}

public static void main(String[] args) {
  String urlString = "http://www.oreilly.com/catalog/learnjava3/";
  if (args.length > 0)
    urlString = args[0];
  new CanisMinor( urlString ).setVisible( true );
}
}
```

JEditorPane is the center of this little application. Passing a URL to setPage( ) causes the JEditorPane to load a new page, either from a local file or from somewhere across the Internet. To go to a new page, enter it in the text field at the top of the window and press Return. This fires an ActionEvent that sets the new page location of the JEditorPane. It can display RTF files, too (RTF is the text or nonbinary storage format for Microsoft Word documents).

Responding to hyperlinks correctly is simply a matter of responding to the HyperlinkEvents thrown by the JEditorPane. This behavior is encapsulated in the LinkActivator inner class. In this case, the only activity we are interested in is when the user "activates" the hyperlink by clicking on it. We respond by setting the location of the JEditorPane to the location given under the hyperlink. Surf away!

Behind the scenes, something called an EditorKit handles displaying documents for the JEditorPane. Different kinds of EditorKits can display different kinds of documents. For

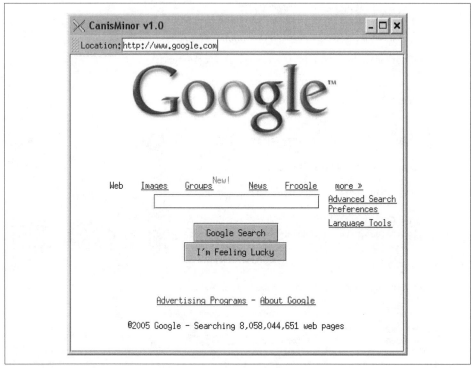

Figure 18-4. The CanisMinor application, a simple web browser

HTML, the HTMLEditorKit class (in the javax.swing.text.html package) handles the display. Currently, this class supports HTML 3.2. Sun says that future enhancements will move the HTMLEditorKit toward the HTML 4.0 standard, but this area hasn't seen much progress. The HTMLEditorKit handles other features of HTML, including HTML forms, in the expected way—automatically submitting results when a submit button is pushed. Java 5.0 added a new API and type of event, FormSubmitEvent, to enable programmatic involvement in form submission.

There's another component here that we haven't covered before—the JToolBar. This nifty container houses our URL text field. Initially, the JToolBar starts out at the top of the window. But you can pick it up by clicking on the little dotted box near its left edge, then drag it around to different parts of the window. You can place this toolbar at the top, left, right, or bottom of the window, or you can drag it outside the window entirely, where it will inhabit a window of its own. This behavior comes for free from the JToolBar class. We only had to create a JToolBar and add some components to it. The JToolBar is just a container, so we add it to the content pane of our window to give it an initial location.

Managing Text Yourself

Swing offers one last subclass of JTextComponent that can do just about anything you want: JTextPane. The basic text components, JTextField and JTextArea, are limited to a single font in a single style. But JTextPane, a subclass of JEditorPane, can display multiple fonts and multiple styles in the same component. It also includes support for a cursor (caret), highlighting, image embedding, and other advanced features.

We'll take a peek at JTextPane by creating a text pane with some styled text. Remember, the text itself is stored in an underlying data model, the Document. To create styled text, we simply associate a set of text attributes with different parts of the document's text. Swing includes classes and methods for manipulating sets of attributes, like specifying a bold font or a different color for the text. Attributes themselves are contained in a class called SimpleAttributeSet; these attribute sets are manipulated with static methods in the StyleConstants class. For example, to create a set of attributes that specifies the color red, you could do this:

```
SimpleAttributeSet redstyle = new SimpleAttributeSet( );
StyleConstants.setForeground(redstyle, Color.red);
```

To add some red text to a document, you would just pass the text and the attributes to the document's insertString( ) method, like this:

```
document.insertString(6, "Some red text", redstyle);
```

The first argument to insertString( ) is an offset into the text. An exception is thrown if you pass in an offset that's greater than the current length of the document. If you pass null for the attribute set, the text is added in the JTextPane's default font and style.

Our simple example creates several attribute sets and uses them to add plain and styled text to a JTextPane, as shown in Figure 18-5:

```
//file: Styling.java
import java.awt.*;
import java.awt.event.*;
import javax.swing.*;
import javax.swing.text.*;

public class Styling extends JFrame {
  private JTextPane textPane;

  public Styling( ) {
    super("Stylin' v1.0");
    setSize(300, 200);

    textPane = new JTextPane( );
    textPane.setFont(new Font("Serif", Font.PLAIN, 24));

    // create some handy attribute sets
    SimpleAttributeSet red = new SimpleAttributeSet( );
    StyleConstants.setForeground(red, Color.red);
```

```
          StyleConstants.setBold(red, true);
          SimpleAttributeSet blue = new SimpleAttributeSet( );
          StyleConstants.setForeground(blue, Color.blue);
          SimpleAttributeSet italic = new SimpleAttributeSet( );
          StyleConstants.setItalic(italic, true);
          StyleConstants.setForeground(italic, Color.orange);

          // add the text
          append("In a ", null);
          append("sky", blue);
          append(" full of people\nOnly some want to ", null);
          append("fly", italic);
          append("\nIsn't that ", null);
          append("crazy", red);
          append("?", null);

          Container content = getContentPane( );  // unnecessary in 5.0+
          content.add(new JScrollPane(textPane), BorderLayout.CENTER);
          setDefaultCloseOperation( JFrame.EXIT_ON_CLOSE );
      }

    protected void append(String s, AttributeSet attributes) {
        Document d = textPane.getDocument( );
        try { d.insertString(d.getLength(), s, attributes); }
        catch (BadLocationException ble) {}
    }

    public static void main(String[] args) {
        new Styling( ).setVisible(true);
    }
}
```

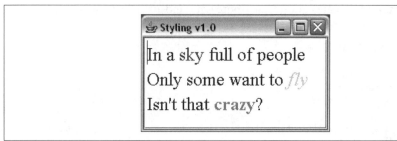

Figure 18-5. Using styled text in a JTextPane

This example creates a JTextPane, which is saved in a member variable. Three different attribute sets are created using combinations of text styles and foreground colors. Then, using a helper method called append( ), text is added to the JTextPane.

The append( ) method tacks a text String on the end of the JTextPane's document, using the supplied attributes. Remember that if the attributes are null, the text is displayed with the JTextPane's default font and style.

You can go ahead and add your own text if you wish. If you place the caret inside one of the differently styled words and type, the new text comes out in the appropriate style. Pretty cool, eh? You'll also notice that JTextPane gives us word-wrapping behavior for free. And since we've wrapped the JTextPane in a JScrollPane, we get scrolling for free, too. Swing allows you to do some really cool stuff without breaking a sweat. Just wait—there's plenty more to come.

This simple example should give you some idea of what JTextPane can do. It's reasonably easy to build a simple word processor with JTextPane, and complex commercial-grade word processors are definitely possible.

If JTextPane still isn't good enough for you, or you need some finer control over character, word, and paragraph layout, you can actually draw text, carets, and highlight shapes yourself. A class in the 2D API called TextLayout simplifies much of this work, but it's outside the scope of this book. For coverage of TextLayout and other advanced text drawing topics, see *Java 2D Graphics* by Jonathan Knudsen (O'Reilly).

Focus Navigation

We've brought up the topic of focus many times in our discussion so far, and we've told you that the handling and user navigation of focus is mostly done automatically. This is largely due to a new focus system introduced in Java 1.4. The new focus system is very powerful and can be heavily customized through the use of "focus traversal policy" objects that control keyboard navigation. For typical application behavior, you won't have to deal with this directly, but we'll explain a few features you should know about.

Swing handles keyboard focus navigation through the KeyboardFocusManager class. This class uses FocusTraversalPolicy "strategy" objects that implement the actual schemes for locating the next component to receive focus. There are two primary FocusTraversalPolicy types supplied with Java. The first, DefaultFocusTraversalPolicy, is part of the AWT package. It emulates the legacy AWT-style focus management that navigated components in the order in which they were added to their container. The next, LayoutFocusTraversalPolicy, is the default for all Swing applications. It examines the layout and attempts to provide the more typical navigation from left to right, top to bottom, based on component position and size.

The focus traversal policy is inherited from containers and oriented around groups of components known as "root cycles." By default, each individual window and JInternalFrame is its own root cycle. In other words, focus traverses all of its child components repeatedly (jumping from the last component back to the first), and won't, by default, leave the container through keyboard navigation.

The default Swing policy uses the following keys for keyboard navigation:

Forward
> Tab or Ctrl-Tab (Ctrl-Tab also works inside text areas)

Back
> Shift-Tab or Ctrl-Shift-Tab (Ctrl-Shift-Tab also works inside text areas)

You can define your own focus traversal keys for forward and back navigation, as well as for navigation across root cycles using the setFocusTraversalKeys( ) method of a container. Here is an example that adds the keystroke Ctrl-N to the list of forward key navigation for components in a Frame:

```
frame.getFocusTraversalKeys(
    KeyboardFocusManager.FORWARD_TRAVERSAL_KEYS );
AWTKeyStroke ks = AWTKeyStroke.getAWTKeyStroke(
    KeyEvent.VK_N, InputEvent.CTRL_DOWN_MASK );
Set new = new HashSet( old );
set.add( ks );
frame.setFocusTraversalKeys(
    KeyboardFocusManager.FORWARD_TRAVERSAL_KEYS,set);
```

Keys are defined by the AWTKeyStroke class, which encapsulates the key and input modifiers, in this case, the Control key. Constants in the KeyboardFocusManager specify forward, back, and up or down root-cycle transfer across windows.

Finally, you can also move focus programmatically using the following methods of KeyboardFocusManager:

```
focusNextComponent( )
focusPreviousComponent( )
upFocusCycle( )
downFocusCycle( )
```

Trees

One of Swing's advanced components is JTree. Trees are good for representing hierarchical information, like the contents of a disk drive or a company's organizational chart. As with all Swing components, the data model is distinct from the visual representation. This means you can do things such as update the data model and trust that the visual component will be updated properly.

JTree is powerful and complex. It's big enough, in fact, that like the text tools, the classes that support JTree have their own package, javax.swing.tree. However, if you accept the default options for almost everything, JTree is very easy to use. Figure 18-6 shows a JTree running in a Swing application that we'll describe later.

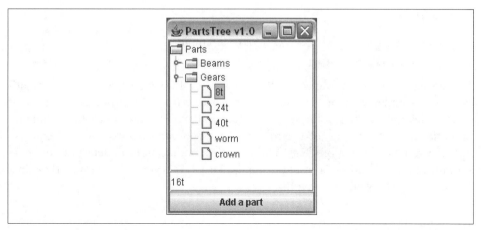

Figure 18-6. The JTree class in action

Nodes and Models

A tree's data model is made up of interconnected nodes. A node has a name, typically, a parent, and some number of children (possibly 0). In Swing, a node is represented by the TreeNode interface. Nodes that can be modified are represented by MutableTreeNode. A concrete implementation of this interface is DefaultMutableTreeNode. One node, called the *root* node, usually resides at the top of the hierarchy.

A tree's data model is represented by the TreeModel interface. Swing provides an implementation of this interface called DefaultTreeModel. You can create a DefaultTreeModel by passing a root TreeNode to its constructor.

You could create a TreeModel with just one node like this:

```
TreeNode root = new DefaultMutableTreeNode("Root node");
TreeModel model = new DefaultTreeModel(root);
```

Here's another example with a real hierarchy. The root node contains two nodes, Node 1 and Group. The Group node contains Node 2 and Node 3 as subnodes.

```
MutableTreeNode root = new DefaultMutableTreeNode("Root node");
MutableTreeNode group = new DefaultMutableTreeNode("Group");
root.insert(group, 0);
root.insert(new DefaultMutableTreeNode("Node 1"), 1);
group.insert(new DefaultMutableTreeNode("Node 2"), 0);
group.insert(new DefaultMutableTreeNode("Node 3"), 1);
```

The second parameter to the insert( ) method is the index of the node in the parent. Once you've got your nodes organized, you can create a TreeModel in the same way as before:

```
TreeModel model = new DefaultTreeModel(root);
```

Save a Tree

Once you have a tree model, creating a JTree is simple:

```
JTree tree = new JTree(model);
```

The JTree behaves like a souped-up JList. As Figure 18-6 shows, the JTree automatically shows nodes with no children as a sheet of paper, while nodes that contain other nodes are shown as folders. You can expand and collapse nodes by clicking on the little knobs to the left of the folder icons. You can also expand and collapse nodes by double-clicking on them. You can select nodes; multiple selections are possible using the Shift and Control keys. And, like a JList, you should put a JTree in a JScrollPane if you want it to scroll.

Tree Events

A tree fires off several flavors of events. You can find out when nodes have been expanded and collapsed, when nodes are about to be expanded or collapsed (because the user has clicked on them), and when selections occur. Three distinct event listener interfaces handle this information.

```
TreeExpansionListener
TreeWillExpandListener
TreeSelectionListener
```

Tree selections are a tricky business. You can select any combination of nodes by using the Control key and clicking on nodes. Tree selections are described by a TreePath, which describes how to get from the root node to the selected nodes.

The following example registers an event listener that prints out the last selected node:

```
tree.addTreeSelectionListener(new TreeSelectionListener() {
  public void valueChanged(TreeSelectionEvent e) {
    TreePath tp = e.getNewLeadSelectionPath( );
    System.out.println(tp.getLastPathComponent( ));
  }
});
```

A Complete Example

This section contains an example that showcases the following tree techniques:

- Construction of a tree model, using DefaultMutableTreeNode
- Creation and display of a JTree
- Listening for tree selection events
- Modifying the tree's data model while the JTree is showing

Here's the source code for the example:

```
//file: PartsTree.java
import java.awt.*;
import java.awt.event.*;
import javax.swing.*;
import javax.swing.event.*;
import javax.swing.tree.*;

public class PartsTree {
  public static void main(String[] args) {
    // create a hierarchy of nodes
    MutableTreeNode root = new DefaultMutableTreeNode("Parts");
    MutableTreeNode beams = new DefaultMutableTreeNode("Beams");
    MutableTreeNode gears = new DefaultMutableTreeNode("Gears");
    root.insert(beams, 0);
    root.insert(gears, 1);
    beams.insert(new DefaultMutableTreeNode("1x4 black"), 0);
    beams.insert(new DefaultMutableTreeNode("1x6 black"), 1);
    beams.insert(new DefaultMutableTreeNode("1x8 black"), 2);
    beams.insert(new DefaultMutableTreeNode("1x12 black"), 3);
    gears.insert(new DefaultMutableTreeNode("8t"), 0);
    gears.insert(new DefaultMutableTreeNode("24t"), 1);
    gears.insert(new DefaultMutableTreeNode("40t"), 2);
    gears.insert(new DefaultMutableTreeNode("worm"), 3);
    gears.insert(new DefaultMutableTreeNode("crown"), 4);

    // create the JTree
    final DefaultTreeModel model = new DefaultTreeModel(root);
    final JTree tree = new JTree(model);

    // create a text field and button to modify the data model
    final JTextField nameField = new JTextField("16t");
    final JButton button = new JButton("Add a part");
    button.setEnabled(false);
    button.addActionListener(new ActionListener() {
      public void actionPerformed(ActionEvent e) {
        TreePath tp = tree.getSelectionPath();
        MutableTreeNode insertNode =
            (MutableTreeNode)tp.getLastPathComponent();
        int insertIndex = 0;
        if (insertNode.getParent() != null) {
          MutableTreeNode parent =
              (MutableTreeNode)insertNode.getParent();
          insertIndex = parent.getIndex(insertNode) + 1;
          insertNode = parent;
        }
        MutableTreeNode node =
            new DefaultMutableTreeNode(nameField.getText());
        model.insertNodeInto(node, insertNode, insertIndex);
      }
    });
```

```
      JPanel addPanel = new JPanel(new GridLayout(2, 1));
      addPanel.add(nameField);
      addPanel.add(button);

      // listen for selections
      tree.addTreeSelectionListener(new TreeSelectionListener( ) {
        public void valueChanged(TreeSelectionEvent e) {
          TreePath tp = e.getNewLeadSelectionPath( );
          button.setEnabled(tp != null);
        }
      });

      // create a JFrame to hold the tree
      JFrame frame = new JFrame("PartsTree v1.0");

      frame.setDefaultCloseOperation( JFrame.EXIT_ON_CLOSE );
      frame.setSize(200, 200);
      frame.getContentPane( ).add(new JScrollPane(tree));
      frame.getContentPane( ).add(addPanel, BorderLayout.SOUTH);
      frame.setVisible(true);
    }
  }
```

The example begins by creating a node hierarchy. The root node is called Parts. It contains two subnodes, Beams and Gears, as shown:

```
MutableTreeNode root = new DefaultMutableTreeNode("Parts");
MutableTreeNode beams = new DefaultMutableTreeNode("Beams");
MutableTreeNode gears = new DefaultMutableTreeNode("Gears");
root.insert(beams, 0);
root.insert(gears, 1);
```

The Beams and Gears nodes contain a handful of items each.

The "Add a part" button inserts a new item into the tree at the level of the current node, and just after it. You can specify the name of the new node by typing it in the text field above the button. To determine where the node should be added, the current selection is first obtained in the anonymous inner class ActionListener:

```
TreePath tp = tree.getSelectionPath( );
MutableTreeNode insertNode =
  (MutableTreeNode)tp.getLastPathComponent( );
```

The new node should be added to the parent node of the current node, so it ends up being a sibling of the current node. The only hitch here is that if the current node is the root node, it won't have a parent. If a parent does exist, we determine the index of the currently selected node, and then add the new node at the next index:

```
int insertIndex = 0;
if (insertNode.getParent( ) != null) {
  MutableTreeNode parent =
      (MutableTreeNode)insertNode.getParent( );
  insertIndex = parent.getIndex(insertNode) + 1;
  insertNode = parent;
```

```
}
MutableTreeNode node =
    new DefaultMutableTreeNode(nameField.getText( ));
model.insertNodeInto(node, insertNode, insertIndex);
```

You must add the new node to the tree's data model, using insertNodeInto( ), not to the MutableTableNode itself. The model notifies the JTree that it needs to update itself.

We have another event handler in this example, one that listens for tree selection events. Basically, we want to enable our "Add a part" button only if a current selection exists:

```
tree.addTreeSelectionListener(new TreeSelectionListener( ) {
  public void valueChanged(TreeSelectionEvent e) {
    TreePath tp = e.getNewLeadSelectionPath( );
    button.setEnabled(tp != null);
  }
});
```

When you first start this application, the button is disabled. As soon as you select something, it is enabled, and you can add nodes to the tree with abandon. If you want to see the button disabled again, you can unselect everything by holding the Control key and clicking on the current selection.

Tables

Tables present information in orderly rows and columns. This is useful for presenting financial figures or representing data from a relational database. Like trees, tables in Swing are incredibly powerful and customizable. If you go with the default options, they're also pretty easy to use.

The JTable class represents a visual table component. A JTable is based on a TableModel, one of a dozen or so supporting interfaces and classes in the javax.swing.table package.

A First Stab: Freeloading

JTable has one constructor that creates a default table model for you from arrays of data. You just need to supply it with the names of your column headers and a 2D array of Objects representing the table's data. The first index selects the table's row; the second index selects the column. The following example shows how easy it is to get going with tables using this constructor:

```
//file: DullShipTable.java
import java.awt.*;
import java.awt.event.*;
import javax.swing.*;
import javax.swing.table.*;
```

```
public class DullShipTable {
  public static void main(String[] args) {
    // create some tabular data
    String[] headings =
      new String[] {"Number", "Hot?", "Origin",
                    "Destination", "Ship Date", "Weight" };
    Object[][] data = new Object[][] {
      { "100420", Boolean.FALSE, "Des Moines IA", "Spokane WA",
          "02/06/2000", new Float(450) },
      { "202174", Boolean.TRUE, "Basking Ridge NJ", "Princeton NJ",
          "05/20/2000", new Float(1250) },
      { "450877", Boolean.TRUE, "St. Paul MN", "Austin TX",
          "03/20/2000", new Float(1745) },
      { "101891", Boolean.FALSE, "Boston MA", "Albany NY",
          "04/04/2000", new Float(88) }
    };

    // create the data model and the JTable
    JTable table = new JTable(data, headings);

    JFrame frame = new JFrame("DullShipTable v1.0");
    frame.getContentPane( ).add(new JScrollPane(table));

    frame.setDefaultCloseOperation( JFrame.EXIT_ON_CLOSE );
    frame.setSize(500, 200);
    frame.setVisible(true);
  }
}
```

This small application produces the display shown in Figure 18-7.

Figure 18-7. A rudimentary JTable

For very little typing, we've gotten some pretty impressive stuff. Here are a few things that come for free:

Column headings

The JTable has automatically formatted the column headings differently than the table cells. It's clear that they are not part of the table's data area.

Cell overflow

If a cell's data is too long to fit in the cell, it is automatically truncated and shown with an ellipses (...). This is shown in the Origin cell in the second row in Figure 18-7.

Row selection

You can click on any cell in the table to select its entire row. This behavior is controllable; you can select single cells, entire rows, entire columns, or some combination of these. To configure the JTable's selection behavior, use the setCellSelectionEnabled( ), setColumnSelectionAllowed( ), and setRowSelectionAllowed( ) methods.

Cell editing

Double-clicking on a cell opens it for editing; you'll get a little cursor in the cell. You can type directly into the cell to change the cell's data.

Column sizing

If you position the mouse cursor between two column headings, you'll get a little left-right arrow cursor. Click and drag to change the size of the column to the left. Depending on how the JTable is configured, the other columns may also change size. The resizing behavior is controlled with the setAutoResizeMode( ) method.

Column reordering

If you click and drag on a column heading, you can move the entire column to another part of the table.

Play with this for a while. It's fun.

Round Two: Creating a Table Model

JTable is a very powerful component. You get a lot of very nice behavior for free. However, the default settings are not quite what we wanted for this simple example. In particular, we intended the table entries to be read-only; they should not be editable. Also, we'd like entries in the *Hot?* column to be checkboxes instead of words. Finally, it would be nice if the *Weight* column were formatted appropriately for numbers rather than for text.

To achieve more flexibility with JTable, we'll write our own data model by implementing the TableModel interface. Fortunately, Swing makes this easy by supplying a class that does most of the work, AbstractTableModel. To create a table model, we'll just subclass AbstractTableModel and override whatever behavior we want to change.

At a minimum, all AbstractTableModel subclasses have to define the following three methods:

```
public int getRowCount( )
public int getColumnCount( )
```
Returns the number of rows and columns in this data model

```
public Object getValueAt(int row, int column)
```
Returns the value for the given cell

When the JTable needs data values, it calls the getValueAt( ) method in the table model. To get an idea of the total size of the table, JTable calls the getRowCount( ) and getColumnCount( ) methods in the table model.

A very simple table model looks like this:

```
public static class ShipTableModel extends AbstractTableModel {
  private Object[][] data = new Object[][] {
    { "100420", Boolean.FALSE, "Des Moines IA", "Spokane WA",
        "02/06/2000", new Float(450) },
    { "202174", Boolean.TRUE, "Basking Ridge NJ", "Princeton NJ",
        "05/20/2000", new Float(1250) },
    { "450877", Boolean.TRUE, "St. Paul MN", "Austin TX",
        "03/20/2000", new Float(1745) },
    { "101891", Boolean.FALSE, "Boston MA", "Albany NY",
        "04/04/2000", new Float(88) }
  };

  public int getRowCount( ) { return data.length; }
  public int getColumnCount( ) { return data[0].length; }

  public Object getValueAt(int row, int column) {
    return data[row][column];
  }
}
```

We'd like to use the same column headings we used in the previous example. The table model supplies these through a method called getColumnName( ). We could add column headings to our simple table model like this:

```
private String[] headings = new String[] {
  "Number", "Hot?", "Origin", "Destination", "Ship Date", "Weight"
};

public String getColumnName(int column) {
  return headings[column];
}
```

By default, AbstractTableModel makes all its cells noneditable, which is what we wanted. No changes need to be made for this.

The final modification is to have the Hot? column and the Weight column formatted specially. To do this, we give our table model some knowledge about the column types. JTable automatically generates checkbox cells for Boolean column types and specially formatted number cells for Number types. To give the table model some intelligence about its column types, we override the getColumnClass( ) method. The JTable calls this method to determine the data type of each column. It may then represent the data in a special way. This table model returns the class of the item in the first row of its data:

```
public Class getColumnClass(int column) {
  return data[0][column].getClass( );
}
```

That's really all there is to do. The following complete example illustrates how you can use your own table model to create a JTable using the techniques just described:

```java
//file: ShipTable.java
import java.awt.*;
import java.awt.event.*;
import javax.swing.*;
import javax.swing.table.*;

public class ShipTable {
  public static class ShipTableModel extends AbstractTableModel {
    private String[] headings = new String[] {
      "Number", "Hot?", "Origin", "Destination", "Ship Date", "Weight"
    };
    private Object[][] data = new Object[][] {
      { "100420", Boolean.FALSE, "Des Moines IA", "Spokane WA",
          "02/06/2000", new Float(450) },
      { "202174", Boolean.TRUE, "Basking Ridge NJ", "Princeton NJ",
          "05/20/2000", new Float(1250) },
      { "450877", Boolean.TRUE, "St. Paul MN", "Austin TX",
          "03/20/2000", new Float(1745) },
      { "101891", Boolean.FALSE, "Boston MA", "Albany NY",
          "04/04/2000", new Float(88) }
    };

    public int getRowCount() { return data.length; }
    public int getColumnCount() { return data[0].length; }

    public Object getValueAt(int row, int column) {
      return data[row][column];
    }

    public String getColumnName(int column) {
      return headings[column];
    }

    public Class getColumnClass(int column) {
      return data[0][column].getClass();
    }
  }

  public static void main(String[] args)
  {
    // create the data model and the JTable
    TableModel model = new ShipTableModel();
    JTable table = new JTable(model);

    table.setAutoResizeMode(JTable.AUTO_RESIZE_OFF);

    JFrame frame = new JFrame("ShipTable v1.0");
    frame.getContentPane().add(new JScrollPane(table));
    frame.setDefaultCloseOperation( JFrame.EXIT_ON_CLOSE );
```

```
        frame.setSize(500, 200);
        frame.setVisible(true);
    }
}
```

The running application is shown in Figure 18-8.

Figure 18-8. Customizing a table

Round Three: A Simple Spreadsheet

To illustrate just how powerful and flexible the separation of the data model from the GUI can be, we'll show a more complex model. In the following example, we'll implement a very slim but functional spreadsheet (see Figure 18-9) using almost no customization of the JTable. All of the data processing is in a TableModel called SpreadSheetModel.

Figure 18-9. A simple spreadsheet

Our spreadsheet does the expected stuff—allowing you to enter numbers or mathematical expressions such as (A1*B2)+C3 into each cell.* All cell editing and updating is driven by the standard JTable. We implement the methods necessary to set and retrieve cell data. Of course, we don't do any real validation here, so it's easy to break our table. (For example, there is no check for circular dependencies, which may be undesirable.)

As you will see, the bulk of the code in this example is in the inner class used to parse the value of the equations in the cells. If you don't find this part interesting, you

---

* You may need to double-click on a cell to edit it.

might want to skip ahead. But if you have never seen an example of this kind of parsing before, we think you will find it to be very cool. Through the magic of recursion and Java's powerful String manipulation, it takes us only about 50 lines of code to implement a parser capable of handling basic arithmetic with arbitrarily nested parentheses.

Here's the code:

```java
//file: SpreadsheetModel.java
import java.util.StringTokenizer;
import javax.swing.*;
import javax.swing.table.AbstractTableModel;
import java.awt.event.*;

public class SpreadsheetModel extends AbstractTableModel {
  Expression [][] data;

  public SpreadsheetModel( int rows, int cols ) {
    data = new Expression [rows][cols];
  }

  public void setValueAt(Object value, int row, int col) {
    data[row][col] = new Expression( (String)value );
    fireTableDataChanged( );
  }

  public Object getValueAt( int row, int col ) {
    if ( data[row][col] != null )
      try { return data[row][col].eval( ) + ""; }
      catch ( BadExpression e ) { return "Error"; }
    return "";
  }
  public int getRowCount( ) { return data.length; }
  public int getColumnCount( ) { return data[0].length; }
  public boolean isCellEditable(int row, int col) { return true; }

  class Expression {
    String text;
    StringTokenizer tokens;
    String token;

    Expression( String text ) { this.text = text.trim( ); }

    float eval( ) throws BadExpression {
      tokens = new StringTokenizer( text, " */+-( )", true );
      try { return sum( ); }
      catch ( Exception e ) { throw new BadExpression( ); }
    }

    private float sum( ) {
      float value = term( );
      while( more( ) && match("+-") )
        if ( match("+") ) { consume( ); value = value + term( ); }
```

```
      else { consume( ); value = value - term( ); }
    return value;
  }
  private float term( ) {
    float value = element( );
    while( more( ) && match( "*/" ) )
      if ( match("*") ) { consume( ); value = value * element( ); }
      else { consume( ); value = value / element( ); }
    return value;
  }
  private float element( ) {
    float value;
    if ( match( "(" ) ) { consume( ); value = sum( ); }
    else {
      String svalue;
      if ( Character.isLetter( token( ).charAt(0) ) ) {
      int col = findColumn( token( ).charAt(0) + "" );
      int row = Character.digit( token( ).charAt(1), 10 );
      svalue = (String)getValueAt( row, col );
      } else
        svalue = token( );
      value = Float.parseFloat( svalue );
    }
    consume( ); // ")" or value token
    return value;
  }
  private String token( ) {
    if ( token == null )
      while ( (token=tokens.nextToken( )).equals(" ") );
    return token;
  }
  private void consume( ) { token = null; }
  private boolean match( String s ) { return s.indexOf( token( ) )!=-1; }
  private boolean more( ) { return tokens.hasMoreTokens( ); }
}

class BadExpression extends Exception { }

public static void main( String [] args ) {
  JFrame frame = new JFrame("Excelsior!");
  JTable table = new JTable( new SpreadsheetModel(15, 5) );
  table.setPreferredScrollableViewportSize( table.getPreferredSize() );
  table.setCellSelectionEnabled(true);
  frame.getContentPane( ).add( new JScrollPane( table ) );
  frame.setDefaultCloseOperation( JFrame.EXIT_ON_CLOSE );
  frame.pack( );
  frame.show( );
}
}
```

Our model extends `AbstractTableModel` and overrides just a few methods. As you can
see, our data is stored in a 2D array of `Expression` objects. The `setValueAt( )` method
of our model creates `Expression` objects from the strings typed by the user and stores

them in the array. The getValueAt( ) method returns a value for a cell by calling the expression's eval( ) method. If the user enters some invalid text in a cell, a BadExpression exception is thrown, and the word "error" is placed in the cell as a value. The only other methods of TableModel we must override are getRowCount( ), getColumnCount( ), and isCellEditable( ) to determine the dimensions of the spreadsheet and to allow the user to edit the fields. That's it! The helper method findColumn( ) is inherited from the AbstractTableModel.

Now on to the good stuff. We'll employ our old friend StringTokenizer to read the expression string as separate values and the mathematical symbols (+-*/( )) one by one. These tokens are then processed by the three parser methods: sum( ), term( ), and element( ). The methods call one another generally from the top down, but it might be easier to read them in reverse to see what's happening.

At the bottom level, element( ) reads individual numeric values or cell names—e.g., 5.0 or B2. Above that, the term( ) method operates on the values supplied by element( ) and applies any multiplication or division operations. And at the top, sum( ) operates on the values that are returned by term( ) and applies addition or subtraction to them. If the element( ) method encounters parentheses, it makes a call to sum( ) to handle the nested expression. Eventually, the nested sum returns (possibly after further recursion), and the parenthesized expression is reduced to a single value, which is returned by element( ). The magic of recursion has untangled the nesting for us. The other small piece of magic here is in the ordering of the three parser methods. Having sum( ) call term( ) and term( ) call element( ) imposes the precedence of operators; i.e., "atomic" values are parsed first (at the bottom), then multiplication, and finally, addition or subtraction.

The grammar parsing relies on four simple helper methods that make the code more manageable: token( ), consume( ), match( ), and more( ). token( ) calls the string tokenizer to get the next value, and match( ) compares it with a specified value. consume( ) is used to move to the next token, and more( ) indicates when the final token has been processed.

Printing JTables

Java 5.0 introduced an API that makes it easy to print JTables. It is now so easy, in fact, that you might program it accidentally. Think we're kidding? If you accept the basic default behavior, all that is required to pop up a print dialog box and print is the following:

```
myJTable.print( );
```

That's it. The default behavior scales the printed table to the width of the page. This is called "fit width" mode. You can control that setting using the PrintMode enumeration of JTable, which has values of NORMAL and FIT_WIDTH:

```
table.print( JTable.PrintMode.NORMAL );
```

The "normal" (ironically, nondefault) mode will allow the table to split across multiple pages horizontally to print without sizing down. In both cases, the table rows may span multiple pages vertically.

Other forms of the JTable print() method allow you to add header and footer text to the page and to take greater control of the printing process and attributes. We'll talk a little more about printing when we cover 2D drawing in Chapter 20.

Desktops

At this point, you might be thinking that there's nothing more that Swing could possibly do, but it just keeps getting better. If you've ever wished that you could have windows within windows in Java, Swing makes it possible with JDesktopPane and JInternalFrame. Figure 18-10 shows how this works.

Figure 18-10. Using internal frames on a JDesktopPane

You get a lot of behavior for free from JInternalFrame. Internal frames can be moved by clicking and dragging the titlebar. They can be resized by clicking and dragging on the window's borders. Internal frames can be iconified, which means reducing them to a small icon representation on the desktop. Internal frames may also be made to fit the entire size of the desktop (maximized). To you, the programmer, the internal frame is just a kind of special container. You can put your application's data inside an internal frame just as with any other type of container.

The following brief example shows how to create the windows shown in Figure 18-10:

```
//file: Desktop.java
import java.awt.*;
import java.awt.event.*;
```

```
import javax.swing.*;
import javax.swing.border.*;

public class Desktop {
  public static void main(String[] args) {
    JFrame frame = new JFrame("Desktop");

    JDesktopPane desktop = new JDesktopPane( );
    for (int i = 0; i < 5; i++) {
      JInternalFrame internal =
          new JInternalFrame("Frame " + i, true, true, true, true);
      internal.setSize(180, 180);
      internal.setLocation(i * 20, i * 20);
      internal.setVisible(true);
      desktop.add(internal);
    }

    frame.setSize(300, 300);
    frame.setDefaultCloseOperation( JFrame.EXIT_ON_CLOSE );
    frame.setContentPane(desktop);
    frame.setVisible(true);
  }
}
```

All we've done here is to create a JDesktopPane and add internal frames to it. When each JInternalFrame is constructed, we specify a window title. The four true values passed in the constructor specify that the new window should be resizable, closable, maximizable, and iconifiable.

JInternalFrames fire off their own set of events. However, InternalFrameEvent and InternalFrameListener are just like WindowEvent and WindowListener with the names changed. If you want to hear about a JInternalFrame closing, just register an InternalFrameListener and define the internalFrameClosing( )method. This is just like defining the windowClosing( ) method for a JFrame.

Pluggable Look-and-Feel

We mentioned before that Swing components can easily change their appearance, like master spies or thespians. Generally, different kinds of components within an application have coordinated appearances that are similar in some way. For example, they probably use the same font and the same basic color scheme. The collection of appearances and common behavior of GUI components is called a look-and-feel (L&F).

Part of the job of designing a GUI for an operating system is designing the L&F. Mac OS, therefore, has its own distinctive L&F, as does Windows. Java offers several different L&F schemes for Swing components. If you're adept at graphic design, you can write your own L&F schemes and easily convince Swing to use them. This chameleon-like ability to change appearance is called *pluggable look-and-feel*, sometimes abbreviated PLAF (don't pronounce that out loud if others are eating).

Seeing is believing. Here's an example that creates a handful of Swing components. Menu items allow you to change the L&F dynamically while the application is running:

```java
//file: QuickChange.java
import java.awt.*;
import java.awt.event.*;
import javax.swing.*;

public class QuickChange extends JFrame {

  public QuickChange() {
    super("QuickChange v1.0");
    createGUI();
  }

  protected void createGUI() {
    setSize(300, 200);

    // create a simple File menu
    JMenu file = new JMenu("File", true);
    JMenuItem quit = new JMenuItem("Quit");
    file.add(quit);
    quit.addActionListener(new ActionListener() {
      public void actionPerformed(ActionEvent e) { System.exit(0); }
    });

    // create the Look & Feel menu
    JMenu lnf = new JMenu("Look & Feel", true);
    ButtonGroup buttonGroup = new ButtonGroup();
    final UIManager.LookAndFeelInfo[] info =
        UIManager.getInstalledLookAndFeels();
    for (int i = 0; i < info.length; i++) {
      JRadioButtonMenuItem item = new
          JRadioButtonMenuItem(info[i].getName(), i == 0);
      final String className = info[i].getClassName();
      item.addActionListener(new ActionListener() {
        public void actionPerformed(ActionEvent ae) {
          try { UIManager.setLookAndFeel(className); }
          catch (Exception e) { System.out.println(e); }
          SwingUtilities.updateComponentTreeUI(QuickChange.this);
        }
      });
      buttonGroup.add(item);
      lnf.add(item);
    }

    // add the menu bar
    JMenuBar mb = new JMenuBar();
    mb.add(file);
    mb.add(lnf);
    setJMenuBar(mb);
```

```
    // add some components
    JPanel jp = new JPanel( );
    jp.add(new JCheckBox("JCheckBox"));
    String[] names =
      new String[] { "Tosca", "Cavaradossi", "Scarpia",
                     "Angelotti", "Spoletta", "Sciarrone",
                     "Carceriere", "Il sagrestano", "Un pastore" };
    jp.add(new JComboBox(names));
    jp.add(new JButton("JButton"));
    jp.add(new JLabel("JLabel"));
    jp.add(new JTextField("JTextField"));
    JPanel main = new JPanel(new GridLayout(1, 2));
    main.add(jp);
    main.add(new JScrollPane(new JList(names)));
    setContentPane(main);
    setDefaultCloseOperation( JFrame.EXIT_ON_CLOSE );
  }

  public static void main(String[] args) {
    new QuickChange( ).setVisible(true);
  }
}
```

The interesting part of this application is creating a menu of the available L&Fs. First, we ask a class called UIManager to tell us all about the available L&Fs on our computer:

```
final UIManager.LookAndFeelInfo[] info =
        UIManager.getInstalledLookAndFeels( );
```

Information about L&Fs is returned as instances of UIManager.LookAndFeelInfo. Despite the long name, there's not much to this class; it just associates a name, such as Metal, and the name of the class that implements the L&F, such as javax.swing. plaf.metal.MetalLookAndFeel. In the QuickChange example, we create a menu item from each L&F name. If the menu item is selected, we tell the UIManager to use the selected L&F class. To make sure all the components are redrawn with the new L&F, we call updateComponentTreeUI( ), a static method in the SwingUtilities class.

The JDK includes several L&Fs: one that resembles Windows, one that resembles Motif, and an original L&F called Metal. Java 5.0 added another original L&F called Ocean; you've been staring at it through all the examples in this and the last chapter. The trend in the industry over the past few years has been toward "flatter" and less visually cluttered interfaces and Ocean follows that trend.

If you're running Swing on Mac OS X, the default L&F is an implementation of Aqua, the UI design for all new Mac applications. Unfortunately, you cannot use this L&F on any other platforms because of licensing issues (the Windows L&F has similar restrictions).

Synth, the Skinnable L&F

Although Swing's pluggable L&F has always been a virtue, writing your own Swing L&F is a fairly tedious, low-level activity. It is not the kind of thing that an end user could do on a whim to beautify one particular application. But a different kind of end-user GUI customization, called "skinning," is growing in popularity. Many applications now allow users to customize the L&F very easily, using only images and simple preferences files to create new appearances. *Skinnability* is not the same as a full-blown pluggable L&F, but it lets you do a lot without any programming required.

Java 5.0 introduced a new skinnable L&F called Synth that acts like an ordinary L&F, but can be customized through the use of images and XML description files to create new looks. For example, the borders of components (such as the shiny metal look of the Metal L&F) can be described by providing an example image and then specifying the offsets of the interior "corners" as well as the method to use (stretch or tile) to cover larger areas. Synth then uses the image to paint the borders of whatever components you specify.

Synth can do quite a lot and even allows you to specify Java objects to be involved in painting, so you can resort to programming again if your L&F gets too complex. Unfortunately we don't have room to truly cover Synth in this book, but you can find a tutorial at *http://www-106.ibm.com/developerworks/java/library/j-synth/*.

Creating Custom Components

In this chapter and the previous, we've worked with different user interface objects. We've used Swing's impressive repertoire of components as building blocks and extended their functionality, but we haven't actually created any new components. In this section, we create an entirely new component from scratch, a *dial*.

Until now, our examples have been fairly self-contained; they generally know everything about what to do and don't rely on additional parts to do processing. Our menu example created a `DinnerFrame` class that had a menu of dinner options, but it included all the processing needed to handle the user's selections. If we wanted to process the selections differently, we'd have to modify the class. A true component separates the detection of user input from the handling of those choices. It lets the user take some action and then informs other interested parties by emitting events.

Generating Events

Since we want our new classes to be components, they should communicate the way components communicate: by generating event objects and sending those events to listeners. So far, we've written a lot of code that listened for events but haven't seen an example that generated its own custom events.

Generating events sounds like it might be difficult, but it isn't. You can either create new kinds of events by subclassing java.util.EventObject, or use one of the standard event types. In either case, you just need to allow registration of listeners for your events and provide a means to deliver events to those listeners. Swing's JComponent class provides a protected member variable, listenerList, you can use to keep track of event listeners. It's an instance of EventListenerList; basically it acts like the maître d' at a restaurant, keeping track of all event listeners, sorted by type.

Often, you won't need to worry about creating a custom event type. JComponent has methods that support firing of generic PropertyChangeEvents whenever one of a component's properties changes. The example we'll look at next uses this infrastructure to fire PropertyChangeEvents whenever a value changes.

A Dial Component

The standard Swing classes don't have a component that's similar to an old fashioned dial—for example, the volume control on your radio. (The JSlider fills this role, of course.) In this section, we implement a Dial class. The dial has a value that can be adjusted by clicking and dragging to "twist" the dial (see Figure 18-11). As the value of the dial changes, DialEvents are fired off by the component. The dial can be used just like any other Java component. We even have a custom DialListener interface that matches the DialEvent class.

Figure 18-11. The Dial component

Here's the Dial code:

```
//file: Dial.java
import java.awt.*;
import java.awt.event.*;
import java.util.*;
import javax.swing.*;

public class Dial extends JComponent {
  int minValue, nvalue, maxValue, radius;

  public Dial() { this(0, 100, 0); }
```

```java
public Dial(int minValue, int maxValue, int value) {
  setMinimum( minValue );
  setMaximum( maxValue );
  setValue( value );
  setForeground( Color.lightGray );

  addMouseListener(new MouseAdapter() {
    public void mousePressed(MouseEvent e) { spin(e); }
  });
  addMouseMotionListener(new MouseMotionAdapter() {
    public void mouseDragged(MouseEvent e) { spin(e); }
  });
}

protected void spin( MouseEvent e ) {
  int y = e.getY( );
  int x = e.getX( );
  double th = Math.atan((1.0 * y - radius) / (x - radius));
  int value=(int)(th / (2 * Math.PI) * (maxValue - minValue));
  if (x < radius)
    setValue( value + (maxValue-minValue) / 2 + minValue);
  else if (y < radius)
    setValue( value + maxValue );
  else
    setValue( value + minValue);
}

public void paintComponent(Graphics g) {
  Graphics2D g2 = (Graphics2D)g;
  int tick = 10;
  radius = Math.min( getSize( ).width,getSize( ).height )/2 - tick;
  g2.setPaint( getForeground( ).darker( ) );
  g2.drawLine( radius * 2 + tick / 2, radius,
      radius * 2 + tick, radius);
  g2.setStroke( new BasicStroke(2) );
  draw3DCircle( g2, 0, 0, radius, true );
  int knobRadius = radius / 7;
  double th = nvalue * (2 * Math.PI) / (maxValue - minValue);
  int x = (int)(Math.cos(th) * (radius - knobRadius * 3)),
  y = (int)(Math.sin(th) * (radius - knobRadius * 3));
  g2.setStroke(new BasicStroke(1));
  draw3DCircle(g2, x + radius - knobRadius,
      y + radius - knobRadius, knobRadius, false );
}

private void draw3DCircle(
    Graphics g, int x, int y, int radius, boolean raised)
{
  Color foreground = getForeground( );
  Color light = foreground.brighter( );
  Color dark = foreground.darker( );
  g.setColor(foreground);
  g.fillOval(x, y, radius * 2, radius * 2);
  g.setColor(raised ? light : dark);
```

```
      g.drawArc(x, y, radius * 2, radius * 2, 45, 180);
      g.setColor(raised ? dark : light);
      g.drawArc(x, y, radius * 2, radius * 2, 225, 180);
    }

    public Dimension getPreferredSize() {
      return new Dimension(100, 100);
    }

    public void setValue( int value ) {
      this.nvalue = value - minValue;
      repaint();
      fireEvent();
    }
    public int getValue()  { return nvalue+minValue; }
    public void setMinimum(int minValue)  { this.minValue = minValue; }
    public int getMinimum()  { return minValue; }
    public void setMaximum(int maxValue)  { this.maxValue = maxValue; }
    public int getMaximum()  { return maxValue; }

    public void addDialListener(DialListener listener) {
      listenerList.add( DialListener.class, listener );
    }
    public void removeDialListener(DialListener listener) {
      listenerList.remove( DialListener.class, listener );
    }

    void fireEvent() {
      Object[] listeners = listenerList.getListenerList();
      for ( int i = 0; i < listeners.length; i += 2 )
        if ( listeners[i] == DialListener.class )
          ((DialListener)listeners[i + 1]).dialAdjusted(
            new DialEvent(this, getValue()) );
    }

    public static void main(String[] args) {
      JFrame frame = new JFrame("Dial v1.0");
      final JLabel statusLabel = new JLabel("Welcome to Dial v1.0");
      final Dial dial = new Dial();
      frame.getContentPane().add(dial, BorderLayout.CENTER);
      frame.getContentPane().add(statusLabel, BorderLayout.SOUTH);

      dial.addDialListener(new DialListener() {
        public void dialAdjusted(DialEvent e) {
          statusLabel.setText("Value is " + e.getValue());
        }
      });

      frame.setDefaultCloseOperation( JFrame.EXIT_ON_CLOSE );
      frame.setSize( 150, 150 );
      frame.setVisible( true );
    }
}
```

Here's DialEvent, a simple subclass of java.util.EventObject:

```
//file: DialEvent.java
import java.awt.*;

public class DialEvent extends java.util.EventObject {
    int value;

    DialEvent( Dial source, int value ) {
        super( source );
        this.value = value;
    }

    public int getValue( ) {
        return value;
    }
}
```

Finally, here's the code for DialListener:

```
//file: DialListener.java
public interface DialListener extends java.util.EventListener {
    void dialAdjusted( DialEvent e );
}
```

Let's start from the top of the Dial class. We'll focus on the structure and leave you to figure out the trigonometry on your own.

Dial's main( ) method demonstrates how to use the dial to build a user interface. It creates a Dial and adds it to a JFrame. Then main( ) registers a dial listener on the dial. Whenever a DialEvent is received, the value of the dial is examined and displayed in a JLabel at the bottom of the frame window.

The constructor for the Dial class stores the dial's minimum, maximum, and current values; a default constructor provides a minimum of 0, a maximum of 100, and a current value of 0. The constructor sets the foreground color of the dial and registers listeners for mouse events. If the mouse is pressed or dragged, Dial's spin( ) method is called to update the dial's value. spin( ) performs some basic trigonometry to figure out what the new value of the dial should be.

paintComponent( ) and draw3DCircle( ) do a lot of trigonometry to figure out how to display the dial. draw3DCircle( ) is a private helper method that draws a circle that appears either raised or depressed; we use this to make the dial look three-dimensional.

The next group of methods provides ways to retrieve or change the dial's current setting and the minimum and maximum values. The important thing to notice here is the pattern of get and set methods for all of the important values used by the Dial. We will talk more about this in Chapter 22. Also, notice that the setValue( ) method does two important things: it repaints the component to reflect the new value and fires the DialEvent signifying the change.

The final group of methods in the `Dial` class provides the plumbing necessary for our event firing. `addDialListener( )` and `removeDialListener( )` take care of maintaining the listener list. Using the `listenerList` member variable we inherited from `JComponent` makes this an easy task. The `fireEvent( )` method retrieves the registered listeners for this component. It sends a `DialEvent` to any registered `DialListeners`.

Model and View Separation

The `Dial` example is overly simplified. All Swing components, as we've discussed, keep their data model and view separate. In the `Dial` component, we've combined these elements in a single class, which limits its reusability. To have `Dial` implement the MVC paradigm, we would have developed a dial data model and something called a UI-delegate that handled displaying the component and responding to user events. For a full treatment of this subject, see the `JogShuttle` example in O'Reilly's *Java Swing*.

In Chapter 19, we'll take what we know about components and containers and put them together using layout managers to create complex GUIs.

CHAPTER 19

Layout Managers

A *layout manager* arranges the child components of a container, as shown in Figure 19-1. It positions and sets the size of components within the container's display area according to a particular layout scheme. The layout manager's job is to fit the components into the available area while maintaining some spatial relationships among them. AWT and Swing come with several standard layout managers that will collectively handle most situations; you can make your own layout managers if you have special requirements.

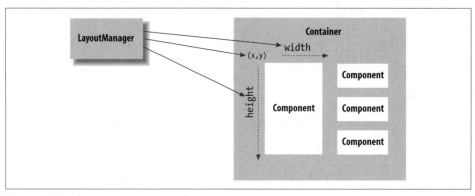

Figure 19-1. A layout manager at work

Every container has a default layout manager. When you make a new container, it comes with a LayoutManager object of an appropriate type. You can install a new layout manager at any time with the setLayout( ) method. For example, we can set the layout manager of a Swing container's content pane to a type called BorderLayout like so:

```
mycontainer.getContentPane().setLayout( new BorderLayout() );
```

Notice that although we have created a BorderLayout, we haven't bothered to save a reference to it. This is typical; after installing a layout manager it usually does its work behind the scenes, interacting with the container. You rarely call the layout manager's methods directly, so you don't usually need a reference (a notable exception is

CardLayout). However, you do need to know what the layout manager is going to do with your components as you work with them.

The LayoutManager is consulted whenever a container's doLayout( ) method is called to reorganize the contents. It does its job by calling the setLocation( ) or setBounds( ) methods of the individual child components to arrange them in the container's display area. A container is laid out the first time it is displayed and thereafter whenever the container's revalidate( ) method is called. Containers that are a subclass of the Window class (Frame, JFrame, and JWindow) are automatically validated whenever they are packed or resized. Calling pack( ) sets the window's size as small as possible while granting all its components their preferred sizes.

Every component provides three important pieces of information used by the layout manager in placing and sizing it: a minimum size, a maximum size, and a preferred size. These sizes are reported by the getMinimumSize( ), getMaximumSize( ), and getPreferredSize( ) methods of Component, respectively. For example, a plain JButton object can normally be changed to any size. However, the button's designer can provide a preferred size for a good-looking button. The layout manager might use this size when there are no other constraints, or it might ignore it, depending on its scheme. If we give the button a label, the button may need a new minimum size to display itself properly. The layout manager should generally respect the button's minimum size and guarantee that it has at least that much space. Similarly, a particular component might not be able to display itself properly if it is too large (perhaps it has to scale up an image); it can use getMaximumSize( ) to report the largest size it considers acceptable.

The preferred size of a Container object has the same meaning as for any other type of component. However, since a Container may hold its own components and want to arrange them in its own layout, its preferred size is a function of its layout manager. The layout manager is, therefore, involved in both sides of the issue. It asks the components in its container for their preferred (or minimum) sizes in order to arrange them. Based on those values, it calculates the preferred size for its own container (which can then be communicated to the container's parent and so on).

When a layout manager is called to arrange its components, it is working within a fixed area. It usually begins by looking at its container's dimensions and the preferred or minimum sizes of the child components. It then doles out screen area and sets the sizes of components according to its scheme and specific constraints.

You can set the minimum, preferred, and maximum sizes for a component with the setMinimumSize( ), setMaximumSize( ), and setPreferredSize( ) methods. Interestingly though, these methods were not added until Java 5.0. Prior to that you had to extend the class and override the corresponding "get" methods to do so. Why were these methods added so late to Java? Because those values normally should be calculated based on the real conditions of the component, not just fixed at a static value that looks good in one particular case. You can override the getMinimumSize( ), getMaximumSize( ), and getPreferredSize( ) methods of your own components to allow them to calculate those values, but you should do this only if you are specializing the component and it has new needs. In general, if you find yourself fighting with a layout manager because it's changing the size of one of your components, you are probably using the wrong kind of layout manager or not composing your user interface properly. Often it's easier to use a number of JPanel objects in a given display, each one with its own LayoutManager. Try breaking down the problem: place related components in their own JPanel and then arrange the panels in the container. When that becomes unwieldy, use a constraint-based layout manager such as GridBagLayout, which we'll discuss later in this chapter.

FlowLayout

FlowLayout is a simple layout manager that tries to arrange components at their preferred sizes, from left to right and top to bottom in the container. A FlowLayout can have a specified row justification of LEFT, CENTER, or RIGHT and a fixed horizontal and vertical padding. By default, a flow layout uses CENTER justification, meaning that all components are centered within the area allotted to them. FlowLayout is the default for JPanels.

The following example adds five buttons to the content pane of a JFrame using the default FlowLayout:

```java
//file: Flow.java
import java.awt.*;
import java.awt.event.*;
import javax.swing.*;

public class Flow extends JPanel {

  public Flow( ) {
    // FlowLayout is default layout manager for a JPanel
    add(new JButton("One"));
    add(new JButton("Two"));
    add(new JButton("Three"));
    add(new JButton("Four"));
    add(new JButton("Five"));
  }

  public static void main(String[] args) {
    JFrame frame = new JFrame("Flow");
    frame.setDefaultCloseOperation( JFrame.EXIT_ON_CLOSE );

    frame.setSize(400, 75);
    frame.setLocation(200, 200);
    Flow flow = new Flow( );
    frame.setContentPane(flow);
    frame.setVisible(true);
  }
}
```

The result is shown in Figure 19-2.

Figure 19-2. A flow layout

Try resizing the window. If it is made narrow enough, some of the buttons will spill over to a second or third row.

GridLayout

GridLayout arranges components into regularly spaced rows and columns. The components are arbitrarily resized to fit the grid; their minimum and preferred sizes are consequently ignored. GridLayout is most useful for arranging identically sized objects—perhaps a set of JPanels, each using a different layout manager.

GridLayout takes the number of rows and columns in its constructor. If you subsequently give it too many objects to manage, it adds extra columns to make the objects fit. You can also set the number of rows or columns to 0, which means that you don't care how many elements the layout manager packs in that dimension. For example, GridLayout(2,0) requests a layout with two rows and an unlimited number of columns; if you put ten components into this layout, you'll get two rows of five columns each.*

The following example sets a GridLayout with three rows and two columns as its layout manager:

```
//file: Grid.java
import java.awt.*;
import java.awt.event.*;
import javax.swing.*;

public class Grid extends JPanel {

  public Grid( ) {
    setLayout(new GridLayout(3, 2));
    add(new JButton("One"));
    add(new JButton("Two"));
    add(new JButton("Three"));
```

---

* Calling new GridLayout(0, 0) causes a runtime exception; either the rows or columns parameter must be greater than zero.

```
      add(new JButton("Four"));
      add(new JButton("Five"));
    }

    public static void main(String[] args) {
      JFrame frame = new JFrame("Grid");
      frame.setDefaultCloseOperation( JFrame.EXIT_ON_CLOSE );
      frame.setSize(200, 200);
      frame.setLocation(200, 200);
      frame.setContentPane(new Grid( ));
      frame.setVisible(true);
    }
  }
```

The results are shown in Figure 19-3.

Figure 19-3. A grid layout

The five buttons are laid out, in order, from left to right, top to bottom, with one empty spot.

BorderLayout

BorderLayout is a little more interesting. It tries to arrange objects in one of five geographical locations, represented by constants in the BorderLayout class: NORTH, SOUTH, EAST, WEST, and CENTER, optionally with some padding between. BorderLayout is the default layout for the content panes of JWindow and JFrame objects. Because each component is associated with a direction, BorderLayout can manage at most five components; it squashes or stretches those components to fit its constraints. As we'll see in the second example, this means that you often want to have BorderLayout manage sets of components in their own panels.

When we add a component to a container with a border layout, we need to specify both the component and the position at which to add it. To do so, we use an overloaded version of the container's add( ) method that takes an additional argument as a *constraint*. The constraint specifies the name of a position within the BorderLayout.

The following application sets a BorderLayout and adds our five buttons again, named for their locations:

```
//file: Border1.java
import java.awt.*;
import java.awt.event.*;
import javax.swing.*;

public class Border1 extends JPanel {

  public Border1( ) {
    setLayout(new BorderLayout( ));
    add(new JButton("North"), BorderLayout.NORTH );
    add(new JButton("South"), BorderLayout.SOUTH );
    add(new JButton("East"), BorderLayout.EAST );
    add(new JButton("West"), BorderLayout.WEST );
    add(new JButton("Center"), BorderLayout.CENTER );
  }

  public static void main(String[] args) {
    JFrame frame = new JFrame("Border1");
    frame.setDefaultCloseOperation( JFrame.EXIT_ON_CLOSE );
    frame.setSize(300, 300);
    frame.setLocation(200, 200);
    frame.setContentPane(new Border1( ));
    frame.setVisible(true);
  }
}
```

The result is shown in Figure 19-4.

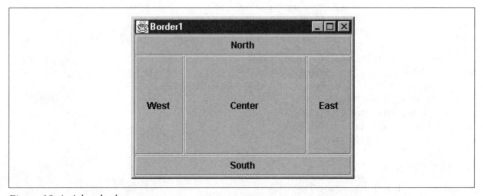

Figure 19-4. A border layout

So, how exactly is the area divided up? Well, the objects at NORTH and SOUTH get their preferred height and fill the display area horizontally. EAST and WEST components, on the other hand, get their preferred width, and fill the remaining area between NORTH and SOUTH vertically. Finally, the CENTER object takes all the rest of the space. As you can see in Figure 19-4, our buttons get distorted into interesting shapes.

What if we don't want BorderLayout messing with the sizes of our components? One option would be to put each button in its own JPanel. The default layout for a JPanel is FlowLayout, which respects the preferred size of components. The preferred sizes of the panels are effectively the preferred sizes of the buttons, but if the panels are stretched, they won't pull their buttons with them. The following application illustrates this approach:

```
//file: Border2.java
import java.awt.*;
import java.awt.event.*;
import javax.swing.*;

public class Border2 extends JPanel {

  public Border2() {
    setLayout(new BorderLayout());
    JPanel p = new JPanel();
    p.add(new JButton("North"));
    add(p, BorderLayout.NORTH);
    p = new JPanel();
    p.add(new JButton("South"));
    add(p, BorderLayout.SOUTH);
    p = new JPanel();
    p.add(new JButton("East"));
    add(p, BorderLayout.E*);
    p = new JPanel();
    p.add(new JButton("West"));
    add(p, BorderLayout.WEST);
    p = new JPanel();
    p.add(new JButton("Center"));
    add(p, BorderLayout.CENTER);
  }

  public static void main(String[] args) {
    JFrame frame = new JFrame("Border2");
    frame.setDefaultCloseOperation( JFrame.EXIT_ON_CLOSE );
    frame.setSize(225, 150);
    frame.setLocation(200, 200);
    frame.setContentPane(new Border2());
    frame.setVisible(true);
  }
}
```

The result is shown in Figure 19-5.

In the example, we create a number of panels, put our buttons inside the panels, and put the panels into the frame window, which has the BorderLayout manager. Now, the JPanel for the CENTER button soaks up the extra space that comes from the BorderLayout. Each JPanel's FlowLayout centers the button in the panel and uses the button's preferred size. In this case, it's all a bit awkward. We'll see how we could accomplish this more directly using GridBagLayout shortly.

Figure 19-5. Another border layout

BoxLayout

Most layout managers are part of the java.awt package and were defined back when Java was first released. Swing adds a couple of new general-purpose layout managers in the javax.swing package; one is BoxLayout. This layout manager is useful for creating simple toolbars or vertical button bars. It lays out components in a single row or column. It is similar to FlowLayout but does not wrap components into new rows.

Although you can use BoxLayout directly, Swing includes a handy container called Box that takes care of the details for you. Every Box uses BoxLayout, but you don't really have to worry about it; the Box class includes some very useful methods for laying out components.

You can create a horizontal or vertical box using Box's static methods.

```
Container horizontalBox = Box.createHorizontalBox();
Container verticalBox = Box.createVerticalBox();
```

Once the Box is created, you can just add( ) components as usual:

```
Container box = Box.createHorizontalBox();
box.add(new JButton("In the"));
```

Box includes several other static methods that create special invisible components that can be used to guide the BoxLayout. The first of these is *glue*; glue is really space between components in the Box. When the Box is resized, glue expands or contracts as more or less space is available. The other special invisible component type is a *strut*. Like glue, a strut represents space between components, but it doesn't resize.

The following example creates a horizontal Box (shown in Figure 19-6) that includes both glue and struts. Play around by resizing the window to see the effect of the glue and the struts.

```
//file: Boxer.java
import java.awt.*;
import java.awt.event.*;
import javax.swing.*;

public class Boxer extends JPanel {
  public static void main(String[] args) {
```

```
      JFrame frame = new JFrame("Boxer");
      frame.setDefaultCloseOperation( JFrame.EXIT_ON_CLOSE );
      frame.setSize(250, 250);
      frame.setLocation(200, 200);
      Container box = Box.createHorizontalBox( );
      box.add(Box.createHorizontalGlue( ));
      box.add(new JButton("In the"));
      box.add(Box.createHorizontalGlue( ));
      box.add(new JButton("clearing"));
      box.add(Box.createHorizontalStrut(10));
      box.add(new JButton("stands"));
      box.add(Box.createHorizontalStrut(10));
      box.add(new JButton("a"));
      box.add(Box.createHorizontalGlue( ));
      box.add(new JButton("boxer"));
      box.add(Box.createHorizontalGlue( ));
      frame.getContentPane( ).add(box, BorderLayout.CENTER);
      frame.pack( );
      frame.setVisible(true);
    }
  }
```

Figure 19-6. Using the Box class

Components are added sequentially for display from left to right or top to bottom with optional "glue" or "strut" constraints placed between them. By default, components simply line up one after another with no space between them. "Glue" acts like a spring, allowing its adjacent components to move to occupy the space evenly. A "strut" imposes a fixed space between adjacent components.

CardLayout

CardLayout is a special layout manager for creating the effect of a "stack" of components. Instead of arranging all of the container's components, it displays only one at a time. You might use this kind of layout to implement a custom-tabbed panel of some kind. In fact, there's probably little reason to use this layout given the Swing JTabbedPane component, described in Chapter 17. We include it here mainly for completeness.

To add a component to a CardLayout, use a two-argument version of the container's add( ) method; the extra argument is an arbitrary string that serves as the card's name:

```
add("netconfigscreen", myComponent);
```

To bring a particular card to the top of the stack, call the CardLayout's show( ) method with two arguments: the parent Container and the name of the card you want to show. There are also methods—first( ), last( ), next( ), and previous( ) for working with the stack of cards. These are all CardLayout instance methods. To invoke them, you need a reference to the CardLayout object itself, not to the container it manages. Each method takes a single argument: the parent Container. Here's an example:

```java
//file: Card.java
import java.awt.*;
import java.awt.event.*;
import javax.swing.*;

public class Card extends JPanel {
  CardLayout cards = new CardLayout( );

  public Card( ) {
    setLayout(cards);
    ActionListener listener = new ActionListener( ) {
      public void actionPerformed(ActionEvent e) {
        cards.next(Card.this);
      }
    };
    JButton button;
    button = new JButton("one");
    button.addActionListener(listener);
    add(button, "one");
    button = new JButton("two");
    button.addActionListener(listener);
    add(button, "two");
    button = new JButton("three");
    button.addActionListener(listener);
    add(button, "three");
  }

  public static void main(String[] args) {
    JFrame frame = new JFrame("Card");
    frame.setDefaultCloseOperation( JFrame.EXIT_ON_CLOSE );
    frame.setSize(200, 200);
    frame.setLocation(200, 200);
    frame.setContentPane(new Card( ));
    frame.setVisible(true);
  }
}
```

We add three buttons to the layout and cycle through them as they are pressed. An anonymous inner class serves as an action listener for each button; it simply calls CardLayout's next( ) method whenever a button is pressed. Card.this refers to the Card object, which is the container in this case. In a more realistic example, we would build a group of panels, each of which might implement some part of a complex user interface and add those panels to the layout. Each panel would have its own layout manager. The panels would be resized to fill the entire area available (i.e., the area of the Container they are in), and their individual layout managers would arrange their internal components.

GridBagLayout

GridBagLayout is a very flexible layout manager that allows you to position components relative to one another using constraints. With GridBagLayout (and a fair amount of effort), you can create almost any imaginable layout. Components are arranged at logical coordinates on an abstract grid. We'll call them "logical" coordinates because they really designate positions in the space of rows and columns formed by the set of components. Rows and columns of the grid stretch to different sizes, based on the sizes and constraints of the components they hold.

A row or column in a GridBagLayout expands to accommodate the dimensions and constraints of the largest component it contains. Individual components may also be told to span more than one row or column. Components that aren't as large as their grid cell can be anchored (positioned to one side) within their cell. They can also be set to fill or to expand their size in either dimension. Extra area in the grid rows and columns can be parceled out according to the weight constraints of the components. In this way, you can control how various components will grow and stretch when a window is resized.

GridBagLayout is much easier to use in a graphical WYSIWYG GUI builder environment. That's because working with GridBag is kind of like messing with the "rabbit ears" antennae on your television. It's not particularly difficult to get the results that you want through trial and error, but writing out hard and fast rules for how to go about it is difficult. In short, GridBagLayout is complex and has some quirks. It is also simply a bit ugly both in model and implementation. Remember that you can do a lot with nested panels and by composing simpler layout managers within one another. If you look back through this chapter, you'll see some examples of composite layouts; it's up to you to determine how far you should go before making the break from simpler layout managers to a more complex all-in-one layout manager like GridBagLayout.

The GridBagConstraints Class

Having said that GridBagLayout is complex and a bit ugly, we're going to contradict ourselves a little and say that its API is surprisingly simple. There is only one constructor with no arguments (GridBagLayout( )), and there aren't a lot of fancy methods to control how the display works.

The appearance of a grid bag layout is controlled by sets of GridBagConstraints, and that's where things get hairy. Each component managed by a GridBagLayout is associated with a GridBagConstraints object. GridBagConstraints holds the following variables, which we'll describe in detail shortly:

int gridx
int gridy

    Controls the position of the component on the layout's grid

int weightx
int weighty

    Controls how additional space in the row or column is allotted to the component

int fill

    Controls whether the component expands to fill the allotted space

int gridheight
int gridwidth

    Controls the number of rows or columns the component spans

int anchor

    Controls the position of the component if there is extra room within the allotted space

int ipadx
int ipady

    Controls padding between the component and the borders of its area

Insets insets

    Controls padding between the component and neighboring components

To make a set of constraints for a component or components, create a new instance of GridBagConstraints and set these public variables to the appropriate values. (There is also a large constructor that takes all 11 arguments.)

The easiest way to associate a set of constraints with a component is to use the version of add( ) that takes both a component object and a layout object as arguments. This puts the component in the container and associates the GridBagConstraints object with it:

```
Container content = getContentPane( );
JComponent component = new JLabel("constrain me, please...");
GridBagConstraints constraints = new GridBagConstraints( );
constraints.gridx = x;
constraints.gridy = y;
...
content.add(component, constraints);
```

You can also add a component to a GridBagLayout using the single argument add( ) method and then calling the layout's setConstraints( ) method directly to pass it the GridBagConstraints object for that component:

```
add(component);
...
myGridBagLayout.setConstraints(component, constraints);
```

In either case, the set of constraints is copied when it is applied to the component. It's the individual constraints that apply to the component, not the GridBagConstraints object. Therefore, you're free to create a single set of GridBagConstraints, modify it as needed, and apply it as needed to different objects. You might want to create a helper method that sets the constraints appropriately, then adds the component, with its constraints, to the layout. That's the approach we'll take in our examples; our helper method is called addGB( ), and it takes a component plus a pair of coordinates as arguments. These coordinates become the gridx and gridy values for the constraints. We could expand upon this later and overload addGB( ) to take more parameters for other constraints that we often change from component to component.

Grid Coordinates

One of the biggest surprises in the GridBagLayout is that there's no way to specify the size of the grid. There doesn't have to be. The grid size is determined implicitly by the constraints of all the objects; the layout manager picks dimensions large enough so that everything fits. Thus, if you put one component in a layout and set its gridx and gridy constraints each to 25, the layout manager creates a virtual 25×25 grid, with rows and columns numbered from 0 to 24. If you then add a second component with a gridx of 30 and a gridy of 13, the virtual grid's dimensions change to 30×25. You don't have to worry about setting up an appropriate number of rows and columns. The layout manager does it automatically as you add components.

With this knowledge, we're ready to create some simple displays. We'll start by arranging a group of components in a cross shape. We maintain explicit x and y local variables, setting them as we add the components to our grid. This is partly for clarity, but it can be a handy technique when you want to add a number of components in a row or column. You can simply increment gridx or gridy before adding each component. This is a simple and problem-free way to achieve relative placement. (Later, we'll describe GridBagConstraints's RELATIVE constant, which does relative placement automatically.) The following code shows the first layout (see Figure 19-7):

```
//file: GridBag1.java
import java.awt.*;
import java.awt.event.*;
import javax.swing.*;

public class GridBag1 extends JPanel {
  GridBagConstraints constraints = new GridBagConstraints();

  public GridBag1() {
    setLayout(new GridBagLayout());
    int x, y;  // for clarity
    addGB(new JButton("North"),  x = 1, y = 0);
    addGB(new JButton("West"),   x = 0, y = 1);
    addGB(new JButton("Center"), x = 1, y = 1);
```

```
      addGB(new JButton("East"),   x = 2, y = 1);
      addGB(new JButton("South"),  x = 1, y = 2);
   }

   void addGB(Component component, int x, int y) {
      constraints.gridx = x;
      constraints.gridy = y;
      add(component, constraints);
   }

   public static void main(String[] args) {
      JFrame frame = new JFrame("GridBag1");
      frame.setDefaultCloseOperation( JFrame.EXIT_ON_CLOSE );
      frame.setSize(225, 150);
      frame.setLocation(200, 200);
      frame.setContentPane(new GridBag1( ));
      frame.setVisible(true);
   }
}
```

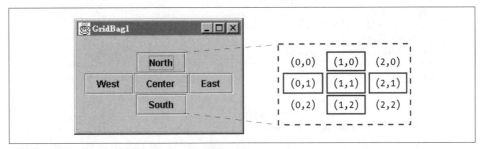

Figure 19-7. A simple GridBagLayout

The buttons in this example are "clumped" together in the center of their display
area. Each button is displayed at its preferred size, without stretching to fill the available
space. This is how the layout manager behaves when the "weight" constraints
are left unset. We'll talk more about weights in the next two sections.

The fill Constraint

Let's make the buttons expand to fill the entire JFrame window. To do so, we must
take two steps: we must set the fill constraint for each button to the value BOTH, and
we must set the weightx and weighty to nonzero values, as shown in this example:

```
//file: GridBag2.java
import java.awt.*;
import java.awt.event.*;
import javax.swing.*;

public class GridBag2 extends JPanel {
   GridBagConstraints constraints = new GridBagConstraints( );
```

```
public GridBag2( ) {
  setLayout(new GridBagLayout( ));
  constraints.weightx = 1.0;
  constraints.weighty = 1.0;
  constraints.fill = GridBagConstraints.BOTH;
  int x, y;  // for clarity
  addGB(new JButton("North"),   x = 1, y = 0);
  addGB(new JButton("West"),    x = 0, y = 1);
  addGB(new JButton("Center"),  x = 1, y = 1);
  addGB(new JButton("East"),    x = 2, y = 1);
  addGB(new JButton("South"),   x = 1, y = 2);
}

void addGB(Component component, int x, int y) {
  constraints.gridx = x;
  constraints.gridy = y;
  add(component, constraints);
}

public static void main(String[] args) {
  JFrame frame = new JFrame("GridBag2");
  frame.setDefaultCloseOperation( JFrame.EXIT_ON_CLOSE );
  frame.setSize(225, 150);
  frame.setLocation(200, 200);
  frame.setContentPane(new GridBag2( ));
  frame.setVisible(true);
}
}
```

Figure 19-8 shows the resulting layout.

Figure 19-8. Making buttons fill the available space

BOTH is one of the constants of the GridBagConstraints class; it tells the component to fill the available space in both directions. Here are the constants you can use to set the fill field:

HORIZONTAL
    Fill the available horizontal space.

VERTICAL
    Fill the available vertical space.

BOTH

Fill the available space in both directions.

NONE

Don't fill the available space; display the component at its preferred size.

We set the weight constraints to 1.0; in this example, it doesn't matter what they are, provided each component has the same nonzero weight. Filling doesn't occur if the component weights in the direction you're filling are 0, which is the default value.

Spanning Rows and Columns

One of the most important features of GridBaglayout is that it lets you create arrangements in which components span two or more rows or columns. To do so, set the gridwidth and gridheight variables of the GridBagConstraints. The following example creates such a display; button one spans two columns vertically, and button four spans two horizontally. Figure 19-9 shows the resulting layout.

```java
//file: GridBag3.java
import java.awt.*;
import java.awt.event.*;
import javax.swing.*;

public class GridBag3 extends JPanel {
  GridBagConstraints constraints = new GridBagConstraints();

  public GridBag3() {
    setLayout(new GridBagLayout());
    constraints.weightx = 1.0;
    constraints.weighty = 1.0;
    constraints.fill = GridBagConstraints.BOTH;
    int x, y;  // for clarity
    constraints.gridheight = 2; // span two rows
    addGB(new JButton("one"),    x = 0, y = 0);
    constraints.gridheight = 1; // set it back
    addGB(new JButton("two"),    x = 1, y = 0);
    addGB(new JButton("three"), x = 2, y = 0);
    constraints.gridwidth = 2; // span two columns
    addGB(new JButton("four"),   x = 1, y = 1);
    constraints.gridwidth = 1; // set it back
  }

  void addGB(Component component, int x, int y) {
    constraints.gridx = x;
    constraints.gridy = y;
    add(component, constraints);
  }

  public static void main(String[] args) {
    JFrame frame = new JFrame("GridBag3");
    frame.setDefaultCloseOperation( JFrame.EXIT_ON_CLOSE );
    frame.setSize(200, 200);
```

```
        frame.setLocation(200, 200);
        frame.setContentPane(new GridBag3());
        frame.setVisible(true);
    }
}
```

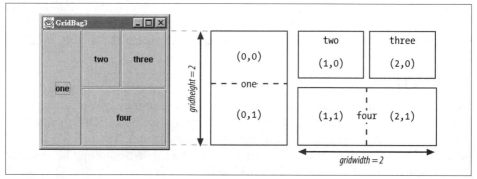

Figure 19-9. Making components span rows and columns

The size of each element is controlled by the `gridwidth` and `gridheight` values of its constraints. For button one, we set `gridheight` to 2; therefore, it is two cells high. Its `gridx` and `gridy` positions are both 0, so it occupies cell (0,0) and the cell directly below it, (0,1). Likewise, button four has a `gridwidth` of 2 and a `gridheight` of 1, so it occupies two cells horizontally. We place this button in cell (1,1), so it occupies that cell and its neighbor, (2,1).

In this example, we set the `fill` to `BOTH` and `weightx` and `weighty` to 1 for all components. By doing so, we tell each button to occupy all the space available and give them all equal weighting. Strictly speaking, this isn't necessary. However, it makes it easier to see exactly how much space each button occupies.

Weighting

The `weightx` and `weighty` variables of a `GridBagConstraints` object determine how "extra" space in the container is distributed among the columns or rows in the layout. As long as you keep things simple, the effect these variables have is fairly intuitive: the larger the weight, the greater the amount of space allocated to the component, relative to its peers. Figure 19-10 shows what happens if we vary the `weightx` constraint from 0.1 to 1.0 as we place three buttons in a row.

Here's the code:

```
//file: GridBag4.java
import java.awt.*;
import java.awt.event.*;
import javax.swing.*;
```

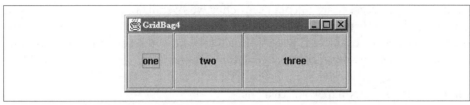

Figure 19-10. Using weight to control component size

```java
public class GridBag4 extends JPanel {
  GridBagConstraints constraints = new GridBagConstraints( );

  public GridBag4( ) {
    setLayout(new GridBagLayout( ));
    constraints.fill = GridBagConstraints.BOTH;
    constraints.weighty = 1.0;
    int x, y; // for clarity
    constraints.weightx = 0.1;
    addGB(new JButton("one"),   x = 0, y = 0);
    constraints.weightx = 0.5;
    addGB(new JButton("two"),   ++x,    y);
    constraints.weightx = 1.0;
    addGB(new JButton("three"), ++x,    y);
  }

  void addGB(Component component, int x, int y) {
    constraints.gridx = x;
    constraints.gridy = y;
    add(component, constraints);
  }

  public static void main(String[] args) {
    JFrame frame = new JFrame("GridBag4");
    frame.setDefaultCloseOperation( JFrame.EXIT_ON_CLOSE );
    frame.setSize(300, 100);
    frame.setLocation(200, 200);
    frame.setContentPane(new GridBag4( ));
    frame.setVisible(true);
  }
}
```

The specific values of the weights are not meaningful; it is only their relative proportions that matter. After the preferred sizes of the components (including padding and insets—see the next section) are determined, any extra space is doled out in proportion to the component's weights. For example, if each of our three components had the same weight, each would receive a third of the extra space. To make this more obvious, you may prefer to express the weights for a row or column as fractions totaling 1.0—for example: 0.25, 0.25, 0.50. Components with a weight of 0 receive no extra space.

The situation is a bit more complicated when there are multiple rows or columns and when there is even the possibility of components spanning more than one cell. In the general case, GridBagLayout calculates an effective overall weight for each row and column and then distributes the extra space to them proportionally. Note that the previous single-row example is just a special case where the columns each have one component. The gory details of the calculations follow.

Calculating the weights of rows and columns

For a given row or column ("rank"), GridBagLayout first considers the weights of all the components contained strictly within that rank—ignoring those that span more than one cell. The greatest individual weight becomes the overall weight of the row or column. Intuitively, this means that GridBagLayout is trying to accommodate the needs of the weightiest component in that rank.

Next, GridBagLayout considers the components that occupy more than one cell and things get a little weird. GridbagLayout wants to evaluate them to see whether they affect the determination of the largest weight in a row or column. However, because these components occupy more than one cell, GridBagLayout divides their weight among the ranks (rows or columns) that they span.

GridBagLayout tries to calculate an effective weight for the portion of the component that occupies each row or column. It does this by trying to divide the weight of the component among the ranks in the same proportions that the length (or height) of the component will be shared by the ranks. But how does it know what the proportions will be before the whole grid is determined? That's what it's trying to calculate after all. It simply guesses based on the row or column weights already determined. GridBagLayout uses the weights determined by the first round of calculations to split up the weight of the component over the ranks that it occupies. For each row or column, it then considers that fraction of the weight to be the component's weight for that rank. That weight then contends for the "heaviest weight" in the row or column, possibly changing the overall weight of that row or column, as we described earlier.

Anchoring

If a component is smaller than the space available for it, it is centered by default. But centering isn't the only possibility. The anchor constraint tells a grid bag layout how to position a component within its cell in the grid. Possible values are GridBagConstraints.CENTER, NORTH, NORTHEAST, EAST, SOUTHEAST, SOUTH, SOUTHWEST, WEST, and NORTHWEST. For example, an anchor of GridBagConstraints.NORTH centers a component at the top of its display area; SOUTHEAST places a component at the bottom-right corner of its area.

Padding and Insets

Another way to control the behavior of a component in a grid bag layout is to use padding and insets. Padding is determined by the ipadx and ipady fields of GridBagConstraints. They specify horizontal and vertical "growth factors" for the component. In Figure 19-11, the West button is larger because we have set the ipadx and ipady values of its constraints to 25. Therefore, the layout manager gets the button's preferred size and adds 25 pixels in each direction to determine the button's actual size. The sizes of the other buttons are unchanged because their padding is set to 0 (the default), but their spacing is different. The West button is unnaturally tall, which means that the middle row of the layout must be taller than the others.

```java
//file: GridBag5.java
import java.awt.*;
import java.awt.event.*;
import javax.swing.*;

public class GridBag5 extends JPanel {
  GridBagConstraints constraints = new GridBagConstraints();

  public GridBag5() {
    setLayout(new GridBagLayout());
    int x, y;  // for clarity
    addGB(new JButton("North"),  x = 1, y = 0);
    constraints.ipadx = 25;  // add padding
    constraints.ipady = 25;
    addGB(new JButton("West"),   x = 0, y = 1);
    constraints.ipadx = 0;   // remove padding
    constraints.ipady = 0;
    addGB(new JButton("Center"), x = 1, y = 1);
    addGB(new JButton("East"),   x = 2, y = 1);
    addGB(new JButton("South"),  x = 1, y = 2);
  }

  void addGB(Component component, int x, int y) {
    constraints.gridx = x;
    constraints.gridy = y;
    add(component, constraints);
  }

  public static void main(String[] args) {
    JFrame frame = new JFrame("GridBag5");
    frame.setDefaultCloseOperation( JFrame.EXIT_ON_CLOSE );

    frame.setSize(250, 250);
    frame.setLocation(200, 200);
    frame.setContentPane(new GridBag5());
    frame.setVisible(true);
  }
}
```

Figure 19-11. Using padding and insets in a layout

Notice that the horizontal padding, ipadx, is added on both the left and right sides of the button. Therefore, the button grows horizontally by twice the value of ipadx. Likewise, the vertical padding, ipady, is added on both the top and the bottom.

Insets add space between the edges of the component and its cell. They are stored in the insets field of GridBagConstraints, which is an Insets object. An Insets object has four fields to specify the margins on the component's top, bottom, left, and right. The relationship between insets and padding can be confusing. As shown in Figure 19-12, padding is added to the component itself, increasing its size. Insets are external to the component and represent the margin between the component and its cell.

Figure 19-12. The relationship between padding and insets

Padding and weighting have an odd interaction with each other. If you use padding, it's best to use the default weightx and weighty values for each component.

Relative Positioning

In all our grid bag layouts so far, we have specified the gridx and gridy coordinates of each component explicitly using its constraints. Another alternative is relative positioning.

Conceptually, *relative positioning* is simple: we simply say, "put this component to the right of (or below) the previous component." To do so, you can set gridx or gridy to the constant GridBagConstraints.RELATIVE. Unfortunately, it's not as simple as this. Here are a couple of warnings:

- To place a component to the right of the previous one, set gridx to RELATIVE *and* use the same value for gridy that you used for the previous component.

- Similarly, to place a component below the previous one, set gridy to RELATIVE *and* leave gridx unchanged.

- Setting both gridx and gridy to RELATIVE places all the components in one row, not in a diagonal line, as you might expect. (This is the default.)

In other words, if gridx or gridy is RELATIVE, you had better leave the other value unchanged. RELATIVE makes it easy to arrange a lot of components in a row or a column. That's what it was intended for; if you try to do something else, you're fighting against the layout manager, not working with it.

GridBagLayout allows another kind of relative positioning in which you specify where, in a row or a column, the component should be placed overall using the gridwidth and gridheight fields of GridBagConstraints. Setting either of these to the constant REMAINDER says that the component should be the last item in its row or column and, therefore, should occupy all the remaining space. Setting either gridwidth or gridheight to RELATIVE says it should be the second to the last item in its row or column. Unfortunately, you can use these constants to create constraints that can't possibly be met; for example, you can say that two components must be the last component in a row. In these cases, the layout manager tries to do something reasonable, but it will almost certainly do something you don't want.

Composite Layouts

Sometimes things don't fall neatly into little boxes. This is true of layouts as well as life. For example, if you want to use some of GridBagLayout's weighting features for part of your GUI, you could create separate layouts for different parts of the GUI and combine them with yet another layout. That's how we'll build the pocket calculator interface in Figure 19-13. We will use three grid bag layouts: one for the first row of buttons (C, %, +), one for the last (0, ., =) and one for the window itself. The master layout (the window's) manages the text field we use for the display, the panels containing the first and last rows of buttons, and the twelve buttons in the middle.*

Figure 19-13. The Calculator application

Here's the code for the Calculator example. It implements only the user interface (i.e., the keyboard); it collects everything you type in the display field until you press C (clear). Figuring out how to connect the GUI to some other code that would perform the operations is up to you. One strategy would be to send an event to the object that does the computation whenever the user presses the equals sign. That object could read the contents of the text field, parse it, do the computation, and display the results.

```java
//file: Calculator.java
import java.awt.*;
import java.awt.event.*;
import javax.swing.*;

public class Calculator extends JPanel implements ActionListener {
  GridBagConstraints gbc = new GridBagConstraints();
  JTextField theDisplay = new JTextField();

  public Calculator() {
    gbc.weightx = 1.0;  gbc.weighty = 1.0;
    gbc.fill = GridBagConstraints.BOTH;
    ContainerListener listener = new ContainerAdapter() {
      public void componentAdded(ContainerEvent e) {
        Component comp = e.getChild();
        if (comp instanceof JButton)
          ((JButton)comp).addActionListener(Calculator.this);
      }
```

---

* If you're curious, this calculator is based on the ELORG-801, encountered in an online "calculator museum"; see *http://www.taswegian.com/MOSCOW/elorg801.html*.

```
      };
      addContainerListener(listener);
      gbc.gridwidth = 4;
      addGB(this, theDisplay, 0, 0);
      // make the top row
      JPanel topRow = new JPanel( );
      topRow.addContainerListener(listener);
      gbc.gridwidth = 1;
      gbc.weightx = 1.0;
      addGB(topRow, new JButton("C"), 0, 0);
      gbc.weightx = 0.33;
      addGB(topRow, new JButton("%"), 1, 0);
      gbc.weightx = 1.0;
      addGB(topRow, new JButton("+"), 2, 0 );
      gbc.gridwidth = 4;
      addGB(this, topRow, 0, 1);
      gbc.weightx = 1.0;  gbc.gridwidth = 1;
      // make the digits
      for(int j=0; j<3; j++)
          for(int i=0; i<3; i++)
              addGB(this, new JButton("" + ((2-j)*3+i+1) ), i, j+2);
      // -, x, and divide
      addGB(this, new JButton("-"), 3, 2);
      addGB(this, new JButton("x"), 3, 3);
      addGB(this, new JButton("\u00F7"), 3, 4);
      // make the bottom row
      JPanel bottomRow = new JPanel( );
      bottomRow.addContainerListener(listener);
      gbc.weightx = 1.0;
      addGB(bottomRow, new JButton("0"), 0, 0);
      gbc.weightx = 0.33;
      addGB(bottomRow, new JButton("."), 1, 0);
      gbc.weightx = 1.0;
      addGB(bottomRow, new JButton("="), 2, 0);
      gbc.gridwidth = 4;
      addGB(this, bottomRow, 0, 5);
  }

  void addGB(Container cont, Component comp, int x, int y) {
    if ((cont.getLayout( ) instanceof GridBagLayout) == false)
      cont.setLayout(new GridBagLayout( ));
    gbc.gridx = x; gbc.gridy = y;
    cont.add(comp, gbc);
  }

  public void actionPerformed(ActionEvent e) {
    if (e.getActionCommand( ).equals("C"))
      theDisplay.setText("");
    else
      theDisplay.setText(theDisplay.getText( )
                          + e.getActionCommand( ));
  }
```

```
        public static void main(String[] args) {
            JFrame frame = new JFrame("Calculator");
            frame.setDefaultCloseOperation( JFrame.EXIT_ON_CLOSE );
            frame.setSize(200, 250);
            frame.setLocation(200, 200);
            frame.setContentPane(new Calculator());
            frame.setVisible(true);
        }
    }
```

Once again, we use an addGB( ) helper method to add components with their constraints to the layout. Before discussing how to build the layout, let's take a look at addGB( ). We said earlier that three layout managers are in our user interface: one for the application panel itself, one for the panel containing the first row of buttons (topRow), and one for the panel containing the bottom row of buttons (bottomRow). We use addGB( ) for all three layouts; its first argument specifies the container to add the component to. Thus, when the first argument is this, we're adding an object to the content pane of the JFrame. When the first argument is topRow, we're adding a button to the first row of buttons. addGB( ) first checks the container's layout manager and sets it to GridBagLayout if it isn't already set properly. It sets the object's position by modifying a set of constraints, gbc, and then uses these constraints to add the object to the container.

We use a single set of constraints throughout the example, modifying fields as we see fit. The constraints are initialized in Calculator's constructor. Before calling addGB( ), we set any fields of gbc for which the defaults are inappropriate. Thus, for the answer display, we set the grid width to 4 and add the answer display directly to the application panel (this). The add( ) method, which is called by addGB( ), makes a copy of the constraints, so we're free to reuse gbc throughout the application.

The first and last rows of buttons motivate the use of multiple GridBagLayout containers, each with its own grid. These buttons appear to straddle grid lines, but you really can't accomplish this using a single grid. Therefore, topRow has its own layout manager, with three horizontal cells, allowing each button in the row to have a grid width of 1. To control the size of the buttons, we set the weightx variables so that the clear and plus buttons take up more space than the percent button. We then add the topRow as a whole to the application, with a grid width of 4. The bottom row is built similarly.

To build the buttons for the digits 1–9, we use a doubly nested loop. There's nothing particularly interesting about this loop, except that it's probably a bit too cute. The minus, multiply, and divide buttons are also simple: we create a button with the appropriate label and use addGB( ) to place it in the application. It's worth noting that we used a Unicode constant to request a real division sign rather than wimping out and using a slash.

That's it for the user interface; what's left is event handling. Each button generates action events; we need to register listeners for these events. We'll make the application panel, the Calculator, the listener for all the buttons. To register the Calculator as a listener, we'll be clever. Whenever a component is added to a container, the container generates a ContainerEvent. We use an anonymous inner class ContainerListener to register listeners for our buttons. This means that the Calculator must register as a ContainerListener for itself and for the two panels, topRow and bottomRow. The componentAdded( ) method is very simple. It calls getChild( ) to find out what component caused the event (i.e., what component was added). If that component is a button, it registers the Calculator as an ActionListener for that button.

actionPerformed( ) is called whenever the user presses any button. It clears the display if the user pressed the C button; otherwise, it appends the button's action command (in this case, its label) to the display.

Combining layout managers is an extremely useful trick. Granted, this example verges on overkill. You won't often need to create a composite layout using multiple grid bags. Composite layouts are common, however, with BorderLayout; you'll frequently use different layout managers for each of a border layout's regions. For example, the CENTER region might be a ScrollPane, which has its own special-purpose layout manager; the EAST and SOUTH regions might be panels managed by grid layouts or flow layouts, as appropriate.

Nonstandard Layout Managers

We've covered the basic layout managers; with them, you should be able to create just about any user interface you like.

But that's not all, folks. If you want to experiment with layout managers that are undocumented, may change, and may not be available locally on all platforms, look in the sun.awt classes. You'll find a HorizBagLayout, a VerticalBagLayout, an OrientableFlowLayout, and a VariableGridLayout. Furthermore, public domain layout managers of all descriptions are on the Net.

Absolute Positioning

It's possible to set the layout manager to null: no layout control. You might do this to position an object on the display at some absolute coordinates. This is usually not the right approach. Components might have different minimum sizes on different platforms, and your interface would not be very portable.

The following example doesn't use a layout manager and works with absolute coordinates instead:

```
//file: MoveButton.java
import java.awt.*;
import java.awt.event.*;
import javax.swing.*;
```

```
public class MoveButton extends JPanel {
  JButton button = new JButton("I Move");

  public MoveButton() {
    setLayout(null);
    add(button);
    button.setSize(button.getPreferredSize( ));
    button.setLocation(20, 20);
    addMouseListener(new MouseAdapter( ) {
      public void mousePressed(MouseEvent e) {
        button.setLocation(e.getX( ), e.getY( ));
      }
    });
  }

  public static void main(String[] args) {
    JFrame frame = new JFrame("MoveButton");
    frame.setDefaultCloseOperation( JFrame.EXIT_ON_CLOSE );
    frame.setSize(250, 200);
    frame.setLocation(200, 200);
    frame.setContentPane(new MoveButton( ));
    frame.setVisible(true);
  }
}
```

Click in the window area, outside of the button, to move the button to a new location. Try resizing the window and note that the button stays at a fixed position relative to the window's upper-left corner.

SpringLayout

The SpringLayout was added in Java 1.4. It supports a combination of absolute positioning and point-to-point attachments between components (kind of like the "glue" of the BoxLayout). SpringLayout is useful in GUI builder applications because it's easy to translate manual user placement into these kinds of constraints.

SpringLayout uses Spring objects to attach edges of components. Springs have a range of motion and can be anchored at a coordinate or at a component's edge. Any two component edges can also be connected by a Spring. The two edges may belong to two different components, in which case, the spring constrains the way the components are placed relative to one another, or they may belong to the same component, in which case, the spring constrains the width or height of the component.

We don't cover SpringLayout here, but you can read about it in O'Reilly's *Java Swing*.

## CHAPTER 20

Drawing with the 2D API

In previous chapters, we looked at the components and component architecture of graphical user interfaces (GUIs) using Java's Swing and AWT packages. Now, we're going to drop down a level and look at the procedural APIs for rendering graphics in Java applications. These APIs are used by components to paint themselves on the screen and to display icons and graphics. This chapter goes into some detail about Java's sophisticated 2D, resolution-independent drawing API and the core tools for loading and displaying images. In the next chapter, we'll explore dynamic image-processing tools in more detail and look at the classes that let you generate and modify image data, pixel by pixel.

The Big Picture

The classes you'll use for drawing come from six packages: java.awt, java.awt.color, java.awt.font, java.awt.geom, java.awt.image, and java.awt.print. Collectively, these classes make up most of the 2D API and cover the drawing of shapes, text, and images. Figure 20-1 shows a bird's-eye view of these classes. There's much more in the 2D API than we can cover in two chapters. For a full treatment, see Jonathan Knudsen's *Java 2D Graphics* (O'Reilly).

An instance of java.awt.Graphics2D is called a *graphics context*. It represents a drawing surface such as a component's display area, a page on a printer, or an offscreen image buffer. A graphics context provides methods for drawing three kinds of graphics objects: shapes, text, and images. Graphics2D is called a graphics context because it also holds contextual information about the drawing area. This information includes the drawing area's clipping region, painting color, transfer mode, text font, and geometric transformation. If you consider the drawing area to be a painter's canvas, you might think of a graphics context as an easel that holds a set of tools and marks off the work area.

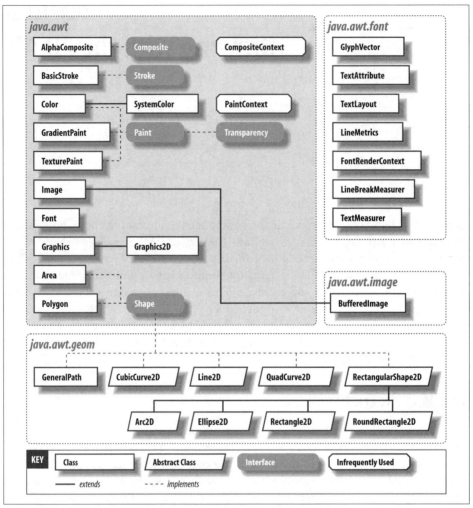

Figure 20-1. Graphics classes of the 2D API

There are four ways to acquire a Graphics2D object. The following list describes them in order from the most common to the least:

From AWT or Swing as the result of a painting request on a component
   In this case, a new graphics context for the appropriate area is created and passed to your component's paint( ) or update( ) method. (The update( ) method really applies only to AWT components, not the newer Swing components.)

Directly from an offscreen image buffer
   In this case, we ask the image buffer for a graphics context directly. We'll use this when we discuss techniques such as double buffering.

By copying an existing Graphics2D object

Duplicating a graphics object can be useful for more elaborate drawing operations; different copies of a Graphics2D object can draw on same area, but with different attributes and clipping regions. A Graphics2D object can be copied by calling the create() method.

Directly from an onscreen component

It's possible to ask a component to give you a Graphics2D object for its display area. However, this is almost always a mistake; if you feel tempted to do this, think about why you're trying to circumvent the normal paint()/repaint() mechanism.

Each time a component's paint() method is called, the windowing system provides the component with a new Graphics2D object for drawing in the display area. This means that attributes set during one painting session, such as the drawing color or clipping region, are reset the next time paint() is called. (Each call to paint() starts with a tidy new easel.) For the most common attributes, such as foreground color, background color, and font, we can set defaults in the component itself. Thereafter, the graphics contexts for painting in that component come with those properties initialized appropriately.

The paint() method can make no assumptions about what is already drawn on the screen. It is responsible for rendering its entire work area. Higher-level APIs are normally responsible for buffering output and limiting the number of times paint() is invoked for a component. AWT components may use an additional method called update(), which allows them to update their appearance under the assumption that their previous artwork is still on the screen. However, this method is not used by Swing components.

For backward compatibility, a graphics context is always passed to the paint() method as an object of type Graphics. If you want to take advantage of the nifty features in the 2D API (as you almost undoubtedly will), you need to cast this reference to a Graphics2D object. You'll see how this works in the upcoming examples.

The Rendering Pipeline

One of the strengths of the 2D API is that shapes, text, and images are manipulated in many of the same ways. In this section, we'll describe what happens to shapes, text, and images after you give them to a Graphics2D object. *Rendering* is the process of taking some collection of shapes, text, and images and figuring out how to represent them by coloring pixels on a screen or printer. Graphics2D supports four rendering operations:

- Draw a shape's outline with the draw() method.
- Fill a shape's interior with the fill() method.

- Draw some text with the `drawString()` method.
- Draw an image with any of the many forms of the `drawImage()` method.

The graphics context represented by a `Graphics2D` object holds the following properties, whose values are controlled by corresponding accessor methods (e.g., `getFont()` and `setFont()`):

paint

The current *paint* (an object of type `java.awt.Paint`) determines what color or pattern will be used to fill a shape. This affects the drawing of shape outlines and text, as well. You can change the current paint using `Graphics2D`'s `setPaint()` method. Note that the `Color` class implements the `Paint` interface, so you can pass `Colors` to `setPaint()` if you want to use solid colors.

stroke

`Graphics2D` uses the *stroke* to determine how to draw the outline of shapes that are passed to its `draw()` method. In graphics terminology, to "stroke" a shape means to take a path defined by the shape and effectively trace it with a pen or brush of a certain size and characteristics. For example, drawing the shape of a circle using a stroke that acts like a solid line would yield a washer or ring shape. The `stroke` object in the Graphics2D API is a little more abstract than that. In actuality it accepts the input shape to be stroked and returns an enclosed shape representing the outline, which `Graphics2D` then fills. You can set the current stroke using `setStroke()`. The 2D API comes with a handy class, `java.awt.BasicStroke`, that implements different line widths, end styles, join styles, and dashing.

font

Text is rendered by creating a shape that represents the characters to be drawn. The current *font* determines what shapes are created for a given set of characters. The resulting text shape is then filled. The current font is set using `setFont()`. The 2D API gives applications access to all the TrueType and PostScript Type 1 fonts that are installed.

transformation

Shapes, text, and images can be geometrically *transformed* before they are rendered. This means that they may be moved, rotated, and stretched. `Graphics2D`'s transformation converts coordinates from "user space" to "device space." By default, `Graphics2D` uses a transformation that maps 72 units in user space to one inch on the output device. If you draw a line from point 0, 0 to point 72, 0 using the default transformation, it will be one inch long, regardless of whether it is drawn on your monitor or your printer. The current transformation can be modified using the `translate()`, `rotate()`, `scale()`, and `shear()` methods.

compositing rule

A *compositing rule* determines how the colors of a new drawing operation are combined with existing colors on the `Graphics2D`'s drawing surface. This attribute is set using `setComposite()`, which accepts an instance of `java.awt.AlphaComposite`.

Compositing allows you to make parts of a drawing or image completely or partially transparent, or to combine them in other interesting ways.

clipping shape

All rendering operations are limited to the interior of the *clipping shape*. No pixels outside this shape are modified. By default, the clipping shape allows rendering on the entire drawing surface (usually, the rectangular area of a Component). However, you can further limit this using any simple or complex shape (for example, text shapes).

rendering hints

There are different techniques that can be used to render graphics primitives. Usually these represent a tradeoff between rendering speed and visual quality or vice versa. Rendering hints (constants defined in the RenderingHints class) specify which techniques to use.

Graphics primitives (shapes, text, and images) pass through the rendering engine in a series of operations called the *rendering pipeline*. Let's walk through the pipeline. It can be reduced to four steps; the first step depends on the rendering operation:

1. Transform the shape. For shapes that will be filled, the shape is simply transformed using the Graphics2D's current transformation. For shapes whose outlines are drawn using draw( ), the current stroke is used to stroke the shape's outline. Then the stroked outline is transformed like any other filled shape. Text is displayed by mapping characters to shapes using the current font. The resulting text shapes are transformed like any other filled shape. Images are also transformed using the current transformation.

2. Determine the colors to be used. For a filled shape, the current *paint* object determines what colors should be used to fill the shape. For drawing an image, the colors are taken from the image itself.

3. Combine the colors with the existing drawing surface using the current *compositing rule*.

4. Clip the results using the current *clipping shape*.

The *rendering hints* are used throughout to control the rendering quality.

A Quick Tour of Java 2D

Next we'll embark on a quick tour of Java 2D, including working with shapes and text. We'll finish with an example of Java 2D in action.

Filling Shapes

The simplest path through the rendering pipeline is filling shapes. For example, the following code creates an ellipse and fills it with a solid color. (This code would live inside a paint( ) method somewhere. We'll present a complete, ready-to-run example a little later.)

```
Shape c = new Ellipse2D.Float(50, 25, 150, 150); // x,y,width,height
g2.setPaint(Color.blue);
g2.fill(c);
```

Here, g2 is our Graphics2D object. The Ellipse2D shape class is abstract but is implemented by concrete inner subclasses called Float and Double that work with float or double precision, respectively. The Rectangle2D class, similarly, has concrete subclasses Rectangle2D.Float and Rectangle2D.Double.

In the call to setPaint( ), we tell Graphics2D to use a solid color, blue, for all subsequent filling operations. Next, the call to fill( ) tells Graphics2D to fill the given shape.

All geometric shapes in the 2D API are represented by implementations of the java.awt.geom.Shape interface. This interface defines methods that are common to all shapes, like returning a rectangle bounding box or testing if a point is inside the shape. The java.awt.geom package is a smorgasbord of useful shape classes, including Rectangle2D, RoundRectangle2D (a rectangle with rounded corners), Arc2D, Ellipse2D, and others. In addition, a few more basic classes in java.awt are Shapes: Rectangle, Polygon, and Area.

Drawing Shape Outlines

Drawing a shape's outline is only a little bit more complicated. Consider the following example:

```
Shape r = new Rectangle2D.Float(100, 75, 100, 100);
g2.setStroke(new BasicStroke(4));
g2.setPaint(Color.yellow);
g2.draw(r);
```

Here, we tell Graphics2D to use a stroke that is four units wide and a solid color, yellow, for filling the stroke. When we call draw( ), Graphics2D uses the stroke to create a new shape, the outline, from the given rectangle. The outline shape is then filled, just as before; this effectively draws the rectangle's outline. The rectangle itself is not filled.

Convenience Methods

Graphics2D includes quite a few convenience methods for drawing and filling common shapes; these methods are actually inherited from the Graphics class. Table 20-1 summarizes these methods. It's a little easier to call fillRect( ) rather than instantiating a rectangle shape and passing it to fill( ).

Table 20-1. Shape-drawing methods in the graphics class

Method	Description
draw3DRect( )	Draws a highlighted, 3D rectangle
drawArc( )	Draws an arc
drawLine( )	Draws a line
drawOval( )	Draws an oval
drawPolygon( )	Draws a polygon, closing it by connecting the endpoints
drawPolyline( )	Draws a line connecting a series of points, without closing it
drawRect( )	Draws a rectangle
DrawRoundRect( )	Draws a rounded-corner rectangle
fill3DRect( )	Draws a filled, highlighted, 3D rectangle
fillArc( )	Draws a filled arc
fillOval( )	Draws a filled oval
fillPolygon( )	Draws a filled polygon
fillRect( )	Draws a filled rectangle
FillRoundRect( )	Draws a filled, rounded-corner rectangle

As you can see, for each of the fill( ) methods in the table, there is a corresponding draw( ) method that renders the shape as an unfilled line drawing. With the exception of fillArc( ) and fillPolygon( ), each method takes a simple x, y specification for the top-left corner of the shape and a width and height for its size.

The most flexible convenience method draws a polygon, which is specified by two arrays that contain the x and y coordinates of the vertices. Methods in the Graphics class take two such arrays and draw the polygon's outline or fill the polygon.

The methods listed in Table 20-1 are shortcuts for more general methods in Graphics2D. The more general procedure is to first create a java.awt.geom.Shape object and then pass it to the draw( ) or fill( ) method of Graphics2D. For example, you could create a Polygon object from coordinate arrays. Since a Polygon implements the Shape interface, you can pass it to Graphics2D's general draw( ) or fill( ) method.

The fillArc( ) method requires six integer arguments. The first four specify the bounding box for an oval—just like the fillOval( ) method. The final two arguments specify what portion of the oval we want to draw, as a starting angular position and an offset, both of which are specified in degrees. The zero-degree mark is at three o'clock; a positive angle is clockwise. For example, to draw the right half of a circle, you might call:

```
g.fillArc(0, 0, radius * 2, radius * 2, -90, 180);
```

draw3DRect( ) automatically chooses shading colors by "darkening" the current color. So you should set the color to something other than black, which is the default (maybe gray or white); if you don't, you'll just get a black rectangle with a thick outline.

Drawing Text

Like drawing a shape's outline, drawing text is just a simple variation on filling a shape. When you ask Graphics2D to draw text, it determines the shapes that need to be drawn and fills them. The shapes that represent characters are called *glyphs*. A font is a collection of glyphs. Here's an example of drawing text:

```
g2.setFont(new Font("Times New Roman", Font.PLAIN, 64));
g2.setPaint(Color.red);
g2.drawString("Hello, 2D!", 50, 150);
```

When we call drawString( ), Graphics2D uses the current font to retrieve the glyphs that correspond to the characters in the string. Then the glyphs (which are really just Shapes) are filled using the current Paint.

Drawing Images

Images are treated a little differently than shapes. In particular, the current Paint is not used to render an image because the image contains its own color information for each pixel (it *is* the paint, effectively). The following example loads an image from a file and displays it:

```
Image i = Toolkit.getDefaultToolkit( ).getImage("camel.gif");
g2.drawImage(i, 75, 50, this);
```

In this case, the call to drawImage( ) tells Graphics2D to place the image at the given location. We'll explain the fourth argument, used for monitoring image loading, later.

Transformations and rendering

Four parts of the pipeline affect every graphics operation. In particular, all rendering is subject to being transformed, composited, and clipped. Rendering hints are used to affect all of Graphics2D's rendering.

This example shows how to modify the current transformation with a translation and a rotation:

```
g2.translate(50, 0);
g2.rotate(Math.PI / 6);
```

Every graphics primitive drawn by g2 will now have this transformation applied to it (a shift of 50 units right and a rotation of 30 degrees counterclockwise). We can have a similarly global effect on compositing:

```
AlphaComposite ac = AlphaComposite.getInstance(
    AlphaComposite.SRC_OVER, (float).5);
g2.setComposite(ac);
```

Now, every graphics primitive we draw will be half transparent; we'll explain more about this later.

All drawing operations are clipped by the current clipping shape, which is any object implementing the Shape interface. In the following example, the clipping shape is set to an ellipse:

```
Shape e = new Ellipse2D.Float(50, 25, 250, 150);
g2.clip(e);
```

You can obtain the current clipping shape using getClip( ); this is handy if you want to restore it later using the setClip( ) method.

Finally, the rendering hints influence all drawing operations. In the following example, we tell Graphics2D to use anti-aliasing, a technique that smoothes out the rough pixel edges of shapes and text:

```
g2.setRenderingHint(RenderingHints.KEY_ANTIALIASING,
    RenderingHints.VALUE_ANTIALIAS_ON);
```

The RenderingHints class contains other keys and values representing other rendering hints. If you really like to fiddle with knobs and dials, this is a good class to check out.

The Whole Iguana

Let's put everything together now, just to show how graphics primitives travel through the rendering pipeline. The following example demonstrates the use of Graphics2D from the beginning to the end of the rendering pipeline. With very few lines of code, we are able to draw some pretty complicated stuff (see Figure 20-2).

Here's the code:

```
//file: Iguana.java
import java.awt.*;
import java.awt.event.*;
import java.awt.geom.*;
import javax.swing.*;

public class Iguana extends JComponent {
  private Image image;
  private int theta;
```

Figure 20-2. Exercising the 2D API

```
public Iguana( ) {
  image = Toolkit.getDefaultToolkit( ).getImage(
      "Piazza di Spagna.small.jpg");
  theta = 0;
  addMouseListener(new MouseAdapter( ) {
    public void mousePressed(MouseEvent me) {
      theta = (theta + 15) % 360;
      repaint( );
    }
  });
}

public void paint(Graphics g) {
  Graphics2D g2 = (Graphics2D)g;

  g2.setRenderingHint(RenderingHints.KEY_ANTIALIASING,
      RenderingHints.VALUE_ANTIALIAS_ON);

  int cx = getSize( ).width / 2;
  int cy = getSize( ).height / 2;

  g2.translate(cx, cy);
  g2.rotate(theta * Math.PI / 180);

  Shape oldClip = g2.getClip( );
  Shape e = new Ellipse2D.Float(-cx, -cy, cx * 2, cy * 2);
  g2.clip(e);

  Shape c = new Ellipse2D.Float(-cx, -cy, cx * 3 / 4, cy * 2);
  g2.setPaint(new GradientPaint(40, 40, Color.blue,
      60, 50, Color.white, true));
  g2.fill(c);
```

```
    g2.setPaint(Color.yellow);
    g2.fillOval(cx / 4, 0, cx, cy);

    g2.setClip(oldClip);

    g2.setFont(new Font("Times New Roman", Font.PLAIN, 64));
    g2.setPaint(new GradientPaint(-cx, 0, Color.red,
        cx, 0, Color.black, false));
    g2.drawString("Hello, 2D!", -cx * 3 / 4, cy / 4);

    AlphaComposite ac = AlphaComposite.getInstance(
        AlphaComposite.SRC_OVER, (float).75);
    g2.setComposite(ac);

    Shape r = new RoundRectangle2D.Float(0, -cy * 3 / 4,
        cx * 3 / 4, cy * 3 / 4, 20, 20);
    g2.setStroke(new BasicStroke(4));
    g2.setPaint(Color.magenta);
    g2.fill(r);
    g2.setPaint(Color.green);
    g2.draw(r);

    g2.drawImage(image, -cx / 2, -cy / 2, this);
  }

  public static void main(String[] args) {
    JFrame frame = new JFrame("Iguana");
    Container c = frame.getContentPane();
    c.setLayout(new BorderLayout());
    c.add(new Iguana(), BorderLayout.CENTER);
    frame.setSize(300, 300);
    frame.setDefaultCloseOperation( JFrame.EXIT_ON_CLOSE );
    frame.setVisible(true);
  }
}
```

The Iguana class is a subclass of JComponent with a very fancy paint( ) method. The main( ) method takes care of creating a JFrame that holds the Iguana component.

Iguana's constructor loads a small image (we'll talk more about this later) and sets up a mouse event handler. This handler changes a member variable, theta, and repaints the component. Each time you click, the entire drawing is rotated by 15 degrees.

Iguana's paint( ) method does some pretty interesting stuff, but none of it is very difficult. First, user space is transformed so that the origin is at the center of the component. The user space is then rotated by theta:

```
    g2.translate(cx, cy);
    g2.rotate(theta * Math.PI / 180);
```

Iguana saves the current (default) clipping shape before setting it to a large ellipse. Then, Iguana draws two filled ellipses. The first is drawn by instantiating an Ellipse2D and filling it; the second is drawn using the fillOval( ) convenience method. (We'll talk about the color gradient in the first ellipse in the next section.) As you can see in Figure 20-2, both ellipses are clipped by the elliptical clipping shape. After filling the two ellipses, Iguana restores the old clipping shape.

Next, Iguana draws some text next (see the section "Using Fonts" later in this chapter). The next action is to modify the compositing rule as follows:

```
AlphaComposite ac = AlphaComposite.getInstance(
    AlphaComposite.SRC_OVER, (float).75);
g2.setComposite(ac);
```

All this means is that we want everything to be drawn with transparency. The AlphaComposite class defines constants representing different compositing rules, much the way the Color class contains constants representing different predefined colors. In this case, we're asking for the *source over destination* rule (SRC_OVER), but with an additional alpha multiplier of 0.75. Source over destination means that whatever we're drawing (the source) should be placed on top of whatever's already there (the destination). The alpha multiplier means that everything we draw will be treated at 0.75, or three quarters, of its normal opacity, allowing the existing drawing to "show through."

You can see the effect of the new compositing rule in the rounded rectangle and the image, which both allow previously drawn elements to show through.

Filling Shapes

Iguana fills its shapes with a number of colors, using the setPaint() method of Graphics2D. This method sets the current color in the graphics context, so we set it to a different color before each drawing operation. setPaint() accepts any object that implements the Paint interface. The 2D API includes three implementations of this interface, representing solid colors, color gradients, and textures.

Solid Colors

The java.awt.Color class represents color in Java. A Color object describes a single color and implements the Paint interface for filling an area with it. You can create an arbitrary Color by specifying the red, green, and blue values, either as integers between 0 and 255 or as floating-point values between 0.0 and 1.0. The (somewhat strange) getColor() method can be used to look up a named color in the system properties table, as described in Chapter 11.

The Color class also defines a number of static final color values; these are what we used in the Iguana example. These constants, such as Color.black and Color.red, provide a convenient set of basic color objects for your drawings.

Color Gradients

A *color gradient* is a smooth blend from one color to another. The GradientPaint class encapsulates this idea in a handy implementation of the Paint interface. All you need to do is specify two points and the color at each point. GradientPaint takes care of the details so that the color fades smoothly from one point to the other. In the previous example, the ellipse is filled with a gradient this way:

```
g2.setPaint(new GradientPaint(40, 40, Color.blue,
    60, 50, Color.white, true));
```

The last parameter in GradientPaint's constructor determines whether the gradient is *cyclic*. In a cyclic gradient, the colors keep fluctuating beyond the two points that you've specified. Otherwise, the gradient just draws a single blend from one point to the other. Beyond each endpoint, the color is solid.

Textures

A *texture* is simply an image repeated over and over like a floor tile. This concept is represented in the 2D API with the TexturePaint class. To create a texture, just specify the image to be used and the rectangle that will be used to reproduce it. To do this, you also need to know how to create and use images, which we'll get to a little later.

Desktop Colors

The Color class makes it easy to construct a particular color; however, that's not always what you want to do. Sometimes you want to match a preexisting color scheme. This is particularly important when you are designing a user interface; you might want your components to have the same colors as other components on that platform and to change automatically if the user redefines his or her color scheme.

That's what the SystemColor class is for. A system color represents the color used by the local windowing system in a certain context. The SystemColor class holds lots of predefined system colors, just like the Color class holds some predefined basic colors. For example, the field activeCaption represents the color used for the background of the titlebar of an active window; activeCaptionText represents the color used for the title itself. menu represents the background color of menu selections; menuText represents the color of a menu item's text when it is not selected; textHighlightText is the color used when the menu item is selected; and so on. You could use the window value to set the color of a Window to match the other windows on the user's screen—whether or not they're generated by Java programs.

```
myWindow.setBackground( SystemColor.window );
```

Because the SystemColor class is a subclass of Color, you can use it wherever you would use a Color. However, the SystemColor constants are tricky. They are constant, immutable objects as far as you, the programmer, are concerned (your code is not allowed to modify them), but they can be modified at runtime by the system. If the user changes his color scheme, the system colors are automatically updated to follow suit; as a result, anything displayed with system colors will automatically change color the next time it is redrawn. For example, the window myWindow would automatically change its background color to the new background color.

The SystemColor class has one noticeable shortcoming. You can't compare a system color to a Color directly; the Color.equals( ) method doesn't return reliable results. For example, if you want to find out whether the window background color is red, you can't call:

```
Color.red.equals(SystemColor.window);
```

Instead, you should use getRGB( ) to find the color components of both objects and compare them, rather than comparing the objects themselves.

Stroking Shape Outlines

Just as a Graphics2D object's current paint determines how its shapes are filled, its current stoke determines how its shapes are outlined. The current stroke determines such drawing features as line thickness, line dashing, and end styles. In the old days, lines were one pixel wide and that was that. With Java 2D, line thickness can be set with floating-point accuracy and the results, like everything else, are subject to the rendering pipeline's transformations and scaling.

To set the current stroke in Graphics2D, call setStroke( ) with any implementation of the Stroke interface. Fortunately, the 2D API includes a BasicStroke class that probably does everything you need. Using BasicStroke, you can create dashed lines, control what decoration is added to line ends, and decide how the corners in an outline should be drawn.

By default, Graphics2D uses a solid stroke with a width of 1. In the previous Iguana example, the line width is changed just before the outline of the rounded rectangle is drawn, like so:

```
g2.setStroke(new BasicStroke(4));
```

Using Fonts

Text fonts in Java are represented by instances of the java.awt.Font class. A Font object is constructed from a name, style identifier, and a point size. We can create a Font object at any time, but it's meaningful only when applied to a particular component on a given display device. Here are a couple of fonts:

```
Font smallFont = new Font("Monospaced", Font.PLAIN, 10);
Font bigFont = new Font("Serif", Font.BOLD, 18);
```

Font names come in three varieties: *family* names, *face* names (also called font names), and *logical* names. Family and font names are closely related. For example, Garamond Italic is a font name for a font whose family name is Garamond.

A *logical name* is a generic name for the font family. The following logical font names should be available on all platforms:

- Serif (generic name for TimesRoman)
- SansSerif (generic name for Helvetica)
- Monospaced (generic name for Courier)
- Dialog
- DialogInput

The logical font name is mapped to an actual font on the local platform. Java's *fonts. properties* file maps the font names to the available fonts, covering as much of the Unicode character set as possible. If you request a font that doesn't exist, you get the default font.

One of the big wins in the 2D API is that it can use most of the fonts you have installed on your computer. The following program prints out a full list of the fonts that are available to the 2D API:

```java
//file: ShowFonts.java
import java.awt.*;

public class ShowFonts {
  public static void main(String[] args) {
    Font[] fonts;
    fonts =
     GraphicsEnvironment.getLocalGraphicsEnvironment().getAllFonts();
    for (int i = 0; i < fonts.length; i++) {
      System.out.print(fonts[i].getFontName() + " : ");
      System.out.print(fonts[i].getFamily() + " : ");
      System.out.print(fonts[i].getName());
      System.out.println();
    }
  }
}
```

Note, however, that the fonts installed on your system may not match the fonts installed on someone else's system. For true portability, you can use one of the logical names (although your application won't look exactly the same on all platforms) or go with the defaults. You can also allow your users to configure the application by choosing fonts themselves.

The static method Font.getFont() looks up a font by name in the system properties list just like Color.getColor(). And as with Color.getColor(), this is interesting but useless. Normally, you'll either choose a Font from one that is available in the environment (as in the ShowFonts example) or use identifiers to describe the font you want in the Font constructor.

The Font class defines three static style identifiers: PLAIN, BOLD, and ITALIC. You can use these values on all fonts. The point size determines the size of the font on a display. If a given point size isn't available, Font substitutes a default size.

You can retrieve information about an existing Font with a number of routines. The getName( ), getSize( ), and getStyle( ) methods retrieve the logical name, point size, and style, respectively. You can use the getFamily( ) method to find out the family name while getFontName( ) returns the face name of the font.

Finally, to actually use a Font object, you can simply specify it as an argument to the setFont( ) method of a Component or Graphics2D object. Subsequent text-drawing commands such as drawString( ) for that component or in that graphics context use the specified font.

Font Metrics

To get detailed size and spacing information for text rendered in a font, we can ask for a java.awt.font.LineMetrics object. Different systems have different real fonts available; the available fonts may not match the font you request. Furthermore, the measurements of different characters within a single font may be different, especially in multilingual text. Thus, a LineMetrics object presents information about a particular set of text in a particular font on a particular system, not general information about a font. For example, if you ask for the metrics of a nine-point Monospaced font, what you get isn't some abstract truth about Monospaced fonts; you get the metrics of the font that the particular system uses for nine-point Monospaced—which may not be exactly nine points or even fixed width.

Use the getLineMetrics( ) method for a Font to retrieve the metrics for text as it would appear for that component. This method also needs to know some information about how you plan to render the text—if you're planning to use anti-aliasing, for instance, which affects the text measurements. This extra information is encapsulated in the FontRenderContext class. Fortunately, you can just ask Graphics2D for its current FontRenderContext rather than having to create one yourself:

```
public void paint(Graphics g) {
    Graphics2D g2 = (Graphics2D)g;
    ...
    FontRenderContext frc = g2.getFontRenderContext( );
    LineMetrics metrics = font.getLineMetrics("Monkey", frc);
    ...
}
```

The Font class also has a getStringBounds( ) method that returns the bounding box of a piece of text:

```
public void paint(Graphics g) {
    Graphics2D g2 = (Graphics2D)g;
```

```
    ...
    FontRenderContext frc = g2.getFontRenderContext( );
    float messageWidth =
        (float)font.getStringBounds("Monkey", frc).getWidth( );
    ...
}
```

The following application, FontShow, displays a word and draws reference lines showing certain characteristics of its font, as shown in Figure 20-3. Clicking in the application window toggles the point size between a small and a large value.

```
//file: FontShow.java
import java.awt.*;
import java.awt.event.*;
import java.awt.font.*;
import javax.swing.*;

public class FontShow extends JComponent
{
  private static final int PAD = 25;    // frilly line padding
  private boolean bigFont = true;
  private String message;

  public FontShow(String message) {
    this.message = message;
    addMouseListener(new MouseAdapter( ) {
      public void mouseClicked(MouseEvent e) {
        bigFont = !bigFont;
        repaint( );
      }
    });
  }

  public void paint(Graphics g)
  {
    Graphics2D g2 = (Graphics2D)g;

    g2.setRenderingHint(RenderingHints.KEY_ANTIALIASING,
        RenderingHints.VALUE_ANTIALIAS_ON);

    int size = bigFont ? 96 : 64;
    Font font = new Font("Dialog", Font.PLAIN, size);
    g2.setFont(font);
    int width = getSize( ).width;
    int height = getSize( ).height;

    FontRenderContext frc = g2.getFontRenderContext( );
    LineMetrics metrics = font.getLineMetrics(message, frc);
    float messageWidth =
        (float)font.getStringBounds(message, frc).getWidth( );

    // center text
    float ascent = metrics.getAscent( );
    float descent = metrics.getDescent( );
```

```
    float x = (width - messageWidth) / 2;
    float y = (height + metrics.getHeight()) / 2 - descent;

    g2.setPaint(getBackground());
    g2.fillRect(0, 0, width, height);

    g2.setPaint(getForeground());
    g2.drawString(message, x, y);

    g2.setPaint(Color.white);   // Base lines
    drawLine(g2, x - PAD, y, x + messageWidth + PAD, y);
    drawLine(g2, x, y + PAD, x, y - ascent - PAD);
    g2.setPaint(Color.green);   // Ascent line
    drawLine(g2, x - PAD, y - ascent,
            x + messageWidth + PAD, y - ascent);
    g2.setPaint(Color.red);      // Descent line
    drawLine(g2, x - PAD, y + descent,
            x + messageWidth + PAD, y + descent);
  }

  private void drawLine(Graphics2D g2,
      double x0, double y0, double x1, double y1) {
    Shape line = new java.awt.geom.Line2D.Double(x0, y0, x1, y1);
    g2.draw(line);
  }

  public static void main(String args[]) {
    String message = "Lemming";
    if (args.length > 0) message = args[0];

    JFrame frame = new JFrame("FontShow");
    frame.setSize(420, 300);
    frame.setDefaultCloseOperation( JFrame.EXIT_ON_CLOSE );
    frame.getContentPane().add(new FontShow(message));
    frame.setVisible(true);
  }
}
```

You can specify the text to be displayed as a command-line argument:

```
% java FontShow "When in the course of human events ..."
```

FontShow may look a bit complicated, but there's really not much to it. The bulk of the code is in paint(), which sets the font, draws the text, and adds a few lines to illustrate some of the font's characteristics (metrics). For fun, we also catch mouse clicks (using an event handler defined in the constructor) and alternate the font size by setting the bigFont toggle variable and repainting.

By default, text is rendered above and to the right of the coordinates specified in the drawString() method. Think of that starting point as the origin of a coordinate system; the axes are the *baselines* of the font. FontShow draws these lines in white. The greatest height the characters stretch above the baseline is called the *ascent* and is shown by a green line. Some fonts also have parts of letters that fall below the baseline.

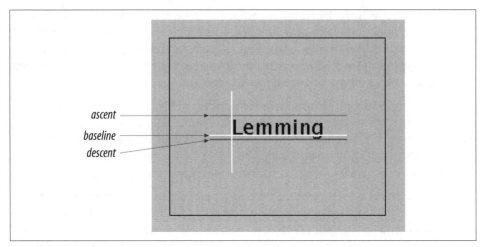

Figure 20-3. The FontShow application

The farthest distance any character reaches below the baseline is called the *descent*, which is illustrated with a red line.

We ask for the ascent and descent of our font with the LineMetrics class's getAscent( ) and getDescent( ) methods. We also ask for the width of our string (when rendered in this font) with Font's getStringBounds( ) method. This information is used to center the word in the display area. To center the word vertically, we use the height and adjust with the descent to calculate the baseline location. Table 20-2 provides a short list of methods that return useful font metrics.

Table 20-2. LineMetrics methods

Method	Description
getAscent( )	Height above baseline
getDescent( )	Depth below baseline
getLeading( )	Standard vertical spacing between lines
getHeight( )	Total line height (ascent + descent + leading)

Leading space is the padding between lines of text. The getHeight( ) method reports the total height of a line of text, including the leading space.

Displaying Images

So far, we've worked with methods for drawing simple shapes and displaying text. For more complex graphics, we'll be working with images. In a typical Swing application, the simplest way to display an image in your application is to use an ImageIcon with a JLabel component. Here, we are talking about working with image data at a lower level, for painting. The 2D API has a powerful set of tools for generating and displaying image data. We'll start with the basics of the java.awt.Image class and see how to load an image into an application and draw it where you want it. The Java AWT toolkit will handle most of the details for us. In the next chapter, we'll go further to discuss how to manage image loading manually as well as how to create and manipulate raw pixel data, allowing you to create any kind of graphics you can dream up.

The core AWT supports images encoded in JPEG, PNG, and GIF. (This includes GIF89a animations so that you can work with simple animations as easily as static images.) If you need to work with other types of images, you can turn to the Java Advanced Imaging javax.imageio framework. We'll mention it briefly here and again in the next chapter when we discuss the BufferedImage class.

The ImageIO framework is bundled with Java 1.4 and later. In many ways, it supercedes and replaces the image handling functionality of the core AWT just as Swing extends and replaces the old AWT components. The ImageIO framework is easily extensible for new image types through plug-ins. However, out of the box, all that it adds is the ability to read bitmap (BMP) and wireless bitmap (WBMP) images. Since most Java code can and does use the original AWT functionality, that is what we'll focus on.

The Image Class

The java.awt.Image class represents a view of an image. The view is created from an image source that produces pixel data. Images can be from a static source, such as a JPEG file, or a dynamic one, such as a video stream or a graphics engine.

AWT Images are created with the getImage( ) and createImage( ) methods of the java.awt.Toolkit class. There are two forms of each method, which accept a URL or plain filename, respectively. createImage( ) can also accept a byte array of image data directly.

When bundling images with your application, you should use the Class class's getResource( ) method (discussed in Chapter 1) to construct a URL reference to the file from the application classpath. getResource( ) allows you to bundle images along with your application, inside JAR files or anywhere else in the classpath. The following code fragment shows some examples of loading images with the getImage( ) method:

```
Toolkit toolkit = Toolkit.getDefaultToolkit( );

// Application resource URL - Best method
URL daffyURL = getClass( ).getResource("/cartoons/images/daffy.gif");
Image daffyDuckImage = toolkit.getImage( daffyURL );

// Absolute URL -
URL monaURL = new URL( "http://myserver/images/mona_lisa.png");
Image monaImage = toolkit.getImage( monaURL );
```

```
// Local file -
Image elvisImage = toolkit.getImage("c:/elvis/lateryears/fatelvis1.jpg" );
```

The createImage( ) method looks just like getImage( ); the difference is that getImage( ) "interns" images and shares them when it receives multiple requests for the same data. The createImage( ) method does not do this (it creates a new Image object every time) and relies on you to cache and share the image. getImage( ) is convenient in an application that uses a limited number of images for the life of the application, but it may not ever release the image data. You should use createImage( ) and cache the Image objects yourself when it's an issue.

The javax.imageio.ImageIO class, similarly, provides several static read( ) methods that can load images from a File, URL, or InputStream:

```
URL daffyURL = getClass( ).getResource("/cartoons/images/daffy.gif");
Image daffyDuckImage = ImageIO.read( daffyURL );
```

We'll discuss image loading with AWT and the ImageIO framework in more detail in Chapter 1.

Once we have an Image object, we can draw it into a graphics context with the drawImage( ) method of the Graphics class. The simplest form of the drawImage( ) method takes four parameters: the Image object, the x, y coordinates at which to draw it, and a reference to a special *image observer* object. We'll show an example involving drawImage( ) soon, but first, let's say a word about image observers.

Image Observers

Images are processed asynchronously, which means that Java performs image operations, such as loading and scaling in the background (allowing the user code to continue). In a typical client application, this might not be important; images may be small for things like buttons, and are probably bundled with the application for almost instant retrieval. However, Java was designed to work with image data over the Web as well as locally, and you will see this expressed in the APIs for working with image data.

For example, the getImage( ) method always returns immediately, even if the image data has to be retrieved over the network from Mars and isn't available yet. In fact, if it's a new image, Java won't even begin to fetch the data until we try to display or manipulate it. The advantage of this technique is that Java can do the work of a powerful, multithreaded image-processing environment for us. However, it also introduces several problems. If Java is loading an image for us, how do we know when it's completely loaded? What if we want to work with the image as it arrives? What if we need to know properties of the image (like its dimensions) before we can start working with it? What if there's an error in loading the image?

These issues are handled by *image observers*, objects that implement the ImageObserver interface. All operations that draw or examine Image objects are asynchronous and take an image observer object as a parameter. The `ImageObserver` monitors the image operation's status and can make that information available to the rest of the application. When image data is loaded from its source by the graphics system, your image observer is notified of its progress, including when new pixels are available, when a complete frame of the image is ready, and if there is an error during loading. The image observer also receives attribute information about the image, such as its dimensions and properties, as soon as they are known.

The `drawImage( )` method, like other image operations, takes a reference to an `ImageObserver` object as a parameter. `drawImage( )` returns a boolean value specifying whether or not the image was painted in its entirety. If the image data has not yet been loaded or is only partially available, `drawImage( )` paints whatever fraction of the image it can and returns. In the background, the graphics system starts (or continues) loading the image data. The image observer object is registered as interested in information about the image. The observer is then called repeatedly as more pixel information is available and again when the entire image is complete. The image observer can do whatever it wants with this information. Most often the information is used to call `repaint( )` to prompt the application to draw the image again with the updated data. In this way, an application or applet can draw the image as it arrives for a progressive loading effect. Alternatively, it could wait until the entire image is loaded before displaying it.

Image observers are covered in Chapter 21. For now, let's avoid the issue by using a prefabricated image observer. The `Component` class implements the `ImageObserver` interface and provides some simple repainting behavior, which means every component can serve as its own default image observer. We can simply pass a reference to whatever component is doing the painting as the image observer parameter of a `drawImage( )` call:

```
public void paint( Graphics g ) {
    g.drawImage( monaImage, x, y, this );
    ...
```

Our component serves as the image observer and calls `repaint( )` for us to redraw the image as necessary. If the image arrives slowly, our component is notified repeatedly as new chunks become available. As a result, the image appears gradually, as it's loaded.*

---

* The `awt.image.incrementaldraw` and `awt.image.redrawrate` system properties control this behavior. `redrawrate` limits how often `repaint( )` is called; the default value is every 100 milliseconds. `incrementaldraw`'s default value, true, enables this behavior. Setting it to `false` delays drawing until the entire image has arrived.

Preloading images

We'll discuss image loading in more detail in the next chapter when we look at MediaTracker, which is a utility for monitoring the load progress of one or more images. However, we'll skip ahead a bit here and show you the easy shortcut for loading a single image and making sure it's complete and ready to draw. You can use the javax.swing.ImageIcon class to do the dirty work for you:

```
ImageIcon icon = new ImageIcon("myimage.jpg");
Image image = icon.getImage();
```

Images loaded by the ImageIO read( ) methods are returned fully loaded. ImageIO provides its own API for monitoring image loading progress. That API follows a more standard event source/listener pattern, but we won't get into it here.

Scaling and Size

Another version of drawImage( ) renders a scaled version of the image:

```
g.drawImage( monaImage, x, y, x2, y2, this );
```

This draws the entire image within the rectangle formed by the points x, y and x2, y2, scaling as necessary. drawImage( ) behaves the same as before; the image is processed by the component as it arrives, and the image observer is notified as more pixel data and the completed image are available. Several other overloaded versions of drawImage( ) provide more complex options: you can scale, crop, and perform some simple transpositions.

Normally, however, for performance you want to make a scaled copy of an image (as opposed to simply painting one at draw-time), and you can use getScaledInstance( ) for this purpose. Here's how:

```
Image scaledDaffy =
  daffyImage.getScaledInstance( 100, 200, Image.SCALE_AREA_AVERAGING );
```

This method scales the original image to the given size; in this case, 100 by 200 pixels. It returns a new Image that you can draw like any other image. SCALE_AREA_AVERAGING is a constant that tells getScaledImage( ) what scaling algorithm to use. The algorithm used here tries to do a decent job of scaling at the expense of time. Some alternatives that take less time are SCALE_REPLICATE, which scales by replicating scan lines and columns (which is fast but probably not pretty). You can also specify either SCALE_FAST or SCALE_SMOOTH and let the implementation choose an appropriate algorithm that optimizes for time or quality. If you don't have specific requirements, you should use SCALE_DEFAULT, which, ideally, would be set by a preference in the user's environment.

If you are going to draw the image more than once (which you almost always will), creating a scaled copy of the image can improve performance dramatically. Otherwise, repeated calls to drawImage( ) with scaling requirements cause the image to be scaled every time, wasting processing time.

The Image getHeight( ) and getWidth( ) methods retrieve the dimensions of an image. Since this information may not be available until the image data is completely loaded, both methods also take an ImageObserver object as a parameter. If the dimensions aren't yet available, they return values of -1 and notify the observer when the actual value is known. We'll see how to deal with these and other problems a bit later. For now, we'll continue to use our Component as the image observer and move on to some general painting techniques.

Drawing Techniques

Now that we've learned about the basic tools, let's put a few of them together. In this section, we'll look at some techniques for doing fast and flicker-free drawing and painting. If you're interested in animation, this is for you. Drawing operations take time, and time spent drawing leads to delays and imperfect results. Our goals are to minimize the amount of drawing work we do and, as much as possible, to do that work away from the eyes of the user. To do this, we use two techniques: clipping and double buffering. Fortunately, Swing now handles double buffering by default. You won't have to implement this logic on your own, but it's useful to understand it.

Our first example, DragImage, illustrates some of the issues in updating a display. Like many animations, it has two parts: a constant background and a changing object in the foreground. In this case, the background is a checkerboard pattern, and the object is a small, scaled image we can drag around on top of it, as shown in Figure 20-4:

```
import java.awt.*;
import java.awt.event.*;
import javax.swing.*;

public class DragImage extends JComponent
    implements MouseMotionListener
{
  static int imageWidth=60, imageHeight=60;
  int grid = 10;
  int imageX, imageY;
  Image image;

  public DragImage(Image i) {
    image = i;
    addMouseMotionListener(this);
  }

  public void mouseDragged(MouseEvent e) {
    imageX = e.getX( );
    imageY = e.getY( );
    repaint( );
  }
  public void mouseMoved(MouseEvent e) {}
```

```java
public void paint(Graphics g) {
  Graphics2D g2 = (Graphics2D)g;

  int w = getSize().width / grid;
  int h = getSize().height / grid;
  boolean black = false;
  for (int y = 0; y <= grid; y++)
    for (int x = 0; x <= grid; x++) {
      g2.setPaint(black ? Color.black : Color.white);
      black = !black;
      g2.fillRect(x * w, y * h, w, h);
    }
  g2.drawImage(image, imageX, imageY, this);
}

public static void main(String[] args) {
  String imageFile = "L1-Light.jpg";
  if (args.length > 0)
    imageFile = args[0];

  // Turn off double buffering
  //RepaintManager.currentManager(null).setDoubleBufferingEnabled(false);

  Image image = Toolkit.getDefaultToolkit().getImage(
      DragImage.class.getResource(imageFile));
  image = image.getScaledInstance(
      imageWidth,imageHeight,Image.SCALE_DEFAULT);
  JFrame frame = new JFrame("DragImage");
  frame.getContentPane().add( new DragImage(image) );
  frame.setSize(300, 300);
  frame.setDefaultCloseOperation( JFrame.EXIT_ON_CLOSE );
  frame.setVisible(true);
}
}
```

Run the application, optionally specifying an image file as a command-line argument. Then try dragging the image around on the pattern.

DragImage is a custom component that overrides the JComponent paint() method to do its drawing. In the main() method we load the image and pre-scale it to improve performance. We then create the DragImage component and place it in the content pane. As the mouse is dragged, DragImage keeps track of its most recent position in two instance variables, imageX and imageY. On each call to mouseDragged(), the coordinates are updated, and repaint() is called to ask that the display be updated. When paint() is called, it looks at some parameters, draws the checkerboard pattern to fill the applet's area and finally paints the small version of the image at the latest coordinates.

Now for a few arcane details about differences between JComponent and a plain AWT Component. First, the default JComponent update() method simply calls our paint() method. Prior to Java 1.4, the AWT Component class's default update() method first

Figure 20-4. The DragImage application

cleared the screen area using a clearRect( ) call before calling paint. Recall that the difference between paint( ) and update( ) is that paint( ) draws the entire area; update( ) assumes the screen region is intact from the last draw. In AWT, update( ) was overly conservative; in Swing it's more optimistic. This is important to know if you are working with an older AWT-based application. In that case, you can simply override update( ) to call paint( ).

A more important difference between AWT and Swing is that Swing components by default perform *double buffering* of the output of their paint( ) method.

Double Buffering

Double buffering means that instead of drawing directly on the screen, Swing first performs drawing operations in an offscreen buffer and then copies the completed work to the display in a single painting operation, as shown in Figure 20-5. It takes the same amount of time to do the drawing work, but, once it's done, double buffering instantaneously updates our display so that the user does not perceive any flickering or progressively rendered output.

You'll see how to implement this technique yourself when we use an offscreen buffer later in this chapter. However, Swing does this kind of double buffering for you whenever you use a Swing component in a Swing container. AWT components do not have automatic double-buffering capability.

It is interesting to take our example and turn off double buffering to see the effect. Each Swing JComponent has a method called setDoubleBuffered( ) that can be set to false to disable the technique. Or you can disable it for all components using a call

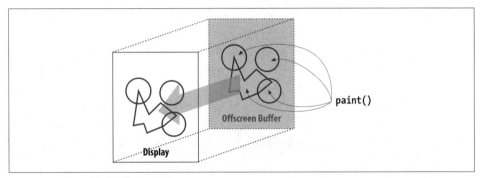

Figure 20-5. Double buffering

to the Swing RepaintManager, as we've indicated in comments in the example. Try uncommenting that line of DragImage and observe the difference in appearance.

The difference is most dramatic when you are using a slow system or doing complex drawing operations. Double buffering eliminates all of the flickering. However, on a slow system, it can decrease performance noticeably. In extreme cases (such as a game), it may be beneficial to provide an option to disable double buffering.

Our example is pretty fast, but we're still doing some wasted drawing. Most of the background stays the same each time it's painted. You might try to make paint( ) smarter, so that it wouldn't redraw these areas, but remember that paint( ) has to be able to draw the entire scene because it might be called in situations when the display isn't intact. The solution is to draw only part of the picture whenever the mouse moves. Next, we'll talk about clipping.

Limiting Drawing with Clipping

Whenever the mouse is dragged, DragImage responds by updating its coordinates and calling repaint( ). But repaint( ) by default causes the entire component to be redrawn. Most of this drawing is unnecessary. It turns out that there's another version of repaint( ) that lets you specify a rectangular area that should be drawn—in essence, a clipping region.

Why does it help to restrict the drawing area? Foremost, drawing operations that fall outside the clipping region are not displayed. If a drawing operation overlaps the clipping region, we see only the part that's inside. A second effect is that, in a good implementation, the graphics context can recognize drawing operations that fall completely outside the clipping region and ignore them altogether. Eliminating unnecessary operations can save time if we're doing something complex, such as filling a bunch of polygons. This doesn't save the time our application spends calling the drawing methods, but the overhead of calling these kinds of drawing methods is usually negligible compared to the time it takes to execute them. (If we were generating an image pixel by pixel, this would not be the case, as the calculations would be the major time sink, not the drawing.)

So we can save some time in our application by redrawing only the affected portion of the display. We can pick the smallest rectangular area that includes both the old image position and the new image position, as shown in Figure 20-6. This is the only portion of the display that really needs to change; everything else stays the same.

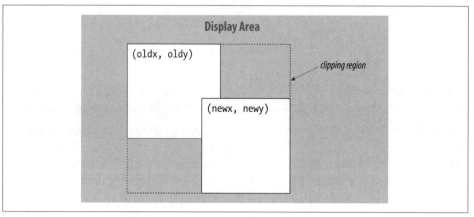

Figure 20-6. Determining the clipping region

A smarter algorithm could save even more time by redrawing only those regions that have changed. However, the simple clipping strategy we've implemented here can be applied to many kinds of drawing and gives good performance, particularly if the area being changed is small.

One important thing to note is that, in addition to looking at the new position, our updating operation now has to remember the last position at which the image was drawn. Let's fix our application so it will use a specified clipping region. To keep this short and emphasize the changes, we'll take some liberties with design and make our next example a subclass of DragImage. Let's call it ClippedDragImage.

```
import java.awt.*;
import java.awt.event.*;
import javax.swing.*;

public class ClippedDragImage extends DragImage {
  int oldX, oldY;

  public ClippedDragImage( Image i ) { super(i); }

  public void mouseDragged(MouseEvent e) {
    imageX = e.getX( );
    imageY = e.getY( );
    Rectangle r = getAffectedArea(
        oldX, oldY, imageX, imageY, imageWidth, imageHeight);
    repaint(r);  // repaint just the affected part of the component
```

```
        oldX = imageX;
        oldY = imageY;
    }

    private Rectangle getAffectedArea(
        int oldx, int oldy, int newx, int newy, int width, int height)
    {
        int x = Math.min(oldx, newx);
        int y = Math.min(oldy, newy);
        int w = (Math.max(oldx, newx) + width) - x;
        int h = (Math.max(oldy, newy) + height) - y;
        return new Rectangle(x, y, w, h);
    }

    public static void main(String[] args) {
        String imageFile = "L1-Light.jpg";
        if (args.length > 0)
            imageFile = args[0];

        // Turn off double buffering
        //RepaintManager.currentManager(null).setDoubleBufferingEnabled(false);

        Image image = Toolkit.getDefaultToolkit().getImage(
            ClippedDragImage.class.getResource(imageFile));
        image = image.getScaledInstance(
            imageWidth,imageHeight,Image.SCALE_DEFAULT);
        JFrame frame = new JFrame("ClippedDragImage");
        frame.getContentPane().add( new ClippedDragImage(image) );
        frame.setSize(300, 300);
        frame.setDefaultCloseOperation( JFrame.EXIT_ON_CLOSE );
        frame.setVisible(true);
    }
}
```

You may or may not find that ClippedDragImage is significantly faster. Modern desktop computers are so fast that this kind of operation is child's play for them. However, the fundamental technique is important and applicable to more sophisticated applications.

What have we changed? First, we've overridden mouseDragged() so that instead of setting the current coordinates of the image, it figures out the area that has changed, using a new, private method. getAffectedArea() takes the new and old coordinates and the width and height of the image as arguments. It determines the bounding rectangle as shown in Figure 20-6, then calls repaint() to draw only the affected area of the screen. mouseDragged() also saves the current position by setting the oldX and oldY variables.

Try turning off double buffering on this example and compare it to the unbuffered previous example to see how much less work is being done. You probably won't see the difference; computers are just too fast nowadays. If you were using the 2D API to do some fancy rendering, it might help a lot.

Offscreen Drawing

In addition to serving as buffers for double buffering, offscreen images are useful for saving complex, hard-to-produce, background information. We'll look at a fun, simple example: the doodle pad. DoodlePad is a simple drawing tool that lets us scribble by dragging the mouse, as shown in Figure 20-7. It draws into an offscreen image; its paint( ) method simply copies the image to the display area.

```java
//file: DoodlePad.java
import java.awt.*;
import java.awt.event.*;
import javax.swing.*;

public class DoodlePad
{
  public static void main(String[] args)
  {
    JFrame frame = new JFrame("DoodlePad");
    Container content = frame.getContentPane( );
    content.setLayout(new BorderLayout( ));
    final DrawPad drawPad = new DrawPad( );
    content.add(drawPad, BorderLayout.CENTER);
    JPanel panel = new JPanel( );
    JButton clearButton = new JButton("Clear");
    clearButton.addActionListener(new ActionListener( ) {
      public void actionPerformed(ActionEvent e) {
        drawPad.clear( );
      }
    });
    panel.add(clearButton);
    content.add(panel, BorderLayout.SOUTH);
    frame.setSize(280, 300);
    frame.setDefaultCloseOperation( JFrame.EXIT_ON_CLOSE );
    frame.setVisible(true);
  }

} // end of class DoodlePad

class DrawPad extends JComponent
{
  Image image;
  Graphics2D graphics2D;
  int currentX, currentY, oldX, oldY;

  public DrawPad( ) {
    setDoubleBuffered(false);
    addMouseListener(new MouseAdapter( ) {
      public void mousePressed(MouseEvent e) {
        oldX = e.getX( );
        oldY = e.getY( );
      }
    });
    addMouseMotionListener(new MouseMotionAdapter( ) {
```

```
    public void mouseDragged(MouseEvent e) {
      currentX = e.getX( );
      currentY = e.getY( );
      if (graphics2D != null)
        graphics2D.drawLine(oldX, oldY, currentX, currentY);
      repaint( );
      oldX = currentX;
      oldY = currentY;
    }
  });
}

public void paintComponent(Graphics g) {
  if (image == null) {
    image = createImage(getSize( ).width, getSize( ).height);
    graphics2D = (Graphics2D)image.getGraphics( );
    graphics2D.setRenderingHint(RenderingHints.KEY_ANTIALIASING,
        RenderingHints.VALUE_ANTIALIAS_ON);
    clear( );
  }
  g.drawImage(image, 0, 0, null);
}

public void clear( ) {
  graphics2D.setPaint(Color.white);
  graphics2D.fillRect(0, 0, getSize( ).width, getSize( ).height);
  graphics2D.setPaint(Color.black);
  repaint( );
}
}
```

Figure 20-7. The DoodlePad application

Give it a try. Draw a nice moose or a sunset. We just drew a lovely cartoon of Bill Gates. If you make a mistake, hit the Clear button and start over.

The parts should be familiar by now. We have made a type of JComponent called DrawPad. The new DrawPad component uses inner classes to supply handlers for the MouseListener and MouseMotionListener interfaces. We have used the JComponent createImage( ) method to create an empty offscreen image buffer to hold our scribble. Mouse-dragging events trigger us to draw lines into the offscreen image and call repaint( ) to update the display. DrawPad's paint( ) method does a drawImage( ) to copy the offscreen drawing area to the display. In this way, DrawPad saves our sketch information.

What is unusual about DrawPad is that it does some drawing outside of paint( ). In this example, we want to let the user scribble with the mouse, so we should respond to every mouse movement. Therefore, we do our work, drawing to the offscreen buffer in mouseDragged( ) itself. As a rule, we should be careful about doing heavy work in event-handling methods because we don't want to interfere with other tasks the windowing system's painting thread is performing. In this case, our line-drawing option should not be a burden, and our primary concern is getting as close a coupling as possible between the mouse movement events and the sketch on the screen. A more elaborate example might push coordinates into a queue for some other drawing thread to consume, thus freeing up the event-handler thread.

In addition to drawing a line as the user drags the mouse, the mouseDragged( ) handler maintains a pair of previous coordinates to be used as a starting point for the next line segment. The mousePressed( ) handler resets the previous coordinates to the current mouse position whenever the user moves the mouse. Finally, DrawPad provides a clear( ) method that clears the offscreen buffer and calls repaint( ) to update the display. The DoodlePad application ties the clear( ) method to an appropriately labeled button through another anonymous inner class.

What if we wanted to do something with the image after the user has finished scribbling on it? As we'll see in the next chapter, we could get the pixel data for the image and work with that. It wouldn't be hard to create a save facility that stores the pixel data and reproduces it later. Think about how you might go about creating a networked "bathroom wall," where people could scribble on your web pages.

Printing

Earlier in this chapter, we hinted at the possibility that you could draw the same stuff on the screen and the printer. It's true; all you really need to do is get a Graphics2D object that represents a printer rather than an area of the screen. Java's printing API provides the necessary plumbing. There isn't room here to describe the whole Printing API, but we will provide you with a short example that will let you get your feet wet (and your paper flowing).

The printing classes are tucked away in the java.awt.print package. You can print anything that implements the Printable interface. This interface has only one method—you guessed it, print( ), which is like the paint( ) methods we've already worked with. It accepts a Graphics object that represents the drawing surface of the printer's page. It also accepts a PageFormat object that encapsulates information about the paper on which you're printing. Finally, print( ) is passed the number of the page that is being rendered. All Swing components implement Printable for you; you can override it in your own components to customize their printed appearance or to do arbitrary printing.

Your print( ) implementation should either render the requested page or state that it doesn't exist. You can do this by returning special values from print( ), either Printable.PAGE_EXISTS or Printable.NO_SUCH_PAGE.

You can control a print job, including showing print and page setup dialogs, using the PrinterJob class. The following class enables you to get something on paper. In this example, we work both sides of the printing equation: implementing a simple Printable interface to generate our data and printing it with the PrinterJob API.

```java
//file: UnbelievablySimplePrint.java
import java.awt.*;
import java.awt.print.*;

public class UnbelievablySimplePrint implements Printable
{
  private static Font sFont = new Font("Serif", Font.PLAIN , 64);

  public int print(Graphics g, PageFormat Pf, int pageIndex)
      throws PrinterException
  {
    if (pageIndex > 0) return NO_SUCH_PAGE;
    Graphics2D g2 = (Graphics2D)g;
    g2.setFont(sFont);
    g2.setPaint(Color.black);
    g2.drawString("Save a tree!", 96, 144);
    return PAGE_EXISTS;
  }

  public static void main(String[] args) {
    PrinterJob job = PrinterJob.getPrinterJob( );
    job.setPrintable(new UnbelievablySimplePrint( ));
    if (job.printDialog( )) {
      try {
        job.print( );
      }
      catch (PrinterException e) {}
    }
    System.exit(0);
  }
}
```

There's not much to this example. We've created an implementation of Printable, called UnbelievablySimplePrint. It has a very simple print( ) method that draws some text.

The rest of the work, in the main( ) method, has to do with setting up the print job. First, we create a new PrinterJob and tell it what we want to print:

```
PrinterJob job = PrinterJob.getPrinterJob( );
job.setPrintable(new UnbelievablySimplePrint( ));
```

Then, we use the printDialog( ) method to show the standard print dialog. If the user presses the OK button, printDialog( ) returns true, and main( ) goes ahead with the printing.

Notice, in the print( ) method, how we perform the familiar cast from Graphics to Graphics2D. The full power of the 2D API is available for printing. In a real application, you'd probably have some subclass of Component that was also a Printable. The print( ) method could simply call the component's paint( ) method to create a component that performs the same rendering to both the screen and the printer.

## CHAPTER 21

Working with Images and Other Media

Until this point, we've confined ourselves to working with the high-level drawing commands of the Graphics2D class, using images in a hands-off mode. In this section, we'll clear up some of the mystery surrounding images and see how they can be created and transformed. The classes in the java.awt.image package handle images and their internals; Figure 21-1 shows the important classes in this package.

First, we'll return to our discussion of image loading and see how we can get more control over image data using an ImageObserver to watch as it's processed asynchronously by GUI components. We'll also see how to use the MediaTracker utility to handle the details for us. Then, we'll move on to the good stuff and have a look at BufferedImage, which is an image whose pixel data is exposed to you through a memory buffer. If you're interested in creating sophisticated graphics, rendered images, or video, this will teach you about the foundations of image construction in Java.

A few notes before we move on: Prior to Java 1.2, creating and modifying images was only possible through the ImageProducer and ImageConsumer interfaces, which, along with ImageObserver, provide low-level, stream-oriented views of the image data. We won't be covering image producers and consumers in this chapter; instead, we'll stick to the new APIs, which are more capable and easier to use in most cases. If you're interested in the older APIs you can find additional coverage and examples using them on the CD accompanying the book.

Looking in the other directions, we will also be referring occasionally to the javax.imageio package, which is part of the Java Advanced Imaging API (JAI). If you need even more advanced capabilities such as image tiling, loading scaled versions of images over the network, and deferred execution of image data processing for working with really large images, you'll want to look at JAI.

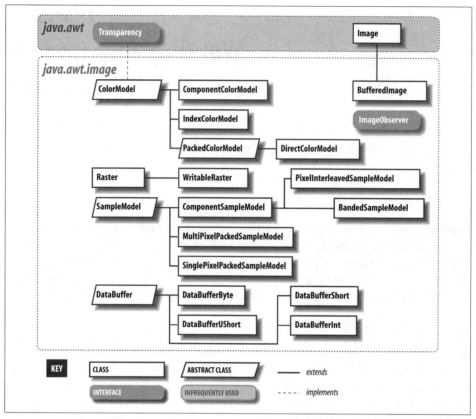

Figure 21-1. The java.awt.image package

Loading Images

One of the challenges in building software for networked applications is that data is not always instantly available. Since some of Java's roots are in Internet applications such as web browsers, its image-handling APIs were designed specifically to accommodate the fact that images might take some time to load over a slow network, providing for detailed information about image-loading progress. While many client applications do not require handling of image data in this way, it's still useful to understand this mechanism if for no other reason than it appears in the most basic image-related APIs. The Swing toolkit adds its own layer of image handling over this with components such as ImageIcon, which encapsulates an image source for you. After reading this chapter, you'll have an understanding of how the layers fit together.

ImageObserver

In the previous chapter, we mentioned that all operations on image data (e.g., loading, drawing, scaling) allow you to specify an "image observer" object as a participant. An image observer implements the ImageObserver interface, allowing it to receive notification as information about the image becomes available. The image observer is essentially a callback that is notified progressively as the image is loaded. For a static image, such as a GIF or JPEG data file, the observer is notified as chunks of image data arrive and also when the entire image is complete. For a video source or animation (e.g., GIF89), the image observer is notified at the end of each frame as the continuous stream of pixel data is generated.

The image observer can do whatever it wants with this information. For example, in the last chapter we used the image observer built into the base Component class. Although you probably didn't see it happen in our examples, the Component image observer invoked repaint( ) for us each time a new section of the image became available so that the picture, if it had taken a long time to load, would have displayed progressively. A different kind of image observer might have waited for the entire image before telling the application to display it; yet another use for an observer might be to update a loading meter showing how far the image loading had progressed.

To be an image observer, you have to implement the single method, imageUpdate( ), defined by the java.awt.image.ImageObserver interface:

```
public boolean imageUpdate(Image image, int flags, int x, int y,
                           int width, int height)
```

imageUpdate( ) is called by the graphics system, as needed, to pass the observer information about the construction of its view of the image. The image parameter holds a reference to the Image object in question. flags is an integer whose bits specify what information about the image is now available. The flag values are defined as static variables in the ImageObserver interface, as illustrated in this example:

```
//file: ObserveImageLoad.java
import java.awt.*;
import java.awt.image.*;

public class ObserveImageLoad {

  public static void main( String [] args)
  {
   ImageObserver myObserver = new ImageObserver( ) {
      public boolean imageUpdate(
        Image image, int flags, int x, int y, int width, int height)
      {
        if ( (flags & HEIGHT) !=0 )
          System.out.println("Image height = " + height );
        if ( (flags & WIDTH ) !=0 )
          System.out.println("Image width = " + width );
```

```
        if ( (flags & FRAMEBITS) != 0 )
          System.out.println("Another frame finished.");
        if ( (flags & SOMEBITS) != 0 )
           System.out.println("Image section :"
                 + new Rectangle( x, y, width, height ) );
        if ( (flags & ALLBITS) != 0 )
          System.out.println("Image finished!");
        if ( (flags & ABORT) != 0 )
          System.out.println("Image load aborted...");
        return true;
      }
    };

    Toolkit toolkit = Toolkit.getDefaultToolkit( );
    Image img = toolkit.getImage( args[0] );
    toolkit.prepareImage( img, -1, -1, myObserver );
  }
}
```

Run the example, supplying an image file as the command-line argument and observe the output. You'll see a number of incremental messages about loading the image.

The flags integer determines which of the other parameters, x, y, width, and height, hold valid data and what that data means. To test whether a particular flag in the flags integer is set, we have to resort to some binary shenanigans (using the & (AND) operator). The width and height parameters play a dual role. If SOMEBITS is set, they represent the size of the chunk of the image that has just been delivered. If HEIGHT or WIDTH is set, however, they represent the overall image dimensions. Finally, imageUpdate( ) returns a boolean value indicating whether or not it's interested in future updates.

In this example, after requesting the Image object with getImage( ), we kick-start the loading process with the Toolkit's prepareImage( ) method, which takes our image observer as an argument. Using an Image API method such as drawImage( ), scaleImage( ), or asking for image dimensions with getWidth( ) or getHeight( ) will also suffice to start the operation. Remember that although the getImage( ) method created the image object, it doesn't begin loading the data until one of the image operations requires it.

The example shows the lowest-level general mechanism for starting and monitoring the process of loading image data. You should be able to see how we could implement all sorts of sophisticated image loading and tracking schemes with this. The two most important strategies (to draw an image progressively, as it's constructed, or to wait until it's complete and draw it in its entirety) are handled for us. We have already seen that the Component class implements the first scheme. Another class, java.awt.MediaTracker, is a general utility that tracks the loading of a number of images or other media types for us. We'll look at it in the next section.

MediaTracker

java.awt.MediaTracker is a utility class that simplifies life if we have to wait for one or more images to be loaded completely before they're displayed. A MediaTracker monitors the loading of an image or a group of images and lets us check on them periodically or wait until they are finished. MediaTracker implements the ImageObserver interface that we just discussed, allowing it to receive image updates.

The following code snippet illustrates using a MediaTracker to wait while an image is prepared:

```java
//file: StatusImage.java
import java.awt.*;
import javax.swing.*;

public class StatusImage extends JComponent
{
  boolean loaded = false;
  String message = "Loading...";
  Image image;

  public StatusImage( Image image ) { this.image = image; }

  public void paint(Graphics g) {
    if (loaded)
        g.drawImage(image, 0, 0, this);
    else {
      g.drawRect(0, 0, getSize().width - 1, getSize().height - 1);
      g.drawString(message, 20, 20);
    }
  }
  public void loaded() {
    loaded = true;
    repaint();
  }
  public void setMessage( String msg ) {
    message = msg;
    repaint();
  }

  public static void main( String [] args ) {
    JFrame frame = new JFrame("TrackImage");
    Image image = Toolkit.getDefaultToolkit().getImage( args[0] );
    StatusImage statusImage = new StatusImage( image );
    frame.getContentPane().add( statusImage );
    frame.setSize(300,300);
    frame.setVisible(true);

    MediaTracker tracker = new MediaTracker( statusImage );
    int MAIN_IMAGE = 0;
    tracker.addImage( image, MAIN_IMAGE );
    try {
        tracker.waitForID( MAIN_IMAGE ); }
```

```
        catch (InterruptedException e) {}
        if ( tracker.isErrorID( MAIN_IMAGE ) )
            statusImage.setMessage( "Error" );
        else
            statusImage.loaded( );
    }
}
```

In this example we have created a trivial component called StatusImage that accepts an image and draws a text status message until it is told that the image is loaded. It then displays the image. The only interesting part here is that we use a MediaTracker to load the image data for us, simplifying our logic.

First, we create a MediaTracker to manage the image. The MediaTracker constructor takes a Component as an argument; this is supposed to be the component onto which the image is later drawn. This argument is somewhat of a hold-over from earlier Java days with AWT. If you don't have the component reference handy, you can simply substitute a generic component reference like so:

```
Component comp = new Component( );
```

After creating the MediaTracker, we assign it images to manage. Each image is associated with an integer identifier we can use later for checking on its status or to wait for its completion. Multiple images can be associated with the same identifier, letting us manage them as a group. The value of the identifier is also meant to prioritize loading when waiting on multiple sets of images; lower IDs have higher priority. In this case, we want to manage only a single image, so we created one identifier called MAIN_IMAGE and passed it as the ID for our image in the call to addImage( ).

Next, we call the MediaTracker waitforID( ) routine, which blocks on the image, waiting for it to finish loading. If successful, we tell our example component to use the image and repaint. Another MediaTracker method, waitForAll( ), waits for all images to complete, not just a single ID. It is possible to be interrupted here by an InterruptedException. We should also test for errors during image preparation with isErrorID( ). In our example, we change the status message if we find one.

The MediaTracker checkID( ) and checkAll( ) methods may be used to poll periodically the status of images loading, returning true or false indicating whether loading is finished. The checkAll( ) method does this for the union of all images being loaded. Additionally, the statusID( ) and statusAll( ) methods return a constant indicating the status or final condition of an image load. The value is one of the MediaTracker constant values: LOADING, ABORTED, ERROR, or COMPLETE. For statusAll( ), the value is the bitwise OR value of all of the various statuses.

This may seem like a lot of work to go through just to put up a status message while loading a single image. MediaTracker is more valuable when you are working with many raw images that have to be available before you can begin parts of an application. It saves implementing a custom ImageObserver for every application. For general

---

Swing application work, you can use yet another simplification by employing the ImageIcon component to use a MediaTracker; this is covered next.

ImageIcon

In Chapter 17, we discussed Swing components that can work with images using the Icon interface. In particular, the ImageIcon class accepts an image filename or URL and can render it into a component. Internally, ImageIcon uses a MediaTracker to fully load the image in the call to its constructor. It can also provide the Image reference back. So, a shortcut to what we did in the last few sections—getting an image loaded fully before using it—would be:

```
ImageIcon icon = new ImageIcon("myimage.jpg");
Image image = icon.getImage( );
```

This quirky but useful approach saves a few lines of typing but uses a component in an odd way and is not very clear. ImageIcon also gives you direct access to the MediaTracker it is using through the getMediaTracker( ) method or tells you the MediaTracker load status through the getImageLoadStatus( ) method. This returns one of the MediaTracker constants: ABORTED, ERROR, or COMPLETE.

ImageIO

As we mentioned in the introduction to Chapter 1, the javax.imageio package is a standard extension that deals with reading and writing many image formats. It is a part of the larger Java Advanced Imaging (JAI) API. This API supports advanced manipulation and display of images. Whereas the AWT has a relatively fixed set of functionality, JAI is an extensible framework that accepts plug-ins for new file formats and features. The imageio portion of JAI is bundled with Java 1.4 and later, so we can take advantage of it on all current Java releases. ImageIO effectively supercedes the APIs we've talked about here with new ones for loading and monitoring image data and although we won't cover it in detail, we will discuss it briefly here for several reasons. First, it is fairly easy to use. Second, ImageIO natively works with BufferedImages and not just plain AWT Images. As we'll discuss throughout the rest of this chapter, buffered images can expose their pixel data for you to read or manipulate. Finally, using ImageIO allows you both to load and save BufferedImages to files. The core AWT has no tools for encoding image data for saving to files.

Previously, we showed how easy it is to load an image with the static read( ) methods of the ImageIO class, which accept either a File, URL, or InputStream:

```
File file = new File("/Users/pat/images/boojum.gif");
BufferedImage bi = ImageIO.read( file );
```

This time we have revealed that the type returned is actually a BufferedImage, which is a subtype of Image. The ImageIO.read( ) method, like the AWT getImage( ) method, automatically detects the image type and decodes it properly. Since ImageIO is extensible, it's useful to be able to list the types of images it can decode. You get this information with the ImageIO.getReaderFormatNames( ) method, which returns an array of strings corresponding roughly to file extensions for the image types it understands. (ImageIO does not rely on file extensions to detect image types but looks at the content of the file.)

Images loaded by the ImageIO.read( ) methods are fully loaded before they are returned, so the method blocks until they are done. If you want more fine-grained information on the progress of image loading, you can use the IIOReadProgressListener interface of the javax.imageio.event package, which roughly corresponds to the AWT ImageObserver. To use it, you must delve a little deeper into the ImageIO API by first looking up an appropriate ImageReader object with which to register the listener:

```
import javax.imageio.*;
import javax.imageio.stream.*;
import javax.imageio.event.*;

File file = new File("image.jpg");
ImageInputStream iis = ImageIO.createImageInputStream( file );

Iterator readers = ImageIO.getImageReaders( iis );
ImageReader reader = (ImageReader)readers.next( ); // choose first one

reader.addIIOReadProgressListener( readProgressListener );
reader.setInput( iis, true );
BufferedImage bi = reader.read( 0/*index*/ );
```

This code is fairly straightforward. The ReadProgressListener is used like any of the AWT or Swing event interfaces we've seen before. You can refer to the Javadoc for the exact methods you must implement.

Finally, in addition to the progress listener, two other listener APIs, IIOReadUpdateListener and IIOReadWarningListener, offer information on pixel changes (e.g., for progressive loading) and loading errors. There are also, of course, "write" versions of all of these tools that handle the flip side, saving image data. We'll return to that topic later in this chapter.

Producing Image Data

There are two approaches to generating image data. The high-level method is to treat the image as a drawing surface and use the methods of Graphics2D to render things into the image. The second way is to twiddle the bits that represent the pixels of the image data yourself. This is harder, but gives you arbitrary control for handling specific formats or mathematically analyzing or creating image data.

Drawing Animations

Let's begin with the simpler approach, rendering on an image through drawing. We'll throw in a twist to make things interesting: we'll build an animation. Each frame will be rendered as we go along. This is very similar to the double buffering we examined in the last chapter, but this time we'll use a timer, instead of mouse events, as the signal to generate new frames.

Swing performs double buffering automatically, so we don't even have to worry about the animation flickering. Although it looks like we're drawing directly to the screen, we're really drawing into an image that Swing uses for double buffering. All we need to do is draw the right thing at the right time.

Let's look at an example, Hypnosis, that illustrates the technique. This example shows a constantly shifting shape that bounces around the inside of a component. When screen savers first came of age, this kind of thing was pretty hot stuff. Hypnosis is shown in Figure 21-2.

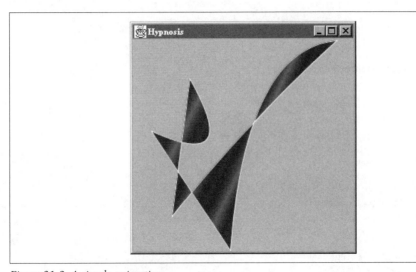

Figure 21-2. A simple animation

Here is its source code:

```
//file: Hypnosis.java
import java.awt.*;
import java.awt.event.*;
import java.awt.geom.GeneralPath;
import javax.swing.*;

public class Hypnosis extends JComponent implements Runnable {
  private int[] coordinates;
  private int[] deltas;
  private Paint paint;
```

```
public Hypnosis(int numberOfSegments) {
  int numberOfCoordinates = numberOfSegments * 4 + 2;
  coordinates = new int[numberOfCoordinates];
  deltas = new int[numberOfCoordinates];
  for (int i = 0 ; i < numberOfCoordinates; i++) {
    coordinates[i] = (int)(Math.random( ) * 300);
    deltas[i] = (int)(Math.random( ) * 4 + 3);
    if (deltas[i] > 4) deltas[i] = -(deltas[i] - 3);
  }
  paint = new GradientPaint(0, 0, Color.blue,
      20, 10, Color.red, true);

  Thread t = new Thread(this);
  t.start( );
}

public void run( ) {
  try {
    while (true) {
      timeStep( );
      repaint( );
      Thread.sleep(1000 / 24);
    }
  }
  catch (InterruptedException ie) {}
}

public void paint(Graphics g) {
  Graphics2D g2 = (Graphics2D)g;
  g2.setRenderingHint(RenderingHints.KEY_ANTIALIASING,
      RenderingHints.VALUE_ANTIALIAS_ON);
  Shape s = createShape( );
  g2.setPaint(paint);
  g2.fill(s);
  g2.setPaint(Color.white);
  g2.draw(s);
}

private void timeStep( ) {
  Dimension d = getSize( );
  if (d.width == 0 || d.height == 0) return;
  for (int i = 0; i < coordinates.length; i++) {
    coordinates[i] += deltas[i];
    int limit = (i % 2 == 0) ? d.width : d.height;
    if (coordinates[i] < 0) {
      coordinates[i] = 0;
      deltas[i] = -deltas[i];
    }
    else if (coordinates[i] > limit) {
      coordinates[i] = limit - 1;
      deltas[i] = -deltas[i];
    }
  }
}
```

```
private Shape createShape( ) {
  GeneralPath path = new GeneralPath( );
  path.moveTo(coordinates[0], coordinates[1]);
  for (int i = 2; i < coordinates.length; i += 4)
    path.quadTo(coordinates[i], coordinates[i + 1],
        coordinates[i + 2], coordinates[i + 3]);
  path.closePath( );
  return path;
}

public static void main(String[] args) {
  JFrame frame = new JFrame("Hypnosis");
  frame.getContentPane( ).add( new Hypnosis(4) );
  frame.setSize(300, 300);
  frame.setDefaultCloseOperation( JFrame.EXIT_ON_CLOSE );
  frame.setVisible(true);
}
}
```

The main( ) method does the usual grunt work of setting up the JFrame that holds our animation component.

The Hypnosis component has a very basic strategy for animation. It holds some number of coordinate pairs in its coordinates member variable. A corresponding array, deltas, holds "delta" amounts that are added to the coordinates each time the figure is supposed to change. To render the complex shape you see in Figure 21-2, Hypnosis creates a special Shape object from the coordinate array each time the component is drawn.

Hypnosis's constructor has two important tasks. First, it fills up the coordinates and deltas arrays with random values. The number of array elements is determined by an argument to the constructor. The constructor's second task is to start up a new thread that drives the animation.

The animation is done in the run( ) method. This method calls timeStep( ), which repaints the component and waits for a short time (details to follow). Each time timeStep( ) is called, the coordinates array is updated and repaint( ) is called. This results in a call to paint( ), which creates a shape from the coordinate array and draws it.

The paint( ) method is relatively simple. It uses a helper method, called createShape( ), to create a shape from the coordinate array. The shape is then filled, using a Paint stored as a member variable. The shape's outline is also drawn in white.

The timeStep( ) method updates all the elements of the coordinate array by adding the corresponding element of deltas. If any coordinates are now out of the component's bounds, they are adjusted, and the corresponding delta is negated. This produces the effect of bouncing off the sides of the component.

createShape() creates a shape from the coordinate array. It uses the GeneralPath class, a useful Shape implementation that allows you to build shapes using straight and curved line segments. In this case, we create a shape from a series of quadratic curves, close it to create an area, and fill it.

BufferedImage Anatomy

So far, we've talked about java.awt.Images and how they can be loaded and drawn. What if you really want to get inside the image to examine and update its data? Image doesn't give you access to its data. You'll need to use a more sophisticated kind of image: java.awt.image.BufferedImage. The classes are closely related—BufferedImage, in fact, is a subclass of Image. BufferedImage gives you all sorts of control over the actual data that makes up the image and provides many capabilities beyond the basic Image class. Because it's a subclass of Image, you can still pass a BufferedImage to any of Graphics2D's methods that accept an Image.

To create an image from raw data, you need to understand exactly how a BufferedImage is put together. The full details can get quite complex—the BufferedImage class was designed to support images in nearly any storage format you can imagine. But, for common operations, it's not that difficult to use. Figure 21-3 shows the elements of a BufferedImage.

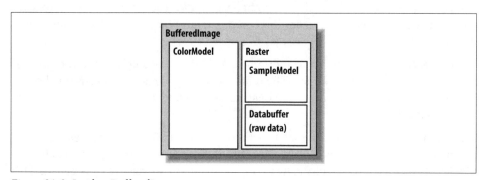

Figure 21-3. Inside a BufferedImage

An image is simply a rectangle of colored pixels, which is a simple enough concept. There's a lot of complexity underneath the BufferedImage class, because there are a lot of different ways to represent the colors of pixels. You might have, for instance, an image with RGB data in which each pixel's red, green, and blue values were stored as the elements of byte arrays. Or you might have an RGB image where each pixel was represented by an integer that contained red, green, and blue component values. Or you could have a 16-level grayscale image with eight pixels stored in each element of an integer array. You get the idea; there are many different ways to store image data, and BufferedImage is designed to support all of them.

A BufferedImage consists of two pieces, a Raster and a ColorModel. The Raster contains the actual image data. You can think of it as an array of pixel values. It can answer the question, "What are the color data values for the pixel at 51, 17?" The Raster for an RGB image would return three values, while a Raster for a grayscale image would return a single value. WritableRaster, a subclass of Raster, also supports modifying pixel data values.

The ColorModel's job is to interpret the image data as colors. The ColorModel can translate the data values that come from the Raster into Color objects. An RGB color model, for example, would know how to interpret three data values as red, green, and blue. A grayscale color model could interpret a single data value as a gray level. Conceptually, at least, this is how an image is displayed on the screen. The graphics system retrieves the data for each pixel of the image from the Raster. Then the ColorModel tells what color each pixel should be, and the graphics system is able to set the color of each pixel.

The Raster itself is made up of two pieces: a DataBuffer and a SampleModel. A DataBuffer is a wrapper for the raw data arrays, which are byte, short, or int arrays. DataBuffer has handy subclasses, DataBufferByte, DataBufferShort, and DataBufferInt, that allow you to create a DataBuffer from raw data arrays. You'll see an example of this technique later in the StaticGenerator example.

The SampleModel knows how to extract the data values for a particular pixel from the DataBuffer. It knows the layout of the arrays in the DataBuffer and is ultimately responsible for answering the question, "What are the data values for pixel x, y?" SampleModels are a little tricky to work with, but, fortunately, you'll probably never need to create or use one directly. As we'll see, the Raster class has many static ("factory") methods that create preconfigured Rasters for you, including their component DataBuffers and SampleModels.

As Figure 21-1 shows, the 2D API comes with various flavors of ColorModels, SampleModels, and DataBuffers. These serve as handy building blocks that cover most common image storage formats. You'll rarely need to subclass any of these classes to create a BufferedImage.

Color Models

As we've said, there are many different ways to encode color information: red, green, blue (RGB) values; hue, saturation, value (HSV); hue, lightness, saturation (HLS); and more. In addition, you can provide full-color information for each pixel, or you can just specify an index into a color table (palette) for each pixel. The way you represent a color is called a *color model*. The 2D API provides tools to support any color model you could imagine. Here, we'll just cover two broad groups of color models: *direct* and *indexed*.

As you might expect, you must specify a color model in order to generate pixel data; the abstract class java.awt.image.ColorModel represents a color model. By default, Java 2D uses a direct color model called ARGB. The A stands for "alpha," which is the historical name for transparency. RGB refers to the red, green, and blue color components that are combined to produce a single, composite color. In the default ARGB model, each pixel is represented by a 32-bit integer that is interpreted as four 8-bit fields; in order, the fields represent the alpha (transparency), red, green, and blue components of the color, as shown in Figure 21-4.

Figure 21-4. ARGB color encoding

To create an instance of the default ARGB model, call the static getRGBdefault() method in ColorModel. This method returns a DirectColorModel object; DirectColorModel is a subclass of ColorModel. You can also create other direct color models by calling a DirectColorModel constructor, but you shouldn't need to unless you have a fairly exotic application.

In an indexed color model, each pixel is represented by a smaller piece of information: an index into a table of real color values. For some applications, generating data with an indexed model may be more convenient. If you are writing an application for an 8-bit display or smaller, using an indexed model may be more efficient, because your hardware is internally using an indexed color model of some form.

Creating an Image

Let's take a look at producing some image data. A picture is worth a thousand words, and, fortunately, we can generate a pretty picture in significantly fewer than a thousand words of Java. If we just want to render image frames byte by byte, you can put together a BufferedImage pretty easily.

The following application, ColorPan, creates an image from an array of integers holding RGB pixel values:

```
//file: ColorPan.java
import java.awt.*;
import java.awt.image.*;
import javax.swing.*;

public class ColorPan extends JComponent {
  BufferedImage image;
```

```
public void initialize( ) {
  int width = getSize( ).width;
  int height = getSize( ).height;
  int[] data = new int [width * height];
  int i = 0;
  for (int y = 0; y < height; y++) {
    int red = (y * 255) / (height - 1);
    for (int x = 0; x < width; x++) {
      int green = (x * 255) / (width - 1);
      int blue = 128;
      data[i++] = (red << 16) | (green << 8 ) | blue;
    }
  }
  image = new BufferedImage(width, height,
      BufferedImage.TYPE_INT_RGB);
  image.setRGB(0, 0, width, height, data, 0, width);
}

public void paint(Graphics g) {
  if (image == null)
      initialize( );
  g.drawImage(image, 0, 0, this);
}

public void setBounds(int x, int y, int width, int height) {
  super.setBounds(x,y,width,height);
  initialize( );
}

public static void main(String[] args) {
  JFrame frame = new JFrame("ColorPan");
  frame.getContentPane( ).add(new ColorPan( ));
  frame.setSize(300, 300);
  frame.setDefaultCloseOperation( JFrame.EXIT_ON_CLOSE );
  frame.setVisible(true);
}
}
```

Give it a try. The size of the image is determined by the size of the application window. You should get a very colorful box that pans from deep blue at the upper-left corner to bright yellow at the bottom right, with green and red at the other extremes.

We create a BufferedImage in the initialize( ) method and then display the image in paint( ). The variable data is a 1D array of integers that holds 32-bit RGB pixel values. In initialize( ), we loop over every pixel in the image and assign it an RGB value. The blue component is always 128, half its maximum intensity. The red component varies from 0 to 255 along the y-axis; likewise, the green component varies from 0 to 255 along the x-axis. This statement combines these components into an RGB value:

```
data[i++] = (red << 16) | (green << 8 ) | blue;
```

The bitwise left-shift operator (<<) should be familiar to anyone who has programmed in C. It simply shoves the bits over by the specified number of positions in our 32-bit value.

When we create the BufferedImage, all its data is zeroed out. All we specify in the constructor is the width and height of the image and its type. BufferedImage includes quite a few constants representing image storage types. We've chosen TYPE_INT_RGB here, which indicates we want to store the image as RGB data packed into integers. The constructor takes care of creating an appropriate ColorModel, Raster, SampleModel, and DataBuffer for us. Then, we simply use the setRGB( )method to assign our data to the image. In this way, we've side-stepped the messy innards of BufferedImage. In the next example, we'll take a closer look at the details.

Once we have the image, we can draw it on the display with the standard drawImage( ) method. We also override the Component setBounds( ) method in order to determine when the frame is resized and reinitialize the drawing image to the new size.

Updating a BufferedImage

BufferedImage can also be used to update an image dynamically. Because the image's data arrays are directly accessible, you can simply change the data and redraw the picture whenever you want. This is probably the easiest way to build your own low-level animation software. The following example simulates the static on an old black-and-white television screen. It generates successive frames of random black and white pixels and displays each frame when it is complete. Figure 21-5 shows one frame of random static.

Figure 21-5. A frame of random static

Here's the code:

```java
//file: StaticGenerator.java
import java.awt.*;
import java.awt.event.*;
import java.awt.image.*;
import java.util.Random;
import javax.swing.*;

public class StaticGenerator extends JComponent implements Runnable {
  byte[] data;
  BufferedImage image;
  Random random;

  public void initialize() {
    int w = getSize().width, h = getSize().height;
    int length = ((w + 7) * h) / 8;
    data = new byte[length];
    DataBuffer db = new DataBufferByte(data, length);
    WritableRaster wr = Raster.createPackedRaster(db, w, h, 1, null);
    ColorModel cm = new IndexColorModel(1, 2,
        new byte[] { (byte)0, (byte)255 },
        new byte[] { (byte)0, (byte)255 },
        new byte[] { (byte)0, (byte)255 });
    image = new BufferedImage(cm, wr, false, null);
    random = new Random();
  }

  public void run() {
    if ( random == null )
        initialize();
    while (true) {
      random.nextBytes(data);
      repaint();
      try { Thread.sleep(1000 / 24); }
      catch( InterruptedException e ) { /* die */ }
    }
  }

  public void paint(Graphics g) {
    if (image == null) initialize();
    g.drawImage(image, 0, 0, this);
  }

  public void setBounds(int x, int y, int width, int height) {
    super.setBounds(x,y,width,height);
    initialize();
  }

  public static void main(String[] args) {
    //RepaintManager.currentManager(null).setDoubleBufferingEnabled(false);
    JFrame frame = new JFrame("StaticGenerator");
    StaticGenerator staticGen = new StaticGenerator();
    frame.getContentPane().add( staticGen );
```

```
      frame.setSize(300, 300);
      frame.setDefaultCloseOperation( JFrame.EXIT_ON_CLOSE );
      frame.setVisible(true);
      new Thread( staticGen ).start( );
   }
}
```

The initialize( ) method sets up the BufferedImage that produces the sequence of images. We build this image from the bottom up, starting with the raw data array. Since we're only displaying two colors here, black and white, we need only one bit per pixel. We want a 0 bit to represent black and a 1 bit to represent white. This calls for an indexed color model, which we'll create a little later.

We'll store our image data as a byte array, where each array element holds eight pixels from our black-and-white image. The array length, then, is calculated by multiplying the width and height of the image and dividing by eight. To keep things simple, we'll arrange for each image row to start on a byte boundary. For example, an image 13 pixels wide actually uses 2 bytes (16 bits) for each row:

```
int length = (w + 7)/8 * h;
```

This calculation rounds upward the number of bytes required to fill a row and then multiplies by the number of rows. Next, the actual byte array is created. The member variable data holds a reference to this array. Later, we'll use data to change the image data dynamically. Once we have the image data array, it's easy to create a DataBuffer from it:

```
data = new byte[length];
DataBuffer db = new DataBufferByte(data, length);
```

DataBuffer has several subclasses, such as DataBufferByte, that make it easy to create a data buffer from raw arrays.

The next step, logically, is to create a SampleModel. We could then create a Raster from the SampleModel and the DataBuffer. Lucky for us, though, the Raster class contains a bevy of useful static methods that create common types of Rasters. One of these methods creates a Raster from data that contains multiple pixels packed into array elements. We simply use this method, supplying the data buffer, the width and height, and indicating that each pixel uses one bit:

```
WritableRaster wr = Raster.createPackedRaster(db, w, h, 1, null/*ul corner*/);
```

The last argument to this method is a java.awt.Point that indicates where the upper-left corner of the Raster should be. By passing null, we use the default of 0, 0.

The last piece of the puzzle is the ColorModel. Each pixel is either 0 or 1, but how should that be interpreted as color? In this case, we use an IndexColorModel with a very small palette. The palette has only two entries, one each for black and white:

```
ColorModel cm = new IndexColorModel(1, 2,
        new byte[] { (byte)0, (byte)255 },
        new byte[] { (byte)0, (byte)255 },
        new byte[] { (byte)0, (byte)255 });
```

The IndexColorModel constructor that we've used here accepts the number of bits per pixel (one), the number of entries in the palette (two), and three byte arrays that are the red, green, and blue components of the palette colors. Our palette consists of two colors: black (0, 0, 0) and white (255, 255, 255).

Now that we've got all the pieces, we just need to create a BufferedImage. This image is also stored in a member variable so we can draw it later. To create the BufferedImage, we pass the color model and writable raster we just created:

```
image = new BufferedImage(cm, wr, false, null);
```

All the hard work is done now. Our paint() method just draws the image, using drawImage().

The init() method starts a thread that generates the pixel data. The run() method takes care of generating the pixel data. It uses a java.util.Random object to fill the data image byte array with random values. Since the data array is the actual image data for our image, changing the data values changes the appearance of the image. Once we fill the array with random data, a call to repaint() shows the new image on the screen.

You can also try turning off double buffering by uncommenting the line involving the RepaintManager. Now it will look even more like an old TV screen flickering and all!

That's about all there is. It's worth noting how simple it is to create this animation. Once we have the BufferedImage, we treat it like any other image. The code that generates the image sequence can be arbitrarily complex. But that complexity never infects the simple task of getting the image on the screen and updating it.

Filtering Image Data

An *image filter* is an object that performs transformations on image data. The Java 2D API supports image filtering through the BufferedImageOp interface. An image filter takes a BufferedImage as input (the *source image)* and performs some processing on the image data, producing another BufferedImage (the *destination image)*.

The 2D API comes with a handy toolbox of BufferedImageOp implementations, as summarized in Table 21-1.

Table 21-1. Image operators in the 2D API

Name	Description
AffineTransformOp	Transforms an image geometrically
ColorConvertOp	Converts from one color space to another
ConvolveOp	Performs a convolution, a mathematical operation that can be used to blur, sharpen, or otherwise process an image
LookupOp	Uses one or more lookup tables to process image values
RescaleOp	Uses multiplication to process image values

Let's take a look at two of the simpler image operators. First, try the following application. It loads an image (the first command-line argument is the filename) and processes it in different ways as you select items from the combo box. The application is shown in Figure 21-6.

Figure 21-6. The ImageProcessor application

Here's the source code:

```
//file: ImageProcessor.java
import java.awt.*;
import java.awt.event.*;
import java.awt.geom.*;
import java.awt.image.*;
import javax.swing.*;

public class ImageProcessor extends JComponent {
  private BufferedImage source, destination;
  private JComboBox options;

  public ImageProcessor( BufferedImage image ) {
    source = destination = image;
    setBackground(Color.white);
    setLayout(new BorderLayout( ));
    // create a panel to hold the combo box
    JPanel controls = new JPanel( );
    // create the combo box with the names of the area operators
    options = new JComboBox(
      new String[] { "[source]", "brighten", "darken", "rotate", "scale" }
    );
    // perform some processing when the selection changes
    options.addItemListener(new ItemListener( ) {
```

```
    public void itemStateChanged(ItemEvent ie) {
      // retrieve the selection option from the combo box
      String option = (String)options.getSelectedItem( );
      // process the image according to the selected option
      BufferedImageOp op = null;
      if (option.equals("[source]"))
        destination = source;
      else if (option.equals("brighten"))
        op = new RescaleOp(1.5f, 0, null);
      else if (option.equals("darken"))
        op = new RescaleOp(.5f, 0, null);
      else if (option.equals("rotate"))
        op = new AffineTransformOp(
            AffineTransform.getRotateInstance(Math.PI / 6), null);
      else if (option.equals("scale"))
        op = new AffineTransformOp(
            AffineTransform.getScaleInstance(.5, .5), null);
      if (op != null) destination = op.filter(source, null);
      repaint( );
    }
  });
  controls.add(options);
  add(controls, BorderLayout.SOUTH);
}

public void paintComponent(Graphics g) {
  int imageWidth = destination.getWidth( );
  int imageHeight = destination.getHeight( );
  int width = getSize( ).width;
  int height = getSize( ).height;
  g.drawImage(destination,
      (width - imageWidth) / 2, (height - imageHeight) / 2, null);
}

public static void main(String[] args) {
  String filename = args[0];

  ImageIcon icon = new ImageIcon(filename);
  Image i = icon.getImage( );

  // draw the Image into a BufferedImage
  int w = i.getWidth(null), h = i.getHeight(null);
  BufferedImage buffImage = new BufferedImage(w, h,
      BufferedImage.TYPE_INT_RGB);
  Graphics2D imageGraphics = buffImage.createGraphics( );
  imageGraphics.drawImage(i, 0, 0, null);

  JFrame frame = new JFrame("ImageProcessor");
  frame.getContentPane( ).add(new ImageProcessor(buffImage));
  frame.setSize(buffImage.getWidth( ), buffImage.getHeight( ));
  frame.setDefaultCloseOperation( JFrame.EXIT_ON_CLOSE );
  frame.setVisible(true);
}
}
```

There's quite a bit packed into the ImageProcessor application. After you've played around with it, come back and read about the details.

How ImageProcessor Works

The basic operation of ImageProcessor is very straightforward. It loads a source image, specified with a command-line argument, in its main( ) method. The image is displayed along with a combo box. When you select different items from the combo box, ImageProcessor performs some image-processing operation on the source image and displays the result (the destination image). Most of this work occurs in the ItemListener event handler that is created in ImageProcessor's constructor (a dubious design because we don't want to tie up event-handling threads for too long, but we'll let it slide here). Depending on what option is selected, a BufferedImageOp (called op) is instantiated and used to process the source image, like this:

```
destination = op.filter(source, null);
```

The destination image is returned from the filter( ) method. If we already had a destination image of the right size to hold the output, we could have passed it as the second argument to filter( ), which would improve the performance of the application a bit. If you just pass null, as we have here, an appropriate destination image is created and returned to you. Once the destination image is created, paint( )'s job is very simple; it just draws the destination image, centered on the component.

Converting an Image to a BufferedImage

Image processing can be performed only on BufferedImages, not Images. Remember that the core AWT tools all work with Image and that only if you are loading images using the ImageIO package will you get BufferedImages. Our ImageProcessor example demonstrates an important technique: how to convert a plain AWT Image to a BufferedImage. You do it by painting into the buffer, effectively copying the data. The main( ) method loads an Image from a file using Toolkit's getImage( ) method:

```
Image i = Toolkit.getDefaultToolkit( ).getImage(filename);
```

Next, main( ) uses a MediaTracker to make sure the image data is fully loaded.

Finally, the trick of converting an Image to a BufferedImage is to draw the Image into the drawing surface of the BufferedImage. Because we know the Image is fully loaded, we just need to create a BufferedImage, get its graphics context, and draw the Image into it:

```
BufferedImage bi = new BufferedImage(w, h,
        BufferedImage.TYPE_INT_RGB);
Graphics2D imageGraphics = bi.createGraphics( );
imageGraphics.drawImage(i, 0, 0, null);
```

Using the RescaleOp Class

Rescaling is an image operation that multiplies all the pixel values in the image by some constant. It doesn't affect the size of the image in any way (in case you thought *rescaling* meant *scaling*), but it does affect the brightness of its pixel's colors . In an RGB image, for example, each of the red, green, and blue values for each pixel would be multiplied by the rescaling multiplier. If you want, you can also adjust the results by adding an offset. In the 2D API, rescaling is performed by the java.awt.image.RescaleOp class. To create such an operator, specify the multiplier, offset, and a set of hints that control the quality of the conversion. In this case, we'll use a zero offset and not bother with the hints (by passing null):

```
op = new RescaleOp(1.5f, 0, null);
```

Here, we've specified a multiplier of 1.5 and an offset of 0. All values in the destination image will be 1.5 times the values in the source image, which has the net result of making the image brighter. To perform the operation, we call the filter( ) method from the BufferedImageOp interface.

Using the AffineTransformOp Class

An Affine Transformation is a kind of 2D transformation that preserves parallel lines; this includes operations like scaling, rotating, and shearing. The java.awt.image. AffineTransformOp image operator geometrically transforms a source image to produce the destination image. To create an AffineTransformOp, specify the transformation you want, in the form of an java.awt.geom.AffineTransform. The ImageProcessor application includes two examples of this operator, one for rotation and one for scaling. As before, the AffineTransformOp constructor accepts a set of hints; we'll just pass null to keep things simple:

```
else if (option.equals("rotate"))
  op = new AffineTransformOp(
      AffineTransform.getRotateInstance(Math.PI / 6), null);
else if (option.equals("scale"))
  op = new AffineTransformOp(
      AffineTransform.getScaleInstance(.5, .5), null);
```

In both cases, we obtain an AffineTransform by calling one of its static methods. In the first case, we get a rotational transformation by supplying an angle. This transformation is wrapped in an AffineTransformOp. This operator has the effect of rotating the source image around its origin to create the destination image. In the second case, a scaling transformation is wrapped in an AffineTransformOp. The two scaling values, .5 and .5, specify that the image should be reduced to half its original size in both the x and y axes.

One interesting aspect of AffineTransformOp is that you may "lose" part of your image when it's transformed. For example, when using the rotate image operator in the ImageProcessor application, the destination image will have clipped some of the original image out. Both the source and destination images have the same origin, so if any part of the image gets transformed into negative x or y space, it is lost. To work around this problem, you can structure your transformations such that the entire destination image would be in positive coordinate space.

Saving Image Data

We've spent a lot of time talking about loading images from files and generating and transforming image data, but nothing about saving it. First, let's remember that saving an image to a file such as a JPG or GIF really implies doing two things: encoding it (highly compressing the data in a way optimized for the type of image) and then writing it to a file, possibly with various metadata. As we mentioned earlier, the core AWT does not provide tools for encoding image data, only decoding it. By contrast, the ImageIO framework has the capability of writing images in any format that it can read.

Writing a BufferedImage is simply a matter of calling the static ImageIO write( ) method:

```
File outFile = new File("/tmp/myImage.png");
ImageIO.write( bufferedImage , "png", outFile );
```

The second argument is a string identifier that names the image type. You can get the list of supported formats by calling ImageIO.getWriterFormatNames( ). We should note that the actual type of the image argument is something called RenderedImage, but BufferedImage implements that interface.

More control over the encoding, for example JPG quality settings, can be had by getting an ImageWriter for the output format and using ImageWriteParams. The process is similar to that in the reader progress listener snippet from the section "ImageIO."

Simple Audio

Now we'll turn from images and open our ears to audio. The Java Sound API became a core API in Java 1.3. It provides fine-grained support for the creation and manipulation of both sampled audio and MIDI music. There's space here only to scratch the surface by examining how to play simple sampled sound and MIDI music files. With the standard Java Sound support bundled with Java you can play a wide range of file formats including AIFF, AU, Windows WAV, standard MIDI files, and Rich Music Format (RMF) files. We'll discuss other formats (such as MP3) along with video media in the next section.

java.applet.AudioClip defines the simplest interface for objects that can play sound. An object that implements AudioClip can be told to play( ) its sound data, stop( ) playing the sound, or loop( ) continuously.

The Applet class provides a handy static method, newAudioClip( ), that retrieves sounds from files or over the network. (And there is no reason we can't use it in a non-applet application.) The method takes an absolute or relative URL to specify where the audio file is located and returns an AudioClip. The following application, NoisyButton, gives a simple example:

```java
//file: NoisyButton.java
import java.applet.*;
import java.awt.*;
import java.awt.event.*;
import javax.swing.*;

public class NoisyButton {

    public static void main(String[] args) throws Exception {
        JFrame frame = new JFrame("NoisyButton");
        java.io.File file = new java.io.File( args[0] );
        final AudioClip sound = Applet.newAudioClip(file.toURL( ));

        JButton button = new JButton("Woof!");
        button.addActionListener(new ActionListener( ) {
            public void actionPerformed(ActionEvent e) { sound.play( ); }
        });

        Container content = frame.getContentPane( );
        content.setBackground(Color.pink);
        content.setLayout(new GridBagLayout( ));
        content.add(button);
        frame.setVisible(true);
        frame.setSize(200, 200);
        frame.setDefaultCloseOperation( JFrame.EXIT_ON_CLOSE );
        frame.setVisible(true);
    }
}
```

Run NoisyButton, passing the name of the audio file you wish to use as the argument. (We've supplied one called *bark.aiff*.)

NoisyButton retrieves the AudioClip using a File and the toURL( )method to reference it as a URL. When the button is pushed, we call the play( ) method of the AudioClip to start things. After that, it plays to completion unless we call the stop( ) method to interrupt it.

This interface is simple, but there is a lot of machinery behind the scenes. Next, we'll look at the Java Media Framework, which supports wider-ranging types of media.

Java Media Framework

Get some popcorn—Java can play movies! To do this, though, we'll need one of Java's standard extension APIs, the Java Media Framework (JMF). The JMF defines a set of interfaces and classes in the javax.media and javax.media.protocol packages. You can download the latest JMF from *http://java.sun.com/products/java-media/ jmf/*. To use the JMF, add *jmf.jar* to your classpath. Or, depending on what version of the JMF you download, a friendly installation program may do this for you.

We'll only scratch the surface of JMF here, by working with an important interface called `Player`. Specific implementations of `Player` deal with different media "container" types, such as Apple QuickTime (*.mov*) and Windows Video (*.avi*). For a full list of supported media types and codecs, consult the latest JMF documentation. There are also players for audio types including MP3. `Players` are handed out by a high-level class in the JMF called `Manager`. One way to obtain a `Player` is to specify the URL of a movie.

What about Windows media player format as well as MP3?

```
Player player = Manager.createPlayer(url);
```

Because video files are so large and playing them requires significant system resources, `Players` have a multistep life cycle from the time they're created to the time they actually play something. We'll look at only one step, *realizing*. In this step, the `Player` finds out (by looking at the media file) what system resources it needs to play the media file.

```
player.realize();
```

The `realize()` method returns right away; it kicks off the realizing process in a separate thread. When the player is finished realizing, it sends out an event. Once you receive this event, you can obtain one of two `Components` from the `Player`. The first is a visual component that, for visual media types, shows the media. The second is a control component that provides a prefab user interface for controlling the media presentation. The control normally includes start, stop, and pause buttons, along with volume controls and attendant goodies.

The `Player` has to be realized before you ask for these components so that it has important information, like how big the component should be. After that, getting the component is easy. Here's an example:

```
Component c = player.getVisualComponent();
```

Now, we just need to add the component to the screen somewhere. We can play the media right away (although this actually moves the `Player` through several other internal states):

```
player.start();
```

The following example, `MediaPlayer`, uses the JMF to load and display a movie or audio file from a specified URL:

```
//file: MediaPlayer.java
import java.awt.*;
import java.net.URL;
```

```
import javax.swing.*;
import javax.media.*;

public class MediaPlayer
{
    public static void main( String[] args ) throws Exception {
        final JFrame frame = new JFrame("MediaPlayer");
        frame.setDefaultCloseOperation( JFrame.EXIT_ON_CLOSE );
        URL url = new URL( args[0] );
        final Player player = Manager.createPlayer( url );

        player.addControllerListener( new ControllerListener() {
            public void controllerUpdate( ControllerEvent ce ) {
                if ( ce instanceof RealizeCompleteEvent )
                {
                    Component visual = player.getVisualComponent();
                    Component control = player.getControlPanelComponent();
                    if ( visual != null )
                        frame.getContentPane().add( visual, "Center" );
                    frame.getContentPane().add( control, "South" );
                    frame.pack();
                    frame.setVisible( true );
                    player.start();
                }
            }
        });

        player.realize();
    }
}
```

This class creates a JFrame that holds the media. Then, it creates a Player from the URL specified on the command line and tells the Player to realize( ). There's nothing else we can do until the Player is realized, so the rest of the code operates inside a ControllerListener after the RealizeCompleteEvent is received.

In the event handler, we get the Player's visual and controller components and add them to the JFrame. We display the JFrame and, finally, we play the movie. It's very simple!

To use the MediaPlayer, pass it the URL of a movie or audio file on the command line. Here are a couple of examples:

```
% java MediaPlayer file:dancing_baby.avi
% java MediaPlayer http://myserver/mp3s/TheCure/KissMe/catch.mp3
```

Figure 21-7 shows the "dancing baby" AVI running in the MediaPlayer. Feel free to dance along, if you want.

Figure 21-7. Image of the dancing baby AVI

## CHAPTER 22

JavaBeans

JavaBeans is a component architecture for Java. It is a set of rules for writing highly reusable software elements that can be linked together in a plug-and-play fashion to build applications. Writing components to the JavaBeans specification means you won't have to write as much custom code to glue them together. It also allows you to leverage JavaBean-aware development tools that can recognize the features of these components automatically. With some integrated development environments (IDEs), it is even possible to build parts of applications just by connecting prefabricated Java beans.

In this chapter, we'll use the NetBeans IDE to create simple applications by connecting Java beans visually. We will also create our own reusable beans to add to the palette of components in the IDE. Although this visual type of application design has never quite reached the level it was expected to (we'll talk about some of the reasons why later), it is still very useful in GUI development. Moreover, the fundamental JavaBeans patterns are firmly entrenched in all aspects of the core Java APIs, so understanding them is important. We will cover all of these aspects in this chapter, including hand-coding with Java beans and some related APIs.

What's a Bean?

What exactly is or are JavaBeans? *JavaBeans* (the architecture) defines a set of rules; *Java beans* are ordinary Java objects that play by these rules. That is, Java beans are Java objects that conform to the JavaBeans API and design patterns. By doing so, they can be recognized and manipulated within visual application builder environments, as well as by hand coding. Beans live and work in the Java runtime system, as do all Java objects. They communicate with their neighbors using events and other normal method invocations.

For examples of Java beans, we need look no further than the javax.swing packages. All the familiar components, such as JButton, JTextArea, JScrollpane, etc., are not only suitable items for beans, but are also, in fact, beans. Much of what you learned in Chapter 16 about the Swing components has prepared you for understanding beans. Although most of the Swing components aren't very useful in isolation, in general, beans can also be large and complex application components, such as spreadsheets or document editors. Sun used to have a HotJavaBrowser bean, a complete web browser whose interface was presented as a Java bean. We'll talk more about exactly what makes a bean a bean in a moment. For now, we want to give you a better sense of how they are used.

The ultimate goal of JavaBeans was to allow components to be manipulated visually within a graphical application builder. Beans can be chosen from a palette of tools and manipulated graphically in an application builder's workspace. In this sense, beans resemble the widgets used in a traditional GUI builder: user interface components that can be assembled to make application "screens." In traditional GUI builders, the result is usually some automatically generated code that provides a skeleton on which you hang the meat of your application. GUI builders generally build GUIs, not entire applications.

In contrast, Java beans can be not only simple UI components, such as buttons and sliders, but also more complex and abstract components. It is easy to get the impression that beans are, themselves, always graphical objects (like the Swing components that we mentioned), but Java beans can implement any part of an application, including "invisible" parts that perform calculations, storage, and communications. Ideally, we would like to be able to snap together a substantial application using prefabricated beans, without ever writing a line of code. Three characteristics of the JavaBeans architecture aim to make it possible to work with application components at this level:

Design patterns

> The most important characteristic of a Java bean is simply a layer of standardization. Design patterns (i.e., coding conventions) let tools and humans recognize the basic features of a bean and manipulate it without knowing how it is implemented. We might say that beans are "self-documenting." By examining a bean, we can tell what events it can fire and receive; we can also learn about its properties (the equivalent of its public variables) and methods. Beans can also provide explicit information about their features tailored specifically for IDEs.

Reflection

> Reflection is an important feature of the Java language. (It's discussed in Chapter 7.) Reflection makes it possible for Java code to inspect and manipulate new Java objects at runtime. In the context of JavaBeans, reflection lets a development tool analyze a bean's capabilities, examine the values of its fields, and invoke its methods. Essentially, reflection allows Java objects that meet at runtime to do all the things that could be done if the objects had been put together at compile time. Even if a bean doesn't come bundled with any "built-in" documentation, we

can still gather information about its capabilities and properties by directly inspecting the class using reflection.

Object serialization

Finally, the Java Serialization API allows us to "freeze-dry" (or "pickle") a live application or application component and revive it later. This is a very important step; it makes it possible to piece together applications without extensive code generation. Rather than customizing and compiling large amounts of Java code to build our application on startup, we can simply paste together beans, configure them, tweak their appearance, and save them. Later, the beans can be restored with all their state and interconnections intact. This makes possible a fundamentally different way of thinking about the design process. It is easy to use serialized objects from handwritten Java code as well, so we can freely mix "freeze-dried" beans with plain old bean classes and other Java code. There is also a "long-term" object serialization mechanism that saves Java beans in an XML format that is very resilient to changes in classes.

How Big Is a Bean?

The bean examples we mentioned have ranged from simple buttons to spreadsheets. Obviously, a button bean would be much less complex than a spreadsheet and would be used at a different level of the application's design. At what level are beans intended to be used? The JavaBeans architecture is supposed to scale well from small to large; simple beans can be used to build larger beans. A small bean may consist of a single class; a large bean may have many. Beans can also work together through their container to provide services to other beans.

Simple beans are little more than ordinary Java objects. In fact, any Java class that has a default (empty) constructor could be considered a bean. A bean should also be serializable, although the JavaBeans specification doesn't strictly require that. These two criteria ensure that we can create an instance of the bean dynamically and that we can later save the bean as part of a group or composition of beans. There are no other requirements. Beans are not required to inherit from a base bean class, and they don't have to implement any special interface.

A useful bean would want to send and receive events and expose its properties to the world. To do so, it follows the appropriate design patterns for naming the relevant methods so that these features can be automatically discovered. Most nontrivial beans intended for use in a visual application builder IDE also provide information about themselves in the form of a BeanInfo class. A BeanInfo class implements the BeanInfo interface, which holds methods that describe a bean's features in more detail, along with extra packaging, such as icons for display to the user. Normally, this "bean info" is supplied by a separate class that is named for and supplied with the bean.

The NetBeans IDE

We can't have a meaningful discussion of beans without spending a little time talking about the builder environments in which they are used. In this chapter, we use the NetBeans IDE Version 4.0 to demonstrate our beans. NetBeans is a popular, pure Java development environment. In this case, the "integrated" in "integrated development environment" means that NetBeans offers powerful source and visual editor capabilities, templates that aid in the creation of various types of Java classes, and the ability to compile, run, and debug applications, all in one tool. In particular, we'll be using the visual development environment of NetBeans to glue together our Java beans and try them out. Other IDEs offer similar capabilities. See Appendix A for a brief comparison of NetBeans and the Eclipse IDE.

Because NetBeans is a full-blown production development environment, it has many features we don't use in these examples. For that reason, we can't really provide a full introduction to it here. We will provide only bare-bones directions here for demonstrating the Java beans in this chapter. But we hope that once you get into the tool and start looking around, you will want to learn more.

Installing and Running NetBeans

You have to install Java 5.0 before you can install NetBeans. If you installed the JDK from Sun's web site, you may have downloaded a combined JDK and NetBeans bundle, so you may already have it installed. Both the JDK and NetBeans are included on the CD-ROM that accompanies this book (view CD content online at *http://examples.oreilly.com/learnjava3/CD-ROM/*). They can also be downloaded from *http://java.sun.com/j2se/* and *http://www.netbeans.org*, respectively.

Follow the simple installation instructions for those packages (you may have to reboot if you installed Java). During the NetBeans installation, it may prompt you for the version of the JDK to use. Choose the Java 5.0 version. When you're all set, launch NetBeans.

When you first start NetBeans, a welcome screen appears. Close it for now by clicking the small x on its tab. (If you want to return to this welcome screen later to take the NetBeans tutorials, choose Help → Welcome Screen.)

Installing our example beans

Before we get started, we'll have to add the example beans used in this chapter to the NetBeans palette. NetBeans installs Java beans in a central location that can be used by multiple projects in the editor. Unfortunately, this obscures the location of the real classes. NetBeans keeps these classes and other configuration information in a directory called *.netbeans* in your home directory (on Windows, the location is */Documents and Settings/<Username>/.netbeans*). If at any time you feel that you've really hosed your environment and want to start fresh, just remove this directory and relaunch NetBeans to get back to square one.

To install our beans, grab our demo beans JAR file, *magicbeans.jar,* from the accompanying CD-ROM or from this book's web site at *http://www.oreilly.com/catalog/ learnjava3/.* Save the file locally and then select Tools → Palette Manager to add the beans. Click Add from Jar, then select the *magicbeans.jar* file and click Next. The wizard then shows you a list of beans that our JAR contains (there should be eight altogether). Select all of them (click the first and shift-click the last), then click Next. NetBeans prompts you for the palette category under which you wish to file these; select Beans, then click Finish and Close. We'll see these beans soon, when we start editing an application.

Creating a project and file

Now, we must create a new project to hold our work. Normally, we'd suggest that you import the examples from the CD or online. In this case, we're going to be doing visual layout and all the action is in the actions, so to speak, so we'll just walk through them as we go. To create a new project, select New Project from the File menu. In the Categories pane of the wizard, select General and in the Projects pane, select Java Application, then click Next. You give your project a name, for example, LearningJava, and specify a location or you can leave the defaults. Uncheck the box labeled Create Main Class since we won't be needing one in our project, then click Finish to complete our empty project. If this is the first time you've created a project in NetBeans, you may see a message that says that NetBeans is scanning project classpaths; this takes a few minutes.

Next, we need to create a class file to put into our project. Select New File from the File menu. NetBeans prompts you with a wizard. In the Categories pane, select Java GUI Forms and in the File Types pane, select JFrame Form. Choosing JFrame Form gives us a Java class file extending JFrame with the basic structure of a GUI application already set up for us. Click Next, then give the file a name, such as LearningJava1. You may leave the package set to the default package if you wish. Now click Finish and the screen looks like Figure 22-1.

The NetBeans workspace

Figure 22-1 shows the NetBeans application. The screen has three main areas with a toolbar at the top. The left area is the explorer window. Tabs in the explorer window can show a Java package and class-oriented view of our project, a filesystem view, or a runtime environment view. With the Files tab selected, the explorer should reveal our *LearningJava1.java* class. In the center area is our workspace with tabs for each open file (currently one). Since we selected a GUI-type file, NetBeans has placed us into GUI editing mode and shows us an empty box where we will place

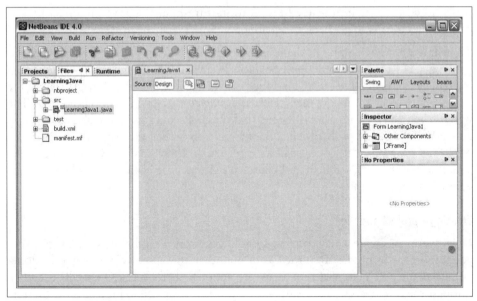

Figure 22-1. The NetBeans workspace

our beans. Click alternately on the Source and Design buttons to switch between the Java source code and this view (try it now).

On the right side is a Palette pane, an Inspector pane, and a Properties pane, which currently shows no properties (that makes sense since we have not yet placed a bean in the workspace). The Palette shows buttons for different groups of beans. The Swing group includes all the standard Swing components. AWT holds AWT components. Layouts holds Java layout managers. Inspector shows a GUI container view of our class, and Properties will show us the configurable features of our beans. Properties changes its contents based on the bean currently selected in the workspace.

Under Palette, select Swing (it may be selected by default) to see some of the available Swing components (they appear as icons at the top of the window). Now select Beans to see the beans we imported earlier. You should see the friendly Dial component bean from Chapter 18, along with a tiny person bean. The rest of our beans have no pretty icons and can't easily be distinguished. That's because these simple example beans aren't packaged as completely as the others. (We'll talk about packaging later in the chapter.) For now, right-click on one of the beans, and select Show Component Names to display the class names of all the beans in the palette. (You may want to resize the pane so you can see more of the beans). Figure 22-2 shows the bean palette.

To place a bean into the workspace, click on it and then click in the workspace. Before you do that, though, you may want to set an appropriate layout manager. The Inspector holds a tree that shows all the components (visible and invisible) in the project. By

Figure 22-2. The bean palette

right-clicking on the JFrame (our top-level container) in either the workspace or the tree, you can select Set Layout to specify the layout manager for the frame. For now, try using AbsoluteLayout, provided by NetBeans. This allows you to arbitrarily place and move beans within the container. You wouldn't want to do this in general, but for our examples it will make life a bit easier. The other layout managers are easy enough to use, but we'll refer you to NetBeans tutorials for that information.

Properties and Customizers

Properties represent the "state" or "data" content of a bean. These features can be manipulated externally to configure the bean. For a bean that's a GUI component, you might expect its properties to include its size, color, and other features of its basic appearance. Properties are similar in concept to an object's public variables. Like a variable, a property can be a primitive type (such as a number or Boolean), or it can be a complex object type (such as a String or a collection of spreadsheet data). Unlike variables, properties are always manipulated using methods to set and get the value; this enables a bean to take action whenever a property changes. By sending an event when a property changes, a bean can notify other interested beans of the change (as discussed later in this chapter).

Let's pull a couple of beans into NetBeans and take a look at their properties. Click on a JButton from the Swing palette, and then click in the workspace. When the JButton is first loaded by NetBeans, it was inspected to discover its properties. When we select an instance of the button, NetBeans displays these properties in the Properties pane and allows us to modify them.

The button has nine basic properties, followed by a few additional groupings. The list called Other Properties adds more detail. There is also a Layout properties section (these are in actuality not properties of the JButton, but are here for convenience) as well as an Accessibility properties list (for components that have accessibility-related properties). The foreground and background properties are colors; their current values are displayed in the corresponding box. font is the font for the label text; an example of the font is shown. text is the text of the button's label. You can also set an image icon for the button, the tooltip text that appears when the mouse hovers over the item, and a keyboard-shortcut identifier, called a *mnemonic*. Try typing something new for the value of the text property, and watch the button label change. Click on the background color to enter a numeric color value, or, better yet, press the "..." button to pop up a color-chooser dialog.

Most of these basic properties will be familiar to you because many GUI beans inherit them from the base JComponent class. The Other Properties section lists almost 50 additional properties inherited from JComponent. NetBeans is making an effort to categorize these for us. As we'll see when we create our own beans, we can limit which properties are included in the Properties pane.

Now place a Juggler bean in the workspace (this is one of Sun's original demonstration Java beans that we have updated). The animation starts, and the juggler begins juggling some roughly drawn beans, as shown in Figure 22-3. If he gets annoying, don't worry; we'll have him under our control soon enough.

You can see that this bean has a different set of properties, including an interesting one called animationRate. It is an integer property that controls the delay in milliseconds between displays of the juggler's frames. Try changing its value. The juggler changes speed as you type each value. Good beans give you immediate feedback when you change their properties. Uncheck the checkbox next to the Boolean juggling property to stop the show if you want.

Notice that the Properties pane provides a way to display and edit each of the different property types. For the foreground and background properties of the JButton, the pane displays the color; if you click on them, a color selection dialog pops up. Similarly, if you click on the font property, you get a font selection dialog. For integer and string values, you can type a new value into the field. NetBeans understands and can edit the most useful basic Java types.

Since the property types are open-ended, NetBeans can't possibly anticipate them all. Beans with more complex property types can supply their own *property editor*. The

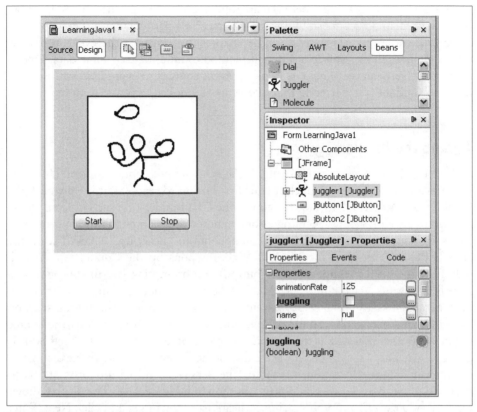

Figure 22-3. Juggling beans

`Molecule` bean that we'll play with in the next section, for example, uses a custom property editor that lets us choose the type of molecule. If it needs even more control over how its properties are displayed, a bean can provide a *customizer*, which allows a bean to provide its own GUI for editing its properties. (For example, a customizer could let you draw an icon for a button.)

Event Hookups and Adapters

Beans use events to communicate. As we mentioned in Chapter 16, events are not limited to GUI components but can be used for signaling and passing information in more general applications. An event is simply a notification; information describing the event and other data are wrapped up in a subclass of `EventObject` and passed to the receiving object by a method invocation. Event sources register listeners that want to receive the events when they occur. Event receivers implement the appropriate listener interface containing the method needed to receive the events. This is Java's general event mechanism in a nutshell.

It's useful to place an adapter between an event source and a listener. An adapter can be used when an object doesn't know how to receive a particular event; it enables the object to handle the event anyway. The adapter can translate the event into some other action, such as a call to a different method or an update of some data. One of the jobs of NetBeans is to help us hook up event sources to event listeners. Another job is to produce adapter code that allows us to hook up events in more complex ways.

Taming the Juggler

Let's face it: jugglers can get annoying. Let's try to get ours under control. Using the Properties pane, change the label of your first button to read "Start." Now click the small Connection Mode icon at the top of the GUI builder (the second icon, showing two items with arrows pointing at one another). After pressing the button, NetBeans is waiting for us to select two components to "hook up." Click first on the Start button and then on the Juggler. NetBeans pops up the Connection Wizard, indicating the source component (the button) and prompting you to choose from a large list of events (see Figure 22-4). Most of them are standard Swing events that can be generated by any kind of JComponent. What we're after is the button's action event. Expand the folder named action, and select actionPerformed as the source event. NetBeans indicates at the bottom the name of an event handler method it is going to generate for us. You can leave the method name as is. Click Next to go to the Specify Target Operation screen for the Juggler. The wizard prompts us to choose a property to set on the Juggler, as shown in Figure 22-5. The display shows three of the Juggler's properties. Choose juggling as the target and click Next. Enter **true** in the Value field and click Finish. NetBeans takes you to the source view and shows you the method it has generated to respond to the button action. We have completed a hookup between the button and the Juggler. When the button fires an action event, the juggling property of the Juggler is set to true.

Scroll around the source view and take a look at the code that NetBeans has generated to make this connection for us. Specifically, in the initComponents( ) method of our template class, it has created an anonymous inner class to serve as the ActionListener for ActionEvents from our button (which it has named jButton1):

```
jButton1.addActionListener(new java.awt.event.ActionListener( ) {
    public void actionPerformed(java.awt.event.ActionEvent evt) {
        jButton1ActionPerformed(evt);
    }
});
```

The adapter calls a private method that sets the property on our Juggler:

```
private void jButton1ActionPerformed(java.awt.event.ActionEvent evt) {
    juggler1.setJuggling(true);
}
```

Figure 22-4. Selecting a source event in the Connection Wizard

Figure 22-5. Specifying a target operation in the Connection Wizard

You'll notice that most of the code that was written for us is shaded light blue to indicate that it is autogenerated and can't be directly modified. The body of the private method is open, however, and we could modify it to perform arbitrary activities when the button is pushed. In NetBeans, the hookup is just a starting point.

This may all seem a little obtuse. After all, if we had made the Juggler an ActionListener in the first place, we would expect to hook it directly to the button. The use of adapters provides a great deal of flexibility, however, as we'll see next.

To complete our example, click the Design button, then repeat the process, adding a second JButton labeled "Stop." Click the Connection Wizard icon; select the Stop button and the Juggler as its target. Again, choose the actionPerformed method as the source, but this time, instead of selecting a property on the Juggler, click the Method call radio button to see a list of available methods on the Juggler bean. Scroll all the way down and select the stopJuggling( ) method. Click Finish to complete the hookup, and look at the generated code if you wish. With this, we have seen an example of hooking up a source of action events to produce an arbitrary method call on a bean.

Running the example

Now, the Juggler will do our bidding. Right-click on the *LearningJava1.java* file in the File tab of the Explorer pane and select Run File. Watch as NetBeans compiles and runs our example. You should be able to start and stop the juggler using the buttons! When you are done, close the juggler application and return to the GUI editor. Close this example by closing its tab in the workspace, and let's move on. (There is no need to save the file explicitly; NetBeans saves automatically as you edit.)

Molecular Motion

Let's look at one more interesting example, shown in Figure 22-6. Create a new file in our project as before, choosing Java GUI Forms from the Categories pane and JFrame Form in the File Types pane. Call this file *LearningJava2*.

Grab a Molecule bean and place it in the workspace. (The default BorderLayout maximizes its area if you place the bean in the center.) If you run the example now, you will see that by dragging the mouse within the image, you can rotate the model in three dimensions. Try changing the type of molecule using the Properties pane: ethane is fun.* Let's see what we can do with our molecule. Grab a Timer bean from the palette. Timer is a clock.† Every so many milliseconds, Timer fires an event. The timer is controlled by an long property called delay, which determines the number of milliseconds between events. Timer is an "invisible" bean; it is not derived from a JComponent and doesn't have a graphical appearance, just as an internal timer in an application doesn't normally have a presence on the screen. NetBeans shows these invisible beans just like any other bean in the Inspector pane. When you wish to select the Timer, click on it in the tree in the Inspector pane.

Let's hook the Timer to our Molecule. Start the Connection Wizard and select the Timer (from the tree) and then the Molecule. Choose the Timer's timerFired( ) event from the list (expand the folder to display it). Click Next and select the Method call

---

* As of this writing, Sun's Molecule example has some problems when used in NetBeans. Selecting a molecule type other than the default causes a compile-time error. You can use the Test Form button on the NetBeans form editor to try the other molecule types.

† A Timer bean used to come with the NetBeans distribution but disappeared in Version 4.0, so we've added our own replacement. We won't discuss it here, but the source code is with the other bean examples and there is nothing special that isn't covered elsewhere.

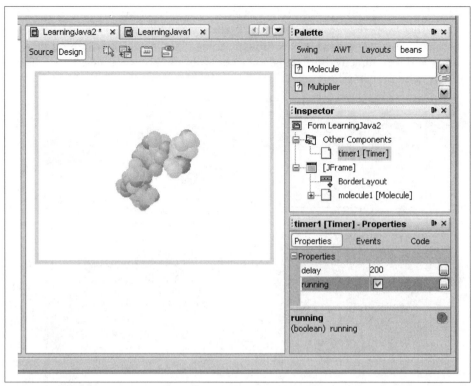

Figure 22-6. The Molecule bean and the Timer

radio button. Find and select the rotateOnX( ) method and click Finish. Run the example. Now the Molecule should turn on its own every time it receives an event from the timer. Try changing the timer's delay property. You can also hook the Timer to the Molecule's rotateOnY( ) method. Use a different instance of Timer and, by setting different delay values, make it turn at different rates in each dimension. There's no end to the fun.

Binding Properties

By using a combination of events and adapters, we can connect beans in many interesting ways. We can even "bind" two beans together so that if a property changes in the first bean, the corresponding property is automatically changed in the second bean. In this scenario, the beans don't necessarily have to be of the same type, but, to make sense, the properties do.

Close the Molecule file and start a new one. Grab two NumericField beans from the palette, drop them in the workspace, and select one of them, as shown in Figure 22-7. You'll probably want to set the AbsoluteLayout again. You can also adjust the width of the fields by dragging them at the sides. You'll notice that a

NumericField has many of the standard properties of a Swing component. If you look in the Other Properties section of the Properties pane, you can find an integer property called value that represents the numeric value of the field. You can set it there or enter a number directly into the field when you run the program. NumericField rejects nonnumeric text.

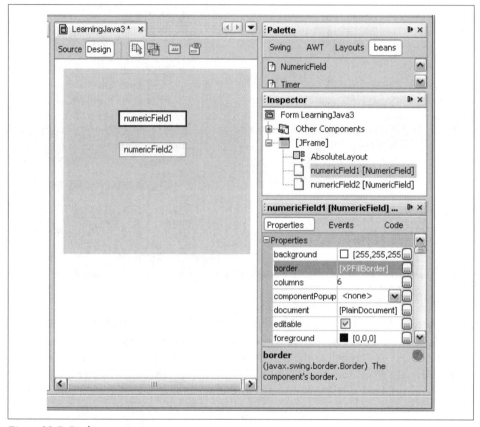

Figure 22-7. Binding properties

Let's bind the value property of one of the fields to the other. Activate the Connection Wizard to create a connection between the two fields. Click first on numericField1 and then on numericField2 so that numericField1 is the source. In the wizard, choose the propertyChange( ) event of the source field. This is the listener method for PropertyChangeEvent, a generic event sent by beans when one of their properties changes. When a bean fires property-change events in response to changes in a particular property, that property is said to be "bound." This means that it is possible to bind the property to another bean through the generic mechanism. In this case, the value property of our NumericField beans is a bound property, so whenever it changes, a PropertyChangeEvent is fired.

Choose Next, and select the value property as the target for numericField2. Click Next again, and select the Property radio button on the Parameters screen. Click the "…" editor button to pop up a Select Property dialog. Select the source numeric field (probably named numericField1, if that is your source button) from the pull-down menu, and then choose the value property. Click Ok and Finish to complete the hookup.

Run the application, and try entering values in the first field (numericField1). The second field should change each time. The second bean's value property has been bound to the first.

Try binding the value property in the other direction as well so that you can change the value in either bean, and the changes are propagated in both directions. (Some simple logic in the beans prevents infinite loops from happening here.)

NetBeans has again generated an adapter for us. This time the adapter listens for PropertyChangeEvents and invokes the setValue( ) method of our target field. We haven't done anything earth-shaking. The PropertyChangeEvent does carry some extra information—the old and new values of the property—but we're not using them here. And with the Connection Wizard, you can use any event source as the impetus to set a property on your target bean. Finally, as we've seen, the property can derive its value from any other bean in the layout. The flexibility of the Connection Wizard is, to some extent, masking the purpose of the events, but that's okay. If we are interested in the specific property that changed, or if we want to apply logic about the value, we can fill in the generated method with our own code.

Many Swing components have bound properties; they are usually documented in the Javadoc for the class.

Constraining Properties

In the previous section, we discussed how beans fire PropertyChangeEvents to notify other beans (and adapters) that a property has changed. In that scenario, the object that receives the event is simply a passive listener as far as the event's source is concerned. JavaBeans also supports *constrained properties*, in which the event listener gets to say whether it will allow a bean to change the property's value. If the new value is rejected, the change is cancelled; the event source keeps its old value.

The concept of constrained properties has not been heavily used in the normal operation of Swing, so we won't cover it in detail here. But it goes something like this. Normally, PropertyChangeEvents are delivered to a propertyChange( ) method in the listener. Constrained properties are implemented by delivering PropertyChangeEvents to a separate listener method called vetoableChange( ). The vetoableChange( ) method throws a PropertyVetoException if it doesn't like a proposed change. In this way, components can govern the acceptable values set by other components.

Building Beans

Now that you have a feel for how beans look from the user's perspective, let's build some. In this section, we will become the Magic Beans Company. We will create some beans, package them for distribution, and use them in NetBeans to build a very simple application. (The complete JAR file, along with all the example code for this chapter, is on the CD-ROM that accompanies this book and at *http://www.oreilly.com/catalog/learnjava3.*)

The first thing we'll remind you of is that absolutely anything can be a bean. Even the following class is a bean, albeit an invisible one:

```
public class Trivial implements java.io.Serializable {}
```

Of course, this bean isn't very useful: it doesn't have any properties, and it doesn't do anything. But it's a bean nonetheless, and we can drag it into NetBeans as long as we package it correctly. If we modify this class to extend JComponent, we suddenly have a graphical bean that be seen in the layout, with lots of standard Swing properties, such as size and color information:

```
public class TrivialComponent extends JComponent {}
```

Next, let's look at a bean that's a bit more useful.

The Dial Bean

We created a nifty Dial component in Chapter 18. What would it take to turn it into a bean? Surprise: it is already a bean! The Dial has a number of properties that it exposes in the way prescribed by JavaBeans. A get method retrieves the value of a property; for example, getValue( ) retrieves the dial's current value. Likewise, a set method (setValue( )) modifies the dial's value. The dial has two other properties, which also have get and set methods: minimum and maximum. This is all the Dial needs to inform a tool such as NetBeans what properties it has and how to work with them. Because Dial is a JComponent, it also has all the standard Swing properties, such as color and size. The JComponent provides the set and get methods for all its properties.

To use our Dial, we'll put it in a Java package named magicbeans and store it in a JAR file that can be loaded by NetBeans. The source code, which can be found on the accompanying CD (view its content online at *http://examples.oreilly.com/learnjava3/CD-ROM/*), includes an Ant build file (see Chapter 15) that compiles the code and creates the final JAR file.

If you were starting from scratch, it would go like this: First, create a directory called *magicbeans* to hold our beans, add a package statement to the source files *Dial.java*, *DialEvent.java*, and *DialListener.java* (from Chapter 18), put the source files into the *magicbeans* directory, and compile them (using the command *javac magicBeans/Dial.java*) to create class files.

Next, we need to create a manifest file that tells NetBeans which of the classes in the JAR file are beans and which are support files or unrelated. At this point, we have only one bean, *Dial.class*, so create the following file, called *magicBeans.manifest*:

```
Name: magicbeans/Dial.class
Java-Bean: True
```

The `Name:` label identifies the class file as it will appear in the JAR: `magicbeans/Dial.class`. Specifications appearing after an item's `Name:` line and before an empty line apply to that item. (See Chapter 3 for more details.) We have added the attribute `Java-Bean: True`, which flags this class as a bean to tools that read the manifest. We will add an entry like this for each bean in our package. We don't need to flag support classes (such as `DialEvent` and `DialListener`) as beans because we won't want to manipulate them directly with NetBeans; in fact, we don't need to mention them in the manifest at all.

To create the JAR file, including our manifest information, enter this command:

```
% jar-cvmf magicbeans.manifest magicbeans.jar magicbeans/*.class
```

If you loaded the precompiled examples as instructed earlier, then you already have the `Dial` bean loaded into NetBeans. The version supplied in the precompiled *magicbeans.jar* file has additional packaging that allows it to appear with a spiffy icon in the palette, as we'll discuss a bit later. (If you haven't loaded the example JAR, you can import the one we just created by selecting Palette Manager from the Tools menu, as described earlier in this chapter.) If you want to replace the `Dial` bean on your palette, you can remove it by right-clicking on the icon and selecting Delete before importing the new JAR. (Actually, NetBeans 4.0 should reload the JAR automatically if you overwrite it.)

You should now have an entry for `Dial` in the bean palette. Drop an instance of the `Dial` bean into a new JFrame Form file in NetBeans.

As Figure 22-8 shows, the `Dial`'s properties—value, minimum, and maximum—appear in the Properties pane and can be modified by NetBeans. If you just created the `Dial` JAR following our minimal instructions, you'll see these properties along with all the Swing properties inherited from the `JComponent` class. The figure shows the `Dial` bean as it appears later in this chapter (with the supplied packaging), after we've learned about the `BeanInfo` class. We're almost there.

Now we're ready to put the `Dial` to use. Reopen the `Juggler` file that we created in the first section of this chapter. Add an instance of our new magic `Dial` bean to the scenario, as shown in Figure 22-9.

Bind the `value` property of the `Dial` to the `animationRate` of the `Juggler`. Use the Connection Wizard, as before, selecting the `Dial` and then the `Juggler`. Select the `DialEvent` source and bind the `animationRate` property, selecting the `Dial`'s value as the property source. When you complete the hookup, you should be able to vary the speed of the juggler by turning the dial. Try changing the maximum and minimum values of the dial to change the range.

Figure 22-8. The Dial component as a bean

Figure 22-9. The Juggler with a dialable animation rate

Design Patterns for Properties

We said earlier that tools such as NetBeans found out about a bean's properties by looking at its get and set methods. The easiest way to make properties visible is to follow these simple design patterns:

- Method for getting the current value of a property:

    ```
    public PropertyType getPropertyName( )
    ```

- Method for setting the value of a property:

    ```
    public void setPropertyName( PropertyType arg )
    ```

- Method for determining whether a Boolean-valued property is currently true:

    ```
    public boolean isPropertyName( )
    ```

The last method is optional and is used only for properties with Boolean values. (You could use the get method for Boolean values as well.)

The appropriate set and get methods for these features of our bean are already in the Dial class, either methods that we added or methods inherited from the java.awt. Component and javax.swing.JComponent classes:

```
// inherited from Component
public Color getForeground( )
public void setForeground(Color c)

public Color getBackground( )
public void setBackground(Color c)

public Font getFont( )
public void setFont(Font f)

// many others from Component and JComponent

// part of the Dial itself
public int getValue( )
public void setValue(int v)

public int getMinimum( )
public void setMinimum(int m)

public int getMaximum( )
public void setMaximum(int m)
```

JavaBeans allows read and write-only properties, which are implemented simply by leaving out the get or set method.

NetBeans uses the Reflection API to find out about the Dial bean's methods; it then uses these naming conventions to learn what properties are available. When we use the properties editor to change a value, NetBeans dynamically invokes the correct set method to change the value.

If you look further at the JComponent class, you'll notice that other methods match the design pattern. For example, what about the setCursor( ) and getCursor( ) pair? NetBeans doesn't know how to display or edit a cursor, and we didn't supply an editor, so it ignores those properties in the properties sheet.

NetBeans automatically pulls the property's name from the name of its accessor methods; it then lowercases the name for display on the properties sheet. For example, the font property is not listed as Font. Later, we'll show how to provide a BeanInfo class that overrides the way these properties are displayed, letting you provide your own friendly property names. Again, if you used the Dial bean from our precompiled example JAR you'll see only our three Dial properties. The JComponent properties are hidden by our special packaging (a BeanInfo class) that presents only the properties we wish to show.

Bean patterns in NetBeans

NetBeans automatically recognizes JavaBeans getter and setter method patterns in classes. In the File or Project Explorer (on the left), expand the folder for our LearningJava1 class and you'll see a Bean Patterns folder. You can add properties to any Java source class by right-clicking on the Bean Patterns folder and selecting Add, then Property. After you supply the name and type of the property, NetBeans automatically creates the necessary getter and setter methods. You can add instance variable and bound property support as well. This can save you a bit of typing if you need to add a lot of properties.

A (Slightly) More Realistic Example

We now have one nifty bean for the Magic Beans products list. Let's round out the set before we start advertising. Our goal is to build the beans we need to make a very simple form. The application performs a simple calculation after data is entered on the form.

A bean for validating numeric data

One component we're sure to need in a form is a text field that accepts numeric data. We're now going to build our NumericField bean that accepts and validates numbers and makes the values available as a property. You should recognize all the parts of the bean:

```
//file: NumericField.java
package magicbeans;

import javax.swing.*;
import java.awt.event.*;

public class NumericField extends JTextField
{
```

```
       private double value;
       static final int defaultSize = 6;

        public NumericField( ) {
          super( defaultSize );
          setInputVerifier( new InputVerifier( ) {
             public boolean verify( JComponent comp ) {
                JTextField field = (JTextField)comp;
                boolean passed = false;
                try {
                   setValue( Double.parseDouble( field.getText( ) ) );
                } catch ( NumberFormatException e ) {
                   comp.getToolkit( ).beep( );
                   field.selectAll( );
                   return false;
                }
                return true;
             }
          } );

          addActionListener( new ActionListener( ) {
             public void actionPerformed( ActionEvent e ) {
                getInputVerifier( ).verify( NumericField.this );
             }
          } );
       }

       public double getValue( ) {
          return value;
       }
       public void setValue( double newValue ) {
          double oldValue = value;
          value = newValue;
          setText( "" + newValue );
          firePropertyChange( "value", oldValue, newValue );
       }
    }
```

NumericField extends the Swing JTextField component. The constructor defaults the
text field to a width of six columns, but you can change its size in NetBeans through
the columns property.

The heart of NumericField is the InputVerifier, which we have implemented as an
anonymous inner class. Our verifier is called to parse the user's entry as a number,
giving it a Double value. We have also added an ActionListener that validates when
the user hits Enter in the field.

If parsing succeeds, we update the value property using our setValue( ) method.
setValue( ) then fires a PropertyChangeEvent to notify any interested beans. If the text
doesn't parse properly as a number, we give feedback to the user by selecting (highlighting) the text.

Earlier we verified the operation of this bean by placing two `NumericFields` in the workspace and binding the value property of one to the other. We saw that we were able to enter a new floating point value in one field and see the change reflected in the other.

An invisible multiplier

Now, let's make an invisible bean that performs a calculation rather than forming part of a user interface. `Multiplier` is a simple invisible bean that multiplies the values of two of its properties (A and B) to produce the value of a third read-only property (C). Here's the code:

```java
//file: Multiplier.java
package magicbeans;

import java.beans.*;

public class Multiplier implements java.io.Serializable {
    private double a, b, c;

    synchronized public void setA( double val ) {
        a = val;
        multiply( );
    }

    synchronized public double getA( ) {
        return a;
    }

    synchronized public void setB( double val ) {
        b = val;
        multiply( );
    }

    synchronized public double getB( ) {
        return b;
    }

    synchronized public double getC( ) {
        return c;
    }

    synchronized public void setC( double val ) {
        multiply( );
    }

    private void multiply( ) {
        double oldC = c;
        c = a * b;
        propChanges.firePropertyChange(
            "c", new Double(oldC) , new Double(c) );
    }
```

```
    private PropertyChangeSupport propChanges =
new PropertyChangeSupport(this);

  public void addPropertyChangeListener(
  PropertyChangeListener listener)
  {
      propChanges.addPropertyChangeListener(listener);
  }
  public void removePropertyChangeListener(
  PropertyChangeListener listener)
  {
      propChanges.removePropertyChangeListener(listener);
  }
}
```

To make a `Multiplier` a source of `PropertyChangeEvents`, we enlist the help of a `PropertyChangeSupport` object. To implement `Multiplier`'s methods for registering property-change listeners, we simply call the corresponding methods in the `PropertyChangeSupport` object. Similarly, a `Multiplier` fires a property change event by calling the `PropertyChangeSupport` object's `firePropertyChange()` method. This is the easiest way to get an arbitrary class to be a source of `PropertyChangeEvents`.

The code is straightforward. Whenever the value of property a or b changes, we call `multiply()`, which multiplies their values and fires a `PropertyChangeEvent`. So, we can say that `Multiplier` supports binding of its c property.

Putting them together

Finally, let's demonstrate that we can put our beans together in a useful way. Arrange three `JLabels`, three `NumericFields`, and a `Multiplier`, as shown in Figure 22-10.

Figure 22-10. TextLabels, NumericFields, and a Multiplier

Bind the values of the first two `NumericFields` to the a and b properties of the `Multiplier`, respectively; bind the c value of the `Multiplier` to the third `NumericField`. Now, we have a simple calculator. Try some other arrangements. Can you build a calculator that squares a number? Can you see how you might build a simple spreadsheet? Well, perhaps not. We'll address some of the limitations in the next section.

Limitations of Visual Design

The last example proved that we can create at least a trivial application by hooking beans together in a mostly visual way. In other development environments, this kind of bean hookup would have been even more streamlined. For example, Sun's "Bean-Box" experimental Java bean container, introduced with Java 1.1, took a different approach from NetBeans. It allowed the developer to work with "live" Java bean instances, dynamically generating adapter code at runtime and relying solely on object serialization to save the resulting work. This kind of design is, in a sense, the real goal of the JavaBeans architecture. It is true "what you see is what you get" (WYSIWYG) programming. However, pure visual design without the ability to integrate handwritten code, as we can do in NetBeans, has not yet proven to scale beyond these kinds of simple applications, and pure visual programming environments have thus far failed to catch on. Meanwhile, Sun is working on a replacement for BeanBox called BeanBuilder. You can learn more about it at *http://java.sun.com/products/javabeans/beanbuilder/*.

Serialization Versus Code Generation

If you've been keeping an eye on the NetBeans source window while we've been working, you may have noticed the code that is being generated when you modify properties of beans. By default, NetBeans generates method calls to set values on beans in the initComponents( ) method. For example, if you set the value of one of your NumericField beans to 42 in the Properties pane, this value gets hardcoded into the application as an initial value of the bean by a call to setValue( ) on the bean object at initialization time. But if you click on the Code button in the Properties pane, you'll see that we have another option. This area holds properties that govern how NetBeans generates the application code. By changing the Code Generation property from Generate Code to Serialize, you change NetBeans' behavior. Instead of generating method calls in the source code, it saves your fully configured bean as a serialized object and then generates the appropriate code to load the freeze-dried bean into the application from a file.

Try changing the code generation property for a Juggler bean to Serialize. Switching to the source-code view and looking at the initComponents( ) method, you'll see a line for that bean that uses the static Beans.instantiate( ) method to load a serialized copy of the bean.

NetBeans treats the serialized bean file as part of the source code and will regenerate it whenever it saves the source file. But to run this example, we have to first do a manual build. Select Build → Build Main Project, then you can run the file as before with the Run File context menu. The reason for the explicit build is to prompt Net-Beans to copy the serialized bean file from the source folder of your source file over to the compiled classes directory (it should be smart enough to do this itself). You should see the serialized bean file, named something like: *LearnJava1_juggler1.ser* alongside your source file (and deployed to the *classes* directory). You can run the example and confirm that it behaves exactly like the code-generated version. (This is pretty neat if you think about it.)

We'll discuss working with serialized beans in more detail later in this chapter and ask you to refer to this stored bean file.

Customizing with BeanInfo

So far, everything NetBeans has known about our beans has been determined by low-level reflection—that is, by looking at the methods of our classes. The java. Beans.Introspector class gathers information on a bean using reflection, then analyzes and describes a bean to any tool that wants to know about it. The introspection process works only if the class follows the JavaBeans naming conventions for its methods; furthermore, it gives us little control over exactly what properties and events appear in NetBeans menus. For example, we've seen that NetBeans by default shows all the stuff we inherit from the base Swing component. We can change that by creating BeanInfo classes for our beans. A BeanInfo class provides the JavaBeans introspector with explicit information about the properties, methods, and events of a bean; we can even use it to customize the text that appears in menus in NetBeans (and in other IDEs).

A BeanInfo class implements the BeanInfo interface. That's a complicated proposition; in most situations, the introspector's default behavior is reasonable. Instead of implementing the BeanInfo interface, we extend the SimpleBeanInfo class, which implements all BeanInfo's methods. We can override specific methods to provide the information we want; when we don't override a method, we'll get the introspector's default behavior.

In the next few sections, we'll develop the DialBeanInfo class that provides explicit information about our Dial bean.

Getting Properties Information

We'll start out by describing the Dial's properties. To do so, we must implement the getPropertyDescriptors() method. This method simply returns an array of PropertyDescriptor objects—one for each property we want to publicize.

To create a PropertyDescriptor, call its constructor with two arguments: the property's name and the class. In the following code, we create descriptors for the Dial's value, minimum, and maximum properties. We next call a few methods of the PropertyDescriptor class to provide additional information about each property. If our methods were bound (generated PropertyChangeEvents when modified), we'd call the setBound( )method of their PropertyDescriptors. Our code is prepared to catch an IntrospectionException, which can occur if something goes wrong while creating the property descriptors, such as encountering a nonexistent method:

```java
//file: DialBeanInfo.java
package magicbeans;
import java.beans.*;

public class DialBeanInfo extends SimpleBeanInfo {

  public PropertyDescriptor[] getPropertyDescriptors() {
    try {
      PropertyDescriptor value =
        new PropertyDescriptor("value", Dial.class);
      PropertyDescriptor minimum =
        new PropertyDescriptor("minimum", Dial.class);
      PropertyDescriptor maximum =
        new PropertyDescriptor("maximum", Dial.class);

      return new PropertyDescriptor [] { value, minimum, maximum };
    }
    catch (IntrospectionException e) {
      return null;
    }
  }
}
```

Perhaps the most useful thing about DialBeanInfo is that by providing explicit information for our properties, we automatically hide other properties introspection might find. After compiling DialBeanInfo and packaging it with the Dial, you'll see that its JComponent properties no longer appear in the NetBeans properties editor. (This has been the case all along if you started with the precompiled example JAR.)

A PropertyDescriptor can provide a lot of other information about a property: the names of the accessor methods (if you decide not to use the standard naming convention), information on whether the property is constrained, and a class to use as a property editor (if the standard property editors aren't sufficient).

Getting events information

The Dial bean defines its own event: the DialEvent. We'd like to tell development tools about this event so that we can build applications using it. The process for telling the world about our event is similar to what we did previously: we add a method to the DialBeanInfo class called getEventSetDescriptors(), which returns an array of EventSetDescriptors.

Events are described in terms of their listener interfaces, not in terms of the event classes themselves, so our getEventSetDescriptors() method creates a descriptor for the DialListener interface. Here's the code to add to the DialBeanInfo class:

```java
public EventSetDescriptor[] getEventSetDescriptors() {
  try {
```

```
    EventSetDescriptor dial = new EventSetDescriptor(
      Dial.class, "dialAdjusted",
      DialListener.class, "dialAdjusted");
    dial.setDisplayName("Dial Adjusted");

    return new EventSetDescriptor [] { dial };
  }
  catch (IntrospectionException e) {
    return null;
  }
}
```

In this method, we create an `EventSetDescriptor` object: `dial`. The constructor for an `EventSetDescriptor` takes four arguments: the class that generates the event, the name of the event (the name that is displayed, by default, by a development tool), the listener class, and the name of the method to which the event can be delivered. (Other constructors let you deal with listener interfaces that have several methods.) After creating the descriptor, we call the `setDisplayName( )` method to provide a friendly name to be displayed by development tools, such as NetBeans. (This overrides the default name specified in the constructor.)

Just as the property descriptors we supply hide the properties that were discovered by reflection, the `EventSetDescriptors` can hide the other events that are inherited from the base component classes. In theory, when you recompile `DialBeanInfo`, package it in a JAR, and load it into NetBeans, you should see only the two events that we have explicitly described: our own `DialEvent` and `PropertyChangeEvent` (displayed as "Dial Adjusted" and "Bound property change"). Unfortunately, the current version of NetBeans ignores this information.

Once we have an `EventSetDescriptor`, we can provide other kinds of information about the event. For example, we can state that the event is *unicast*, which means that it can have only one listener.

Supplying icons

Some of the beans that come with NetBeans are displayed on the palette with a cute icon. This makes life more pleasant for everyone. To supply an icon for the `BeanInfo` object we have been developing, we have it implement the getIcon( ) method. You may supply up to four icons, with sizes of 16×16 or 32×32, in either color or monochrome. Here's the getIcon( ) method for `DialBeanInfo`:

```
public class DialBeanInfo extends SimpleBeanInfo {
  ...
  public java.awt.Image getIcon(int iconKind) {

    if (iconKind == BeanInfo.ICON_COLOR_16x16) {
      return loadImage("DialIconColor16.gif");
    } else
    if (iconKind == BeanInfo.ICON_COLOR_32x32) {
      return loadImage("DialIconColor32.gif");
```

```
    } else
    if (iconKind == BeanInfo.ICON_MONO_16x16) {
      return loadImage("DialIconMono16.gif");
    } else
    if (iconKind == BeanInfo.ICON_MONO_32x32) {
      return loadImage("DialIconMono32.gif");
    }
    return null;
  }
```

This method is called with a constant, indicating what kind of icon is being requested; for example, BeanInfo.ICON_COLOR_16x16 requests a 16 × 16 color image. If an appropriate icon is available, it loads the image and returns an Image object. If the icon isn't available, it returns null. For convenience, you can package the images in the same JAR file as the bean and its BeanInfo class.

Though we haven't used them here, you can also use a BeanInfo object to provide information about other public methods of your bean (for example, array-valued properties) and other features.

Creating customizers and property editors

JavaBeans lets you provide a *customizer* for your beans. Customizers are objects that do advanced customization for a bean as a whole; they let you provide your own GUI for tweaking your bean. We won't show you how to write a customizer; it's not too difficult, but it's beyond the scope of this chapter. Suffice it to say that a customizer must implement the java.beans.Customizer interface and should extend Component (or JComponent) so that it can be displayed.

A *property editor* isn't quite as fancy as a customizer. Property editors are a way of giving the properties sheet additional capabilities. For example, you would supply a property editor to let you edit a property type that is specific to your bean. You could provide a property editor that would let you edit an object's price in dollars and cents. We've already seen a couple of property editors: the editor used for Color-valued properties is fundamentally no different from a property editor you might write yourself. In addition, the Molecule bean uses a property editor to specify its moleculeName property.

Again, describing how to write a property editor is beyond the scope of this chapter. Briefly, a property editor must implement the PropertyEditor interface; it usually does so by extending the PropertyEditorSupport class, which provides default implementations for most of the methods.

Hand-Coding with Beans

So far, we've seen how to create and use beans within a bean application builder environment. That is the primary motivation for JavaBeans, at least in GUI development.

But beans are not limited to being used by automated tools. There's no reason we can't use beans in handwritten code. You might use a builder to assemble beans for the user interface of your application and then load that serialized bean or a collection of beans in your own code, just as NetBeans does when told to use object serialization. We'll give an example of that in a moment.

Bean Instantiation and Type Management

Beans are an abstraction over simple Java classes. They add, by convention, features that are not part of the Java language. To enable certain additional capabilities of JavaBeans, we have to use some special tools that take the place of basic language operations. Specifically, when working with beans, we are provided with replacements for three basic Java operations: creating an object with new, checking the type of an object with the instanceof operator, and casting a type with a cast expression. In place of these, use the corresponding static methods of the java.beans.Beans class, shown in Table 22-1.

Table 22-1. Methods of the java.beans.Beans class

Operator	Equivalent
New	Beans.instantiate(classloader, name)
Instanceof	Beans.isInstanceOf(object, class)

Beans.instantiate() is the new operation for beans. It takes a class loader and the name of a bean class or serialized bean as arguments. Its advantage over the plain new operator is that it can also load beans from a serialized form. If you use instantiate(), you don't have to specify in advance whether you will provide the bean as a class or as a serialized object. The instantiate() method first tries to load a resource file based on the name bean, by turning package-style names (with dots) into a path-style name with slashes and then appending the suffix *.ser*. For example, magicbeans.NumericField becomes *magicbeans/NumericField.ser*. If the serialized form of the bean is not found, the instantiate() method attempts to create an instance of the class by name.[*]

Beans.isInstanceOf() and Beans.getInstanceOf() do the jobs of checking a bean's type and casting it to a new type. These methods were intended to allow one or more beans to work together to implement "virtual" or dynamic types. They are supposed to allow beans to take control of this behavior, providing different "views" of themselves. However, they currently don't add any functionality and aren't widely used.

---

[*] This feature would seemingly be applicable to XML-serialized Java beans using the XMLOutputStream as well, but it is not currently implemented for them. This is another sign that the JavaBeans APIs have stagnated.

Working with Serialized Beans

Remember the `Juggler` we serialized a while back? Well, it's time to revive him, just like Han Solo from his "Carbonite" tomb in Star Wars. We'll assume that you saved the `Juggler` by flipping on the Serialization property while working with the `LearnJava1` class and that NetBeans, therefore, saved him in the file *LearnJava1_juggler1.ser*. If you didn't do this, you can use the following snippet of code to serialize the bean to a file of your choice:

```
// Serialize a Juggler instance to a file...
import magicbeans.sunw.demo.juggler.Juggler;
import java.io.*;

public class SerializeJuggler {
   public static void main( String [] args ) throws Exception
   {
      Juggler duke = new Juggler( );
      ObjectOutputStream oout = new ObjectOutputStream(
         new FileOutputStream("juggler.ser") );
      oout.writeObject( duke );
      oout.close( );
   }
}
```

Once you have the frozen Juggler, compile the following small application:

```
//file: BackFromTheDead.java
import java.awt.Component;
import javax.swing.*;
import java.beans.*;

public class BackFromTheDead extends JFrame {

  public BackFromTheDead( String name ) {
    super("Revived Beans!");
    try {
      Object bean = Beans.instantiate(
        getClass( ).getClassLoader( ), name );

      if ( Beans.isInstanceOf( bean, JComponent.class) ) {
        JComponent comp = (JComponent)
          Beans.getInstanceOf(bean, JComponent.class);
        getContentPane( ).add("Center", comp);
      } else {
          System.out.println("Bean is not a JComponent...");
      }
    } catch ( java.io.IOException e1 ) {
      System.out.println("Error loading the serialized object");
    } catch ( ClassNotFoundException e2 ) {
      System.out.println(
          "Can't find the class that goes with the object");
    }
  }
```

```
    public static void main(String [] args) {
      JFrame frame = new BackFromTheDead( args[0] );
      frame.pack( );
      frame.setVisible(true);
    }
  }
```

Run this program, passing the name of your serialized object as an argument and making sure that our *magicbeans.jar* file is in your classpath. The name should *not* include the *.ser* extension in the name; the Beans.instantiate( ) method adds this automatically in its search for the serialized or class version. The juggler should spring back to life, juggling once again as shown in Figure 22-11.

Figure 22-11. The restored Juggler

In BackFromTheDead, we use Beans.instantiate( ) to load our serialized bean by name. We then check to see whether it is a GUI component using Beans.isInstanceOf( ). (It is, because the Juggler is a subclass of java.awt.Component.) Finally, we cast the instantiated object to a Component with Beans.getInstanceOf( ) and add it to our application's JFrame. Notice that we still need a static Java cast to turn the Object returned by getInstanceOf( ) into a JComponent. This cast may seem gratuitous, but it is the bridge between the dynamic beans lookup of the type and the static, compile-time view of the type.

Everything we've done here could be done using the plain java.io.ObjectInputStream discussed in Chapter 12. But these bean management methods are intended to shield the user from details of how the beans are implemented and stored.

One more thing before we move on. We blithely noted that when the Juggler was restored, the bean began juggling again. This implies that threads were started when the bean was deserialized. Serialization doesn't automatically manage transient resources such as threads or even loaded images, but it's easy to take control of the process to finish reconstructing the bean's state when it is deserialized. Have a look at the Juggler source code (provided with the examples) and refer to Chapter 12 for a discussion of object deserialization using the readObject( ) method.

Runtime Event Hookups with Reflection

We've discussed reflection largely in terms of how design tools use it to analyze classes. Today, reflection is frequently finding its way into applications to perform dynamic activities that wouldn't be possible otherwise. In this section, we'll look at a dynamic event adapter that can be configured at runtime.

In Chapter 16, we saw how adapter classes could be built to connect event firings to arbitrary methods in our code, allowing us to cleanly separate GUI and logic in our applications. In this chapter, we have seen how NetBeans interposes this adapter code between beans to do this for us.

The AWT/Swing event model reduces the need to subclass components to perform simple hookups. If we start relying heavily on special adapter classes, we can quickly end up with as many adapters as components. Anonymous inner classes let us hide these classes, but they're still there. A potential solution for large or specialized applications is to create *generic* event adapters that serve a number of event sources and targets simultaneously.

Java 1.4 added a tool to the `java.beans` package: the `EventHandler` is a dynamic event dispatcher that simply calls methods in response to events.[*] What makes the `EventHandler` unique in Java (so far) is that it is the first standard utility to use reflection to allow us to specify the method by *name*. In other words, you ask the `EventHandler` to direct events to a handler by specifying the handler object and the string name of the method to invoke on that object. This is a big change from the normal style of coding in Java and comes with some associated risks. We'll talk more about those later.

We can use the `create()` method of `EventHandler` to get an adapter for a specified type of event listener, specifying a target object and method name to call when that event occurs. The target object doesn't have to be a listener for the particular event type or any other particular kind of object. The following application, `DynamicHookup`, uses the `EventHandler` to connect a button to a `launchTheMissiles()` method in our class:

```
//file: DynamicHookup.java
import javax.swing.*;
import java.awt.event.*;
import java.beans.EventHandler;

public class DynamicHookup extends JFrame {
  JLabel label = new JLabel( "Ready...", JLabel.CENTER );
  int count;
```

---

[*] Prior to Java 1.3, we developed our own dynamic event adapter in this chapter. That example is still instructive if you want to work with beans using reflection. You can find it in the file *DynamicActionAdapter.java* in the examples on the accompanying CD-ROM (view CD content online at *http://examples.oreilly.com/learnjava3/CD-ROM/*).

```
    public DynamicHookup( ) {
      JButton launchButton = new JButton("Launch!");
      getContentPane( ).add( launchButton, "South" );
      getContentPane( ).add( label, "Center" );
        launchButton.addActionListener(
              (ActionListener)EventHandler.create(
                    ActionListener.class, this, "launchTheMissiles"));
    }
    public void launchTheMissiles( ) {
      label.setText("Launched: "+ count++ );
    }

    public static void main(String[] args) {
      JFrame frame = new DynamicHookup( );
        frame.setDefaultCloseOperation( JFrame.EXIT_ON_CLOSE );
      frame.setSize(150, 150);
      frame.setVisible( true );
    }
  }
```

Here, we call the EventHandler's create( ) method, passing it the ActionListener class, the target object (this), and a string with the name of the method to invoke on the target when the event arrives. EventHandler internally creates a listener of the appropriate type and registers our target information. Not only do we eliminate an inner class, but the implementation of EventHandler may allow it to share adapters internally, producing very few objects.

This example shows how we would call a method that takes no arguments, but the EventHandler can actually do more, setting JavaBeans properties in response to events. The following form of create( ) tells EventHandler to call the launchTheMissiles( ) method, passing the "source" property of the ActionEvent as an argument:

```
EventHandler.create(
    ActionListener.class, target, "launchTheMissiles", "source")
```

All events have a source property (via the getSource( )) method, but we can go further, specifying a chain of property "gets" separated by dots, which are applied before the value is passed to the method. For example:

```
EventHandler.create(
    ActionListener.class, target, "launchTheMissiles", "source.text")
```

The source.text parameter causes the value getSource( ).getText( ) to be passed as an argument to launchTheMissiles( ). In our case, that would be the label of our button. Other forms of create( ) allow more flexibility in selecting which methods of a multimethod listener interface are used and other options. We won't cover every detail of the tool here.

Safety implications

The EventHandler is a powerful tool, but it was, in actuality, primarily intended for use by IDEs, not developers. Reflection allows you to do things at runtime that you couldn't do otherwise. Therein lies the problem with this technique: by using reflection to locate and invoke methods, we abandon Java's strong typing and head off in the direction of scripting languages. We add power at the expense of safety. If the method name specified to EventHandler doesn't exist, or if it exists but wants the wrong type of arguments, you may receive a runtime exception, or worse, it may be silently ignored.

How it works

The EventHandler uses the java.lang.reflect.Proxy, which is a factory that can generate adapters implementing any type of interface at runtime. By specifying one or more event listener interfaces (e.g., ActionListener), we get an adapter that implements those listener interfaces generated for us on the fly. The adapter is a specially created class that delegates all the method calls on its interfaces to a designated InvocationHandler object. See Chapter 1 for more information about proxy classes.

BeanContext and BeanContextServices

So far we've talked about some sophisticated mechanisms for connecting Java beans together at design time and runtime. However, we haven't talked at all about the environment in which Java beans live. To build advanced, extensible applications, we'd like a way for Java beans to find each other or "rendezvous" at runtime. The java.beans.beancontext package provides this kind of container environment. It also provides a generic "services" lookup mechanism for beans that wish to advertise their capabilities. These mechanisms have existed for some time, but they haven't found much use in the standard Java packages. Still, they are interesting and important facilities that you can use in your own applications.

You can find a full explanation and example of how to use the bean context to find beans and listen for services in the expanded material on the CD-ROM that comes with the book or on this book's web site.

The Java Activation Framework

The Java Activation Framework (JAF) is a standard extension that can be used by beans that work with many external data types, such as media retrieved from files and streams. It is essentially a generalized content/protocol handler mechanism for JavaBeans. The JAF is an extensible set of classes that wrap arbitrary, raw data sources to provide access to their data as streams or objects, identify the MIME type of the data, and enumerate a registered set of "commands" for operating on the data.

The JAF provides two primary interfaces: DataSource and DataHandler. The DataSource acts like the protocol handlers we discussed in Chapter 14. It wraps the data source and determines a MIME type for the data stream. The DataHandler acts like a content handler, except it provides a great deal more than access to the data. A `DataHandler` is constructed to wrap a `DataSource` and interpret the data in different forms. It also provides a list of command operations that can be used to access the data. `DataHandler` also implements the `java.awt.datatransfer.Transferable` interface, allowing data to be passed among application components in a well-defined way.

The JAF hasn't been used much outside the JavaMail API, but you can find out more about JAF from Sun at *http://java.sun.com/beans/glasgow/jaf.html*.

Enterprise JavaBeans

Enterprise JavaBeans is a very big topic, and we can't do more than provide a few paragraphs of insight here. If you want more information, see *Enterprise JavaBeans* by Richard Monson-Haefel (O'Reilly). The thrust of EJB is to take the JavaBeans philosophy of portable, pluggable components and extend it to the server side to accommodate the sorts of things that multitiered, networked and database-centric applications require. Although EJB pays homage to the basic JavaBeans concepts, it is much larger and more specialized. It doesn't have a lot in common with the kinds of things we've been talking about in this chapter. EJBs are server-side components for networked applications. EJBs and plain Java beans are both reusable, portable components that can be deployed and configured for specific environments. But in the case of EJBs, the components encapsulate access to business logic and database tables instead of GUI and program elements.

EJB ties together a number of other Java enterprise-oriented APIs, including database access, transactions, and name services, into a single component model for server applications. EJB imposes a lot more structure on how you write code than plain old Java beans. It does so to allow the server-side *EJB container* to take on a lot of responsibility and optimize your application's activities without you having to write a lot of code. Here are a few things Enterprise JavaBeans tackles:

- Object life cycle and remote access
- Container-managed persistence
- Transaction management
- Server resource pooling and management
- Deployment configuration

EJB divides the world into two camps: *entity beans*, which represent data in a database, and *session beans*, which implement services and operations over entity beans. These correspond well to the second and third tiers in a three-tiered business application. "Business logic" is represented by session bean services, and database access is made transparent through automated object mapping by entity beans.

Many aspects of EJB behavior can be controlled through "deployment descriptors" that customize bean behavior for the target environment. The result is a high level of abstraction over ordinary business-specific code. It allows powerful, networked business application components to be packaged and reused in the sort of way that ordinary beans are reused to build client-side applications.

Sun has created a reference EJB platform as part of Java 2 Enterprise Edition (J2EE), but currently, the most robust EJB implementations are provided by third parties. Usually, the EJB container is packaged as part of a more general application server that performs other duties, such as running web services, servlets, and JSPs. There are many vendors of commercial EJB servers. Two popular alternatives are BEA's WebLogic, an application server with many high-end features, and JBoss, an open source application server and implementation of the J2EE APIs. JBoss can be downloaded from *http://www.jboss.org*.

## CHAPTER 23

Applets

One of the original promises of Java was that applications could be delivered over the network to your computer as needed. Instead of buying a shrink-wrapped box containing a word processor, installing it, and upgrading it every few years, it should be possible to use the software directly from the Internet, safely and on any platform. This new model of software distribution would be a boon for both free software and for commercial products that could offer a new pay-per-use sales model. Unfortunately, this revolutionary idea has been hampered by the realities of a slow Internet and the uneven progress of Java on the client side (for reasons both technical and political). Even so, Java has maintained a toehold in this arena through small downloadable applications called applets.

An *applet* is a Java program that runs in the context of a web page. Like an image or hyperlink it "owns" some rectangular area of the user's screen. It can draw whatever it wants and respond to keyboard and mouse events in that area. When the web browser loads a page that contains a Java applet, it knows how to load the classes of the applet and run them.

This chapter describes how applets work and how to incorporate them into web pages. We'll also describe how to use Sun's Java Plug-in to take advantage of the latest Java features. Finally, we'll cover the details of creating signed applets, which can step outside the typical applet security restrictions to do client-side things, such as reading and writing files.

The Politics of Applets

The potential for applets to add dynamic content to web pages was one of the driving forces behind the spread of the Java programming language. Prior to Java's introduction in 1994, there was really no standard way to do this; even the now ubiquitous animated GIF images were not yet widely supported. Sun's HotJava Java-based web browser was the first to support applets. It was Java's original "killer application." Later, in 1995, Netscape announced that it would support the Applet

API in its browsers, and soon after that Microsoft jumped on the bandwagon. For a while, it seemed that Java would flourish on the Web. But there have been some bumps along the road.

Many problems, both technical and political, plagued the early years of Java's use in client-side applications. Performance issues were to be expected in such a young language. But what really crippled Java early on was the nonportable and buggy AWT, Java's original GUI toolkit. Many people overlook the fact that Java's success as a portable language is in large part a result of just how much of the Java API is implemented *in* Java. You might be surprised to learn just how many Java internals involve no native code—everything from cryptography to DNS is done in Java—requiring no porting for new platforms. Similarly, the renaissance of Java GUI applications seen in recent years is due almost entirely to the introduction of the pure Java Swing GUI toolkit. In contrast, the original AWT system was based on native code, which had to be ported to each new system, taking into account subtle and tricky platform dependencies. AWT was effectively a large, graphical C program that Java talked to through a set of interfaces and Java was, to some extent, unfairly painted as nonportable and buggy by association.

Java faced other, less technical obstacles as well. Netscape forced the original AWT upon the world when it insisted that Java be released with "native look and feel" in lieu of a less capable, but portable initial toolkit. Later, Microsoft effectively stuck us with this by freezing the level of the Applet API in its browsers at Java 1.1. Applets have been stuck with AWT while lawsuits between Sun and Microsoft have dragged on. The result is that support for applets in web browsers is a mess. There are a lot of applets on the Web today, but they only hint at Java's original promise. There is, however, some light on the horizon.

Sun has made an attempt to insulate Java from the browser battles with the introduction of the Java Plug-in. The Plug-in allows applets to run in an up-to-date Java VM, identically, in all major browsers. But for most browsers, it requires installation by the user, which is less than desirable. More recently, versions of Netscape and Firefox have supported the latest version of Java using the Plug-in directly. As these browsers gain market share, applets become more capable. Newer APIs such as Java Web Start also offer the alternative of simple, zero administration, local installation of Java applications. The latest version of the Java runtime for Java 5.0 consolidates Java Web Start and the Java Plug-in into one package and control panel for the Windows operating system. A relatively painless, one-time install is now all that is necessary to open a variety of options for deploying Java applications to clients.

The JApplet Class

A JApplet is something like a Swing JPanel with a mission. It is a GUI container that has some extra structure to allow it to be used in an "alien" environment, such as a browser. Applets also have a life cycle that lets them act more like an application than a static component, such as a paragraph of text or an image. Although applets tend to be relatively simple, there's no inherent restriction on their complexity, other than download speed. There's no reason you couldn't write a big application like a word processor as an applet (but that would probably be better suited for Java Web Start, which installs and manages versions locally).

The `java.applet.Applet` class defines the core functionality of an applet. It was used early on with AWT. The `javax.swing.JApplet` class is a simple extension of `Applet` that adds the plumbing necessary for Swing.

Structurally, an applet is a sort of wrapper for your Java code. In contrast to a stand-alone graphical Java application, which starts up from a `main( )` method and creates a GUI, an applet itself is a component that expects to be dropped into someone else's GUI. Thus, an applet can't run by itself; it runs in the context of a web browser or a special applet-viewer program (which we'll talk about later). Instead of having your application create a `JFrame` to hold your GUI, you stuff your application inside a `JApplet` (itself is a `Container`) and let someone else add your applet to their GUI.

Applets are placed on web pages with the `<applet>` HTML tag, which we'll cover later in this chapter. At its simplest, you just specify the name of the applet class and a size in pixels for the applet:

```
<applet code="AnalogClock" width="100" height="100"></applet>
```

Pragmatically, an applet is an intruder into someone else's environment and therefore has to be treated with suspicion. The web browsers that run applets impose restrictions on what the applet is allowed to do. The restrictions are enforced by an applet security manager. The browser provides everything the applet needs through an applet context—the API the applet uses to interact with its environment.

A `JApplet` expects to be embedded in a page and used in a viewing environment that provides it with resources. In all other respects, however, applets are just ordinary `Panel` objects. As Figure 23-1 shows, an applet is a kind of `Panel`. Like any other `Panel`, a `JApplet` can contain user-interface components and use all the basic drawing and event-handling capabilities of the `Component` class. You can draw on a `JApplet` by overriding its `paint( )` method and respond to events in the `JApplet`'s display area by providing the appropriate event listeners. Applets also have additional structure that helps them interact with the browser environment.

Aside from the top-level structure and the security restrictions, there is no difference between an applet and an application. If your application can live within the limits imposed by a browser's security manager, you can easily structure it to function as both an applet and a standalone application. Normally, you'll use your applet class itself only as a thin wrapper to manage the life cycle and appearance of your application—create the GUI, start, and stop. So, the bulk of your code should be easily adaptable to either a standalone or applet deployment.

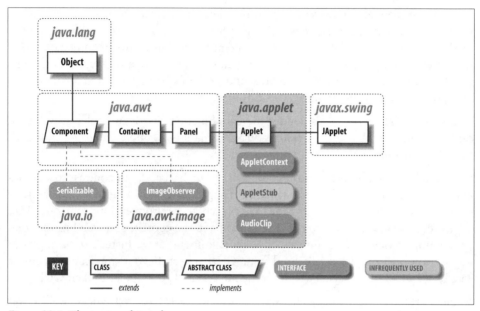

Figure 23-1. The java.applet package

Applet Life Cycle

The Applet class contains four methods that can be overridden to guide it through its life cycle. The init( ), start( ), stop( ), and destroy( ) methods are called by the appletviewer or web browser to direct the applet's behavior. init( ) is called once, after the applet is created. The init( ) method is where you perform basic setup such as parsing parameters, building a user interface, and loading resources.

By convention, applets don't provide an explicit constructor to do any setup. The reason for this is that the constructor is meant to be called by the applet's environment, for simple creation of the applet. This might happen before the applet has access to certain resources, such as information about its environment. Therefore, an applet doesn't normally do any work there; instead it should rely on the default constructor for the JApplet class and do its initialization in the init( ) method.

The start( ) method is called whenever the applet becomes visible; it shouldn't be a surprise then that the stop( ) method is called whenever the applet becomes invisible. init( ) is called only once in the life of an applet, but start( ) and stop( ) can be called any number of times (although always in the logical sequence). The start( ) method is called when the applet is displayed, such as when it scrolls onto the screen; stop( ) is called if the applet scrolls off the screen, or the viewer leaves the document. start( ) tells the applet it should be active. The applet may want to create threads, animate, or otherwise perform useful (or annoying) activity. stop( ) is called to let the applet know it should go dormant. Applets should cease CPU-intensive or wasteful activity when they are stopped and resume it when (and if) they are restarted. However, there's no requirement that an invisible applet stop computing; in some applications, it may be useful for the applet to continue running in the background. Just be considerate of your user, who doesn't want an invisible applet dragging down system performance.

Finally, the destroy( ) method gives the applet a last chance to clean up before it's removed—some time after the last call to stop( ). For example, an applet might want to gracefully close down suspended communications channels at this time. Exactly when destroy( ) is called depends on the browser; Netscape calls destroy( ) just prior to deleting the applet from its cache. This means that although an applet can cling to life after being told to stop( ), how long it can go on is unpredictable. If you want to maintain an applet as the user progresses through other pages of activities, you may have to put it in an HTML frame, so that it remains visible and won't be told to stop( ). See "Applet Persistence and Navigation" later in this chapter.

If you've been through the rest of this book, you've already seen a couple of applets that snuck in among other topics. In Chapter 9, we created a simple clock applet, and in Chapter 13, we used an applet to send packets of information from a web browser. Now let's try a simple Swing-based example using JApplet. The following example, shown in Figure 23-2, ShowApplet, does nothing special, but you can use it to test the version of Java that's running in your browser (and see if the Plug-in is installed) and to see when the applet is started and stopped. It's a good reference.

```java
import javax.swing.*;
import java.awt.event.*;

public class ShowApplet extends JApplet {
    JTextArea text = new JTextArea( );
    int startCount;

    public void init( ) {
        JButton button = new JButton("Press Me");
        button.addActionListener( new ActionListener( ) {
            public void actionPerformed( ActionEvent e ) {
                text.append("Button Pressed!\n");
            }
        } );
        getContentPane( ).add( "Center", new JScrollPane( text ) );
        JPanel panel = new JPanel( );
        panel.add( button );
        getContentPane( ).add( "South", panel );
        text.append( "Java Version: "
            +System.getProperty("java.version")+"\n" );
        text.append( "Applet init( )\n" );
    }
    public void start( ) {
        text.append( "Applet started: "+ startCount++ +"\n" );
    }
```

```
   public void stop( ) {
      text.append( "Applet stopped.\n" );
   }
}
```

Figure 23-2. ShowApplet

After compiling the applet, we have to create an HTML page in which to embed it. The following will do:

```
<html><head><title>ShowApplet</title></head>
<body>
<applet code="ShowApplet" width="300" height="300">
   Your browser does not understand Java.</applet>
</body>
</html>
```

We'll discuss the applet tag and other issues related to embedding applets in documents in detail later in this chapter. For now, just save this in a file called *showapplet.html*. Load the file with your favorite web browser (we suggest Firefox or Netscape 6.2 or later, which comes with a recent version of Java) and see what happens. If you have access to a web server, you can use it. Otherwise, you can open the file locally using either the browser's Open File menu option or a URL such as:

```
file://localhost/c:/somedirectory/showapplet.html
```

The applet shows the version of Java running it and prints messages when its button is pressed. If you have installed the latest Java Plug-in you should see "Java version: 1.5.0" in the box, regardless of which browser you are using (including Microsoft Internet Explorer). The applet prints messages when its start( ) and stop( ) methods are called, along with a count. You can use this to experiment with different browsers and page-layout configurations to see when your applet is reloaded or restarted. If your browser fails to display the applet with the correct version of Java, don't despair. Later in this chapter, we'll talk about how to convert the HTML to force the browser to use the Java Plug-in explicitly.

The Applet Security Sandbox

Applets are quarantined within the browser by an applet `SecurityManager`. The `SecurityManager` is part of the web browser or `appletviewer` application. It is installed before the browser loads any applets and implements the basic restrictions that let the user run untrusted applets (loaded over the Internet) safely. Remember, there are no inherent security restrictions on a standalone Java application. It is the browser that limits what applets are allowed to do using a security policy.

Most browsers impose the following restrictions on untrusted applets:

- Untrusted applets can't read or write files on the local host.
- Untrusted applets can open network connections (sockets) only to the server from which they originated.
- Untrusted applets can't start other processes on the local host.
- Untrusted applets can't have native methods.

The motivation for these restrictions should be fairly obvious: you clearly wouldn't want a program coming from some random Internet site to access your files or run arbitrary programs. Although untrusted applets can't directly read and write files on the client side or talk to arbitrary hosts on the network, applets can work with servers to store data and communicate. For example, an applet can use Java's RMI facility to do processing on its server. An applet can communicate with other applets on the Net by proxy through its server.

Trusted applets

We've been using the term *untrusted applet*, so it should come as no surprise that it is also possible to have such a thing as a *trusted applet*. Applets become trusted through the use of digital signatures, by *signing* the JAR file containing your applet code. Because a signature identifies the applet's origin unambiguously, we can now distinguish between trusted applets (i.e., applets that come from a site or person you trust not to do anything harmful) and run-of-the-mill untrusted applets. In browser environments that support signing, trusted applets can be granted permission to "go outside" of the applet security sandbox. Trusted applets can be allowed to do all of the things that standalone Java applications can do: read and write files, open network connections to arbitrary machines, and interact with the local operating system by starting processes. Trusted applets still can't have native methods, but including native methods in an applet would destroy its portability anyway.

Chapter 3 discussed how to package your applet's class files and resources into a JAR file. Later in this chapter, we'll show you how to sign an applet JAR with your digital signature.

Getting Applet Resources

An applet must communicate with its browser or applet viewer. For example, it may need configuration parameters from the HTML document in which it appears. An applet may also need to load images, audio clips, and other items. It may also want to ask the viewer about other applets on the same HTML page in order to communicate with them. To get resources from the environment, applets use the AppletStub and AppletContext interfaces, provided by the browser.

Applet parameters

An applet can get configuration parameters from <param> tags placed inside the <applet> tag in the HTML document, as we'll describe later. You can retrieve these parameters using Applet's getParameter( ) method. For example, the following code reads parameters called imageName and sheep from its HTML page:

```
String imageName = getParameter( "imageName" );
try {
    int numberOfSheep = Integer.parseInt( getParameter( "sheep" ) );
} catch ( NumberFormatException e ) { /* use default */ }
```

There is an API that allows an applet to provide information (help) about the parameters it accepts. The applet's getParameterInfo( ) can return an array of string arrays, listing and describing the applet's parameters. However, it's unclear who, if anyone, uses this API.

Applet resources

An applet can find out where it lives using the getDocumentBase( ) and getCodeBase( ) methods. getDocumentBase( ) returns the base URL of the document in which the applet appears; getCodeBase( ) returns the base URL of the Applet's class files (these two are often the same). An applet can use these methods to construct relative URLs from which to load other resources from its server, such as images, sounds, and other data. The getImage( ) method takes a URL and asks for an image from the viewer environment. The image may be cached or loaded when later used. The getAudioClip( ) method, similarly, retrieves sound clips.

The following example uses getCodeBase( ) to construct a URL and load a properties configuration file, located in the same remote directory on the web server as the applet's class file:

```
Properties props = new Properties( );
try {
  URL url = new URL( getCodeBase( ), "appletConfig.props" );
  props.load( url.openStream( ) );
} catch ( IOException e ) { /* failed */ }
```

A better way to load resources is by calling the getResource( ) and getResourceAsStream( ) methods of the Class class, which search the applet's JAR files (if any) as well as its codebase, which is an extension of the classpath for applets. The following code loads the same properties file in a more portable way:

```
Properties props = new Properties();
try {
  props.load( getClass().getResourceAsStream( "appletConfig.props") );
} catch ( IOException e ) { /* failed */ }
```

An applet can ask its viewer to retrieve an image by calling the getImage( ) method. The location of the image to be retrieved is given as a URL, either absolute or fetched from an applet's resources:

```
public class MyApplet extends javax.swing.JApplet {
  public void init( ) {
    try {
      // absolute URL
      URL monaURL =
          new URL( "http://myserver/images/mona_lisa.gif");
      Image monaImage = getImage( monaURL );
      // applet resource URL
      URL daffyURL =
          getClass().getResource("cartoons/images/daffy.gif");
      Image daffyDuckImage = getImage( daffyURL );
    }
    catch ( MalformedURLException e ) {
        // unintelligable url
    }
  }
  // ...
}
```

Again, using getResource( ) is preferred; it looks for the image in the applet's JAR file (if there is one), before looking elsewhere in the applet's classpath on the server (We'll talk more later about how classes are located for applets).

Driving the browser

The *status line* is a blurb of text that usually appears somewhere in the web browser's display, indicating a current activity. An applet can request that some text be placed in the status line with the showStatus( ) method. (The browser isn't required to do anything in response to this call, but most browsers will oblige you.)

An applet can also ask the browser to show a new document. To do this, the applet makes a call to the showDocument(url) method of the AppletContext. You can get a reference to the AppletContext with the applet's getAppletContext( ) method. Calling showDocument(url) replaces the currently showing document, which means that your currently running applet will be stopped.

Another version of showDocument( ) takes an additional String argument to tell the browser where to display the new URL:

```
getAppletContext().showDocument( url, name );
```

The name argument can be the name of an existing labeled HTML frame; the document referenced by the URL is displayed in that frame. You can use this method to create an applet that "drives" the browser to new locations dynamically but keeps itself active on the screen in a separate frame. This is common for applets that act like navigation controls or menus. If the named frame doesn't exist, the browser creates a new top-level window to hold it. Alternatively, name can have one of the following special values:

self
> Show in the current frame

_parent
> Show in the parent of our frame

_top
> Show in outermost (top-level) frame

_blank
> Show in a new top-level browser window

Both showStatus( ) and showDocument( ) requests may be ignored by a cold-hearted viewer or web browser. Nothing in browser-land is ever really certain.

Inter-applet communication

Although it's not very common, applets that are embedded in documents loaded from the same location on a web site can use a simple mechanism to locate one another and coordinate their activities on a page. Once an applet has a reference to another applet, it can communicate with it, just as with any other object, by invoking methods and sending events. The getApplet( ) method of the applet context looks for an applet by name:

```
Applet clock = getAppletContext( ).getApplet("theClock");
```

Give an applet a name within your HTML document using the name attribute of the <applet> tag. Alternatively, you can use the getApplets( ) method to enumerate all the available applets in the pages.

The tricky thing with applet communications is that applets run inside the security sandbox. An untrusted applet can "see" and communicate only with objects that were loaded by the same class loader. Currently, the only reliable criterion for when applets share a class loader is when they share a common base URL. For example, all the applets contained in web pages loaded from the base URL of *http://foo.bar.com/mypages/* should share a class loader and should be able to see each other. This includes documents such as *mypages/foo.html* and *mypages/bar.html*, but not *mypages/morestuff/foo.html*.

When applets do share a class loader, other techniques are possible, too. As with any other class, you can call static methods in applets by name. So you could use static methods in one of your applets as a "registry" to coordinate your activities.

Applet persistence and navigation

One of the biggest shortcomings of the Applet API is the lack of a real context for coordinating their activities during navigation across a multipage document or web application. The Applet API simply wasn't designed for this. Although an applet's life cycle is well-defined in terms of its API, it is not well-defined in terms of management by the browser or scope of visibility. As we described in the previous section, applets loaded from the same codebase can rendezvous at runtime using their name attributes. But there are no guarantees about how long an applet will live—or whether it will be stopped as opposed to being destroyed—once it is out of view. If you experiment with our ShowApplet in various browsers and in the Java Plug-in (which we'll discuss later), you'll see that, in some cases, the applet is stopped and restarted when the user leaves the page, but more often the applet is reinitialized from scratch. This makes designing multipage applications that work in all browsers difficult.

One solution has been to use static methods as a shared "registry," as mentioned earlier. However, the details governing how classes loaded by applets are managed are even less well-defined than the management of the applet's themselves. In Java 1.4, a new pair of methods was added to the AppletContext to support short-term applet persistence: setStream( ) and getStream( ). With these methods, an applet can ask the context to save a stream of byte data by a key value and return it later. The notion of providing the state to the context as a stream is a little odd but easy enough to accommodate. Here is an example:

```
getAppletContext.setStream("myStream",
    new ByteArrayInputStream( "This is some test data...".getBytes( ) ) );
```

Later, the stream data can be retrieved:

```
InputStream in = getAppletContext.getStream( "myStream" );
```

Currently, the data is retained only as long as the browser is running. But it's possible that a longer-term persistence API will come about in the future. If you need more complex state and navigation capabilities, you might consider using a signed applet to write to a file or taking advantage of the new Java Web Start API to install your application locally.

Applets versus standalone applications

The following are the methods of the Applet API. The first list is from the AppletStub interface:

```
boolean isActive( );
URL getDocumentBase( );
URL getCodeBase( );
String getParameter(String name);
AppletContext getAppletContext( );
void appletResize(int width, int height);
```

The second list is from the `AppletContext` interface:

```
AudioClip getAudioClip(URL url);
Image getImage(URL url);
Applet getApplet(String name);
Enumeration getApplets();
void showDocument(URL url);
public void showDocument(URL url, String target);
void showStatus(String status);
```

These are the methods provided by the applet-viewer environment. If your applet doesn't use any of them, or if you can provide alternatives to handle common cases (such as loading images), your applet can function as a standalone application as well as an applet. Again, it's best to structure your code so that both the applet and an alternative "Main" application class contain as little environment-specific code as possible and share implementation classes.

Applets are embedded in HTML documents with the `<applet>` tag. The `<applet>` tag resembles the HTML `<img>` image tag. It contains attributes that identify the applet to be displayed and, optionally, give the web browser hints about how it should be shown.[*]

The standard image tag sizing and alignment attributes, such as height and width, can be used inside the applet tag. However, unlike images, applets have both an opening `<applet>` and a closing `</applet>` tag. Sandwiched between these can be any number of `<param>` tags that contain configuration data to be passed to the applet:

```
<applet attribute attribute ... >
    <param parameter >
    <param parameter >
    ...
</applet>
```

Attributes

Attributes are name/value pairs that are interpreted by a web browser or applet viewer. Attributes of the `<applet>` tag specify general features that apply to any applet, such as size and alignment. The definition of the `<applet>` tag lists a fixed set of recognized attributes; specifying an incorrect or nonexistent attribute should be considered an HTML error.

Three attributes are required in the `<applet>` tag. Two of these attributes, width and height, specify the space the applet occupies on the screen. The third required attribute must be either code or object; you must supply one of these attributes, and you can't specify both. The code attribute specifies the class file from which the

---

[*] If you aren't familiar with HTML or other markup languages, you may want to refer to *HTML and XHTML: The Definitive Guide* by Chuck Musciano and Bill Kennedy (O'Reilly) for a complete reference on HTML and structured web documents.

applet is loaded; the object attribute specifies a serialized representation of an applet. Most often, you'll use the code attribute.

The following is an HTML fragment for a simple clock applet that takes no parameters and requires no special HTML layout:

```
<applet code="AnalogClock" width="100" height="100"></applet>
```

The HTML file that contains this <applet> tag must be stored in the same directory as the *AnalogClock.class* class file. The applet tag is not sensitive to spacing in the HTML, so the previous tag could be also be formatted a little more readably like so:

```
<applet
    code="AnalogClock"
    width="100"
    height="100">
</applet>
```

Parameters

Parameters are analogous to command-line arguments; they provide a way to pass information to an applet. Each <param> tag contains a name and a value that are passed as string values to the applet:

```
<param name = "parameter_name" value = "parameter_value">
```

Parameters provide a means of embedding application-specific data and configuration information within an HTML document. Our AnalogClock applet, for example, might accept a parameter that selects between local and universal time:

```
<applet code="AnalogClock" width="100" height="100">
    <param name="zone" value="GMT">
</applet>
```

Presumably, this AnalogClock applet is designed to look for a parameter named zone with a possible value of GMT.

Parameter names and values should be quoted and can contain spaces and other whitespace characters. The parameters a given applet expects are, of course, determined by the developer of that applet. There is no standard set of parameter names or values; it's up to the applet to interpret the parameter name/value pairs that are passed to it. Any number of parameters can be specified, and the applet may choose to use or ignore them as it sees fit.

¿Habla Applet?

Web browsers are supposed to ignore tags they don't understand; if the web browser doesn't know about the <applet> or <param> tags, we would expect them to disappear, and any HTML between the <applet> and </applet> tags to appear normally. By convention, Java-enabled web browsers ignore any extra HTML between the <applet> and </applet> tags. Combined, this means we can place some alternative

HTML inside the <applet> tag, which is displayed only by web browsers that can't run the applet.

For our AnalogClock example, we could display a small text explanation and an image of the clock applet as a teaser:

```
<applet code="AnalogClock" width="100" height="100">
    <param name="zone" value="GMT">
    <strong>If you see this, you don't have a Java-enabled Web
    browser. Here's a picture of what you are missing.</strong>
    <img src="clockface.gif">
</applet>
```

The Complete <applet> Tag

We'll now spell out the complete syntax for the <applet> tag:

```
<applet
    code = class_name
```

or:

```
    object = serialized_applet_name

    width = pixels_high
    height = pixels_wide

    [ codebase = location_URL ]
    [ archive = comma_separated_list_of_archive_files ]
    [ name = applet_instance_name ]
    [ alt = alternate_text ]
    [ align = style ]
    [ vspace = vertical_pad_pixels ]
    [ hspace = horizontal_pad_pixels ]
>
    [ <param name = parameter_name value = parameter_value> ]
    [ <param ...   ]

    [ HTML code for non-Java-aware browsers ]
</applet>
```

Either the code attribute or the object attribute must be present to specify the applet to run. The code attribute specifies the applet's class file; you'll see this most frequently. The object attribute specifies a serialized representation of an applet. When you use the object attribute to load an applet, the applet's init( ) method is not called. However, the serialized applet's start( ) method is called.

The width, height, align, vspace, and hspace attributes determine the preferred size, alignment, and padding, respectively. The width and height attributes are required.

The codebase attribute specifies the base URL to be searched for the applet's class files. If this attribute isn't present, the browser looks in the same location as the HTML file. The archive attribute specifies a list of JAR or ZIP files in which the applet's class files are located. To put two or more files in the list, separate the filenames with commas; for example, the following attribute tells the browser to load and search three archives for the applet's classes:

```
archive="Part1.jar,Part2.jar,Utilities.jar"
```

The archive files listed by the archive tag are loaded from the codebase URL. When searching for classes, a browser checks the archives before searching any other locations on the server.

The alt attribute specifies alternate text that is displayed by browsers that understand the <applet> tag and its attributes but have Java disabled or don't run applets. This attribute can also describe the applet because, in this case, any alternate HTML between <applet> and </applet> is, by convention, ignored by Java-enabled browsers.

The name attribute specifies an instance name for the executing applet. This is a name specified as a unique label for each copy of an applet on a particular HTML page. For example, if we include our clock twice on the same page (using two applet tags), we should give each instance a unique name to differentiate them:

```
<applet code="AnalogClock" name="bigClock" width="300" height="300">
</applet>
<applet code="AnalogClock" name="smallClock" width="50" height="50">
</applet>
```

Applets can use instance names to recognize and communicate with other applets on the same page. We could, for instance, create a "clock setter" applet that knows how to set the time on an AnalogClock applet and pass it the instance name of a particular target clock on this page as a parameter. This might look something like:

```
<applet code="ClockSetter">
    <param name="clockToSet" value="bigClock">
</applet>
```

Loading Class Files

The code attribute of the <applet> tag should specify the name of an applet. This is either a simple class name or a package path and class name. For now, let's look at simple class names; we'll discuss packages in a moment. By default, the Java runtime system looks for the class file in the same location as the HTML document that contains it. This location is known as the *base URL* for the document.

Consider an HTML document, *clock.html*, that contains our clock applet example:

```
<applet code="AnalogClock" width="100" height="100"></applet>
```

Let's say we retrieve the document at the following URL:

```
http://www.time.ch/documents/clock.html
```

Java tries to retrieve the applet class file from the same base location:

```
http://www.time.ch/documents/AnalogClock.class
```

The codebase attribute of the <applet> tag specifies an alternative base URL for the class file search. Let's say our HTML document now specifies codebase, as in the following example:

```
<applet
    codebase="http://www.joes.ch/stuff/"
    code="AnalogClock"
    width="100"
    height="100">
</applet>
```

Java now looks for the applet class file at:

```
http://www.joes.ch/stuff/AnalogClock.class
```

Packages

For "loose" applet class files that are not packaged into archives, Java uses the standard package name to directory path mapping to locate files on the server. The only difference is that the requests are not local file lookups but requests to the web server at the applet's codebase URL. Before a class file is retrieved from a server, its package-name component is translated by the client into a relative path name under the applet's codebase.

Let's suppose that our AnalogClock has been placed into a package called time.clock (a subordinate package for clock-related classes, within a package for time-related classes). The fully qualified name of our class is time.clock.AnalogClock. Our simple <applet> tag would now look like:

```
<applet code="time.clock.AnalogClock" width="100" height="100"></applet>
```

Let's say the *clock.html* document is once again retrieved from:

```
http://www.time.ch/documents/clock.html
```

Java now looks for the class file in the following location:

```
http://www.time.ch/documents/time/clock/AnalogClock.class
```

The same is true when specifying an alternative codebase:

```
<applet
    codebase="http://www.joes.ch/stuff/"
    code="time.clock.AnalogClock"
    width="100"
    height="100">
</applet>
```

Java now tries to find the class in the corresponding path under this base URL:

```
http://www.joes.ch/stuff/time/clock/AnalogClock.class
```

appletviewer

Sun's SDK comes with an applet-viewer program, aptly called *appletviewer*. To use *appletviewer*, specify the URL of the document on the command line. For example, to view our (still only theoretical) AnalogClock at the URL shown earlier, use the following command:

```
% appletviewer http://www.time.ch/documents/clock.html
```

appletviewer retrieves all applets in the specified document and displays each one in a separate window. *appletviewer* isn't a web browser; it doesn't attempt to display HTML. It was primarily useful before the Java Plug-in as a way to test an applet in a specific version of the Java runtime.

Using the Java Plug-in

The disadvantage of the <applet> tag is that you generally have to rely on the browser's Java interpreter. This is bad for two reasons:

- The version of Java that is included in popular browsers lags the current version of Java by years and Java has never been fully supported in Internet Explorer (IE).

- Historically, Microsoft's version of Java has had its own bugs and idiosyncrasies, which were different from the bugs and idiosyncrasies of Sun's version. Microsoft is also in the process of dropping its support for Java in general, so it is unclear what the future holds for IE.

At the time of this writing, most common versions of Netscape and IE are stuck with a Java 1.1 environment. Modern versions of the Netscape and Firefox web browsers as well as Mac OS X's Safari support current versions of Java when they are installed. However, Mac OS X will not support Java 5.0 until its 10.4 release. As a developer, you will want to use modern features of Java including Swing, Collections, etc., on all platforms. So what can we do?

What Is the Java Plug-in?

We might take the state of Java in the browser to indicate that applets are dead. But the Java Plug-in might just save the day. A *plug-in* is simply a loadable application module that is used to support new content types in a web browser. All major browsers have a *plug-in* mechanism that allows the browser to be extended in this way.

You're probably familiar with plug-ins of one type or another. The browser gives control for a part of a web page to another piece of code. For example, you can view movies in your browser using Apple's QuickTime plug-in. You can view interactive multimedia with Macromedia's Shockwave plug-in. The idea is very similar to applets; basically the browser hands-off responsibility for some rectangular area on the screen to someone else's code. The Java Plug-in is simply a Java runtime environment implemented as a browser plug-in.

Applets that use the Java Plug-in can take advantage of the very latest Java platform features. With the Plug-in, Java developers can specify the version of Java they require, and their applets should run in exactly the same way in any browser using it. The browser isn't even really running the applet anymore; the Plug-in takes care of it.

This is nifty technology, but it does come with a small hurdle for deployment. Users who want to use the Java Plug-in to run applets have to download and install it first. While this is not a huge burden, it is a barrier to universal acceptance. With Java 5.0, the Java Plug-in is installed automatically when the Java Runtime Environment (JRE) is installed, so users have one-stop shopping for Java. But with the wide installed base of browser versions by both Microsoft and Netscape, installation will be an issue for some time to come.

Messy Tags

The HTML for web pages that contain Plug-in applets is much messier than the <applet> tag you've already seen. Part of the problem is that you have to use specialized tags for different browsers (primarily IE). Netscape, Firefox, and Safari use the <embed> tag for plug-ins while IE uses the <object> tag. However, there are some tricks involving fitting the <embed> tag inside the <object> tag that should allow all browsers to recognize and run the same document correctly.

These tags have their own syntax, but, basically, you're still providing the same information to the browser. You specify the size of the applet, the class name to use, the location of additional classes, and parameters that should be passed to the applet itself. Fortunately, you don't have to worry too much about the details. Sun provides a handy utility, the HTML Converter, which converts <applet> tags to the appropriate <embed> and <object> tags. Assuming you've set up your <applet> tag correctly, you should have no trouble converting your HTML page to use the Java Plug-in. This utility is available for download at *http://java.sun.com/products/plugin/*.

Suppose, for example, that you create a web page called *ShowOff.html*. Once you have the <applet> tag set up the way you want (you can test it with a reliable browser or *appletviewer*), you can use the HTML Converter to set up your web page to use the Plug-in. The HTML Converter runs as a Swing application. To run it, navigate to the directory where you installed the HTML Converter and type the following:

```
C:\> java HTMLConverter
```

The utility is pretty self-explanatory. You can convert all HTML files in a directory or just convert a single HTML file. The conversion is done "in-place," which means that your original HTML is overwritten with the new stuff. The Converter automatically backs up your old files unless you tell it otherwise.

You can perform different kinds of conversions, represented by different templates. By default, the HTML Converter uses the "standard" template that produces a page that works with Netscape and Internet Explorer on Windows and Solaris. If you choose "extended," it tries to produce a more elaborate version that should work on a wider set of browsers. In addition to adding the <embed> and <object> tags, the "extended" template preserves the original <applet> tag. This has the added benefit that you'll still be able to test your applet with *appletviewer*.

Applets in Internet Explorer

We should also note that as of Version 1.4, the Java Plug-in for Windows has a new feature: once installed, the Plug-in takes over control of the regular <applet> for IE so that, by default, all applets begin to use the Plug-in. Once the Plug-in installation is boot-strapped, all applets benefit from it, regardless of whether the page uses the special tags. This is why if, after installing the Java Plug-in, you run the ShowApplet from our earlier example, it should show the latest Java version even without using special markup. The main advantage of the HTML Converter in this case is for users who have not yet installed the plug-in. In that case, the special HTML instructs them that they need to install it, instead of simply running the degenerate version of Java.

Viewing Plug-in Applets

What actually happens when users browse to a page with HTML that requires the Plug-in for an applet? It depends, of course, on which browser you're using and what has been installed. If you are on a "virgin" system, IE asks the user for permission to download and run the Java Plug-in to display the applet. Older versions of Netscape direct the user to the JRE download page. (The Java Plug-in is distributed as part of the JRE.) In either case, the download and installation times vary. Depending on network speed and user comfort level, you can expect that most Internet users will have to spend five to ten minutes downloading and installing the JRE.

The good news is that the installation needs to be done only once. When JRE is installed and running, you can view Plug-in applets immediately (at least as soon as the browser loads the Plug-in). The only time the user needs to install a new Plug-in is when a new version of Java comes out. The current version of the Plug-in can automatically check for updates on a periodic basis, like most modern software.

Despite the price of installation and HTML tag messiness, the Plug-in is powerful medicine indeed. No longer do you have to wait for browser vendors to implement the latest Java platform features; the Plug-in makes the latest Java releases available to applets immediately, and it provides a more hospitable environment for applets, regardless of what browser displays them.

Java Web Start

The Java Web Start API is an interesting alternative to using applets. Java Web Start uses the Java Network Launching Protocol (JNLP) to transparently download and install Java applications locally. All the user has to do is to click on the install link on a web page. The installed applications can then be launched just like any installed application, by clicking on an icon on the desktop or through the Start menu, but they continue to be managed by the Java security policy unless authorized otherwise by the user. Web Start applications also automatically check for upgrades and update themselves over the net. Java Web Start is a form of *zero administration* client installation, which implies that the client doesn't have to do any work to install or maintain the application. JNLP applications may be signed, allowing the user to grant them fine-grained privileges, or unsigned. But even unsigned JNLP applications can take advantage of standard APIs that prompt the user for permission to perform basic operations, such as opening files and printing.

Packaging your application to use JNLP is relatively easy, but we won't get into it here. The process mainly involves creating a JNLP deployment file that lists your JARs and specifies any special permission they require. You must then include an appropriate link in your web page that uses Web Start. The first time a user tries to install a JNLP application, they will have to install the Java Plug-in. Thereafter, the Java Web Start component manages all JNLP installs. See *http://java.sun.com/products/javawebstart/* for more information.

Using Digital Signatures

Digital signatures provide a way to authenticate documents and other data. They solve one of the Internet's biggest problems: given that you've received a message from Ms. X, how do you know that the message really came from Ms. X and not an imposter? Just as important for Java, let's say that you've downloaded a great new applet written by your favorite author, Pat Niemeyer, and you'd like to grant it some additional privileges, so that it can do something cool for you. You trust that this particular author wouldn't intentionally distribute something harmful. But how do you know that this person really is who he says he is? And what if you downloaded the applet from a third-party location, like an archive? How can you be sure that someone hasn't modified the applet since the author wrote it? With Java's default security policies for web browsers, such an applet can't do anything serious, but when we're talking about granting additional privileges to applets coming from trusted sites, you would be in for trouble—if it weren't for digital signatures.

Like their inky analogs, digital signatures associate a name with an item in a way that is difficult to forge. In reality, a digital signature is much more difficult to forge than a traditional signature. Furthermore, digital signatures provide another benefit: they allow you to authenticate the *contents* of a document, proving that it hasn't been altered in transit. In other words, you know who the sender is, and that the data you received is exactly what the sender sent. Some malicious person can't clip out a digital signature, modify the original document (or applet), and attach the old signature to the result. And he can't generate a new signature; at least, he can't generate a signature claiming that the document came from its original sender. (He could, of course, attach his own signature, but that would be like signing the stick-up note you hand to the bank teller.)

Digital signatures are based on public-key cryptography, which is well beyond the scope of this book. However, the basics are important and interesting.* In a public-key system, there are two pieces of information: a public key and a private one. The keys have a special, asymmetric relationship, such that a message encrypted with one key can only be decrypted with the other key. Furthermore, if you know only one key, it is very difficult to compute the other. Therefore, if I give you my public key, you can use it to create an encrypted message that only I can read. No one else, including you, has enough information to go through the process of decrypting the encoded message, so it's safe to send it over untrusted networks. Furthermore, I can (and probably will) give my public key to anyone in the world, since the public key only lets people send me messages; it doesn't let them read my messages.

Digital signatures are based on the reverse process. If I encrypt something with my private key, anyone can use my public key to read the message. That may not sound very useful, since I already said that I'd give my public key away to anyone who wants it. But in this case, we're not trying to keep the message secret, we're trying to prove that I'm the only one who could have sent the message. And that's exactly what it does. No one else has my private key, so no one else can send a message that can be decrypted with my public key. Therefore, only the real me could have sent the message.

We've simplified the process in one crucial way. Encrypting a large message with complex algorithms takes a long time, even with fast computers. And some public-key algorithms just aren't suitable for encrypting large amounts of data for other reasons, as well. For digital signatures, then, we don't usually encrypt the entire message. First, we use a standard algorithm to create a "hash" or "message digest." To produce the signature, we then encrypt the (relatively small) message digest with the private key. The recipient can then decrypt the signature with the public key and check whether the resulting message digest matches the message he received. If it does, the recipient knows the message hasn't been altered, and the sender is who he claims to be.

Digital signatures can be used to authenticate Java class files and other types of data sent over the network. The author of an object signs the data with his or her digital

---

* See Bruce Schneier's encyclopedic *Applied Cryptography* (John Wiley & Sons) or Jonathan Knudsen's *Java Cryptography* (O'Reilly).

signature, and we use the author's public key to authenticate that signature after we retrieve it. We don't have to communicate with anyone in order to verify the authenticity of the data. We don't even have to make sure that the communications by which we received the data are secure. We simply check the signature after the data arrives. If it is valid, we know that we have the authentic data and that it hasn't been tampered with. Or do we?

There is a larger problem digital signatures alone don't solve: verifying identity. If the signature checks out, we know that only the person (or entity) that published the public key could have sent the data. But how do we know that the public key really belongs to whomever we think it does? How do we associate an identity with that public key in the first place? We've made it more difficult to counterfeit a message, but it's not impossible. A forger could conceivably create a counterfeit Java class, sign it with his own private key, and try to trick you into believing that his public key is that of the real author or the trusted web site. In this case, you'll download the bad applet, then use the wrong public key to verify the applet, and be tricked into thinking that there's nothing wrong. This is where *certificates* and *certificate authorities* come into play.

Certificates

A certificate is a document that lists a name and a public key. By a name, we mean some real-world information describing a person or entity. For example, a certificate might contain your full name and address or the name of a company and the location of its headquarters. We'll consider the combination of a name and a public key in this way to make up an *identity*. If we have valid information for a particular identity, we can verify data that the identity has signed.

A certificate is signed with the digital signature of a certificate authority (CA)—the entity that issued the certificate. The certificate is, in effect, a proclamation by the CA that the identity listed is valid—in other words, that the listed public key really does belong to the entity named. If we decide to trust the CA, we can then believe the identities contained in the certificates it issues are valid. The certificate acts as a sort of electronic ID card, backed up by the credentials of the CA. Of course, we no longer issue certificates on fancy vellum scrolls, as shown in Figure 23-3; the digital format for modern certificates is described by a standard called X.509.

Certificate authority certificates

This is all well and good, but the original problem remains: in order to verify the authenticity of a certificate, we need to verify its signature. To do that we need to know the CA's public key; rather than solving the problem, we simply seem to have shifted the problem to a new front. If a counterfeiter could substitute her public key for the public key of one entity, she might be able to do the same for the CA. But shifting the problem helps quite a bit. We have reduced the number of public keys

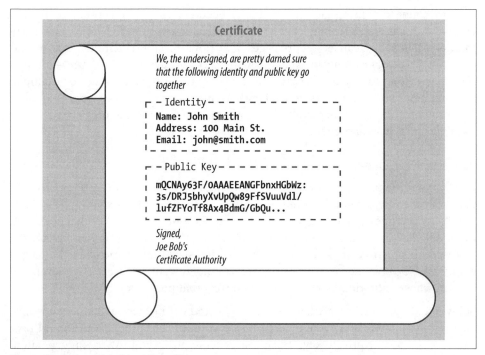

Figure 23-3. An old-fashioned certificate

we need to know from an unlimited number (all the identities we might ever encounter) to a very small number: one for each CA. We have chained our trust of the identity to the trust of the CA's identity. Chaining can be allowed to extend further, to an arbitrary depth, allowing CAs to back up lower CAs, and so on. At some point, of course, the chain has to stop, and that usually happens with a "self-signed" or *certificate authority certificate*; that is, a certificate that is issued by the CA for itself, containing its own public key. "What good is that?" you might ask.

As for the authenticity of the top-level CAs themselves, we have to rely on strong, well-known certificates that we have acquired by very secure or perhaps very tangible means. Web browsers typically come with CA certificates for several popular CAs. Netscape and MSIE are, for example, shipped with a CA certificate for Veri-Sign (*http://www.verisign.com*), so that you can safely verify any certificates signed by VeriSign, wherever you encounter them. So, if all is working, we've reduced the problem to just that of your getting your copy of the web-browser software securely the first time. As far as maintenance goes, browsers like Netscape let you download new CA certificates dynamically, using a secure connection.

Site certificates

Certificates are presented to your web browser for verification when you encounter signed objects (signed JAR files). They are also issued by web servers when you make a secure connection using the HTTPS (HTTP Secure Sockets Layer) protocol. Browsers like Netscape and IE may save these certificates encountered from third-party locations so that you can assign privileges or attributes to those identities and so that they can be recognized again. We'll call these certificates *site certificates*—though they may belong to any third party, like a person or an organization. For example, you might declare that objects signed by a certain site are allowed to write local files. The browser then saves that site's certificate, marking it with the privileges (writing local files) that it should grant.

User (signer) certificates

Finally, you, the user, can have your own identity and your own certificates to validate your identity. Browsers store *user certificates* that can identify you to third parties. A user certificate is associated with a private key—the private key that goes with the public key in the certificate. When you use a private key to sign an object, the corresponding certificate is shipped as part of the signature. Remember, the recipient needs the public key in your certificate to validate your signature. The certificate says on whose authority the recipient should trust that public key.

So, where do you get private keys, public keys, and certificates validating your public keys? As for the keys, you generate those yourself. No other party should ever have access to your private key, much less generate it for you. After you generate a public and private key pair, you send your public key to the CA to request that they certify you. The CA can make you jump through whatever hoops are necessary; when they are satisfied that you are who you say you are, they grant you a certificate.

The Java SDK supplies the *keytool* utility to create and manage keys and certificates. We'll talk about it next.

The keytool Utility

keytool is the standard Java utility for managing a database of identities. With it, you can generate or import key pairs and certificates. You can then use these keys and certificates to sign JAR files used by the Java Plug-in.

The packages that implement cryptography in Java are part of the Java Cryptography Extension (JCE). As of Java 1.4, the JCE is bundled with the standard edition of Java. Prior to that, it was an optional package (and subject to export restrictions). The JCE provides both framework and implementations of algorithms. The implementations are called "provider" packages; Sun's security provider package comes with the SDK by default. Other packages can be installed to provide additional or alternate implementations of the cryptographic algorithms. By default, *keytool* uses the implementations found in Sun's provider package, though it can use other packages if any are available.

The user interface to *keytool* is awkward. It's a good bet that someone will implement a key management utility with a friendlier GUI; maybe it will be supplied with a future version of Java. In any event, we won't spend a great deal of time discussing the details of *keytool*; it's more important to understand the concepts.

What about Netscape and Internet Explorer?

Before the debut of the Java Plug-in, Netscape and Microsoft both invented their own code-signing schemes. As a result, signed applets in the Java 1.1 world were a disaster. There were three different ways to sign and deploy code, one each for Netscape, Sun's HotJava, and Microsoft's IE. Unless you knew in advance that you had only one kind of browser worry about, you were pretty much out of luck.

The Java Plug-in levels the field for signed applets, because the packaging and deployment strategy is the same for all browsers.

The TestWrite example

Before we dive into the details, let's look at an example to show that the process really works with the Java Plug-in. Use your browser to navigate to *http://examples. oreilly.com/learnjava3/TestWrite/Unsigned.html*. (At the time of this writing, on the Mac, this example works in Safari. Other browsers on the Mac should catch up with the Java 5.0 release for OS X.) You'll see the applet shown in Figure 23-4. When you push the button, this applet attempts to write a harmless file on the local host. Give it a try. The applet should fail with a security exception and display a message.

Figure 23-4. An unsigned applet violating security policy

Now try a web page that displays the same applet: *http://examples.oreilly.com/ learnjava3/TestWrite/Signed.html*. (Again, currently on the Mac, this example only works with the Safari web browser on OS X.) The only difference is that we've signed the JAR file containing the applet, with a key and certificate generated using *keytool*.

When the Java Plug-in loads the applet's JAR file, it examines the signature. What happens next depends on whether you're using the latest Java Plug-in. With Java 1.4 or later, the Plug-in prompts the user to decide whether or not to trust the code. In that case, you get a dialog like Figure 23-5.

Figure 23-5. Signed applet prompt

The dialog informs you that the applet is signed, in this case, by Pat Niemeyer, and asks if you want to grant access to it. You can get information about the certificate used to sign the JAR by clicking on View Certificate. The two fields of interest are Issuer and Subject. In this case, we have signed the JAR file with our own *self-issued* certificate; the issuer and subject (or signer) are both identified as "Pat Niemeyer." After pondering our trustworthiness, you can grant the TestWrite applet permissions or deny them. You can also specify whether the permissions last for one session or are remembered until the certificate expires. If you deny permissions, the applet may still run; it depends on what it tries to do and how it handles being denied access. In this case, the applet prints the security exception when it tries to write the file. If you granted the applet permissions, hitting the button should show a successful write. In the next section, we'll look at how we created our certificate and signed this JAR.

If you have an older version of the Plug-in (Java 1.3 or lower), Java informs you it can't verify the signature because it doesn't know about our certificate, and older versions didn't prompt the user to accept unknown signers. We could manually install our certificate in the local Java environment, but this procedure is complicated. Fortunately, with the Plug-in, we can specify the version required if we want to. (If you are interested in learning how to install keys manually for older versions of Java, you can find out all about it in the expanded material included on the accompanying CD and on this book's web site.)

Keystores, Keys, and Certificates

The SDK supports *keystores* that hold identities along with their public keys, private keys, and certificates. It includes the utility we covered earlier, *keytool*. We'll use this database as a repository while we create and work with our identity locally.

An identity can be a person, an organization, or perhaps a logical part of an organization. Before it can be used, an identity must have a public key and at least one certificate validating its public key. *keytool* refers to entities in the local database by IDs or aliases. These names are arbitrary and are not used outside the keystore (and possibly local Java security policy files that reference the keystore). Identities that have a private key stored locally in the keystore, as well as a public key, are called *signers*. These identities can be used to sign JAR files.

The default location for a keystore is the file *.keystore* in the user's home directory. On a single user system, the Java installation directory is used instead of the user's home directory. The default keystore location is used by *keytool* unless you specify another keystore with the -keystore option.

If you are going to maintain any private keys in a keystore (if you will have any signers), you must take special care to keep the keystore file safe (and not publicly readable). Private keys must be kept private.

Public and private keys

We can create a new entry in the default keystore, complete with a key pair, with the following *keytool* command:

```
C:\> keytool -genkey -alias Pat -keyalg DSA -keysize 1024 -dname "CN=Pat Niemeyer, \
OU=Technical Publications, O=O'Reilly & Associates, C=US" -keypass secure \
-storepass boofa
```

There are a lot of options to explain. The most important one is *-genkey*, which tells *keytool* to create a new key pair for this entry. A key pair enables this entry to sign code. The *-alias* option supplies an alias for this entry, Pat. The *-keyalg* argument, DSA, is the algorithm for which we are going to generate the keys. Java supports at minimum DSA, the Digital Signature Algorithm, which is a U.S. government standard for signing. Check the documentation for your Java installation to see what other algorithms may be supplied with it. The *-keysize* argument is the key length in bits. For most algorithms, larger key sizes provide stronger encryption. DSA supports keys of either 512 or 1,024 bits. You should use the latter, unless you have a specific reason to do otherwise.

keytool generates the keys and places them in the default keystore. Private keys are specially protected using the *-keypass* option. To retrieve Pat's private key, you need the correct key password. The integrity of the keystore as a whole is protected by the *-storepass* option. You need to supply the same keystore password to retrieve data from this keystore later.

Once we've created a keystore entry, we can display it with the command:

```
C:\> keytool -list -alias Pat -storepass boofa
```

To see more detail, add the -*v* option (for "verbose"):

```
C:\> keytool -list -alias Pat -v -storepass boofa
```

We can also list the entire contents of the database:

```
C:\> keytool -list -storepass boofa
```

Certificates

Now that we have keys, we want a certificate in which to wrap our public key for distribution. Ideally, at this point, we'd send a public key to a trusted CA and receive a certificate in return. *keytool* can generate such a request in a standard format called a Certificate Signing Request (CSR). To generate a signing request for the entry we just created, you would do this:

```
C:\> keytool -csr -alias Pat -file Pat.csr -keypass secure -storepass boofa
```

You need to specify the alias for the entry you want, a filename where the CSR will be written, and the password for the private key. The output file will contain the public key, along with the name and organizational information you provided. Once you've generated the CSR file, you can send it off to your favorite Certificate Authority. After they've performed some identity checks on you, and once you pay them, they will send a certificate back to you. Suppose they send it back in a file called *Pat. x509*. You can then use *keytool* to import this certificate as follows:

```
C:\> keytool -import -alias Pat -file Pat.x509 -keypass secure -storepass boofa
```

However, to demonstrate the features of *keytool*, we can serve as our own authority (as we did in the example) and use our own self-signed certificate. It turns out that *keytool* already did this for us when we created keys! A self-signed certificate already exists in the keystore; all we have to do is export it as follows:

```
C:\> keytool -export -alias Pat -file Pat.cer -storepass boofa
```

The jarsigner Utility

If we have a signer keystore entry, initialized with its private and public keys, we are ready to sign JAR files. This is accomplished using another command-line utility, *jarsigner*. All we need to do is specify which keystore entry should do the signing, which JAR needs to be signed, and the keystore password:

```
C:\> jarsigner -storepass boofa testwrite.jar Pat
```

If we list the archive, we see that *jarsigner* has added two files to the *META-INF* directory: *PAT.SF* and *PAT.DSA*. *PAT.SF* is the signature file; it's like the manifest file for this particular signature. The signature file lists the objects that were signed and the signature algorithms. *PAT.DSA* is the actual binary signature. That's it!

We've now created a JAR file that could only have come from us. Signed JAR files with the Java Plug-in level the playing field for Java applications by allowing them to do anything that a regular Java application could do, safely.

Conclusion

In this chapter, we covered some of the events that led to the current, fractured applet world and set the scene as it is. The Java Plug-in is currently your best option for running Java in the browser. New technologies such as Java Web Start are starting to provide alternatives for client-side deployment that may also be appealing. Although it is tempting to try to use minimalist Java 1.1 applets as a workaround for deployment issues, it's really a losing proposition. It's best to take control of the issue from the start and use the plug-in unless you have total control of the browser environment of your users.

CHAPTER 24

XML

Every now and then, an idea comes along that in retrospect seems just so simple and obvious that everyone wonders why it hadn't been seen all along. Often when that happens, it turns out that the idea isn't really all that new after all. The Java revolution began by drawing on ideas from all the programming languages that came before it. XML—the Extensible Markup Language—does for content what Java did for programming: providing a portable language for describing data.

XML is a simple, common format for representing structured information as text. The concept of XML follows the success of HTML as a universal document presentation format and generalizes it to handle any kind of data. In the process, XML has not only recast HTML but is transforming the way that businesses think about their information. In the context of a world driven more and more by documents and data exchange, XML's time has come.

A Bit of Background

XML and HTML are called markup languages because of the way they add structure to plain-text documents—by surrounding parts of the text with tags that indicate structure or meaning, much as someone with a pen might highlight a sentence and add a note. While HTML predefines a set of tags and their structure, XML is a blank slate in which the author gets to define the tags, the rules, and their meanings.

Both XML and HTML owe their lineage to Standard Generalized Markup Language (SGML)—the mother of all markup languages. SGML has been used in the publishing industry for many years (including at O'Reilly). But it wasn't until the Web captured the world that it came into the mainstream through HTML. HTML started as a very small application of SGML, and if HTML has done anything at all, it has proven that simplicity reigns.

HTML flourished but eventually showed its limitations. Documents using HTML have an unhealthy mix of both structural information (such as <head> and <body>)

and presentation information (for an egregious example, `<blink>`). Mixing the model and the user interface in this way limits the usefulness of HTML as a format for data exchange; it's hard for a machine to understand. XML documents consist purely of structure, and it is up to the reader of the document to apply meaning. As we'll see in this chapter, several related languages exist to help interpret and transform XML for presentation or further processing.

Text Versus Binary

When Tim Berners-Lee began postulating the Web back at CERN in the late 1980s, he wanted to organize project information using hypertext.[*] When the Web needed a protocol, HTTP—a simple, text-based client-server protocol—was invented. So, what exactly is so enchanting about the idea of plain text? Why, for example, didn't Tim turn to the Microsoft Word format as the basis for Web documents? Surely a binary, non-human-readable format and protocol would be more efficient? Since the Web's inception, there have now been literally trillions of HTTP transactions. Was it really a good idea for them to use (English) words like "GET" and "POST"?

The answer, as we've all seen, is yes! What humans can read, human developers can work with more easily. There is a time and place for a high level of optimization (and obscurity), but when the goal is universal acceptance and cross-platform portability, simplicity and transparency are paramount. This is the first, fundamental proposition of XML.

A Universal Parser

Using text to exchange data is not exactly a new idea, either, but historically, for every new document format that came along, a new *parser* would have to be written. A parser is an application that reads a document and understands its formatting conventions, usually enforcing some rules about the content. For example, the Java `Properties` class has a parser for the standard properties file format (Chapter 11). In our simple spreadsheet in Chapter 18, we wrote a parser capable of understanding basic mathematical expressions. As we've seen, depending on complexity, parsing can be quite tricky.

With XML, we can represent data without having to write this kind of custom parser. This isn't to say that it's reasonable to use XML for everything (e.g., typing math expressions into our spreadsheet), but for the common types of information that we exchange on the Net, we should no longer have to write parsers that deal with basic syntax and string manipulation. In conjunction with document-verifying components (Document Type Definitions [DTDs] or XML Schema), much of the

---

[*] To read Berners-Lee's original proposal to CERN, go to *http://www.w3.org/History/1989/proposal.html*.

complex error checking is also done automatically. This is the second fundamental proposition of XML.

The State of XML

The APIs we'll discuss in this chapter are powerful and popular. They are being used around the world to build enterprise-scale systems today. Unfortunately, the current slate of XML tools bundled with Java only partially remove the burden of parsing from the developer. Although we have taken a step up from low-level string manipulation to a common, structured document format, the standard tools still generally require the developer to write relatively low-level code to traverse the content and interpret the string data manually. The resulting programs remain somewhat fragile, and much of the work can be tedious. The next step, as we'll discuss later in this chapter, is to begin to use generating tools that read a description of an XML document (an XML DTD or Schema in some form) and generate Java classes or bind existing classes to XML data automatically. As these APIs grow, so does their complexity, and XML begins to lose some of its charm. Nonetheless, the promise of a seamless blending of XML documents and Java objects is one worth pursuing.

The XML APIs

In Java 1.4, all the basic APIs for working with XML were bundled with the standard release of Java. This included the javax.xml standard extension packages for working with Simple API for XML (SAX), Document Object Model (DOM), and Extensible Stylesheet Language (XSL) transforms. In Java 5.0, several enhancements were made and some important new APIs were introduced, including validation, XPath, and XInclude. These new APIs expose more of the power of XML through Java in a completely portable way. If you are using an older version of Java, you can still use many of these tools, but you will have to download packages separately from *http://java.sun.com/xml/* or find alternative implementations.

XML and Web Browsers

Microsoft (IE) was the first web browser to support XML explicitly. If you load an XML document in IE 5.0 or greater, it is displayed as a tree using a special stylesheet. The stylesheet uses dynamic HTML to allow you to collapse and expand nodes (like an outline) while viewing the document. Displaying the XML is mainly for debugging, but IE also supports client-side XSL transformation directly in the browser. XSL is a language for transforming XML into other documents; we'll talk about it later in this chapter. Recent versions of Netscape and Firefox support XML viewing and transformation as well.

A few exceptions remain. At the time of this writing, on the otherwise stellar Mac OS X operating system, the native Safari browser does not display XML in this way, nor does it apply stylesheets for transformation. Browsers that do not explicitly format XML for viewing simply display the text of the document with all the tags (structural information) stripped off. This is the prescribed behavior for working with unknown XML markup in a viewing environment. Remember that you can always use the "view source" option to display the text of a file in your browser, if you want to see the original source.

XML Basics

The basic syntax of XML is extremely simple. If you've worked with HTML, you're already halfway there. As with HTML, XML represents information as text using *tags* to add structure. A tag begins with a name sandwiched between less-than (<) and greater-than (>) characters. Unlike HTML, XML tags must always be *balanced*; in other words, an opening tag must always be followed by a closing tag. A closing tag looks just like the opening tag but starts with a less-than sign and a slash (</). An opening tag, closing tag, and any content in between are collectively referred to as an *element* of the XML document. Elements can contain other elements, but they must be properly nested (all tags started within an element must be closed before the element itself is closed). Elements can also contain plain text or a mixture of elements and text (called mixed content). Comments are enclosed between <!-- and --> markers. Here are a few examples:

```
<!-- Simple -->
<Sentence>This is text.</Sentence>

<!-- Element -->
<Paragraph><Sentence>This is text.</Sentence></Paragraph>

<!-- Mixed -->
<Paragraph>
        <Sentence>This <verb>is</verb> text.</Sentence>
</Paragraph>

<!-- Empty -->
<PageBreak></PageBreak>
```

An empty tag can be written more compactly with a single tag ending with a slash and a greater-than sign (/>):

```
<PageBreak/>
```

Attributes

An XML element can contain *attributes*, which are simple name-value pairs supplied inside the start tag.

```
<Document type="LEGAL" ID="42">...</Document>
<Image name="truffle.jpg"/>
```

The attribute value must always be enclosed in quotes. You can use double (") or single (') quotes. Single quotes are useful if the value contains double quotes.

Attributes are intended to be used for simple, unstructured properties or compact identifiers associated with the element data. It is always possible to make an attribute into a child element so, strictly speaking, there is no real need for attributes. But they often make the XML easier to read and more logical. In the case of the Document element in our snippet above, the attributes type and ID represent metadata about the document. We might expect that a Java class representing the Document would have an enumeration of document types such as LEGAL. In the case of the Image element, the attribute is simply a more compact way of including the filename. As a rule, attributes should be compact, with little significant internal structure (URLs push the envelope); by contrast, child elements can have arbitrary complexity.

XML Documents

An XML document begins with a header like the following and one *root element*:

```
<?xml version="1.0" encoding="UTF-8"?>
<MyDocument>
</MyDocument>
```

The header identifies the version of XML and the character encoding used. The root element is simply the top of the element hierarchy, which can be considered a tree. If you omit this header or have XML text without a single root element (as in our earlier simple examples), technically what you have is called an XML *fragment*.

Encoding

The default encoding for an XML document is UTF-8, the ASCII-friendly 8-bit Unicode encoding. This encoding preserves ASCII values, so English text is unaltered by it. It also allows Unicode values to be stored in a reasonably efficient way. An XML document may specify another encoding using the encoding attribute of the XML header.

Within an XML document, certain characters are necessarily sacrosanct: for example, the < and > characters that indicate element tags. When you need to include these in your text, you must encode them. XML provides an escape mechanism called "entities" that allows for encoding special structures. XML has five predefined entities in, as shown in Table 24-1.

Table 24-1. XML entities

Entity	Encodes
&amp;	& (ampersand)
&lt;	< (less than)

Table 24-1. XML entities (continued)

Entity	Encodes
>	> (greater than)
"	" (quotation mark)
'	' (apostrophe)

An alternative to encoding text in this way is to use a special "unparsed" section of text called a character data (CDATA) section. A CDATA section starts with the cryptic string `<![CDATA[` and ends with `]]>`, like this:

```
<![CDATA[  Learning Java, O'Reilly & Associates ]]>
```

The CDATA section looks a little like a comment, but the data is still part of the document, just opaque to the parser.

In the Java 5.0 XML APIs, another alternative is possible. You can use a special `<include>` directive to include the contents of a URL or file either as pre-escaped text or as parsed XML. This new feature is very convenient and we'll talk about it later in this chapter.

Namespaces

You've probably seen that HTML has a `<body>` tag that is used to structure web pages. Suppose for a moment that we are writing XML for a funeral home that also uses the tag `<body>` for some other, more macabre, purpose. This could be a problem if we want to mix HTML with our mortuary information.

If you consider HTML and the funeral home tags to be languages in this case, the elements (tag names) used in a document are really the vocabulary of those languages. An XML *namespace* is a way of saying whose dictionary you are using for a given element, allowing us to mix them freely. (Later we'll talk about XML Schemas, which enforce the grammar and syntax of the language.)

A namespace is specified with the `xmlns` attribute, whose value is a Uniform Resource Identifier (URI) that uniquely defines the set (and usually the meaning) of tags from that namespace:

```
<element xmlns="namespaceURI">
```

Recall from Chapter 14 that a URI is not necessarily a URL. URIs are more general than URLs. In practical terms, a URI is to be treated as a unique string. Often, the URI is, in fact, also a URL for a document describing the namespace, but that is only by convention.

An `xmlns` namespace attribute can be applied to an element and affects all its (nested) children; this is called a default namespace for the element:

```
<body xmlns="http://funeral-procedures.org/">
```

But more often it is desirable to mix and match namespaces on a tag-by-tag basis. To do this, we can use the xmlns attribute to define a special identifier for the namespace and use that identifier as a prefix on the tags in question. For example:

```
<funeral xmlns:fun="http://funeral-procedures.org/">
    <html><head></head><body>
    <fun:body>Corpse #42</fun:body>
</funeral>
```

In the above snippet of XML, we've qualified the body tag with the prefix "fun:" that we defined in the `<funeral>` tag. In this case, we should also qualify the root tag as well, reflexively:

```
<fun:funeral xmlns:fun="http://funeral-procedures.org/">
```

In the history of XML, support for namespaces is relatively new. Not all parsers support them. To accommodate this, the XML parser factories supplied with Java have a switch to specify whether you want a parser that understands namespaces. As of Java 5.0, this switch is still off by default.

```
parserFactory.setNamespaceAware( true );
```

We'll talk more about parsing in the sections on SAX and DOM later in this chapter.

Validation

A document that conforms to the basic rules of XML, with proper encoding and balanced tags, is called a *well-formed* document. Just because a document is syntactically correct, however, doesn't mean that it makes sense. Two related sets of tools, DTDs and XML Schemas, define ways to provide a grammar for your XML elements. They allow you to create syntactic rules, such as "a City element can appear only once inside an Address element." XML Schema goes further to provide a flexible language for describing the validity of data content of the tags, including both simple and compound data types made of numbers and strings.

XML Schema is a newer and far more complete solution (it includes data validation and not just rules about elements), but it is still not as widely used as the simpler DTDs. The standard (World Wide Web Consortium [W3C] approved) language for XML Schema is also fairly heavy and complex. For this reason, the Java validation APIs in Java 5.0 can support other schema languages for validating XML. We'll talk about the options later in this chapter.

A document that is checked against a DTD or XML Schema description and follows the rules is called a *valid* document. A document can be well-formed without being valid, but not vice versa.

HTML to XHTML

To speak very loosely, we could say that the most popular and widely used form of XML in the world today is HTML. The terminology is loose because HTML is not really well-formed XML. HTML tags violate XML's rule forbidding unbalanced elements; the common <p> tag is typically used without a closing tag, for example. HTML attributes also don't require quotes. XML tags are also case-sensitive; <P> and <p> are two different tags in XML. We could generously say that HTML is "forgiving" with respect to details like this, but as a developer, you know that sloppy syntax results in ambiguity. XHTML is an alternate, strict XML version of HTML that is clear and unambiguous. This form of HTML works in most modern browsers. Fortunately, if you want to switch, you don't have to manually clean up all your HTML documents; Tidy (*http://tidy.sourceforge.net*) is an open source program that automatically converts HTML to XHTML, validates it, and corrects common mistakes.

SAX

SAX is a low-level, event-style API for parsing XML documents. SAX originated in Java but has been implemented in many languages. We'll begin our discussion of the Java XML APIs here, at this lower level, and work our way up to higher-level (and sometimes more convenient) APIs as we go.

The SAX API

To use SAX, we'll be drawing on classes from the org.xml.sax package, standardized by the W3C. This package holds mainly interfaces common to all implementations of SAX. To perform the actual parsing, we'll need the javax.xml.parsers package, which is the standard Java package for accessing XML parsers. The java.xml.parsers package is part of the Java API for XML Processing (JAXP), which allows different parser implementations to be used with Java in a portable way.

To read an XML document with SAX, we first register an org.xml.sax.ContentHandler class with the parser. The ContentHandler has methods that are called in response to parts of the document. For example, the ContentHandler's startElement() method is called when an opening tag is encountered, and the endElement() method is called when the tag is closed. Attributes are provided with the startElement() call. Text content of elements is passed through a separate method called characters(). The characters() method can be invoked repeatedly to supply more text as it is read, but it often gets the whole string in one bite. The following are the method signatures of these methods of the ContentHandler class.

```
public void startElement(
    String namespace, String localname, String qname, Attributes atts );
public void characters(
    char[] ch, int start, int len );
```

```
public void endElement(
    String namespace, String localname, String qname );
```

The qname parameter is the *qualified name* of the element. This is the element name, prefixed with namespace if it has one. When working with namespaces, the namespace and localname parameters are also supplied, providing the namespace and unqualified name separately. (Java 5.0 introduced a new javax.xml.namespace package that holds concrete classes representing namespaces and qualified names. The SAX API doesn't use them yet, however.)

The ContentHandler interface also contains methods called in response to the start and end of the document, startDocument( ) and endDocument( ), as well as those for handling namespace mapping, special XML instructions, and whitespace that can be ignored. We'll confine ourselves to the three methods above for our examples. As with many other Java interfaces, a simple implementation, org.xml.sax.helpers.DefaultHandler, is provided for us that allows us to override just the methods we're interested in.

JAXP

To perform the parsing, we'll need to get a parser from the javax.xml.parsers package. JAXP abstracts the process of getting a parser through a *factory pattern*, allowing different parser implementations to be plugged into the Java platform. The following snippet constructs a SAXParser object and then gets an XMLReader used to parse a file:

```
import javax.xml.parsers.*;

SAXParserFactory factory = SAXParserFactory.newInstance( );
SAXParser saxParser = factory.newSAXParser( );
XMLReader parser = saxParser.getXMLReader( );

parser.setContentHandler( myContentHandler );
parser.parse( "myfile.xml" );
```

You might expect the SAXParser to have the parse method. The XMLReader intermediary was added to support changes in the SAX API between 1.0 and 2.0. Later we'll discuss some options that can be set to govern how XML parsers operate. These options are normally set through methods on the parser factory (e.g., SAXParserFactory) and not the parser itself. This is because the factory may wish to use different implementations to support different required features.

SAX's strengths and weaknesses

The primary motivation for using SAX instead of the higher-level APIs that we'll discuss later is that it is lightweight and event-driven. SAX doesn't require maintaining the entire document in memory. If, for example, you need to grab the text of just a few elements from a document, or if you need to extract elements from a large stream of XML, you can do so efficiently with SAX. The event-driven nature of SAX also allows you to take actions as the beginning and end tags are parsed. This can be useful for directly manipulating your own models without first going through another representation. The primary weakness of SAX is that you are operating on a tag-by-tag level with no help from the parser to maintain context. We'll talk about how to overcome this limitation next. Later, we'll also talk about the new XPath API, which combines much of the benefits of both SAX and DOM in a form that is easier to use.

Building a Model Using SAX

The ContentHandler mechanism for receiving SAX events is very simple. It should be easy to see how one could use it to capture the value or attributes of a single element in a document. What may be harder to see is how one could use SAX to populate a real Java object model. Creating or pushing data into Java objects from XML is such a common activity that it's worth considering how the SAX API applies to this problem. The following example, SAXModelBuilder, does just this, reading an XML description and creating Java objects on command. This example is a bit unusual in that we resort to using reflection to do the job, but this is a case where we're trying to interact with Java objects dynamically. Later, we'll discuss more powerful, standard tools for statically generating and building models for XML documents.

In this section, we'll start by creating some XML along with corresponding Java classes that serve as the model for this XML. The final step in this example is to create the generic model builder that reads the XML and populates the model classes with their data. The idea is that the developer is creating only XML and model classes—no custom code—to do the parsing. You might use code like this to read configuration files for an application or to implement a custom XML "language" for describing workflows. The advantage is that there is no parsing code in the application at all, only in the generic builder tool.

Creating the XML file

The first thing we'll need is a nice XML document to parse. Luckily, it's inventory time at the zoo! The following document, *zooinventory.xml*, describes two of the zoo's residents, including some vital information about their diets:

```
<?xml version="1.0" encoding="UTF-8"?>
<!-- file zooinventory.xml -->
<Inventory>
    <Animal animalClass="mammal">
        <Name>Song Fang</Name>
        <Species>Giant Panda</Species>
        <Habitat>China</Habitat>
        <Food>Bamboo</Food>
        <Temperament>Friendly</Temperament>
    </Animal>
    <Animal animalClass="mammal">
```

```
        <Name>Cocoa</Name>
        <Species>Gorilla</Species>
        <Habitat>Central Africa</Habitat>
        <FoodRecipe>
            <Name>Gorilla Chow</Name>
            <Ingredient>Fruit</Ingredient>
            <Ingredient>Shoots</Ingredient>
            <Ingredient>Leaves</Ingredient>
        </FoodRecipe>
        <Temperament>Know-it-all</Temperament>
    </Animal>
</Inventory>
```

The document is fairly simple. The root element, <Inventory>, contains two <Animal> elements as children. <Animal> contains several simple text elements for things like name, species, and habitat. It also contains either a simple <Food> element or a compound <FoodRecipe> element. Finally, note that the <Animal> element has one attribute (animalClass) that describes the zoological classification of the creature.

The model

Now let's make a Java object model for our zoo inventory. This part is very mechanical—easy, but tedious to do by hand. We simply create objects for each of the complex element types in our XML, using the standard JavaBeans property design patterns ("setters" and "getters") so that our builder can automatically recognize them later. (We'll prove the usefulness of these patterns later when we see that these same model objects can be understood by the Java XMLEncoder tool.) For convenience, we'll have our model objects extend a base SimpleElement class that handles text content for any element, but you could eliminate this requirement easily.

```java
public class SimpleElement {
    StringBuffer text = new StringBuffer();
    public void addText( String s ) { text.append( s ); }
    public String getText() { return text.toString(); }
    public void setAttributeValue( String name, String value ) {
        throw new Error( getClass( )+": No attributes allowed");
    }
}
public class Inventory extends SimpleElement {
    List<Animal> animals = new ArrayList<Animal>();
    public void addAnimal( Animal animal ) { animals.add( animal ); }
    public List<Animal> getAnimals() { return animals; }
    public void setAnimals( List<Animal> animals ) { this.animals = animals; }
}

public class Animal extends SimpleElement {
    public final static int MAMMAL = 1;
    int animalClass;
    String name, species, habitat, food, temperament;
    FoodRecipe foodRecipe;
```

```
        public void setName( String name ) { this.name = name ; }
        public String getName(  ) { return name; }
        public void setSpecies( String species ) { this.species = species ; }
        public String getSpecies(  ) { return species; }
        public void setHabitat( String habitat ) { this.habitat = habitat ; }
        public String getHabitat(  ) { return habitat; }
        public void setFood( String food ) { this.food = food ; }
        public String getFood(  ) { return food; }
        public void setFoodRecipe( FoodRecipe recipe ) {
            this.foodRecipe = recipe; }
        public FoodRecipe getFoodRecipe(  ) { return foodRecipe; }
        public void setTemperament( String temperament ) {
            this.temperament = temperament ; }
        public String getTemperament(  ) { return temperament; }

        public void setAnimalClass( int animalClass ) {
            this.animalClass = animalClass; }
        public int getAnimalClass(  ) { return animalClass; }
        public void setAttributeValue( String name, String value ) {
            if ( name.equals("animalClass") && value.equals("mammal") )
              setAnimalClass( MAMMAL );
            else
                throw new Error("Invalid attribute: "+name);
        }
        public String toString(  ) { return name +"("+species+")"; }
    }

    public class FoodRecipe extends SimpleElement {
        String name;
        List<String> ingredients = new ArrayList<String>();
        public void setName( String name ) { this.name = name ; }
        public String getName() { return name; }
        public void addIngredient( String ingredient ) {
            ingredients.add( ingredient ); }
        public void setIngredients( List<String> ingredients ) {
            this.ingredients = ingredients; }
        public List<String> getIngredients(  ) { return ingredients; }
        public String toString() { return name + ": "+ ingredients.toString(  ); }
    }
```

The SAXModelBuilder

Let's get down to business and write our builder tool. The SAXModelBuilder we create in this section receives SAX events from parsing an XML file and constructs classes corresponding to the names of the tags. Our model builder is simple, but it handles the most common structures: elements with text or simple element data. We handle attributes by passing them to the model class, allowing it to map them to their own identifiers (perhaps Animal.MAMMAL). Here is the code:

```
import org.xml.sax.*;
import org.xml.sax.helpers.*;
import java.util.*;
import java.lang.reflect.*;
```

```java
public class SAXModelBuilder extends DefaultHandler
{
    Stack<SimpleElement> stack = new Stack<SimpleElement>( );
    SimpleElement element;

    public void startElement(
        String namespace, String localname, String qname, Attributes atts )
        throws SAXException
    {
        SimpleElement element = null;
        try {
            element = (SimpleElement)Class.forName(qname).newInstance( );
        } catch ( Exception e ) { }
        if ( element == null )
            element = new SimpleElement( );
        for(int i=0; i<atts.getLength( ); i++)
            element.setAttributeValue( atts.getQName(i), atts.getValue(i) );
        stack.push( element );
    }

    public void endElement( String namespace, String localname, String qname )
        throws SAXException
    {
        element = stack.pop( );
        if ( !stack.empty( ) )
        try {
            setProperty( qname, stack.peek( ), element );
        } catch ( Exception e ) { throw new SAXException( "Error: "+e ); }
    }

    public void characters(char[] ch, int start, int len ) {
        String text = new String( ch, start, len );
        stack.peek( ).addText( text );
    }

    void setProperty( String name, Object target, Object value )
        throws SAXException
    {
        Method method = null;
        try {
            method = target.getClass( ).getMethod("add"+name, value.getClass( ));
        } catch ( NoSuchMethodException e ) { }
        if ( method == null ) try {
            method = target.getClass( ).getMethod("set"+name, value.getClass( ));
        } catch ( NoSuchMethodException e ) { }
        if ( method == null ) try {
            value = ((SimpleElement)value).getText( );
            method = target.getClass( ).getMethod( "add"+name, String.class );
        } catch ( NoSuchMethodException e ) { }
        try {
            if ( method == null )
                method = target.getClass( ).getMethod("set"+name, String.class);
```

```
            method.invoke( target, value );
        } catch ( Exception e ) { throw new SAXException( e.toString() ); }
    }

    public SimpleElement getModel() { return element; }
}
```

The `SAXModelBuilder` extends `DefaultHandler` to help us implement the `ContentHandler` interface. We use the `startElement()`, `endElement()`, and `characters()` methods to receive information from the document.

Because SAX events follow the structure of the XML document, we use a simple stack to keep track of which object we are currently parsing. At the start of each element, the model builder attempts to create an instance of a class with the same name as the element and push it onto the top of the stack. Each nested opening tag creates a new object on the stack until we encounter a closing tag. Upon reaching an end of the element, we pop the current object off the stack and attempt to apply its value to its parent (the enclosing element), which is the new top of the stack. The final closing tag leaves the stack empty, but we save the last value in the result variable.

Our `setProperty()` method uses reflection and the standard JavaBeans naming conventions to look for the appropriate property "set" method to apply a value to its parent object. First, we check for a method named add<Property> or set<Property>, accepting an argument of the child element type (for example, the `addAnimal( Animal animal )` method of our `Inventory` object). Failing that, we look for an "add" or "set" method accepting a `String` argument and use it to apply any text content of the child object. This convenience saves us from having to create trivial classes for properties containing only text.

The common base class `SimpleElement` helps us in two ways. First, it provides a method allowing us to pass attributes to the model class. Next, we use `SimpleElement` as a placeholder when no class exists for an element, allowing us to store the text of the tag.

Test drive

Finally, we can test-drive the model builder with the following class, `TestModelBuilder`, which calls the SAX parser, setting an instance of our `SAXModelBuilder` as the content handler. The test class then prints some of the information parsed from the *zooinventory.xml* file:

```
import org.xml.sax.*;
import org.xml.sax.helpers.*;
import javax.xml.parsers.*;

public class TestModelBuilder
{
    public static void main( String [] args ) throws Exception
    {
```

```
SAXParserFactory factory = SAXParserFactory.newInstance( );
SAXParser saxParser = factory.newSAXParser( );
XMLReader parser = saxParser.getXMLReader( );
SAXModelBuilder mb = new SAXModelBuilder( );
parser.setContentHandler( mb );
parser.parse( "zooinventory.xml" );

Inventory inventory = (Inventory)mb.getModel( );
System.out.println("Animals = "+inventory.getAnimals( ));
Animal cocoa = (Animal)(inventory.getAnimals( ).get(1));
FoodRecipe recipe = cocoa.getFoodRecipe( );
System.out.println( "Recipe = "+recipe );
    }
  }
```

The output should look like this:

```
Animals = [Song Fang(Giant Panda), Cocoa(Gorilla)]
Recipe = Gorilla Chow: [Fruit, Shoots, Leaves]
```

In the following sections, we'll generate the equivalent output using different tools.

Limitations and possibilities

To make our model builder more complete, we could use more robust naming conventions for our tags and model classes (taking into account packages and mixed capitalization, etc.). But more generally, we might not want to name our model classes strictly based on tag names. And, of course, there is the problem of taking our model and going the other way, using it to generate an XML document. Furthermore, as we've said, writing the model classes in this way is tedious and error-prone. All this is a good indication that this area is ripe for auto-generation of classes. We'll discuss tools that do that later in the chapter.

XMLEncoder/Decoder

Java includes a standard tool for serializing JavaBeans classes to XML. The java.beans package XMLEncoder and XMLDecoder classes are analogous to java.io ObjectInputStream and ObjectOutputStream. Instead of using the native Java serialization format, they store the object state in a high-level XML format. We say that they are analogous, but the XML encoder is not a general replacement for Java object serialization. Instead, it is specialized to work with objects that follow the JavaBeans design patterns, and it can only store and recover the state of the object that is expressed through a bean's public properties in this way (using getters and setters).

When you call it, the XMLEncoder attempts to construct an in-memory copy of the graph of beans that you are serializing, using only public constructors and JavaBean properties. As it works, it writes out the steps required as "instructions" in an XML format. Later, the XMLDecoder executes these instructions and reproduces the result. The primary advantage of this process is that it is highly resilient to changes in the class implementation. While standard Java object serialization can accommodate many kinds of "compatible changes" in classes, it requires some help from the developer to get it right. Because the XMLEncoder uses only public APIs and writes instructions in simple XML, it is expected that this form of serialization will be the most robust way to store the state of JavaBeans. The process is referred to as "long-term persistence" for JavaBeans.

Give it a whirl. You can use the model-builder example to create the beans and compare the output to our original XML. You can add this bit to our TestModelBuilder class, which will populate the beans for us before we write them out:

```
import java.beans.XMLEncoder;
...
XMLEncoder xmle = new XMLEncoder( System.out );
xmle.writeObject( inventory );
xmle.close( );
```

Fun!

Further thoughts

It might seem at first like this would obviate the need for our SAXModelBuilder example. Why not simply write our XML in the format that XMLDecoder understands and use it to build our model? Although XMLEncoder is very efficient at eliminating redundancy, you can see that its output is still very verbose (about two to three times larger than our original XML) and not very human-friendly. Although it's possible to write it by hand, this XML format wasn't designed for that. Finally, although XMLEncoder can be customized for how it handles specific object types, it suffers from the same problem that our model builder does, in that "binding" (the namespace of tags) is determined strictly by our Java class names. As we've said before, what is really needed is a more general tool to generate classes or to map our own classes to XML and back.

DOM

In the last section, we used SAX to parse an XML document and build a Java object model representing it. In that case, we created specific Java types for each of our complex elements. If we were planning to use our model extensively in an application, this technique would give us a great deal of flexibility. But often it is sufficient (and much easier) to use a "generic" model that simply represents the content of the XML in a neutral form. The Document Object Model (DOM) is just that. The DOM API parses an XML document into a full, memory-resident representation consisting of classes such as Element and Attribute that hold their own values.

As we saw in our zoo example, once you have an object model, using the data is a breeze. So a generic DOM would seem like an appealing solution, especially when working mainly with text. The only catch in this case is that DOM didn't evolve first as a Java API, and it doesn't map well to Java. DOM is very complete and provides access to every facet of the original XML document, but it's so generic (and language-neutral) that it's cumbersome to use in Java. In our example, we'll start by making a couple of helper methods to smooth things over. Later, we'll also mention a native Java alternative to DOM called JDOM that is more pleasant to use.

The DOM API

The core DOM classes belong to the org.w3c.dom package. The result of parsing an XML document with DOM is a Document object from this package (see Figure 24-1). The Document is a factory and a container for a hierarchical collection of Node objects, representing the document structure. A node has a parent and may have children, which can be traversed using its getChildNodes( ), getFirstChild( ), or getLastChild( ) methods. A node may also have "attributes" associated with it, which consist of a named map of nodes.

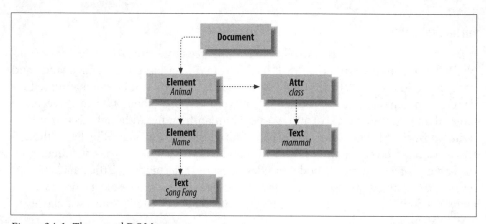

Figure 24-1. The parsed DOM

Subtypes of Node—Element, Text, and Attr—represent elements, text, and attributes in XML. Some types of nodes (including these) have a text "value." For example, the value of a Text node is the text of the element it represents. The same is true of an attribute, cdata, or comment node. The value of a node can be accessed by the getNodeValue( ) and setNodeValue( ) methods.

The Element node provides "random" access to its child elements through its getElementsByTagName( ) method, which returns a NodeList (a simple collection type). You can also fetch an attribute by name from the Element using the getAttribute( ) method.

The javax.xml.parsers package contains a factory for DOM parsers, just as it does for SAX parsers. An instance of DocumentBuilderFactory can be used to create a DocumentBuilder object to parse the file and produce a Document result.

Test-Driving DOM

Let's use DOM to parse our zoo inventory and print the same information as our model-builder example. Using DOM saves us from having to create all those model classes and makes our example much shorter. But before we even begin, we're going to make a couple of utility methods to save us a great deal of pain. The following class, DOMUtil, covers two very common operations on an element: retrieving a simple (singular) child element by name and retrieving the text of a simple child element by name. Here is the code:

```java
import org.w3c.dom.*;

public class DOMUtil
{
    public static Element getFirstElement( Element element, String name ) {
        NodeList nl = element.getElementsByTagName( name );
        if ( nl.getLength() < 1 )
            throw new RuntimeException(
                "Element: "+element+" does not contain: "+name);
        return (Element)nl.item(0);
    }

    public static String getSimpleElementText( Element node, String name )
    {
        Element namedElement = getFirstElement( node, name );
        return getSimpleElementText( namedElement );
    }

    public static String getSimpleElementText( Element node )
    {
        StringBuffer sb = new StringBuffer();
        NodeList children = node.getChildNodes();
        for(int i=0; i<children.getLength(); i++) {
            Node child = children.item(i);
            if ( child instanceof Text )
                sb.append( child.getNodeValue() );
        }
        return sb.toString();
    }
}
```

With that out of the way, we can present our TestDOM class:

```java
mport javax.xml.parsers.*;
import org.w3c.dom.*;

public class TestDOM
{
    public static void main( String [] args ) throws Exception
    {
        DocumentBuilderFactory factory = DocumentBuilderFactory.newInstance();
        DocumentBuilder parser = factory.newDocumentBuilder();
        Document document = parser.parse( "zooinventory.xml" );
```

```
Element inventory = document.getDocumentElement( );
NodeList animals = inventory.getElementsByTagName("Animal");

System.out.println("Animals = ");
for( int i=0; i<animals.getLength( ); i++ ) {
    String name = DOMUtil.getSimpleElementText(
        (Element)animals.item(i),"Name" );
    String species = DOMUtil.getSimpleElementText(
        (Element)animals.item(i), "Species" );
    System.out.println( "  "+ name +" ("+species+")" );
}

Element foodRecipe = DOMUtil.getFirstElement(
    (Element)animals.item(1), "FoodRecipe" );
String name = DOMUtil.getSimpleElementText( foodRecipe, "Name" );
System.out.println("Recipe = " + name );
NodeList ingredients = foodRecipe.getElementsByTagName("Ingredient");
for(int i=0; i<ingredients.getLength( ); i++)
    System.out.println( "   " + DOMUtil.getSimpleElementText(
        (Element)ingredients.item(i) ) );
    }
}
```

TestDOM creates an instance of a DocumentBuilder and uses it to parse our *zooinventory.xml* file. We use the Document getDocumentElement( ) method to get the root element of the document, from which we will begin our traversal. From there, we ask for all the Animal child nodes. The getElementbyTagName( ) method returns a NodeList object, which we then use to iterate through our creatures. For each animal, we use our DOMUtil.getSimpleElementText( ) method to retrieve the basic name and species information. Next, we use the DOMUtil.getFirstElement( ) method to retrieve the element called FoodRecipe from the second animal. We use it to fetch a NodeList for the tags matching Ingredient and print them as before. The output should contain the same information as our SAX-based example. But as you can see, the tradeoff in not having to create our own model classes is that we have to suffer through the use of the generic model and produce code that is harder to read.

Generating XML with DOM

Thus far, we've used the SAX and DOM APIs to parse XML. But what about generating XML? Sure, it's easy to generate trivial XML documents simply by emitting the appropriate strings. But if we plan to create a complex document on the fly, we might want some help with all those quotes and closing tags. We may also want to validate our model against an XML DTD or Schema before writing it out. What we can do is to build a DOM representation of our object in memory and then transform it to text. This is also useful if we want to read a document and then make some alterations to it. To do this, we'll use of the java.xml.transform package. This package does a lot more than just printing XML. As its name implies, it's part of a general transformation facility. It includes the XSL/XSLT languages for generating one XML document from another. (We'll talk about XSL later in this chapter.)

We won't discuss the details of constructing a DOM in memory here, but it follows fairly naturally from what you've learned about traversing the tree in our previous example. The following example, PrintDOM, simply parses our *zooinventory.xml* file to a DOM and then prints it back to the screen:

```
import javax.xml.parsers.*;
import org.w3c.dom.*;
import javax.xml.transform.*;
import javax.xml.transform.dom.DOMSource;
import javax.xml.transform.stream.StreamResult;

public class PrintDOM {
    public static void main( String [] args ) throws Exception
    {
        DocumentBuilder parser =
            DocumentBuilderFactory.newInstance( ).newDocumentBuilder( );
        Document document=parser.parse( "zooinventory.xml" );
        Transformer transformer =
            TransformerFactory.newInstance( ).newTransformer( );
        Source source = new DOMSource( document );
        Result output = new StreamResult( System.out );
        transformer.transform( source, output );
    }
}
```

Note that the imports are almost as long as the entire program! Here, we are using an instance of a Transformer object in its simplest capacity to copy from a source to an output. We'll return to the Transformer later when we discuss XSL, at which point, it will be doing a lot more work for us.

JDOM

As we promised earlier, we'll now describe an easier DOM API: JDOM, created by Jason Hunter and Brett McLaughlin, two fellow O'Reilly authors (*Java Servlet Programming* and *Java and XML*, respectively). It is a more natural Java DOM that uses real Java collection types such as List for its hierarchy and provides more streamlined methods for building documents. You can get the latest JDOM from *http:// www.jdom.org/*. Here's the JDOM version of our standard "test" program:

```
import org.jdom.*;
import org.jdom.input.*;
import org.jdom.output.*;
import java.util.*;

public class TestJDOM {
    public static void main( String[] args ) throws Exception {
        Document doc = new SAXBuilder( ).build("zooinventory.xml");
        List animals = doc.getRootElement( ).getChildren("Animal");
```

```
            System.out.println("Animals = ");
            for( int i=0; i<animals.size(); i++ ) {
                String name = ((Element)animals.get(i)).getChildText("Name");
                String species = ((Element)animals.get(i)).getChildText("Species");
                System.out.println( "   "+ name +" ("+species+")" );
            }
            Element foodRecipe = ((Element)animals.get(1)).getChild("FoodRecipe");
            String name = foodRecipe.getChildText("Name");
            System.out.println("Recipe = " + name );
            List ingredients = foodRecipe.getChildren("Ingredient");
            for(int i=0; i<ingredients.size(); i++)
                System.out.println( "   "+((Element)ingredients.get(i)).getText() );
        }
    }
```

JDOM has its own convenience methods that take the place of our homemade DOM helper methods. Namely, the JDOM `Element` class has `getChild( )` and `getChildren( )` methods as well as a `getChildText( )` method for retrieving node text.

Now that we've covered the basics of SAX and DOM, we're going to look at a new API that, in a sense, straddles the two. XPath allows us to target only the parts of a document that we want and gives us the option of getting at those components in DOM form.

XPath

XPath is an expression language for addressing parts of an XML document. You can think of XPath expressions as sort of like regular expressions for XML. They let you "pull out" parts of an XML document based on patterns. In the case of XPath, the patterns are more concerned with structural information than with character content and the values returned may be either simple text or "live" DOM nodes. With XPath, we can query an XML document for all of the elements with a certain name or in a certain parent-child relationship. We can also apply fairly sophisticated tests or *predicates* to the nodes, which allows us to construct complex queries such as this one: give me all of the `Animals` with a `Weight` greater than the number 400 and a `Temperament` of irritable whose `animalClass` attribute is mammal.

The full XPath specification has many features and includes both a compact and more verbose syntax. We won't try to cover it all here, but the basics are easy and it's important to know them because XPath expressions are at the core of XSL transformations and other APIs that refer to parts of XML documents. The full specification does not make great bedtime reading but can be found at *http://www.w3.org/TR/xpath*.

Nodes

An XPath expression addresses a Node in an XML document tree. The node may be an element (possibly with children) like `<Animal>...</Animal>` or it may be a lower-level document node representing an attribute (e.g., `animalClass="mammal"`), a CDATA block, or even a comment. All of the structure of an XML document is accessible through the XPath syntax. Once we've addressed the node, we can either reduce the content to a text string (as we might with a simple element like Name) or we can access it as a proper DOM tree to further read or manipulate it.

Table 24-2 shows the most basic node-related syntax.

Table 24-2. Basic node-related syntax

Syntax	Example	Description
/Name	/Inventory/Animal	All Animal nodes under /Inventory
//Name	//Animal	All Animal nodes anywhere in document. A FoodRecipe/Animal would also match
Name/*	/Inventory/*	All child nodes of Inventory (Animals and any other elements directly under Inventory)
@Name	//Animal/@animalClass	All animalClass attributes of Animals
.	/Inventory/Animal/.	The current node (all Animals)
..	/Inventory/Animal/..	The parent node (Inventory)

Nodes are addressed with a slash-separated path based on name (e.g., /Inventory/Animal refers to the set of all Animal nodes under the Inventory node). If we want to list the names of all Animals, we would use /Inventory/Animal/Name. The // syntax matches a node anywhere in a document, at any level of nesting, so //Name would match the name elements of Animals, FoodRecipes, and possibly many other elements. We could be more specific, using //Animal/Name to match only Name elements whose parent is an Animal element. The at sign (@) matches attributes. This becomes much more useful with predicates, which we describe next. Finally, the familiar . and .. notation can be used to "move" relative to a node; read on to see how this is used.

Predicates

Predicates let us apply a test to a node. Nodes that pass the test are included in the result set or used to select other nodes (child or parent) relative to them. There are many types of tests available in XPath. Table 24-3 lists a few examples.

Table 24-3. Predicates

Syntax	Example	Description
[n]	/Inventory/Animal[1]	Select the *n*th element of a set. (Starts with 1 rather than 0.) For example, select the first Animal in the Inventory.
[@name=value]	//Animal[@animalClass="mammal"]	Match nodes with the specified attribute value. For example, Animals with the animalClass attribute "mammal".
[element=value]	//Animal[Name="Cocoa"]	Match nodes with a child node whose text value is specified. For example, match the Animal with a Name element containing the simple text "Cocoa".
= != > <	//Animal[Weight > 400]	Predicates may also test for inequality and numeric greater-/lesser-than value.
and, or	//Animal[@animalClass= "mammal" or @class="reptile"]]	Predicates may use logical AND and OR to test. For example, Animals whose animalClass is mammal or reptile.

Predicates can be compounded (AND'ed) using this syntax or simply by adding more predicates, like so:

```
//Animal[@animalClass="mammal"][Weight > 400]
```

Here, we've asked for Animals with a class attribute of "mammal" and a Weight element containing a number greater than 400.

We can now also see the usefulness of the .. operator. Suppose we want to find all of the Animals with a FoodRecipe that uses Fruit as an ingredient:

```
//Animal/FoodRecipe[Ingredient="Fruit"]/..
```

The .. means that instead of returning the matching FoodRecipe node itself, we return its parent—the Animal element. The . operator is useful in other cases where we use XPath functions to manipulate values in more refined ways. We'll say a few words about functions next.

Functions

The XPath specification includes not only the basic node traversal and predicate syntax we've shown but also the ability to invoke more open-ended functions that operate on nodes and the node context. These XPath functions cover a wide range of duties and we'll just give a couple of examples here. The functions fall into a few general categories.

Some functions select node types other than an element. For example, there is no special syntax for selecting an XML comment. Instead you invoke a special method called comment( ), like this:

```
/Inventory/comment( )
```

This expression returns any XML comment nodes that are children of the Inventory element. XPath also offers functions that duplicate all of the (compact) syntax we've discussed, including methods like child( ) and parent( ) (corresponding to . and ..).

Other functions look at the context of nodes, for example, last( ) and count( ).

```
/Inventory/Animal[last( )]
```

This expression selects the last Animal child element of Inventory in the same way that [n] selects the nth.

```
//FoodRecipe[count(Ingredient)>2]
```

This expression matches all of the FoodRecipe elements with more than two ingredients. (Cool, eh?)

Finally, there are many string-related functions. Some are useful for simple tests, but others are really useful only in the context of XSL, where they help out the language (in an awkward way) with basic formatting and string manipulation. For example, the contains( ) and starts-with( )methods can be used to look at the text values inside XML documents:

```
//Animal[starts-with(Name,"S")]
```

This expression matches Animals whose Name starts with the character S (e.g., Song Fang). The contains( ) method, similarly, can be used to look for a substring in text.

The XPath API

Now that we've got a taste for the syntax, let's look at how to use the API. XPath has been around for a while now, but the API for using it directly in Java was just introduced in Java 5.0. The pattern is similar to that of the Java regular expression API for strings. We use a factory to create an XPath object. We can then either evaluate expressions with it or "compile" an expression down to an XPathExpression for better performance if we're going to use it more than once.

```
XPath xpath = XPathFactory.newInstance( ).newXPath( );
InputSource source = new InputSource( filename );

String result = xpath.evaluate( "//Animal/Name", source );
// Song Fang
```

We've used the simplest form of the evaluate( ) method, which returns only the first match and takes the value as a string. This method is useful for pulling simple text values from elements. However, if we want the full set of values (the names of all the

Animals matched by this expression), we need to return the results as a set of Node objects instead.

The return type of evaluate( ) is controlled by identifiers of the XPathConstants class. We can get the result as one of the following: STRING, BOOLEAN, NUMBER, NODE, or NODESET. The default is STRING, which strips out child element tags and returns just the text of the matching nodes. BOOLEAN and NUMBER are conveniences for getting primitive types. NODE and NODESET return org.w3c.dom.Node and NodeList objects, respectively. We need the NodeList to get all the values.

```
NodeList elements = (NodeList)xpath.evaluate(
    expression, inputSource, XPathConstants.NODESET );
```

Next, let's put this together in a useful example.

XMLGrep

This simple example can be used as a command-line utility, such as *grep*, for testing XPath expressions against a file. It applies an XPath expression and then prints the resulting elements as XML text using the same technique we used in our PrintDOM example. Nodes that are not elements (e.g., attributes, comments, and so on) are simply printed with their toString( ) method, which normally serves well enough to identify them, but you can expand the example to your taste. Here it is:

```
import org.w3c.dom.*;
import org.xml.sax.InputSource;
import javax.xml.xpath.*;
import javax.xml.transform.*;
import javax.xml.transform.dom.DOMSource;
import javax.xml.transform.stream.StreamResult;

public class XMLGrep {

    public static void printXML( Element element ) throws TransformerException
    {
        Transformer transformer =
            TransformerFactory.newInstance( ).newTransformer( );
        transformer.setOutputProperty( OutputKeys.OMIT_XML_DECLARATION, "yes" );
        Source source = new DOMSource( element );
        Result output = new StreamResult( System.out );
        transformer.transform( source, output );
        System.out.println( );
    }

    public static void main( String [] args ) throws Exception
    {
        if ( args.length != 2 ) {
            System.out.println( "usage: PrintXPath expression file.xml" );
            System.exit(1);
        }
        String expression = args[0], filename = args[1];
```

```
        XPath xpath = XPathFactory.newInstance( ).newXPath( );
        InputSource inputSource = new InputSource( filename );

        NodeList elements = (NodeList)xpath.evaluate(
            expression, inputSource, XPathConstants.NODESET );

        for( int i=0; i<elements.getLength( ); i++ )
            if ( elements.item(i) instanceof Element ) {
                printXML( (Element)elements.item(i) );
            } else
                System.out.println( elements.item(i) );
    }

}
```

There are again a lot of imports in this example. The transform code in our printXML( ) method is drawn from the PrintDOM example with one addition. We've set a property on the transformer to omit the standard XML declaration that would normally be output for us at the head of our document. Since we may print more than one element, the output is not well-formed XML anyway.

Run the example by passing an XPath expression and the name of an XML file as arguments:

```
% java XMLGrep "//Animal[starts-with(Name,'C')]" zooinventory.xml
```

This example really is useful for trying out XPath. Please give it a whirl. Mastering these expressions (and learning more) will give you great power over XML documents and, again, form the basis for learning about XSL transformations.

XInclude

XInclude is a very simple but sorely needed "import" facility for XML documents. Like XPath, the ability to use the XInclude standard from Java just arrived in Java 5.0. With the XInclude directive, you can easily include one XML document in another either as XML or as plain (and escaped) text. This means that you can break down your documents into as many files as you see fit and reference the pieces in a simple, standard way. We should note that it has been possible to do this in the past, in a way, using XML entity declarations, but they were fraught with problems. XInclude is simpler and does what its name implies, including the specified document at the current location; you just have to declare the proper namespace for the new <include> element. Here is an example:

```
<Book xmlns:xi="http://www.w3.org/2001/XInclude">
  <Title>Learning Java</Title>
  <xi:include href="chapter1.xml"/>
  <xi:include href="chapter2.xml"/>
  <xi:include href="chapter3.xml"/>
  ...
</Book>
```

We've used the namespace identifier xi to qualify the <include> elements that we use to import the chapters of our book. By default, the file is imported as XML content, which means that the parser incorporates the included document as part of our document. The resulting DOM or SAX view will show the merged documents as one. Alternatively, we can use the parse attribute to specify that we want the target included as text only. In this case, the text is automatically escaped for us like a CDATA section. For example, we could use it to include an XML example in our book without danger of corrupting our file:

```
<Example>
  <Title>The Zoo Inventory Example</Title>
  <xi:include parse="text " href="zooinventory.xml"/>
</Example>
```

Here, the entire *zooinventory.xml* file will be included as nicely escaped text for us (not added to our document as XML).

XInclude also allows for "fallback" content to be specified using a nested fallback element. The fallback element may point to another file or simply hold XML to be used if the included file can't be found. For example:

```
<xi:include parse="text " href="zooinventory.xml">
    <xi:fallback href="filenotfound.xml"/>
</xi:include>

<xi:include parse="text" href="example.xml">
    <xi:fallback>This example is missing...</xi:fallback>
</xi:include>
```

In the first case, if *zooinventory.xml* is not found, the *filenotfound.xml* file will be included. In the second case, the "missing" text will be included instead of the file. If there is no fallback specified, a parse-time fatal error occurs. An empty fallback element can be used to suppress any error. Fallbacks may also be nested within fallbacks to combine these behaviors.

Enabling XInclude

Getting XInclude to work for us requires simply turning on a couple of flags before we begin parsing our file. First, since the XInclude facility uses namespaces, we have to turn on namespace processing in our parser factory. Second, we have to explicitly tell the parser to interpret the include directives. To modify our PrintDOM example to perform the includes before printing the result, we turn on these flags on the factory, before creating a DocumentBuilder instance:

```
DocumentBuilderFactory factory = DocumentBuilderFactory.newInstance( );

// enable XInclude processing
factory.setNamespaceAware( true );
factory.setXIncludeAware( true );
```

```
DocumentBuilder parser = factory.newDocumentBuilder( );
Document document = parser.parse( input );
```

We should also mention before we move on that XInclude can make use of XPath expressions (via an API called XPointer) in order to include just selected parts of an XML document.

Validating Documents

"Words, words, mere words, no matter from the heart."
—William Shakespeare, *Troilus and Cressida*

In this section, we talk about DTDs and XML Schema, two ways to enforce rules in an XML document. A DTD is a simple grammar for an XML document, defining which tags may appear where, in what order, with what attributes, etc. XML Schema is the next generation of DTD. With XML Schema, you can describe the data content of the document as well as the structure. XML Schemas are written in terms of primitives, such as numbers, dates, and simple regular expressions, and also allow the user to define complex types in a grammar-like fashion. The word *schema* means a blueprint or plan for structure, so we'll refer to DTDs and XML Schema collectively as schema where either applies. The term XML Schema is also a bit overloaded because there are now several competing languages (syntaxes) for describing XML in addition to the official W3C XML Schema standard.

DTDs, although much more limited in capability, are still currently more widely used. This may be partly due to the complexity involved in writing XML Schemas by hand. The W3C XML Schema standard is verbose and cumbersome, which may explain why several alternative syntaxes have sprung up. In Java 5.0, a new `javax.xml.validation` API was added to standardize XML validation in a pluggable way. Out of the box, Java 5.0 supports only DTDs and W3C XML Schema, but new schema languages can be added in the future.

Using Document Validation

XML's validation of documents is a key piece of what makes it useful as a data format. Using a schema is somewhat analogous to the way Java classes enforce type checking in the language. A schema defines document types. Documents conforming to a given schema are often referred to as *instance documents* of the schema.

This type safety provides a layer of protection that eliminates having to write complex error-checking code. However, validation may not be necessary in every environment. For example, when the same tool generates XML and reads it back, validation should not be necessary in normal operation. It is invaluable, though, during development. Often, document validation is used during development and turned off in production environments.

DTDs

The DTD language is fairly simple. A DTD is primarily a set of special tags that define each element in the document and, for complex types, provide a list of the elements it may contain. The DTD `<!ELEMENT>` tag consists of the name of the tag and either a special keyword for the data type or a parenthesized list of elements.

```
<!ELEMENT Name ( #PCDATA )>
<!ELEMENT Document ( Head, Body )>
```

The special identifier `#PCDATA` (parsed character data) indicates a string. When a list is provided, the elements are expected to appear in that order. The list may contain sublists, and items may be made optional using a vertical bar (|) as an OR operator. Special notation can also be used to indicate how many of each item may appear; two examples of this notation are shown in Table 24-4.

Table 24-4. DTD notation defining occurrences

Character	Meaning
*	Zero or more occurrences
?	Zero or one occurrences

Attributes of an element are defined with the `<!ATTLIST>` tag. This tag enables the DTD to enforce rules about attributes. It accepts a list of identifiers and a default value:

```
<!ATTLIST Animal animalClass (unknown | mammal | reptile) "unknown">
```

This `ATTLIST` says that the `Animal` element has a `class` attribute that can have one of three values: unknown, mammal, or reptile. The default is unknown.

We won't cover everything you can do with DTDs here. But the following example will guarantee *zooinventory.xml* follows the format we've described. Place the following in a file called *zooinventory.dtd* (or grab this file from the CD-ROM or web site for the book):

```
<!ELEMENT Inventory ( Animal* )>
<!ELEMENT Animal (Name, Species, Habitat, (Food | FoodRecipe), Temperament)>
<!ATTLIST Animal animalClass (unknown | mammal | reptile) "unknown">
<!ELEMENT Name ( #PCDATA )>
<!ELEMENT Species ( #PCDATA )>
<!ELEMENT Habitat ( #PCDATA )>
<!ELEMENT Food ( #PCDATA )>
<!ELEMENT FoodRecipe ( Name, Ingredient+ )>
<!ELEMENT Ingredient ( #PCDATA )>
<!ELEMENT Temperament ( #PCDATA )>
```

The DTD says that an `Inventory` consists of any number of `Animal` elements. An `Animal` has a `Name`, `Species`, and `Habitat` tag followed by either a `Food` or `FoodRecipe`. `FoodRecipe`'s structure is further defined later.

Normally, to use a DTD, we associate it with the XML document. We can do this by placing a DOCTYPE declaration in the XML document itself. In Java 5.0, the new validation API can be used to validate arbitrary XML (whether it be an in-memory DOM representation or a file stream) against any kind of schema, including DTDs. We'll cover that API after we discuss XML Schema.

In this case, when a validating parser encounters the DOCTYPE, it attempts to load the DTD and validate the document. There are several forms the DOCTYPE can have, but the one we'll use is:

```
<!DOCTYPE Inventory SYSTEM "zooinventory.dtd">
```

Both SAX and DOM parsers can automatically validate documents as they read them, provided that the documents contain a DOCTYPE declaration. However, you have to explicitly ask the parser factory to provide a parser that is capable of validation. To do this, just set the validating property of the parser factory to true before you ask it for an instance of the parser. For example:

```
SAXParserFactory factory = SAXParserFactory.newInstance( );
factory.setValidating( true );
```

This setValidating( ) method is an older, simplistic way to enable validation of documents that contain DTD references. As you can see, it is tied to the parser. The new validation package that we'll discuss later is independent of the parser and more flexible. You should not use the parser-validating method in combination with the new validation API unless you want to validate documents twice for some reason.

Try inserting the setValidating( ) line in our model builder example after the factory is created. Abuse the *zooinventory.xml* file by adding or removing an element or attribute and see what happens when you run the example. You should get useful error messages from the parser indicating the problems and parsing should fail. To get more information about the validation, we can register an org.xml.sax.ErrorHandler object with the parser, but by default, Java installs one that simply prints the errors for us.

XML Schema

Although DTDs can define the basic structure of an XML document, they don't provide a very rich vocabulary for describing the relationships between elements and say very little about their content. For example, there is no reasonable way with DTDs to specify that an element is to contain a numeric type or even to govern the length of string data. The XML Schema standard addresses both the structural and data content of an XML document. It is the next logical step and it or one of the competing schema languages with similar capabilities should replace DTDs in the future.

XML Schema brings the equivalent of strong typing to XML by drawing on many predefined primitive element types and allowing the user to define new complex types of her own. These schemas even allow for types to be extended and used polymorphically, like types in the Java language. Although we can't cover XML Schema in any detail, here's the equivalent W3C XML Schema for our *zooinventory.xml* file:

```xml
<?xml version="1.0" encoding="UTF-8"?>
<xs:schema xmlns:xs="http://www.w3.org/2001/XMLSchema">

<xs:element name="Inventory">
  <xs:complexType>
    <xs:sequence>
      <xs:element maxOccurs="unbounded" ref="Animal"/>
    </xs:sequence>
  </xs:complexType>
</xs:element>

<xs:element name="Name" type="xs:string"/>

<xs:element name="Animal">
  <xs:complexType>
    <xs:sequence>
      <xs:element ref="Name"/>
      <xs:element name="Species" type="xs:string"/>
      <xs:element name="Habitat" type="xs:string"/>
      <xs:choice>
        <xs:element name="Food" type="xs:string"/>
        <xs:element ref="FoodRecipe"/>
      </xs:choice>
      <xs:element name="Temperament" type="xs:string"/>
    </xs:sequence>

    <xs:attribute name="animalClass" default="unknown">
      <xs:simpleType>
        <xs:restriction base="xs:token">
          <xs:enumeration value="unknown"/>
          <xs:enumeration value="mammal"/>
          <xs:enumeration value="reptile"/>
        </xs:restriction>
      </xs:simpleType>
    </xs:attribute>
  </xs:complexType>
</xs:element>

<xs:element name="FoodRecipe">
  <xs:complexType>
    <xs:sequence>
      <xs:element ref="Name"/>
      <xs:element maxOccurs="unbounded" name="Ingredient" type="xs:string"/>
    </xs:sequence>
  </xs:complexType>
</xs:element>

</xs:schema>
```

This schema would normally be placed into an XML Schema Definition file, which has a *.xsd* extension. The first thing to note is that this schema file is a normal, well-formed XML file that uses elements from the W3C XML Schema namespace. In it we use nested `element` declarations to define the elements that will appear in our document. As with most languages, there is more than one way to accomplish this task. Here, we have broken out the "complex" `Animal` and `FoodRecipe` elements into their own separate element declarations and referred to them in their parent elements using the `ref` attribute. In this case, we did it mainly for readability; it would have been legal to have one big, deeply nested element declaration. However, referring to elements by reference in this way also allows us to reuse the same element declaration in multiple places in the document, if needed. Our `Name` element is a small example of this. Although it didn't do much for us here, we have broken out the `Name` element and referred to it for both the `Animal/Name` and the `FoodRecipe/Name`.

Control directives like `sequence` and `choice` allow us to define the structure of the child elements allowed and attributes like `minOccurs` and `maxOccurs` let us specify cardinality (how many instances). The `sequence` directive says that the enclosed elements should appear in the specified order (if they are required). The `choice` directive allows us specify alternative child elements like `Food` or `FoodRecipe`. We declared the legal values for our `animalClass` attribute using a `restriction` declaration and `enumeration` tags.

Simple types

Although we've not really exercised it here, the `type` attribute of our elements touches on the standardization of types in XML Schema. All of our "text" elements specify a type `xs:string`, which is a standard XML Schema string type (kind of like PCDATA in our DTD). There are many other standard types covering things such as dates, times, periods, numbers, and even URLs. These are called *simple types* (though some of them are not so simple) because they are standardized or "built-in." Table 24-5 lists W3C Schema simple types and their corresponding Java types. The correspondence will become useful later when we talk about JAXB and automated binding of XML to Java classes:

Table 24-5. W3C Schema simple types

Schema element type	Java type	Example
xsd:string	java.lang.String	"This is text"
xsd:boolean	boolean	true, false, 1, 0
xsd:byte	byte	
xsd:unsignedByte	short	
xsd:integer	java.math.BigInteger	
xsd:int	int	
xsd:unsignedInt	long	
xsd.long	long	
xsd:short	short	

Table 24-5. W3C Schema simple types (continued)

Schema element type	Java type	Example
xsd:unsignedShort	int	
xsd:decimal	java.math.BigDecimal	
xsd:float	float	
xsd:double	double	
xsd:Qname	javax.xml.namespace.QName	funeral:corpse
xsd:dateTime	java.util.Calendar	2004-12-27T15:39:05.000-06:00
xsd:base64Binary	byte[]	PGZv
xsd:hexBinary	byte[]	FFFF
xsd:time	java.util.Calendar	15:39:05.000-06:00
xsd:date	java.util.Calendar	2004-12-27
xsd:anySimpleType	java.lang.String	

For example, suppose we want to add a floating point `Weight` element like this to our `Animal`:

```
<Weight>400.5</Weight>
```

We could now validate it in our schema by inserting the following entry at the appropriate place:

```
<xs:element name="Weight" type="xs:double"/>
```

In addition to enforcing that the content of elements matches these simple types, XML Schema can give us much more control over the text and values of elements in our document using simple rules and regular expression-like patterns.

Complex types

In addition to the predefined simple types listed in Table 24-5, we can define our own, *complex types* in our schema. Complex types are element types that have internal structure and possibly child elements. Our `Inventory`, `Animal`, and `FoodRecipe` elements all have complex types and their content must be declared with the `complexType` tag in our schema. Complex type definitions can be reused, similar to the way that element definitions can be reused in our schema. That is, we can break out a complex type definition and give it a name. We can then refer to that type by name in the type attributes of other elements. Since all of our complex types were only used once, in their corresponding elements, we didn't give them names. They were considered *anonymous type definitions*, declared and used in the same spot. For example, we could have separated our `Animal`'s type from its element declaration:

```
<xs:element name="Inventory">
  <xs:complexType>
    <xs:sequence>
      <xs:element name="Animal" maxOccurs="unbounded" type="AnimalType"/>
```

```
      </xs:sequence>
    </xs:complexType>
  </xs:element>

  <xs:complexType name="AnimalType">
    <xs:sequence>
      <xs:element ref="Name"/>
      <xs:element name="Species" type="xs:string"/>
      <xs:element name="Habitat" type="xs:string"/>
      ...
```

Declaring the `AnimalType` separately from the instance of the `Animal` element declaration would allow us to have other, differently named elements with the same internal structure. For example, our `Inventory` element may hold another element, `MainAttraction`, which is a type of `Animal` with a different tag name. The distinction between elements and their type definitions will also be important later when working with JAXB.

There's a lot more to say about W3C XML Schema and they can get quite a bit more complex than our simple example. However, you can do a lot with the few pieces we've shown above. Some tools are available to help you get started. We'll talk about one called Trang in a moment. For more information about XML Schema, see the W3C's site (*http://www.w3.org/XML/Schema*) or *XML Schema* by Eric van der Vlist (O'Reilly). In the next section, we'll show how to validate a file or DOM against the XML Schema we've just created, using the new validation API.

Trang

Many tools can help you write XML Schema. One helpful tool is called Trang (*http://www.thaiopensource.com/relaxng/trang.html*). It is part of an alternative schema language project called RELAX NG (which we mention later in this chapter), but Trang is very useful in and of itself. It is an open source tool that cannot only convert between DTDs and XML Schema but also create a rough DTD or XML Schema by reading "example" XML documents. This is a great way to sketch out a basic, example schema for your documents.

The Validation API

To use our example XML schema, we need to exercise the new `javax.xml.validation` API. As we said earlier, the validation API is an alternative to the simple, parser-based validation supported through the `setValidating( )` method of the parser factories. To use the validation package, we create an instance of a `SchemaFactory`, specifying the schema language. We can then validate a DOM or stream source against the schema.

The following example, Validate, is another simple command-line utility that you can use to test our your XML and schemas. Just give it the XML filename and an XML Schema file (*.xsd* file) as arguments:

```java
import javax.xml.XMLConstants;
import javax.xml.validation.*;
import org.xml.sax.*;
import javax.xml.transform.sax.SAXSource;
import javax.xml.transform.Source;
import javax.xml.transform.stream.StreamSource;

public class Validate
{
    public static void main( String [] args ) throws Exception
    {
        if ( args.length != 2 ) {
            System.err.println("usage: Validate xmlfile.xml xsdfile.xsd");
            System.exit(1);
        }
        String xmlfile = args[0], xsdfile = args[1];

        SchemaFactory factory =
            SchemaFactory.newInstance( XMLConstants.W3C_XML_SCHEMA_NS_URI);
        Schema schema = factory.newSchema( new StreamSource( xsdfile ) );
        Validator validator = schema.newValidator();

        ErrorHandler errHandler = new ErrorHandler() {
            public void error( SAXParseException e ) { System.out.println(e); }
            public void fatalError( SAXParseException e ) { System.out.println(e); }
            public void warning( SAXParseException e ) { System.out.println(e); }
        };
        validator.setErrorHandler( errHandler );

        try {
            validator.validate( new SAXSource(
                new InputSource("zooinventory.xml") ) );
        } catch ( SAXException e ) {
            // Invalid Document, no error handler
        }
    }
}
```

The schema types supported initially are listed as constants in the XMLConstants class. Right now, only W3C XML Schema is implemented but DTDs should be and there is also another intriguing type in there that we'll mention later. Our validation example follows the pattern we've seen before, creating a factory, then a Schema instance. The Schema represents the grammar and can create Validator instances that do the work of checking the document structure. Here, we've called the validate( ) method on a SAXSource, which comes from our file, but we could just as well have used a DOMSource to check an in-memory DOM representation:

```java
validator.validate( new DOMSource(document) );
```

Any errors encountered will cause the validate method to throw a SAXException, but this is just a coarse means of detecting errors. More generally, and as we've shown in this example, we'd want to register an ErrorHandler object with the validator. The error handler can be told about many errors in the document and convey more information. When the error handler is present, the exceptions are given to it and not thrown from the validate method.

The errors generated by these parsers can be a bit cryptic. Hopefully, they will improve in the future. Keep in mind that these errors may not be able to give you line numbers because the validation is not necessarily being done against a stream.

Alternative schema languages

In addition to DTDs and W3C XML Schema, several other popular schema languages are being used today. One interesting alternative that is tantalizingly referenced in the XMLConstants class is called RELAX NG. This schema language offers the most widely used features of XML Schema in a more human-readable format. In fact, it offers both a very compact, non-XML syntax and a regular XML-based syntax. RELAX NG doesn't offer the same text pattern and value validation that W3C XML Schema do. Instead these aspects of validation are left to other tools (many people consider this to be "business logic," not properly done here anyway). If you are interested in exploring other schema languages be sure to check out RELAX NG and its useful schema conversion utility, Trang.

JAXB and Code Generation

We've said that the ultimate goal of XML is automated binding of XML to Java classes. With automated binding, no fragile parsing code is created by the developer and just one schema is used for both the document and the object models. While many tools do just this, none is really ideal in terms of capabilities and ease of use. This is not entirely the fault of the tool vendors. Many aspects of mapping XML to Java constructs and back are tricky. For example, if an XML document can contain one of several types of elements at some point, what is the best way to represent that in Java?

Several tools available today bridge XML and Java. The one we'll discuss here is the standard Java API for XML Binding (JAXB, not to be confused with JAXP, the parser API). JAXB is a standard extension that is provided as part of the Java Web Services Developer Pack (JWSDP), though it is also useful outside of the web services arena. You can download JAXB from *http://java.sun.com/xml/jaxb*. Compiling the examples in this section requires several of the JAR files from the JAXB lib and JWSDP "shared" lib directories to be in your classpath. To simplify this, we've provided an Ant build file along with the example code for these examples. You can find this and all of the source code on the CD accompanying this book.

JAXB generates Java source code. It can work with either DTDs or XML Schema and generates Java classes that match the structure of the XML. At runtime, JAXB-generated classes can read an XML document and parse it into the object model it has defined or you can go the other way, populating your object model and then writing it out to XML. In both cases, JAXB can validate the data to make sure it matches the schema. This may sound like the DOM interface, but, in this case, we're not using generic classes—we're using classes custom-generated for our model. For example, in the case of our *zooinventory.xml* file, we'll have classes like Inventory, Animal, and FoodRecipe to work with, each having the expected setter and getter methods. This means that our workflow centers more around writing the XML Schema, with the job of creating the classes done for us.

As you might guess, the question of how to customize these generated classes or map them to your own classes if you already have them is a big topic. JAXB defines its own additional "binding" language that allows a great deal of flexibility in these areas as well as in naming of methods, etc. We'll just use the default behavior here. Things don't line up exactly with our previous model, but they are close enough for our purposes.

Generating the Model

Everything in JAXB begins with the schema. We'll be using our W3C XML Schema, but other schema languages may be supported in the future. After installing JAXB, run the JAXB schema compiler, *xjc*, found in *JWSDP_HOME/jaxb/bin* on our schema file.

```
% xjc.sh -p com.learningjava zooinventory.xsd
```

The *-p* option tells *xjc* the name of a Java package into which to place the generated classes. Alternately, you can use the Ant build file to do this:

```
% ant jaxb
```

We use the package name com.learningjava so that our generated files end up in a *com/learningjava/* directory.

```
com/learningjava/Animal.java
com/learningjava/AnimalType.java
com/learningjava/FoodRecipe.java
com/learningjava/FoodRecipeType.java
com/learningjava/Inventory.java
com/learningjava/InventoryType.java
com/learningjava/Name.java
com/learningjava/ObjectFactory.java
com/learningjava/impl/...
```

The first thing to note is that JAXB has generated interfaces for us in com.learningjava and a separate subpackage, impl, which holds the implementation classes. There is an interface for each of the "top-level" elements in our schema. Providing interfaces in this way makes for a clean separation of the API relating to our schema from the particular generated code that JAXB produces to fulfill that API. You only have to work with the interfaces in your code. The objects will be produced by a factory pattern, either created for us when reading a document or by us using the generated ObjectFactory.

The next thing to note is that each of our elements has two interfaces: an *element type* and *content type* interface (for example, Animal and AnimalType). These correspond to the difference between the elements and their complex types as we described earlier in this chapter in "XML Schema." Although our schema uses types "anonymously" in only one location, JAXB has automatically created type interfaces for them and named them by appending the suffix Type to the interfaces. AnimalType holds the actual interface of our Animal element (for example, the getName( ) and setName( ) methods).

```
public interface AnimalType {
    java.lang.String getFood();
    void setFood(java.lang.String value);
    double getWeight();
    void setWeight(double value);
    java.lang.String getHabitat();
    void setHabitat(java.lang.String value);
    java.lang.String getSpecies();
    void setSpecies(java.lang.String value);
    java.lang.String getAnimalClass();
    void setAnimalClass(java.lang.String value);
    java.lang.String getTemperament();
    void setTemperament(java.lang.String value);
    java.lang.String getName();
    void setName(java.lang.String value);
    com.learningjava.FoodRecipeType getFoodRecipe();
    void setFoodRecipe(com.learningjava.FoodRecipeType value);
}
```

The Animal interface extends AnimalType and also the javax.xml.bind.Element flag interface, which indicates that it is an element type. As we described earlier, more than one element may have the same content type. The get methods of the generated classes generally return the "Type" content interface. You can see this in the getFoodRecipe( ) method above. If we had two elements in our example that used a "food recipe" schema type, they could have different element class names but return the same FoodRecipeType. When you are constructing your model to write out XML, you must create the correct element types, using the object factory, at the correct locations. You'll see this in the following examples.

Unmarshaling from XML

Taking an object model and writing it out to XML is called *marshaling* the objects to XML. Doing the converse and parsing an XML file into an object model is called *unmarshaling* the document. The following example unmarshals our *zooinventory.xml* file and prints the same bits of information as our previous examples:

```java
import javax.xml.bind.*;
import com.learningjava.*;
import java.io.File;
import java.util.*;

public class TestJAXBUnmarshall
{
    public static void main( String [] args ) throws JAXBException
    {
        JAXBContext jbcontext = JAXBContext.newInstance("com.learningjava");
        Unmarshaller unmarshaller = jbcontext.createUnmarshaller( );

        Inventory inventory =
            (Inventory)unmarshaller.unmarshal( new File("zooinventory.xml") );

        System.out.println( "Animals = " );
        List<AnimalType> animals = inventory.getAnimal( );
        for( AnimalType animal : animals )
            System.out.println( "\t"+animal.getName( ) );
        AnimalType cocoa = (AnimalType)(inventory.getAnimal( ).get(1));
        FoodRecipeType recipe = cocoa.getFoodRecipe( );
        System.out.println( "Recipe = " + recipe.getName( ) );
        List<String> ingredients = recipe.getIngredient( );
        for( String ingredient : ingredients )
            System.out.println( "\t"+ingredient );
    }

}
```

Note how similar this code is to the hand-written code we created for our SAXModelBuilder example. The main difference is the naming of the classes. Here we refer to the content types—e.g., AnimalType—to read the data. The elements that hold collections return Lists, as in our own model. JAXB does not pluralize the setter and getter method names for us, so we have a getAnimal( ) method on our Inventory, which returns the collection of AnimalType objects. The list is mutable and this is how we add and remove Animals.

The process for unmarshaling is simple. We create a JAXBContext object representing our generated classes' package, in this case com.learningjava. We then ask it for an unmarshaler and parse the file. The unmarshaler returns the object corresponding to the root element of our document, Inventory. That's really about all there is to it. If we'd wanted to validate the document while parsing it, we could turn on validation in the unmarshaler:

```java
unmarshaller.setValidating(true);
```

To compile and run the TestJAXBUnmarshall program and our generated classes requires all of the jars of the *JWSDP_HOME/jaxb/lib* directory, as well as the directory containing our examples and generated code to be in the classpath. The Ant build file also has a compile target that will compile the source for you.

The output of our program is as we'd expect:

```
Animals =
         Song Fang
         Cocoa
Recipe = Gorilla Chow
         Fruit
         Shoots
         Leaves
```

Marshaling to XML

Let's go the other way. In this example, we'll start by building our object model and then marshal it out to XML.

```java
import javax.xml.bind.*;
import com.learningjava.*;
import java.io.File;
import java.util.*;

public class TestJAXBMarshall
{

    public static void main( String [] args ) throws JAXBException
    {
        ObjectFactory factory = new ObjectFactory( );

        Inventory inventory = factory.createInventory( );
        Animal fang = factory.createAnimal( );
        fang.setName("Song Fang");
        fang.setSpecies("Giant Panda");
        fang.setHabitat("China");
        fang.setFood("Bamboo");
        fang.setTemperament("Friendly");
        inventory.getAnimal( ).add( fang );

        JAXBContext jbcontext = JAXBContext.newInstance("com.learningjava");
        Marshaller marshaller = jbcontext.createMarshaller( );
        marshaller.setProperty(Marshaller.JAXB_FORMATTED_OUTPUT, Boolean.TRUE);
        marshaller.marshal( inventory, System.out );
    }
}
```

To create our objects, we use the generated ObjectFactory that was created for us in the com.learningjava package. It has a set of methods for creating each of our complex element types. Here, we created an Inventory (it uses its own implementation) and one Animal to populate it. When we've got our model, we use the JAXBContext to get a marshaler object and write it out. We've set a property on the marshaler, JAXB_FORMATTED_OUTPUT, to indicate that we want nicely indented, human-readable XML.

Again, to compile and run the `TestJAXBMarshall` program and our generated classes requires all of the JARs of the *JWSDP_HOME/jaxb/lib* directory as well as the directory containing our examples and generated code to be in the classpath. The Ant build file can compile the classes for you with the `compile` target.

The output of the marshaler looks as you'd expect:

```
<?xml version="1.0" encoding="UTF-8" standalone="yes"?>
<Inventory>
    <Animal>
        <Name>Song Fang</Name>
        <Species>Giant Panda</Species>
        <Habitat>China</Habitat>
        <Food>Bamboo</Food>
        <Temperament>Friendly</Temperament>
    </Animal>
</Inventory>
```

Again, that's about all there is to it for this simple case. Of course, to do real work, you will probably want to customize the generated classes in some ways. This can be done in JAXB through the use of special binding descriptor files or through special annotations placed in the XML Schema.

JAXB does, as promised, achieve the goal of binding XML to Java objects without requiring you to write low-level XML code. Although taking the tool beyond these simple examples is not as easy as we'd like, the benefits for a large project can be enormous. There are also other XML binding tools to consider. A popular alternative is Castor (*http://www.castor.org*), which works in much the same way with XML Schema.

Having worked our way through the options for bridging XML to Java, we'll turn our attention to transformations on XML itself with XSL, the styling language for XML.

Transforming Documents with XSL/XSLT

Earlier in this chapter, we used a `Transformer` object to copy a DOM representation of an example back to XML text. We mentioned that we were not really tapping the potential of the `Transformer`. Now, we'll give you the full story.

The `javax.xml.transform` package is the API for using the XSL/XSLT transformation language. XSL stands for Extensible Stylesheet Language. Like Cascading Stylesheets for HTML, XSL allows us to "mark up" XML documents by adding tags that provide presentation information. XSL Transformation (XSLT) takes this further by adding the ability to completely restructure the XML and produce arbitrary output. XSL and XSLT together comprise their own programming language for processing an XML document as input and producing another (usually XML) document as output. (From here on in, we'll refer to them collectively as XSL.)

XSL is extremely powerful, and new applications for its use arise every day. For example, consider a web portal that is frequently updated and which must provide access to a variety of mobile devices, from PDAs to cell phones to traditional browsers. Rather than recreating the site for these and additional platforms, XSL can transform the content to an appropriate format for each platform. More generally, rendering content from XML is simply a better way to preserve your data and keep it separate from your presentation information. XSL can be used to render an entire web site in different styles from files containing "pure data" in XML, much like a database. Multilingual sites also benefit from XSL to lay out text in different ways for different audiences.

You can probably guess the caveat that we're going to issue: XSL is a big topic worthy of its own books (see, for example, O'Reilly's *Java and XSLT* by Eric Burke, a fellow St. Louis author), and we can only give you a taste of it here. Furthermore, some people find XSL difficult to understand at first glance because it requires thinking in terms of recursively processing document tags. Don't be put off if you have trouble following this example; just file it away and return to it when you need it. At some point, you will be interested in the power transformation can offer you.

XSL Basics

XSL is an XML-based standard, so it should come as no surprise that the language is based on XML. An XSL *stylesheet* is an XML document using special tags defined by the XSL namespace to describe the transformation. The most basic XSL operations include matching parts of the input XML document and generating output based on their contents. One or more XSL *templates* live within the stylesheet and are called in response to tags appearing in the input. XSL is often used in a purely input-driven way, where input XML tags trigger output in the order that they appear, using only the information they contain. But more generally, the output can be constructed from arbitrary parts of the input, drawing from it like a database, composing elements and attributes. The XSLT transformation part of XSL adds things like conditionals and iteration to this mix, enabling truly any kind of output to be generated based on the input.

An XSL stylesheet contains as its root element a stylesheet tag. By convention, the stylesheet defines a namespace prefix xsl for the XSL namespace. Within the stylesheet are one or more template tags containing a match attribute describing the element upon which they operate.

```
<xsl:stylesheet
    xmlns:xsl="http://www.w3.org/1999/XSL/Transform" version="1.0">

    <xsl:template match="/">
      I found the root of the document!
    </xsl:template>

</xsl:stylesheet>
```

When a template matches an element, it has an opportunity to handle all the children of the element. The simple stylesheet above has one template that matches the root of the input document and simply outputs some plain text. By default, input not matched is simply copied to the output with its tags stripped (HTML convention). But here we match the root so we consume the entire input and nothing but our message appears on the output.

The match attribute can refer to elements using the XPath notation that we described earlier. This is a hierarchical path starting with the root element. For example, match="/Inventory/Animal" would match only the Animal elements from our *zooinventory.xml* file. In XSL, the path may be absolute (starting with "/") or relative, in which case, the template detects whenever that element appears in any subcontext (equivalent to "//" in XPath).

Within the template, we can put whatever we want, as long as it is well-formed XML (if not, we can use a CDATA section or XInclude). But the real power comes when we use parts of the input to generate output. The XSL value-of tag is used to output the content of an element or a child of the element. For example, the following template would match an Animal element and output the value of its Name child element:

```
<xsl:template match="Animal">
    Name: <xsl:value-of select="Name"/>
</xsl:template>
```

The select attribute uses an XPath expression relative to the current node. In this case, we tell it to print the value of the Name element within Animal. We could have used a relative path to a more deeply nested element within Animal or even an absolute path to another part of the document. To refer to the "current" element (in this case, the Animal element itself), a select expression can use "." as the path. The select expression can also retrieve attributes from the elements it references.

If we try to add the Animal template to our simple example, it won't generate any output. What's the problem? If you recall, we said that a template matching an element has the opportunity to process all its children. We already have a template matching the root ("/"), so it is consuming all the input. The answer to our dilemma—and this is where things get a little tricky—is to delegate the matching to other templates using the apply-templates tag. The following example correctly prints the names of all the animals in our document:

```
<xsl:stylesheet
    xmlns:xsl="http://www.w3.org/1999/XSL/Transform" version="1.0">

    <xsl:template match="/">
        Found the root!
        <xsl:apply-templates/>
    </xsl:template>
```

```
<xsl:template match="Animal">
    Name: <xsl:value-of select="Name"/>
</xsl:template>

</xsl:stylesheet>
```

We still have the opportunity to add output before and after the apply-templates tag. But upon invoking it, the template matching continues from the current node. Next, we'll use what we have so far and add a few bells and whistles.

Transforming the Zoo Inventory

Your boss just called, and it's now imperative that your zoo clients have access to the zoo inventory through the Web, today! After reading Chapter 15, you should be thoroughly prepared to build a nice "zoo portal." Let's get you started by creating an XSL stylesheet to turn our *zooinventory.xml* into HTML:

```
<xsl:stylesheet
    xmlns:xsl="http://www.w3.org/1999/XSL/Transform" version="1.0">

    <xsl:template match="/Inventory">
        <html><head><title>Zoo Inventory</title></head>
        <body><h1>Zoo Inventory</h1>
        <table border="1">
        <tr><td><b>Name</b></td><td><b>Species</b></td>
        <td><b>Habitat</b></td><td><b>Temperament</b></td>
        <td><b>Diet</b></td></tr>
            <xsl:apply-templates/>
                <!-- Process Inventory -->
        </table>
        </body>
        </html>
    </xsl:template>
    <xsl:template match="Inventory/Animal">
        <tr><td><xsl:value-of select="Name"/></td>
            <td><xsl:value-of select="Species"/></td>
            <td><xsl:value-of select="Habitat"/></td>
            <td><xsl:value-of select="Temperament"/></td>
            <td><xsl:apply-templates select="Food|FoodRecipe"/>
                <!-- Process Food,FoodRecipe--></td></tr>
    </xsl:template>

    <xsl:template match="FoodRecipe">
        <table>
        <tr><td><em><xsl:value-of select="Name"/></em></td></tr>
        <xsl:for-each select="Ingredient">
            <tr><td><xsl:value-of select="."/></td></tr>
        </xsl:for-each>
        </table>
    </xsl:template>

</xsl:stylesheet>
```

The stylesheet contains three templates. The first matches /Inventory and outputs the beginning of our HTML document (the header) along with the start of a table for the animals. It then delegates using apply-templates before closing the table and adding the HTML footer. The next template matches Inventory/Animal, printing one row of an HTML table for each animal. Although there are no other Animal elements in the document, it still doesn't hurt to specify that we will match an Animal only in the context of an Inventory, because, in this case, we are relying on Inventory to start and end our table. (This template makes sense only in the context of an Inventory.) Finally, we provide a template that matches FoodRecipe and prints a small (nested) table for that information. FoodRecipe makes use of the "for-each" operation to loop over child nodes with a select specifying that we are only interested in Ingredient children. For each Ingredient, we output its value in a row.

There is one more thing to note in the Animal template. Our apply-templates element has a select attribute that limits the elements affected. In this case, we are using the "|" regular expression-like syntax to say that we want to apply templates for only the Food or FoodRecipe child elements. Why do we do this? Since we didn't match the root of the document (only Inventory), we still have the default stylesheet behavior of outputting the plain text of nodes that aren't matched anywhere else. We take advantage of this behavior to print the text of the Food element. But we don't want to output the text of all of the other elements of Animal that we've already printed explicitly, so we process only the Food and FoodRecipe elements. Alternatively, we could have been more verbose, adding a template matching the root and another template just for the Food element. That would also mean that new tags added to our XML would, by default, be ignored and not change the output. This may or may not be the behavior you want, and there are other options as well. As with all powerful tools, there is usually more than one way to do something.

XSLTransform

Now that we have a stylesheet, let's apply it! The following simple program, XSLTransform, uses the javax.xml.transform package to apply the stylesheet to an XML document and print the result. You can use it to experiment with XSL and our example code.

```
import javax.xml.transform.*;
import javax.xml.transform.stream.*;

public class XSLTransform
{
    public static void main( String [] args ) throws Exception
    {
        if ( args.length < 2 || !args[0].endsWith(".xsl") ) {
            System.err.println("usage: XSLTransform file.xsl file.xml");
```

```
        System.exit(1);
    }
    TransformerFactory factory = TransformerFactory.newInstance(  );
    Transformer transformer =
        factory.newTransformer( new StreamSource( args[0] ) );
    StreamSource xmlsource = new StreamSource( args[1] );
    StreamResult output = new StreamResult( System.out );
    transformer.transform( xmlsource, output );
  }
}
```

Run XSLTransform, passing the XSL stylesheet and XML input, as in the following command:

```
% java XSLTransform zooinventory.xsl zooinventory.xml > zooinventory.html
```

The output should look like Figure 24-2.

Zoo Inventory

Name	Species	Habitat	Temperament	Diet
Song Fang	Giant Panda	China	Friendly	Bamboo
Cocoa	Gorilla	Central Africa	Know-it-all	*Gorilla Chow* Fruit Shoots Leaves

Figure 24-2. Image of the zoo inventory table

Constructing the transform is a similar process to that of getting a SAX or DOM parser. The difference from our earlier use of the TransformerFactory is that this time we construct the transformer, passing it the XSL stylesheet source. The resulting Transformer object is then a dedicated machine that knows how to take input XML and generate output according to its rules.

One important thing to note about XSLTransform is that it is not guaranteed thread-safe. In our example, we run the transform only once. If you are planning to run the same transform many times, you should take the additional step of getting a Templates object for the transform first, then using it to create Transformers.

```
Templates templates =
    factory.newTemplates( new StreamSource( args[0] ) );
Transformer transformer = templates.newTransformer();
```

The Templates object holds the parsed representation of the stylesheet in a compiled form and makes the process of getting a new Transformer much faster. The transformers themselves may also be more highly optimized in this case. In Java 5.0, the XSL transformer actually generates bytecode for very efficient "translets" that implement the transform. This means that instead of the transformer reading a description of what to do with your XML, it actually produces a small compiled program to execute the instructions!

XSL in the Browser

With our XSLTransform example, you can see how you'd go about rendering XML to an HTML document on the server side. But as mentioned in the introduction, modern web browsers support XSL on the client side as well. Internet Explorer 5.x and above, Netscape 6.x, and FireFox can automatically download an XSL stylesheet and use it to transform an XML document. To make this happen, just add a standard XSL stylesheet reference in your XML. You can put the stylesheet directive next to your DOCTYPE declaration in the *zooinventory.xml* file:

```
<?xml-stylesheet type="text/xsl" href="zooinventory.xsl"?>
```

As long as the *zooinventory.xsl* file is available at the same location (base URL) as the *zooinventory.xml* file, the browser will use it to render HTML on the client side.

Web Services

As we saw in our web services examples in Chapters 14 and 15, one of the most interesting directions for XML is web services. A web service is simply an application service supplied over the network, making use of XML to describe the request and response. Normally, web services run over HTTP and use an XML-based protocol called SOAP (Simple Object Access Protocol), an evolving W3C standard. The combination of XML and HTTP provides a universally accessible interface for services.

SOAP and other XML-based remote procedure call mechanisms can be used in place of Java RMI for cross-platform communications and as an alternative to CORBA. There is a lot of excitement surrounding web services, and it is likely that they will grow in importance in coming years. To learn more about Java APIs related to web services, check out the networking chapters of this book and take a look at *http://java.sun.com/webservices/*.

That's it for our brief introduction to XML. There is a lot more to learn about this exciting new area, and many of the APIs are evolving rapidly. We hope we've given you a good start.

The End of the Book

With this chapter, we also wrap up the main part of our book. We hope that you've enjoyed *Learning Java*. This, the third edition of *Learning Java*, is really the fifth edition of the series that began almost ten years ago with *Exploring Java*. It's been a long and amazing trip watching Java develop in that time and we thank those of you who have come along with us over the years. As always, we welcome your feedback to help us keep making this book better in the future. Ready for another 10 years of Java?

The Eclipse IDE

This is a book about the Java language and as such we've tried to avoid talking too much about specific tools and applications. But of course, we've had to make some exceptions where the real world of Java programming and de facto standards dictate. An example of this is the Apache Ant build tool that we discussed briefly in Chapter 15. Ant has become a de facto standard for building Java applications and something that every Java programmer should at least be aware of. A more challenging topic to cover is that of Java integrated development environments (IDEs).

A wide array of Java IDEs are available, with greatly varying features. Like all applications with a great deal of interest, IDEs are constantly changing and improving. Throughout this book, rather than distract from the topic at hand with screenshots of one IDE or another, we've chosen to refer only to simple command-line tools. In the real world, many if not most Java developers now use IDEs, so our approach paints a bit of a skewed picture of the process. We aim to rectify the situation here by introducing the Eclipse IDE and showing how to use it to load and explore all of the example code from this book.

IDEs offer many benefits as well as a few drawbacks, especially for the new Java programmer. The benefits include an all-in-one view of Java source code with syntax highlighting, navigation help, source control, integrated documentation, building, refactoring, and deployment all at your fingertips. The downside, historically at least, has been that the all-in-one tool tends to become an all-or-nothing tool that locks users into the product and makes them all but helpless without it. IDEs tend to encourage an overly simplistic project layout with no structure or partitioning to help humans understand it. IDEs can also become hairballs of state and information about the project that cannot be easily shared with other developers or across projects. Many of these problems are being addressed by the latest generation of IDEs, and, for most people, the benefits far outweigh the negatives.

The IDE Wars

Comparing IDEs on features alone is futile because all modern IDEs are based on a plug-in architecture that allows new tools to be added by third parties. Saying that an IDE has feature X is just an invitation for someone to retort that their IDE has plug-ins for X and Y. Still, it is worth taking a moment to draw some comparisons here (if we dare). In this book, we have used both the NetBeans 4.x and Eclipse 3.x editors. How do they stack up? The short answer is that at the time of this writing, Eclipse is more popular and a bit more polished at the expense of being platform-dependent whereas the latest release of NetBeans offers a few more advanced features out of the box.

A big distinction between the two is that Eclipse is not a pure-Java application. It has native code for each platform, which means that it won't necessarily look and feel the same on all platforms. The upside is that Eclipse on the PC is very polished. The downside is that on other platforms, things may not be as smooth and some features and plug-ins are not available. NetBeans, on the other hand, is a pure-Java application. It may lack some subtle niceties on some platforms, but, in general, it should behave the same everywhere. Another difference is that Eclipse is based on an alternative Java graphics toolkit called SWT that uses native components. Some people use SWT in their own applications as a Swing alternative to get improved performance.

Out of the box, NetBeans also offers two features that Eclipse doesn't: a visual application builder and a web application development environment. Of course, you can add those to Eclipse, but you must choose from (possibly pay-ware) alternatives. Another important feature of NetBeans 4.x is that it uses a fully externalized Ant build process. This means that you can build your application inside or outside of the IDE in exactly the same way. This is an important advance and it will be interesting to see if Eclipse adopts it in the future. With that said, let's move on to Eclipse....

Getting Started with Eclipse

Let's get started. First, you'll need to install Eclipse. You can get Version 3.1 from the CD accompanying this book or you can download the latest version from *http://eclipse.org/*. Simply unpack the zip file to a location of your choice and then launch the application.

The first time you run Eclipse you'll be prompted to select a workspace. This is a root directory to hold new projects that you create within Eclipse. The default location is inside the application's folder itself, probably not what you want. Pick a location and click OK.

Eclipse greets you with the Welcome Screen. Close this window by closing the Welcome tab within the application. If you want to come back later and go through the

Eclipse tutorials and related help topics, you can get this window back by choosing Help → Welcome.

One last thing before we move on: Eclipse stores all of its configuration information in the *configuration* folder inside the Eclipse installation directory. If, at any point in this introduction, you feel that things are not right and you want to start from scratch, you can quit the application and remove this folder. You may also wish to remove your workspace items as they hold per-project state. Less drastically, if you wish to reset all of the application windows to their default locations, you can choose Window → Reset Perspective. We'll talk more about perspectives later.

Importing the Learning Java Examples

Before we talk about the IDE itself, let's load the examples from this book. You can find a ZIP file containing all of the examples from this book nicely packaged as an Eclipse project on the CD accompanying this book or at *http://www.oreilly.com/ catalog/learnjava3*. The Eclipse version of the examples is called *examples-eclipse.zip*. (The file *examples.zip* holds the same examples but packaged slightly differently and without the Eclipse project files.)

First, create a new project to hold the examples using the File → New Project menu item. In the New Project wizard, select Java Project as the project type and click Next. Give the project a name (we used LearningJava). The default location for the project folder will be in the workspace area that you designated earlier, but you can change this if you wish. Click Finish when you're done. (If Eclipse asks if you wish to set the "project compliance settings" to Java 5.0, you should answer Yes.)

Next, we'll import the examples zip file. Choose File → Import to open the Import wizard. Select Archive File as the source and click Next. Click the Browse button and choose the *eclipse-examples.zip* file. Check the "Overwrite existing files without warning" button so that our Eclipse-specific project file will overwrite the empty one in your new project. The Import wizard should look like Figure A-1 (we've expanded the folder tree so that you can see the examples). Click Finish.

Eclipse will now import all of the files from the archive and immediately begin building the source in the background (a small progress bar at the bottom of the screen will show this).

Using Eclipse

The first thing we need to do is set up the IDE for browsing and editing our Java source code. Choose Window → Open Perspective → Java to put Eclipse into the Java editing perspective. A perspective in Eclipse is an arrangement of different tools, menu bars, and shortcuts geared toward a particular kind of task, such as Java editing or CVS repository browsing. You can open additional tools and move things

Figure A-1. The import projects dialog box

around to your liking, but the predefined perspectives give you a good start. Now the *Learning Java* examples appear in Eclipse, as shown in Figure A-2.

On the left is the Package Explorer. It shows a tree view of the Java packages, libraries, and resources of our project. Click the folder handles to expand the tree and see source folders for each chapter in the book.

The bottom area holds tabs related to Java editing. The tab that is open in Figure A-2, Problems, shows errors and warnings associated with our project code. Eclipse has already compiled our code in the background. In general, you don't have to tell it to do so. You'll also notice red Xs on some of the source folders and files. These files have errors. We'll talk about why some of our examples are being flagged in a moment. The other tabs, Javadoc and Declaration, give information about the file we're editing or the source code item selected. The Declaration tab can show a preview of the source for an item selected in the main editor window without requiring you to open it explicitly.

To clear up some of those red Xs, we need to make sure Eclipse is in Java 5.0–compatible mode. Choose Window → Preferences → Java → Compiler and set the Compiler

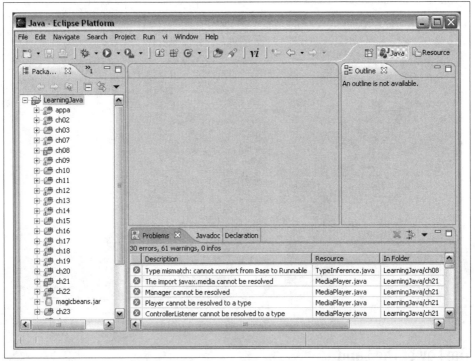

Figure A-2. Learning Java examples in Eclipse's Java editing perspective

Compliance Level to 5.0. Click OK and select Yes to rebuild the source. (It is also possible to set the compiler level on a per-project basis through the project preferences.)

If there are still some red Xs left, double-click the *README-Eclipse.txt* file in the project tree to read the latest explanations for these issues. Some of these issues relate to generating source code or installing additional libraries to make the examples work properly.

Getting at the Source

Let's navigate to a source file. Go to the *Calculator.java* file located in the *ch19/ default package*. Double-click it to open the source, as shown in Figure A-3.

When you're expanding the source folder tree, you can actually continue "deeper" than the Java source file level, expanding elements of the file itself. By moving into the source file in the explorer, you can expose parts of the Java source like methods, variables, and inner classes. By double-clicking these elements, you can open the file and jump right to the corresponding line. This is similar to the outline view that we'll see in the next section.

Figure A-3. Opening Calculator.java

The Lay of the Land

In the center of the screen, the open file is displayed in a new editor tab. The editor is, of course, the center of much of the action in a Java IDE. Note the color-coded syntax highlighting. Also, notice the little arrows immediately to the left of the source code. These are *folds*. A fold groups a section of Java code, such as a Java method or comment, and allows you to collapse or expand it like an outline. For example, the import statements in the file are folded by default. Click the blue arrow to the left of the import line to expand them and see all of the imports.

Next, warnings and errors are highlighted in the column to the left of the folds column. Try making a small error in the file. For example, try changing the `javax.swing` import to `javax.boofa` and see what happens. Note all the red Xs indicating problems. When you hover over a red X, you get a pop-up report of the problem. The column on the right of the scrollbar provides a view of the location of warnings and errors. Clicking on these areas takes you to the corresponding line of code. The *problems area* in the bottom tab is also linked; clicking on a problem report opens the corresponding file at the correct line.

On the right side of the IDE is the *outline pane* that shows a structured view of the Java code similar to what we saw by expanding the source file tab in the project browser. By clicking on a field, method, or inner class, you jump to the corresponding line in the source editor. Options at the top of the pane let you filter which members are shown for quick access.

Running the Examples

To run the Calculator example, select the source file and choose Run → Run As → Java Application. The Calculator runs, as shown in Figure A-4.

Figure A-4. Running the calculator

We chose Run As to tell Eclipse that this file actually is a standalone class with a main( ) method. Normally, a project has a lot of code and only one or a few main( ) methods. In that case, the Run menu option (and large green "play" button icon on the toolbar) can be configured to launch the default class for the overall application. An individual file can also be launched from its context menu, which you display by right-clicking on the file (control-click on the Mac). If we had chosen an application that printed output to System.out, Eclipse would have opened a Console tab in the bottom panel to capture the output. To see this in action, run the *ch10/PrintExamples.java* example. To run an example that requires arguments, you choose the more general Run option from the Run menu instead. This option pops up a dialog box that lets you configure, among other things, command-line arguments for the launch. The Run menu also includes a Run History option with recent launches so you can run them again quickly.

Building the Ant-Based Examples

Some of the chapters include components that must be built with the supplied Ant build file. For example, the JavaBeans JAR in Chapter 22 and the Web Application WAR file in Chapter 15 have Ant builds. You can run Ant from within Eclipse simply by right-clicking the *build.xml* file in the folder and selecting Run-As → Ant Build. There are two Ant Build options. The first runs the default target for the build while the second lets you choose a target (analogous to Run-As and Run in the Run menu). For example, to build the *magicbeans.jar* file from Chapter 22, navigate to *ch22/learningjava/build.xml*, right-click, and select Run-As → Ant Build (the first option).* You may have to use the File → Refresh option to see new files generated by the Ant build in the project tree.

Loner Examples

Some of the examples in the book may be a little easier to deal with outside of Eclipse, at least until you get immersed in the IDE. For example, some of the networking examples may be easier run on the command line. There's no reason to stay in the IDE for everything. Get comfortable in both environments.

Eclipse Features

Eclipse has too many interesting features to really do them justice here, but we'll mention a few to show you why people love this IDE.

Coding Shortcuts

Of course, you've noticed all the color coding and meta-information present when viewing Java source code in Eclipse. You can customize all of this behavior to suit your taste through the Window → Preferences → Java → Editor → Syntax Coloring panel. Many other options can be set through the Window → Preferences → Java → Code Style and Editor panes.

What may not be immediately obvious is that editing is also enhanced. When typing, try pressing Ctrl-Space to attempt autocompletion or have Eclipse present you with relevant options. For example, instead of typing JButton, try typing JBu plus Ctrl-Space. Eclipse completes the name for you. If the portion of the name you type is ambiguous, a drop-down list appears, similar to that shown in Figure A-5.

---

* If you had previously installed the Java JRE alongside the JDK, you may get an error indicating com.sun.tools.javac.Main not being in the classpath. To resolve this bug in Eclipse, open the Windows → Preferences → Ant → Runtime → Classpath tab to add the external JAR *tools.jar* from the JDK to the Ant classpath.

Figure A-5. Using completion in Eclipse

Eclipse also provides abbreviations for common items. Try typing sysout and pressing Crtl-Space. Eclipse expands this to System.out.println( ) and places the cursor in the parentheses automatically. If you type a quotation mark, Eclipse closes the quotation for you. Note the green bar it places after the closing quote. Pressing Tab takes you to that point so that you don't have to use the arrow keys. Pressing Tab again takes you to the next green bar spot, the end of the line.

Auto-Correction

Eclipse can offer fixes for simple problems in your code when it detects them. To see suggested fixes, click on the red X next to a problem line. Eclipse presents a drop-down menu of possible fixes for the problem. Selecting an option shows you the code changes Eclipse will make before you choose it.

For example, try changing the name of one of the JButtons in our Calculator to JBButton. Now, click the red X and a screen similar to Figure A-6 appears. Eclipse offers several possible corrections; the best one is to fix the misspelling and change it back to JButton. Of course, if we'd really meant to refer to a new kind of button, we could choose the option to create the new class right there and Eclipse would help us do that by creating a skeleton for us.

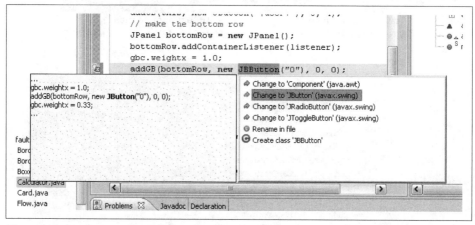

Figure A-6. Autocorrection in Eclipse

Refactoring

Eclipse offers a number of tools under the collective title "refactoring." These include the ability to rename and move members, automatically tracking down references to them and changing them throughout the project. More advanced options allow you to do things like create an interface for your class by copying all of its public methods or add a factory pattern to your code to encapsulate all object creation for a type. You can even encapsulate access to a variable, changing the code to use an accessor method instead. These tools can save you a lot of typing (or retyping, as the case may be).

For an example, let's look at our Calculator again. Click on the addGB( ) method in the outline or select the method definition yourself. We use this method a lot, so let's give it a better name. Select Refactor → Rename and change the name to addToGridBag. If you want to see what it's going to do in advance, press the preview button to get a diff view of the code. By selecting OK, Eclipse changes the name and all references to the method in your project (in this case that would include all of the source directories for all chapters). You can also refactor methods in order to change the method signature and add or remove arguments.

Diff'ing Files

Eclipse provides the ability to quickly diff two files. Select two files simultaneously in the Package Explorer. Right-click the first file to display a context menu and select Compare With → Each Other. Eclipse opens a dual-source view editor pane that shows the differences between the files graphically. You can even resolve conflicts by copying differences from one file to the other with the arrows at the top of the pane. For example, open *ch15/learningjava/all-web.xml* and *ch15/learningjava/filters-web.xml* and view the differences. You can also review changes made to a file using the Compare With → Local History option that lets you compare the current state of the file with previous saves in the project. These are very useful tools.

Organizing Imports

Eclipse can tidy up the import statements in your source code. Selecting Source → Organize Imports causes Eclipse to turn package imports into single class imports. Eclipse automatically determines exactly which classes from each package are used and breaks the package imports into individual imports. This makes the code a little more explicit, but some people prefer package imports when too many classes are used.

Formatting Source Code

Eclipse can autoformat your source code using the Source → Format option. This applies standard Java conventions and indentation. The style is highly customizable; choose Window → Preferences → Java → Code Style → Formatter to see the available options.

Conclusion

This appendix provides the briefest of introductions to the sorts of things that you can do in Eclipse and other Java IDEs. Please investigate more on your own to learn what these tools can do to increase your productivity as a Java developer. You should also compare Eclipse, NetBeans, and other editing environments such as jEdit (*http://jedit.org*) to see which you prefer. And don't forget to read more about Apache Ant, the de facto standard for building Java applications.

BeanShell: Simple Java Scripting

In this book, we (in this case, I, Pat) have avoided talking about many third-party tools that aren't part of the standard JDK. I'm going to make an exception here to mention a nifty, free Java tool called BeanShell. As its name suggests, BeanShell can be used as a Java "shell." It allows you to type standard Java syntax—statements, expressions, and even classes—on the command line and see the results immediately. With BeanShell, you can try out bits of code as you work through the book. (The current release of BeanShell doesn't support all of the new Java 5.0 syntax, but check for updates that will.) You can access all Java APIs and even create graphical user interface components and manipulate them "live." BeanShell uses only reflection, so there is no need to compile class files.

I wrote BeanShell while developing the examples for this book, and I think it makes a good companion to have along on your journey through Java. BeanShell is an open source software project, so the source code is included on the CD-ROM that accompanies this book (view CD content online at *http://examples.oreilly.com/learnjava3/CD-ROM/*). You can always find the latest updates and more information at its official home: *http://www.beanshell.org*. In recent years, BeanShell has become fairly popular. It is part of the Java Development Environment for Emacs (JDEE) and has been distributed with the NetBeans and Sun Java Studio IDEs as well as BEA's WebLogic application server. I hope you find it both useful and fun!

Running BeanShell

All you need to run BeanShell is the Java runtime system (Version 1.1 or greater) and the *bsh* JAR file. Under Windows, you can launch a graphical desktop for BeanShell by simply double-clicking the JAR file icon. More generally, you can add the JAR to your classpath:

```
Unix:     export CLASSPATH=$CLASSPATH:bsh.jar
Windows:  set classpath %classpath%;bsh.jar
```

You can then run BeanShell interactively in either a GUI or command-line mode:

```
java bsh.Console      // run the graphical desktop
java bsh.Interpreter  // run as text-only on the command line
```

Running BeanShell with the GUI console brings up a simple, Swing-based, desktop that allows you to open multiple shell windows with basic command history, line editing, and cut-and-paste capability. There are some other GUI tools available as well, including a simple text editor and class browser. Alternately, you can run Bean-Shell on the command line, in text-only mode.

You can run BeanShell scripts from files, like so:

```
% java bsh.Interpreter myfile.bsh
```

Within some versions of the NetBeans and Sun Java Studio IDEs, you can create BeanShell script files using the New File wizard or run any file with a *.bsh* extension just as you would execute Java code.

Java Statements and Expressions

At the prompt or in a BeanShell script, you can type standard Java statements and expressions. Statements and expressions are all of the normal things that you'd include in a Java method: variable declarations and assignments, method calls, loops, and conditionals. You can declare classes in the usual way if you want to, but BeanShell allows you to write statements outside of a class or method in an unstructured way as well.

You can type statements exactly as they would appear in Java. You also have the option of working in a more scripting-language-like fashion, with "loosely typed" variables and arguments. That is, you can simply be lazy and not declare the types of variables that you use (both primitives and objects). BeanShell will still give you an error if you attempt to misuse the actual contents of the variable. If you do declare types of variables or primitives, BeanShell will enforce them.

Here are some examples:

```
foo = "Foo";
four = (2 + 2)*2/2;
print( foo + " = " + four );   // print() is a bsh command
// do a loop
for (i=0; i<5; i++)
    print(i);
// pop up an AWT frame with a button in it
button = new JButton("My Button");
frame = new JFrame("My Frame");
frame.getContentPane().add( button, "Center" );
frame.pack();
frame.setVisible( true );
```

If you don't like the idea of "loosening" Java syntax at all, you can turn off this feature of BeanShell with the following command:

```
setStrictJava( true );
```

Imports

By default, BeanShell imports all of the core Java packages for you. You can import your own classes using the standard Java import declaration:

```
import mypackage.*;
```

In addition to regular package, class, and static imports, BeanShell can also import the methods and variables of an object instance into the current context using the importObject( ) command. For example:

```
Map map = new HashMap( );
importObject( map );
put("foo", "bar");
print( get("foo") ); // "bar"
```

BeanShell Commands

BeanShell comes with a number of useful built-in commands in the form of Java methods. These commands are implemented as BeanShell scripts, and are supplied in the *bsh* JAR file. You can make your own commands by defining methods in your own scripts or adding them to your classpath. See the BeanShell user's manual for more information.

One important BeanShell command is print( ), which displays values. print( ) does pretty much the same thing as System.out.println( ) except it ensures the output always goes to the command line (if you have multiple windows open). print( ) also displays some types of objects (such as arrays) more verbosely than Java would. Another very useful command is show( ), which toggles on and off automatic printing of the result of every line you type. (You can turn this on if you want to see every result value.)

Here are a few other examples of BeanShell commands:

source( ), run( )
    Reads a script into this interpreter, or runs it in a new interpreter

frame( )
    Displays an AWT or Swing component in a frame

load( ), save( )
    Loads or saves serializable objects (such as JavaBeans)

```
cd( )
cat( )
dir( )
pwd( )
etc.
```
Unix-like shell commands

```
exec( )
```
Runs a native application

```
addClassPath( )
reloadClasses( )
```
Modifies the classpath or reload classes

```
javap( )
```
Prints a javap-style class description for the class or object specified

See the BeanShell user's manual for a full list of commands.

Scripted Methods and Objects

You can declare and use methods in BeanShell, just as you would inside a Java class:

```
int addTwoNumbers( int a, int b ) {
    return a + b;
}
sum = addTwoNumbers( 5, 7 );  // 12
```

BeanShell methods may also have dynamic (loose) argument and return types.

```
add( a, b ) {
    return a + b;
}
foo = add(1, 2);              // 3
foo = add("Hello ", "Kitty");  // "Hello Kitty"
```

In BeanShell, as in JavaScript and Perl, method *closures* can take the place of classes for scripting objects (but in BeanShell you can also use the regular class syntax). You can turn the context of a method call into an object reference by having the method return the special value this. You can then use the this reference to refer to any variables that were set during the method call. To be useful, an object may also need methods; so in BeanShell, methods may also contain methods at any level. Here is a simple example:

```
user( n ) {
    name = n;
    reset() {
        print( "Reset user:"+name );
    }
    return this;  // return user as object
}
bob = user("Bob" );
```

```
print( bob.name ); // "Bob"
bob.reset();       // prints "Reset user: Bob"
```

This example assigns the context of the user( ) method to the variable bob and refers to the field bob.name and the method bob.reset( ).

If you find this strange, don't worry. The most common reason you'd want to script an object is to implement a Java interface, and you can do that using the standard Java anonymous inner class syntax, as we'll discuss next or just use a regular class. BeanShell gives you a lot of options.

Scripting Interfaces and Adapters

One of the most powerful features of BeanShell is that you can "script" any interface type (provided you are running Java 1.3 or greater). BeanShell-scripted objects can automatically implement any required interface type. All you have to do is implement the necessary method (or at least the ones that are going to be invoked). You can use this feature either by explicitly referring to a BeanShell script using a this-style reference as described earlier, or by using the standard Java anonymous inner class syntax. Here is an example:

```
actionPerformed( event ) { print( event ); }
button = new JButton("Press Me!");
button.addActionListener( this );
frame( button );
```

You can type this code right on the command line and press the button to see the events it generates. In this case, the this reference refers to the current context, just as in a method. BeanShell automatically implements the ActionListener interface and delegates calls to its actionPerformed( ) method to our scripted method.

Alternately, we could use the anonymous inner class syntax to create an ActionListener for our button:

```
button = new JButton("Press Me!");
button.addActionListener( new ActionListener(  ) {
    actionPerformed( event ) { print( event ); }
} );
frame( button );
```

In this case the "anonymous inner class" is actually a BeanShell script that implements the ActionListener interface for us in the same way as the previous example.

One more thing: we hinted earlier that you only have to implement those methods of the interface that you want to use. If you don't script a method, it's okay as long as it's not invoked (in which case, you'd get an exception). For convenience in implementing a large interface, you can define the special invoke( ) method, which handles calls to scripted methods that don't exist:

```
invoke( name, args ) { print("Method: "+name+" invoked!"); }
```

This `invoke( )` method will handle method calls for methods that are not defined and simply print their names. See the user manual for more details.

Changing the Classpath

Within BeanShell, you can add to your classpath and even reload classes:

```
addClassPath("mystuff.jar");
addClassPath("http://examples.oreilly.com/learnjava3/magicbeans.jar");
```

To reload all classes in the classpath, simply use:

```
reloadClasses( );
```

You can do more elaborate things as well, such as reloading individual classes, if you know what you're doing. See the user manual for more details.

Learning More...

BeanShell has many more features than I've described here. You can embed Bean-Shell into your applications as a lightweight scripting engine, passing live Java objects into and out of scripts. You can even run BeanShell in a remote server mode, which lets you work in a shell inside your running application, for debugging and experimentation. There is also a BeanShell servlet that can be used for running scripts inside an application server.

BeanShell is small (only about 200 KB) and it's free, licensed under the GNU Library General Public License and the Sun Public License. You can learn more by checking out the full user's manual and FAQ on the web site. If you have ideas, bug fixes, or improvements, please consider joining the developer's mailing list.

Please feel free to send feedback, using the book's web page, *http://www.oreilly.com/catalog/learnjava3*. Enjoy!

Glossary

abstract

The abstract keyword is used to declare abstract methods and classes. An abstract method has no implementation defined; it is declared with arguments and a return type as usual, but the body enclosed in curly braces is replaced with a semicolon. The implementation of an abstract method is provided by a subclass of the class in which it is defined. If an abstract method appears in a class, the class is also abstract.

annotations

Metadata added to Java source code using the @ tag syntax. Annotations can be used by the compiler or at runtime to augment classes, provide data or mappings, or flag additional services.

Ant

A popular, XML-based build tool for Java applications. Ant builds can compile, package, and deploy Java source code as well as generate documentation and perform other activities through pluggable "targets."

API (Application Programmer Interface)

An API consists of the methods and variables programmers use to work with a component or tool in their applications. The Java language APIs consist of the classes and methods of the java.lang, java.util, java.io, java.text, and java.net packages and many others.

applet

An embedded Java application that runs in the context of an applet viewer, such as a web browser.

<applet> tag

An HTML tag that embeds an applet within a web document.

appletviewer

Sun's application that runs and displays Java applets outside of a web browser.

application

A Java program that runs standalone, as compared with an applet.

apt (Annotation Processing Tool)

A frontend for the Java compiler that processes annotations via a pluggable factory architecture, allowing users to implement custom compile-time annotations.

assertion

A language feature used to test for conditions that should be guaranteed by program logic. If a condition checked by an assertion is found to be false, a fatal error is thrown. For added performance, assertions can be disabled when an application is deployed.

atomic

Discrete or transactional in the sense that an operation happens as a unit, in an all-or-nothing fashion. Certain operations in the Java virtual machine (VM) and provided by the Java concurrency API are atomic.

AWT (Abstract Window Toolkit)

Java's original platform-independent windowing, graphics, and user interface toolkit.

BeanShell

An open source, lightweight, Java-compatible scripting language that can be used for Java experimentation, teaching, application extension, configuration, and debugging.

Boojum

The mystical, spectral, alter-ego of a Snark. From the Lewis Carroll poem "*The Hunting of the Snark*," 1876.

Boolean

A primitive Java data type that contains a true or false value.

bounds

In Java generics, a limitation on the type of a type parameter. An upper bound specifies that a type must extend (or is assignable to) a specific Java class. A lower bound is used to indicate that a type must be a supertype of (or is assignable from) the specified type.

boxing

Wrapping of primitive types in Java by their object wrapper types. See also *unboxing*.

byte

A primitive Java data type that's an 8-bit two's-complement signed number.

callback

A behavior that is defined by one object and then later invoked by another object when a particular event occurs. The Java event mechanism is a kind of callback.

cast

The changing of the apparent type of a Java object from one type to another, specified type. Java casts are checked both statically by the Java compiler and at runtime.

catch

The Java catch statement introduces an exception-handling block of code following a try statement. The catch keyword is followed by an exception type and argument name in parentheses and a block of code within curly braces.

certificate

An electronic document using a digital signature to assert the identity of a person, group, or organization. Certificates attest to the identity of a person or group and contain that organization's public key. A certificate is signed by a certificate authority with its digital signature.

certificate authority (CA)

An organization that is entrusted to issue certificates, taking whatever steps are necessary to verify the real-world identity for which it is issuing the certificate.

char

A primitive Java data type; a variable of type char holds a single 16-bit Unicode character.

class

1. The fundamental unit that defines an object in most object-oriented programming languages. A class is an encapsulated collection of variables and methods that may have privileged access to one another. Usually a class can be instantiated to produce an object that's an instance of the class, with its own unique set of data.

2. The class keyword is used to declare a class, thereby defining a new object type.

classloader

An instance of the class java.lang.ClassLoader, which is responsible for loading Java binary classes into the Java VM. Classloaders help partition classes based on their source for both structural and security purposes and can also be chained in a parent-child hierarchy.

class method

See *static method*.

classpath

The sequence of path locations specifying directories and archive files containing compiled Java class files and resources, which are searched in order to find components of a Java application.

class variable

See *static variable*.

client

The consumer of a resource or the party that initiates a conversation in the case of a networked client/server application. See also *server*.

Collections API

Classes in the core `java.util` package for working with and sorting structured collections or maps of items. This API includes the `Vector` and `Hashtable` classes as well as newer items such as `List`, `Map`, and `Queue`.

compilation unit

The unit of source code for a Java class. A compilation unit normally contains a single class definition and, in most current development environments, is simply a file with a *.java* extension.

compiler

A program that translates source code into executable code.

component architecture

A methodology for building parts of an application. It is a way to build reusable objects that can be easily assembled to form applications.

composition

Combining existing objects to create another, more complex object. When you compose a new object, you create complex behavior by delegating tasks to the internal objects. Composition is different from inheritance, which defines a new object by changing or refining the behavior of an old object. See also *inheritance*.

constructor

A special method that is invoked automatically when a new instance of a class is created. Constructors are used to initialize the variables of the newly created object. The constructor method has the same name as the class and no explicit return value.

content handler

A class that is called to parse a particular type of data and that converts it to an appropriate object.

datagram

A packet of data normally sent using a connectionless protocol such as UDP, which provides no guarantees about delivery or error checking and provides no control information.

data hiding

See *encapsulation*.

deep copy

A duplicate of an object along with all of the objects that it references, transitively. A deep copy duplicates the entire "graph" of objects, instead of just duplicating references. See also *shallow copy*.

DOM (Document Object Model)

An in-memory representation of a fully parsed XML document using objects with names like `Element`, `Attribute`, and `Text`. The Java XML DOM API binding is standardized by the World Wide Web Consortium (W3C).

double

A Java primitive data type; a `double` value is a 64-bit (double-precision) floating-point number.

DTD (Document Type Definition)

A document containing specialized language that expresses constraints on the structure of XML tags and tag attributes. DTDs are used to validate an XML document and can constrain the order and nesting of tags as well as the allowed values of attributes.

EJB (Enterprise JavaBeans)

A server-side business component architecture named for, but not significantly related to, the JavaBeans component architecture. EJBs represent business services and database components and provide declarative security and transactions.

encapsulation

The object-oriented programming technique of limiting the exposure of variables and methods to simplify the API of a class or package. Using the private and protected keywords, a programmer can limit the exposure of internal ("black box") parts of a class. Encapsulation reduces bugs and promotes reusability and modularity of classes. This technique is also known as *data hiding*.

enum

The Java keyword for declaring an enumerated type. An enum holds a list of constant object identifiers that can be used as a typesafe alternative to numeric constants that serve as identifiers or labels.

enumeration

See *enum*.

erasure

The implementation technique used by Java generics in which generic type information is removed (erased) and distilled to raw Java types at compilation. Erasure provides backward compatibility with nongeneric Java code, but introduces some difficulties in the language.

event

1. A user's action, such as a mouse-click or key press.

2. The Java object delivered to a registered event listener in response to a user action or other activity in the system.

exception

A signal that some unexpected condition has occurred in the program. In Java, exceptions are objects that are subclasses of Exception or Error (which themselves are subclasses of Throwable). Exceptions in Java are "raised" with the throw keyword and handled with the catch keyword. See also catch, throw, and throws.

exception chaining

The design pattern of catching an exception and throwing a new, higher level, or more appropriate exception that contains the underlying exception as its *cause*. The "cause" exception can be retrieved if necessary.

extends

A keyword used in a class declaration to specify the superclass of the class being defined. The class being defined has access to all the public and protected variables and methods of the superclass (or, if the class being defined is in the same package, it has access to all non-private variables and methods). If a class definition omits the extends clause, its superclass is taken to be java.lang.Object.

final

A keyword modifier that may be applied to classes, methods, and variables. It has a similar, but not identical, meaning in each case. When final is applied to a class, it means that the class may never be subclassed. java.lang.System is an example of a final class. When final is applied to a variable, the variable is a constant—i.e., it can't be modified.

finalize

A reserved method name. The finalize( ) method is called by the Java VM when an object is no longer being used (i.e., when there are no further references to it) but before the object's memory is actually reclaimed by the system. A finalizer should perform cleanup tasks and free system resources before the object is discarded by Java's garbage-collection system.

finally

A keyword that introduces the finally block of a try/catch/finally construct. catch and finally blocks provide exception handling and routine cleanup for code in a try block. The finally block is optional and appears after the try block, and after zero or more catch blocks. The code in a finally block is executed once, regardless of how the code in the try block executes. In normal execution, control reaches the end of the try block and proceeds to the finally block, which generally performs any necessary cleanup.

float

A Java primitive data type; a float value is a 32-bit (single-precision) floating-point number represented in IEEE 754 format.

garbage collection

The process of reclaiming the memory of objects no longer in use. An object is no longer in use when there are no references to it from other objects in the system and no references in any local variables on the method call stack.

generics

The syntax and implementation of parameterized types in the Java language, added in Java 5.0. Generic types are Java classes that are parameterized by the user on one or more additional Java types to specialize the behavior of the class. Generics are sometimes referred to as templates in other languages.

generic class

A class that uses the Java generics syntax and is parameterized by one or more type variables, which represent class types to be substituted by the user of the class. Generic classes are particularly useful for container objects and collections that can be specialized to operate on a specific type of element.

generic method

A method that uses the Java generics syntax and has one or more arguments or return types that refers to type variables representing the actual type of data element the method will use. The Java compiler can often infer the types of the type variables from the usage context of the method.

graphics context

A drawable surface represented by the java.awt.Graphics class. A graphics context contains contextual information about the drawing area and provides methods for performing drawing operations in it.

GUI (graphical user interface)

A traditional, visual user interface consisting of a window containing graphical items such as buttons, text fields, pull-down menus, dialog boxes, and other standard interface components.

hashcode

A random-looking identifying number, based on the data content of an object, used as a kind of signature for the object. A hashcode is used to store an object in a hashtable (or hash map). See also *hash table*.

hash table

An object that is like a dictionary or an associative array. A hash table stores and retrieves elements using key values called hashcodes. See also *hashcode*.

hostname

The human-readable name given to an individual computer attached to the Internet.

HotJava

An early web browser written in Java, capable of downloading and running Java applets.

HTTP (Hypertext Transfer Protocol)

The protocol used by web browsers or other clients to talk to web servers. The simplest form of the protocol uses the commands GET to request a file and POST to send data.

IDE (Integrated Development Environment)

A GUI tool such as NetBeans or Eclipse that provides source editing, compiling, running, debugging, and deployment functionality for developing Java applications.

implements

A keyword used in class declarations to indicate that the class implements the named interface or interfaces. The implements clause is optional in class declarations; if it appears, it must follow the extends clause (if any). If an implements clause appears in the declaration of a non-abstract class, every method from each specified interface must be implemented by the class or by one of its superclasses.

import

The import statement makes Java classes available to the current class under an abbreviated name or disambiguates classes imported in bulk by other import statements. (Java classes are always available by their fully qualified name, assuming the appropriate class file can be found relative to the CLASSPATH environment variable and that the class file is readable. import doesn't make the class available; it just saves typing and makes your code more legible.) Any number of import statements may appear in a Java program. They must appear, however, after the optional package statement at the top of the file, and before the first class or interface definition in the file.

inheritance

An important feature of object-oriented programming that involves defining a new object by changing or refining the behavior of an existing object. Through inheritance an object implicitly contains all of the non-private variables and methods of its superclass. Java supports single inheritance of classes and multiple inheritance of interfaces.

inner class

A class definition that is nested within another class or a method. An inner class functions within the lexical scope of another class.

instance

An occurrence of something, usually an object. When a class is instantiated to produce an object, we say the object is an instance of the class.

instance method

A non-static method of a class. Such a method is passed an implicit this reference to the object that invoked it. See also *static*; *static method*.

instanceof

A Java operator that returns true if the object on its left side is an instance of the class (or implements the interface) specified on its right side. instanceof returns false if the object isn't an instance of the specified class or doesn't implement the specified interface. It also returns false if the specified object is null.

instance variable

A non-static variable of a class. Each instance of a class has an independent copy of all of the instance variables of the class. See also *class variable*; *static*.

int

A primitive Java data type that's a 32-bit two's-complement signed number.

interface

1. A keyword used to declare an interface.

2. A collection of abstract methods that collectively define a type in the Java language. Classes implementing the methods may declare that they implement the interface type and instances of them may be treated as that type.

internationalization

The process of making an application accessible to people who speak a variety of languages. Sometimes abbreviated I18N.

interpreter

The module that decodes and executes Java bytecode. Most Java bytecode is not, strictly speaking, interpreted any longer but compiled to native code dynamically by the Java VM.

introspection

The process by which a JavaBean provides additional information about itself, supplementing information learned by reflection.

ISO 8859-1

An 8-bit character encoding standardized by the ISO. This encoding is also known as Latin-1 and contains characters from the Latin alphabet suitable for English and most languages of western Europe.

JavaBeans

A component architecture for Java. It is a way to build interoperable Java objects that can be manipulated easily in a visual application builder environment.

Java beans

Java classes that are built following the JavaBeans design patterns and conventions.

JavaScript

A language developed early in the history of the Web by Netscape for creating dynamic web pages. From a programmer's point of view, it's unrelated to Java, although some of its syntax is similar.

JAXB (Java API for XML Binding)

A Java API that allows for generation of Java classes from XML DTD or Schema descriptions and the generation of XML from Java classes.

JAXP (Java API for XML Parsers)

The Java API that allows for pluggable implementations of XML and XSL engines. This API provides an implementation-neutral way to construct parsers and transforms.

JAX-RPC

The Java API for XML Remote Procedure Calls, used by web services.

JDBC (Java Database Connectivity)

The standard Java API for talking to an SQL (structural query language) database.

JDOM

A native Java XML DOM created by Jason Hunter and Brett McLaughlin. JDOM is easier to use than the standard DOM API for Java. It uses the Java collections API and standard Java conventions. Available at *http://www.jdom.org/*.

JWSDP (Java Web Services Developer Pack)

A bundle of standard extension APIs packaged as a group with an installer from Sun. The JWSDP includes JAXB, JAX-RPC, and other XML and web services–related packages.

Latin-1

A nickname for ISO 8859-1.

layout manager

An object that controls the arrangement of components within the display area of a Swing or AWT container.

lightweight component

A pure Java GUI component that has no native peer in the AWT.

local variable

A variable that is declared inside a method. A local variable can be seen only by code within that method.

Logging API

The Java API for structured logging and reporting of messages from within application components. The Logging API supports logging levels indicating the importance of messages, as well as filtering and output capabilities.

long

A primitive Java data type that's a 64-bit two's-complement signed number.

message digest

A cryptographically computed number based on the content of a message, used to determine whether the message's contents have been changed in any way. A change to a message's contents will change its message digest. When implemented properly, it is almost impossible to create two similar messages with the same digest.

method

The object-oriented programming term for a function or procedure.

method overloading

Provides definitions of more than one method with the same name but with different argument lists. When an overloaded method is called, the compiler determines which one is intended by examining the supplied argument types.

method overriding

Defines a method that matches the name and argument types of a method defined in a superclass. When an overridden method is invoked, the interpreter uses "dynamic method lookup" to determine which method definition is applicable to the current object. In Java 5.0, overridden methods can have different return types, with restrictions.

Model-View-Controller (MVC) framework

A user-interface design that originated in Smalltalk. In MVC, the data for a display item is called the "model." A "view" displays a particular representation of the model, and a "controller" provides user interaction with both. Java incorporates many MVC concepts.

modifier

A keyword placed before a class, variable, or method that alters the item's accessibility, behavior, or semantics. See also *abstract*; *final*; *native*; *private*; *protected*; *public*; *static*; *synchronized*.

NaN (not-a-number)

This is a special value of the `double` and `float` data types that represents an undefined result of a mathematical operation, such as zero divided by zero.

native method

A method that is implemented in a native language on a host platform, rather than being implemented in Java. Native methods provide access to such resources as the network, the windowing system, and the host filesystem.

new

`new` is a unary operator that creates a new object or array (or raises an `OutOfMemoryException` if there is not enough memory available).

NIO

The Java "new" I/O package. A core package introduced in Java 1.4 to support asynchronous, interruptible, and scalable I/O operations. The NIO API supports non-threadbound "select" style I/O handling.

null

`null` is a special value that indicates a reference-type variable doesn't refer to any object instance. Static and instance variables of classes default to the value `null` if not otherwise assigned.

object

1. The fundamental structural unit of an object-oriented programming language, encapsulating a set of data and behavior that operates on that data.

2. An instance of a class, having the structure of the class but its own copy of data elements. See also *instance*.

<object> tag

An HTML tag used to embed media objects and applications into web browsers like the `<applet>` tag.

package

The package statement specifies the Java package for a Java class. Java code that is part of a particular package has access to all classes (`public` and non-`public`) in the package, and all non-private methods and fields in all those classes. When Java code is part of a named package, the compiled class file must be placed at the appropriate position in the `CLASSPATH` directory hierarchy before it can be accessed by the Java interpreter or other utilities. If the package statement is omitted from a file, the code in that file is part of an unnamed default package. This is convenient for small test programs run from the command line, or during development because it means the code can be interpreted from the current directory.

<param> tag

An HTML tag used within `<applet>` ... `</applet>` to specify a named parameter and string value to an applet within a web page.

parameterized type

A class, using Java generics syntax, that is dependent on one or more types to be specified by the user. The user-supplied parameter types fill in type values in the class and adapt it for use with the specified types.

plug-in

A modular application component for a web browser designed to extend the browser's capabilities to handle a specific type of data (MIME type). The Java Plug-in supports Java applets in browsers that do not have up-to-date Java runtime support.

polymorphism

One of the fundamental principles of an object-oriented language. Polymorphism states that a type that extends another type is a "kind of" the parent type and can be used interchangeably with the original type, but augmenting or refining its capabilities.

Preferences API

The Java API for storing small amounts of information on a per-user or systemwide basis across executions of the Java VM. The Preferences API is analogous to a small database or the Windows registry.

primitive type

One of the Java data types: `boolean`, `char`, `byte`, `short`, `int`, `long`, `float`, `double`.

Primitive types are manipulated, assigned, and passed to methods "by value" (i.e., the actual bytes of the data are copied). See also *reference type*.

printf

A style of text formatting originating in the C language, relying on an embedded identifier syntax and variable-length argument lists to supply parameters.

private

The private keyword is a visibility modifier that can be applied to method and field variables of classes. A private method or field is not visible outside its class definition and cannot be accessed by subclasses.

protected

A keyword that is a visibility modifier; it can be applied to method and field variables of classes. A protected field is visible only within its class, within subclasses, and within the package of which its class is a part. Note that subclasses in different packages can access only protected fields within themselves or within other objects that are subclasses; they cannot access protected fields within instances of the superclass.

protocol handler

A URL component that implements the network connection required to access a resource for a type of URL scheme (such as HTTP or FTP). A Java protocol handler consists of two classes: a StreamHandler and a URLConnection.

public

A keyword that is a visibility modifier; it can be applied to classes and interfaces and to the method and field variables of classes and interfaces. A public class or interface is visible everywhere. A non-public class or interface is visible only within its package. A public method or variable is visible everywhere its class is visible. When none of the private, protected, or public modifiers are specified, a field is visible only within the package of which its class is a part.

public-key cryptography

A cryptographic system that requires public and private keys. The private key can decrypt messages encrypted with the corresponding public key, and vice versa. The public key can be made available to the public without compromising security and used to verify that messages sent by the holder of the private key must be genuine.

queue

A list-like data structure normally used in a first-in-first-out fashion to buffer work items.

raw type

In Java generics, the plain Java type of a class without any generic type parameter information. This is the true type of all Java classes after they are compiled. See also *erasure*.

reference type

Any object or array. Reference types are manipulated, assigned, and passed to methods "by reference." In other words, the underlying value is not copied; only a reference to it is. See also *primitive type*.

reflection

The ability of a programming language to interact with structures of the language itself at runtime. Reflection in Java allows a Java program to examine class files at runtime to find out about their methods and variables, and to invoke methods or modify variables dynamically.

regular expression

A compact yet powerful syntax for describing a pattern in text. Regular expressions can be used to recognize and parse most kinds of textual constructs allowing for wide variation in their form.

Regular Expression API

The core java.util.regex package for using regular expressions. The regex package can be used to search and replace text based on sophisticated patterns.

Remote Method Invocation (RMI)

RMI is a native Java distributed object system. With RMI, you can pass references to objects on remote hosts and invoke methods in them as if they were local objects.

SAX (Simple API for XML)

SAX is an event-driven API for parsing XML documents in which the client receives events in response to activities such as the opening of tags, character data, and the closing of tags.

Schema

XML Schemas are a replacement for DTDs. Introduced by the W3C, XML Schema is an XML-based language for expressing constraints on the structure of XML tags and tag attributes, as well as the structure and type of the data content. Other types of XML schema languages have different syntaxes.

SDK (Software Development Kit)

A package of software distributed by Sun Microsystems for Java developers. It includes the Java interpreter, Java classes, and Java development tools: compiler, debugger, disassembler, applet viewer, stub file generator, and documentation generator. Also called the JDK.

SecurityManager

The Java class that defines the methods the system calls to check whether a certain operation is permitted in the current environment.

serialize

To serialize means to put in order or make sequential. A serialized object is an object that has been packaged so that it can be stored or transmitted over the network. Serialized methods are methods that have been synchronized with respect to threads so that only one may be executing at a given time.

server

The party that provides a resource or accepts a request for a conversation in the case of a networked client/server application. See also *client*.

servlet

A Java application component that implements the `javax.servlet.Servlet` API allowing it to run inside a servlet container or web server. Servlets are widely used in web applications to process user data and generate HTML or other forms of output.

servlet context

In the Servlet API, it is the web application environment of a servlet that provides server and application resources. The base URL path of the web application is also often referred to as the servlet context.

shadow

To declare a variable with the same name as a variable defined in a superclass. We say the variable "shadows" the superclass's variable. Use the super keyword to refer to the shadowed variable or refer to it by casting the object to the type of the superclass.

shallow copy

A copy of an object that duplicates only values contained in the object itself. References to other objects are repeated as references and are not duplicated themselves. See also *deep copy*.

short

A primitive Java data type that's a 16-bit two's-complement signed number.

signature

1. Referring to a digital signature. A combination of a message's message digest, encrypted with the signer's private key, and the signer's certificate, attesting to the signer's identity. Someone receiving a signed message can get the signer's public key from the certificate, decrypt the encrypted message digest, and compare that result with the message digest computed from the signed message. If the two message digests agree, the recipient knows that the message has not been modified and that the signer is who he or she claims to be.

2. Referring to a Java method. The method name and argument types and possibly return type, collectively uniquely identifying the method in some context.

signed applet

An applet packaged in a JAR file signed with a digital signature, allowing for authentication of its origin and validation of the integrity of its contents.

signed class

A Java class (or Java archive) that has a signature attached. The signature allows the recipient to verify the class's origin and that it is unmodified. The recipient can therefore grant the class greater runtime privileges.

sockets

A networking API originating in BSD Unix. A pair of sockets provide the endpoints for communication between two parties on the network. A server socket listens for connections from clients and creates individual server-side sockets for each conversation.

spinner

A GUI component that displays a value and a pair of small up and down buttons that increment or decrement the value. The Swing JSpinner can work with number ranges and dates as well as arbitrary enumerations.

static

A keyword that is a modifier applied to method and variable declarations within a class. A static variable is also known as a class variable as opposed to non-static instance variables. While each instance of a class has a full set of its own instance variables, there is only one copy of each static class variable, regardless of the number of instances of the class (perhaps zero) that are created. static variables may be accessed by class name or through an instance. Non-static variables can be accessed only through an instance.

static import

A statement, similar to the class and package import, that imports the names of static methods and variables of a class into a class scope. The static import is a convenience that provides the effect of global methods and constants.

static method

A method declared static. Methods of this type are not passed implicit this references and may refer only to class variables and invoke other class methods of the current class. A class method may be invoked through the class name, rather than through an instance of the class.

static variable

A variable declared static. Variables of this type are associated with the class, rather than with a particular instance of the class. There is only one copy of a static variable, regardless of the number of instances of the class that are created.

stream

A flow of data, or a channel of communication. All fundamental I/O in Java is based on streams. The NIO package uses channels, which are packet oriented.

String

A sequence of character data and the Java class used to represent this kind of character data. The String class includes many methods for operating on string objects.

subclass

A class that extends another. The subclass inherits the public and protected methods and variables of its superclass. See also *extends*.

super

A keyword used by a class to refer to variables and methods of its parent class. The special reference super is used in the same way as the special reference this is used to qualify references to the current object context.

superclass

A parent class, extended by some other class. The superclass's public and protected methods and variables are available to the subclass. See also *extends*.

synchronized

A keyword used in two related ways in Java: as a modifier and as a statement. First, it is a modifier applied to class or instance methods. It indicates that the method modifies the internal state of the class or the internal state of an instance of the class in a way that is not thread-safe. Before running a synchronized class method, Java obtains a lock on the class, to ensure that no other threads can modify the class concurrently. Before running a synchronized instance method, Java obtains a lock on the instance that invoked the method, ensuring that no other threads can modify the object at the same time.

Java also supports a synchronized statement that serves to specify a "critical section" of code. The synchronized keyword is followed by an expression in parentheses and a statement or block of statements. The expression must evaluate to an object or array. Java obtains a lock on the specified object or array before executing the statements.

TCP (Transmission Control Protocol)

A connection-oriented, reliable protocol. One of the protocols on which the Internet is based.

this

Within an instance method or constructor of a class, this refers to "this object"— the instance currently being operated on. It is useful to refer to an instance variable of the class that has been shadowed by a local variable or method argument. It is also useful to pass the current object as an argument to static methods or methods of other classes.

There is one additional use of this: when it appears as the first statement in a constructor method, it refers to one of the other constructors of the class.

thread

An independent stream of execution within a program. Since Java is a multi-threaded programming language, more than one thread may be running within the Java interpreter at a time. Threads in Java are represented and controlled through the Thread object.

thread pool

A group of "recyclable" threads used to service work requests. A thread is allo-

cated to handle one item and then returned to the pool.

throw

The throw statement signals that an exceptional condition has occurred by throwing a specified Throwable (exception) object. This statement stops program execution and passes it to the nearest containing catch statement that can handle the specified exception object.

throws

The throws keyword is used in a method declaration to list the exceptions the method can throw. Any exceptions a method can raise that are not subclasses of Error or RuntimeException must either be caught within the method or declared in the method's throws clause.

try

The try keyword indicates a guarded block of code to which subsequent catch and finally clauses apply. The try statement itself performs no special action. See also *catch* and *finally* for more information on the try/catch/finally construct.

type instantiation

In Java generics, the point at which a generic type is applied by supplying actual or wildcard types as its type parameters. A generic type is instantiated by the user of the type, effectively creating a new type in the Java language specialized for the parameter types.

type invocation

See *type instantiation*. The term "type invocation" is sometimes used by analogy with the syntax of method invocation.

UDP (User Datagram Protocol)

A connectionless unreliable protocol. UDP describes a network data connection based on datagrams with little packet control.

unboxing

Unwrapping a primitive value that is held in its object wrapper type and retrieving the value as a primitive.

Unicode

A universal standard for text character encoding, accommodating the written forms of almost all languages. Unicode is standardized by the Unicode Consortium. Java uses Unicode for its char and String types.

UTF-8 (UCS transformation format 8-bit form)
An encoding for Unicode characters (and more generally, UCS characters) commonly used for transmission and storage. It is a multibyte format in which different characters require different numbers of bytes to be represented.

variable-length argument list
A method in Java may indicate that it can accept any number of a specified type of argument after its initial fixed list of arguments. The arguments are handled by packaging them as an array.

varargs
See *variable-length argument list*.

vector
A dynamic array of elements.

verifier
A kind of theorem prover that steps through the Java bytecode before it is run and makes sure that it is well-behaved and does not violate the Java security model. The bytecode verifier is the first line of defense in Java's security model.

WAR file (Web Applications Resources file)
A JAR file with additional structure to hold classes and resources for web applications. A WAR file includes a *WEB-INF* directory for classes, libraries, and the *web.xml* deployment file.

web application
An application that runs on a web server or application server, normally using a web browser as a client.

web service
An application-level service that runs on a server and is accessed in a standard way using XML for data marshaling and HTTP as its network transport.

wildcard type
In Java generics, a "*" syntax used in lieu of an actual parameter type for type instantiation to indicate that the generic type represents a set or supertype of many concrete type instantiations.

XInclude
An XML standard and Java API for inclusion of XML documents.

XML (Extensible Markup Language)
A universal markup language for text and data, using nested *tags* to add structure and meta-information to the content.

XPath
An XML standard and Java API for matching elements and attributes in XML using a hierarchical, regex-like expression language.

XSL/XSLT (Extensible Stylesheet Language/XSLTransformations)
An XML-based language for describing styling and transformation of XML documents. Styling involves simple addition of markup, usually for presentation. XSLT allows complete restructuring of documents, in addition to styling.

Index

We'd like to hear your suggestions for improving our indexes. Send email to *index@oreilly.com*.

ActionListener interface *(continued)*
  pop-up menus, 606
  program registration, 586
actionPerformed( ) method, 54, 556, 592,
      606, 624
activeCount( ) method, 277
adapter classes
  anonymous, 190
  EventHandler, creating with, 782
  generic adapter for ActionEvents, 782
  listening for PropertyChangeEvents, 765
adapters
  BeanShell, 880
  classes, 580
  dummy, 582
  dynamic interface, 209
  inner classes as, 184
  JavaBeans, 759–763
  threads, 254
adaptive compilation, 6
add( ) method, 216
  Calendar class, 597
  Container class, 53
  GridBagConstraints class, 673
  List interface, 360
  Set interface, 360
addCookie( ) method, 519
addElement( ) method, 139
addGB( ) method, 674, 686
addHeader( ) method, 509
addImage( ) method, 728
adding static variables, 129
addMouseListener( ) method, 46
addMouseMotionListener( ) method, 48
addObserver( ) method, 387
addresses (IP), 438
addTab( ) method, 611
ad-hoc polymorphism, 142
AdjustmentEvents class, 615
administration (see management)
AffineTransformOp operator, 741
algorithms
  DSA, 813
  for garbage collection, 148
  image scaling, 711
align attribute (HTML), 800
aligning text, 317
allocate( ) method, 427
allocating
  memory, 13
  objects, 143–147

alpha RGB (ARGB) color model, 736
AlphaComposite class, 427, 692, 700
alt attribute (HTML), 801
alternation in patterns, 331
anchoring components, 680
animations, 731
  creating and starting threads for, 251
  delta arrays, 733
  double buffering, 731
  drawing, 731
  GIF89a files, 708
  juggling beans, 758
  running threads with adapters, 254
annotations, 211–213
  accessing, 208
  facility, 86
anonymous arrays, 122
anonymous inner classes, 182, 188, 771, 782
  ActionListener, implementing with, 588
  in BeanShell, 880
  implementing Runnable interface, 255
  listeners for action events, 760
anonymous type definitions, 848
Ant, 540–543
  Eclipse IDEs, 872
Apache Project, Tomcat server, 502
APIs (application programming
      interfaces), 883
  2D API, 689
    drawing, 712–720
    filling shapes, 700
    fonts, 702–707
    navigating, 693–700
    printing, 720
    rendering pipelines, 691–693
    stroking shapes, 702
    viewing images, 707–712
  JAI, 729
  java.util.regex, 335
  javax.xml.validation, 849
  JAXB, 851–856
  logging, 379–386
  Preferences, 376–379
  ServletContext API, 520
  text-related, 299
  XPath, 839
append( ) method, 636
  JTextArea class, 624
  StringBuffer class, 307
appending data to existing files, 411
Apple QuickTime (.mov) Player, 748

ARGB (alpha RGB) color model, 736
arguments
    annotations, 212
    command-line, 33
    declaring for methods, 35
    instance variables versus, 43
    numbers, 318
    references, 136
    types, 240
    variable-length lists, 140
arithmetic expressions, 342
arithmetic utilities, 342–346
ArithmeticException class, 342
arraycopy( ) method (System class), 122
arrays, 13, 56, 118–124
    { } construct, using, 120
    animation, use in, 733
    anonymous, 122
    Array class, 207
    ArrayIndexOutOfBoundsException, 121
    ArrayStoreException, 181
    base type of, 91, 118
    byte, 301
        ByteArray class, 427
        copying string characters into, 305
        encoding, 301
    of characters, 301
    classes, 124, 181
    collections, 354, 358, 364
    creating and initializing, 119
    deltas (animation), 733
    generics, 243–246
    image data, updating, 738
    other Java objects versus, 118
    length of, 57, 118, 121
    multidimensional, 123
    new operator, 118
    objects, 56
    raw data, creating data buffer from, 740
    references, 13, 56, 91
    of strings, 69
    triangular, 124
    types, 244
    unchecked exceptions and, 110
ascent and descent (fonts), 706
ASCII, Unicode character compatibility, 84
asList( ) method, 358

aspersions, casting, 166
assertions, 115–118
    applying, 116
    enabling and disabling, 116
    helper methods for, 117
asShortBuffer( ) method, 426
assignment
    += operator, 92
    expressions, 101
    local variables, 135
    operators used in, 100
    roles to users, 528
asyncExecute( ) method, 470
atomic operations, 280, 295
attach( ) method, 477, 481
attachment( ) method, 481
attributes
    align (HTML), 800
    <applet> tag, 798
    applets, 798
    ARCHIVE, 74
    archive, 800
    code (HTML), 798, 800
    default for color and font, setting in
        components, 691
    defining, 844
    name (HTML), 801
    objects, 798, 800
    session, getting and setting, 515
    sets, 635
    XML, 819
    xmlns, 821
audio
    images, 746
    loading clips for applets, 794
    players for, 748
AudioClip interface, 746
authentication
    users, 530
    web applications, 528
@Author annotation, 212
auto-correction (Eclipse IDEs), 873
autoboxing primitive types, 139
available( ) method
    FileInputStream class, 409
    InputStream class, 394
availableCharsets( ) method, 428

AWT (Abstract Window Toolkit), 41, 49,
    569, 884
  double buffering and, 714
  early problems with, 788
  graphics context, acquiring, 690
  update( ) method, 713
AWT Robot, 583
AWTKeyStroke class, 638

B

backing store (for preferences), 378
BackingStoreException, 378
BadExpression exception, 651
base directory, URL name and, 468
base type of arrays, 91, 118
base URLs, 484, 801
baselines of fonts, 706
basic access modifiers, 178
BasicStroke class, 692, 702
BeanBox development environment, 774
BeanBuilder development environment, 774
BeanInfo
    customizing, 775–778
    interface, 753, 775
beans, 753, 779
    hand-coding with, 778–784
    NumericField, 770
    state, 757
    (see also JavaBeans)
Beans class, 779
BeanShell script, 211, 876–881
    classpath, changing, 881
    commands, 878
    interfaces and adapters, 880
    online user's manual and FAQ, 881
Beans.instantiate( ) method, 774
Berners-Lee, Tim, 817
big endian, 427
BigDecimal class, 344
BigInteger class, 344
binary search trees, 365
bind( ) method
    Naming class, 466
    ServerSocketChannel class, 481
binding
    JavaBean properties, 763–765
    JAXB, 851–856
    overriden methods and, 160
    static methods, 160
black-and-white images, 740

BlockingQueue interface, 361, 367
blocks
    initializer, 146
    nonstatic code, 146
<body> tag, 821
Booleans, 43
    blinkState variable, 62
    parsing, 311
    property values, 769
    system property, getting, 376
BorderLayout, 666–668
borders, Swing components, 598–600
    Border interface, 598
    BorderFactory class, 598
    Borders class (example), 599
    implementation classes, 598
BOTH constant, 676
boundaries, words, 329
bounds
    generics, 230–232
    lower, 234
    wildcards, 233
Box class, 669
boxing primitive types, 139
BoxLayout, 669
break statements, 97, 98
browsers, 5
    access to user filesystem, 412
    building, using JEditorPane HTML
        display, 632
    CA certificates, 809
    caching, 150
    content and protocol handlers, 488
    displaying, 22
    driving browser with, 795
    editors, using in, 633
    HotJava web, 20, 412
    HotJavaBrowser Bean, 752
    Java, support for, 803
    lacking cookie support, rewriting URLs
        for, 516
    POST method, 510
    redirecting to different URL, 509
    responding to unknown tags, 799
    running in context of, 789
    support for, 787
    XML, 818, 862
    XSL in, 862
    (see also interfaces)
bsh JAR files, 876
bubbling up (exceptions), 107

object creation, 102
order of evaluation, 92
XPath, 836–843
(see also regular expressions)
extending interfaces, 173
Extensible Markup Language (see XML)
Extensible Stylesheet Language (see XSL)
extent parameter, 615
extra paths, 510

F

-f (file) option (jar utility), 75
face (or font) names, retrieving, 704
factory methods, 135
factory patterns, 824
false values, 88
family names (fonts), 703
features of Eclipse IDE, 872–875
Field class, 201
fields, 32
    access, 203
    accessor methods, 126, 203
    HTTP headers, 494
    updating, 297
FileChannel class
    concurrent access, 430
    direct data transfers, 432
    file locking, 431
    MapMode static inner classes, 432
    transferTo( ) method, 482
FileHandler class, 381
file (-f) option (jar utility), 75
files
    bsh JAR, 876
    build.xml, 541
    diff'ing (Eclipse IDEs), 874
    File class, 405
    FileNotFoundException, 409
    FileReader class, 410
    fonts, 703
    images, 708
    input/output, 404–415
    JAR, 74–78
    localizing path with JFileDialog class, 406
    locking, 423
    memory, 423, 431
    NetBeans, creating, 755
    nonexistent on server, 487
    RandomAccessFile class, 411
    read-only, 412
    read/write, 430
    restricting access to, 447

source code, .java extension, 72
source files (Eclipse IDEs), 869, 875
streams, 391
uploading and removing with HTTP, 506
video, 748
WAR, 505, 521–532
    Ant, 540–543
    deployment, 505
web.xml, 522
welcome, 526
fill constraints (GridBagLayout), 675, 678
fill( ) method, 691
filling shapes, 693, 699
filter( ) method, 744
FilterBypass class, 628
filtering
    AffineTransformOp class, 745
    declaring, 535
    documents, 627
    FilterInputStream class, 397, 404
    images, 741–746
    input to formatted text components, 626,
        628
    mapping, 535
    RescaleOp class, using, 745
    servlets, 532–540
final modifier
    combining with static modifier, 130
    String class, 142
finalization, 148
finally clauses, 113
FindResources class, 414
fireEvent( ) method, 661
first( ) method
    CardLayout class, 671
    SortedSet class, 360
fixed delay, 286
fixed rate, 286
flags
    ImageObserver interface, 725
    interest set, for selection keys, 475
    ready set, for selector keys, 476
    in regular expression matching, 332
    strings, 320
    threads, using with, 256
    windows from untrusted applications, 20
Flanagan, David, 8
flip( ) method, 425
Float class, 694
float data type, 89
FloatBuffer class, 426
floating-point data types, 88, 138, 319, 342

JTree class, 638–643
jugglers, 760
justifying text, 317
just-in-time compilation, 6
JWDSP (Java Web Services Developer's Pack), 851
JWindow, 565

K

key values (hash codes), 367
KeyboardFocusManager class, 637
keyboards, 556
  events, 45
  shortcuts
    copying, pasting, and cutting text, 624
    menus, 601
    mnemonics for, 603, 758
KeyEvent class, 46, 603
KEYGEN extension to HTML, 810
keys() method, 478
keys, modifiers, 574
keySet() method, 362
keystores, 813
KeyStroke class, 603
keytool
  generating public/private key pairs with, 813
  user interface awkwardness, 811
keywords
  assert, 115
  class, 126
  extends, 37
  interface, 169
  interfaces, 174
  return, 132
  synchronized, 15, 370
  void, 132
Knudsen, Jonathan, 637

L

labels
  combining with JavaBeans, 773
  frame windows, creating with JLabel, 34
  JLabel class, 588
  split panes, 610
  swing, 586–590
  tick marks in sliders, 615
languages
  codes, 308
  strings, 303
last() method, 671

lastIndexOf() method, 304, 306
lastModified() method, 407, 409
late-binding programming languages, 12
layout managers, 563, 662–664
  BorderLayout, 666–668
  BoxLayout, 669
  CardLayout, 670
  FlowLayout, 664
  GridBagLayout, 672–687
  GridLayout, 665
  nonstandard, 687
  SpringLayout, 688
LayoutFocusTraversalPolicy class, 637
Lea, Doug, 281
leading spaces, 317, 707
leftmost bounds, 231
legacy code, 231
length() method, 409
  CharSequence interface, 427
  File class, 407, 409
  RandomAccessFile class, 412
  String class, 101, 300, 306
length of arrays, 118, 121
levels, logging, 382
lexical comparison of strings, 303
L&Fs (look-and-feels), 26, 653, 655
life cycle of applets, 790
lightweight components (Swing), 889
limit and value pairs for numerical ranges, 323
limitations
  on inner classes (in methods), 187
  of JavaBeans, 774
  of parameter types, 222, 229
  of serialization, 460
  of XML, 830
LineMetrics class, 707
lines (shape outlines), 692, 702
linked lists, 137, 364
links
  generating with LinkResponseFilter (example), 538
  HyperlinkEvent class, 632
  responding to, 633
LinkWriter class, 540
Linux, support for Java, 28
Lisp programming language
  dynamic data typing, 11
  Java, comparison to, 7
list() method, 409
  File class, 407
  Properties class, 375

methods *(continued)*
   getParent( ), 409
   getPassword( ), 629
   getPath( ), 409
   getPercentInstance( ), 322
   getPreferredSize( ), 595, 663
   getProperty( ), 374
   getPropertyDescriptors( ), 775
   getProtocol( ), 485
   getRequestURI( ), 513, 516
   getResource( ), 74, 708, 794
   getResourceAsStream( ), 794
   getResponseCode( ), 494
   getRGBdefault( ), 736
   getRowCount( ), 646
   getScaledInstance( ), 711
   getSelectedText( ), 625
   getSelectedValues( ), 594
   getSelection( ), 592
   getSession( ), 515
   getSimpleElementText( ), 834
   getSoTimeout( ), 448
   getSource( ), 55
   getStackTraceI( ) (Throwable), 109
   getState( ), 273
   getStringBounds( ), 704
   getTargetException( ), 206
   getTcpNoDelay( ), 448
   getText( ), 624
   getTimeInstance( ), 350
   getValue( ), 518, 625
   getValueAt( ), 646, 651
   getWheelRotation( ), 576
   getWidth( ), 712
   getWriter( ), 508, 539
   group( ), 446
   hashCode( ), 365, 368
      Object class, 194
      String class, 305
   hasMoreElements( ), 359
   hasMoreTokens( ), 314
   hasNext( ), 358
   helper methods for assertions, 117
   HttpServletResponse encodeURL( ), 516
   ImageIO write( ), 746
   imageUpdate( ), 725
   importPreference( ), 379
   indexOf( ), 304
   init( )
      Applet class, 454, 790
      Servlet class, 505
   initialize( ), 737, 740

inner classes within, 186
input, validating, 117
insert( ), 307
insertNodeInto( ), 643
insertString( )
   Document class, 635
   DocumentFilter class, 628
instance, 127, 204
instantiate( ), 779
interestOps( ), 477, 481
interface, 48, 170
intern( ), 303, 306
internalFrameClosing( ), 653
interrupt( )
   Thread class, 255, 257
   UpdateApplet class, 260
invalidate( ), 516
invoke( )
   InvocationHandler class, 210
   Method class, 204, 206
invoking, 102
isAbsolute( ), 406, 409
isAcceptable( ), 477
isCommitted( ), 510
isConnectable( ), 477
isDirectory( ), 406, 409
isEmpty( ), 356
isError( ), 429
isErrorID( ), 728
isFile( ), 406, 409
isHidden( ), 409
isLoggable( ), 386
isNaN( ), 343
isReadable( ), 477
isSelected( ), 592
isShared( ), 431
isSupported( ), 428
isUnderflow( ), 429
iterator( ), 356
JComponent, 561
join( ), 255
keys, 478
keySet( ), 362
last( ), 671
lastIndexOf( ), 304, 306
lastModified( ), 407, 409
late-binding in Java, 12
length( ), 409
   CharSequence interface, 427
   File class, 407, 409
   RandomAccessFile class, 412
   String class, 101, 300, 306

---

methods *(continued)*
    writeInt( ), 397
    writeObject( ), 416, 460
    yield( ), 276
Microsoft
    applets, history of use, 788
    C# language and .NET initiative, 3
    IE, 28
    Java version, problems with, 803
    Word, use of RTF in documents, 633
    (see also IE)
MIME types (Multipurpose Internet Mail
        Extensions), 486
    DataSource, determining for data
        stream, 784
    determining for servlet output, 508
MissingResourceException class, 309
mkdir( ) method, 407, 409
mkdirs( ) method, 409
mnemonics, 601, 758
modal dialogs, 616
mode of files (read/write), specifying, 411
models, colors, 735
Model-View-Controller framework (see MVC
        framework)
modification times, 73
modifiers, 574
    abstract, 168
    basic access, 178
    InputEvents class, 574
    interfaces
        methods, 170
        variables, 172
    keys, 574, 638
    private, 16, 41, 155
    protected, 179, 196
    public, 41, 128
        combining with static modifier, 69
        interface, 170
        methods and variables, 178
    security, 203
    static (see static modifiers)
    strictfp class, 88
    synchronized, 57, 65, 144
    transient, 415
    visibility (see visibility modifiers)
modifying Swing, 585
monitors, 14, 261
Monson-Haefel, Richard, 785
months, setting, 347

mouse, 556, 569, 575, 582
    events
        DrawPad application (example), 720
        getting x and y coordinates of
            position, 46
        inner classes supplying handlers
            for, 720
        MouseEvent class, 46
        MouseMotionListener interface, 48,
            54
        pop-up menus and, 606
    InputEvents class, 574
    wheels, scrolling with, 575, 609
mouseDragged( ) method, 45, 48, 713, 717,
    720
mouseMoved( ) method, 45
mousePressed( ) method, 606
mouse-wheel, 575
movies, 747
multicast sockets, 437
multicasting events, 573
multidimensional arrays, 123
multiline (m) mode, regular expression
        matching, 332
multimedia, 747
multiple inheritance, 155
multiplicity, 329
Multipurpose Internet Mail Extensions (see
        MIME types)
multithreading, 60
    Swing, 584
MutableTreeNode interface, 639
MVC (Model-View-Controller)
        framework, 387, 558, 622, 631

N

Nagle's algorithm, turning off, 448
names
    applets, 802
    attribute (HTML), 801
    binding/rebinding names to registry, 466
    domains, 520
    files, localization of, 406
    fonts, 703
    fully qualified, 39, 68
    HTML frames for displaying
        documents, 795
    inner classes, 186
    Naming class, 464
    packages, 175

variables (*continued*)
  weighty, 678
  (see also instance variables)
vectors, 354
verbose (-v) option (jar utility), 75
verbose mode, jar utility, 75
verifier( ) method, 9
verifiers, bytecode, 17
verify( ) method, 629
VERITCAL constant, 676
versions, troubleshooting, 66
vertical scrollbars, display policy, 609
vetoableChange( ) method, 765
video files, 748
viewers for applets
  appletviewer program, 803
  creating, 798
viewing
  applets, 805
  appletviewer program, 803
  images, 707–712
  Plug-in applets, 805
views (components), 631
virtual machines, 4–7, 31
virtual memory, 431
virtual methods (C++), 159
visibility
  applets, 790
  basic access modifiers, 178
  classes, 15, 175
  inheritance and, 155
  invisible components in BoxLayout, 669
  of methods and variables, 178–181
  security, 192
  shortcomings in API, 797
  subclasses and, 180
visibility modifiers
  access to class members, controlling, 128
  constructors, 144
  private, 16, 56
  protected, 891
  public, classes in source code files, 72
  static inner classes, 188
visual development environments, 24
void return type, 132, 206

W

W3C schema simple types, 847
wait conditions, 266
wait( ) method, 255, 264
waitForAll( ) method, 728

waitforID( ) method, 728
WaitServlet, 534
wakeup( ) method, 477
waking up threads blocked in I/O
    operations, 423
WAR files, 505, 521–532
  Ant, 540–543
  deployment, 505
@WarningMessage annotation, 212
weak references, 149, 371
weakCompareAndSet( ) method, 297
WeakHashMap class, 371
web applications, 504
  communicating with, 490–496
  filters, 532–540
  frameworks, 504
  HttpURLConnection, 494
  Java Servlets API, 27
  JSPs, 503
  reloading, 526
  security, 528
  servlets, 504–521
  technologies, 502–504
  URLs, URNs, and URIs, 495–500
  WAR files, 521–532
  XML, 504
  (see also applications)
web browsers, 5
  POST method, 510
  (see also browsers)
web pages, dynamic content, 787
web services, 862
  applying, 549
  data types, 546
  deploying, 548
  implementing, 543–551
  XML, 862
Web Services Description Language
    (WSDL), 497
Web Services Developer Pack, 497
Web Start API, 79
Web Start (Java), 806
webapps directory, 526
WEB-INF directory, 522
WebNFS Java extension, 413
web.xml files, 505, 522, 541
weighting (GridBagLayout), 675, 678, 682
weightx variable, 678
weighty variable, 678
welcome files, 526
well-formed documents (XML), 822

Z

About the Authors

Patrick Niemeyer (*pat@pat.net*) became involved with Oak (Java's predecessor) while working at Southwestern Bell Technology Resources. He is currently an independent consultant, author, and active member of the Java community process, which helps define new APIs for the Java platform. Pat is the creator of BeanShell, a popular Java scripting language, and various other free goodies on the Net. In recent years, Pat has been developing enterprise architecture and applications for the financial industry. He currently lives in the Central West End area of St. Louis with his wife Ellen and various creatures.

Jonathan Knudsen is the author of several books, including *Wireless Java: Developing with J2ME*, Second Edition (APress); *The Unofficial Guide to LEGO MINDSTORMS Robots* (O'Reilly); and *Java 2D Graphics* (O'Reilly). Jonathan has written extensively about Java and Lego robots for JavaWorld, EXE, NZZ Folio, and the O'Reilly Network. Jonathan holds a degree in mechanical engineering from Princeton University.

Colophon

Our look is the result of reader comments, our own experimentation, and feedback from distribution channels. Distinctive covers complement our distinctive approach to technical topics, breathing personality and life into potentially dry subjects.

The animals on the cover of *Learning Java*, Third Edition are a Bengal tigress and her cubs. The Bengal tiger (*Panthera tigris*) lives in Southern Asia. It has been hunted practically to extinction, principally for its bone, which is reputed to have medicinal value. It now lives mostly in natural preserves and national parks, where it is strictly protected. It's estimated that there are fewer than 3,000 Bengal tigers left in the wild.

The Bengal tiger is reddish orange with narrow black, gray, or brown stripes, generally in a vertical direction. Males can grow to nine feet long and weigh as much as 500 pounds; they are the largest existing members of the cat family. Preferred habitats include dense thickets, long grass, or tamarisk shrubs along river banks. Maximum longevity can be 26 years but is usually only about 15 years in the wild.

Tigers most commonly conceive after the monsoon rains; the majority of cubs are born between February and May after a gestation of three and a half months. Females bear single litters every two to three years. Cubs weigh under three pounds at birth and are striped. Litters consist of one to four cubs, with occasionally as many as six, but it's unusual for more than two or three to survive. Cubs are weaned at four to six months but depend on their mother for food and protection for another two years. Female tigers are mature at three to four years, males at four to five years.

Their white ear spots may help mothers and cubs to keep track of each other in the dim forests at night.

Matt Hutchinson was the production editor for *Learning Java*, Third Edition. Octal Publishing, Inc. provided production services. Darren Kelly, Sanders Kleinfeld, and Claire Cloutier provided quality control.

Hanna Dyer designed the cover of this book, based on a series design by Edie Freedman. The cover image is an original engraving from the book *Forest and Jungle: An Illustrated History of the Animal Kingdom* by P.T. Barnum (1899). Karen Montgomery produced the cover layout with Adobe InDesign CS using Adobe's ITC Garamond font, and designed the CD label.

David Futato designed the interior layout. This book was converted by Andrew Savikas to FrameMaker 5.5.6 with a format conversion tool created by Erik Ray, Jason McIntosh, Neil Walls, and Mike Sierra that uses Perl and XML technologies. The text font is Linotype Birka; the heading font is Adobe Myriad Condensed; and the code font is LucasFont's TheSans Mono Condensed. The illustrations that appear in the book were produced by Robert Romano, Jessamyn Read, and Lesley Borash using Macromedia FreeHand MX and Adobe Photoshop CS. The tip and warning icons were drawn by Christopher Bing. This colophon was written by Mary Anne Weeks Mayo.

Better than e-books

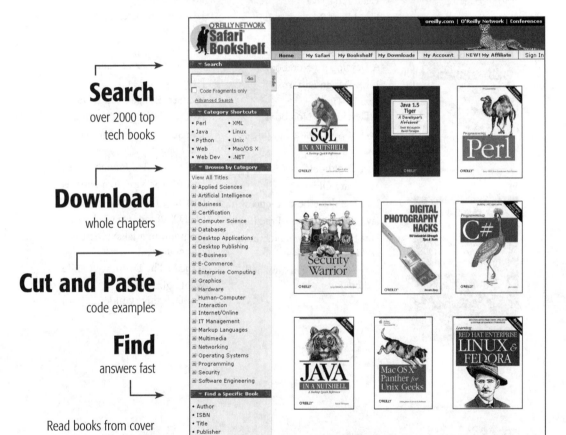

Search
over 2000 top
tech books

Download
whole chapters

Cut and Paste
code examples

Find
answers fast

Read books from cover
to cover. Or, simply click
to the page you need.

**Search Safari! The premier electronic reference
library for programmers and IT professionals**

Addison
Wesley

O'REILLY®

AdobePress

Sun
microsystems

SAMS

ALPHA

New
Riders

Java

Cisco Press

Microsoft
Press

QUE®

macromedia
PRESS

Peachpit
Press

PRENTICE
HALL
PTR

Related Titles Available from O'Reilly

Java

Ant: The Definitive Guide

Better, Faster, Lighter Java

Eclipse

Eclipse Cookbook

Enterprise JavaBeans,
4th Edition

Hardcore Java

Head First Java

Head First Servlets & JSP

Head First EJB

Hibernate:
A Developer's Notebook

J2EE Design Patterns

Java 1.5 Tiger:
A Developer's Notebook

Java & XML Data Binding

Java & XML

Java Cookbook, *2nd Edition*

Java Data Objects

Java Database Best Practices

Java Enterprise Best Practices

Java Enterprise in a Nutshell,
2nd Edition

Java Examples in a Nutshell,
3rd Edition

Java Extreme Programming
Cookbook

Java in a Nutshell, *4th Edition*

Java Management Extensions

Java Message Service

Java Network Programming,
2nd Edition

Java NIO

Java Performance Tuning,
2nd Edition

Java RMI

Java Security, *2nd Edition*

JavaServer Faces

Java ServerPages, *2nd Edition*

Java Servlet & JSP Cookbook

Java Servlet Programming,
2nd Edition

Java Swing, *2nd Edition*

Java Web Services in a Nutshell

Learning Java, *2nd Edition*

Mac OS X for Java Geeks

Programming Jakarta Struts
2nd Edition

Tomcat: The Definitive Guide

WebLogic:
The Definitive Guide

O'REILLY®

Our books are available at most retail and online bookstores.
To order direct: 1-800-998-9938 • *order@oreilly.com* • *www.oreilly.com*
Online editions of most O'Reilly titles are available by subscription at *safari.oreilly.com*

Keep in touch with O'Reilly

1. Download examples from our books

To find example files for a book, go to:

www.oreilly.com/catalog

select the book, and follow the "Examples" link.

2. Register your O'Reilly books

Register your book at *register.oreilly.com*

Why register your books?
Once you've registered your O'Reilly books you can:

*   Win O'Reilly books, T-shirts or discount coupons in our monthly drawing.

*   Get special offers available only to registered O'Reilly customers.

*   Get catalogs announcing new books (US and UK only).

*   Get email notification of new editions of the O'Reilly books you own.

3. Join our email lists

Sign up to get topic-specific email announcements of new books and conferences, special offers, and O'Reilly Network technology newsletters at:

elists.oreilly.com

It's easy to customize your free elists subscription so you'll get exactly the O'Reilly news you want.

4. Get the latest news, tips, and tools

www.oreilly.com

*   "Top 100 Sites on the Web"—PC Magazine
*   CIO Magazine's Web Business 50 Awards

Our web site contains a library of comprehensive product information (including book excerpts and tables of contents), downloadable software, background articles, interviews with technology leaders, links to relevant sites, book cover art, and more.

5. Work for O'Reilly

Check out our web site for current employment opportunities:

jobs.oreilly.com

6. Contact us

O'Reilly & Associates
1005 Gravenstein Hwy North
Sebastopol, CA 95472 USA

TEL: 707-827-7000 or 800-998-9938
       (6am to 5pm PST)

FAX: 707-829-0104

order@oreilly.com
For answers to problems regarding your order or our products. To place a book order online, visit:

www.oreilly.com/order_new

catalog@oreilly.com
To request a copy of our latest catalog.

booktech@oreilly.com
For book content technical questions or corrections.

corporate@oreilly.com
For educational, library, government, and corporate sales.

proposals@oreilly.com
To submit new book proposals to our editors and product managers.

international@oreilly.com
For information about our international distributors or translation queries. For a list of our distributors outside of North America check out:

international.oreilly.com/distributors.html

adoption@oreilly.com
For information about academic use of O'Reilly books, visit:

academic.oreilly.com